Converging Methods

for Understanding

Reading and Dyslexia

Converging Methods

for Understanding

Reading and Dyslexia

edited by
Raymond M. Klein
and
Patricia McMullen

The MIT Press
Cambridge, Massachusetts
London, England

Library of Congress Cataloging-in-Publication Data

Converging methods for understanding reading and dyslexia / edited by Raymond M. Klein and Patricia A. McMullen.
    p. cm. -- (Language, speech, and communication)
Includes bibliographical references and index.
ISBN 0-262-11247-7 (alk. paper)
1. Dyslexia. 2. Reading--Remedial teaching. I. Klein, Raymond M. II. McMullen, Patricia A. III. Series.
LB1050.5 .C662 1999
371.91'44--dc21   99-045493

This book is dedicated to the pursuit of education
for its own sake which our parents taught us and we
hope to pass on to our students

Contents

Acquired Dyslexia

Brain Imaging of Reading Subprocesses

Computational Modeling of Reading, Dyslexia, and Remediation

Integrating Themes in Reading Research

Preface

We had two goals in editing this book: to illustrate different approaches used by scientists to understand the complex skill of reading and its breakdown, and to stimulate thought about how converging evidence from these approaches can lead to new insights and advances.

Leaders in the field of reading research and its remediation have contributed state-of-the-art chapters. The focus is on the application of useful and innovative techniques for understanding how the normal reading system develops and functions in adulthood, breaks down after brain damage, and is subsequently remediated.

This book is unique because the themes of normal and disrupted reading and remediation, approached from a wide variety of methods (normal performance, development, brain imaging, cognitive neuropsychology, and computational modeling), have rarely been so comprehensively covered at this level. This is important because understanding reading, particularly its breakdown, is crucial to optimizing the function of society today. It is timely because recent technological advances in brain imaging of cognitive operations and in computational modeling now concretely indicate where and how reading is performed by the brain.

This book will be of special interest to all researchers and many practitioners in the area of reading. It is ideal for graduate and upper-level undergraduate seminars. More broadly, it will be of general interest to individuals in the fields of cognitive psychology, neuropsychology, cognitive neuroscience, computational modeling of cognitive processes, developmental psycholinguistics, cognitive development, and behavioral neurology.

We thank the Natural Sciences & Engineering Research Council of Canada, the Toronto Hospital for Sick Children's Foundation and the National Health and Research Development Program for conference grants that made this book possible. We are grateful for the assistance of Amelia Hunt for her work on the indices. Marilyn Klein's assiduous efforts converting figures, tables, chapters, and eventually the entire book into a publishable form are deeply appreciated.

Introduction: The Reading Brain

Raymond M. Klein
Patricia McMullen

Less than 500 years ago reading was an activity confined to monks and a handful of scholars. Invention of the printing press in the fifteenth century began a revolution that has led to the nearly universal use of reading as a method of information and cultural transmission. In the information age, reading is one of the most important cognitive skills an individual acquires. As such, a scientific understanding of this skill to help optimize its acquisition and performance is imperative.

Reading was of interest to the earliest psychologists, but it was not until the publication of Huey's (1908) book, *The Psychology and Pedagogy of Reading* (which includes a review of the history of reading and writing and of reading methods, texts, and hygiene) that the subject received its first comprehensive treatment. This book still makes for interesting reading because Huey foreshadowed many contemporary themes and presented ingenious experiments whose findings remain pertinent (see Rayner, chapter 1, this volume). Huey also realized that mental processes involved in reading broadly represented mental processes in general. Within this context, he anticipated the current role that reading plays in psychological research when he noted that understanding reading "would almost be the acme of a psychologist's achievements." He also clearly recognized the artificial nature of reading, which he called "the most remarkable specific performance that civilization has learned in all its history." Reading is a recently developed cognitive skill that involves connecting visual input in the form of arbitrary symbols (orthography) to linguistic representations (meaning). As such, reading is too recent a human invention to have been directly shaped by evolution. Nonetheless, the human brain does contain language and visual pattern recognition modules, as delineated by Fodor (1983), which have been honed by evolutionary pressures and are used in reading.

Readers of this book will notice an emphasis upon the reading of single words, often summarized by the phrase "access to the lexicon." Yet, we usually read phrases, sentences, and paragraphs to actively construct the ideas in a message. Once a visually presented word has activated representations in the mental lexicon, however, subsequent processes leading to understanding are more or less the same when we are listening to speech or reading text. These include the use of context to constrain semantic interpretation, the role of syntax in parsing, demands upon short-term memory and other comprehension processes. Since there are many good treatments of these topics from a reading perspective (e.g., Rayner and Pollatsek, 1989), and we are primarily interested in processes unique to reading printed text, this book focuses on processes involved in single word recognition.

The book can be divided into five subject groupings, including normal adult reading and its development, developmental dyslexia, varieties of brain-damaged reading, neuroimaging, and computational modeling. An overview of each of these sections follows. The final chapter of the book provides an integrative summary.

Normal Adult Reading and Its Development

Reading is an information processing activity, "one in which an arbitrary conventional set of symbols is used to transfer information from one mind to another" (Huey, 1908). This nearly century-old description has a very contemporary ring. Many of the questions posed and topics covered in Huey's book provide a suitable introduction for this section.

How do the eyes pick up information from the printed page? We may feel that our eyes glide smoothly along the printed line or page, but in fact the eye movements made during reading are jerky saccades, or rapid changes in fixation. The typical reader makes about 3 or 4 such movements per second (each movement lasts between 30 to 40 ms, and the eyes remain fixated for about 200 to 300 ms). Moreover, about 15% of the eye movements made by typical college students are regressive, meaning they go back to material previously fixated. This much was known a century ago. Rayner's chapter illustrates how technological advances for presenting text together with those for on-line recording of eye position have provided an incredible window on the cognitive processes that operate when we read.

What is the nature of the processes and codes that operate during reading? The dual-route model of word recognition (see Ellis, 1984) captures the distinction between "reading by ear" and "reading by eye" first anticipated by Huey. Unskilled readers or skilled readers reading unfamiliar words may rely on auditory images, whereas visual images may suffice when skilled readers read familiar words. Huey also anticipated the importance of automatization, "whereby well-practiced events are run off with less and less conscious control." This frees the mind of the reader to work on the task of constructing the meaning of a message. When reading is not fully automatic, word recognition demands so much capacity that there is not enough left for this important integrative function.

Rayner and his colleagues asked subjects to read while real-time recordings of their eye movements (saccades) and fixations were made. Along with this naturalistic observation he implemented on-line manipulations of the text being read (such as the moving window) to determine how much information is gleaned in a typical fixation and what role, if any, the to-be-foveated text plays in normal reading. Rayner describes the normal behavior of the eyes during reading of standard and modified text and shows how one can draw inferences about the perceptual and cognitive processes involved. He also connects this methodology to the study of dyslexia, and he argues that if there are abnormal eye movement patterns by dyslexics while reading (and this, itself, is debatable), these patterns reflect rather than cause their reading problems.

Normal adult reading is usually acquired in childhood. For this reason, understanding the acquisition of reading depends as much upon cognitive development as it does upon learning to read per se. This interaction is the general theme of the chapters by Goswami and Levy. Eschewing the notion of stages in reading acquisition, in chapter 2 Goswami emphasizes that an appreciation of the phonological structure of language constrains acquisition of the orthography of language. This results in an interaction between reading acquisition and phonological knowledge. While acknowledging the importance of linguistic representations, Levy emphasizes the importance of general learning principles such as practice on reading acquisition in chapter 3. Although she does not specifically allude to Hebb (1949), his idea that the formation of cell assemblies, the building blocks of cognitive (perceptual and conceptual) representations, depends on repeated and correlated firing of a set of neurons, appears to be quite pertinent here. The neuroscientific nature regarding this assumption is nicely captured in the rhyme: "neurons that fire together wire together." Behaviorally the changes associated with the formation of these assemblies may be reflected in the adage "practice makes perfect."

Following the lead of Huey, LaBerge and Samuels (1974) make the important point that practice until performance is error free is not sufficient to support high levels of skilled performance. To accomplish this, pathways must be automatic or activated in response to sensory inputs without requiring conscious attention. Automaticity frees cognitive resources for the more difficult task of integration and comprehension. If attention and effort are devoted to low-level processes, like decoding the pronunciation of a letter string, there may be insufficient resources to execute processes needed for comprehension.

Goswami first describes different levels of phonological awareness: syllabic and subsyllabic, with the latter emphasizing larger units of onsets and rimes, or smaller units of phonemes. Awareness of syllables, onset and rime emerges at about three or four years of age, long before children go to school. In contrast, awareness of phonemes emerges around ages six to seven, after children have been reading for about a year. Goswami describes three findings that lead her to hypothesize that phonological skills needed to discriminate onset-rimes are very important in early stages of learning to read English: (1) Bradley and Bryant's classic (1983) finding of a positive relationship between awareness of rhyme in three- to four-year olds and reading ability five years later, (2) delayed readers are worse than reading matched controls at a rhyme oddity task, and (3) remediation focused on rimes leads to significant improvements in reading and spelling.

Goswami notes some of the unique properties of mapping spelling-to-sound in English such as nontransparency, which is exemplified as irregular spelling combinations or spelling patterns with more than one pronunciation or more than one spelling pattern associated with the same sound. Considering that children who learn to read English deal with these irregular and inconsistent spelling-sound correspondences, the importance of phonology might be questioned. Goswami points to research, however, showing that when the unit of analysis is rime rather than phoneme, there is a considerable increase in the "transparency" of written English (Treiman et al., 1995). Hence, the initial use of onset-rime parsing may make the English spelling system easier to learn. Goswami supports the notion that this is how children parse words when learning to read by showing that they generalize by analogy from words they know to new ones.

As an alternative to traditional stage models of reading acquisition (e.g., Frith, 1985), Goswami proposes an "interactive analogy" model in which initial attempts at the visual analysis of words are strongly constrained by phonological knowledge, which she argues is knowledge of onsets and rimes. In Goswami's model, orthographic representations are formed by analogy with phonological knowledge; this strategy operates automatically during the entire acquisition process and results in spelling units that are larger than single letters being used throughout acquisition. Finally, Goswami describes converging evidence for her interactive theory from cross-linguistic studies of reading by analogy using carefully constructed nonsense words in languages that differ in their degree of transparency.

Another approach (used by Levy) to understanding the acquisition of an artificial skill such as reading is to explore the effectiveness of training programs in which different component subskills are emphasized. Appropriately, her chapter begins with a review of the training literature. Although the literature provides "no consistent advice for teachers on the appropriate orthographic unit" to use in teaching the new reader, Levy does.

Her own research compares whole-word repetition with segmentation training in which either phonemes, onsets or rimes are emphasized. All the training methods were superior to a control condition, but generally the whole-word method was inferior to the methods that used segmentation, and of the segmentation methods, those using onsets or rimes were generally superior to the phoneme training. These findings were obtained for both new readers and readers described as reading delayed. Levy next shows that whole-word repetition is important for reducing reading times and that further repetitions, even when reading speed is asymptotic, are important for preserving the gains in reading speed over time. Although Levy refers to this process of repetition as leading to enhanced automaticity, it should be noted that merely showing that mental operations have been made more rapid is not sufficient to demonstrate their automaticity. This requires converging evidence from dual task or interference paradigms.

Developmental Dyslexia

It is important to recognize that processing deficits leading to difficulties in the acquisition of reading skill can occur in children regardless of their level of intellectual ability (Stanovich and Siegel, 1994). Nevertheless, the "idealized" developmental dyslexic has difficulty acquiring the skill of reading while demonstrating at least normal intelligence, vision, language, and performance in most cognitive domains other than reading.

Given such a definition, should we expect developmental dyslexia to be a homogeneous disorder? Our thinking on this issue leads to two answers that can both be right, depending on the interpretation of the definition. First, if we strictly adhere to the criterion that the dyslexic should be perfectly normal in the performance of all cognitive tasks except reading, then, the problem in developmental dyslexia must be in a stage(s) of processing that is needed only for reading. One culprit could be the module that performs orthographic-to-phonological conversion. Indeed, many developmental dyslexics have trouble performing this function. Second, even normal readers are not "perfectly" normal in the performance of all tasks. Suppose we examine language ability or visual perception with very subtle measuring devices. We may then find individuals who have imperfect functioning of language or pattern recognition modules but who are still able to perform everyday tasks requiring the functions these modules implement. These imperfections may not disturb tasks performed primarily within these modules because evolution has designed them to be robust through highly redundant coding schemes. As noted above and in Carr's chapter 14, however, reading has not been performed long enough to be crafted by evolutionary forces. If either the language or visual pattern recognition module is only slightly compromised, this weakness may be multiplied when performance depends on transmission across sparse connections to the other system thus producing a reading problem (see Plaut, chapter 11, this volume). Using this logic, a reading difficulty could be rooted primarily in a subtle problem with language (Liberman and Shankweiler, 1985) or vision (Lovegrove, Martin, and Slaghuis, 1986) or some combination of both (Boder, 1971; Castles and Coltheart, 1993).

It has been suggested recently (Paula Tallal is the primary advocate, but see Farmer and Klein's, 1995, review) that a deficit in rapid temporal processing may directly cause phonological and linguistic problems that consequently are indirectly responsible for dyslexia. Farmer and Klein reviewed the literature and showed conclusively that there was an association between the occurrence of dyslexia and temporal processing deficits in both the visual and auditory modalities. Although the existence of such an association cannot be used to assert a causal connection (this requires converging evidence of a different nature) Farmer and Klein did delineate plausible causal links from both a visual temporal processing deficit and an auditory temporal processing deficit to dyslexia (see figure I.1). If this reasoning is accepted, an auditory temporal processing deficit results in a degraded representation of the phonology of language, primarily because most of the information that distinguishes among consonants occurs very rapidly. This deficit causes reading problems that are akin to acquired phonological dyslexia, which is characterized by poor ability to decode and therefore deal with infrequent words or nonwords, while sight vocabulary for high-frequency words is nearly normal. If there is a visual temporal processing deficit, this may result in poor "erasure" of the visual representation extracted during the previous fixation when the eyes move to the next position on the printed page (Breitmeyer, 1989; Lovegrove et al., 1986). This would directly disrupt reading and might make the activity unpleasant or difficult. Even in the presence of adequate phonological representations, reading avoidance could lead to a pattern akin to surface dyslexia that is characterized by poor sight vocabulary, especially for irregular words. Of course, some individuals may have temporal processing problems in both modalities, in which case their dyslexia would appear "mixed."

It is interesting to consider the recent data from Tallal and Merzenich (Tallal et al., 1996; Merzenich et al., 1996) as it pertains to the notion that the relative success of different remediation strategies can inform us about the underlying nature of a disorder. They have shown that a training program in which rapid spectral changes that comprise stopped consonants were slowed down ("stretched" speech) produced a remarkable improvement in the language functioning of children who suffer from severe language impairments. Importantly, a subsequent study (Tallal et al., 1996) demonstrated that although the same training with normal speech also produced improvements, the improvements were much more dramatic with the "stretched" speech. Even children whose language ability was in the "nor-

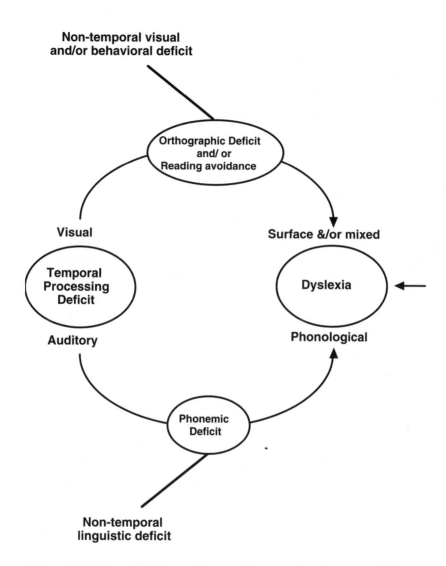

Figure I.1 A simplified view of the possible causaal pathways to dyslexia including those from a temporal processing deficit in either the auditory or visual modality (from Farmer and Klein, 1995).

mal" range showed improvements with the program. This finding suggests the need for one more piece of evidence before one can conclude that the success of this program demonstrates a causal link between an auditory temporal processing deficit and the language problem: It must be shown that the advantage conferred by "stretching" speech is greater for language-impaired than for normal children (conversely the normal children should benefit more from the remainder of the training program than the language impaired children).

Chapters 4 and 5 by Lovett and Olson et al., apply two different strategies to understanding developmental dyslexia: remediation effectiveness and behavioral-genetic analysis.

Lovett begins by noting that the core deficit in most children who are reading disabled is poor phonological awareness. In addition she notes two other deficits that characterize this group: a difficulty in rapidly naming visually presented material even when the names are known and a difficulty in strategy selection and implementation, particularly when different strategies must occur in rapid succession. She describes a large-scale remediation study in which the performance of a control group was compared to two dyslexic treatment groups. One treatment was aimed at phonological awareness via basic word segmentation and sound blending skills. The other emphasized the acquisition, implementation, and monitoring of effective word identification strategies, including identification by analogy, trying different vowel pronunciations, looking for familiar parts or embedded words, and stripping off suffixes and prefixes. Both treatments were significantly better than receiving attention with no formal reading remediation. Moreover, the improvements were not confined to the training materials; significant transfer to new items occurred. As might be expected, the group given phonological awareness training was much improved on phonological processing skills and showed improvements on nonword reading and reading untrained regular words. In contrast, the "strategy" training transferred both to regular and exception words, but not to nonwords. It appears likely that the choice of remediation strategy should depend on the nature of the performance deficit shown by the dyslexic reader (phonological versus surface) and that perhaps with some disabled readers using a combination of both methods would be most fruitful.

To what degree does heredity versus environment contribute to reading skill and disability? In Chapter 5, Olson and colleagues compare reading by identical and fraternal twins using sophisticated regression tools to answer these fascinating and important questions. Phonological coding and orthographic coding (which are correlated with each other) each show significant heritability and a smaller influence of environment. Olson et al. demonstrate independent genetic contributions to phonological coding and orthographic coding. By separating the twins into subgroups on the basis of an IQ-derived score, it was also demonstrated that heritability of word recognition deficits is higher for individuals with a large discrepancy between IQ and reading ability. Whereas, environmental factors such as the frequency of printed words contributed much greater variance to the reading of the so-called "garden variety" poor readers who have a small discrepancy between their IQ and reading ability. In light of the remediation data of Tallal and Merzenich described above, it would be a logical next step for twin studies such as these to include measures of temporal processing.

Finally Olson et al. point to recent DNA analyses that suggest a significant linkage among reading, phonological, and orthographic coding and genes on the short arm of chromosome 6. Further exploration of the genetic bases of dyslexia will provide a valuable tool for clinicians and scientists alike. Olson et al. caution the reader, however, that knowing there is a genetic basis to dyslexia should not discourage attempts at remediation.

Acquired Dyslexia

The rationale behind cognitive neuropsychology is that an accurate characterization of how a system malfunctions can provide insight into how it functions when intact. Reciprocally, a more complete knowledge of the functioning of an intact system can guide researchers and clinicians toward more efficacious techniques for rehabilitating the cognitive functions disturbed by damage to that system. This latter approach was followed by Behrmann (see chapter 6, this volume) when a therapy regime was constructed for a brain-damaged patient who could only read words on a letter-by-letter basis. With the knowledge that normal readers process letters at the beginning and ends of words before other letters, the patient was asked to report the first and last letters of words as they increased in length. This regime was adopted to encourage parallel processing of words in a more normal fashion. Although the patient showed improvement as a result of therapy in the time to read words overall, she, alas, continued to read words on a letter-by-letter basis.

In addition to guiding rehabilitation therapies, valid models of normal cognitive function ought to make predictions about the patterns of performance we can expect to see in neuropsychological patients. When these patterns are exhibited by patients, the model is confirmed. Failure to find patients who exhibit these patterns, however, does not necessarily disconfirm the model. They may be found in the future and researchers should be actively looking for them. The history of the discovery of conduction aphasia is a classic example of how a model of normal cognitive function, in this case language, successfully predicted patient performance.

Long before such patients had been described, some models of normal language predicted an impaired performance pattern in which spoken phrases could not be repeated despite the ability to comprehend these phrases.

Criticism has been leveled against cognitive neuropsychology as a means of testing models of normal cognition (e.g., Bay, 1953; Bender and Feldman, 1972). After all, apparent deficits of specific functions might be due to general impairments of intelligence or elementary visual function. Hence, it is important to rule out these possibilities with full clinical neurological and neuropsychological assessments. More recently, single neuropsychological case reports have been criticized on the grounds of problems with replicability and generalizability (see Caramazza, 1986; Shallice, 1981; 1988). Nevertheless, cognitive neuropsychology has weathered these storms and gained greater acceptance as evidenced by the number of new journals devoted to this pursuit. The marriage of functional imaging techniques that can pinpoint the location of cognitive functions in the brain and a cognitive neuropsychology that can determine the functional deficits associated with damage to those locations provides a powerful convergence. Combining the outcome of this convergence with a working computational neural network of the function under study can offer the what, where, and how of any cognitive function we care to study. As Demb, Poldrack and Gabrieli (chapter 9, this volume) note, patterns of performance from brain-damaged patients are critical in revealing which neuroanatomical loci implicated in a cognitive function by positron emission tomography (PET) and functional magnetic resonance imaging (fMRI), express that function or are merely reflecting a correlated activity. Neuroimaging methods will reveal areas of the brain that are active during a particular mental function whether or not that activation is necessary for the execution of that function. Therefore, areas that "light up" but which, when damaged, do not interfere with performance are likely involved in correlated activity. In contrast when damage to a brain region, that is active during performance of a function interferes with that function, then we can be confident that the brain region is part of the neural substrate necessary for that function. Thus evidence from neuroimaging and neuropsychology, when considered together, provide a more complete account than either can when considered alone.

Much consistency has been found between what we know about normal reading and what we know about brain-damaged reading. Notably, the independence of orthography, semantics, and phonology has been confirmed with both populations. Both brain-damaged and normal reading performance have also supported a third route to reading aloud that supplements the well-established semantic and rule-based routes (see Besner, chapter 13, this volume; Schwartz, Saffran, and Marin, 1980). Progress can also follow from inconsistencies. When results from brain-damaged reading are inconsistent with extant models of normal reading, we are forced to reconsider the assumptions underlying these models and amend them in ways that satisfy the constraints imposed by both normal and brain-damaged functioning. Indeed, the history of the third route to reading aloud is one in which brain-damaged patient performance (i.e., a patient who could read aloud an irregularly pronounced word that she could not comprehend, Schwartz et al., 1980) predicted a third route that was only later confirmed with normal readers (Buchanan and Besner, 1993).

Perhaps cognitive neuropsychology's biggest contribution is its ability to show functional dissociations. Many dissociations between component processes are more pronounced with brain-damaged performance than with normal performance. One reason for this may be the existence of emergent cognitive functions (Farah, 1994). As Marr (1976) noted, any large system should be split into subparts that are as computationally independent as possible. This design avoids the problem of a change, such as brain damage, having consequences in many places. Instead, a modular system can sustain damage to a restricted subsystem. This has been a strong argument for modularity for years. Farah (1994) has challenged this doctrine, however, in asking, what if some cognitive functions do rely on a completely intact system? Surely, as Marr suggested, these functions would be particularly susceptible to the effects of brain damage. Farah has suggested that these cognitive functions emerge from the system in toto and as such are not localizable. Farah, O'Reilly, and Vecera (1993) showed that explicit memory, or at least explicit memory for faces, may be such a vulnerable, emergent function. Finally, in chapter 8, Farah postulates yet another such emergent function; one that underlies letter identification.

In fact, explicit knowledge itself may be a function that emerges from a larger, intact memory system. Brain-damaged individuals frequently demonstrate performance of functions implicitly in the absence of explicit performance. Under the same conditions, normal subjects demonstrate these functions both explicitly and implicitly. This pattern might tempt us to postulate a separate explicit memory component. An alternative interpretation is that explicit memories emerge from an intact general memory system that underlies both implicit and explicit memory. As an emergent property or function, explicit memory may be particularly susceptible to damage to any part of the general memory system. A clear example of the apparent dissociation between implicit and explicit memory in individuals with reading impairments due to brain damage is described in chapter 7 by Buchanan, Hildebrandt, and MacKinnon. They show that deep dyslexic readers can implicitly process the phonology of words by a route thought to be damaged on the basis of their impaired explicit phonological performance.

Two broad classes of brain-damaged reading can be distinguished: the so-called peripheral dyslexias such as letter-by-letter reading, attentional dyslexia, and neglect dyslexia and the so-called central dyslexias such as phonological, surface, and deep dyslexia. As such, the chapters in this section of the book address a representative peripheral dyslexia: letter-by-letter reading (Farah and Behrmann) and a representative central dyslexia: deep dyslexia (Buchanan et al.).

Deep dyslexia holds a special place in the history of the cognitive neuropsychology of reading as the first well-studied disorder (Coltheart, Patterson, and Marshall, 1980). Three hypotheses have been presented to account for this syndrome: (1) reading with the right hemisphere (Coltheart et al., 1987), (2) reading with a normal isolated semantic route, and (3) reading with a severely damaged rule-based route and damage to at least one of three sites in the semantic route (Shallice, 1988). All three hypotheses assume damaged phonology. Based on their demonstration of intact implicit phonological processing in these patients, Buchanan et al. suggest a new hypothesis: reading with a damaged phonological selection mechanism.

Both Behrmann and Farah attempt to determine the damaged mechanism responsible for letter-by-letter reading. In so doing, they come to the same conclusion: letter-by-letter readers have a general visual deficit for the rapid identification of multiple forms that manifests most acutely with orthographic material. Using a self-organizing, neural network model, Farah accounts for the sensitivity of this deficit to letter processing based on the connectedness of letters to each other within an emergent computational "letter space." This space is presumably selectively susceptible to damage. Within this space, abstract letter identities may also be represented and so damage to them may also contribute to letter-by-letter reading via the same mechanism responsible for the defect in rapid identification of multiple forms. Since this orthographic space is subsumed within an area of the brain that is specialized for the representation of all types of multiple shapes, some degree of impairment with nonorthographic material is predicted and has been found by both Behrmann (Behrmann, Plaut, and Nelson, 1998; Sekuler and Behrmann, 1996) and Farah (Farah and Wallace, 1991).

A plethora of theories have been postulated to account for letter-by-letter reading. Indeed, there are almost as many theories as patients studied. So we must caution that several mechanisms may contribute to each of the types of reading disorders we study. Furthermore, within this individual differences theme, it has become apparent that the same patient may use different reading strategies, sometimes parallel and sometimes piecemeal, depending on the task (see Carr, chapter 14, this volume). Given these caveats, it is encouraging that Behrmann and Farah have come to similar conclusions regarding letter-by-letter reading, despite studying different patients who performed different tasks.

The study of individual differences is itself a powerful methodology to help converge on a model of normal reading. Variation in the performance of normal adult and children's reading ought to reflect the extreme forms of individual differences in reading performance demonstrated by brain-damaged readers (see Carr, chapter 14). Strong support for this hypothesis has come from developmental studies of normal children who show reading pattern subtypes that parallel the reading disorders seen as a result of brain-damage (Castles and Coltheart, 1993).

Brain Imaging of Reading Subprocesses

Cognitive neuroscience is currently one of the hottest areas in science and this is primarily due to new technologies that allow us to visualize the anatomy of the brain and more importantly the neuroanatomical structures activated during specific mental functions (see Posner and Raichle, 1994). Not long ago, brain structures could only be viewed from the kind of brain slices seen in gross anatomy class. With the advent of computerized axial tomography (CAT) scans, nuclei can be distinguished from neural pathways with x-ray technology and the entire brain can be reconstructed as many "slices" or views stacked upon each other. Better resolution and less patient risk was achieved with magnetic resonance imaging (MRI). It was with positron emission tomography (PET) scans or single-photon emission computed tomograpahy (SPECT), however, that we first glimpsed the interaction between mental function and neuranatomy. More recently, fMRI provides low-risk, functional localization, and high-resolution structural information. Both PET and fMRI provide functional localization information based on the fact that areas of the brain that are active during task performance show increased blood flow.

Equally important to information about the location of mental processes is information about the time course of mental operations during the performance of a task (Posner, 1978). Task analyses in cognitive psychology carve a performance into a sequence of processes. How can we confirm the validity of these sequences, know how long each process takes and locate the brain systems responsible for each process? Event related potentials or recordings of electrical (ERPs) or magneto-encephalography (MEG) activity from the scalp of the task performer have proven invaluable in this enterprise. This technology provides more accurate timing information than PET or fMRI because changes in electrical activity reflect brain function in real time, whereas the changes in blood flow detected via PET and fMRI happen seconds later. Yet recordings of electrical and magnetic activity are not as accurate at localizing brain sites that are the sources of this activity. Ideally, we want the best information about both the time course and the brain areas involved in each mental process. The joint consideration of data from electromagnetic recording of brain activity (ERP or MEG) with that from PET or fMRI holds great promise (Heinze et al., 1994; Liu, Belliveau, and Dale, 1998) for achieving this ideal.

Neuroimaging studies are particularly important in the exploration of exclusively human mental activities such as reading. Clearly, no animal models of these functions can be obtained. Hence, we lack the brain localization and timing information that are available for the study of other mental operations, such as object recognition and attention, from single brain cell recordings in awake monkeys. Both Demb et al. and Posner and McCandliss cautiously guide us through the current problems and successes in using PET, fMRI, and ERPs in the study of reading.

Demb et al. focus on localization information gained from fMRI and PET studies as it relates to the primary mental components involved in reading: orthography, semantics, and phonology. As an earlier process in the task of reading, it is not surprising that orthographic tasks such as passively viewing words versus nonwords, activate early visual processing centers such as left-medial extrastriate cortex and left-lateral temporal cortex. Phonological tasks such as passively listening to speech versus noise bursts appear to converge on brain centers related to auditory such as posterior temporal and superior temporal cortices. Motor centers such as the fronto-orbital and premotor areas are also activated. Finally, semantic tasks such as the generation of words activate more frontal areas such as left prefrontal and the anterior cingulate. In an attempt to isolate the parts of the brain that characterize developmental dyslexia, they suggest that left perisylvian activity may be abnormal when elicited by phonological tasks, while left-hemisphere regions involved in semantics may be normal.

Posner and McCandliss (chapter 10, this volume) focus on orthography and semantics. Many areas active during fMRI and PET are also active during ERP when tasks of orthography and semantics are employed. In particular, support for a word-form system located in the left posterior cortex that is active within 150 ms of the presentation of a word was found. Posner and McCandliss describe three other aspects of reading: priming, practice, and acquisition. They conclude that priming takes less than 100 ms, and so it is early, bottom-up, automatic, and relies on posterior cortical regions. Effects of repetition priming are relatively posterior while semantic priming effects are relatively more anterior. During the acquisition of the reading skill, children's ERP components are larger and slower than those in adult, skilled readers.

We believe that the combined use of fMRI and high-density ERP recordings will lead to major advances in cognitive neuroscience. By collecting precise spatial data using fMRI and precise temporal information using ERPs during the same tasks, we anticipate that scientists will be able to generate data that show how different functional modules in the brain are orchestrated to perform a task. Many interesting questions about the activation of different codes during reading, about the nature of dyslexic reading, about the mechanisms of reading acquisition, and reading remediation will be illuminated by the convergence of these two imaging techniques.

Computational Modeling of Reading, Dyslexia and Remediation

Understanding is captured in a theory, and a good theory will account for a wide body of empirical relationships. In our effort to develop an understanding of reading we might ask, what kind of theoretical framework should we use to construct our theory? Should we stick with information processing models of reading and word recognition, like those of LaBerge and Samuels (1974) and Morton (1968, 1969), that are characterized by localist representations? Or should we abandon these to artificial neural network (ANN) models, like those of Seidenberg and McClelland (1989), where the emphasis is upon parallel distributed processing (PDP)? The answer should be decided by the ability of the two classes of theory to reflect and explain reading behavior: its development, breakdown, and remediation.

In this section, computational models of reading based on a neural network architecture are highlighted. Such models have tremendous appeal (but see Broadbent, 1985; Massaro, 1990), in part because they are cast in terms of neuron-like units and hence hold the promise of explanation at a conceptual level while reflecting how the computations might be implemented in the brain. As will be seen, we can learn as much from their failures to simulate a wide range of reading behaviors as from their successes.

Plaut begins by describing different views of how word recognition proceeds in a nonsystematic domain (nontransparent), emphasizing the contrast between a distributed connectionist framework and dual-route theories: "...the essence of dual-route theory is not that it has two pathways from print to sound...rather, it is the claim that the mechanism that processes nonwords is functionally distinct from, and operates according to different principles than, the mechanism that processes exception words." The distributed connectionist approach of Plaut (and others) rejects this dual-route view. Three core concepts of the distributed connectionist framework are introduced: distributed representation, structure-sensitive learning, and interactivity, and then this framework is applied to normal reading, acquired dyslexia, and remediation.

In a PDP model with orthographic input, phonological output and intermediary semantic units, reading aloud (activation of the correct phonological output units) can proceed via direct connections between orthographic and phonological units (as in the original Seidenberg and McClelland model) or via semantic mediation. After training this model, a surface dyslexic pattern is apparent following damage to the semantic units. Interestingly, there is a kind of tradeoff in training, such that, if one pathway contributes more to learning then there is less pressure for the other to learn. This opens the door to the possibility of premorbid individual differences in reading style (Castles and Coltheart, 1993) which, in the model's behavior are seen as "individual differences" in the effect of otherwise equivalent "lesions." The notion of premorbid differences in reading holds tremendous potential for understanding the dramatic differences in reading breakdown following apparently similar lesions. Although this is equally true whether the premorbid differences are conceptualized within a localist or a distributed architecture, Plaut has provided a compellingly simple demonstration of the way it might occur within a distributed architecture.

He then moves on to deep and phonological dyslexia, where extensions to the seminal work of Hinton and Shallice are presented. Normal reading and reading by the model are both better for concrete than abstract words (in the model, because concrete words were assigned more semantic features). One important finding here is that damaging connections that implement attractors at the semantic level produces better reading of abstract than concrete words (an unusual pattern that has been reported only once in the literature). Plaut suggests that this finding demonstrates that the typical implication of double dissociations (separate modules) is not necessarily warranted, because here the double dissociation is obtained by damaging different parts of the same distributed network. Although this does appear to challenge the use of double dissociations as a marker for independent modules, a less theoretically stringent and perhaps more typical conclusion—that there are different parts of a system with different functional roles—is still warranted.

Besner (chapter 13, this volume) defends the notion of multiple and distinct routines in word recognition by showing how the three-route model succeeds and PDP models fail. First he discusses the evolution of the PDP framework from Seidenberg and McClelland's single route PDP into the dual-route PDP model of Plaut et al. (1996). He notes how this model deals with the criticisms of the previous model, and he claims that its proponents believe it is a model of what humans do when they read (not merely an existence proof that they might read this way).

Besner then asks, how well do the different models predict the time to name letter strings from human readers? Neither the Seidenberg and McClelland (1989) nor the Plaut et al. (1996) models account for more than about 3% of the variance in human naming times. Moreover, substantial increases in variance accounted for can be obtained by entering a second step: word frequency, length, and number of neighbors. This is damaging to the extant PDP models because these variables are supposed to be represented in the network after learning. Besner notes that a similar finding has been recently reported by Spieler and Balota (1997). In comparison, naming times obtained from the three-route model accounted for 13% of the variance, and adding the variables discussed above in a second step only increased the variance accounted for by about 3%. Clearly, however successful PDP models are in accounting for the global influence of certain manipulations upon word recognition, they must do better at the level of accounting for the relative difficulty of individual pronunciations. In the end, Besner is not disputing the fruitfulness of PDP modeling. In his view, a satisfactory model of reading will need to incorporate three different routes, whether distributed or localist representations are used. This is clearly different from Plaut's view.

To model context effects in a distributed memory system, Masson (chapter 12, this volume) implements a three-level (orthographic, phonological, semantic), small-scale, Hopfield network in which connection weights are modified following the Hebb rule. He then shows how this model naturally accommodates some findings in the literature and has difficulty with others. For example, localist models (spreading activation) predict that the onset of priming and asymptotic priming should be delayed for weakly related items, when in fact the evidence shows there is no effect on timing, only the amount of priming. In contrast, these aspects of the time course of priming are accounted for naturally in the model. Masson also shows that his model, which does not include any top-down influences from semantics or phonology onto the orthographic input layer, matches data from studies of human performance in which context, in the form of semantic priming, improves signal detectability (d') in lexical decision and other tasks. This finding directly challenges Farah's (1989) claim that d' measures reflect perceptual processing whereas effects due to attentional and semantic processing will be reflected in measures of bias. Because Masson emphasizes tasks for which activation in the phonological and semantic systems may contribute to the decision, the importance of his simulations for the claim that there is a top-down influence from, say semantics, onto low-level perceptual representations is muted. Semantic priming studies using a task in which high level representations can make no direct contribution (see Christie and Klein, 1995, 1996) would seem to be required here. Another possibility would be to examine early components of the ERP as a function of prime relatedness.

Masson ends with a very useful discussion of the strengths and weakness of

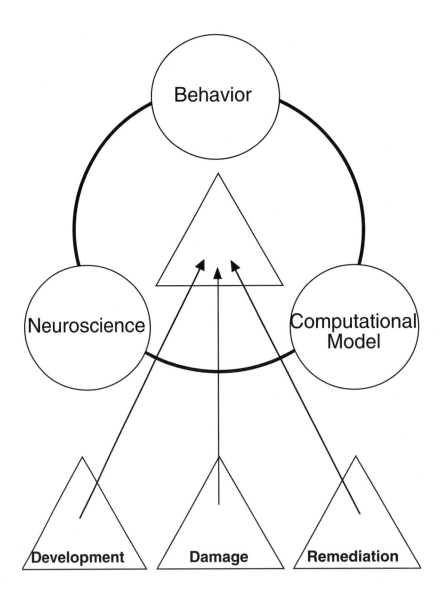

Figure I.2 A strategy for interdisciplinary research and converging methodologies (adapted from Klein, 1996).

distributed memory models in general, including the one implemented in his chapter. For example, noting that task performance can be mediated by activation from different subsystems and even different levels within a system, Masson, like Besner, raises the issue of flexibility in processing. This point is reminiscent of a prediction made by Broadbent (best known for the cognitive "hardware" implicit in his filter theory) concerning the importance of cognitive "software" (the effects of task variables and individual differences in strategy selection). "In the long run, psychology will, like computer science, become an ever-expanding exploration of the merits and disadvantages of alternative cognitive strategies." (1980, p. 69).

Converging Methodologies

The interdisciplinary research strategy for linking brain and behavior that we advocate in this book is illustrated in figure I.2. The outer circular pathway represents two-way links between behavioral evidence, neuroscientific evidence, and a computationally explicit theoretical framework (e.g., artificial neural network). Evidence from a variety of domains can be used to improve, test, and constrain our understanding of how a cognitive function like reading is performed by the brain. Normal performance, development, problems in the acquisition of reading, performance following brain damage, remediation, and genetic analysis have been emphasized in this book. But this is not an exclusive list; other approaches such as an effort to understand individual differences in reading ability will also be valuable. Let us take brain damage as an example: performance of a computational model of reading following "lesions" to it should mirror performance of people following accidental damage to the brain. Moreover, to the extent a model of reading is accurate, the model's response to remedial training following damage should predict or mimic the response to remediation of individuals with real damage (see Plaut). Chapter 14 of the book, by Tom Carr, emphasizes such integrative themes and points toward exciting interdisciplinary research in which the methods illustrated in the preceding chapters are combined.

References

Bay, E. (1953). Disturbances of visual perception and their examination. *Brain, 76,* 515–530.

Behrmann, M., Plaut, D.C., and Nelson, J. (1998). A literature review and new data supporting an interactive account of letter-by-letter reading. *Cognitive Neuropsychology, 15,* 7–51.

Bender, M.B., and Feldman, M. (1972). The so–called visual agnosias. *Brain, 95,* 173–186.

Bradley, L., and Bryant, P.E. (1983). Categorizing sounds and learning to read: A causal connection. *Nature, 301,* 419–421.

Boder, E. (1971). Developmental dyslexia: Prevailing diagnostic concepts and a new diagnostic approach. In H. Myklebust (ed.) *Progress in Learning Disabilities* (vol 2, pp. 293–321). New York: Grune and Stratton.

Breitmeyer, B.G. (1989). A visually based deficit in specific reading disability. *The Irish Journal of Psychology, 10,* 534–541.

Broadbent, D.E. (1985). A question of levels: Comment on McClelland and Rumelhart. *Journal of Experimental Psychology: General, 114,* 189–192.

Buchanan, L., and Besner, D. (1993). Reading aloud: Evidence for the use of a whole word nonsemantic pathway. *Canadian Journal of Experimental Psychology, 47,* 133–152.

Caramazza, A. (1986). On drawing inferences about the structure of normal cognitive systems from the analysis of patterns of impaired performance: The case for single-patient studies. *Brain and Cognition, 5,* 41–66.

Castles, A., and Coltheart, M. (1993). Varieties of developmental dyslexia. *Cognition, 47,* 149–180.

Christie, J. and Klein, R.M., (1995). Familiarity and attention: Does what we know affect what we notice? *Memory and Cognition, 23,* 547–550.

Christie, J. and Klein, R.M., (1996). Assessing the evidence for novel popout. *Journal of Experimental Psychology: General, 125,* 201–207.

Coltheart, M., Patterson, K.E., and Marshall, J.C. (1987). Deep dyslexia since 1980. In M. Coltheart, K.E. Patterson, and J.C. Marshall (eds.), *Deep Dyslexia* (pp. 381–406). London: Routledge and Kegan Paul.

Ellis, A.W. (1984). *Reading, Writing and Dyslexia: A Cognitive Analysis.* Hillsdale, NJ: Lawrence Erlbaum Associates.

Farah, M.J. (1989). Semantic and perceptual priming: How similar are the underlying mechanisms? *Journal of Experimental Psychology: Human Perception and Performance, 15,* 188–194.

Farah, M.J. (1994). Neuropsychological inference with an interactive brain: A critique of the "locality" assumption. *Behavioral and Brain Sciences, 17,* 43–104.

Farah, M.J., O'Reilly, R.C., and Vecera, S.P. (1993). Dissociated overt and covert recognition as an emergent property of a lesioned neural network. *Psychological Review, 100,* 571–588.

Farah, M.J., and Wallace, M.A. (1991). Pure alexia as a visual impairment: A reconsideration. *Cognitive Neuropsychology, 8,* 313–334.

Farmer, M.E. and Klein, R.M. (1995). The evidence for a temporal processing deficit linked to dyslexia: A review. *Psychonomic Bulletin and Review, 2,* 460–493.

Fodor, J. (1983). *The Modularity of Mind.* Cambridge, Mass.: MIT Press.

Frith, U. (1985). Beneath the surface of developmental dyslexia. In K. Patterson, M.

Coltheart and J. Marshall (eds.) *Surface Dyslexia.* (pp. 301–330). Cambridge: Academic Press.

Hebb, D.O. (1949). *The Organization of Behavior: A Neuropsychological Theory.* New York: Wiley.

Heinze, H.J., Mangun, G.R., Burchert, W., Hinrichs, H., Scholz, M., Munte, T.E., Gos, A., Scherg, M., Johannes, S., Hundeshagen, H., Gazzaniga, M.S., and Hillyard, S.A. (1994). Combined spatial and temporal imaging of brain activity during visual selective attention in humans. *Nature, 372,* 543–546.

Huey, E.B. (1908). *The Psychology and Pedagogy of Reading.* New York: Macmillan.

Klein, R.M. (1996). Attention: Yesterday, today and tomorrow [review of Baddeley and Weiskrantz (eds.) *Attention: Perception, Selection, Awareness and Control: A tribute to Donald Broadbent* .London: Oxford U. Press] *American Journal of Psychology, 109,* 159–171.

LaBerge, D., and Samuels, S.J. (1974). Toward a theory of automatic information processing reading. *Cognitive Psychology, 6,* 297–328.

Liberman, I.Y., and Shankweiler, D. (1985). Phonology and the problem of learning to read. *Remedial and Special Education, 6,* 8–17.

Liu, A.K., Belliveau, J.W., and Dale, A.M. (1998). Spatiotemporal imaging of human brain activity using functional MRI constrained magnetoencephalography data: Monte Carlo simulations. *Proceedings of the National Academy of Sciences. USA, 95,* 8945–8950.

Lovegrove, W., Martin, F., and Slaghuis, W. (1986). A theoretical and experimental case for a visual deficit in specific reading disability. *Cognitive Neuropsychology, 3,* 225–267.

Marr, D. (1976). Early processing of visual information. *Philosophical Transactions of the Royal Society of London B, 275,* 483–524.

Massaro, D.W. (1990). Psychology of connectionism. *Behavioral and Brain Sciences, 13,* 403–406.

Merzenich, M.M., Jenkins, W.M., Johnston, P., Schreiner, C., Miller, S.L., and Tallal, P. (1996). Temporal processing deficits of language-learning impaired children ameliorated by training. *Science, 271,* 77–80.

Morton, J. (1968). Grammar and computation in language behaviour. In J.C. Catford (ed.), *Studies in Language and Language Behaviour.* Centre for Research in Language and Language Behavior. Progress report no. VI. Ann Arbor, MI.: University of Michigan.

Morton, J. (1969). Interaction of information in word recognition. *Psychological Review, 76,* 165–178.

Plaut, D.C., McClelland, J.L., Seidenberg, M.S., and Patterson, K.E. (1996). Understanding normal and impaired word reading: Computational principles in quasiregular domains. *Psychological Review, 103,* 56–115.

Posner, M.I. (1978). *Chronometric Explorations of Mind.* Hillsdale, NJ.: Lawrence Erlbaum Associates.

Posner, M.I. and Raichle, M.E. (1994). *Images of Mind.* New York: Scientific American Library.

Rayner, K., and Pollatsek, A. (1989). *The Psychology of Reading.* Englewood Cliffs, NJ: Prentice Hall.

Schwartz, M.F., Saffran, E.M., and Marin, O.S.M. (1980). Fractionating the reading process in dementia: Evidence for word specific print to sound associations. In M. Coltheart, K.E. Patterson, and J.C. Marshall (eds.), *Deep Dyslexia* (pp. 259–269). London: Routledge and Kegan Paul.

Seidenberg, M.S., and McClelland, J.L. (1989). A distributed, developmental model of word recognition and naming. *Psychological Review, 96,* 523–568.

Sekuler, E., and Behrmann, M. (1996). Perceptual cues in pure alexia. *Cognitive Neuropsychology, 13,* 941–974.

Shallice, T. (1981). Neurological impairment of cognitive processes. *British Medical Bulletin, 37,* 187–192.

Shallice, T. (1988). *From Neuropsychology To Mental Structure.* Cambridge: Cambridge University Press.

Stanovich, K.E., and Siegel, L.S. (1994). Phenotypic performance profile of children with reading disabilities: A regression–based test of the phonological-core variable-difference model. *Journal of Educational Psychology, 86,* 24–53.

Spieler, D.H., and Balota, D.A. (1997). Bring computational models of word naming down to the item level. *Psychological Science, 8,* 411–416.

Tallal, P., Miller, S.L., Bedi, G., Byma, G., Wang, X., Nagarajan, S.S., Schreiner, C., Jenkins, W.M., and Merzenich, M.M. (1996). Language comprehension in language-learning impaired children improved with acoustically modified speech. *Science, 271,* 81–84

Treiman, R., Mullennix, J., Bijeljac–Babic, R., and Richmond-Welty, E.D. (1995). The special role of rimes in the description, use and acquisition of English orthography. *Journal of Experimental Psychology: General, 124,* 107–136.

1
What Have We Learned about Eye Movements during Reading?

Keith Rayner

The use of eye movement data to study reading has a rich tradition within experimental psychology dating back to a classic book written by Huey (1908) entitled *The Psychology and Pedagogy of Reading*. Following an introductory chapter, Huey's second and third chapters dealt with eye movements and were titled "The work of the eye in reading" and "The extent of reading matter perceived during a reading pause." In the fourth and fifth chapters, Huey appealed on numerous occasions to eye movement data to differentiate among alternative accounts of word recognition. The work reported by Huey and his contemporaries (Dearborn, Dodge, Javal, and others) during this first era of eye movement research has formed the basis for much of what we know about the basic characteristics of eye movements during reading. Despite the fact that their work relied on relatively crude types of eye movement recording systems, most of their findings have stood the test of time.

Following the early research, eye movements in reading were intensively studied during a second era by Buswell (1922), Tinker (1958), and others. While a great deal of descriptive information was gathered about eye movements during reading by Buswell, Tinker, and their contemporaries, in retrospect their work does not appear as informative about basic cognitive and perceptual processes in reading as does the work from the first era. Perhaps the onset of the behaviorist revolution in the early 1900s contributed to research being more descriptive than analytical with respect to cognitive processes. Tinker, who wrote a number of review articles on eye movements in reading (see Tinker, 1936, 1946, 1958), concluded his final review in the *Psychological Bulletin* on the rather pessimistic note that almost everything that could be learned about reading from eye movements had been discovered. Perhaps that opinion was widely held, because between the late 1950s and the mid-1970s very little research on eye movements and reading was undertaken. Historically, it is also interesting to note that the first edition of the classic book *Experimental Psychology* by Woodworth (1938) contained an entire chapter on reading (with a large section devoted to eye movements) whereas in the second edition of the work (Woodworth and Schlosberg, 1954), the discussion of reading was relegated to a small section in a chapter on eye movements.

Beginning around 1975, a third era of eye movement research began in which a great deal has been learned about reading from eye movement data (see Rayner, 1978, 1998; Rayner and Pollatsek, 1987, 1989). This resurgence has been due to three factors. First, there have been improvements in eye movement recording systems, that have allowed measurements to be more accurate and more easily obtained. Second, eye movement recording systems are now routinely interfaced with computers so that large amounts of data can be collected and analyzed. In addition, computers have made it possible to do research using eye-contingent display changes (see below). And third, the development of more detailed theories of language processing has allowed researchers to use eye movement data for critical examinations of the cognitive processes underlying reading. Indeed, eye-movement data often become the final source in adjudicating among alternative empirical findings obtained via different methods typically used to infer something about the reading process (see Just and Carpenter, 1987; Rayner and Pollatsek, 1989).

In my view, we have learned a great deal about reading from eye-movement data. Indeed, it is my impression that we have learned as much about reading from eye-movement studies as from any other source of data. The vast array of studies dealing with word recognition are potentially quite informative concerning the reading process. Since words are presented in isolation in such studies, however, one is never really sure of the extent to which the results generalize to the more complex and dynamic process of reading. One can also raise questions about the generalizability of the findings from most of the tasks that have been devised to study various aspects of reading since there is almost always a mismatch between what subjects are asked to do in the task and what they do when they read. Eye movements, on the other hand, are a normal part of reading, so there are fewer concerns about the ecological validity of results obtained via examinations of eye movements.

There are four reasons why researchers have been very interested in eye movements during reading. First, there are a number of important questions about perceptual processes during reading that can best be examined via investigations using eye movements. For example, how much information do readers acquire during each eye fixation? What kind of information is integrated across eye movements? What controls where readers fixate? If we are to understand reading, we need to know the answers to questions such as these. Second, eye movements per se are an interesting topic of investigation. If we can understand eye movement control in reading, we will have learned something important about motor control processes. Third, eye movement data can be used to investigate cognitive processes in reading. Fixation times on words (and phrases) and the pattern of eye movements can be very informative in terms of inferring something about moment-to-moment comprehension processes. Fourth, eye movements may inform us about the difficulties encountered in reading by dyslexic readers. Each of these four issues will be discussed in turn in this chapter. Prior to discussing each of these issues, however, I will describe some basic facts about eye movements in reading.

Basic Facts about Eye Movements in Reading

When we read, our phenomenological impression is that our eyes move smoothly across the line of text. This impression is illusory, however, since we make a series of eye movements (*saccades*) separated by periods of time when the eyes are relatively still (*fixations*). The two eyes move pretty much in synchrony with each other across the line, but the progress is not continuous since the saccades are separated by fixations. Furthermore, no useful information is obtained during the saccades because vision is suppressed while the eyes are moving (Wolverton and Zola, 1983). The pattern of information extraction during reading is thus somewhat like seeing a slide show. We see a "slide" during a fixation, then there is a brief "off time" while the eyes move, and then a new slide of a different view of the page. The other way in which our subjective impression is illusory is that the eyes do not move forward in the text as relentlessly as we might think. While most saccades in reading move forward, about 10 to 15% of the time we move our eyes back in the text to look at material our eyes have already passed over (*regressions*).

We move our eyes so frequently during reading because of the acuity limitations of the visual system. A line of text falling on the retina of a reader can be divided into three regions. The foveal region, in the center of vision, extends 1 degree of visual angle (3 or 4 letter spaces for normal sized text held at a normal reading distance) to the left and right of fixation. The *parafoveal* region extends from the foveal region to about 5 degrees of visual angle from the fixation point. Beyond the parafoveal region, the remainder of the line consists of the *peripheral* region. Although acuity is very good in the center of vision, our ability to discriminate letters deteriorates very rapidly from the foveal region to the parafoveal and peripheral regions. To clearly see the letters and words we wish to process next, therefore, we move our eyes so as to place the fovea over the next unprocessed region of the text.

The average fixation duration in reading is 200 to 250 ms, the average saccade length is roughly 8 letter spaces, and about 10 to 15% of the time we make regressions back to read text that we looked at earlier (regressions are sometimes back to lines above where we are currently reading, but often they are to the immediately preceding word on the line we are currently on). It is important to note that these values for fixation duration, saccade length, and regression frequency are averages; if the eye movements of twenty skilled readers were recorded, the average fixation would be between 200 and 250 ms, the average saccade length would be about 8 letter spaces, and the average regression frequency would be around 10 to 15%. There is considerable between-subject variability, however, in these measures. Some readers' average fixation durations are around 200 ms, some around 250, and some around 300; some readers' average saccade length is 6 letter spaces, some 8, and some 10 (as well as 7 and 9); and some readers regress rather infrequently while others regress much more often. Reading rate is a combination of the average fixation time and the number of fixations (which is also reflected by the average saccade length), as well as the frequency of regressions. Readers with average fixations of 200 ms and average saccades of 10 letter spaces read at a faster rate than readers with average fixations of 300 ms and average saccades of 7 letter spaces. The more skilled the reader, the shorter the average fixation time, the longer the average saccade length, and the smaller percentage of regressions in comparison to less skilled readers.

While the variability in eye movement measures that exists among readers is quite interesting, the variability that exists within readers is even more interesting. That is, for a given reader, there is considerable variability in fixation duration and saccade length as fixation durations can range from under 100 ms to over 500 ms and saccade lengths can range from 1 letter space to over 15 letter spaces (though long saccades are typically movements following regressions to get the reader back to the original place in the text) within the same passage of text. It is now clear that much of the variability associated with these eye movement measures is due to the ease or difficulty that the reader has processing the text. In this vein, it is important to note that text difficulty has a powerful influence on eye movement measures: as the text gets more difficult, fixations get longer, saccades get shorter, and regressions increase.

There are two other important points to note with respect to fixation durations and saccade lengths. It has now become quite apparent that the measure *average fixation duration* is not very informative on questions about cognitive processes during reading. This measure is useful only as a global measure of processing and when eye fixations on specific target words are examined, more analytic measures are necessary (see Blanchard, 1985; Rayner, 1998; Rayner and Pollatsek, 1989). Thus, most current reports of eye movement data typically report measures such as (1) *first fixation duration* (Inhoff, 1984), which is the duration of the first fixation on a word, (2) *gaze duration* (Just and Carpenter, 1980), which is the sum of all fixations on a word before moving to another word, (3) *single fixation duration* (Rayner, Sereno, and Raney, 1996), which is the duration of fixations when only one fixation is made on a target word, and (4) *total fixation duration*, which is the sum of all fixations on a word (including regressions). When discussing saccade length, it is also clear that the appropriate metric is letter spaces (and not visual angle) since the distance the eyes move remains fairly constant despite variations in the number of letters falling within a degree of visual angle (Morrison and Rayner, 1981) as long as the size of the print is fairly normal.

In the next four sections, I will discuss research related to the four areas identified as being important reasons that researchers have been interested in eye movements during reading: (1) perceptual processes in reading, (2) eye-movement control, (3) eye movements and cognitive processes, and (4) eye movements and dyslexia.

Perceptual Processes in Reading

Two issues will be discussed in this section: (1) research dealing with the size of the effective visual field or perceptual span (the region from which readers obtain useful information during an eye fixation) in reading, and (2) research dealing with the type of information that is integrated across successive eye movements in reading.

The perceptual span.

How much useful information are we able to obtain on each eye fixation? This question has intrigued researchers interested in reading since the time of Huey (1908). Many experimental paradigms have been used to address this issue, but they all are either unlike normal reading or make overly simplistic assumptions (see Rayner, 1978 for discussion of these criticisms). A number of years ago, George McConkie and I developed the eye-contingent display change technique to determine how much useful information is acquired during eye fixations in normal reading. With this technique, readers' eye movements are monitored every millisecond via an accurate eye-tracking system that is interfaced with a computer, which in turn is interfaced with a display monitor (with a rapidly decaying phosphor) from which the reader reads. Changes in the text are made at precise times contingent on the location of the reader's eye.

The first type of eye-contingent display technique, the *moving window* paradigm (McConkie and Rayner, 1975), was developed to study the size of the effective visual field. With this technique, a portion of the text around the reader's fixation is available for processing on each fixation. Outside of this window area, however, the text is replaced by other letters or by xs (see figure 1.1). When an eye movement is made, the window moves with the eyes: wherever the reader looks, there is readable text within the window while outside of the window, the text is mutilated in some way. The rationale is that when the window is as large as the region from which a reader can normally obtain information, reading will not be different from when there is no window present.

A number of studies using the moving window paradigm have led to the conclusion that the span of effective vision for readers of English extends to about 14 to 15 letter spaces to the right of fixation (McConkie and Rayner, 1975; Rayner, 1986; Rayner and Bertera, 1979; Rayner, Inhoff, Morrison, Slowiaczek, and Bertera, 1981; Rayner, Well, Pollatsek, and Bertera, 1982). Similar results have been obtained with French (O'Regan, 1979) and Dutch readers (DenBuurman, Boersema, and Gerrisen, 1981). The span is asymmetric, however, in that information is obtained from the currently fixated word, but no more than 3 or 4 letter spaces to the left of fixation (McConkie and Rayner, 1976; Rayner, Well, and Pollatsek, 1980). For readers of Hebrew (which is read from right-to-left), the span is asymmetric in the opposite direction, so that it extends further to the left than to the right of fixation (Pollatsek, Bolozky, Well, and Rayner, 1981). Characteristics of the orthography also influence the size of the span in that more densely packed orthographies, like Chinese and Japanese, yield smaller spans (Ikeda and Saida, 1978; Inhoff and Liu, 1998; Osaka, 1992) than English; Hebrew, which is more densely packed than English also yields a smaller span (Pollatsek et al., 1981). Finally, reading ability affects the size of the span: beginning readers have a smaller span than skilled readers. The span extends to about 11 letter spaces to the right of fixation for children at the end of the first grade, but is asymmetric (Rayner, 1986). The span also appears to be somewhat smaller for dyslexic readers than normal readers (Rayner,

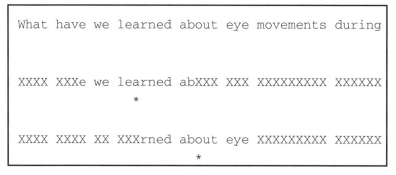

Figure 1.1 An example of the moving window paradigm. The first line shows a normal line of text. The next two lines show an example of two successive fixations with a window of 15 letter spaces. The fixation location is marked with an asterisk.

Murphy, Henderson, and Pollatsek, 1989). The smaller span is most likely due to the fact that beginning readers and dyslexic readers have so much difficulty processing the foveal word that they cannot effectively utilize parafoveal information (Inhoff, Pollatsek, Posner, and Rayner, 1989; Rayner, 1986).

Do readers acquire useful information from below the line they are reading? Research on this question has indicated that they do not (Inhoff and Briihl, 1991; Inhoff and Topolski, 1992; Pollatsek, Raney, LaGasse, and Rayner, 1993). It appears that information below the line of fixation can interfere with reading and that readers focus their attention on the fixated line so as to ignore information on other lines. This does not mean that readers are incapable of obtaining information below the line of text: if the task is changed from reading to visual search (using text, with the task to locate a specific target word), subjects can obtain information from below the fixated line (Pollatsek et al., 1993; Prinz, 1984).

Research utilizing the moving window paradigm has provided important information on the overall size of the span of effective vision. It has not been very diagnostic, however, of what type of information is obtained within the span. A second type of eye-contingent display change technique, the *boundary* paradigm (Rayner, 1975), has been much more diagnostic about the type of information that is acquired within the span. With this technique, a boundary location is specified in the computer and when the reader's eye movement crosses the invisible boundary, an initially displayed word or letter string is replaced by a target word (see figure 1.2). The amount of time that the reader looks at the target word (the first fixation duration and gaze duration) is then computed as a function of (1) the relationship between the initially displayed stimulus and the target word and (2) the

```
What have we studied about eye movements during
        *


What have we learned about eye movements during
            *
```

Figure 1.2 An example of the boundary paradigm. The first line shows text prior to a display change with fixation location marked by an asterisk. When the reader's eye movement crosses an invisible boundary (the letter e in we), an initially displayed word (studied) is replaced by the target word (learned) as shown in the second line. The change occurs during the saccade so that the reader does not see the change.

distance that the reader was from the target word prior to launching the saccade that crossed the boundary. Research using the boundary paradigm has demonstrated that the span of word identification is smaller than the span of effective vision: readers acquire information used to identify words from the fixated word and sometimes the word to the right of fixation. If three short words occur in succession, readers can identify all three words on the current fixation. In general, it appears that the span of word identification extends to about 8 letter spaces to the right of fixation (Henderson and Ferreira, 1990; Rayner and Pollatsek, 1987; Underwood and McConkie, 1985), though the span is somewhat variable depending on the length of the fixated word and the next word.

A third eye-contingent technique, the *moving mask* paradigm (which is a variation of the moving window paradigm), in which a mask moves with the eyes (see figure 1.3) has also yielded important information about the type of information obtained within the perceptual span region (Rayner and Bertera, 1979; Rayner, Morrison, Inhoff, Slowiaczek, and Bertera, 1981; Slowiaczek and Rayner, 1987). When the mask is larger than 7 letters, readers are unable to use foveal vision when reading (resulting in an artificial foveal scotoma). Results from these experiments have demonstrated that skilled readers find it very difficult, if not impossible, to read when foveal vision is masked. More interestingly, when the mask was 13 letters or larger (so that it extended 6 letter spaces to the right of fixation), readers made many errors as they tried to read; these errors suggest that readers obtain only partial information about words in parafoveal vision. The errors are also informative about the type of information that is acquired. For example, the sentence "The pretty

```
What have we learned about eye movements during


What have weXXXXXXXd about eye movements during
                  *


What have we learnedXXXXXXXeye movements during
                        *
```

Figure 1.3 An example of the foveal mask paradigm. The first line shows a normal line of text. The lower two lines show two successive fixations with a mask of 7 letter spaces. Fixation location is marked by an asterisk. As in the moving window paradigm, the mask moves in synchrony with the eyes.

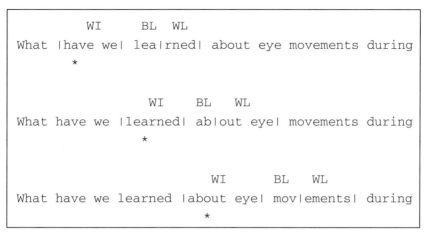

Figure 1.4 An example of information obtained within the perceptual span. Three fixations are shown with the type of information obtained indicated by the vertical lines. Fixation location is marked by an asterisk. WI = word identification region; BL = beginning letter information; WL = word length information.

bracelet attracted much attention" was read as "The priest brought much ammunition." It appears that the reader was obtaining information about the beginning and ending letters of words and trying to construct a meaningful representation on the basis of the information acquired.

In summary, research dealing with the size of the perceptual span has indicated that the area of effective vision is quite limited on each fixation. It appears that readers acquire information out to about 14 to 15 character spaces to the right of fixation. Furthermore, the span is asymmetric as readers obtain information from the currently fixated word, but no more than 3 to 4 letters to the left of fixation. The area from which words are identified is somewhat variable, but appears to extend no more than about 8 letter spaces to the right of fixation. Beyond the word identification area, readers obtain some letter information and word length information. Finally, little or no information is obtained below the fixated line. Figure 1.4 summarizes the types of information that are obtained within the perceptual span.

Integration of information across fixations

Results from experiments using the moving window and the boundary paradigms have demonstrated a preview benefit in which information obtained about a parafoveal word (the word to the right of the fixated word) on fixation n is combined with information on fixation $n+1$ to speed the identification of that word when it is subsequently fixated. In a number of different experiments using the boundary paradigm, orthographic, phonological, and semantic similarity between the initially displayed stimulus and the target word have been varied to determine the basis of the preview effect. The results of these experiments (Balota, Pollatsek, and Rayner, 1985; Briihl and Inhoff, 1995; Henderson and Ferreira, 1990; Kennison and Clifton, 1995; Lima, 1987; Rayner, 1975; Rayner, McConkie, and Ehrlich, 1978; Rayner, McConkie, and Zola, 1980) have indicated that the facilitation in processing is due to orthographic similarity: chest facilitates the processing of chart. The facilitation is not due to strictly visual similarity, however, since the case of letters can change from fixation to fixation (ChArT on fixation *n* would be cHaRt on fixation *n+1*) with little effect on reading behavior (McConkie and Zola, 1979; Rayner et al., 1980). Thus, the facilitation appears to be due to an abstract letter code associated with the first few letters of word *n+1* (Rayner, McConkie, and Zola, 1980; Rayner, Well, Pollatsek, and Bertera, 1982). Although morphological factors can influence fixation time on a word, they are not the source of the preview benefit (Briihl and Inhoff, 1995; Lima, 1987). A number of experiments by Inhoff and colleagues (Inhoff, 1989; 1990; Inhoff and Tousman, 1990) have demonstrated that some information is obtained from other parts of word *n+1* besides beginning letter information. It appears that the bulk of the preview effect, however, comes from the beginning letters. Inhoff's research also shows that the effect is not simply due to spatial proximity since there is facilitation from the beginning letters of words when readers are asked to read sentences from right-to-left, but with the letters within words printed from left-to-right.

In other boundary paradigm experiments, Pollatsek, Lesch, Morris, and Rayner (1992) and Henderson, Dixon, Petersen, Twilley, and Ferreira (1995) demonstrated that phonological codes are used to preserve information across saccades. For example, Pollatsek et al. found that a preview of *beach* facilitated the processing of *beech* (more than a preview of a visual control word like *bench*) and a preview of *chute* facilitated the processing of *shoot* in a boundary experiment. Finally, there is no facilitation due to semantic similarity since Rayner, Balota, and Pollatsek (1986) found that *song* as the initial preview stimulus did not facilitate the processing of *tune* during reading even though the semantically related pairs of words yielded facilitation under typical priming conditions.

In summary, research on the type of information integrated across fixations has yielded some important conclusions about perceptual processes during reading. Importantly, while readers obtain preview information about to-be-fixated words, the information is not semantic, but appears to consist of abstract letter information and phonological codes associated with the first few letters of the next word.

Eye Movement Control

What determines where we look next? What determines when we move our eyes? It appears that decisions about where to move next and about when to move the eyes are independent processes (Rayner and McConkie, 1976; Rayner and Pollatsek, 1981). Fixation locations within words in text are determined by low-level visual information obtained in parafoveal vision: the length of a yet-to-be fixated word in parafoveal vision strongly influences where a reader initially fixates in that word (Blanchard, Pollatsek, and Rayner, 1989; Hyönä, 1995; O'Regan, 1979, 1980, 1981; Rayner and Morris, 1992; Rayner, Fischer, and Pollatsek, 1998; Rayner et al., 1996) and perturbing word-boundary information (using the eye-contingent technique) also has a major effect on eye movement patterns since readers do not move their eyes as far when space information is not available or perturbed in some manner (Morris, Rayner, and Pollatsek, 1990; Pollatsek and Rayner, 1982; Rayner and Pollatsek, 1996).

One important finding is that where readers fixate in individual words is quite systematic: the initial fixation on a word tends to be about halfway between the beginning and middle of a word (McConkie, Kerr, Reddix, and Zola, 1988; McConkie, Kerr, Reddix, Zola, and Jacobs, 1989; O'Regan, 1981; Rayner, 1979; Rayner and Fischer, 1996; Rayner et al. 1996, 1998; Vitu, O'Regan, and Mittau, 1990; Vitu, O'Regan, Inhoff, and Topolski, 1995). This phenomenon was labeled the *preferred viewing location* by Rayner (1979). O'Regan and Levy-Schoen (1987) later made a distinction between the preferred viewing location and what O'Regan (1981) originally termed the *convenient viewing location* when describing a related phenomenon. The distinction that has been made is that the preferred viewing location is where the eyes land in the word, whereas the convenient viewing location or *optimal viewing position* (as O'Regan and colleagues now refer to it) is the location in the word where readers can obtain maximal information about the word. Thus, the optimal viewing position is a bit to the right of the preferred viewing location and closer to the center of the word. The reason for this could be due to some inherent property of the oculomotor system so that the eyes typically undershoot targets, or it could be due to the preview effect discussed above. Readers may often move their eyes to a position in a word that coincides with the point at which they need to get further information about the word given that they have already processed the words' first few letters on the prior fixation. Thus, if the first two letters of a seven-letter word were identified parafoveally on fixation n, the reader would move to the third or fourth letter of the word on fixation $n+1$ to obtain the maximal amount of information. The position the eye lands on need not strictly coincide with the point at which new information is needed because readers can acquire information to the left of fixation (Rayner et al., 1980; Binder, Pollatsek, and Rayner, 1999).

Whereas the landing position effect is quite robust, more controversial is the idea that some type of semantic preprocessing affects where the eyes land in words. Some research reported by Underwood and his colleagues (Everatt and Underwood, 1992; Hyönä, Niemi, and Underwood, 1989; Underwood, Bloomfield, and Clews, 1988; Underwood, Clews, and Everatt, 1990) has suggested that semantic information obtained from a parafoveal word influences where the reader's initial fixation lands in a word. They reported that the eyes move farther into word $n+1$ when the informative portion of the word is at the end rather than at the beginning of the word. In this situation, presumably the reader's attention would move from the currently fixated word to the next word and assess where the informative information is located. Neither Rayner and Morris (1992) nor Hyönä (1995), however, replicated the effect (and the effect was often either very small or not present in the experiments reported by Underwood and colleagues). At this point, it seems prudent to assume that semantic preprocessing of this sort does not occur.

The type of model of eye movement control consistent with most of the data is one in which parafoveally obtained word length information is the primary determinant of where to look next. Thus, the critical information obtained parafoveally is sublexical and presemantic. Lexical and semantic information are clearly involved, however, in eye movement control during reading. According to a model proposed by Morrison (1984) and subsequently modified by Rayner and Balota (1989) and Pollatsek and Rayner (1990), lexical access of the fixated word serves as the trigger for an eye movement. In this model, when the fixated word is identified, attention shifts to the next word, and a saccade follows in a time-locked fashion to a fixation location based on word-length cues. Words can occasionally be identified without direct fixation (they are identified parafoveally), however, and when they are, the fixation prior to skipping the word is inflated (Hogaboam, 1983; Pollatsek, Rayner, and Balota, 1986). In addition, factors such as contextual constraint can influence the process because more parafoveal preview is obtained from parafoveal words that are highly predictable (Balota et al., 1985). Finally, when the fixated word is difficult to process, little or no preview benefit is obtained because foveal processing takes precedence over parafoveal processing (Henderson and Ferreira, 1990; Inhoff, Pollatsek, Posner, and Rayner, 1989; Rayner, 1986).

An interesting fact about Morrison's model is that it was able to account for short fixations in text during reading. Given the reaction time of the eyes (see Rayner, Slowiaczek, Clifton, and Bertera, 1983), fixations under 140 ms should not occur in reading. Fixations as short as 50 ms, however, are occasionally noted during reading. Morrison's model accounted for these short fixations by assuming that sometimes the reader identifies word $n+1$ while still fixating on word n but is so far into the program of the next saccade that it cannot be aborted. In such instances, the program for a second saccade is initiated to word $n+2$ while the reader is still fixated on word n. Morrison's concept of parallel programming of saccades thus accounts for short fixations.

Whereas other models of eye movement control exist (see O'Regan, 1990), I subscribe to the view that the decision about where to fixate next is largely made on the basis of low-level visual cues obtained parafoveally, and the decision about when to move the eyes is based primarily on cognitive processes associated with comprehending the fixated word. The decision about where to fixate next, however, can be influenced by lexical processing if the parafoveal word to the right of fixation is identified and skipped by the ensuing saccade. As noted earlier, if two (or three) short words are in the center of fixation, they may all be identified on the current fixation. In such a situation, word length information about the next unidentified parafoveal word would be the basis for deciding where to fixate next. With respect to the decision about when to move the eyes, processes that are higher level than lexical access can also influence the decision of when to move (see Pollatsek and Rayner, 1990, for further discussion).

Recently, we (Rayner, Reichle, and Pollatsek, 1998; Reichle, Pollatsek, Fisher, and Rayner, 1998) developed a more formal model of eye movement control in reading that builds upon Morrison's model. Along the way it has been necessary to modify it, however, for two reasons. First, Morrison's model cannot account for certain findings in the literature. For example, the model cannot account for the "foveal difficulty" effect (Henderson and Ferreira, 1990; Rayner, 1986) discussed above: that less information is processed in the parafovea when the foveal material is difficult. Another limitation of Morrison's model is that it does not attempt to deal with the details of fixations within words. Second, in the process of trying to simulate eye-movement behavior it became apparent to us that Morrison's model is an oversimplification of the processes that are involved. Thus, while we have preserved the basic conception of Morrison's model and assumed that readers attend to only one word at a time and the signal to shift attention to the next word is lexical access of the attended word, we have also complicated the model in a number of ways. For example, we have postulated a familiarity check process, prior to lexical access, which is the signal to program an eye movement. The rationale for this process is that the reader might not want to wait until lexical access is complete before deciding to move the eyes because eye movement latencies are relatively long (150 to 175 ms), even for very simple stimuli (Rayner et al., 1983). Thus, using a prior signal that indicates that lexical access is imminent (with high probability) might make for more efficient reading. We envision this familiarity stage to be related to lexical access and its completion may be triggered when the level of total excitation in the lexicon exceeds a certain threshold.

In our modeling, both the lexical access stage (which controls attention shifts) and the familiarity check stage (which controls eye movement programing) are decreasing linear functions of the log frequency of a word in the language, and the difference between them is also a decreasing linear function of log frequency. The latter assumption allows us to account for the foveal difficulty effect: as the difference between the initiation of the eye-movement program and the attention shift increases, the reader spends more time processing the foveal word after the eye-movement program has been laid down and thus there is less preview benefit.

It is beyond the scope of this chapter to further discuss this work. A number of variations of the model (which we call the *E-Z reader* model) have been instantiated (see Reichle et al., 1998 for details) and we can account for both fixation times (first fixation duration, single fixation duration, and gaze duration) and the probability that a word will be skipped with very high accuracy; specifically, there is a very good fit between the predicted data and the observed data (collected from subjects actually reading). Our modeling work is at the beginning stages, but the endeavor has been successful because we can account for the observed data so well. But the work is also important because in the course of modeling the data we have observed effects that the model predicted that have not previously been reported. For example, the model predicted that when a word is skipped there should be an increase in both the fixation prior to the skip and after the skip. While the first effect had been previously reported, the second had not. Careful examination of the data, however, revealed that when readers skip a word, the duration of the following fixation is increased. My guess is that attempts to model eye movement behavior during reading will increase in the near future. The fact that we have so much data about eye movement control from empirical studies will undoubtedly aid this activity.

Eye Movements and Cognitive Processes

To what extent do eye movements reflect cognitive processes in reading? According to some views (Bouma and deVoogd, 1974; Kolers, 1976), there is a significant lag in processing (generally called the *eye-mind span*) such that information obtained on a given eye fixation is not available for higher level cognitive processing until the eyes have moved to another location. A considerable amount of research (see Just and Carpenter, 1980; Rayner, 1998; Rayner and Pollatsek, 1981; Rayner and Pollatsek, 1989, for further details), however, suggests that the link between the eye and the mind is fairly tight. The reason why the link is fairly tight is because readers typically have a preview of word *n+1* prior to fixating it (as discussed earlier in this chapter) and readers can extract information from text very quickly during each eye fixation. On the latter point, Rayner, Inhoff, Morrison, Slowiaczek, and Bertera (1981; see also Slowiaczek and Rayner, 1987; Ishida and Ikeda, 1989) presented a visual mask at various points after the onset of a fixation and found that if readers had 50 ms to process the text prior to the onset of the mask that reading proceeded quite normally. If the text was masked earlier than that, reading was disturbed. While readers may typically acquire the visual information needed for reading during the first 50 ms of a fixation, it is also clear that they can obtain information at other times during the fixation as needed (Blanchard, McConkie, Zola, and Wolverton, 1984). The fact that information needed for reading is obtained so early in a fixation, however, means that there is time left over during a fixation for cognitive processes to influence the fixation time (since the reader also programs where to move next in parallel with comprehending the fixated word).

Other research demonstrates more directly that the eye-mind span is quite tight. For example, effects due to eye-contingent display changes appear immediately on the fixation following a display change and are not delayed for a couple of fixations. It is also the case that when word length is controlled, low-frequency words yield longer fixation times than high frequency words (Altarriba, Kroll, Sholl, and Rayner, 1996; Just and Carpenter, 1980; Inhoff and Rayner, 1986; Raney and Rayner, 1995; Rayner and Duffy, 1986; Rayner and Fischer, 1996; Rayner and Raney, 1996; Rayner et al., 1996, 1998; Rayner, Sereno, Morris, Schmauder, and Clifton, 1989). Specifically, first fixation durations and single fixation durations are typically about 30 ms longer on low frequency words than on high frequency words, and gaze durations are typically about 80 ms longer. In addition, words that are highly constrained or predictable given the context are fixated for less time than words that are not constrained or predictable (Altarriba et al., 1996; Balota, Pollatsek, and Rayner, 1985; Ehrlich and Rayner, 1981; Morris, 1994; Rayner and Well, 1996; Schustack, Ehrlich, and Rayner, 1987; Zola, 1984). Specifically, gaze durations are typically about 30 ms shorter on highly constrained words than on unconstrained words. If there were an appreciable eye-mind lag, effects such as these would not show up on the current fixation, but would be delayed.

Using eye movements to infer cognitive processes

The general finding that the area of effective vision and the word identification span are small (so that readers typically identify only the fixated word) coupled with the conclusion that there is no appreciable eye-mind span has led to considerable optimism concerning the use of eye movement data to investigate cognitive processes during reading. Indeed, during the past few years, there has been a considerable amount of research using eye-movement data to investigate (1) how readers parse sentences containing temporary syntactic ambiguities (see Altmann, Garnham, and Dennis, 1992; Ferreira and Clifton, 1986; Ferreira and Henderson, 1990; Frazier and Rayner, 1982; Rayner, Carlson, and Frazier, 1983; Rayner, Garrod, and Perfetti, 1992; Trueswell, Tanenhaus, and Kello, 1993), (2) the processing of lexically ambiguous words (see Binder and Morris, 1995; Binder and Rayner, 1998; Dopkins, Morris, and Rayner, 1992; Duffy, Morris, and Rayner, 1988; Rayner and Duffy, 1986; Rayner and Frazier, 1989; Rayner, Pacht, and Duffy, 1994), (3) the processing of phonologically ambiguous words (see Daneman and Reingold, 1993; Daneman, Reingold, and Davidson, 1995; Folk and Morris, 1995; Rayner, Pollatsek, and Binder, 1998;) and (4) anaphora and inferencing during reading (see Duffy and Rayner, 1990; Ehrlich and Rayner, 1983; Garrod, Freudenthal, and Boyle, 1994; Garrod, O'Brien, Morris, and Rayner, 1990; O'Brien, Raney, Albrecht, and Rayner, 1997; O'Brien, Shank, Myers, and Rayner, 1988). These studies have yielded highly informative results (see Rayner and Sereno, 1994; and Rayner et al., 1989 for further discussion). The point is that eye movement data have revealed a great deal of important information about moment-to-moment cognitive processes during the reading process. Variations in how long readers look at certain target words or phrases in text have been shown to be due to the ease or difficulty associated with processing those words.

The study of eye movements during reading is important for what it can tell us about some basic perceptual processes during reading and for what it can tell us about eye movements per se during reading. As the data I reviewed earlier have indicated, a great deal of information has been learned about the perceptual span in reading, the type of information that is integrated across successive eye movements and eye-movement control. But, a great deal has also been learned about the reading process in general by examinations of eye movement data. Rather than summarizing all of this data (and because I have done so in other places, see Rayner and Sereno, 1994; Rayner et al., 1989, 1995), let me simply mention one test case.

The issue of how readers parse temporarily ambiguous sentences has attracted a great deal of recent attention. The earliest studies dealing with this topic relied on rather gross measures (such as total reading time). It is important for theoretical reasons (see Frazier and Rayner, 1982), however, to know exactly when the reader became aware of the ambiguity. While many researchers interested in this issue have used eye-movement data (because there is a great deal of precision available when eye movements are recorded), some investigators have relied on self-paced reading techniques to examine the issue. It has become increasingly apparent, however, that to have temporal precision and to know exactly when the reader made a regression (while reading a garden path sentence), or paused for a long time to resolve the ambiguity, that eye movement recording is necessary. Thus, eye-movement data have been the primary source of evidence for adjudicating between alternative theoretical views (see Rayner and Sereno, 1994).

One way then in which eye movements can be used to infer cognitive processes during reading involves recording readers' eye movements as they read text in which variables of interest are manipulated. Another way that eye movements can be used to infer cognitive processes involves the use of eye-contingent display change techniques. The research I reviewed previously here documents how eye-contingent techniques can be used to examine parafoveal word processing. Eye-contingent techniques, in particular the *fast priming* technique developed by Sereno and Rayner (1992), can also be used to examine the time course of foveal word processing. The fast priming paradigm is very much like the boundary paradigm described earlier (see figure 1.5) except that the initially displayed stimulus is a random string of letters. When the readers' eye movement crosses the boundary loca-

```
What have we rtsgelk about eye movements during
        *


What have we studied about eye movements during
              *


What have we learned about eye movements during
            *
```

Figure 1.5 An example of the fast priming paradigm. The first line shows text prior to a display change with fixation location marked by an asterisk. The target location is initially occupied by a random string of letters. When the reader's eye crosses an invisible boundary (the letter e in we), the random string of letters changes to a prime word (studied) which is presented for about 30-35 ms. The prime is then replaced by the target word (learned) which remains for the rest of the trial.

tion, the random string of letters (which is used to preclude any efficient preview of the target word) is replaced by a prime word that is presented for a brief duration. The prime word is then replaced by the target word for the remainder of the trial.

Using the fast priming technique, Sereno and Rayner (1992) demonstrated semantic priming effects when the prime was presented for about 30 to 35 ms. The technique has been used to examine how early in a fixation phonological codes are activated (Lee, Binder, Kim, Pollatsek, and Rayner, 1999; Rayner, Sereno, Lesch, and Pollatsek, 1995) and to examine the processing of lexically ambiguous words (Sereno, 1995). My guess is that this technique will prove very useful in examining other questions related to the time course of processing.

In summary, a great deal of research now shows that there is a rather tight link between eye fixations and cognitive processes. Given that the perceptual span is quite small and that the eye-mind span is quite tight, eye movement data can be used to study many important questions about on-line language processing.

Eye Movements and Dyslexia

What can eye movements tell us about developmental dyslexia? Are eye movements a contributing causative factor in developmental dyslexia? From a practical standpoint, if an eye movement control deficit were at the root of the dyslexic's problem, the disability could be diagnosed via simple oculomotor tests. In addition, perhaps dyslexics could be helped by training programs designed to improve their reading by focusing on eye movement control exercises. Related to this, it has often been assumed that skilled readers and dyslexic readers differ in that the former execute smooth, efficient eye movements whereas the latter have highly erratic and unpredictable eye movement patterns. The suggestion that good readers execute regular eye movement patterns, however, and that therefore poor readers can be trained to be better readers by teaching them to make smooth consistent eye movements is not supported by the data. As noted earlier, good readers are highly variable in both how long the fixation lasts and how far they move their eyes.

Although readers with some type of oculomotor disturbance such as saccade intrusion (Ciuffreda, Kenyon, and Stark, 1983) or congenital jerk nystagmus (Ciuffreda, 1979) have difficulty reading, most of the data currently available suggest that eye movements are a reflection of the processing activities associated with reading and not a cause of reading problems. It is well-known that developmental dyslexics' eye movements while reading are quantitatively different from those of normal readers (Rayner, 1978, 1985, 1998). In comparison to normal readers, dyslexic readers' average fixation durations are longer, their average saccade length is shorter, and the average number of regressions is much larger. But, such differences could be attributed to a number of different causal factors, including (1) difficulty processing the words in the text, (2) visual persistence from prior fixations (as suggested by Farmer and Klein, 1995; see below), or (3) faulty control of the saccadic eye movement system (as suggested by Pavlidis, 1981, 1985). The point is that we cannot tell merely by examining eye movements of dyslexic readers while they read.

On this last point, Pavlidis (1981) noted that any study based on reading experiments alone would be open to a number of interpretations, and he reasoned that if the cause of dyslexia is due to an attentional or sequential processing difficulty (manifesting itself in faulty eye movements), one would expect that such a disability should manifest itself not only in reading but in other tasks in which sequencing and eye movements are important. Thus, he conducted some studies (Pavlidis, 1981, 1985, 1991) in which he found that when dyslexic and normal readers were asked to sequentially fixate on targets that stepped across a display screen, the dyslexics had much more difficulty doing so than normal readers (particularly when the target moved from left-to-right). He concluded that erratic eye movements (moving from right-to-left when the task calls for movements from left-to-right) are characteristic of dyslexic readers.

Pavlidis' results are consistent with some case studies (Ciuffreda, Bahill, Kenyon, and Stark, 1976; Pirozzolo and Rayner, 1978; Zangwill and Blakemore, 1972) in which dyslexic readers have been described as having a tendency to move their eyes from right-to-left during reading. On the basis of Pavlidis' (1981) original report, however, a number of attempts were undertaken to confirm his findings. None of these studies (Black, Collins, DeRoach, and Zubrick, 1984; Brown, Haegerstrom-Portnoy, Adams, Yingling, Galin, Herron, and Marcus, 1983; Olson, Kliegl, and Davidson, 1983; Stanley, Smith, and Howell, 1983) were able to replicate Pavlidis' findings: there was no indication in any of these studies that dyslexic readers differed from normals in the frequency of regressions when moving their eyes from left-to-right in his task. Other studies (Adler-Grinberg and Stark, 1978; Eskenazi and Diamond, 1983; Stanley et al., 1983) have also failed to find differences between normal and dyslexic readers' eye movement patterns in a visual search task. Perhaps the easiest way to account for the discrepant findings between Pavlidis' research and the others is that his subject-selection process somehow resulted in a larger number of dyslexic readers with visual deficits in his sample than is typical of the population of dyslexics (Pollatsek, 1983; Rayner, 1985). Some of the studies that failed to replicate Pavlidis' findings did report that a few subjects yielded results like those reported by Pavlidis.

Another interesting proposal concerning eye movements and dyslexia was made by Farmer and Klein (1995) who suggested that dyslexics may have visual persistence from a prior fixation interfering with processing of the current fixation. This implies that dyslexic readers' eye fixations when reading text should be longer than those of normal readers and/or they should make more fixations than normal readers. As noted above, both are true of dyslexic readers, but the reason for this is not clear and could be due to a number of factors. When dyslexic readers are given age-appropriate reading material, their eye movement characteristics do not differ from normal readers of that age (Pirozzolo, 1979), whereas when normal readers are given text that is too difficult, their eye-movement characteristics look very much like those of dyslexic readers (Rayner, 1986). Furthermore, when dyslexic readers' eye movements during reading are compared to reading-age controls, their average fixation times and eye-movement characteristics do not differ (Hyönä and Olson, 1994, 1995). Finally, Hyönä and Olson found that fixation durations of dyslexics and normal readers did not differ in a visual search task. If visual persistence (or some other low-level visual factor) were the problem, one would expect dyslexics' eye-movement patterns to be different from normal readers regardless of the difficulty of the text. Thus, the most likely explanation for most dyslexic readers' longer fixation durations when reading is that they are having difficulty processing individual words.

Farmer and Klein (1995) also suggested that dyslexic readers may process less parafoveal information on each fixation than normal readers. On this issue, there are some relevant data using the eye-contingent moving window paradigm. Rayner, Murphy, Henderson, and Pollatsek (1989) compared the reading performance of dyslexic and normal readers. Although the dyslexic readers reached asymptote in reading rate with a two-word window (i.e., the fixated word and the word to the right of fixation were both available within the window) whereas the normal readers did not reach asymptote until the window was three words (i.e., the fixated word plus the next two words were available), the general pattern of the data was quite similar. The data thus suggest that the perceptual span for dyslexic readers might be a bit smaller than that of normal readers. The data do not necessarily mean, however, that there is a parafoveal processing deficit in dyslexic readers. When the fixated word is difficult to process, readers obtain less parafoveal information than when the fixated word is easy to process (Rayner, 1986; Henderson and Ferreira, 1990). In other words, processing difficulty associated with the fixated word shrinks the size of the perceptual span. Thus, while the perceptual span may be somewhat smaller for dyslexic readers than normal readers, it may not be because they process parafoveal information less effectively than normal readers but rather may be due to the difficulty they have processing the fixated word (see Rayner, Pollatsek, and Bilsky, 1995).

With respect to parafoveal processing, Geiger and Lettvin (1987) have reported a finding that appears opposite to the idea of Farmer and Klein (1995). Specifically, Geiger and Lettvin (1987) reported some experiments in which they found that dyslexic readers process parafoveal information more effectively than normal readers and suggested that the dyslexics' efficient parafoveal processing interferes with foveal processing, leading to their reading problem. Indeed, Geiger, Lettvin, and Fahle (1994) argued that dyslexic readers can markedly increase their reading ability by cutting a small window in an index card and then moving the card across the text reading the material inside the window. There is considerable controversy, however, concerning the basic result that dyslexic readers process parafoveal information more effectively than normal readers. Whereas Perry, Dember, Warm, and Sacks (1989) reported results consistent with Geiger and Lettvin, others (Goolkasian and King, 1990; Klein, Berry, Briand, D'Entremont, and Farmer, 1990; Slaghuis, Lovegrove, and Freestun, 1992) were unable to obtain consistent results. One dyslexic reader reported by Rayner et al. (1989) did show characteristics that were similar to those of Geiger and Lettvin's subjects: he could identify parafoveal words and letters better than normal readers. In addition, when reading with an eye-contingent moving window, he read better with a small window than with larger windows; all other normal and dyslexic readers tested had faster reading rates with large windows (three words) than with small windows (one word). Rayner et al. concluded that the dyslexic reader has a selective attention deficit that makes it difficult for him to focus attention on the fixated word; however, he is undoubtedly atypical of dyslexic readers.

A number of other claims have been made about the relationship between some aspect of eye movements and dyslexia. For example, in some studies (see Eden, Stein, Wood, and Wood, 1994) a high percentage of dyslexics have been found to have difficulty holding their eyes steady (as is necessary in reading). In other studies (Fischer, Biscaldi, and Otto, 1993; Fischer and Weber, 1990) a high percentage of dyslexics have been found to make more express saccades (short-latency eye movements) than do normal readers. At this point, it is too early to evaluate the reliability of these findings as systematic attempts to replicate them in other labs are either not widespread or undertaken at all. Given the controversy surrounding the findings of Pavlidis (1981) and Geiger and Lettvin (1987), however, it would seem appropriate to be quite cautious about accepting these findings.

In summary, quite a bit of attention has been devoted to the relationship between eye movements and dyslexia. From my point of view, it appears clear that there are many underlying factors contributing to dyslexia (see Farmer and Klein, 1995; Rayner and Pollatsek, 1989). But more relevant here, it seems that the most appropriate conclusion is that eye movements are not a cause of dyslexia but rather reflect the processing difficulties that dyslexic readers have processing text.

Conclusions

We have learned a great deal about the reading process by examining readers' eye movements. Indeed, my assertion is that we have learned as much about reading from studies of eye movements as from any other source of data. While many different techniques have been used to study the reading process, for the most part one has to question the extent to which results obtained from tasks that differ from normal silent reading are generalizable to the reading process. Eye movements, on the other hand, are a normal part of silent (and oral) reading. When eye movement data represent the dependent variable in a reading study, readers presumably read in the same manner as they normally do outside of the laboratory. Indeed, data collected by Tinker (1939) many years ago show quite clearly that reading rate and comprehension are the same when readers' eye movements are recorded in an eye-movement laboratory and when they read in a soft easy chair outside of the laboratory.

Eye movement data can be obtained in relatively unobtrusive ways and one need not rely on secondary tasks (which may lead to unusual processing strategies) nor make questionable generalizations from tasks (such as lexical decision, naming, categorization, and tachistoscopic identification) that may or may not resemble reading. Eye-movement data also provide for finer resolutions than can be obtained from more gross measures (such as reading time or question answering): specific effects can be localized at precise points in the text.

Here, I have sketched out some of the findings that have been obtained from studies of eye movements and reading. We have learned a lot about issues such as (1) the size of the effective visual field in reading, (2) what kind of information is integrated across fixations, (3) where readers fixate in words, and (4) eye movement control in reading. As important as the findings concerning these issues are, perhaps even more important is the fact that eye movement data are being used to successfully examine a number of issues related to cognitive and perceptual processes during reading. Since the size of the effective visual field is small and the eye-mind span is quite tight, it has become apparent that eye movement data can be used in many ways to examine a number of important issues concerning moment-to-moment processes in reading.

While there is therefore considerable optimism concerning the use of eye-movement data to study the reading process, I am considerably less optimistic about using eye-movement data to infer something important about developmental dyslexia. Eye-movement patterns (where readers look and how long they look at particular words) primarily reflect the processes associated with comprehending the fixated words. While dyslexic readers have longer fixations and more forward and regressive fixations, the eye movements per se are not the cause of the reading deficit. Rather, eye movements reflect the problems that dyslexic readers have comprehending text. To the extent that eye movements are used to infer processing difficulties of dyslexic readers (see Rayner et al, 1989), they are useful measures. But erratic eye movements in reading and nonreading situations do not appear to characterize most dyslexic readers. Finally, given that we now have a lot of data on the characteristics of eye movements during reading, it appears appropriate that more quantitative models of eye movements during reading should be developed. An attempt to do this is currently underway in my laboratory.

Acknowledgments

The author's research is supported by Grants HD17246 and HD26765 from the National Institute of Child Health and Human Development, by Grant DBS-9121375 from the National Science Foundation, and by a Research Scientist Award from the National Institute of Mental Health.

References

Adler–Grindberg, D., and Stark, L. (1978). Eye movements, scanpaths, and dyslexia. *American Journal of Optometry and Physiological Optics, 55,* 557–70.

Altarriba, J., Kroll, J.F., Sholl, A., and Rayner, K. (1996). The influence of lexical and conceptual constraints on reading mixed–language sentences: Evidence from eye fixations and naming times. *Memory and Cognition, 24,* 477–492.

Altmann, G.T.M., Garnham, A., and Dennis, Y. (1992). Avoiding the garden path: Eye movements in context. *Journal of Memory and Language, 31,* 685–712.

Balota, D.A., Pollatsek, A., and Rayner, K. (1985). The interaction of contextual constraints and parafoveal visual information in reading. *Cognitive Psychology, 17,* 364–390.

Binder, K.S., and Morris, R.K. (1995). Eye movements and lexical ambiguity resolution: Effects of prior encounter and discourse type. *Journal of Experimental Psychology: Learning, Memory, and Cognition, 21,* 1186–1196.

Binder, K.S., Pollatsek, A., and Rayner, K. (1999). Extraction of information to the left of the fixated word in reading. *Journal of Experimental Psychology: Human Perception and Performance, 25*, 1162–1172.

Binder, K.S., and Rayner, K. (1998). Contextual strength does not modulate the subordinate bias effect: Evidence from eye fixations and self–paced reading. *Psychonomic Bulletin and Review, 5*, 271–276.

Black, J.L., Collins, D.W.K., DeRoach, J.N., and Zubrick, S. (1984). A detailed study of sequential saccadic eye movements for normal and poor reading children. *Perceptual and Motor Skills, 59*, 423–434.

Blanchard, H.E. (1985). A comparison of some processing time measures based on eye movements. *Acta Psychologica, 58*, 1–15.

Blanchard, H.E., McConkie, G.W., Zola, D., and Wolverton, G.S. (1984). Time course of visual information utilization during fixations in reading. *Perception and Psychophysics, 10*, 75–89.

Blanchard, H.E., Pollatsek, A., and Rayner, K. (1989). The acquisition of parafoveal word information in reading. *Perception and Psychophysics, 46*, 85–94.

Bouma, H., and deVoogd, A.H. (1974). On the control of eye saccades in reading. *Vision Research, 14*, 273–284.

Briihl, D., and Inhoff, A.W. (1995). Integrating information across fixations in reading: The use of orthographic bodies and of exterior letters.*Journal of Experimental Psychology: Learning, Memory , and Cognition, 21*, 55–63.

Brown, B., Haegerstrom–Portnoy, G., Adams, A.J., Yingling, C.D., Galin, D., Herron, J., and Marcus, M. (1983). Predictive eye movements do not discriminate between dyslexic and control children. *Neuropsychologia, 21*, 121–128.

Buswell, G.T. (1922). *Fundamental Reading Habits: A Study of Their Development.* Chicago: Chicago University Press.

Ciuffreda, K.J. (1979). Jerk nystagmus: Some new findings. *American Journal of Optometry and Physiological Optics, 53*, 389–395.

Ciuffreda, K.J., Kenyon, R.W., and Stark, L. (1983). Saccadic intrusions contributing to reading difficulty: A case report. *American Journal of Optometry and Physiological Optics, 60*, 242–249.

Ciuffreda, K.J., Bahill, A.T., Kenyon, R.V., and Stark, L. (1976). Eye movements during reading: Case studies. *American Journal of Optometry and Physiological Optics, 53*, 389–395.

Daneman, M., and Reingold, E. (1993). What eye fixations tell us about phonological recoding during reading. *Canadian Journal of Experimental Psychology, 47*, 153–178.

Daneman, M., Reingold, E., and Davidson, M. (1995). Time course of phonological activation during reading: Evidence from eye fixations. *Journal of Experimental Psychology: Learning, Memory, and Cognition, 21*, 884–898.

DenBuurman, R., Boersema, T., and Gerrisen, J.F. (1981). Eye movements and the perceptual span in reading. *Reading Research Quarterly, 16*, 227–235.

Dopkins, S., Morris, R.K., and Rayner, K. (1992). Lexical ambiguity and eye fixations in reading: A test of competing models of lexical ambiguity resolution. *Journal of Memory and Language, 31*, 461–477.

Duffy, S.A., Morris, R.K., and Rayner, K. (1988). Lexical ambiguity and fixation times in reading. *Journal of Memory and Language, 27*, 429–446.

Duffy, S.A., and Rayner, K. (1990). Eye movements and anaphor resolution: Effects of antecedent typicality and distance. *Language and Speech, 33*, 103–119.

Eden, G.F., Stein, J.F., Wood, H.M., and Wood, F.B. (1994). Differences in eye movements and reading problems in dyslexic and normal children. *Vision Research, 34*, 1345–1358.

Ehrlich, K., and Rayner, K. (1983). Pronoun assignment and semantic integration during reading: Eye movements and immediacy of processing. *Journal of Verbal Learning and Verbal Behavior, 22*, 75–87.

Ehrlich, S.F., and Rayner, K. (1981). Contextual effects on word perception and eye movements during reading. *Journal of Verbal Learning and Verbal Behavior, 20*, 641–655

Eskenazi, D., and Diamond,S.P. (1983). Visual exploration of non–verbal material by dyslexic children. *Cortex, 19*, 353–370

Everatt, J., and Underwood, G. (1992). Parafoveal guidance and priming effects during reading: A special case of the mind being ahead of the eyes. *Consciousness and Cognition, 1*, 186–197.

Farmer, M.E., and Klein, R. (1995). The evidence for a temporal processing deficit linked to dyslexia: A review. *Psychonomic Bulletin and Review, 2*, 460–493.

Ferreira, F., and Clifton, C. (1986). The independence of syntactic processing. *Journal of Memory and Language, 25*, 75–87.

Ferreira, F., and Henderson, J.M. (1990). The use of verb information in syntactic parsing: A comparison of evidence from eye movements and word–by–word self–paced reading. *Journal of Experimental Psychology: Learning, Memory, and Cognition, 16*, 555–568.

Fischer, B., Biscaldi, M., and Otto, P. (1993). Saccadic eye movements of dyslexic adult subjects. *Neuropsychologia, 31*, 887–906.

Fischer, B., and Weber, H. (1990). Saccadic reaction times of dyslexic and age–matched normal subjects. *Perception, 19*, 805–818.

Folk, J.R., and Morris, R.K. (1995). Multiple lexical codes in reading: Evidence from eye movements, naming time, and oral reading. *Journal of Experimental Psychology: Learning, Memory, and Cognition, 21*, 1412–1429.

Frazier, L., and Rayner, K. (1982). Making and correcting errors during sentence comprehension: Eye movements in the analysis of structurally ambiguous sentences. *Cognitive Psychology, 14,* 178–210.

Garrod, S., Freudenthal, D., and Boyle, E. (1994). The role of different types of anaphora in the on–line resolution of sentences in discourse. *Journal of Memory and Language, 33,* 39–68.

Garrod, S., O'Brien, E., Morris, R.K., and Rayner, K. (1990). Elaborative inferencing as an active or passive process. *Journal of Experimental Psychology: Learning, Memory, and Cognition, 16,* 250–257.

Geiger, G., and Lettvin, J.Y. (1987). Peripheral vision in persons with dyslexia. *New England Journal of Medicine, 316,* 1238–1243.

Geiger, G., Lettvin, J.Y., and Fahle, M. (1994). Dyslexic children learn a new visual strategy for reading: A controlled experiment. *Vision Research, 34,* 1223-1233.

Goolkasian, P., and King, J. (1990). Letter identification and lateral masking in dyslexic and average readers. *American Journal of Psychology, 103,* 519–538.

Henderson, J.M., Dixon, P., Petersen, A., Twilley, L.C., and Ferreira, F. (1995). Evidence for the use of phonological representations during transsaccadic word recognition. *Journal of Experimental Psychology: Human Perception and Performance, 21,* 82–97.

Henderson, J.M., and Ferreira, F. (1990). Effects of foveal processing difficulty on the perceptual span in reading: Implications for attention and eye movement control. *Journal of Experimental Psychology: Learning, Memory, and Cognition, 16,* 417–429.

Hogaboam, T.W. (1983). Reading patterns in eye movement data. In K. Rayner (ed.), *Eye Movements in Reading: Perceptual and Language Processes.* New York: Academic Press.

Huey, E.B. (1908). *The Psychology and Pedagogy of Reading.* New York: Macmillan.

Hyönä, J. (1995). Do irregular letter combinations attract readers' attention? Evidence from fixation locations in words. *Journal of Experimental Psychology: Human Perception and Performance, 21,* 68–81.

Hyönä, J., Niemi, P., and Underwood, G. (1989). Reading long words embedded in sentences: Informativeness of word parts affects eye movements. *Journal of Experimental Psychology: Human Perception and Performance, 15,* 142–152.

Hyönä, J., and Olson, R.K. (1994). Dyslexic and normal readers' eye movement patterns in reading, visual search, and tracking. In Ygge and G. Lennerstrand (eds.), *Eye Movements in Reading.* London: Pergamon Press.

Hyönä, J., and Olson, R.K. (1995). Eye fixation patterns among dyslexic and normal readers: Effects of word length and word frequency. *Journal of Experimental Psychology: Learning, Memory, and Cognition, 21,* 1430–1440.

Ikeda, M., and Saida, S. (1978). Span of recognition in reading. *Vision Research, 18,* 83–88.

Inhoff, A.W. (1984). Two stages of word processing during eye fixations in the reading of prose. *Journal of Verbal Learning and Verbal Behavior, 23*, 612–624.

Inhoff, A.W. (1989). Lexical access during eye fixations in reading: Are word codes used to integrate lexical information across interword fixations? *Journal of Memory and Language, 28*, 444–461.

Inhoff, A.W. (1990). Integrating information across eye fixations in reading: The role of letter and word units. *Acta Psychologica, 73*, 281–297.

Inhoff, A.W., and Briihl, D. (1991). Semantic processing of unattended text during selective reading: How the eyes see it. *Perception and Psychophysics, 49*, 289–294.

Inhoff, A.W., and Liu, W. (1998). The perceptual span and oculomotor activity during the reading of Chinese sentences. *Journal of Experimental Psychology: Human Perception and Performance, 24*, 20–34.

Inhoff, A.W., Pollatsek, A., Posner, M.I., and Rayner, K. (1989). Covert attention and eye movements during reading. *Quarterly Journal of Experimental Psychology, 41A*, 63–89.

Inhoff, A.W., and Rayner, K. (1986). Parafoveal word processing during eye fixations in reading: Effects of word frequency. *Perception and Psychophysics, 40*, 431–439.

Inhoff, A.W., and Topolski, R. (1992). Lack of semantic activation from unattended text during passage reading. *Bulletin of the Psychonomic Society, 30*, 365–366.

Inhoff, A.W., and Tousman, S. (1990). Lexical priming from partial–word previews. *Journal of Experimental Psychology: Learning, Memory, and Cognition, 16*, 825–836.

Ishida, T., and Ikeda, M. (1989). Temporal properties of information extraction in reading studied by a text–mask replacement technique. *Journal of the Optical Society of America A, 6*, 1624–1632.

Just, M.A., and Carpenter, P.A. (1980). A theory of reading: From eye fixations to comprehension. *Psychological Review, 87*, 329–354.

Just, M.A., and Carpenter, P.A. (1987). *The Psychology of Reading and Language Processing*. Newton, MA.: Allyn and Bacon.

Kennison, S.M., and Clifton, C. (1995). Determinants of parafoveal preview benefit in high and low working memory capacity readers: Implications for eye movement control. *Journal of Experimental Psychology: Learning, Memory, and Cognition, 21*, 68–81.

Klein, R., Berry, G., Briand, K., D'Entremont, B., and Farmer, M. (1990). Letter identification declines with increasing retinal eccentricity at the same rate for normal and dyslexic readers. *Perception and Psychophysics, 47*, 601–606.

Kolers, P.A. (1976). Buswell's discoveries. In R.A. Monty and J.W. Senders (eds.), *Eye Movements and Psychological Processes*. Hillsdale, NJ: Erlbaum.

Lee, Y., Binder, K.S., Kim, J., Pollatsek, A., and Rayner, K. (1999). Activation of phonological codes during eye fixations in reading. *Journal of Experimental Psychology: Human Perception and Performance, 25,* 948–964.

Lima, S.D. (1987). Morphological analysis in reading. *Journal of Memory and Language, 26,* 84–99.

McConkie, G.W., Kerr, P.W., Reddix, M.D., and Zola, D. (1988). Eye movement control during reading: I. The location of initial eye fixations on words. *Vision Research, 28,* 1107–1118.

McConkie, G.W., Kerr, P.W., Reddix, M.D., Zola, D., and Jacobs, A.M. (1989). Eye movement control during reading: II. Frequency of refixating a word. *Perception and Psychophysics, 46,* 245–253.

McConkie, G.W., and Rayner, K. (1975). The span of the effective stimulus during a fixation in reading. *Perception and Psychophysics, 17,* 578–586.

McConkie, G.W., and Rayner, K. (1976). Asymmetry of the perceptual span in reading. *Bulletin of the Psychonomic Society, 8,* 365–368.

McConkie, G.W., and Zola, D. (1979). Is visual information integrated across successive fixations in reading? *Perception and Psychophysics, 25,* 221–224.

Morris, R.K. (1994). Lexical and message–level sentence context effects on fixation times in reading. *Journal of Experimental Psychology: Learning, Memory, and Cognition, 20,* 92–103.

Morris, R.K., Rayner, K., and Pollatsek, A. (1990). Eye movement guidance in reading: The role of parafoveal letter and space information. *Journal of Experimental Psychology: Human Perception and Performance, 16,* 268–281.

Morrison, R.E. (1984). Manipulation of stimulus onset delay in reading: Evidence for parallel programming of saccades. *Journal of Experimental Psychology: Human Perception and Performance, 10,* 667–682.

Morrison, R.E., and Rayner, K. (1981). Saccade size in reading depends upon character spaces and not visual angle. *Perception and Psychophysics, 30,* 395–396.

O'Brien, E.J., Raney, G.E., Albrecht, J.E., and Rayner, K. (1997). Processes involved in the resolution of explicit anaphors. *Discourse Processes, 23,* 1–24.

O'Brien, E.J., Shank, D.M., Myers, J.L., and Rayner, K. (1988). Elaborative inferences during reading: Do they occur on–line? *Journal of Experimental Psychology: Learning, Memory, and Cognition, 14,* 410–420.

Olson, R.K., Kliegl, R., and Davidson, B.J. (1983). Dyslexic and normal readers' eye movements. *Journal of Experimental Psychology: Human Perception and Performance, 9,* 816–825.

O'Regan, J.K. (1979). Eye guidance in reading: Evidence for the linguistic control hypothesis. *Perception and Psychophysics, 25,* 501–509.

O'Regan, J.K. (1980). The control of saccade size and fixation duration in reading. *Perception and Psychophysics, 28,* 112–117.

O'Regan, J.K. (1981). The convenient viewing hypothesis. In D.F. Fisher, R.A. Monty, and J.W. Senders (eds.), *Eye Movements: Cognition and Visual Perception*. Hillsdale, NJ.: Erlbaum.

O'Regan, J.K. (1990). Eye movements and reading. In E. Kowler (ed.), *Eye Movements and Their Role in Visual and Cognitive Processes*. Amsterdam: Elsevier.

O'Regan, J.K., and Levy–Schoen, A. (1987). Eye movement strategy and tactics in word recognition and reading. In M. Coltheart (ed.), *Attention and Performance 12: The Psychology of Reading*. Hillsdale, NJ: Erlbaum.

Osaka, N. (1992). Size of saccade and fixation duration of eye movements during reading: Psychophysics of Japanese text processing. *Journal of the Optical Society of America A, 9*, 5–13.

Pavlidis, G.T. (1981). Do eye movements hold the key to dyslexia? *Neuropsychologia, 19*, 57–64.

Pavlidis, G.T. (1985). Eye movement differences between dyslexics, normal and slow readers while sequentially fixating digits. *American Journal of Optometry and Physiological Optics, 62*, 820–822.

Pavlidis, G.T. (1991). Diagnostic significance and relationship between dyslexia and erratic eye movements. In J. F. Stein (ed.), *Vision and Vsual Dyslexia*. London: Macmillan.

Perry, A.R., Dember, W.N., Warm, J.S., and Sacks, J.G. (1989). Letter identification in normal and dyslexic readers: A verification. *Bulletin of the Psychonomic Society, 27*, 445–448.

Pirozzolo, F.J. (1979). *The Neuropsychology of Developmental Reading Disorders*. New York: Praeger.

Pirozzolo, F.J., and Rayner, K. (1978). The normal control of eye movements in acquired and developmental reading disorders. In H. Avakian–Whitaker and H.A. Whitaker (eds.), *Advances in Neurolinguistics and Psycholinguistics*. New York: Academic Press.

Pirozzolo, F.J., and Rayner, K. (1978). Disorders of oculomotor scanning and graphic orientation in developmental Gerstmann syndrome. *Brain and Language, 5*, 119–126.

Pollatsek, A. (1983). What can eye movements tell us about dyslexia? In K. Rayner (ed.), *Eye Movements in Reading: Perceptual and Language Processes*. New York: Academic Press.

Pollatsek, A., Bolozky, S., Well, A.D., and Rayner, K. (1981). Asymmetries in the perceptual span for Israeli readers. *Brain and Language, 14*, 174–180.

Pollatsek, A., Lesch, M.F., Morris, R.K. and Rayner, K. (1992). Phonolgical codes are used in intergrating information across saccades in word identification and reading. *Journal of Experimental Psychology: Human Perception and Performance, 18*, 148–162.

Pollatsek, A., Raney, G.E., LaGasse, L., and Rayner, K. (1993). The use of information below fixation in reading and in visual search. *Canadian Journal of Experimental Psychology, 47,* 179–200.

Pollatsek, A., and Rayner, K. (1982). Eye movement control in reading: The role of word boundaries. *Journal of Experimental Psychology: Human Perception and Performance, 8,* 817–833.

Pollatsek, A., and Rayner, K. (1990). Eye movements and lexical access in reading. In D.A. Balota, G.B. Flores d'Arcais, and K. Rayner (eds.), *Comprehension Processes in Reading.* Hillsdale, NJ: Erlbaum.

Pollatsek, A., Rayner, K., and Balota, D.A. (1986). Inferences about eye movement control from the perceptual span in reading. *Perception and Psychophysics, 40,* 123–130.

Prinz, W. (1984). Attention and sensitivity in visual search. *Psychological Research, 45,* 355–366.

Raney, G.E., and Rayner, K. (1995). Word frequency effects and eye movements during two readings of a text. *Canadian Journal of Experimental Psychology, 49,* 151–172.

Rayner, K. (1975). The perceptual span and peripheral cues in reading. *Cognitive Psychology, 7,* 65–81.

Rayner, K. (1978). Eye movements in reading and information processing. *Psychological Bulletin, 85,* 618–660.

Rayner, K. (1979). Eye guidance in reading: Fixation locations in words. *Perception, 8,* 21–30.

Rayner, K. (1985). Do faulty eye movements cause dyslexia? *Developmental Neuropsychology, 1,* 3–15.

Rayner, K. (1986). Eye movements and the perceptual span in beginning and skilled readers. *Journal of Experimental Child Psychology, 41,* 211–236.

Rayner, K. (1998). Eye movements in reading and information processing: Twenty years of research. *Psychological Bulletin, 124,* 372–422.

Rayner, K., and Balota, D.A. (1989) Parafoveal preview effects and lexical access during eye fixations in reading. In W. Marlsen–Wilson (ed.), *Lexical Representation and Process.* Cambridge, MA: MIT Press.

Rayner, K., Balota, D.A., and Pollatsek, A. (1986). Against parafoveal semantic preprocessing during eye fixations in reading. *Canadian Journal of Psychology, 40,* 473–478.

Rayner, K., and Bertera, J.H. (1979). Reading without a fovea. *Science, 206,* 468–469.

Rayner, K., Carlson, M., and Frazier, L. (1983). The interaction of syntax and semantics during sentence processing: Eye movements in the analysis of semantically biased sentences. *Journal of Verbal Learning and Verbal Behavior, 22,* 358–374.

Rayner, K., and Duffy, S.A. (1986). Lexical complexity and fixation times in reading: Effects of word frequency, verb complexity, and lexical ambiguity. *Memory and Cognition, 14,* 191–201.

Rayner, K., and Fischer, M.H. (1996). Mindless reading revisited: Eye movements during reading and scanning are different. *Perception and Psychophysics, 58,* 734–747.

Rayner, K., Fischer, M.H., and Pollatsek, A. (1998). Unspaced text interferes with both word identification and eye movement control. *Vision Research, 38,* 1129–1144.

Rayner, K., and Frazier, L. (1989). Selection mechanisms in reading lexically ambiguous words. *Journal of Experimental Psychology: Learning, Memory, and Cognition, 15,* 779–790.

Rayner, K., Garrod, S., and Perfetti, C.A. (1992). Discourse influences during parsing are delayed. *Cognition, 45,* 103–139.

Rayner, K., Inhoff, A.W., Morrison, R.E., Slowiaczek, M.L., and Bertera, J.H. (1981). Masking of foveal and parafoveal vision during eye fixations in reading. *Journal of Experimental Psychology: Human Perception and Performance, 7,* 169–179.

Rayner, K., and McConkie, G.W. (1976). What guides a reader's eye movements? *Vision Research, 16,* 829–837.

Rayner, K., McConkie, G.W., and Ehrlich, S.F. (1978). Eye movements and integrating information across fixations. *Journal of Experimental Psychology: Human Perception and Performance, 4,* 529–544.

Rayner, K., McConkie, G.W., and Zola, D. (1980). Integrating information across eye movements. *Cognitive Psychology, 12,* 206–226.

Rayner, K., and Morris, R.K. (1992). Eye movement control in reading: Evidence against semantic preprocessing. *Journal of Experimental Psychology: Human Perception and Performance, 18,* 163–172.

Rayner, K., Murphy, L.A., Henderson, J.M., and Pollatsek, A. (1989). Selective attentional dyslexia. *Cognitive Neuropsychology, 6,* 357–378.

Rayner, K., Pacht, J.M., and Duffy, S.A. (1994). Effects of prior encounter and discourse bias on the processing of lexically ambiguous words: Evidence from eye fixations. *Journal of Memory and Language, 33,* 527–544.

Rayner, K., and Pollatsek, A. (1981). Eye movement control during reading: Evidence for direct control. *Quarterly Journal of Experimental Psychology, 33A,* 351–373.

Rayner, K., and Pollatsek, A. (1987). Eye movements in reading: A tutorial review. In M. Coltheart (ed.), *Attention and Performance 12: The Psychology of Reading.* Hillsdale, NJ: Erlbaum.

Rayner, K., and Pollatsek, A. (1989). *The Psychology of Reading.* Englewood Cliffs, NJ: Prentice Hall.

Rayner, K., and Pollatsek, A. (1996). Reading unspaced text is not easy: Comments on the implications of Epelboim et al.'s (1994) study for models of eye movement control in reading. *Vision Research, 36,* 461–470.

Rayner, K., Pollatsek, A., and Bilsky, A.B. (1995). Can a temporal processing deficit account for dyslexia? *Psychonomic Bulletin and Review, 2,* 501–507.

Rayner, K., Pollatsek, A., and Binder, K.S. (1998). Phonological codes and eye movements in reading. *Journal of Experimental Psychology: Learning, Memory, and Cognition, 24,* 476–497.

Rayner, K., and Raney, G.E. (1996). Eye movement control in reading and visual search: Effects of word frequency. *Psychonomic Bulletin and Review, 3,* 238–244.

Rayner, K., Raney, G.E., and Pollatsek, A. (1995). Eye movements and discourse processing. In R.F. Lorch and E.J. O'Brien (eds.), *Sources of Coherence in Reading.* Hillsdale, NJ: Erlbaum.

Rayner, K., Reichle, E.D., and Pollatsek, A. (1998). Eye movement control in reading: An overview and a model. In G. Underwood (ed.), *Eye Guidance in Reading and Scene Perception* (pp 243–268). Oxford: Elseveir.

Rayner, K., and Sereno, S.C. (1994). Eye movements in reading: Psycholinguistic studies. In M. A. Gernsbacher (ed.), *Handbook of Psycholinguistics.* San Diego, CA: Academic Press.

Rayner, K., Sereno, S.C., Lesch, M.F., and Pollatsek, A. (1995). Phonological codes are automatically activated during reading: Evidence from an eye movement priming paradigm. *Psychological Science, 6,* 26–32.

Rayner, K., Sereno, S.C. and Raney, G.E. (1996). Eye movement control in reading: A comparison of two types of models. *Journal of Experimental Psychology: Human Perception and Performance, 22,* 1188–1200.

Rayner, K., Sereno, S.C., Morris, R.K., Schmauder, A.R., and Clifton, C. (1989) Eye movements and on–line language comprehension processes. *Language and Cognitive Processes, 4* (special issue), 21–50.

Rayner, K., Slowiaczek, M.L., Clifton, C., and Bertera, J.H. (1983). Latency of sequential eye movements: Implications for reading. *Journal of Experimental Psychology: Human Perception and Performance, 9,* 912–922.

Rayner, K., and Well, A.D. (1996). Effects of contextual constraints on eye movements in reading: A further examination. *Psychonomic Bulletin and Review, 3,* 504–509.

Rayner, K., Well, A.D., and Pollatsek, A. (1980). Asymmetry of the effective visual field in reading. *Perception and Psychophysics, 27,* 537–544.

Rayner, K., Well, A.D., Pollatsek, A., and Bertera, J.H. (1982). The availability of useful information to the right of fixation in reading. *Perception and Psychophysics, 31,* 537–550.

Reichle, E., Pollatsek, A., Fisher, D.L., and Rayner, K. (1998) Toward a model of eye movement control in reading. *Psychological Review, 105,* 125–157.

Schustack, M.W., Ehrlich, S.F., and Rayner, K. (1987). The complexity of contextual facilitation in reading: Local and global influences. *Journal of Memory and Language, 26,* 322–340.

Sereno, S.C. (1995). The resolution of lexical ambiguity: Evidence from an eye movement priming paradigm. *Journal of Experimental Psychology: Learning, Memory, and Cognition, 21,* 582–595.

Sereno, S.C., and Rayner, K. (1992). Fast priming during eye fixations in reading. *Journal of Experimental Psychology: Human Perception and Performance, 18,* 173–184.

Slaghuis, W.L., Lovegrove, W.J., and Freestun, J. (1992). Letter recognition in peripheral vision and metacontrast masking in dyslexic and normal readers. *Clinical Vision Sciences, 7,* 53–65.

Slowiaczek, M.L., and Rayner, K. (1987). Sequential masking during eye fixations in reading. *Bulletin of the Psychonomic Society, 25,* 175–178.

Stanley, G., Smith, G.A., and Howell, E.A. (1983). Eye–movements and sequential tracking in dyslexic and control children. *British Journal of Psychology, 74,* 181–187.

Tinker, M.A. (1936). Eye movements in reading. *Journal of Educational Research, 30,* 241–277.

Tinker, M.A. (1939). Reliability and validity of eye–movement measures of reading. *Journal of Experimental Psychology, 19,* 732–746.

Tinker, M.A.(1946).The study of eye movements in reading. *Psychological Bulletin, 43,* 93–120.

Tinker, M.A. (1958). Recent studies of eye movements in reading. *Psychological Bulletin, 55,* 215–231.

Trueswell, J.C., Tanenhaus, M.K., and Kello, C. (1993). Verb–specific constraints in sentence processing: Separating effects of lexical preference from garden–paths. *Journal of Experimental Psychology: Learning, Memory, and Cognition, 19,* 528–553.

Underwood, G., Bloomfield, R., and Clews, S. (1988). Information influences the pattern of eye fixations during sentence comprehension. *Perception, 17,* 267–278.

Underwood, G., Clews, S. and Everatt, J. (1990). How do readers know where to look next? Local information distributions influence eye fixations. *Quarterly Journal of Experimental Psychology, 42A,* 39–65.

Underwood, N.R., and McConkie, G.W. (1985). Perceptual span for letter distinctions during reading. *Reading Research Quarterly, 20,* 153–162.

Vitu, F., O'Regan, J.K., and Mittau, M. (1990). Optimal landing position in reading isolated words and continuous text. *Perception and Psychophysics, 47,* 583–600.

Vitu, F., O'Regan, J.F., Inhoff, A.W., and Topolski, R. (1995). Mindless reading: Eye–movement characteristics are similar in scanning letter strings and reading texts. *Perception and Psychophysics, 57,* 352–364.

Wolverton, G.S., and Zola, D. (1983). The temporal characteristics of visual information extraction during reading. In K. Rayner (ed.), *Eye Movements in Reading: Perceptual and Language Processes.* New York: Academic Press.

Woodworth, R.S. (1938). *Experimental Psychology.* New York: Holt.

Woodworth, R.S., and Schlosberg, H. (1954). *Experimental Psychology.* New York: Holt.

Zangwill, O.L., and Blakemore, C. (1972). Dyslexia: Reversal of eye movements during reading. *Neuropsychologia, 10,* 117–126.

Zola, D. (1984). Redundancy and word perception during reading. *Perception and Psychophysics, 36,* 277–284.

2

Integrating Orthographic and Phonological Knowledge as Reading Develops: Onsets, Rimes and Analogies in Children's Reading.

Usha Goswami

For a long time, studies of reading development have formed an encapsulated research literature. Although studies of how reading develops should be of great interest to those who study the strategies used by skilled readers, to those who attempt to model the developed lexicon, and to those who study damage to the developed system, there have been relatively few points of contact between developmental researchers and those who study adult cognition. Recently, however, a noticeable degree of convergence has been emerging over the nature of the key issues in skilled reading and reading development. This chapter focuses on three such issues: the importance of phonological factors in reading, the nature of orthographic representations, and the interactive relationship between phonology and orthography in the pronunciation of printed words.

Phonological Skills and Learning to Read

Studies of the factors governing reading development in young children have achieved a remarkable degree of consensus over the past two decades (e.g., Bradley and Bryant, 1983; Fox and Routh, 1975; Juel, 1988; Lundberg, Olofsson, and Wall, 1980; Perfetti, Beck, Bell, and Hughes, 1987; Snowling, 1980; Stanovich, Cunningham, and Cramer, 1984; Tunmer and Nesdale, 1985; Vellutino and Scanlon, 1987; Wagner, 1988). This consensus concerns the causal role of phonological skills in young children's reading progress. Children who have good phonological skills, or good "phonological awareness", become good readers and good spellers. Children with poor phonological skills progress more poorly. In particular, those who have a specific phonological deficit are likely to be classified as dyslexic by the time that they are 9 or 10 years old.

Levels of Phonological Awareness

Phonological skills in young children can be measured at a number of different levels. The term *phonological awareness* is a global one, and refers to a deficit in recognizing smaller units of sound within spoken words. Developmental work has shown that this deficit can be at the level of syllables, of onsets and rimes, or of phonemes. For example, a 4-year-old child might have difficulty in recognising that a word like *valentine* has three syllables, suggesting a lack of *syllabic* awareness (Liberman, Shankweiler, Fischer, and Carter, 1974). A 5-year-old might have difficulty in recognising that the odd word out in the set of words *fan, cat, hat, mat* is *fan* (Bradley and Bryant, 1983). This task requires an awareness of the sub-syllabic units of the *onset* and the *rime* (Treiman, 1988). The onset corresponds to any initial consonants in a syllable, and the rime corresponds to the vowel and to any following consonants. Rimes correspond to rhyme in single-syllable words, and so the rime in *fan* differs from the rime in *cat, hat,* and *mat.* In longer words, rime and rhyme may differ. The onsets in *valentine* are /v/ and /t/, and the rimes correspond to the spelling patterns *al, en,* and *ine.*

A 6-year-old might have difficulty in recognising that *plea* and *pray* begin with the same initial sound (Treiman and Zukowski, 1991). This is a *phonemic* judgment. Although the initial phoneme /p/ is shared between the two words, in *plea* it is part of the onset *pl,* and in *pray* it is part of the onset *pr.* Until children can segment the onset (or the rime), such phonemic judgments are difficult for them to make. In fact, a recent survey of different developmental studies has shown that the different levels of phonological awareness appear to emerge sequentially (Goswami and Bryant, 1990). The awareness of syllables, onsets, and rimes appears to emerge at around the ages of 3 and 4, long before most children go to school. The awareness of phonemes, on the other hand, usually emerges at around the age of 5 or 6, when children have been taught to read for about a year. An awareness of onsets and rimes thus appears to be a precursor of reading, whereas an awareness of phonemes at every serial position in a word only appears to develop as reading is taught. The onset-rime and phonemic levels of phonological structure, however, are not distinct. Many onsets in English are single phonemes, and so are some rimes (e.g., *sea, go, zoo*).

The Temporal Priority of Onset-Rime Knowledge

The early availability of onsets and rimes is supported by studies that have compared the development of phonological awareness of onsets, rimes, and phonemes in the same subjects using the same phonological awareness tasks. For example, the study by Treiman and Zukowski used a same-different judgment task based on the beginning or the end sounds of words. In the beginning sound task, the words either began with the same onset, as in *plea* and *plank*, or shared only the initial phoneme, as in *plea* and *pray*. In the end sound task, the words either shared the entire rime, as in *spit* and *wit*, or shared only the final phoneme, as in *rat* and *wit*. Treiman and Zukowski showed that 4- and 5-year-old children found the onset-rime version of the same/different task significantly easier than the version based on phonemes (see also Treiman and Zukowski, 1996). Only the 6-year-olds, who had been learning to read for about a year, were able to perform both versions of the task with an equal level of success.

A similar developmental result was reported by Kirtley, Bryant, Maclean, and Bradley (1989), using a version of the oddity task referred to earlier. In this task, children have to select the odd word out by its difference in sound to other words. This task can also be performed at either an onset-rime or a phonemic level. If children are given word triples like *top*, *rail*, and *hop*, then the odd word out can be chosen on the basis of the whole rime. If they are given triples like *mop*, *lead*, and *whip*, then the odd word out must be selected on the basis of the final phoneme. When Kirtley et al. gave these versions of the task to 4-, 5- and 6-year-old children, they found that every age group tested showed a selective deficit in the phoneme version of the task. Again, these results support the view that the development of onset-rime awareness precedes the development of an awareness of phonemes that are not onsets.

Rhyme Awareness and the Development of Reading

This developmental progression in phonological skills might be expected to affect the development of reading in some interesting ways. In particular, we might predict a special relationship between rhyming and reading. Such a special relationship indeed appears to exist, at least for the English orthography.

First of all, we know that phonological awareness, measured at both the onset-rime and the phonemic level, is a good predictor of reading development. Studies of very young children however, have suggested a particular causal link between an early awareness of rhyme and the development of reading in English. For example, Bradley and Bryant (1983) reported the results of a large-scale study of approximately 400 schoolchildren in Oxford, England, whose rhyming skills were measured at the age of 4 to 5 years, and whose progress in reading was followed up when they were 8 and 9 years old. This study found a strong predictive link between early rhyme awareness and later reading development, and this link held even after controlling for other variables such as IQ and memory (see also Bryant, Maclean, Bradley, and Crossland, 1990; Maclean, Bryant, and Bradley, 1987). This suggests a strong and specific link between early rhyme awareness and later reading progress. A much weaker (although still significant) relationship between rhyme and reading has been found in more transparent languages such as Swedish and Norwegian (e.g., Hoien, Lundberg, Stanovich, and Bjaalid, 1995; Lundberg, Olofsson, and Wall, 1980).

Second, children who have reading difficulties are known to have selective difficulties in tasks requiring rhyme awareness. For example, when Bradley and Bryant (1978) gave the oddity task to 10-year-old backward readers reading at the 7-year level, they found that the backward readers were much worse at choosing the odd word out than normal 7-year-old readers. This study used a reading level match design in which reading level is held constant and age is varied rather than vice versa. The reading level match thus makes the older children's deficit in rhyme a particularly striking one, as they had higher mental ages than the control children as well as three more years of general experience in taking tests. A rhyming deficit in dyslexia has since been found in other studies conducted in English using the stringent reading level match design (e.g., Bowey, Cain, and Ryan, 1992; Holligan and Johnston, 1988).

Third, training children's rhyming skills can have a significant impact on their reading progress. Bradley and Bryant (1983) took the 60 children in their cohort of 400 who had performed most poorly in the oddity task and gave them two years of intensive training in grouping words on the basis of phonological units such as rhymes. This was largely done by a picture sorting task in which the children learned to group words by sound, for example placing a picture of a *hat*, a *rat*, a *mat* and a *bat* together. A taught control group learned to sort the same pictures by semantic category. For example, if the category was farmyard animals, the control children might learn to group the *rat* with a *pig* and a *cow*.

The experimental group spent the second year of the study learning how the similarities in sound in words like *hat*, *rat*, and *mat* were reflected in shared spelling. The children used plastic letters for this task, learning to spell a word like *hat*, and then to change it into *rat* by discarding the onset and retaining the rime. Following training, the children in the experimental group were eight months further along in reading than the children in the taught control group and a year further on in spelling. Compared to children who had spent the intervening period in an additional unseen control group, they were an astonishing two years further along in spelling and twelve months in reading. Thus there is a clear connection between training children about how the alphabet is used to represent onsets, rimes, and phonemes, and reading and spelling development.

The Rhyme Hypothesis

These different research findings, which have been replicated by other research groups working in English, suggest a hypothesis about rhyme awareness and early reading. The hypothesis is that phonological skills at the onset-rime level might be very important for progress in reading, at least for children learning to read English. Children with good rhyming skills may be better equipped for learning to read. The rhyme hypothesis clearly fits well with what we know about the development of phonological skills and the early availability of onset-rime units. It may appear to fit less well, however, with the fact that English is an alphabetic orthography.

In fact, it can be shown that spelling patterns that correspond to rimes are important spelling units in English. Although the English spelling system depends on the alphabet, and many grapheme-phoneme correspondences in English are regular, written English is not very consistent (or transparent) at the grapheme-phoneme level. The simple 1:1 correspondence between graphemes and phonemes found in transparent languages like Spanish, German and Norwegian is absent in written English, largely because of irregularities in the pronunciation of vowels. This holds true even when larger vowel graphemic units like the digraphs *ea* and *oo* are considered. The skilled reading literature has long recognised the importance of both regularity and consistency for word pronunciation (e.g., Andrews, 1982), but the developmental literature has been slow to follow. The English child will meet many irregularities in the pronunciation of identical graphemes, as in *cat* and *car*, where the pronunciation of the vowel changes because of a change in the final consonant. Thus although a purely phonemic approach to learning to read might pay big dividends for a young child learning to read a highly transparent orthography like German or Spanish (e.g., Goswami, Gombert, and De Barrera, 1998; Wimmer and Goswami, 1994), it may be less successful for a young child who is learning to read English. The English child has to contend with both inconsistency and irregularity.

Recent research in psycholinguistics has shown that there is a considerable gain in the orthographic transparency of written English when spelling units that correspond to rime units are considered. In an analysis of patterns of redundancy in the English spelling system, Treiman, Mullennix, Bijeljac-Babic, and Richmond-Welty (1995) demonstrated that there is considerably less orthographic redundancy at the onset-rime juncture than at any other point in the letter string. Treiman et al. carried out a statistical analysis of the links between spellings and sounds in all the words with a consonant-vowel-consonant (CVC) phonological structure in English. They found that orthographic units consisting of a V and final C (VC_2) had more stable pronunciations than either individual vowel graphemes or initial consonant plus vowel (C_1V) units. For example, whereas 77% of CVC words sharing a rime (VC_2) spelling had a consistent pronunciation, only 51% of CVC words sharing a vowel spelling and 52% of CVC words sharing a C_1V spelling had a consistent pronunciation (by token). An equivalent pattern held by type, the figures being 80%, 62% and 55%, respectively. Treiman et al. suggested that the characteristics of the English orthography itself could encourage readers to use an onset-rime parsing when reading words. Stanback (1992), in an analysis of the rime patterns in the 43,041 syllables making up the 17,602 words in the Carroll, Davis, and Richman (1971) word frequency norms for children, has shown that the entire corpus can be described by 824 rimes of which 616 occur in rime families. This link between orthographic structure and phonology is no accident as the writing system was designed to encode the spoken language. Statistical analyses of phonological structure have shown that rimes are also salient phonological units in spoken English (Kessler and Treiman, 1997). These analyses are consistent with the hypothesis that phonological skills at the onset-rime level might be very important ones for progress in learning to read English.

Orthographic Analogies and Reading Development

Evidence that young children do use knowledge about rimes when learning to read English comes from a series of studies that have examined the kinds of analogies that children make between the spelling patterns of words. Consider a child who learns the spelling pattern for the word *beak*. That child could use the spelling-sound correspondences in *beak* as a basis for reading new words like *peak* and *weak* (rime analogies), for reading new words like *bean* and *bead* (onset-vowel analogies), and for reading new words like *heap* and *mean* (vowel analogies). The first kind of analogy depends on making a prediction about shared sound based on a shared spelling pattern for the rime (*beak-peak*), a unit for which phonological awareness develops relatively early. The second and third kind of analogies depend on shared spelling units that require segmentation of the rime, either by attaching the onset to the vowel, as in *beak-bean*, or by deleting the onset and segmenting the rime, as in *beak-heap*. These latter analogies depend on phonemic knowledge, which we know develops as reading is taught.

If early reading behavior is intimately linked to a child's phonological skills, then rime analogies (*beak-peak*) might be expected to emerge prior to analogies based on other spelling units like the onset and the vowel (*beak-bean*). According to the rhyme hypothesis, rime analogies should be relatively easy for young children to use and should emerge first developmentally. On the other hand, if phonological knowledge plays no special role in children's analogies, then the development of analogy might depend on some kind of visual factor such as the proportion of the spelling pattern that is shared between two words. On a visual hypothesis, rime analogies (*beak-peak*) and onset-vowel analogies (*beak-bean*) would be expected to emerge concurrently, as both types of analogy depend on shared spelling units of three letters. These analogies, however, might be expected to precede analogies based on shared spelling units of two letters, like *beak-heap*.

Most of the analogy studies conducted to date have depended on the clue word method, which is a measure of transfer. To avoid the problem of the child having no basis for an analogy, the children in these studies are first taught to read a clue word, like *beak*, which remains available on a card as their clue. They are then shown other words that share part of the spelling pattern with *beak*, either analogous words like *peak*, *bean* and *heap*, or non-analogous control words that are matched in frequency to these words, like *bank* and *lake*. In some clue word experiments, the children are selected because they cannot read any of these test words, both analogous and control (e.g., Goswami, 1988). In others, pretest knowledge of these words is compared to reading performance in an analogy test when the children have a clue word available to help them (e.g., Goswami, 1986).

The findings from such studies have been very consistent (Goswami, 1986, 1988, 1990a, 1993). The most robust analogies, and those that emerge first developmentally, are rime analogies like *beak-peak*. Onset-vowel analogies (*beak-bean*) and vowel digraph analogies (*beak-heap*) emerge somewhat later, typically during the first year of learning to read, and at around the same time as each other (Goswami, 1993). This pattern of analogizing, with rime analogies preceding the use of analogies based on single phonemes or on groups of phonemes, supports the hypothesis that analogies depend on phonological skills rather than on some other factor such as visual similarity. Furthermore, rime analogies do not reflect a letter position effect. If analogies between shared consonant blends in words are compared, then more analogies are found between shared consonant blends at the beginnings of words (*trim-trap*), which correspond to onsets, than between shared consonant blends at the ends of words (*west-dust*), which correspond to part of the rime (Goswami, 1991).

Finally, it has been demonstrated that rime analogies are not an artifact of phonological priming. If young children are taught a clue word like *head*, then they make significantly more analogies to rhyming words like *bread* than to rhyming words like *said*, which have a different rime spelling pattern (Goswami, 1990a). This supports the claim that analogies in early reading depend on shared orthography. Children's orthographic analogies appear to reflect the application of phonological (onset-rime) knowledge to the spelling system of English. Indeed, as the rhyme hypothesis would predict, the number of analogies that children make is related to the level of their phonological skills. Children with good rhyming skills make more rime analogies than children with poor rhyming skills (Goswami, 1990b), whereas children who have reading difficulties (and who are likely to have a rhyme deficit) find rime analogies very difficult (see Lovett, chapter 4, this volume).

The analogy research thus provides one reason for thinking that rime-based coding is very important for young children who are learning to read English. The argument is not that rime-based coding will be used instead of phonemic coding. Rather, the hypothesis is that learning the correspondence between onsets and rimes and shared spelling patterns will help children to learn the spelling system of English, which reflects the rime. We can speculate that the weaker relationship between rhyme and reading found in more transparent orthographies such as Norwegian reflects the fact that the spelling system of such orthographies does not accord functional significance to rime units. For languages that are highly consistent at the grapheme-phoneme level, rime-based coding confers no particular advantage in learning to read.

Theoretical Models of Rhyme and Analogy in Reading Development

To develop a theoretical framework to describe these research findings on the role of rhyme and analogy in beginning reading, Goswami and Bryant (1990) suggested that the process of learning to read could be characterized as a series of causal connections. Three causal connections were proposed, a connection between preschool awareness of rime and alliteration and later progress in reading and spelling mediated by analogy, a connection between tuition at the level of the phoneme and the development of phonemic awareness (which was suggested to be rapid following such tuition), and a connection between progress in spelling and progress in reading (and vice versa). These connections were not meant to represent separate stages that were causally sequential, as the first two connections were claimed to be in play as soon as children began to read and spell. The first two connections were also claimed to be linked as rhyming ability was a predictor of children's ability to detect phonemes. It was argued, however, that preschool awareness of rhyme and alliteration and the phonemic awareness that emerged as a consequence of direct tuition at the level of the phoneme might make separate contributions to reading development.

In an effort to describe the first causal connection between preschool awareness of rime and alliteration and later progress in reading and spelling in more detail, Goswami proposed an interactive analogy model of reading (Goswami, 1993).

This model argued that the phonological knowledge that children brought with them to reading played an important role in establishing orthographic recognition units from the earliest phases of development. The early visual analysis of words was thought to be founded in phonological knowledge (see also Stuart and Coltheart, 1988), and it was suggested that larger spelling units were functionally important in decoding from the beginning of the recognition process. The interactive analogy model assumed that children could use analogies between the spelling patterns in words from the earliest phases of learning to read, as long as they had a basis for analogy available in the form of a sight word vocabulary or a clue word. It was argued that analogical processes played a role in the development of reading throughout acquisition. Analogy use was conceived of as an automatic process, driven by the level of a child's phonological knowledge and by the nature of the orthographic-phonological relations that operated in a particular orthography. The argument was not that young readers of English would rely only on rime analogies early in learning to read, but rather that rime-based coding should play an important role in the development of orthographic knowledge via a continuous interaction between phonological and orthographic knowledge. The interactive analogy model of learning to read mirrors connectionist accounts of reading in terms of the kind of automatic learning mechanism that was being proposed (see Plaut, chapter 11, this volume, and Zorzi, Houghton, and Butterworth, 1998, for a localist connectionist model of reading development that demonstrates the benefits of onset-rime coding). Goswami's (1993) model, however, did not include an account of the impact of teaching methods on reading development (see Goswami and East, 1998).

More recently, these theoretical views have been refined to take account of a new distinction in the phonological awareness literature between epilinguistic knowledge and the metalinguistic control over phonological structures that emerges as a consequence of teaching (Gombert, 1992). Epilinguistic knowledge is linguistic knowledge that is used as a basis for linguistic behaviour but is not yet accessible to conscious inspection. The child gains conscious access to linguistic knowledge via the acquisition of metalinguistic control, which is driven by external factors such as tuition in literacy and the structure of the orthography being learned. On the basis of research evidence in many languages, Gombert argued that epilinguistic knowledge represents syllables and rimes. As the acquisition of metalinguistic control depends on the phonological units highlighted in literacy tuition (which are often phoneme-level correspondences), Gombert argued that the child might gain metalinguistic control over phonemes prior to gaining metalinguistic control over rimes (see Duncan, Seymour, and Hill, 1997; Goswami and East, 1998, for empirical evidence relating to this proposal).

Gombert's representational framework has important implications for
Goswami and Bryant's (1990) model. In the light of this framework, Goswami and
Bryant's first causal connection between preschool awareness of rhyme and alliteration and later progress in reading can be seen as a connection between *epilinguistic*
knowledge and reading development (see Goswami, 1998, in press a, for fuller discussions). This connection works largely through analogies. As these analogies are
based on the child's epilinguistic knowledge about rime, they are initially nonstra-
tegic and implicit, in line with the proposals made by Goswami's (1993) interactive analogy model of reading. The second causal connection between tuition at
the level of the phoneme and the development of phonemic awareness can be seen
as a more general connection between direct tuition in literacy and the emergence
of metalinguistic control over phonological structures. If literacy tuition emphasizes grapheme-phoneme correspondences, metalinguistic control will emerge at the
phonemic level of linguistic structure. If literacy tuition also emphasizes onsets and
rimes, metalinguistic control will also emerge at the onset-rime level of linguistic
structure. The emergence of metalinguistic control in either case should be rapid
following such direct tuition, and in either case should lead the child to apply phonological knowledge strategically and consciously to reading (for example, by using alphabetic strategies like sounding out words and by intentionally using rime
analogies). The third connection between spelling and reading can also be seen in
the light of achieving metalinguistic control over phonological structures. Spelling
requires the explicit representation of phonological knowledge. Thus spelling in itself
necessitates the development of metalinguistic control over phonological structures
and this in turn enables further reading and spelling progress.

Cross-Linguistic Studies of Analogy Use

If analogy use is indeed at first the automatic process assumed by Goswami's (1993)
model and is also at first driven by the level of a child's phonological knowledge
and by the nature of the writing system that is being learned, then analogies in reading should be found to operate in every orthography. In a very transparent orthography, such as Spanish or German, analogies would be expected to reflect grapheme-phoneme relations because of the nature of the writing system and because children are taught grapheme-phoneme correspondences in a highly structured fashion. In a less transparent orthography, such as English, analogies would be expected
to reflect rime-based coding as well as and possibly more frequently than grapheme-phoneme relations. The more transparent the orthographic system, the more
that analogy use will reflect the grapheme-phoneme code, and the easier and the
faster that this code should be mastered by the novice (although rime analogies may

in fact be used as frequently in the acquisition of a transparent code like German as in the acquisition of a nontransparent code like English, the use of rime analogies would be less visible in German than in English and consequently not very amenable to experimental investigation (see Gombert, Bryant, and Warrick, 1997; Wimmer and Goswami, 1994).

A recent series of cross-cultural studies of children's use of analogies in learning to read different orthographies has investigated some of these proposals (Goswami, Gombert, and Fraca de Barrera, 1998; Goswami, Porpodas, and Wheelwright, 1997). In these studies, nonsense word reading in English, French, Spanish, and Greek was used as a basis for measuring analogies. Nonsense word reading was felt to be the best means of comparing code acquisition at different reading levels across the different orthographies even though prior studies of children's nonsense word reading in English have produced mixed results[1]. To compare rime analogies and grapheme-phoneme analogies in different orthographies, nonsense words were created that reflected the orthographic-phonological relations in each orthography at either the onset-rime level or at the grapheme-phoneme level. In addition, the familiarity of the orthographic-phonological relations used as a basis for the different nonsense words was varied.

The logic behind this design will be described using the English stimuli. At least three kinds of nonsense word are possible in English. One type reflects orthographic-phonological relations at both the onset-rime and the grapheme-phoneme level, as in *dake* and *murn*. These nonsense words can either be decoded by using rime units from real word neighbours (*cake, turn*) or via knowledge of grapheme-phoneme correspondences. They will be designated O+P+ nonsense words, as they share both orthography (O) and phonology (P) at the level of the rime with real English words. A second kind of nonsense word is O+P- words, like *daik* and *mirn*. These words share phonology with real English words at the level of the rime (*cake, turn*), but they use orthographic rime sequences that are found in no English words. They can still be decoded, however, by using knowledge of grapheme-phoneme correspondences. Hence if English children find it easier to read nonsense words like *dake* than matched nonsense words like *daik*, this would support the idea that young readers of English represent information about rime units when developing visual recognition units for words.

Finally, nonsense words can be designed that share neither orthography nor phonology at the level of the rime with real English words. Examples of such O-P- words are nonsense words like *faish* and *zoip*. Although these nonsense words can also be decoded by using grapheme-phoneme correspondences, not only are the sequences of grapheme-phoneme correspondences that constitute their rimes unfamiliar from the traditional orthography, their phonological rimes are also unfamiliar from real-word phonology. If O+P+ nonsense words like *dake* are easier to read than O-P- nonsense words like *zoip*, then this would imply that young children are learning something specific about the orthographic-phonological relations that operate in their particular orthography. This advantage for O+P+ nonsense words would be expected in all orthographies, but might be greater in an orthography with low transparency like English in which the grapheme-phoneme relations are more variable.

The first kind of comparison—that between O+P+ and O-P+ nonsense words like *dake* and *daik*—enables us to measure the benefits of rime analogies to young readers of different orthographies. The less transparent the orthography the more that rime-based coding might be expected to be used by young learners, and the bigger the difference in accuracy that might be predicted in reading the O+P+ vs. the O-P+ nonsense words. To test this prediction, O+P+ and O-P+ nonsense words like *dake* and *daik* were given to English and French 7-, 8- and 9-year-old readers (matched on reading age) and college students (Goswami et al., 1998). The two nonsense word types were matched for lower level orthographic familiarity using mean positional bigram frequencies. Examples of the French stimuli are *fanche* (O+P+ - manche), and *fenche* (O-P+). Note that a comparison between O+P+ and O-P+ nonsense words is impossible to make in an extremely regular orthography like Spanish, as there is only one possible way of spelling any particular rime. The results of this first cross-linguistic comparison are given in table 2.1 which shows that an advantage in reading the O+P+ nonsense words occurred in both orthographies. The size of this effect, however, was much larger in English. The younger English children read around 20% more of the O+P+ nonsense words correctly

Table 2.1
Accuracy of nonsense word reading:
O+P+ words versus O-P+ words

List type	English		French		Age(years)
	O+P+	O-P+	O+P+	O-P+	
Example	DAKE	DAIK	FANCHE	FENCHE	
	MURN	MIRN	ROILE	ROALE	
% correct	56.3	36.2	83.1	77.9	7
	64.1	48.2	89.8	84.6	8
	91.7	78.9	94.3	87.8	9
	93.8	85.4	95.8	91.4	23

compared to the O-P+ nonsense words. This suggests that rime-based coding is more important for reading development in English than in French. A similar comparison between English and Greek based on bi- and tri-syllables has shown almost no reliance on rhyme-based coding in this highly transparent orthography (Goswami et al., 1997).

The second kind of comparison, that between O+P+ and O-P- nonsense words like *dake* and *zoip*, enables us to measure the combined effects of orthographic and phonological familiarity on reading printed words, and to compare the benefits of this familiarity to young readers who are learning different orthographies that vary in transparency. Whereas nonsense words like *dake* are familiar at the rime level in both orthography and phonology, nonsense words like *zoip* require phonemic decoding of an unfamiliar sequence of rime graphemes to produce an unfamiliar phonological rime. This might be more difficult in less transparent orthographies as even an unfamiliar sequence of rime graphemes will have a very predictable pronunciation in a highly transparent orthography.

To test this second prediction, O+P+ and O-P- nonsense words like *faish* and *zoip* were given to new groups of English, French, and Spanish 7-, 8- and 9-year-old readers (Goswami et al., 1998). Examples of the French stimuli are *fanche* (O+P+ - manche), and *chenfe* (O-P-); examples of the Spanish stimuli are *duez* (O+P+) and *muet* (O-P-). The results of this second cross-linguistic comparison are given in table 2.2. The table shows that an advantage in reading the O+P+ nonsense words occurred in all orthographies. The size of this effect, however, varied with orthographic

Table 2.2
Accuracy of nonsense word reading:
O+P+ words versus O-P- words

Language	List Type		Age
	O+P+	O-P-	
% correct			
English	28.7	11.8	7
	66.2	33.3	8
	59.9	50.7	9
French	71.4	52.9	7
	80.5	68.5	8
	82.0	73.4	9
Spanish	95.8	94.3	7
	94.3	94.3	8
	94.8	92.2	9

transparency. The effect was extremely small (0 to 3%) in Spanish and relatively large (10 to 20%) in English and French. The Spanish children showed a significant effect of familiarity in reading speed, however, taking longer to read the O-P- nonsense words than the O+P+ nonsense words. Greek children given O-P- nonsense words behaved in a very similar fashion to the Spanish children (Goswami et al., 1997).

In fact, nonsense word reading accuracy also varied remarkably with orthographic transparency (see figure 2.1). The Spanish children were close to ceiling on the nonsense word reading task at every age studied. If nonsense word reading is accepted as a useful means of comparing code acquisition across different orthographies, then this result suggests that code acquisition in Spanish is extremely rapid. The orthographic-phonological relations in this very transparent orthography are acquired to a high level of accuracy in the first year of learning to read. In French and English, however, code acquisition proceeds at a slower developmental pace. Even so, the more transparent orthographic-phonological relations in French appear to be acquired at a faster rate than the less transparent orthographic-phonological relations in English. Thus orthographic transparency as well as orthographic familiarity can affect the orthographic representations developed by young readers who are learning different orthographies (Goswami, in press b).

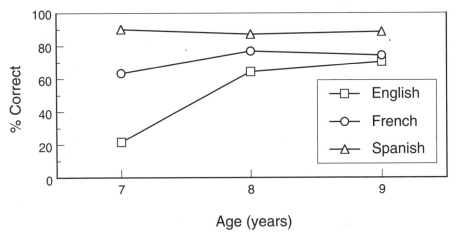

Figure 2.1 Nonsense word reading, accuracy (O+P and O-P-
combined) in English, French, and Spanish 7-, 8-, 9-year olds.

Conclusion

Studies of nonsense word reading thus support studies of transfer (analogy) in suggesting that rime-based coding plays an important role in learning to read in English. The importance of rimes in reading development in English appears to reflect the operation of both phonological and orthographic factors. Rhyming ability is a particularly strong predictor of later reading development in English (e.g., Bradley and Bryant, 1983), and the English orthography is most easily parsed into onset-rime units (e.g., Treiman et al., 1995). Furthermore, children's early orthographic analogies show a priority for the rime (e.g., Goswami, 1993). These findings suggest that reading development can usefully be modeled as an interactive process in which phonological knowledge and the early development of orthographic representations are intimately linked (akin to the operation of PDP models, see also Ehri, 1992; Perfetti, 1992). The current challenge for such interactive accounts is how to incorporate the effects of direct teaching on the developing orthographic lexicon, given that such teaching may involve different levels of phonological structure. Nevertheless, we can discern clear continuities between developmental processes and skilled reading. College students, like young children, show increased reading accuracy when nonsense words contain familiar rimes (see table 2.1), and phonological activation in adult reading appears to be mandatory rather than optional (e.g., van Orden, Pennington, and Stone, 1990), as appears to be the case in children. There are clearly many points of continuity in the factors that influence reading across the life span. Future research in skilled reading and in the neuropsychology of reading will surely benefit from taking these points of continuity into account.

Notes

1. While some studies of nonsense word reading have suggested that grapheme-phoneme decoding precedes rime-based decoding of nonsense words (e.g., Coltheart and Leahy, 1992), others have suggested that rime analogies are available from the beginning of learning to read (Bowey and Hansen, 1994; Treiman, Goswami ,and Bruck, 1990). These discrepancies in results appear to reflect the degree of regularity and consistency of the real word analogues chosen as a basis for generating the nonsense words. The present study used nonsense words based only on regular and consistent real words.

References

Andrews, S. (1982). Phonological recoding: Is the regularity effect consistent? *Memory and Cognition, 10,* 565–575.

Bowey, J.A. (1990). Orthographic onsets and rimes as functional units of reading. *Memory and Cognition, 18,* 419–427.

Bowey, J.A., Cain, M.T., and Ryan, S.M. (1992). A reading-level design study of phonological skills underlying fourth-grade children's word reading difficulties. *Child Development, 63,* 999–1011.

Bowey, J.A., and Hansen, J. (1994). The development of orthographic rimes as units of word recognition. *Journal of Experimental Child Psychology, 58,* 465–488.

Bradley, L., and Bryant, P.E. (1978). Difficulties in auditory organisation as a possible cause of reading backwardness. *Nature, 271,* 746–747.

Bradley, L., and Bryant, P.E. (1983). Categorising sounds and learning to read: A causal connection. *Nature, 310,* 419–421.

Bryant, P.E., Maclean, M., Bradley, L., and Crossland, J. (1990). Rhyme, alliteration, phoneme detection, and learning to read. *Developmental Psychology, 26,* 429–438.

Carroll, J.B., Davies, P., and Richman, B. (1971). *Word Frequency Book.* New York: American Heritage Publishing Company.

Coltheart, V., and Leahy, J. (1992). Children's and adult's reading of nonwords: Effects of regularity and consistency. *Journal of Experimental Psychology, LMC, 18,* 718–729.

Duncan, L.G., Seymour, P.H.K., and Hill, S. (1997). How important are rhyme and analogy in beginning reading? *Cognition, 63,* 171–208.

Ehri, L.C. (1992). Reconceptualising sight word reading. In P.B. Gough, L.C. Ehri, and R. Treiman (eds)., *Reading Acquisition,* pp. 107–143. Hillsdale, NJ: Lawrence Erlbaum Associates.

Fox, B., and Routh, D.K. (1975). Analysing spoken language into words, syllables and phonemes: A developmental study. *Journal of Psycholinguistic Research, 4,* 331–342.

Gombert, J.E. (1992). *Metalinguistic Development.* Hemel Hempstead, Herts: Havester Wheatsheaf.

Gombert, J.E., Bryant, P., and Warrick, N. (1997). Children's use of analogy in learning to read and to spell. In C.A. Perfetti, M. Fayol and L. Rieben (eds,), *Learning to Spell,* pp. 221–235. New Jersey: Erlbaum.

Goswami, U. (1986). Children's use of analogy in learning to read: A developmental study. *Journal of Experimental Child Psychology, 42,* 73–83.

Goswami, U. (1988). Orthographic analogies and reading development. *Quarterly Journal of Experimental Psychology, 40A,* 239–268.

Goswami, U. (1990a). Phonological priming and orthographic analogies in reading. *Journal of Experimental Child Psychology, 49,* 323–340.

Goswami, U. (1990b). A special link between rhyming skills and the use of orthographic analogies by beginning readers. *Journal of Child Psychology and Psychiatry, 31,* 301–311.

Goswami, U. (1991). Learning about spelling sequences: The role of onsets and rimes in analogies in reading. *Child Development, 62,* 1110–1123.

Goswami, U. (1993). Toward an interactive analogy model of reading development: Decoding vowel graphemes in beginning reading. *Journal of Experimental Child Psychology, 56,* 443–475.

Goswami, U. (1998). *Rhyme and analogy theory and beginning reading: More recent research and implications for teaching.* Manuscript submitted for publication.

Goswami, U. (in press, a). Phonological development and reading by analogy: Epilinguistic and metalinguistic issues. To appear in: J. Oakhill and R. Beard (eds), *Reading Development and the Teaching of Reading: A Psychological Perspective.* Cambridge: Cambridge University Press.

Goswami, U. (in press, b). The relationship between phonological awareness and orthographic representations in different orthographies. To appear in M. Harris and G. Hatano (eds), *A Cross–Linguistic Perspective on Learning to Read.* Cambridge: Cambridge University Press.

Goswami, U. and Bryant, P.E. (1990). *Phonological Skills and Learning to Read.* Hillsdale, NJ: Lawrence Erlbaum.

Goswami, U., and East, M. (1998). *Epilinguistic and metalinguistic factors in rhyme and analogy in beginning reading: The importance of teaching.* Manuscript submitted for publication.

Goswami, U., Gombert, J.E., and Fraca de Barrera, L. (1998). Children's orthographic representations and linguistic transparency: Nonsense word reading in English, French and Spanish. *Applied Psycholinguistics, 19,* 19–52.

Goswami, U., Porpodas, C., and Wheelwright, S. (1997). Children's orthographic representations in English and Greek. *European Journal of Psychology of Education, 12* (3), 273–292.

Hoien, T., Lundberg, L., Stanovich, K.E., and Bjaalid, I.K. (1995). Components of phonological awareness. *Reading and Writing, 7,* 171–188.

Holligan, C., and Johnston, R.S. (1988). The use of phonological information by good and poor readers in memory and reading tasks. *Memory and Cognition, 16,* 522–532.

Juel, C. (1988). Learning to read and write: A longitudinal study of 54 children from first through fourth grades. *Journal of Educational Psychology, 80,* 437–447.

Kessler, B., and Treiman, R. (in press). Syllable structure and phoneme distribution. *Journal of Memory and Language.*

Kirtley, C., Bryant, P., MacLean, M., and Bradley, L. (1989). Rhyme, rime and the onset of reading. *Journal of Experimental Child Psychology, 48,* 224–245.

Liberman, I.Y., Shankweiler, D., Fischer, F.W., and Carter, B. (1974). Explicit syllable and phoneme segmentation in the young child. *Journal of Experimental Child Psychology, 18,* 201–212.

Lundberg, I., Olofsson, A., and Wall, S. (1980). Reading and spelling skills in the first school years predicted from phonemic awareness skills in kindergarten. *Scandanavian Journal of Psychology, 21*, 159–173.

MacLean, M., Bryant, P.E., and Bradley, L. (1987). Rhymes, nursery rhymes and reading in early childhood. *Merrill–Palmer Quarterly, 33*, 255–282.

Perfetti, C. (1992). The representation problem in reading acquisition. In P.B. Gough, L.C. Ehri, and R. Treiman (eds), *Reading Acquisition*, (pp.145–174). Hillsdale, NJ: Lawrence Erlbaum Associates.

Perfetti, C., Beck, I., Bell, L., and Hughes, C. (1987). Phonemic knowledge and learning to read are reciprocal: A longitudinal study of first grade children. *Merrill Palmer Quarterly, 33*, 283–319.

Snowling, M.J. (1980). The development of grapheme–phoneme correspondence in normal and dyslexic readers. *Journal of Experimental Child Psychology, 29*, 294–305.

Stanback, M.L. (1992). Syllable and rime patterns for teaching reading: Analysis of a frequency–based vocabulary of 17,602 words. *Annals of Dyslexia, 42*, 196–221.

Stanovich, K.E., Cunningham, A.E., and Cramer, B.R. (1984). Assessing phonological awareness in kindergarten: Issues of task comparability. *Journal of Experimental Child Psychology, 38*, 175–190.

Stuart, M., and Coltheart, M. (1988). Does reading develop in a sequence of stages? *Cognition, 30*, 139–181.

Treiman, R. (1988). The internal structure of the syllable. In G. Carlson and M. Tanenhaus (eds), *Linguistic Structure in Language Processing* (pp. 27–52). Dordrecht, The Netherlands: Kluger.

Treiman, R., Goswami, U., and Bruck, M. (1990). Not all nonwords are alike: Implications for reading development and theory. *Memory and Cognition, 18*, 559–567.

Treiman, R., Mullennix, J., Bijeljac–Babic, R., and Richmond–Welty, E.D. (1995). The special role of rimes in the description, use and acquisition of English orthography. *Journal of Experimental Psychology, General, 124*, 107–136.

Treiman, R., and Zukowski, A. (1991). Levels of phonological awareness. In S. Brady and D. Shankweiler (eds) *Phonological Processes in Literacy*. Hillsdale, NJ: Erlbaum.

Treiman, R., and Zukowski, A. (1996). Children's sensitivity to syllables, onsets, rimes and phonemes. *Journal of Experimental Child Psychology, 61*, 193–215.

Tunmer W.E., and Nesdale A.R. (1985). Phonemic segmentation skill and beginning reading. *Journal of Educational Psychology, 77*, 417–527.

van Orden, G.C., Pennington, B.F., and Stone, G.O. (1990). Word indentification in reading and the promise of subsymbolic psycholinguistics. *Psychological Review, 97*, 488–522.

Vellutino, F.R., and Scanlon, D.M. (1987). Phonological coding, phonological awareness and reading ability: Evidence from a longitudinal and experimental study. *Merrill–Palmer Quarterly, 33*, 321–363.

Wagner, R.K. (1988). Causal relations between the development of phonological processing abilities and the acquisition of reading skills: A meta–analysis. *Merrill–Palmer Quarterly, 34*, 261–279.

Wimmer, H., and Goswami, U. (1994). The influence of orthographic consistency on reading development: Word recognition in English and German children. *Cognition, 51*, 91–103.

Zorzi, M., Houghton, G., and Butterworth, B. (1998). The development of spelling–sound relationships in a model of phonological reading. *Language and Cognitive Processes, 13*, 337–371.

3
Whole Words, Segments, and Meaning: Approaches to Reading Education

Betty Ann Levy

There has been a long-standing controversy in education regarding the best way to start children down the road to reading. While the main task in reading is clearly to extract meaning from the printed display, the first task confronting the child is how to decode the visual orthography so as to reveal the message hidden in the script. The often heated debate surrounding skill-based versus meaning-based curricula for beginning readers focused on whether children should first be taught to read words in isolation, prior to reading them in text, or whether word recognition should be taught in the context of reading texts. There is general agreement, however, that children should not be asked to read text unless they are familiar with 80 to 90% of the words on a page (Adams, 1990), so that attention can be focused on message comprehension rather than on struggling with unknown words. Therefore, before the child can begin to read more than simple short sentences, he or she must establish a considerable reading vocabulary. The important question is how to get the beginning reader to this stage where he or she can rapidly recognize a reasonable number of printed words. Until that time, reading for meaning is hampered by the resource drains of slow word recognition processes (Lesgold and Perfetti, 1978).

I argue here that there are several aspects of reading development that often become confused in the educational debates. The methods debate frequently queries which is the best or the optimal instructional approach for beginning readers. I will argue that the instructional methods that have been at the center of the educational debate (whole word, phonics, whole language) all contribute to an important but different aspect of reading development. Our concern should not be which one; rather, we should consider how to amalgamate the best aspects of these techniques so as to optimally meet the needs of individual young readers. I will first discuss the problem of developing an initial reading vocabulary and describe two of our recent experiments that explored different training regimes for acquiring such vocabulary both for beginning non-readers and for children who failed to show normal reading development in the first grade. But early reading is hampered by more than just skill in "getting words off the page." To develop reading fluency, the child must be able to read the words within milliseconds. Are the processes that facilitate the setting up of initial reading vocabulary the same as those that lead to rapid, more fluent word recognition and reading? In the second part of the chapter, I will summarize our work on word recognition speed in the context of recent literature on developing reading speed. In the final section of the chapter, I will explore how context facilitates word recognition and reading fluency through recent research on text rereading gains. Throughout the chapter, I will focus on the learning mechanisms that underlie the gains observed for each training task. Only when we understand how training tasks influence basic learning mechanisms can we begin to make intelligent instructional choices that will address specific reading problems and specific needs of individual young readers.

Beginning Word Recognition

Even though English is an alphabetic language, with a set of rules relating the spoken and written forms, learning to read written English is hampered by irregularities in the spelling to sound mappings. Words in spoken English are expressed using about 46 phonemes, but these phonemes must be mapped onto only 26 letters in written English. Consequently, many consonants have more than one pronunciation (e.g., *c* and *g*) and all vowels have both long and short sounds, with some representing multiple phonemes (e.g., *a, e*). This multiple mapping of sounds onto letters makes reading even regular words difficult, but the difficulty is enhanced further by the existence of irregular words (e.g., *pint, island*) where the spelling to sound regularities are violated. We have words in English that look alike (e.g., *pint, mint; couch, touch*) but do not rhyme, and words that rhyme but have different orthographies (e.g., *mate, eight*). Consequently, the beginning reader experiences difficulty in grasping the grapheme to phoneme correspondence of English. This difficulty led some researchers to advocate the use of whole word reading, without breaking the words into linguistic segments that might lead to irregular mappings and difficulties in blending the segments back into whole word pronunciations.

While whole word learning appears to have some advantages, this method makes no use of the alphabetic nature of English and reduces reading to a logographic form. Unfortunately, the written letters of English were not designed to form distinctive visual forms when they are combined into words, so that English words often look remarkably similar (e.g., *cat, rat, oat*). This visual similarity should produce considerable confusion for beginning readers, particularly when their attention is focused on the whole word. The orthographic regularities in English stem from rules guiding letter sequencing, but the orthographic regularities are not marked by visual distinctiveness. Thus it is not clear that English words can be more easily processed as whole word forms than through grapheme to phoneme regularities. Consequently, we have the continuing debate between educators advocating whole word versus phonics approaches to early reading instruction.

If education is to be informed by scientific findings, we must examine the nature of the learning that occurs when children learn to read with instruction that teaches segmentation versus whole word repetition. While there is ample evidence indicating that reading development is best predicted by the phonemic awareness of the preschool or kindergarten child (e.g., Bradley and Bryant, 1983; Tunmer, Herriman, and Nesdale, 1988; Bryant, MacLean, Bradley, and Crossland, 1990; see Adams, 1990 for a thorough review), the instructional significance of this relationship is not obvious. Phonemic awareness is measured by a variety of tests (rhyme generation, oddity tasks, phoneme deletion, etc.) that may tap more than one basic skill. It is unclear how phonemic awareness develops or exactly what skills are involved. As Barron (1991) argued, phonemic awareness "is not a homogeneous skill that emerges naturally during the later stages of oral language development; instead, it is a heterogeneous skill and its acquisition involves a complex pattern of interactions between print and speech both before and after children learn to read and spell" (p. 243). There is now evidence that phonemic awareness is influenced by the prereading and the beginning reading experiences of the child and that beginning literacy experiences may be critical to the development of phonological sensitivities. This creates a "chicken or egg" dilemma; is phonemic awareness a precursor to beginning reading or a result of initial experiences with print (Mann, 1986, Barron, 1990)? Barron suggested there are protoliteracy skills that develop spontaneously from the child's early experiences with rhyming and alliteration; this protoliteracy then relates to sensitivity to orthographic units that are larger than phonemes. Print experience is necessary, however, to develop sensitivity to single phonemes, in Barron's view. The educator needs to know which language skills are precursors to developing reading, and he or she needs to understand how early listening skills relate to different types of orthographic units, so that the child can see units that are acoustically familiar.

While there is a considerable literature on training beginning readers, the optimal orthographic unit to use has not become apparent. Bryant and Bradley (1985) reported a two-year training study that began when the children were six years old. One group of children with poor phonemic awareness skill received sound-based training for two years, while the other group, who also had poor phonemic awareness, received the same sound-based training that was supplemented in the second year with training using plastic letters to relate spoken sounds to their letter representations. Both groups were reliably superior on reading and spelling following the two-year training regime, when compared with matched control groups who received only classroom instruction or training on semantic classification. The addition of plastic letters to teach spelling-sound correspondence reliably enhanced reading compared with the sound only group. These results suggest that phonemic awareness training leads to enhanced reading development, and that teaching grapheme-phoneme correspondence once awareness has developed further accelerates reading achievement. These children were six when training began, however, so they already had considerable literacy experience. Furthermore, there were no comparisons with other methods to gauge relative success as a first instructional methodology.

Roth and Beck (1987) used two computerized methods to help children become aware of the segments of written English. Very delayed fourth graders received eight months of training on a hint-and-hunt or a construct-a-word task that showed them how to form words from beginning and end segments and by changing the vowel to form new words. These tasks emphasized segment recognition and recombination skills. Training gains were indicated by improved standardized reading scores. Despite the success of this segmentation training, Roth and Beck suggested that such techniques should not be used for normal beginning readers, but rather were useful for delayed readers who need long periods of direct instruction to acquire skills that normal children develop spontaneously in the course of early literacy experience. The special difficulties of young dyslexic readers was also shown by Lovett, Warren-Chaplin, Ransby, and Borden (1990). They reported that dyslexic children read both regular and irregular words better than controls, following training with a whole word repetition method and following phonics instruction that sounded out and blended sounds in individual words. The control group received a nonreading skills program. Interestingly, the training gains were not greater for regular than for irregular words, even for the phonics group. This suggests that the phonics regime did not lead to reliance on grapheme-phoneme correspondence because that would have enhanced the reading of regular, relative to irregular, words. Furthermore, neither the phonics nor the whole word trained dyslexic readers were superior to controls in reading new words. There was improved spelling of new regular and irregular words for both groups, with the whole word group being reliably superior to the phonics group on spelling irregular words. Lovett et al. suggested that these reader have specific deficits in phonemic processing that might require intensive training to rectify.

In a recent paper, Lovett, Borden, DeLuca, Lacerenza, Benson and Brackstone (1994) reported generalization of training to the reading of new words from two training programs. PHAB emphasized phonological analysis and blending skills, while WIST taught word attack strategies (analogy to other words, seeking known parts, peeling prefixes and suffices, trying variable vowel pronunciations). WIST and PHAB showed equally good generalization to reading new regular words, but WIST trained dyslexics were better than PHAB-trained dyslexics in reading irregular words. These results may indicate that attending to units larger than the phoneme and/or reading by analogy may be most useful for very deficient readers.

In a more direct analysis of the benefits of phonic versus whole word methods, Vellutino and Scanlon (1986) trained poor and normal readers in grades two and six to read nonsense words composed from a novel regular alphabet. Children were trained with one of three methods: (1) by a phonics method that consisted of breaking words into component phonemes and sounding them out; (2) by a look-say, whole word method that also associated each word with a cartoon character to add meaning to the word; or (3) by a combination of both the phonic and whole word methods. While both methods by themselves led to better reading of new nonwords on a transfer test, compared with a classroom control group, the single methods did not differ from each other and the combined method yielded superior reading compared with either method by itself. Analyses of reading errors led Vellutino and Scanlon to argue that whole word training led to a more global word attack strategy and the phonics method to a more analytic strategy. They argued that both strategies are required for fluent reading and that optimal early instruction might focus first on whole words to start the reading process and then introduce phonics to improve analytic skills.

Despite this evidence that poor readers benefit from both whole word and phonics training, it is not clear whether either of these methods is the best one for introducing new print vocabulary to beginning normal readers. Goswami (1986, 1988, 1990a, b) has shown that preschoolers are sensitive to onset-rime segments of words even before they can respond to phonemes. The onset is the consonant or consonant cluster preceding the vowel, while the rime consists of the vowel and the subsequent consonant or consonant cluster. These units are said to be more discriminable than phonemes in spoken language for very young children (Kirtley, Bryant, MacLean, and Bradley, 1989; Treiman, 1985, 1992), and Goswami and Bryant (1990) have argued that rhyming and alliteration skills are causally related to reading development through the increase in sensitivity to these larger orthographic units during beginning reading. Goswami has suggested that knowledge of these larger units allows young readers to decipher unknown regular and irregular words through analogy to known words that share onsets or rimes.

Testing this view that beginning readers might benefit from segmentation into orthographic units larger than phonemes but smaller than whole words, Olson and Wise (1992) summarized their findings from two phases of the Colorado remediation project that compared training with different size units. Their sample consisted of poor readers whose functioning was anywhere from severely deficient to very near the national norm. They used a DECtalk computer system to provide both spoken and visual feedback when children were unable to read a word. Children read texts presented on the computer screen and with the aid of a mouse or a pen they were able to query particular words they could not read. For one group of readers, the query led the computer to highlight the word and give the word's pronunciation. For another group the computer feedback consisted of the word being broken into syllables and the syllables being individually pronounced—the syllable was isolated orthographically and pronounced as a unit. Finally, for a third group the words were broken into onset-rime segments and these were the units pronounced by the computer. A control group received regular, whole language classroom instruction while their trained peers were logged onto the computer.

During phase I of the study, 27 children received an average of 6.4 hours of computerized reading training with considerable supervision to ensure that words were appropriately targeted. In phase II of the study, a larger population of 111 children received training but with less initial training and supervision on the task, as was required to accommodate the larger sample. These children spent about 8.1 hours in computerized training. During phase I, children receiving onset-rime feedback showed the greatest gains in reading skill following training, while children in the whole word condition showed the weakest gains. With the larger sample, however, who may not have received enough supervision from teachers to preform the task optimally, the whole word group performed better at post-test than controls and the onset-rime feedback led to the worst performance. When Olson and Wise combined the two samples and then looked at the poorest readers versus the best readers in the two phases of their study, they found that onset-rime segmentation led to the smallest reading gains for the most severely disabled readers, but led to the largest reading gains for the least disabled readers. These results may suggest that these larger units are optimal only for children who are in the normal beginning reader population, but the result must be interpreted cautiously because the treatment differences were not large.

Some very recent studies have suggested limitations in the use of onset-rime segmentation as a way to learn to read new words. Goswami (1986, 1988) showed that when children are told how to read a word (e.g., *cat*) and then are shown *rat* while *cat* is still visible, they are able to read *rat* by analogy to *cat*. Thus, she argued that children can read new words by analogy to known words with shared onsets or rimes. Muter, Snowling, and Taylor (1994) reported that reading by analogy, however, is much reduced if the analogy word is not present when the new word is encountered. This suggests that such analogy processing would be of limited use in reading, where the known analogies are rarely also visible on the printed page. Further, Ehri and Robbins (1992) demonstrated that only if the child is already a "decoder", as indicated by the ability to read some nonwords, is reading by analogy observed in beginning readers. Children who could not read nonwords also failed to read new words even when the known analogy word was visible. These results again question the general use of onset-rime segmentation as a first orthographic unit for acquiring alphabetic knowledge about English print.

Haskell, Foorman, and Swank (1992) reported a study that directly compared whole word, phonemic, and onset-rime training given to 48 first grade children. Four groups of twelve children each were given pre- and post-tests requiring them to read 40 regular and 20 irregular words. The control group received only classroom experience during the six weeks between pre- and posttests, but the other three groups received fifteen 20-minute training sessions. The phonics group received training on phoneme segmentation and blending, the onset-rime group were taught to break words into these segments, while the whole word group read complete words for practice. While the four groups had been equivalent on the pre-test, only the phonics and onset-rime groups outperformed the controls at post-test. The phonics and onset-rime groups were not different. Haskell et al. concluded that both segmentation methods were superior to whole word reading for beginning reader, but the segment size matters little. There was a trend for the phonics group to read more regular words correctly than the onset-rime group, while the latter group did better than their phonics colleagues on the irregular words. The differences, however, were small and unreliable.

In contrast, training with onset-rime and phonemic segmentation did not lead to equivalent gains in a study reported by Bruck and Treiman (1992) who also studied first grade readers. They studied 39 grade 1 children attending normal classes with a whole-language reading curriculum. These children were accepted for study only if they already knew basic letter-sound relations, so they were decoders by the Ehri and Robbins (1992) criterion. They were then taught to read 10 target words by analogy to cue words. For each target there were three types of cue words, with different training groups defined by the type of cue they received. One group was first taught to read 10 cues that shared rimes with the 10 target words. They then attempted to read the 10 targets, using the Goswami analogy method, but where the rime unit of the cue and the target were also color highlighted to emphasize the unit similarity. For a second group the cues and targets shared onset plus vowels, and these were colored during the attempts to read the targets. For the third group the cues and targets had the same vowel sound but differed in other phonemes. Again, the similar vowels were color highlighted. Children attempted to read the list of 10 targets until they read 8 out of 10 correctly on two successive trials. After that, the colored highlighting was removed and the children read the targets in the presence of the cues but in black ink to the same criterion as above. The day after criterion was met, the cues were removed and the children's retention was tested by reading the targets without their analogy cues. Finally, all children were asked to read 20 CVC nonwords that were derived from the cue words, such that one nonword shared the rime of the cue and one shared the onset plus vowel. This was a generalization test to assess the specificity of the units learned in training. The basic result was that the rime group learned to read the 10 target words faster than the onset plus vowel and vowel only groups, but the rime group was worse than the other two on the retention test without the cue words, and it was the vowel only group who read the most words on the generalization. These mixed results offered no support for onset-rime over phoneme segmentation as the best training regime.

The available literature appears to offer no consistent advice for teachers on the appropriate orthographic unit for introducing reading vocabulary to beginning readers. The methodologies and duration of the interventions for the various studies as well as the populations used, however, were very different, making it difficult to draw good comparisons across studies. In our own recent studies (Levy and Lysynchuk, 1997) we contrasted learning via whole word repetition, with learning through segmentation training, using either phonemes or onset-rime units as the basic orthographic segment. Our interest was in the speed of acquisition of a set of new words, the retention of training over a week and even months, and the generalization of training to the reading of new words that contained the trained segments. In the first experiment we studied the success of these method for nonreaders in kindergarten and grade 1. In the second experiment we studied a grade 2 population who had failed to show the expected reading bloom in the latter half of the first grade. Our interest here was in whether the same methods were optimal for delayed readers as for normal beginning readers, because delayed readers may have particular difficulty with abstract segments rather than whole words (Roth and Beck, 1987; Lovett et al.,1990).

In experiment 1, 100 children (83 in Grade 1 and 17 in kindergarten), were selected from a larger population of 150 children from two schools of the Hamilton-Wentworth Separate School Board. Selection for the study was based on performance on the word identification subtest of the Woodcock Reading Mastery Test and the word identification subtest of the Wide Range Achievement Test (revised edition), as well as a pretest reading of all of the target words to be used in training. Only children who read very few words on any of these tests were included in the study sample. The grade 1 children were tested first, with the kindergartners added in the spring of that year, so that they were about to go into grade 1. Time of year effects were balanced across groups by assigning children equally to all conditions throughout the school year.

Twenty children were randomly assigned to each of five conditions. The control group received the pretests, the retention tests, and the generalization tests, but they received only regular classroom instruction in the five-week period during which their peers received training. The schools involved adhered to a whole-language curriculum. The pretests for all groups consisted of a battery of letter knowledge tests and tests of phonemic sensitivity as well as four subtests of the WISC-R (vocabulary, picture arrangement, similarities, and block design) and the Peabody Picture Vocabulary Tests. All children scored within the normal range on the WISC-R and the Peabody and there were no differences among the five groups on these measures. The letter tasks required the child to name all 26 letters of the alphabet and to provide one sound made by each letters. The phonemic sensitivity tasks consisted of *rhyme generation* where the child gave as many words as possible that rhymed with each of 10 target words; an *oddity* task where the child chose the word from a set of four spoken words that differed in the beginning, middle or end sound; a *syllable deletion* task where the child read 20 words after deleting the initial syllable; a *phoneme deletion* task that required deleting the first phoneme and then saying each of 20 words; and a *phoneme counting* task where the child laid out poker chips for each phoneme of a set of 20 words. Analyses of variance indicated that the five groups did not differ on any of the pretest measure. The letter and phonemic sensitivity measures were later correlated with the outcome measures for each training regime, as an index of the prereading skills that best relate to training success.

Following the pretest, four groups of children began training. All groups learned the same set of 32 words. As table 3.1 shows, these words could be divided into sets of 4 words that shared rimes (across rows) or that shared onsets and vowels (down columns). In the *rime* condition, sets of 4 words that shared a rime were shown together on cards, with their rime segment highlighted in colored ink to indicate the similar orthography. On the first trial the experimenter pronounced the rime and then read each word, emphasizing the onset-rime segments (*c-at, r-at ; b-at,* etc.). The child then attempted to read the set of 32 words, once a day for the next 15 days or until he or she read all 32 words correctly on two consecutive readings. If the child was unable to read a word, the experimenter read it with the on-

Table 3.1
Training words used in experiment 1

fit	bit	wit	pit
fig	big	wig	pig
fin	bin	win	pin
fill	bill	will	pill
cap	flap	map	rap
can	flan	man	ran
cash	flash	mash	rash
cat	flat	mat	rat

set-rime segmentation. After 15 trials or after criterion was met, the child then read the 32 words again, but this time without the colored highlighting, for another 10 trials or until a criterion of two perfect readings was achieved. For the *onset* condition, the procedure was identical but the 4 words of a set shared the onset and vowel and these were in colored highlighting for the first 15 trials or until criterion was met. For the *phoneme* condition, the four words shown together were unrelated but each phoneme of every word was highlighted in a different color and the experimenter sounded out and blended the phonemes. Criteria for colored and black-white trials were as above. In the *whole word* condition, the words were unrelated and were always printed in black ink. The experimenter read each word and then the child read them on 15 trials or until two perfect readings in succession. After that there were 10 further readings or until criterion was met again. Feedback for errors or misses was always the word name with no segmentation.

After the end of training the children received two generalization tests. First they were asked to read 48 new words, 24 that began with onset plus vowels that had occurred in the training set and 24 that ended in rimes that occurred in training. Then, they were asked to read 48 nonwords—24 with trained onsets and 24 with trained rimes. Finally, one week after the end of training, all 100 children again attempted to read the 32 trained words to gauge the retention of training for each condition. After the first six months of testing, the teachers asked us to retest all of the children again to see whether they could still read the words. This retention test was four to six months post training. Thus the data from the study indicate the speed of acquisition, the retention of training after one week and after four to six months as well as generalization of training to new words and nonwords that shared the trained units. An ideal method for first instruction would be one that led to the most rapid learning, but that also led to good retention and generalization to reading new items with similar orthographies.

The important findings can be easily summarized. The onset and rime conditions led to the fastest acquisition, followed by the phoneme condition, with the whole word condition being the slowest (see figure 3.1). The onset and rime conditions were reliably superior to the whole word condition, but the phoneme condition was intermediate and not reliably different from either extreme. Another way to examine learning is to look at the number of children who met criterion by the end of the 15 color trials in each condition. Of the 20 children per group, 15 in the onset, 18 in the rime, 15 in the phoneme, but only 7 in the whole word, conditions met this criterion. Again, the segmentation conditions were clearly superior to the whole word group. Table 3.2 contains the mean proportion read correctly after one week and after four to six months. The most striking thing to note is that retention was good for all training methods, indicating that if training is extensive then retention is good irrespective of training method. After one week, however, the onset and rime groups were reliably superior to the whole word group with the phoneme group again not differing from either extreme. After four to six months the four trained groups were still reliably better than the control group, but only the phoneme group was reliably better than whole word. These differences in retention must be qualified however. These differences occur only when all 20 children in each group are included in the analyses. When retention is analysed only

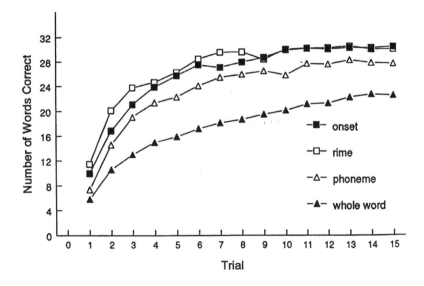

Figure 3.1   Mean number of words read correctly by each
    training group of beginning readers on the first 15 days of training (from
    Levy and Lysynchuk, 1997).

Table 3.2

Mean proportion of words read correctly (M) and
standard deviations (SD) on retention tests

		One week	4 to 6 months
Onset	M	.89	.81
	SD	.19	.30
Rime	M	.92	.75
	SD	.20	.30
Phoneme	M	.83	.86
	SD	.28	.18
Whole word	M	.68	.70
	SD	.34	.27
Control	M	.15	.40
	SD	.22	.33

Source: Levy and Lysynchuk (1997).

for children who met the criterion of perfect learning, then no differences due to method of learning occur. All training groups are better than controls on the retention test, but the groups differences are entirely due to the children who failed to fully acquire the word set during training. Clearly, retention is determined by the degree of learning. When the word set is well learned, irrespective of method of acquisition, then retention is excellent.

Finally, table 3.3 shows the mean proportion of generalization words and nonwords read correctly. The data are separated into words that shared trained onsets and trained rimes because for the shared onset words all four trained groups were reliably superior to the control group, indicating generalization of learning, but the onset group was also superior to the whole word group, indicating a specific benefit for the trained segment. For the words with trained rimes, all groups were again superior to the control group, but in addition all three segmentation groups were superior to the whole word group. Again, these data show good generalization to new words, and training with any size segments appears to lead to knowledge of the larger rime unit, compared with the whole word training. As in retention, however, these differences in generalization disappear if data for only children who met the criterion of perfect learning are analyzed. Method of acquisition is irrelevant when the entire word set was perfect acquired. The data for nonwords are not broken into shared segment because there was no interaction involving that variable. Rather, for all 48 generalization nonwords the four trained groups were superior to controls, with no reliable differences among training conditions. The most strik-

Table 3.3

Mean proportion (M) and standard deviations (SD) for new words read correctly on the first encounter on generalization tests

| | Word | | | | Nonword | |
| | Shared onset | | Shared rime | | | |
	M	SD	M	SD	M	SD
Onset	.40	.21	.53	.30	.57	.27
Rime	.34	.23	.47	.32	.43	.29
Phoneme	.36	.23	.52	.29	.51	.31
Whole word	.26	.26	.30	.31	.40	.35
Control	.05	.15	.07	.16	.09	.21

Source: Levy and Lysynchuk (1997).

ing aspect of table 3.3 is that these children read 40 to 50 percent of the new words and nonwords on their first encounter with them after their training experiences. Clearly, knowledge about word parts was acquired even with whole word exposure for these word sets that contained word families with repeated segments. Taking the word and nonword data together, while all training regimes led to generalization, there was again an advantage for the segmentation training over the whole word repetition, but this advantage was due to the better learning that occurred during segmentation training.

Taking the acquisition, retention, and generalization data together, there is clear superiority of segmentation training over whole word repetition as a means to rapidly acquire new reading vocabulary. Even whole word reading led to significant gains, however, that generalized to reading new words and nonwords, indicating that normally progressing children abstract orthographic units as they learn new words, even if these are not specifically taught. While the differences between segmenting into phonemes versus onset-rime units were sometimes not significant, the onset-rime performance was consistently better than the phoneme performance. The onset-rime groups were almost always reliably better than the whole word group while the phoneme group was not. The overall pattern suggests an advantage for these normal beginning readers when the larger units are taught first. Regression analyses of the training outcome measures with the pretests of letter knowledge and phonemic sensitivity indicated that knowing letter names and/or sounds was the best predictor of training success, irrespective of training method. The phonemic sensitivity measure often added some additional predictive power, but letter knowledge appears to be the most important prerequisite skill for early readers.

Given this outcome for normal beginning readers, we next asked whether the same advantage of segmentation methods over whole word repetition would be found for children who failed to make the expected progress in reading during grade 1. In the second half of grade 1, most children show a reading 'bloom' whereby they begin to read beyond the single word level. Some children enter grade 2, however, already behind their peers in reading skill. Phonemic sensitivity measures have been shown to reliably predict these early reading problems (see Adams, 1990, or Carr and Levy, 1990, for reviews) and it has been suggested that these children have specific problems with segmentation skills. Is this a subset of children who may benefit more from an initial training regime that used whole word reading rather than forcing them to read with the word segments that may tax their phonological skills?

To address this issue we conducted another study using the same five-group design as in the beginning nonreader study. The trained words were again 32 words that could be divided into sets of 4 words with shared onsets or shared rimes, but these words contained more consonant clusters to accommodate the grade 2 level. Training again consisted of 15 colored trials, followed by 10 black and white trials, or until criterion was met in both phases. Retention was tested after one week and generalization was tested the day after training. Again 48 words and 48 nonwords that shared onsets and rimes with the training set were tested in generalization. The participants in this study were 125 grade 2 children, 25 randomly assigned to each group, from 16 schools in the same school system. Their mean score on the Woodcock Reading Mastery Test word identification subtest was at the grade 1.2 level and in the preschool range of the reading subtest of the Wide Range Achievement Test. On average they read only 3 or 4 words on a pretest of the training words. These children, then, were selected for study because they were the most deficient readers in these sixteen schools that were scattered over a broad geographic area and covered a broad range of socioeconomic classes.

Figure 3.2 shows that mean proportion of words read correctly on the 15 colored trials. The most important result is the speed with which these poor readers learned the 32 word set, irrespective of training technique. Clearly, when shown word families, these children acquired reading vocabulary quickly. Analyses of variance, however, indicated that there were reliable differences in acquisition among the training conditions, even though these differences decreased as all groups approached ceiling performance after the first five or six trials. The rime group was reliably superior to the whole word and the phoneme groups, and the onset group was reliably superior to the whole word group. Thus, while all training methods led to rapid learning, the onset-rime segmentation methods again showed an advantage. By the fifteenth trial, 24 rime, 25 onset, 20 phoneme, and 19 whole word

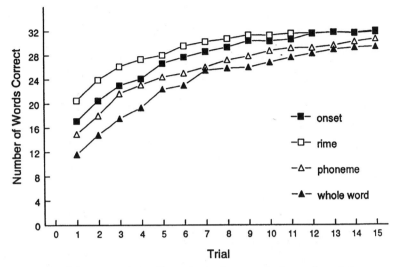

Figure 3.2 Mean number of words read correctly by each training group
        of problem readers on the first 15 days of training. (from Levy and
        Lysynchuk, 1997).

subjects had all reached the criterion of two successive perfect readings. Thus most
of these poor readers learned the set within three weeks.

Table 3.4 shows that retention of the trained set over a week-long interval was
around 90%, with no reliable differences due to method, but all trained subjects
were superior to the control readers who received only classroom experience. Table
3.5 contains the mean proportion of new words and nonwords read correctly on
the generalization test. The word data are broken into words that had shared rimes
versus those with shared onsets. When all 125 children were included in the analyses, the onset trained group outperformed their whole-word peers on the onset
generalization words. No other differences occurred among the four trained groups.
All trained groups were superior, however, to the control group on both word and
nonword reading, even when only those who met the perfect learning criterion were
included, but the specific advantage for the onset trained group on onset words
disappeared when only children who met criterion during learning were included
in the analyses. That is, all types of training led to good generalization to reading
the new words and nonwords. The excellent generalization for these poor readers
indicates that when taught to read word families these children were able to learn
orthographic segments, even if these were not emphasized in training. Overall, there
was again an advantage in efficiency of learning for the onset-rime segmentation
methods, but the differences were smaller than in the nonreader study and these

Table 3. 4
Mean proportion (M) and standard deviations (SD) of
words read correctly on the retention tests after one week

	M	SD
Onset	.88	.18
Rime	.90	.21
Phoneme	.92	.16
Whole word	.88	.16
Control	.49	.33

Source: Levy and Lysynchuk (1997).

children showed remarkable ability to learn new reading vocabulary, given that they were the poorest readers in their schools. Perhaps more reading of related words, as in word families, is important in establishing the orthographic "neighborhoods" that may be critical for generalization in reading development.

The findings of the Levy and Lysynchuk studies suggest that it is important to continue training until all words are well learned. Learning must be well consolidated to avoid the problems of poor retention and generalization that plagued the Bruck and Treiman (1992) study. We also suggest that the Goswami single-word analogy method may not be a good way to establish the larger onset-rime discriminations needed for spontaneous use of these segments. Reading by analogy relies on easy memorial access to a neighborhood of words with similar segments that can be retrieved to assist in reading by analogy. Single analogy words may be insufficient, but our word families appeared to be beneficial in establishing knowledge of these units that could be used to read new words and nonwords, even when the trained words were not visible. Our findings suggest that for most beginning readers, training with segmentation methods leads to optimal learning, retention and generalization compared with whole word repetition. Even whole word repetition of words from word families, however, led to rapid learning and good generalization, particularly for the poor grade 2 readers. The popularity of Dr. Seuss books with young readers may stem partly from the manner in which they teach word families through rhyme play in a meaningful context. Our studies lead me to recommend the use of onset-rime segmentation as the initial method of instruction for setting up new reading vocabulary, with these larger units gradually broken into their phonemic segments for the child. If a child does not respond to these

Table 3.5

Mean proportions (M) and standard deviations (SD)
for new words read correctly on the first encounter on the
generalization test

| | Word | | | | Nonword | |
| | Shared onset | | Shared rime | | | |
	M	SD	M	SD	M	SD
Onset	.52	.20	.45	.23	.63	.27
Rime	.43	.23	.40	.22	.53	.21
Phoneme	.49	.24	.44	.24	.63	.23
Whole word	.39	.24	.43	.24	.54	.27
Control	.20	.20	.23	.18	.34	.23

Source: Levy and Lysynchuk (1997).

segments, however, the teacher should remember that whole word repetition also led to rapid learning and good generalization when word families were studied.

Developing Reading Fluency

The training studies just described suggested that early direct instruction on orthographic-phonological segmentation aids the child in establishing initial reading vocabulary and provides word attack skills that can be used to decipher new words. There is more to early reading development, however, than just setting up the reading lexicon. Through reading practice the child must learn to identify written words within milliseconds so that reading does not become resource-limited. Practice acts to automate word recognition processes, thus freeing resources or attentional capacity for higher-order linguistic analyses (Laberge and Samuels, 1974). There is now reasonable agreement that the child who struggles to slowly get the words from the page suffers from the need to focus at the word level, disrupting the smooth integration of ideas that is needed to fluently comprehend text. To compensate for these slow word recognition processes, some children rely on context and attempt to guess the word rather than decipher the print (Stanovich, 1981a). While it has been argued that such contextual reliance is a signature of fluent readers (e.g., Goodman, 1970, 1985), there is evidence showing that fluent readers process words so rapidly that the slow speed of contextual guessing would actually hinder their reading progress (Perfetti and Roth, 1981; Stanovich, 1981b). These researchers argue that it is rapid word recognition, not contextual guessing, that best characterizes the fluent reader. Practice or repetition is needed to develop automatized word recognition, but what processes are involved in the improved speed observed with reading practice?

Most of the research on word recognition speed comes from studies that measure naming times for visually presented stimuli. There is a well-established correlation between reading ability and naming times for words and pseudowords (Perfetti, Finger, and Hogaboam, 1978; Stanovich, 1981b). There has been dispute, however, about whether there is a more general deficit in naming time that extends to nonalphabetic items. Levy and Hinchley (1990) found a strong relationship between word and pseudoword reading times and reading ability for children in grades 3 through 6. While the magnitude of the reading time difference between good and poor readers was smaller for the older children, the difference was still reliable in grade 6. Regression analyses indicated that naming time was the main predictor of reading ability, when reading speed was used as a criterion variable. Even when good and poor readers were selected largely on the basis of text comprehension skill, naming times still contributed to prediction of reading ability. Further, in every grade good readers named pictures of objects about 200 msec faster than poorer readers, suggesting that there was a more global deficit in visual access times for poor readers. Recently Bowers and Swanson, (1991, see also Bowers, 1995) showed a relationship between digit naming speed and reading ability. This variance in reading ability captured by the digit naming task was independent of variance attributable to phonemic awareness. Bowers and Wolf (1993) suggested that digit naming time may act as a marker of poor orthographic processing. They suggested that children who name digits slowly are those who have a general deficit in the speed of sequential visual processing. This problem relates to poor skill in grasping the orthographic patterns that allow more fluent readers to read words in larger orthographic units, like syllables and even words. They argued that fluency requires automating visual access to larger orthographic units so that the reader is not required to decode words in an algorithmic fashion as skill develops.

Similarly, Perfetti (1992), in discussing the development of representations used in reading, suggested that decoding processes may play a role in setting up the representations used in reading, but that "as words become represented in the lexicon, decoding becomes only indirectly important" (p.155). He suggested that the letter constituents of words are automatically activated during the access process, but that the critical representations are of words not subword units. Like Ehri (1992), Perfetti presented a view of "sight word" reading that suggests an interactive dependency with orthographic and phonological processes. That is, whole word reading is not through direct access from visual word forms to meaning. Rather, access is buttressed by the activation of orthographic and phonological associations such that the whole word becomes activated. As Ehri (1992) says, " At some point the reader's memory for that specific word should take over and eliminate the need for phonological recoding" (p. 113).

What experiences lead to this freeing of the reader from the need to decode on every occurrence? What automates the word recognition process so that naming times fall within the millisecond range needed for fluent reading? An obvious candidate is reading practice. One advantage that early readers have over their reading-delayed peers is that they read for pleasure. Their reading practice does not depend only on school instruction. Good readers read, thus automating their word recognition skills, and perhaps also setting up the automatic access to word representations as discussed by Perfetti and by Ehri. Poor readers read only when forced by teachers or parents because it is a slow and laborious task. Consequently, they miss the hundreds of hours of practice that their good reading peers gain through reading outside of the classroom. This lack of practice leads to slow laborious access because the buttressing associations to support access to whole word representations are not formed. The notion that simple practice in reading words changed the access to familiar word representations led Lemoine, Levy, and Hutchinson (1993) to explore the effects of repeated reading on the speed of naming visually presented words. Our interest was in the variables that determined long term benefits of practice and also in the nature of the mechanism that mediated such benefits.

The naming time task was presented to children as a "stop the clock" game. A word appeared on a computer monitor and the child attempted to name it as rapidly as possible. Visual feedback allowed the child to attempt to better his or her speed on each trial. The child's voice triggered a voice key attached to the computer so that the computer recorded naming time and accuracy for each trial. In our first study, 40 good and 40 poor readers in grade 3 classrooms were given practice in naming either 50 regular words or 50 exception words. The words were chosen to be familiar to most grade 3 children, so that we could study speed changes for words already represented in the child's visual lexicon. For each word type, subsets of the words were practiced 5, 10, 15, 20 or 25 times over the week of training. One week after the completion of training, the words were retested to evaluate the long-term retention of training benefits.

Figure 3.3 shows the mean median reading times for regular and irregular words, for good and poor readers, over the 25 training repetitions. For good readers there was no difference in naming times for regular and irregular words and the reliable repetition effect was due to a gain of about 100 msec over the first 3 repetitions. For poor readers, on the other hand, there were large gains in naming speed

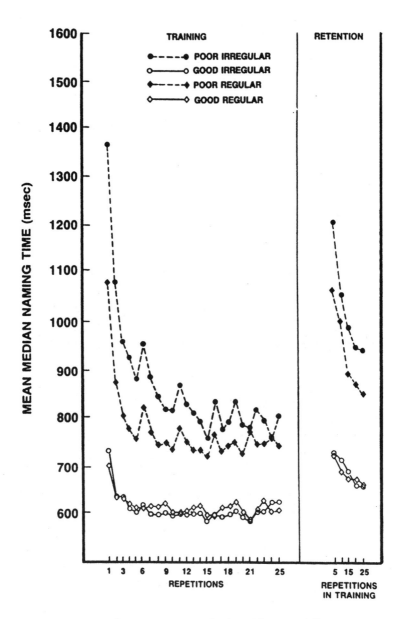

Figure 3.3 Mean median naming time (ms) as a function of repetitions for regular and irregular words (adapted from Lemoine, Levy and Hutchinson, 1993).

over the first 9 or 10 repetitions, after which naming times stabilized. The difference between naming times for regular versus irregular words also became smaller over these trials. Basically, the poor readers showed rapid learning of both types of words even though their naming times never became as rapid as those of the good readers. While the acquisition function flattened after the first 10 repetitions, leading one to think that there were no further training benefits, the functions in the retention panel of figure 3.3 show that this conclusion is unwarranted. The retention functions show the mean median naming times for words given 5, 10, 15, 20, or 25 repetitions during training. It is clear from the figure that if training had been stopped after 10 repetitions, the gains in naming times would have been lost over the week-long retention interval. The more repetitions in training, the better the consolidation of those gains over the retention interval. The accuracy data mirrored the naming time results. The good readers made almost no errors. The poor readers made a few errors on the irregular words, but accuracy was perfect by trial 10.

The main points to be taken from this study are that repetition leads to very rapid gains in word recognition speed for both regular and irregular words, and these gains can be made stable by overlearning, in that retention was better when training was continued well beyond the point where changes in naming times levelled off. The fact that the naming time gains were just as large for the irregular as for the regular words led us to suspect that orthographic-phonological mechanisms were not critical to the repetition benefits. Lovett et al. (1990) also reported training gains due to word repetition that were similar for regular and irregular words, for very delayed readers. To further explore the dependence of the repetition benefit on mechanisms that segmented words into regular units, we conducted a second study using word families. Using the naming time game just described, we trained 36 poor readers in grade 3 to name 40 words—4 members of 10 word families—where the words of a family shared the rime. For half of the subjects the four family members always occurred together on each repetition (blocked presentation), while for the other half of the subjects the 40 words were scrambled so that no two family members ever occurred in succession (scrambled presentation). The logic of this manipulation was that if the naming time benefit across repetitions was mediated by a mechanism that relied on orthographic regularity, then the blocked presentation would highlight the rime regularity, and consequently learning and retention would be better for blocked than for scrambled presentation conditions. Retention of training gains was tested four and seven days posttraining. Figure 3.4 shows the acquisition and retention functions.

While figure 3.4 shows a small advantage for blocked over scrambled presentation in the first few trials, there was no reliable effect of blocking in the analysis.

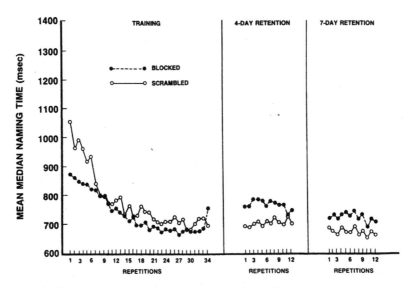

Figure 3.4 Mean median naming time (ms) as a function of repetitions
during acquisition and retention after 4 and 7 days (from Lemoine,
Levy and Hutchison, 1993).

The only reliable effect during acquisition was the decrease in naming time over
the 34 repetitions that was equivalent for the two presentation conditions. Thus
the learning gains did not appear to be mediated by a mechanism that was sensitive to the spelling-sound regularity that was made so obvious in the blocked condition. As the two retention panels of figure 3.4 indicate, after 34 repetitions during learning the naming time gain was stable over the week interval. No further
decrease in naming times occurred with repetitions during the retention test. There
was no retention loss of this newly acquired naming skill. Thus the effects of practice in making word recognition more fluent are rapid and can be made stable with
only 34 repetitions.

Knowing that practice had such a large effect on naming time, and that the
first two studies showed no effect of manipulations of the orthographic to phonological regularities, we tried an even stronger manipulation of the blocking of word
families by using larger word families in the next study. This time we trained 42
words, that were 6 exemplars of only 7 families. In the blocked condition all six
members of a family always occurred together, whereas in the scrambled condition
no two family siblings could occur in succession. Thirty-two poor readers in grade
4 participated in the training sessions, and then in a generalization test four days
after training. During the generalization test, all children attempted first to read 42
new words that contained the trained rimes, 6 exemplars of the 7 rime families. They

read this set four times so that we could also see savings in learning. After the same rime test, the children then read, four times, a set of 42 new words that had rimes that had not occurred in training. The purpose of these generalization tests was to examine benefits to trained units that are smaller than the whole word, in this case the rimes that had occurred in the training set.

Figure 3.5 shows the acquisition and generalization data for blocked and scrambled presentation conditions. With these larger word families, there was a reliable advantage in acquisition for the blocked presentation condition. While the repetition effect was reliable in both conditions, the learning slope was much flatter when the family words were blocked. Clearly, children in the blocked condition were relying on the rime similarities to enhance their naming speed. Despite this use of the rime overlap during learning, however, there was no generalization of the speed gain to the naming of new words that shared the trained rimes during generalization. The generalization data in figure 3.5 show the naming times for same

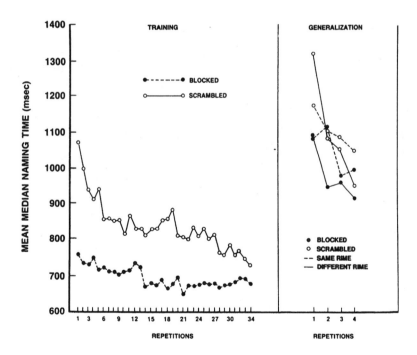

Figure 3.5 Mean median naming time (ms) as a function of repetitions during acquisition and generalization to new words (from Lemoine, Levy and Hutchison, 1993).

versus different rime words for children trained in the blocked versus scrambled conditions. In the generalization test all family rime words were scrambled. A quick glance indicates that the same rime words were named no faster than the different rime words, even after blocked training where family resemblance had been used to speed naming during training. These data indicate again that the fluency gains in word recognition that occur with practice do not appear to be mediated by mechanisms that are sensitive to units smaller than words and that the gains are specific to the trained items. This type of learning looks like "sight word" acquisition, but this does not mean it has no relation to alphabetic principles. As Ehri (1992) and Perfetti (1992) have suggested, once the reading lexicon is established, practice acts to free access from the need to actively decode when a known word is encountered. The word representation is activated, but this is an interactive consequence of the known orthographic and phonological representations that buttress the words representation. Unlike our earlier training studies with unknown words described in the first section, the effects of practice on speed gains appear to be centered on the entire lexical unit with no generalization to words that share a smaller orthographic segment, in this case the rime.

The main point of this section of the paper was to emphasize that whole word repetition or reading practice also plays an important role in early reading development. Once an item is represented in the reading lexicon, practice leads to its automatic activation during reading, without the need to actively decode it into its orthographic segments on each occurrence. This type of practice should be used to enhance reading fluency or reading speed even when the child can decipher the print. The teacher's job is not finished when the child can manage to decode print; access must become fluent and automatic. Whole word practice appears to provide the experience necessary to meet this need.

Reading in Context

All of the research discussed so far focused on word recognition when the words were out of context. While there is a strong relationship between reading words out of context and in context, we must still consider the benefits of contextual reading. In fact, the "whole language" philosophy of reading instruction advocates almost exclusive use of contextual reading. This emphasis on the use of contextual reading stems from Goodman's (1970; 1985) notion of top-down guidance of reading. In his view, context provides the key to reducing the processing load of reading. He viewed fluent reading as a psycholinguistic guessing game (Goodman, 1970), whereby the fluent reader did not have to "plod through the print", left to right down the page. Rather, the fluent reader was a problem solver who used context and knowledge to constrain word recognition. The cognitive system provided hypotheses on the meaning being conveyed and the printed text needed to be sampled only enough to confirm these message-level hypotheses. Goodman believed that reading every word was a nonfluent form of reading. The constraints of linguistic structure, general knowledge, and text context freed the fluent reader from a need to fully analyze all of the printed display. This notion led some educators to advocate contextual guessing as the mainstay of initial reading instruction. Rather than spending much of the limited instructional time teaching word attack strategies, the emphasis was moved to teaching the child to figure out the concept (even if the wrong word was finally read) from verbal and nonverbal context. As long as the meaning remained coherent and consistent with the text's intent, correction of word errors was often considered unimportant.

Irrespective of ones view of this instructional technique for use with young children, there is evidence that contextual reading aids in reading development. I will focus here on the use of repeated readings as a remedial technique for children with reading problems and ask what mechanisms lead to the benefits observed from repeatedly reading a text. Dahl (1979) used repeated reading to help poor readers in grade 2. During daily 20 minute sessions over an eight-month period, children read passages over and over until they met a criterion reading speed of 100 words/minute When criterion was met, a new story was chosen and repeated readings continued. Later tests of word identification ability, and of comprehension using a cloze measure, indicated that children trained with repeated reading outperformed a control group given regular classroom experience as well as a group that was trained for eight months on single-word identification. This latter group was no better than the classroom control. Dahl argued that the repeated readings experience provided the practice needed for the development of reading fluency. " Using repeated practice in meaningful context gives the child the opportunity to integrate the subskills." (p. 62). Basically, she argued that reading words in context did more than just automate word recognition skills. It allowed the reader to integrate word recognition with comprehension skills.

While Samuels (1979) reported similar benefits for poor readers trained with the repeated readings technique, he credited the benefits to automating word recognition so that processing resources became available for comprehension. This position is questioned, however, by the work of Fleisher, Jenkins, and Pany (1979). These researchers first trained poor readers to rapidly identify words out of context. They then asked the children to read texts containing these words. While the word-trained children read the texts faster than untrained children, their comprehension of the texts was no better. That is, improving word recognition did not lead to improved reading comprehension as suggested by Samuel's argument. Rather, contextual reading appears to provide benefits, at the text level, as suggested by Dahl. What are these benefits? One possibility is that when a text is read repeatedly, a representation is formed in memory that can then be used to guide subsequent reading. Goodman's view might suggest that the prior reading provided knowledge about the text that can then be used for hypothesis generation, so that the child need not "plod through the print." The improved fluency across readings results from the child now being able to sample, rather than fully analyse the print, so that resources can then be focused on comprehension.

In a study by Levy, Nicholls, and Kohen (1993), we tested this explanation of the repeated reading benefit. Good and poor readers in grades 3 to 5 read stories four times each. While they read they also crossed out any misspelled words they noticed. On each reading there were 20 misspelled words on the page. Ten misspellings were pronounceable nonwords, formed by changing one letter in a word, such that the visual envelope of the word was not altered. The other 10 misspellings were word substitutions that were visually similar to the correct word, but that did not make sense in the sentence context. These 20 misspellings were randomly distributed across the page. An important point was that on each of the four readings of a story the 20 misspelled words were different. The logic here was that over the four readings, reading times should get faster and faster. If this improved reading fluency resulted from the use of memorial knowledge from prior readings to guide reading, as suggested by Goodman (1970), then this top-down guidance should free the reader from the need to analyze every word. If that were true, then on the later readings the child should read faster but he or she should also miss more of the misspellings because not all of the print would be sampled.

The data did not support this view. As figure 3.6 shows, for every grade level there was a graceful decline in reading times over the four readings, indicating a build up of fluency with practice. The figure shows this effect for stories that were at grade level and for stories that were one grade above and one grade below grade level. The new data points represent reading of unpracticed stories at the end of the experiment. These data points indicate the generalizability of the training effects. While good readers read faster than poor readers, the poor readers actually improved more over the four readings than the good readers. Thus, as Dahl and Samuels have shown, repeated readings improve reading fluency, particularly for poor readers. Importantly, this improved reading fluency over repeated readings was accompanied by improved, not worse, detection of misspellings, particularly word misspellings (see figures 3.7 and 3.8 for detection of nonword and word errors respectively). The word errors could only be detected by realizing that the sentences

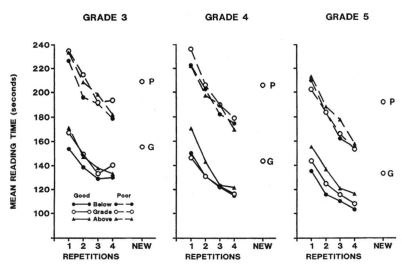

Figure 3.6 Mean reading time in seconds across reading repetitions (from Levy, Nicholls and Kohen, 1993).

in which they occurred were incoherent, so the better detection as the children read faster on these later readings indicated that they were still reading for meaning. That is, children were not scanning or sampling on the later readings, rather than reading all of the print as they read for meaning, because scanning or sampling would have led to missing the word errors that could only be detected at the syntactic-semantic level. Thus, improved speed was accompanied by improved word recognition, not scanning and guessing as Goodman's view suggests. Finally, the childrens' comprehension, as measured by question answering, also improved over the four readings, again suggesting that repetitions led to faster reading and better understanding of the story.

This study reinforced the view that repeated text reading is a good remedial technique, but not because it allowed children to act as "contextual guessers." Rather, practice improved both word recognition and comprehension skills. In a further study of the mechanisms involved in the benefits observed from repeatedly reading a text, Faulkner and Levy (1994) manipulated the similarity of stories read in succession. Two successive stories could be identical repetitions, or they could be paraphrases of each other such that they conveyed the same message but with different wording, or they could have many of the same words but convey different messages. Comparisons among these three conditions allowed us to determine the separate and joint contributions of repeated words and of repeated meanings of two stories to the reading speed and accuracy gains on the second reading. Basically we

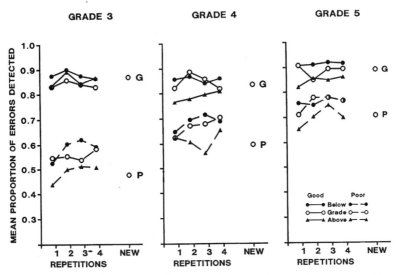

Figure 3.7 Mean proportion of nonword errors detected across reading
repetitions (from Levy, Nicholls and Kohen, 1993).

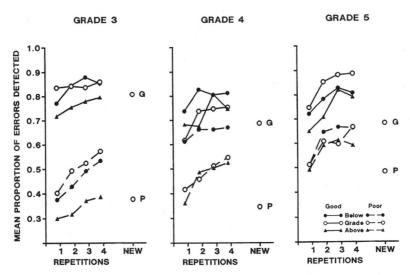

Figure 3.8 Mean proportion of word errors detected across reading
repetitions (from Levy, Nicholls and Kohen, 1993).

wanted to know whether the faster and more accurate reading of the second story was mediated by a lexical or a meaning-based representation. In the first two studies the important findings were that for good readers, the second story was read faster and more accurately when both wording and meaning were the same as in first story (i.e., the repetition condition). There was also a smaller but reliable benefit, however, when the meaning but not the wording were the same (paraphrase condition). There was no benefit when the second story used a lot of the words from the first story but to convey an unrelated message (word overlap condition). Good readers, then, appear to rely on meaning based representations that may contain lexical information, but word representations themselves, out of the meaning context, could not mediate the rereading benefit. For poor readers, on the other hand, while the repetition condition was again reliably superior to the other two, there was also a reliable rereading benefit when only the meaning or only the words were repeated in the second story. (See table 3.6 for mean reading times for these conditions for children in grades 1 and 3) The important point here is that poor readers appear to learn individual words in texts and these new words are accessed when read in an entirely new context. Thus for poor readers, the text representation is not so tightly integrated around meaning, and these children gain word recognition practice even in text contexts.

Table 3.6
Mean reading times (in seconds) for the second stories

		Repetition	Word Overlap	Paraphrase	Unrelated
Grade 1					
Good readers	M	66.88	77.12	74.80	78.93
	SD	10.43	15.81	12.79	15.22
Poor Readers	M	119.21	135.90	140.34	148.22
	SD	22.84	27.37	28.33	32.87
Grade 3					
Good readers	M	75.29	82.69	79.49	86.22
	SD	16.11	18.08	14.12	20.67
Poor readers	M	131.66	147.79	152.84	165.67
	SD	34.65	38.13	39.18	39.39

Source: Faulkner and Levy (1994)

These results are qualified in the later studies of the Faulkner and Levy (1994) paper, in that it is not reader skill per se that determines whether word level representations can contribute independently to rereading benefits. Rather, it is the relationship between the reader's skill and the text's difficulty such that the independent word level effects are observed when the materials are difficult for that reader's skill level. When the reader must focus at the word recognition level, then word recognition gains are observed. When the text is easy for the reader, then higher-order text mechanisms consume the rereading benefits (see also Faulkner and Levy, 1999). These studies suggest that both Samuels and Dahl were partly correct in the mechanisms that underlie rereading gains, particularly for poor readers. The representations formed during reading for poor readers are less well organized around the message than are those formed by good readers. Practice can then improve the automaticity of word recognition while it also helps the subskill integration that leads to fluent text reading (see Levy, 1993; Levy, Abello, and Lysynchuk, 1997; Bourassa, Levy, Dowin, and Casey, 1998). Bowers (1993) reported a study of repeated reading of text and demonstrated that the gains in reading speed are related to digit naming speed, the variable that she has shown to be a marker of orthographic processing. She argued that the speed gains in repeated readings are fluency gains unrelated to phonemic awareness that is usually viewed as the prime developmental indicator of skill. Again, the point is that more than one process is important to early reading development. From the teacher's perspective, the results described here suggest that he or she should not view reading in context as a guessing task. Rather, contextual reading provides an opportunity for practice that automates skills and integrates word and comprehension subskills so as to mediate fluent reading. Contextual reading may not be a good way to rapidly acquire new words, but it is a good way to improve fluency and comprehension.

Conclusions

The research discussed in this chapter shows that educational debates that focus on one versus another method, as the sole form of first reading instruction, are wrong-headed. Each type of reading experience contributes to the development of reading ability. Understanding the orthographic to phonological regularities helps the child to quickly set up a reading lexicon with knowledge that can be used to help in deciphering new unknown words. Whole word practice frees the reader from the need to actively decode on each reading encounter, fostering the development of reading fluency or speed. Contextual reading adds to this arsenal of instructional tools by providing further practice that is particularly useful in automating and integrating the skills of word recognition and of message comprehension. Fluent reading is a complex and highly skilled act. Children must be provided with educational opportunities to improve all aspects of this difficult skill.

Acknowlegments

Preparation of this manuscript and all of the studies from my laboratory described here werre supported by grants from the Ontario Mental Health Association. I am grateful for the foundation's support and for the support of the Hamilton-Wentworth Catholic Separate School Board in opening their schools to us. The teachers, parents, and children in these schools have made the work possible and enjoyable, and we thank them for their participation. Through cooperative efforts of researchers and school systems, we hope that all children can benefit.

References

Adams, M.J. (1990). *Beginning to Read: Thinking and Learning about Print*. Cambridge, MA:MIT Press.

Barron, R. (1991). Proto-literacy, literacy and the acquisition of phonological awareness. *Learning and Individual Differences, 3*, 243–255.

Bourassa, D.C., Levy, B.A., Dowin, S., and Casey, A. (1998). Transfer effects across contextual and linguistic boundaries: Evidence from poor readers. *Journal of Experimental Child Psychology, 71*, 45–61.

Bowers, P.G. (1993). Text reading and rereading: Determinants of fluency beyond word recognition. *Journal of Reading Behavior, 25*, 133–153.

Bowers, P.G. (1995). A speculative account of several factors affecting the development of orthographic skill. *Paper presented at the annual AERA meeting, San Francisco*.

Bowers, P.G, and Swanson, L.B. (1991). Naming speed deficits in reading disability: Multiple measures of a single process. *Journal of Experimental Child Psychology, 51*, 195–219.

Bowers, P.G., and Wolf, M. (1993). Theoretical links among naming speed, precise timing mechanisms and orthographic skill in dyslexia. *Reading and Writing: An Interdisciplinary Journal, 5*, 69–85.

Bradley, L., and Bryant, P.E. (1983). Categorising sounds and learning to read – a causal connection. *Nature, 301*, 419–421

Bryant, P.E., and Bradley, L. (1985). *Children's Reading Problems*. Oxford: Blackwell.

Byrant, P.E., MacLean, M., Bradley, L., and Crossland, J. (1990). Rhyme and alliteration, phoneme detection and learning to read. *Developmental Psychology, 26*, 429–438.

Bruck, M., and Treiman, R. (1992). Learning to pronounce words: The limitations of analogies. *Reading Research Quarterly, 27*, 375–388.

Carr, T.H., and Levy, B.A. (1990). *Reading and Its Development: Component Skills Approaches.* New York: Academic Press.

Dahl, P.R. (1979). An experimental program for teaching high speed word recognition and comprehension skills. In J.E. Button, T.C. Lovitt, and T.D. Rowland (eds.), *Communications Research in Learning Disabilities and Mental Retardation* (pp. 33–65). Baltimore, MD: University Park Press

Ehri, L.C. (1992). Reconceptualizing the development of sight word reading and its relationship to recoding. In P.B. Gough, L.C. Ehri, and R. Treiman (eds.) *Reading Acquisition* (pp.107–143), Hillsdale NJ: Erlbaum.

Ehri, L.C., and Robbins, C. (1992). Beginners need some decoding skill to read words by analogy. *Reading Research Quarterly, 27,* 13–26.

Faulkner, H.J., and Levy, B.A. (1994). How text difficulty and reader skill interact to produce differential reliance on word and content overlap in reading transfer. *Journal of Experimental Child Psychology, 58,* 1–24.

Faulkner, H.J., and Levy, B.A.(1999). Fluent and nonfluent forms of transfer in reading: Words and their message. *Psychonomic Bulletin and Review, 6,* 111–116.

Fleisher, L.S., Jenkins, J.R., and Pany, D. (1979). Effects on poor readers' comprehension of training in rapid decoding. *Reading Research Quarterly, 15,* 30–48.

Goodman, K.S. (1970). Reading: A psycholinguistic guessing game. In H. Singer and R.B. Ruddell (eds.), *Theoretical Models and Processes of Reading,* (1st. edition, pp. 259–272.) International Reading Association.

Goodman, K.S. (1985). A linguistic study of cues and miscues in reading. In H. Singer and R.B. Ruddell (eds.), *Theoretical Models and Processes of Reading,* (3rd.edition, pp.129–134) International Reading Association.

Goswami, U. (1986). Children's use of analogy in learning to read: A developmental study. *Journal of Experimental Child Psychology, 42,* 73–83.

Goswami, U. (1988). Orthographic analogies and reading development. *Quarterly Journal of Experimental Psychology, 40A,* 239–268.

Goswami, U. (1990a). A special link between rhyming skill and the use of orthographic analogies by beginning readers. *Journal of Child Psychology and Psychiatry, 31,* 301–311.

Goswami, U. (1990b). Phonological priming and orthographic analogies in reading. *Journal of Experimental Child Psychology, 49,* 323–340.

Goswami, U., and Bryant, P.E. (1990). *Phonological Skills and Learning To Read.* Hillsdale,.NJ: Erlbaum.

Haskell, D.W., Foorman, B.R., and Swank, P.R. (1992). Effects of three orthographic/phonological units on first-grade reading. *Remedial and Special Education, 13,* 40–49.

Kirtley, C., Bryant, P.E., MacLean, M.,and Bradley, L. (1989). Rhyme, rime and the onset of reading. *Journal of Experimental Child Psychology,48*, 224–245.

Laberge, D., and Samuels, S.J. (1974). Toward a theory of automatic information processing in reading. *Cognitive Psychology, 6*, 293–323.

Lemoine, H.E., Levy, B.A., and Hutchinson, A. (1993). Increasing the naming speed of poor readers: Representations formed across repetitions. *Journal of Experimental Child Psychology, 55*, 297–328.

Levy, B.A. (1993). Fluent rereading: An implicit indicator of reading skill development. In P. Graf and M.E.J. Masson (eds.) *Implicit Memory: New Directions in Cognition, Development and Neuropsychology* (pp. 49–73). Hillsdale, NJ: Erlbaum

Levy, B.A., Abello, B., and Lysynchuk, L. (1997). Transfer from word training to reading in context: Gains in reading fluency and comprehension. *Learning Disability Quarterly, 20*, 173–188.

Levy, B.A., and Hinchley, J. (1990). Individual and developmental differences in the acquisition of reading skill. In. T.H. Carr and B.A. Levy (eds.), *Reading and Its Development: Component Skills Approaches*. San Diego:Academic Press.

Levy, B.A., and Lysynchuk, L. (1997). Beginning word recognition: Benefits of training by segmentation and whole word methods. *Scientific Studies of Reading, 1*, 359–387.

Levy, B.A., Nicholls, A., and Kohen, D. (1993). Repeated read–ings: Process benefits for good and poor readers. *Journal of Experimental Child Psychology, 56*, 303–327.

Lesgold, A.M., and Perfetti, C.A. (1978). Interactive processes in reading comprehension. *Discourse Processes, 1*, 323–336.

Lovett, M.W., Warren-Chaplin, P.M., Ransby, M.J., and Borden, S.L. (1990). Training the word recognition skills of reading disabled children: Treatment and transfer effects. *Journal of Educational Psychology, 82*, 769–780.

Lovett, M.W., Borden, S.L., DeLuca, T., Lacerenza, L., Benson, N.J., and Brackstone, D. (1994). Treating the core deficits of developmental dyslexia: Evidence of transfer of learning after phonological and strategy-based reading training programs. *Developmental Psychology, 30*, 805–822.

Mann, V.A. (1986). Phonological awareness: The role of reading experience. *Cognition, 24*, 65–92.

Muter, V., Snowling, M., and Taylor, S. (1994). Orthographic analogies and phonological awareness: Their role and significance in early reading development. *Journal of Experimental Psychology and Psychiatry, 35*, 293–310.

Olson, R.K., and Wise, B.W. (1992) Reading on the computer with orthographic and speech feedback. *Reading and Writing: An Interdisciplinary Journal, 4*, 107–144.

Perfetti, C.A. (1992). The representation problem in reading acquisition. In. P.B. Gough, L.C. Ehri and R. Treiman (eds.). *Reading Acquisition*. Hillsdale, NJ: Erlbaum.

Perfetti, C.A., Finger, E., and Hogaboam, T. (1978). Sources of vocalization latency differences between skilled and less skilled young readers. *Journal of Educational Psychology, 70,* 730–739.

Perfetti, C.A., and Roth, S.F. (1981). Some of the interactive processes in reading and their role in reading skill. In A.M. Lesgold and C.A. Perfetti (eds.), *Interactive Processes in Reading* (pp.269–297). Hillsdale, NJ: Erlbaum.

Roth, S.F., and Beck, I.L. (1987). Theoretical and instructional implications of the assessment of two microcomputer word recognition programs. *Reading Research Quarterly, 22,* 197–218.

Samuels, S.J. (1979). The method of repeated readings. *The Reading Teacher, 32,* 403–408.

Stanovich, K.E. (1981a). Attentional and automatic context effects in reading. In A.M. Lesgold and C.A.Perfetti (eds.), *Interactive Processes in Reading* (pp. 341–267). Hillsdale, NJ: Erlbaum.

Stanovich, K.E. (1981b). Relationship between word de–cod–ing speed, general name retrieval ability, and reading progress in first-grade children. *Journal of Educational Psychology, 73,* 809–815.

Treiman, R. (1985). Onset and rimes as units of spoken syllables: Evidence from children. *Journal of Experimental Child Psychology, 39,* 161–181.

Treiman, R. (1992). The role of intrasyllabic units in learning to read and spell. In P. Gough, L. Ehri, and R. Treiman (eds.), *Reading Acquisition.*(pp. 65–106). Hillsdale, NJ: Erlbaum.

Tumner, W.E., Herriman, M.L, and Nesdale, A.R. (1988). Metalinguistic abilities and beginning reading. *Reading Research Quarterly, 23,* 134–158.

Vellutino, F.R. and Scanlon, D.M. (1986). Experiment,al evidence for the effects of instructional bias on word identification. *Exceptional Children, 53,* 145–155.

4
Defining and Remediating the Core Deficits of Developmental Dyslexia: Lessons from Remedial Outcome Research with Reading Disabled Children

Maureen W. Lovett

It has been recognized for more than a century that a sizeable minority of otherwise intelligent, healthy children fail to acquire basic literacy skills. It is conservatively estimated that 3 to 6% of children unexpectedly fail to learn to read at age-appropriate levels (Hynd and Cohen, 1983; Rutter, 1978; Stanovich, 1986). Hinshelwood (1895) referred to the phenomenon as *visual word blindness*, Orton (1925; 1928) as *strephosymbolia*, and the World Federation of Neurology (Critchley, 1970) as *specific developmental dyslexia*. In the 1990s, the same phenomenon of unexpected reading acquisition failure is labeled *developmental reading disability*, and it is recognized to exist independent of estimated intellectual potential. Reading disability is now acknowledged to involve the same defining processing deficits in disabled readers of high and low estimated intellectual abilities (Fletcher, Shaywitz, Shankweiler, et al., 1994; Stanovich and Siegel, 1994).

The most reliable indicator of developmental reading disability is a failure to develop rapid, context-free word recognition skills (Gough and Tunmer, 1986; Lovett, 1992; 1997; Perfetti, 1985; Stanovich, 1986; 1994). Reading disabled individuals experience difficulty with connected text at the levels of word identification accuracy, reading speed, and text comprehension; but the defining feature of their reading disorder involves severe developmental failures of word identification learning and deficits in processing components within the word identification domain.

Developmental Reading Disability: What Are the Core Deficits?

Childhood reading disabilities often appear to have precursors in specific aspects of speech and language development. This has led some authors to describe developmental reading disability as "the index symptom of a developmental language disorder too subtle to lead to referral of the child in preschool life" (Denckla, 1979, p. 550). A number of prospective empirical studies confirm the relationship between very specific speech and language deficits and later reading disability (Bishop and Adams, 1990; Gathercole and Baddeley, 1987; Scarborough, 1990). Within the past two decades, there has been overwhelming evidence that a core linguistic deficit associated with reading acquisition failure involves an area of metalinguistic competence called "phonological awareness." Although defined in different ways by different authors, phonological awareness can be described as "the ability to reflect explicitly on the sound structure of spoken words" (Snowling and Hulme, 1993).

Awareness of the sound structure of spoken language is acknowledged to be a multifaceted ability (Barron, 1998), with different levels of sound analysis and sound awareness developing at different rates (Goswami and Bryant, 1990). Longitudinal studies of kindergarten children have been conducted to define the latent abilities inherent to phonological processing abilities in young children. Wagner, Torgesen, and Rashotte (1994) described five distinct yet correlated abilities, including phonological awareness (analysis), phonological awareness (synthesis), phonological coding in working memory, isolated naming, and serial naming functions. These abilities exhibited different developmental rates and were associated with stable individual differences over time in their longitudinal sample.

There is good evidence indicating that reading acquisition success in the early grades can be best predicted by measuring phonological processing abilities in kindergarten (Bradley and Bryant, 1983; Wagner, Torgesen, Laughon, et al., 1993; Wagner, Torgesen, and Rashotte, 1994). Wagner et al. (1997) subsequently examined the relative causal influences of an abbreviated set of latent phonological processing variables on reading development by studying many of the 1994 subjects over a five-year period. Phonological analysis and synthesis were combined to render a single latent phonological awareness variable and the naming variable consisted only of serial naming.

The phonological awareness, memory, and naming variables all appeared consistent across the five years in their ability to predict word recognition performance when each variable was examined individually. When predictive relationships were assessed simultaneously, however, with all variables considered, only the phonological awareness variable proved a unique predictor of word reading skill at every time interval over the five-year study period; in these analyses, the autoregressive effect of word reading ability in the earlier grades was removed. Serial naming speed was also a unique predictor of word reading skill from kindergarten to grade 3, however, and an estimate of vocabulary knowledge emerged as a unique predictor for grades 1, 2, and 3. In contrast, the phonological memory measure did not emerge as having a unique causal influence across the five years.

A recent review of several longitudinal studies predicting successful reading development reveals findings generally consistent with those of Wagner, Torgesen, and their colleagues (Scarborough, 1997). Other investigators report evidence that rapid serial naming measures are predictive of reading achievement only for impaired readers, but not for normal reader samples (Meyer, Wood, Hart, and Felton, 1998).

Because some level of phonological awareness and phonological processing skill are considered prerequisites to learning and using letter-sound correspondence patterns and acquiring an alphabetic code–achievements that are persistently diffi-cult for many disabled readers–the phonological skills of reading disabled individuals have been extensively studied for more than two decades. Several different aspects of phonological awareness and phonological processing have been demonstrated to be deficient in reading disabled samples, including the ability to segment or differ-entiate individual sounds in words, to blend individual speech sounds together to form a spoken word, and to use phonological codes as an aid to working memory (Liberman and Mattingly, 1985; Mann, 1986; Stanovich, 1991; 1994; Wagner and Torgesen, 1987). Recent classification research has revealed multiple profiles of reading disability in childhood, with all but one subtype characterized as sharing impairments in phonological processing skill (Morris, Stuebing, Fletcher, et al., 1998). The significance of these speech processing difficulties for disabled readers is emphasized with the finding that phonological processing deficits persist into adulthood–even when adults with childhood diagnoses of dyslexia were demon-strated to have achieved reasonable standards of literacy (Bruck, 1992).

Children with reading disabilities also have been demonstrated to be charac-terized reliably by another highly specific deficit in speech and language develop-ment–the ability to name visually presented material rapidly–a set of complex abili-ties tapped by serial naming tasks and one which is uniquely predictive of reading acquisition success in the early grades (Wagner et al., 1997). Many disabled readers have significant difficulty rapidly retrieving and accessing names for visual mate-rial, even though the relevant names are known to them (Bowers, Steffy, and Tate, 1988; Bowers and Swanson, 1991; Wolf, 1982; 1991; Wolf, Bally, and Morris, 1986; Wolf and Obregon, 1992). Some investigators suggest the visual naming speed deficit to be a component of phonological processing ability (Wagner, Torgesen, and Rashotte, 1994); but others, notably Wolf, Bowers, and their col-leagues (Bowers, 1995a; Wolf, 1997; Wolf, Bowers, and Biddle, in press), argue that the deficits in visual naming speed and phonological processing are distinct and dissociable core deficits in separate aspects of speech, language, and visible language development. Different subgroups of single and double-deficit disabled readers can be identified demonstrating different diagnostic profiles (Bowers, 1995b; Lovett, Steinbach, and Frijters, in press; Manis and Doi, in press; Wolf and Bowers, in press) and somewhat different response to treatment (Lovett, Steinbach, and Frijters, in press).

Similar to the phonological core deficit, the visual naming speed problem persists over time, characterizing disabled readers from kindergarten (Wolf, Bally, and Morris, 1986) through adulthood (Felton and Brown, 1990; Wolff, Michel, and Ovrut, 1990; Wolff, Michel, Ovrut, et al., 1990). Visual naming speed deficits have been demonstrated in disabled readers of other languages (Novoa, 1988; Wolf, Pfeil, Lotz, et al., 1994; Yap and Van der Liej, 1993), and are also suggested to be causally implicated in the disabled reader's failure to acquire rapid, context-free word identification skill (Bowers and Wolf, 1993; Wolf, 1991; Wolf, Bowers, and Biddle, in press). Bowers and Wolf (1993) suggest that slow naming speed may be considered (1) a "marker variable" indexing difficulties in the amalgamation of phonological and orthographic codes during reading acquisition; or (2) evidence of an impaired timing mechanism affecting the quality of orthographic codes acquired and represented in memory during learning.

According to the "double deficit hypothesis" (Wolf, 1997; Wolf and Bowers, in press; Wolf, Bowers, and Biddle, in press), developmental reading disabilities can be caused by one or both of two highly specific core deficits in separate aspects of speech, language, and visible language development: (1) problems in the ability to represent, access, and manipulate individual speech sounds in words; and (2) difficulty in rapidly accessing and retrieving names for visual symbols. Both of these core deficits impede language and visible language processing at lexical and sublexical levels, and they begin to explain why the defining feature of reading disability appears to be a failure to acquire rapid, context-free word identification skill.

Reading Disabilities and Cognitive Strategy Use: Another Contributing Factor?

In addition to the specific core processing deficits in the speech and language domain, many disabled readers are handicapped by more general difficulties in cognitive and metacognitive strategy use in several academic areas. Once described as "inactive learners" (Torgesen and Licht, 1983), many learning disabled children are now considered to be instead "actively inefficient learners" (Swanson, 1989), with poorly developed repertoires of learning and self-regulatory strategies. Successful learners routinely use a variety of strategies to acquire, retain, and use new information in the course of learning (Meltzer, 1996; Pressley, Borkowski, Forrest-

Pressley, et al., 1993; Pressley, Simmons, Snyder, et al., 1989). Children with reading and other learning disabilities, however, appear to have difficulties reliably organizing and coordinating different strategies and operations, especially if they occur in rapid succession (Meltzer, 1996; Swanson, 1989), knowing when and how to change strategies flexibly (Meltzer and Reid, 1994; Swanson, 1989; 1991), and evaluating and monitoring their own performance (Meltzer, 1996; Short and Ryan, 1984; Swanson, 1989).

These deficiencies in cognitive strategy use affect word identification learning when reading disabled children fail to use whatever they do know about words and letter-sound mappings to help them decode new words (Gaskins, Downer, Anderson, et al., 1988). Reading disabled children taught to read the words *meat* and *heat* will not necessarily be able to use that new learning to help them identify *seat* or *feat* (Lovett, 1991; Lovett, Warren-Chaplin, Ransby, et al., 1990). The ability to identify new words independently–and thus to be free to read independently for information or entertainment–depends upon some level of phonological processing ability, consolidated and ready-to-use letter-sound knowledge, effective and flexible word identification strategies, and an ability to exert some control over the metacognitive decoding process (Lovett, 1997). All of these conditions pose challenges to children with developmental reading disabilities in the course of attempting to acquire basic literacy skills.

Issues in the Effective Remediation of Developmental Reading Disability

Evidence that some of the core speech and language deficits of developmental dyslexia appear to be life-long complaints (Bruck, 1985; 1992; Felton and Brown, 1990) has focused attention on the question of whether the specific core deficits identified above can be effectively remediated. Some authors, impressed by the persistence and severity of core phonological processing deficits, have suggested that there may be a developmental window beyond which the phonological deficits associated with developmental dyslexia are unlikely to be effectively treated (Lyon, 1995).

More consensus exists in the literature about the nature of the associated cognitive impairment than about how and whether reading disabilities can be effectively remediated. Although methods of assessment and instruction for developmental reading disability have existed for much of this century, it has only been in the past 10 to 15 years that properly controlled studies have attempted to evaluate and compare the relative benefits of one treatment approach over another (Gittelman, 1983; Hewison, 1982; Lovett, 1992). Evidence over the past decade has been encouraging in demonstrating, through controlled intervention or training studies, that the reading and reading-related abilities of dyslexic or poor-reader samples can be substantially improved with intensive and focused instructional efforts (Foorman, Francis, Fletcher, et al., 1998; Lovett, Ransby, and Barron, 1988; Lovett, Ransby, Hardwick, et al., 1989; Lovett, et al., 1990; Olson, Wise, Conners, et al., 1990; Olson and Wise, 1992; Olson, Wise, Ring, and Johnson, 1997; Roth and Beck, 1987; Torgesen, Wagner, and Rashotte, 1997; Vellutino, Scanlon, Sipay et al., 1996; Wise, Olson, and Treiman, 1990; Wise and Olson, 1991). As Torgesen, Wagner, and Rashotte suggest, however, "it is clear there is still a great deal to learn about effective intervention methods for children with the most severe phonologically-based reading disabilities" (1997, p.122).

In the pages to follow, I will describe ongoing studies from our laboratory classrooms and clinical research program at The Hospital for Sick Children in Toronto. I will summarize positive findings obtained from samples of such disabled readers and demonstrate that children with severe developmental reading disorders are able to benefit from specific forms of literacy training that address directly some of the core processing deficits discussed above.

Our early intervention studies at The Hospital for Sick Children yielded both treatment successes and treatment failures; and the latter proved quite valuable in providing a window on the core acquisition difficulties of children with developmental reading disabilities (Lovett, Benson, and Olds, 1990; Lovett, Ransby, and Barron, 1988; Lovett, et al., 1989; Lovett, et al., 1990). We found that children with severe reading disabilities experienced inordinate difficulty abstracting grapheme-phoneme (letter-sound) pattern invariance even in situations where letter-sounds were directly taught and practiced in word family patterns. In a central study, we demonstrated that reading disabled children often fail to show significant transfer to uninstructed reading words, even in situations where training on very similar instructed words has been demonstrated to be effective (Lovett, et al., 1990). In this study, subjects experienced success on training words such as *line* and *mark,* but were not reliably improved in their identification of uninstructed words with the same spelling pattern (i.e., *fine* and *dark*). Reading disabled children effectively doubled their estimated reading vocabularies, demonstrating a positive response to intensive remedial reading programs; yet the children appeared to have acquired specific lexical knowledge rather than systematic letter-sound knowledge that could be used to facilitate their identification of new, unknown words (Lovett, 1991; 1997).

This phenomenon in dyslexic reading acquisition appears to reflect a basic failure in transfer-of-learning during the course of instruction, an interpretation consistent with disabled readers' performance on experimental learning paradigms

(Benson, Lovett, and Kroeber, 1997). We have attributed these transfer-of-learning difficulties in word identification learning to basic processing problems in parsing syllables into subsyllabic units. Reading disabled children are precluded from acquiring reliable word identification skills if they cannot extract either large units (e.g., rime–i.e., the vowel and what comes after it, as the *ain* in *rain*) or smaller units (letter-sound, letter-cluster-sound mappings). An ability to abstract spelling-to-sound patterns when acquiring new reading vocabulary is fundamental to the successful acquisition of word identification skill. We have suggested that the disabled readers' difficulties in large- and small-unit extraction of spelling-to-sound patterns is a consequence of the first core deficit described earlier–the phonemic awareness deficits known to characterize the most prevalent forms of developmental reading disability. Other authors have suggested that these difficulties may be attributed to the nature and/or accessability of the lexical representations laid down in memory during the course of word identification learning in these disabled readers (Lemoine, Levy, and Hutchinson, 1993; Perfetti, 1991).

Two approaches to remediating the word identification learning and transfer deficits of severely reading disabled children

In a subsequent intervention study, we addressed two of the three core deficits identified at the beginning of this chapter as contributing to the word identification learning difficulties facing reading disabled children. In this study, interventions were selected for their potential to ameliorate transfer-of-learning difficulties in the course of word identification learning. To date, more than 200 children with severe developmental reading disability have been randomly assigned to one of two forms of word identification training, both designed to promote transfer-of-learning, or to a study skills control program. Data described below are based on an analysis of results from the first 166 subjects who range from 7 to 13 years of age at referral. These children are, on average, between 9 and 10 years old, and they are of average intelligence on both verbal and nonverbal estimates of intellectual functioning. At entry the children are performing, on average, more than two standard deviations below age-norm expectations on multiple standardized reading and spelling achievement measures, with half the sample consistently below the first percentile for age on these standardized achievement measures. These subjects, therefore, constitute a severely reading disabled sample.

Both of the reading intervention programs consisted of intensive, systematic word identification training. The goal of both programs was to help the disabled reader acquire reliable decoding and word identification skills and an expanded reading vocabulary. Both word identification training programs taught procedures for identifying unknown words and focussed on print training primarily at the word and subword levels. The programs differed, however, in their remedial approach. Both programs used an identical corpus of words during instruction with virtually all words having regular spelling-to-sound correspondences. A total of thirty five sessions were conducted in each program, with children randomly assigned to an intervention program and to a particular teacher. The children were taught in a 2:1 or 3:1 ratio in special laboratory classrooms at The Hospital for Sick Children or in affiliated satellite schools in the greater Toronto area. The teaching sessions were 60 minutes in duration and were held four times a week.

Direct Phonological Training.

The first word identification training program focused on remediating basic phonological analysis and blending deficits. This program was undertaken based on the belief that transfer-of-learning deficits during the course of word identification learning could only be effectively remediated if basic phonological and subsyllabic segmentation problems were effectively remediated. Simply put, improved transfer performance was hypothesized to depend upon improved phonological processing skills. The first program, the Phonological Analysis and Blending/Direct Instruction Program (PHAB/DI), used direct instructional materials developed by Engelmann and his colleagues at the University of Oregon to train phonological analysis, blending, and letter-sound association skills (Engelmann and Bruner, 1988; Engelmann, Carnine, and Johnson, 1978; 1988). In direct instruction, content is introduced in a carefully graduated sequence of small steps, with multiple opportunities for overlearning of content and skills—a necessary condition for transfer-of-learning to occur according to some verbal learning theorists (Ausubel, 1967).

The PHAB/DI program emphasized instruction in word segmentation and sound-blending skills. At the oral level, sound segmentation and sound blending are considered prerequisite skills for successful word identification learning. In the PHAB/DI program, the disabled readers were taught to say each sound in a word slowly, one-at-a-time, in a left-to-right sequence. Segmentation activities were designed to allow the children to hear individual sounds in words and to develop awareness that there are subsyllabic units within spoken words. Blending training taught the children how to put individual speech sounds together to form words. At the same time, the children were taught individual letter-sound correspondences in a manner that provided a carefully structured basis for blending sounds when reading printed words. Letter-sounds were introduced in a specified, highly systematic order. The focus of the letter-sound training in the PHAB/DI program is on small units and individual sounds within words, with some limited use of rhyming to allow a small amount of subsyllabic segmentation at the level of onsets and rimes.

Training of Metacognitive Decoding Strategies

The second intervention program, the Word Identification Strategy Training Program (WIST), trained disabled readers in the acquisition, use, and monitoring of effective word identification strategies. In the adoption and development of this program, it was speculated that improved transfer would depend on two factors—a combination of reliable letter-sound knowledge together with some metacognitive control over word identification processes. In the WIST program, disabled readers were taught four explicit decoding strategies, with the overall goal of helping them use what they do know in attempts to decode unfamiliar words. Part of the WIST program is based on an excellent strategy training program developed by Irene Gaskins and her colleagues at the Benchmark school; the key words, dialogue structure, and one word identification strategy (compare/contrast) are based on the Benchmark School Word Identification/Vocabulary Development program (Gaskins, et al., 1988; Gaskins, Downer, and Gaskins, 1986). In WIST, however, the children were taught four decoding strategies: word identification by analogy (Benchmark's compare/contrast strategy), seeking the part of the word that is known, attempting variable vowel pronunciations, and peeling off prefixes and suffixes in multisyllabic words.

The first part of every WIST lesson was devoted to some basic skill-building instruction, teaching prerequisite skills needed to implement the four strategies. Successful use of the strategies, for example, depends upon knowledge of a set of key words that exemplify 120 high-frequency spelling patterns in the English language. The key words were taught by a whole word approach and, once learned, were displayed on a wall chart organized by vowel sound and rime pattern. The skill building part of the lesson also involved instruction in vowel pronunciations, variant vowel combinations (e.g., *ea, oo, ow, ie*) and familiarity with affixes (e.g., *pre, re, un, ing, ly, ment*). The remainder of the lesson was devoted to explicit strategy instruction and practice, and guided discussion on strategy implementation and strategy monitoring.

The first strategy, "word identification by analogy," trained the child to compare an unfamiliar word to an already known or just learned word (specifically a key word); the idea was to help the children use what they do know to help them decode the new word, thereby addressing the general strategy use deficits noted to characterize children with developmental reading disability. The key words *kick* and *her* would be used, for example, to decode the new word *bicker*. Rhyming and abstraction of rime patterns provide an important basis for successful implementation of this strategy, and they are central to word identification learning in the WIST program.

The second strategy, "vowel variations," teaches flexibility in word identification. Disabled readers are taught that vowels have multiple pronunciations, with the pronunciations determined by surrounding letters. The children are trained to attempt different vowel pronunciations in a new word, seeing which sound results in a real word that they know (e.g., for the word *find*, the reader first tries the short vowel sound *i*, determines that it does not yield a word he/she knows, and then attempts another pronunciation using the long vowel sound for *i*).

The third strategy is called "seek the part you know" or SPY. Disabled readers are taught to look for small words or word parts that are familiar (e.g., identifying *bun* and *dan* helps in the decoding of *abundance*).

The final strategy, "peeling off," is used on multisyllabic words with Latin or Greek bases. The disabled readers are taught to segment prefixes and suffixes at the beginning and end of words, reducing unfamiliar words to smaller root words. The children then apply one of the other practiced strategies to decode the word and subsequently blend together prefix, root, and suffix.

Evaluating Remedial Outcome

The effectiveness of both word identification training programs was compared with that of a control treatment in which disabled readers received the same amount of clinic time and individual professional attention as did those in the word training programs. Instead of remedial reading instruction, however, the control group received the Classroom Survival Skills program (CSS) which delivered training in the areas of classroom etiquette, life skills, organizational strategies, academic problem-solving, study, and self-help techniques. For issues of experimental design, the use of an alternative treatment control condition ensures that any positive treatment effects obtained for the WIST or PHAB/DI programs may be attributed to specific programing content rather than to involvement in an active remedial program or to the benefits of individualized attention from an experienced teacher. Children in the control treatment received 35 hours of remedial reading instruction after all posttesting was complete.

A comprehensive pre- and posttest battery was administered to all subjects to assess training and transfer-of-learning outcomes. Different types of outcome measures were used. These included measures of specifically trained content (e.g., key words, letter-sound identification), transfer-of-learning measures varying in their distance from specifically trained content and skills (ranging from transfer test words varying in systematic ways from the 120 key word spelling patterns to a more distant measure of transfer, regular and exception words that were uninstructed and bore no relationship to trained content), and a set of standardized achievement and phonological processing measures, including oral measures of sound analysis and sound blending, and two separate measures of nonword reading. A final outcome measure was an experimental strategy test assessing subjects' ability to select, apply, and self-monitor systematic decoding strategies to identify a set of 10 unknown, low-frequency words.

Results from the first 62 participants in this study have been published in a separate report that also includes greater detail on the design and content of the teaching programs (Lovett, Borden, DeLuca, et al., 1994). Additional empirical papers are available–one describing results from a detailed analysis of 122 subjects to examine differential effectiveness by age at intervention (Lovett and Steinbach, 1997), and another assessing potential subgroup differences in remedial outcomes for children with different profiles of phonological and visual naming speed deficits (Lovett, Steinbach, and Frijters, in press). The reader is directed to these reports for a more complete presentation and discussion of the results.

The Effectiveness of the PHAB/DI and WIST Approaches

The results from this work have been important in providing positive evidence of transfer-of-learning in the treatment of severe developmental reading disability. Both the PHAB/DI and the WIST intervention programs were associated with sizeable gains in the word identification and word attack skills of severely disabled readers. Probably the most critical finding of this research was the controlled demonstration that the phonological processing deficits associated with severe reading disability were, in fact, amenable to systematic and intense treatment. These data indicated that the phonological segmentation, blending, and letter-sound learning abilities of disabled readers could be significantly improved with well-designed phonological training interventions. The persistent phonological processing deficits of these disabled readers, seen on both speech- and print-based measures, were not completely ameliorated after only 35 hours of training. Both speech- and print-based phonological skills, however, were clinically and statistically significantly improved and closer to age-appropriate levels after intensive and systematic phonological intervention.

The second and equally significant finding of these studies was that sizeable transfer-of-learning effects were obtained following both the WIST and the PHAB/DI intervention programs. The two programs were associated with different patterns of transfer, but graduates of both training programs were able to successfully identify previously unknown and uninstructed words varying in their similarity to and distance from training words specifically taught in the remedial programs. The transfer successes of both PHAB/DI- and WIST-trained children ranged from orthographic relatives of instructed regular words (test of transfer words) to completely unrelated regular and exception words (unrelated to instructed key words and spelling patterns) and difficult multisyllabic words. These results are obviously different from those obtained in a previous study (Lovett, et al., 1990) in which children doubled their estimated reading vocabularies but failed to abstract systematic letter-sound knowledge and demonstrate significant transfer-of-learning.

As might be expected, based on their differing remedial approaches, a different pattern of transfer was obtained following the two intervention programs. PHAB/DI-trained children enjoyed greater transfer success within the phonological domain with their transfer of learning evident on unknown, uninstructed words of varying complexity , two measures of nonword reading, and two speech-based measures of phonological processing. The generalized training successes associated with this phonologically oriented program emphasized regular word reading and appeared largely dependent upon phonologically based decoding processes. The transfer-of-learning achieved by the PHAB/DI-trained disabled readers appeared based upon successful training of what is considered the first core deficit of developmental reading disability–deficient phonological processing and nonword reading skill.

In comparison, the transfer-of-learning successes of the WIST graduates revealed greater generalized effects across the domain of real English words. The success extended to improved identification of both uninstructed regular and exception words and superior outcomes on the identification of difficult multisyllabic words. Both intervention programs focused on orthographically regular words in their training corpus, with the WIST program segmenting larger subsyllabic units within the printed word and teaching the child to look for a match between the decoded product and a known word from the child's spoken vocabulary. This metacognitive decoding approach appeared to provide an improved basis for attempting a wide array of printed words with improved success, including particularly difficult-to-decode words like multisyllabic words and words that are exceptions to spelling-to-sound patterns.

The success of both PHAB/DI and WIST suggest that different routes of subsyllabic segmentation are possible in the effective remediation of severe reading disability in children. The PHAB/DI program emphasized subsyllabic segmentation at the level of individual letter-sound correspondences, while the WIST approach segmented within the syllable according to onset and rime units, emphasizing the vowel and what comes after. It is important to recognize that both approaches were associated with improved word identification and decoding skills in this design. What is critical to recognize is that some level of segmentation within the syllable is essential to facilitate transfer from a just learned word to a similarly spelled word during the course of word identification learning. Unless subsyllabic segmentation is explicitly trained and practiced during word identification learning, most disabled readers will fail to transfer new word learning and, thus, be prevented from becoming independent readers.

Continuing Issues and Future Directions for Remediation Research

Results from the research summarized above indicate that both metacognitive strategy training and phonologically based interventions are of merit in the remediation of developmental reading disability. Data from our laboratory classrooms suggest that only systematic, deficit-directed remediation will allow severely disabled readers to overcome core processing deficits and avoid transfer-of-learning failures in the course of word identification learning. To be effective, it appears that remedial programs for children with reading disability must address the issue of transfer-of-learning in every remedial lesson, and they must be designed in a proactive way to offer intensive, systematic remediation of the core processing deficits contributing to reading acquisition failure in these children.

Other investigators also have reported new encouraging results identifying some key components of effective intervention for children with reading problems and young children at risk for reading failure. Work by Vellutino, Scanlon, and their colleagues (Scanlon and Vellutino, 1997; Vellutino et al., 1996), Foorman, Francis, Fletcher et al. (1998), and Torgesen, Wagner, and Rashotte (1997) have converged in providing convincing evidence that phonological decoding skills are "teachable aspects of reading for most children" (Moats and Foorman, 1997, p.188) and that substantial gains can be achieved with explicit phonologically based instruction.

A number of issues remain to be addressed, however, concerning the generalization or transfer of skill improvements in the phonological domain to other aspects of reading skill acquisition. After two and one half years of preventive intervention with at-risk kindergarten children, Torgesen, Wagner, and Rashotte (1997) reported that subjects who received the most intense forms of oral-motor phonological awareness and synthetic phonics training were superior to other groups on nonword reading and phonological awareness measures but their advantage was not consistently established on word identification and reading comprehension measures. In a commentary on this and other intervention studies, Moats and Foorman observe that "the generalization and transfer of decoding proficiency to fluent word recognition and better reading comprehension was not automatic and constitutes a next phase of remediation that needs…additional study" (1997, p. 188).

In our own clinical research studies described above, we have demonstrated generalization to word identification but not to text comprehension performance. Reading comphension per se is not easily assessed, however, in any of the disabled reader samples discussed here. Passage comprehension measures are usually administered with the assumption that the subject is able to accurately decode the text's words and thus have access to its content—an assumption rarely met by the disabled readers in our clinical samples. With a few exceptions, only experimental training studies specifically designed to assess the relationships among word identification speed, reading fluency, and text comprehension, have been able to demonstrate interpretable gains in text comprehension and these studies have generally been conducted with far less severely impaired readers (e.g., Levy, Abello, and Lysynchuk, 1997).

Collectively, the results summarized above indicate that effective remedial techniques are available to address two of the core deficits of developmental reading disability—the deficits in phonological processing and in cognitive strategy use. Currently, there is increased commitment to evaluate the positive effects of phonological training interventions for disabled readers and ongoing research pursuing phonological awareness training for at-risk young children as a preventative intervention. The success of our strategy-based WIST intervention and evidence of the generalizability of its effects across the domain of real English words—those of regular and exceptional orthography—emphasizes the value of metacognitive interventions particularly when meeting the challenge of generalizability of gains.

As more treatment-specific effects are reported and evidence converges as to the critical elements of intervention for children at different stages of reading development and with different degrees of reading impairment, opportunities to define the most efficacious treatment components and combinations for particular groups of disabled readers will be greater. Ongoing NICHD-funded research by Robin Morris, Maryanne Wolf, and the present author is designed to evaluate, among other goals, the type of disabled reader who demonstrates optimal remedial response to phonological and metacognitive interventions in combination (PHAB + WIST) and to phonological training in combination with a new program designed to address issues of rate and automaticity (RAVE-O: Wolf, Miller, and Donnelly, in press). As the consequences of a double-deficit model for understanding developmental dyslexia become better understood (Bowers and Wolf, 1993; Wolf, 1997; Wolf and Bowers, in press; Wolf, Bowers, and Biddle, in press), remedial interventions that address visual naming speed deficits and their specific sequelae in reading acquisition will be developed and evaluated. The new RAVE-O intervention developed by Wolf and her colleagues represents progress conceptually and therapeutically for individuals with these different profiles of processing deficit.

With the increased methodological sophistication of new intervention research and the adoption of more rigourous data analysis models, there should be an abundance of new opportunities to use remedial outcome data to provide a better window on key processing operations in reading disabled children. In the decade to come, we will become better informed about the nature and malleability of the central deficits limiting the literacy skill acquisition of reading disabled children.

Acknowledgments

The research described in this chapter has been supported by operating grants from the Ontario Mental Health Foundation and the Social Sciences and Humanities Research Council of Canada. Preparation of this manuscript has been supported, in part, by Grant HD30970 from the US National Institute of Child Health and Human Development.

References

Ausubel, D.P. (1967). A cognitive structure theory of school learning. In L. Siegel (ed.), *Instruction from Contemporary Viewpoints*. San Francisco, CA: Chandler.

Barron, R.W. (1998). Proto-literate knowledge: Antecedents and influences on phonological awareness and literacy. In C. Hulme and R.M. Joshi (eds.), *Reading and Spelling: Development and Disorders* (153–173). Mahwah, NJ: Lawrence Erlbaum Associates.

Benson, N.J., Lovett, M.W., and Kroeber, C.L. (1997). Training and transfer-of-learning effects in disabled and normal readers: Evidence of specific deficits. *Journal of Experimental Child Psychology, 64*, 343–366.

Bishop, D.V.M., and Adams, C. (1990). A prospective study of the relationship between specific language impairment, phonological disorders and reading retardation. *Journal of Child Psychology and Psychiatry, 31*(7), 1027–1050.

Bowers, P.G. (1995a). Tracing symbol naming speed's unique contributions to reading disabilities over time. *Reading and Writing: An Interdisciplinary Journal, 7*, 189–216.

Bowers, P.G. (April 1995b). Re-examining selected reading research from the viewpoint of the double-deficit-hypothesis, *Society for Research in Child Development*, Indianapolis.

Bowers, P.G., Steffy, R.A., and Tate, E. (1988). Comparison of the effects of IQ control methods on memory and naming speed predictors of reading disability. *Reading Research Quarterly, 23*, 304–319.

Bowers, P.G., and Swanson, L.B. (1991). Naming speed deficits in reading disability: Multiple measures of a singular process. *Journal of Experimental Child Psychology, 51*, 195–219.

Bowers, P.G., and Wolf, M. (1993). Theoretical links between naming speed, precise mechanisms, and orthographic skill in dyslexia. *Reading and Writing: An Interdisciplinary Journal, 5*, 69–85.

Bradley, L., and Bryant, P.E. (1983). Categorizing sounds and learning to read—a causal connection. *Nature, 301*, 419–421.

Bruck, M. (1985). The adult functioning of children with specific learning disabilities: A follow-up study. In I.E. Siegel (ed.), *Advances in Applied Developmental Psychology, vol. 1* (91–129). Norwood, NJ: Ablex.

Bruck, M. (1992). Persistence of dyslexics' phonological awareness deficits. *Developmental Psychology, 28*, 874–886.

Critchley, M. (1970). *The Dyslexic Child.* Springfield, IL: Charles C. Thomas.

Denckla, M.B. (1979). Childhood learning disabilities. In K.M. Heilman and E. Valenstein (eds.), *Clinical Neuropsychology.* New York: Oxford University Press.

Engelmann, S., and Bruner, E.C. (1988). *Reading Mastery I/II Fast Cycle: Teacher's Guide.* Chicago: Science Research Associates, Inc.

Engelmann, S., Carnine, L., and Johnson, G. (1978). *Corrective Reading: Word Attack Basics, Decoding A.* Chicago: Science Research Associates, Inc.

Engelmann, S., Carnine, L., and Johnson, G. (1988). *Corrective Reading, Word Attack Basics, Decoding A.* Chicago: Science Research Associates, Inc.

Felton, R.H., and Brown, I.S. (1990). Phonological processes as predictors of specific reading skills in children at risk for reading failure. *Reading and Writing: An Interdisciplinary Journal, 2*, 39–59.

Fletcher, J.M., Shaywitz, S.E., Shankweiler, D.P., Katz, L., Liberman, I.Y., Stuebing, K.K., Francis, D.J., Fowler, A.E., and Shaywitz, B.A. (1994). Cognitive profiles of reading disability: Comparisons of discrepancy and low achievement definitions. *Journal of Educational Psychology, 86*(1), 6–23.

Foorman, B.R., Francis, D.J., Fletcher, J.M., Schatschneider, C., and Mehta, P. (1998). The role of instruction in learning to read: Preventing reading failure in at-risk children. *Journal of Educational Psychology, 90*(1), 37–55.

Gaskins, I.W., Downer, M.A., Anderson, R.C., Cunningham, P.M., Gaskins, R.W., Schommer, M., and Teachers of the Benchmark School. (1988). A metacognitive approach to phonics: Using what you know to decode what you don't know. *Remedial and Special Education, 9*, 36–41, 66.

Gaskins, I.W., Downer, M.A., and Gaskins, R.W. (1986). *Introduction to the Benchmark*

School Word Identification/Vocabulary Development Program. Media, PA: Benchmark School.

Gathercole, S.E., and Baddeley, A.D. (1987). The processes underlying segmental analysis. *European Bulletin of Cognitive Psychology, 7,* 462–464.

Gittelman, R. (1983). Treatment of reading disorders. In M. Rutter (ed.), *Developmental Neuropsychiatry* (pp. 520–541). New York: Guilford Press.

Goswami, U., and Bryant, P.E. (1990). *Phonological Skills and Learning to Read.* Hillsdale, NJ: Erlbaum.

Gough, P.B., and Tunmer, W.E. (1986). Decoding, reading, and reading disability. *Remedial and Special Education, 7,* 6–10.

Hewison, J. (1982). The current status of remedial intervention for children with reading problems. *Developmental Medicine and Child Neurology, 24,* 183–186.

Hinshelwood, J. (1895). Word blindness and visual memories. *Lancet, 2,* 1566–1570.

Hynd, G.W., and Cohen, M. (1983). *Dyslexia: Neuropsychological Theory, Research, and Clinical Differentiation.* New York: Grune and Stratton.

Lemoine, H.E., Levy, B.A., and Hutchinson, A. (1993). Increasing the naming speed of poor readers: Representations formed across repetitions. *Journal of Experimental Child Psychology, 55,* 297–328.

Levy, B.A., Abello, B., and Lysynchuk, L. (1997). Transfer from word training to reading in context: Gains in reading fluency and comprehension. *Learning Disability Quarterly, 20 (3),* 173–188.

Liberman, A., and Mattingly, I.G. (1985). The motor theory of speech perception revised. *Cognition, 21,* 1–36.

Lovett, M.W. (1991). Reading, writing, and remediation: Perspectives on the dyslexic learning disability from remedial outcome data. *Learning and Individual Differences, 3,* 295–305.

Lovett, M.W. (1992). Developmental dyslexia. In I. Rapin and S.J. Segalowitz (eds.), *Handbook of Neuropsychology, vol. 7, Child Neuropsychology* (pp. 163–185). Amsterdam: Elsevier Science.

Lovett, M.W. (1997). Developmental reading disorders. In T.E. Feinberg and M.J. Farah (eds.), *Behavioral Neurology and Neuropsychology.* (pp773–787) New York: McGraw-Hill.

Lovett, M.W., Benson, N.J., and Olds, J. (1990). Individual difference predictors of treatment outcome in the remediation of developmental dyslexia. *Learning and Individual Differences, 2*(3), 284–314.

Lovett, M.W., Borden, S.L., DeLuca, T., Lacerenza, L., Benson, N.J., and Brackstone, D. (1994). Treating the core deficits of developmental dyslexia: Evidence of transfer-of-learning following phonologically- and strategy-based reading training programs. *Developmental Psychology, 30*(6), 805–822.

Lovett, M.W., Ransby, M.J., and Barron, R.W. (1988). Treatment, subtype, and word type effects in dyslexic children's response to remediation. *Brain and Language, 34*, 328–349.

Lovett, M.W., Ransby, M.J., Hardwick, N., Johns, M.S., and Donaldson, S.A. (1989). Can dyslexia be treated? Treatment-specific and generalized treatment effects in dyslexic children's response to remediation. *Brain and Language, 37*, 90–121.

Lovett, M.W., and Steinbach, K.A. (1997). The effectiveness of remediation for reading disabled children of different ages: Is there decreased benefit for older children? *Learning Disability Quarterly, 20(3)*, 189–210.

Lovett, M.W., Steinbach, K.A., and Frijters, I.C. (in press). Remediating the core deficits of developmental reading disability: A double deficit perspective. *Journal of Learning Disabilities.*

Lovett, M.W., Warren-Chaplin, P.M., Ransby, M.J., and Borden, S.L. (1990). Training the word recognition skills of reading disabled children: Treatment and transfer effects. *Journal of Educational Psychology, 82*, 769–780.

Lyon, G.R. (1995). Research initiatives in learning disabilities: Contributions from scientists supported by the National Institute of Child Health and Human Development. *Journal of Child Neurology, 10*(1), S120–S126.

Manis, F.R., and Doi, L. (in press). Naming speed, phonological awareness and orthographic knowledge in second graders. *Journal of Learning Disabilities.*

Mann, V. (1986). Why some children encounter reading problems. In J. Torgesen and B. Wong (eds.), *Psychological and Educational Perspectives on Learning Disabilities* (pp. 133–159). New York: Academic Press.

Meltzer, L.J. (1996). Strategic learning in LD students: The role of students' self-awareness and self-perceptions. In T.E. Scruggs and M. Mastropieri (eds.), *Advances in Learning and Behavioral Disabilities, vol 10*. Greenwich CT: JAI.

Meltzer, L.J., and Reid, D. (1994). New directions in the assessment of students with special needs: The shift toward a constructivist perspective. *Journal of Special Education, 28*(3), 338–355.

Meyer, M.S., Wood, F.B., Hart, L.A., and Felton, R.H. (1998). Selective predictive value of rapid automatized naming in poor readers. *Journal of Learning Disabilities, 31(2)*, 106–118.

Moats, L.C. and Foorman, B.R. (1997). Introduction to special issue of SSR: Components of effective reading instruction. *Scientific Studies of Reading, 1(3)*, 187–189.

Morris, R.D., Stuebing, K.K., Fletcher, J.M., Shaywitz, S.E., Lyon, G.R., Shankweiler, D.P., Katz, L., Francis, D.J., and Shaywitz, B.A. (1998). Subtypes of reading disability: Variability around a phonological core. *Journal of Educational Psychology, 90(3)*, 1–27.

Novoa, L. (1988). Word retrieval process and reading acquisition and development in bilingual and monolingual children: Harvard University, Cambridge, MA.

Olson, R.K., Wise, B.W., Ring, J. and Johnson, M. (1997). Computer-based remedial training in phoneme awareness and phonological decoding: Effects on the posttraining development of word recognition. *Scientific Studies of Reading, 1(3)*, 235–254.

Olson, R.K., Wise, B., Conners, F., and Rack, J. (1990). Organization, heritability, and remediation of component word recognition and language skills in disabled readers. In T. Carr and B.A. Levy (eds.), *Reading and its Development: Component Skills Approaches* (pp. 261–322). San Diego, CA: Academic Press.

Olson, R.K., and Wise, B.W. (1992). Reading on the computer with orthographic and speech feedback. *Reading and Writing: An Interdisciplinary Journal, 4*, 107–144.

Orton, S.T. (1925). 'Word-blindness' in school children. *Archives of Neurology and Psychiatry, 14*, 581–615.

Orton, S.T. (1928). Specific reading disability–strephosynbolia. *Journal of the American Medical Association, 90*, 1095–1099.

Perfetti, C.A. (1985). *Reading Ability.* New York: Oxford University Press.

Perfetti, C.A. (1991). Representations and awareness in the acquisition of reading competence. In L. Rieben and C.A. Perfetti (eds.), *Learning to Read: Basic Research and its Implications* (33–44). Hillsdale, NJ: Erlbaum.

Pressley, M., Borkowski, J.G., Forrest-Pressley, D., Gaskins, I., and Wile, D. (1993). Closing thoughts in strategy instruction for individuals with learning disabilities: The good information processing perspective. In L.J. Meltzer (ed.), *Strategy Assessment and Instruction for Students with Learning Disabilities: From Theory to Practice* (355–377). Austin, TX: Pro-ed.

Pressley, M., Simmons, S., Snyder, B.L., and Cariglia-Bull, T. (1989). Strategy instruction research comes of age. *Learning Disabilities Quarterly, 12*, 16–30.

Roth, S.F., and Beck, I.L. (1987). Theoretical and instructional implications of the assessment of two microcomputer word recognition programs. *Reading Research Quarterly, 22*, 197–218.

Rutter, M. (1978). Prevalence and types of dyslexia. In A. Benton and D. Pearl (eds.), *Dyslexia: An Appraisal of Current Knowledge.* New York: Oxford University Press.

Scanlon, D.M., and Vellutino, F.R. (1997). A comparison of the instructional backgrounds and cognitive profiles of poor, average, and good readers who were initially identified as at risk for reading failure. *Scientific Studies of Reading, 1(3)*, 191–216.

Scarborough, H.S. (April 1997). Predicting the predictors of reading: Early precursors to phonological awareness, naming, and letter-sound knowledge in kindergarten. Paper presented to the biennial meetings of the Society for Research on Child Development, Washington D.C.

Scarborough, H.S. (1990). Very early language deficits in dyslexic children. *Child Development, 61*, 1728–1743.

Short, E.J., and Ryan, E.B. (1984). Metacognitive differences between skilled and less-skilled readers: Remediating deficits through story grammar and attribution training. *Journal of Educational Psychology, 76*, 225–235.

Snowling, M., and Hulme, C. (1993). Developmental dyslexia and language disorders. In G. Blanken, J. Dittmann, H. Grimm, J.C. Marshall, and C.W. Wallesch (eds.), *Linguistic Disorders and Pathologies: An International Handbook* (724–732). New York: Walter de Gruyter.

Stanovich, K.E. (1986). Matthew effects in reading: Some consequences of individual differences in the acquisition of literacy. *Reading Research Quarterly, 21*, 360–407.

Stanovich, K.E. (1991). Changing models of reading and reading acquisition. In L. Rieben and C.A. Perfetti (eds.), *Learning to Read: Basic Research and Its Implications* (19–31). Hillsdale: Erlbaum.

Stanovich, K.E. (1994). Annotation: Does dyslexia exist? *Journal of Child Psychology and Psychiatry, 55*(4), 579–595.

Stanovich, K.E., and Siegel, L.S. (1994). Phenotypic performance profile of children with reading disabilities: A regression-based test of the phonological-core variable-difference model. *Journal of Educational Psychology, 86*(1), 24–53.

Swanson, H.L. (1991). A subgroup analysis of learning-disabled and skilled readers' working memory: In search of a model for reading. In L.V. Feagans, E.J. Short, and L.J. Meltzer (eds.), *Subtypes of Learning Disabilities: Theoretical Perspectives and Research* (209–228). Hillsdale: Lawrence Erlbaum Associates, Inc.

Swanson, L.B. (1989). Analyzing naming speed-reading relationships in children: Unpublished doctoral dissertation, University of Waterloo, Waterloo, Ontario, Canada.

Torgesen, J.K., and Licht, B. (1983). The learning disabled child as an inactive learner: Retrospects and prospects. In J. McKinney and L. Feagans (eds.), *Current Topics in Learning Difficulties, vol. 1* (3–31). Norwood, NJ: Ablex.

Torgesen, J.K., Wagner, R.K., and Rashotte, C.A. (1997). Prevention and remediation of severe reading disabilities: Keeping the end in mind. *Scientific Studies of Reading, 1 (3)*, 217–234.

Vellutino, F.R., and Scanlon, D.M. (1987). Phonological coding, phonological awareness, and reading ability: Evidence from a longitudinal and experimental study. *Merrill-Palmer Quarterly, 33*(3), 321–363.

Vellutino, F.R., Scanlon, D.M., Sipay, E.R., Small, S.G., Pratt, A., Chen, R., and Denckla, M.B. (1996). Cognitive profiles of difficult-to-remediate and readily remediated poor readers: Early intervention as a vehicle for distinguishing between cognitive and experiential deficits as basic causes of specific reading disability. *Journal of Educational Psychology, 88*(4), 601–638.

Wagner, R.K., and Torgesen, J.K. (1987). The nature of phonological processing and its causal role in the acquisition of reading skills. *Psychological Bulletin, 101*, 192–212.

Wagner, R.K., Torgesen, J.K., Laughon, P., Simmons, K., and Rashotte, C.A. (1993). Development of young readers' phonological processing abilities. *Journal of Educational Psychology, 85*(1), 83–103.

Wagner, R.K., Torgesen, J.K., and Rashotte, C.A. (1994). Development of reading-related phonological processing abilities: New evidence of bidirectional causality from a latent variable longitudinal study. *Developmental Psychology, 30*(1), 73–87.

Wagner, R.K., Torgesen, J.K., Rashotte, C.A., Hecht, S.A., Barker, T.A., Burgess, S.R., Donahue, J., and Garon, T. (1997). Changing relations between phonological processing abilities and word-level reading as children develop from beginning to skilled readers: A five-year longitudinal study. *Developmental Psychology, 33(3)*, 468–479.

Wise, B., Olson, R.K., and Treiman, R. (1990). Subsyllabic units in computerized reading instruction: Onset-rime vs. post-vowel segmentation. *Journal of Experimental Child Psychology, 24*, 234–267.

Wise, B.W., and Olson, R.K. (1991). Remediating reading disabilities. In J.E. Obrzut and G.W. Hynd (eds.), *Neuropsychological Foundations of Learning Disabilities: A Handbook of Issues, Methods, and Practice* (631–658). San Diego, CA: Academic Press.

Wolf, M. (1982). The word retrieval process and reading in children and aphasics. In K. Nelson (ed.), *Children's Language, vol. 3* (473–493). Hillsdale, NJ: Erlbaum.

Wolf, M. (1991). Naming speed and reading: The contribution of the cognitive neurosciences. *Reading Research Quarterly, 26*, 123–141.

Wolf, M. (1997) A provisional integrative account of phonological and naming speed deficits in dyslexia: Implication for diagnosis and intervention. In B. Blachman (ed.), *Cognitive and Linguisitic Foundations of Reading Acquisition: Implications for Intervention Research (67–92)*. Hillsdale, NJ: Lawrence Erlbaum Associates.

Wolf, M., Bally, H., and Morris, R. (1986). Automaticity, retrieval processes, and reading: A longitudinal study in average and impaired readers. *Child Development, 57*(4), 988–1000.

Wolf, M. and Bowers, P.G. (in press). The question of naming speed deficits in developmental reading disabilities: An introduction to the double deficit hypothesis. *Journal of Learning Disabilities.*

Wolf, M., Bowers, P.G., and Biddle, K. (in press). Naming speed processes, timing, and reading: A review. *Journal of Learning Disabilities.*

Wolf, M., Miller, L., and Donnelly, K. (in press). (RAVE-O): A comprehensive, fluency-based reading intervention program. *Journal of Learning Disabilities.*

Wolf, M., and Obregon, M. (1992). Early naming deficits, developmental dyslexia, and a specific deficit hypothesis. *Brain and Language, 42*, 219–247.

Wolf, M., Pfeil, C., Lotz, R., and Biddle, K. (1994). Towards a more universal understanding of the developmental dyslexias: The contribution of orthographic factors. In V.W. Berninger (ed.), *The Varieties of Orthographic Knowledge, I* (137–171). Dordrecht: Kluwer Academic Press.

Wolff, P.H., Michel, G., and Ovrut, M. (1990). Rate variables and automatized naming in developmental dyslexia. *Brain and Language, 39*, 556–575.

Wolff, P.H., Michel, G., Ovrut, M., and Drake, C. (1990). Rate and timing precision of motor coordination in developmental dyslexia. *Developmental Psychology, 26*, 349–359.

Yap, R., and Van der Liej, A. (1993). Word processing in dyslexia: An automatic coding deficit? *Reading and Writing: An Interdisciplinary Journal, 5*, 261–279.

5
A Behavioral-Genetic Analysis of Reading Disabilities and Component Processes

Richard K. Olson, Helen Datta, Javier Gayan, and
John C. DeFries

The genetic and environmental etiology of reading disabilities and related cognitive deficits is being studied through the comparison of identical and fraternal twins in Colorado (DeFries, Filipek, Fulker, Olson, Pennington, Smith, and Wise, 1997). Earlier analyses based on a relatively small number of twins established the presence of a significant genetic etiology for the group deficit in a composite measure consisting of reading comprehension, word recognition, and spelling (DeFries, Fulker, and Labuda, 1987), and in related skills in phoneme awareness and phonological decoding (Olson, Wise, Conners, Rack, and Fulker, 1989). Now the twin sample has increased in size so we can begin to address more complex and interesting questions about bivariate and differential genetic etiology. We have begun to explore the genetic and environmental covariation between different reading and language skills as well as their independent genetic and environmental influences. We have also begun to explore potentially important subtype differences in genetic etiology within the reading disabled population. Some results from these preliminary analyses are reviewed in this chapter.

We will focus primarily on deficits in printed word recognition, which is usually the core deficit in normally intelligent children with reading disability (Stanovich, 1986). We will also consider several related component skills in reading and language. In the following section, we review the results of recent behavioral-genetic analyses on group deficits in these skills. In the third section, we review bivariate behavioral-genetic analyses to assess both common and independent genetic influences on orthographic and phonological skills in word recognition. In the fourth section, we explore the question of differences in genetic etiology among disabled readers related to IQ, general processing speed, and "phonological-surface" subtype dimensions. In the fifth section, the results of DNA linkage analyses will suggest that a major gene or genes on the short arm of chromosome 6 may be involved in the etiology of many reading disabilities. We end the chapter with a discussion of the implications of our behavior-genetic results for the prevention and remediation of reading disabilities.

Behavioral-Genetic Analyses of Group Deficits

Twin pairs from the third through twelfth grades who speak English as their first language are identified from school records in 27 Colorado school districts. If at least one member of a pair has some indication of a reading problem in their school records (based on low test scores if available or information from teachers), both twins are invited to participate in a weekend testing session at the University of Colorado. A smaller comparison sample of twins with no evidence of reading problems in their records is also tested, although a small percentage of these twins show a significant reading deficit in our measures. Twins with IQ scores below 85 on both verbal and performance subscales of the Wechsler (1974) or neurological signs such as seizures are usually excluded from the analyses.

Our behavioral-genetic analyses are based on the comparison of identical and fraternal twin-pair similarities: Identical or one-egg (monozygotic, MZ) twins share the same genes while fraternal or two-egg (dizygotic, DZ) twins share only half their segregating genes on average (Plomin, DeFries, and McClearn, 1990). With the assumption of equal shared environment for the MZ and DZ pairs, contrasts between within-pair similarities for MZ and same-sex DZ pairs provide evidence regarding the relative influence of genetic factors and shared-environment factors, while within-pair differences for MZ twins (who share the same genes and home environment) provide evidence for the influence of nonshared environment, including test error.

Behavioral-genetic analyses of the broad range of individual differences in the general population typically compare the correlations or covariance matrices for MZ and DZ twins, yielding estimates of the proportion of individual variation due to genetic factors (h^2), shared environment (c^2), and nonshared environment (e^2). This approach focuses on individual differences across the general population and not specifically on a deviant group. It is quite possible that the genetic influence on deviant group membership is different from the genetic influence on individual differences across the general population.

A different behavioral-genetic analysis is appropriate for assessing the heritability of deviant group ($_g$) membership (e.g., reading disabled) when twins are selected from the extreme low end of the normal distribution. The twin(s) of a pair who is (are) deviant enough on the reading dimension to be classified as reading disabled is (are) called the *proband(s)*, and the other member of the pair is called the *cotwin* (who may or may not also be a proband). If both members of a twin pair meet the classification criterion for deficit-group membership, they are entered twice in the analysis (see below), with twin members exchanging proband and cotwin status. Thus, within-pair twin differences below the criterion are canceled out. For a genetically influenced group deficit, this "double entry" procedure will happen more often for MZ pairs. The standard errors for the estimates are based on the actual number of twin pairs in the analyses.

The genetic (h^2_g) and shared-environment (c^2_g) proportional influence on the probands' group membership in the low tail (commonly < -1.5 standard deviation in our analyses) of the reading dimension can be assessed by comparing the amount of regression toward the population mean for the MZ and DZ cotwins. For an extreme example, if the probands' group reading deficit was entirely due to genetic influence ($h^2_g = 1$) and there was no test error, MZ cotwins would show no regression to the normal population mean while DZ cotwins would regress half way to the population mean on average, because they share half their segregating genes on average.

DeFries and Fulker (1985) developed a regression model for twin data to derive estimates and their standard errors for genetic h^2_g influences on deviant group membership:

$$C = B_1 P + B_2 R + A \qquad (1)$$

where the cotwin's (C) score is predicted from the proband's (P) score and the coefficient of relationship (R = 1 for MZ twins and .5 for DZ twins, A is the regression constant). B_1 provides an estimate of average MZ and DZ twin-pair similarity while B_2 estimates twice the difference between the means of the MZ and DZ cotwins, that is,. a test of the extent to which the deficit of probands is due to genetic influence. When the data are properly transformed, B_2 yields a direct estimate of the proportion of genetic influence on deviant-group membership ($h^2 g$) (DeFries and Fulker, 1988). As we will see in later sections of the chapter, this basic regression model has been extended to assess the degree to which the genetic influence on group membership may vary depending on within-group subtype and to assess common genetic influences on group deficits in different but phenotypically correlated skills.

A broad range of reading and language skills are positively correlated in our twin sample, as they are in nontwin samples (Stanovich, 1986), but there is also significant independent variance for some measures (Olson, Forsberg, and Wise, 1994). Therefore, we separately select probands (affected twins) for each variable to be at least 1.5 standard deviation units below the normal mean (e.g., below the tenth percentile) on that variable. As a result, a proband for one measure of reading (e.g., word recognition) may not necessarily be a proband for another measure (e.g., reading comprehension). The less than perfect phenotypic correlations among different reading and related cognitive skills allows the possibility of significantly different estimates of genetic ($h^2{}_g$) and shared environment ($c^2{}_g$) influences on the group deficit across different measures.

For example, a behavioral-genetic analysis by Olson et al. (1994) yielded rather different estimates for the group deficits on the word recognition and reading comprehension subtests of the Peabody Individual Achievement Test (PIAT) (Dunn and Markwardt, 1970). For the group deficit in PIAT word recognition, $h^2{}_g$ = .46(.10); $c^2{}_g$ = .45(.11) (standard errors of the estimates are in parentheses). In contrast, the group deficit in PIAT reading comprehension appeared to be less heritable ($h^2{}_g$ = .27(.12)) and more due to shared-environment influences ($c^2{}_g$ = .52(.11)). We hypothesized that the world knowledge needed to understand the vocabulary and concepts in the more difficult PIAT comprehension questions may have depended largely on the twins' shared educational and home environment, while basic processes (phonological and orthographic coding) associated with the development of word recognition were more constrained by genetic factors.

Beginning with our initial phenotypic studies of reading disability (Olson, Kliegl, Davidson, and Foltz, 1985), we have examined two component processes in word recognition. The phonological decoding component is assessed primarily through the timed oral reading of nonwords, although similar results are found in a silent nonword reading task (see Olson, Forsberg, Wise, and Rack, 1994, for a detailed discussion of these and other measures mentioned below). The group deficit in phonological decoding was highly heritable ($h^2{}_g$ = .59(.12); $c^2{}_g$ = .27(.12)). A similarly high genetic influence was found for the group deficit in phoneme awareness, as measured by an oral language game similar to "pig latin" ($h^2{}_g$ = .60(.17); $c^2{}_g$ = .20(.16))(Olson, Forsberg, and Wise, 1994).

The focus on phonological decoding and phoneme awareness in reading disability has often been justified by the apparent deficit in these skills when groups of older disabled readers are matched to younger normal children whose level of word recognition is similar (the "reading-level-match" comparison). The results of our reading-level-match comparisons (Conners and Olson, 1990; Olson, 1985; Olson, Wise, Conners, Rack, and Fulker, 1989) have been consistent with those of most other studies (see Rack, Snowling, and Olson, 1992, for a review). The results suggest that unique deficits in phonological decoding and/or phoneme awareness may play a causal role in most cases of reading disability, but we are mindful of the cautions raised by Jackson and Butterfield (1989) and the need for experimental confirmation of what essentially is a causal hypothesis based on correlational evidence (Berninger, 1995).

A second component skill in word recognition—orthographic coding—has gained more attention over the past decade. The measures of this construct have varied as have the results in reading-level-match comparisons (see Olson et al. 1994, for a review). Our operational definition of subjects' skill in orthographic coding is their ability to access words' specific orthographic patterns accurately and quickly. We measure skill in orthographic coding by having subjects quickly choose between a word and a homophonic nonword (e.g., *rain rane*) or between two homonyms following a priming sentence (which one lives in the woods? *bear bare*). Earlier genetic analyses on a small sample of twins found no significant genetic influence on the group deficit in orthographic coding (Olson et al., 1989), but it is now clear in a larger sample and different analyses that there is substantial genetic influence on the group deficit in orthographic coding (h^2_g = .56(.13); c^2_g = .29(.13))(Olson et al., 1994). In the next section, we examine the common and independent genetic variance for orthographic and phonological coding skills.

Bivariate Analyses of Shared and Independent Genetic Influence

The fact that two moderately correlated variables (e.g., orthographic and phonological coding) are both significantly heritable does not imply that their genetic influences are due to the same genes. Their moderate phenotypic correlation could be due to shared-environmental influences instead. Fortunately, the DeFries and Fulker (1985) regression procedure can be extended to the bivariate case, where probands are selected on one variable and cotwin regression is assessed on a different but phenotypically correlated variable. Olson et al. (1994) reported from this type of analysis that the phenotypic correlations between probands' group deficits in word recognition, phonological decoding, phoneme awareness, and orthographic coding were largely due to the same genes, with bivariate h^2_gs ranging from .58 to .85 after being divided by the phenotypic regressions among the variables. The phenotypic correlations among variables, however, are substantially less than 1, and latent-trait modeling (confirmatory factor analysis) has shown that the independent variance is not simply due to test error. Are there significant independent genetic effects (different genes) for this independent phenotypic variance across different reading-related variables?

This question has been addressed in a series of new behavioral-genetic analyses. The main focus has been on the independent variance in orthographic and phonological skills. The first set of analyses regressed subjects' orthographic scores on their phonological decoding scores and vice versa. This yielded a phonological deficit score that was independent from the subject's orthographic score and an orthographic deficit score that was independent from the subject's phonological score. Subsequent analysis of these scores in the DeFries and Fulker (1985) basic model indicated that both were significantly heritable at about $h^2_g = .4$. We are still evaluating this regression procedure, however, to assure ourselves of its validity.

Because the phonological and orthographic variables are normally distributed within the combined proband and cotwin sample (of course the mean of this distribution is below that of the normal-range comparison sample), it is possible to use the classic genetic model employing MZ and DZ covariance matrices to assess h^2, c^2, and e^2 for individual differences across the sample range, rather than for the probands' group deficit. Of particular interest is the heritability of the independent variance in phonological decoding and orthographic coding. Neale and Cardon (1992) described a multivariate "Cholesky decomposition" procedure which yields estimates of the genetic and environmental influences on a first variable, genetic and environmental influences that are shared with a second variable, and finally genetic and environmental influences on the second variable that are independent from those of the first variable. The underlying mechanism of this decomposition is essentially that of hierarchical regression.

We recently employed the Cholesky decomposition procedure to isolate the independent genetic and environmental effects on phonological decoding and orthographic coding. The results of these analyses of data from 243 MZ and 181 DZ twin pairs are presented in figure 5.1. The numbers next to the path arrows are path coefficients. The squares of the values on the A, C, and E paths are estimates of h^2 (genetic), c^2 (shared environment), and e^2 (nonshared environment) respectively. Figure 5.1a shows the results of entering phonological decoding first and orthographic coding second. Figure 5.1b shows the results of entering orthographic coding first and phonological decoding second. The overall fit of both genetic models was very good (X^2 (11) = 8.33, p = .68, AIC = -13.7). Their fit was slightly improved by dropping from the model paths C_1 (shared-environment influence that is the same for both variables) and C_2 (shared-environment influence that is specific to the last-entered variable)(X^2 (14) = 8.41, p = .87, AIC = -19.6).

Note the significant independent heritability of orthographic coding in path A_2 of figure 5.1a ($h^2 = .6^2 = .36$), and the independent heritability of phonological decoding in path A_2 of figure 5.1b ($h^2 = .62^2 = .38$). A similar pattern of independent genetic influence for phonological and orthographic coding was found when these models were applied to data from the normal-range control twin sample.

Hohnen and Stevenson (1995) recently reported a Cholesky decomposition for a second "orthographic" reading factor in their unselected sample of 13-year-old London twins. This factor also showed independent genetic variance after accounting for variance in a first "phonological" factor. The "orthographic" factor was

Cholesky Decomposition of Genetic (A), Shared Environment (C), and Non-shared Environment (E)

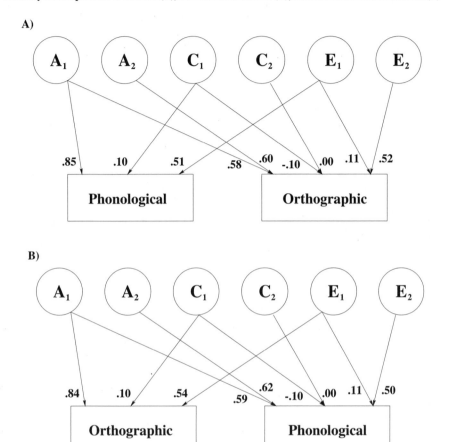

Figures 5.1 The A1 paths indicate the proportional genetic influence on individual differences in first (left-side) variable and shared genetic influences on the second (right-side) variable. A2 indicates the proportional independent genetic influence on the second variable. The same relations hold for the shared-environment paths (C1, C2) and the non shared environment paths (E1, E2).

mostly due to variance in the same-different matching of letter strings that were different in case, so it is not clear that this factor is tapping the same skills as our orthographic choice tasks.

The significant independent genetic variance for both phonological decoding and orthographic coding adds new understanding to our prior knowledge of their partial phenotypic independence (Barker, Wagner, and Torgesen, 1992; Olson et al., 1994). Stanovich and West (1989) and Olson et al. have linked part of the independent orthographic variance to differences in print exposure measured by the recognition of popular book titles in children's literature. Recent behavioral-genetic analyses of the group deficit in print exposure have revealed a strong and significant influence from shared environment (c^2_g = .60 (.13)), but no significant genetic influence (h^2_g = .21 (.13)). Therefore, the present twin analyses reveal a significant genetic basis for the independent variance in orthographic coding.

Etiology of Reading-Disability Subtypes

Individual differences among disabled readers has been a long-term concern in the field of learning disabilities and it is a major focus of our research at both the phenotypic and genotypic levels of analysis. DeFries and Fulker (1985) noted that an extension of their basic model for determining h^2_g would allow a test for differential heritability in relation to subtype variables. The extension simply requires the inclusion of the probands' subtype designation (S) and the product of the coefficient of relationship and subtype designation (RS):

$$C = B_1P + B_2R + B_3S + B_4PS + B_5RS \quad (2)$$

B_5 provides a test of the significance of differences in h^2g as a function of the subtype variable. Subtype variables in the model can range from dichotomous groups, such as gender, to continuously distributed variables such as age, and IQ.

IQ and the Heritability of the Group Deficit in Word Recognition

Many have argued that a discrepancy between reading level and IQ is essential to the classification of dyslexia or specific reading disability but this argument has recently been reconsidered. One reason for this reconsideration is that disabled readers with reading-discrepant and nonreading-discrepant IQ scores tend to have similar phonological deficits (Siegel, 1989; Stanovich and Siegel, 1994). In addition, difficulties in reading may ultimately cause lower IQ (Stanovich, 1986; Shaywitz, Holford, Holahan, Fletcher, Steubing, Francis, and Shaywitz, 1995). Here we consider the possibility that disabled readers' relative level of IQ may be related to the genetic etiology of their deficit in word recognition.

In an earlier study we failed to find significant differences in genetic etiology for poor reading defined by ability or IQ-discrepancy levels, but we noted that these definitions were highly correlated (r = .93) (Pennington, Gilger, Olson, and DeFries, 1992). In our most recent unpublished analyses, we increased the IQ range by relaxing the minimum verbal or performance IQ criterion from 90 to 85 (the lowest full-scale IQ score was 77) and focused on group deficits in a highly reliable measure of word recognition. In addition, we increased the twin sample size to 279 MZ and 334 DZ pairs by relaxing the proband deficit severity criterion to -1 SD on word recognition and by adding opposite-sex DZ twins.

We defined a residual full-scale IQ-subtype variable that was not confounded with level of word recognition among the reading disabled probands. The reason for using the residual IQ variable rather than an unadjusted IQ score is as follows. There was a broad range of proband deficits in word recognition below the -1 SD criterion and a broad range of full-scale IQ scores (77 to 133). The word recognition and IQ variables are significantly correlated within the proband sample (r = .23). The use of unadjusted IQ scores as the subtype dimension, therefore, would lead to a more severe proband deficit in word recognition in a low versus high IQ group. Any difference in the heritability of deficits in word recognition along the IQ subtype dimension could be due to differences in IQ and/or differences in the severity of probands' word-recognition deficit. Instead, we regress IQ on word recognition and then create an adjusted IQ subtype variable based on the deviation of subjects' IQ scores from the regression line for word recognition. This residual IQ variable is then uncorrelated with the severity of the probands' deficit in word recognition. The procedure is similar to approaches that distinguish "garden variety" from "dyslexic" readers based on differences in standard scores for reading and IQ (see Stanovich, 1986). Dyslexic readers would be those whose IQ is relatively high compared to their reading level, while garden-variety poor readers would have IQ standard scores that are closer to or even below their reading level.

The residual IQ variable was tested for the significance of its interaction with level of heritability (h^2_g) for the group deficit in word recognition. The interaction term (B5 in table 5.1) has now reached an acceptable level of significance (p = .05, two tailed). Earlier analyses by Olson, Rack, Conners, DeFries, and Fulker (1991) and by DeFries and Light (1996) had reported similar but nonsignificant trends in the same direction with other reading measures. The direction of the IQ interaction with the heritability of probands' deficits in word recognition is indicated in table 5.1 by dividing subjects along the residual IQ dimension into three nearly equal sized groups. The resulting groups had similar mean proband deficits in word recognition, but different mean full-scale IQ scores of 89 (range = 77 to 99), 99 (range = 92 to 106), and 110 (range = 96 to 133). (The IQ ranges for each group overlap because the groups were divided along the adjusted IQ dimension described above.) Heritability levels for the group deficit were then separately assessed within each of the subgroups. It is clear that with increasing levels of IQ, heritability level increases and shared-environment decreases. The low-IQ group has a very low level of genetic etiology and a high level of shared-environment influence on the group deficit in word recognition. The opposite pattern was found for the high-IQ group.

We have examined the relations between the IQ-subtype dimension and many other variables to try to understand the related differences in genetic and shared-environment etiology. The percentage of female probands is higher (57%) in the low-IQ group than in the high-IQ group (39%), but males (h^2_g = .40) and females (h^2_g = .36) in this analysis were nearly the same in their group heritability levels for word-recognition deficits. Not surprisingly, the low-IQ group had significantly lower scores in reading comprehension (Conners and Olson, 1990). There were no IQ-subtype relations to a number of birth-problem indices that might have accounted for a strong shared-environment effect on both MZ and DZ twins. There were small but statistically significant differences in mothers' years of education and in number of books in the home (lower in the low-IQ group) that might be linked to a poorer shared environment for reading development. The groups did not differ on parent reports about frequency of reading to their children.

General Processing Speed and h^2g for Word Recognition

A general processing-speed dimension was defined by subjects' z scores on four measures that loaded on a common factor similar to a mental abilities factor called "perceptual speed" in John Carroll's (1993) review. The highest loading measure,identical pictures (IP) (French, Ekstrom, and Price, 1963), required subjects to find the match for a picture (e.g., a house) among similar foils (e.g., houses with slight variations in detail). WISC-R coding (Wechsler, 1974) required the rapid mapping of symbols with numbers based on a key. Colorado Perceptual Speed (DeFries, Singer, Foch, and Lewitter, 1978) followed the IP procedure but with patterns of letters and numbers (e.g., *bhsf*). Finally, the Denckla and Rudel (1976) rapid automatic naming (RAN) test for numbers and letters also loaded on the speed factor.

When the individual speed tasks (regressed on word recognition) were used as subtype variables, each showed a similar pattern for differential genetic influence on word recognition: The slowest third of the sample showed a relatively low level of genetic etiology for word recognition and high shared-environment influence. The opposite pattern was seen for the high-speed group. The subtype interaction was statistically significant, however, only for the IP task (see table 5.1). Therefore, a composite speed dimension was created by adding the z scores for the four tasks. A similar pattern of differential h^2_g was found for the combined measure, and the subtype interaction was statistically significant (p = .05, two tailed; see table 5.1).

When comparing the speed-subtype groups on other variables, we found strong differences in the rapid naming of pictures and colors (not used to form the

Table 5.1. Genetic (h^2_g) and shared-environment (c^2_g) influence on group deficits (< -1.0 SD) in word recognition depending on subjects' adjusted full-scale Wechsler IQ, Colorado perceptual speed (CPS), identical pictures (IP), rapid automatic naming (RAN), the coding subscale of the WISC-R, and a composite of CPS, IP, RAN, and WISC-R coding

Subtype level	h^2_g (SE)	B5 signif.	c^2_g
Low IQ	.32 (.13)*		.63
Medium IQ	.39 (.12)*	$p = .05$*	.56
High IQ	.54 (.16)*		.37
Low CPS	.28 (.14)*		.67
Medium CPS	.38 (.14)*	$p = .18$	.60
High CPS	.58 (.16)*		.31
Low IP	.10 (.16)		.84
Medium IP	.43 (.13)*	$p = .04$*	.52
High IP	.61 (.16)*		.33
Low RAN	.26 (.16)		.69
Medium RAN	.38 (.13)*	$p = .30$	.56
High RAN	.52 (.17)*		.40
Low WISC coding	.33 (.15)*		.62
Medium WISC coding	.22 (.14)	$p = .19$	.73
High WISC coding	.70 (.16)*		.22
Low-speed composite	.20 (.15)		.76
Mid-speed composite	.47 (.14)*	$p = .05$*	.48
High-speed composite	.52 (.15)*		.40

Note: All subtype variables were adjusted for their relation to word recognition before being used to divide the groups. The significance of group differences in heritability depending on subtype (B5) was assessed by an extension of DeFries and Fulker's (1985) basic model (see text).

speed dimension), modest but significant differences in IQ (although no differences in reading comprehension), a significant deficit for the slow-speed group in the orthographic coding tasks, and no significant differences in mothers' years of education or books in the home. Bowers and Wolf (1993) have speculated that naming speed for letters and numbers is related to precise timing mechanisms that have been proposed by Tallal (1980) as the primary basis for reading disability. Unfortunately, we have no measures in our battery that could be used to test this hypothesis.

In view of the low heritability for word-recognition deficits in the slow group, we wondered if genetic influence on the same subjects' speed deficits would be similarly low. In fact, the heritability for the group deficit (< -1.5) in the composite speed measure was low and nonsignificant (h^2_g = .18 (.13)) while shared-environment influence was highly significant (c^2_g = .65 (.12)). This result mirrors the low heritability and high shared environment for word recognition in the slow-speed group. It suggests that some shared environment factor or factors may be causing this subgroup's slow speed and poor word recognition.

Further research is needed to understand the broad implications of the IQ and speed-subtype dimensions for the etiology and remediation of different reading disabilities. At present there is limited evidence for shared-environmental deprivation (slightly lower print exposure and maternal education) that may jointly lead to depressed IQ and reading. These variables, however, were not significantly related to deficits in the speed tasks. We may have to search more broadly for other shared-environmental effects such as maternal nutrition, illness, or lead exposure. In future analyses we plan to compare the behavioral-genetic subtype results with those from genetic linkage analyses of individual's patterns of DNA (see the fifth section) and from MRI studies of individuals' brain morphology.

Phonological-Orthographic Profiles

A third dimension of individual differences among disabled readers, the relative levels of phonological and orthographic skills, has a long history (e.g., Boder, 1973; Gjessing, 1953), and renewed attention in two recent papers (Castles and Coltheart, 1993; Manis, Seidenberg, Doi, McBride-Chang, and Peterson, 1996). Here we add to our understanding of this dimension by assessing its interaction with the heritability of probands' deficits in word recognition, by assessing its genetic basis, and by relating it to other dimensions of reading and language.

The subtraction of subjects' z scores for orthographic coding from their z scores for phonological coding yielded a normally distributed dimension that was not significantly correlated with their word recognition scores. Consistent with historical and current subtype terminology (Castles and Coltheart, 1993; Manis et al., 1996), we will refer to "phonological dyslexics" who were low on this dimension with relatively poor phonological coding, and "surface dyslexics" who were high on the dimension with relatively poor orthographic coding. The test-retest reliability for the subtype dimension was assessed in a longitudinal study (average test interval of five years) of 150 probands and cotwins. This correlation was .7, indicating a substantial reliability and longitudinal consistency for the measure.

Gayan, Forsberg, and Olson (1994) reported that the interaction between the phonological-surface subtype dimension and h^2_g for probands' group word-recognition deficit below -1.5 SD was not significant. More recently, we relaxed the minimum proband deficit criterion to -1 SD and found a slightly stronger but still nonsignificant interaction. The trend of this nonsignificant interaction suggested that the phonological dyslexic group word-recognition deficit (h^2_g = .53) might be more heritable than that of the surface dyslexic group (h^2_g = .30). The difference in heritability, however, was much smaller when the subtype variable was based on percent correct in the phonological and orthographic tasks or when probands' deficits in word recognition were more severe (at least -2.0 SD).

Even though the interaction between h^2_g for word recognition and the phonological-surface subtype dimension was not significant, this does not imply that there is no significant genetic contribution to the subtype dimension itself. The possibility of at least partially different genetic mechanisms for phonological and surface subtypes is suggested by the previously discussed results showing significant genetic influence on the independent variance in phonological and orthographic coding. Gayan et al. (1994) assessed the group heritability of disabled readers' extreme positions on the normally distributed subtype dimension by selecting probands who were one standard deviation above the mean ("surface dyslexics") or below the mean ("phonological dyslexics") and then observing their cotwin regression to the sample mean. Group membership in both the phonological (h^2_g = .68 (.32)) and surface (h^2_g = .65 (.34)) subtypes proved to be significantly heritable.

After establishing the long-term stability and partial genetic basis for the phonological-surface subtype dimension, we have begun to explore its phenotypic relations with other variables. To understand how various speed measures are related to the dimension, we recreated the dimension based only on relative accuracy in the phonological decoding and orthographic coding tasks rather than the combination of accuracy and speed used in the measures discussed earlier. We then looked at differences in performance for a number of variables depending on the disabled readers' (n = 307) membership in the lower (phonological dyslexic) or upper (surface dyslexic) half of the dimension.

Although the phonological dyslexics were less accurate in nonword reading, they were significantly ($p < .05$) faster on correct responses and their errors were more frequently words. They were also faster in two measures of orthographic coding and in a timed word-recognition test. The phonological dyslexics were significantly lower in their accuracy on several oral language measures of phonological awareness, including phoneme deletion and a "pig-latin" game. They were also significantly lower on a rhyme generation task. The groups did not differ, however, in the RAN task or in verbal IQ.

The groups did not differ significantly on the IP test discussed earlier, although a trend favored the phonological dyslexics. In contrast, the phonological dyslexics were significantly worse on a perceptual organization factor derived from the Wechsler subscales. This latter result suggested to us that there might be a significant gender difference between the subtypes. In fact, proportionally more females were on the phonological dyslexic side of the dimension. This was largely due, however, to the females' superior performance on the orthographic tasks (and on a measure of timed word recognition). Males and females did not differ significantly on phonological decoding or on the language measures of phonological awareness, although the females were significantly faster in the RAN task. Thus, there are complex interactions among gender, subtype dimension, and related variables. Further research is needed to fully understand these interactions.

While genetic factors appear to play a significant role in phonological and surface subtype membership and in related language skills, we should not overlook the possible role of environmental factors, particularly those related to methods of early reading instruction, remediation, and print exposure (Manis et al., 1996; Wise and Olson, 1995). Unfortunately we have not been successful in obtaining reliable information on the twins' reading instruction, but we have collected parent reports on number of books in the home and we have used the book title recognition test (Stanovich and West, 1989) to assess individual differences in print exposure. Both of these measures indicate significantly higher levels of print exposure for the phonological dyslexics who had relatively high orthographic accuracy. Print exposure may play a significant role, along with genetic factors, establishing rapidly assessable and accurate orthographic codes for words.

Implications for Specific Genetic and Environmental Effects on Individuals: Linkage and Training Studies

Our behavioral-genetic data indicate that there is a significant genetic basis *and* significant shared environment for the group deficit in word recognition. Behavioral-genetic analyses, however, cannot determine the relative balance of genetic and environmental influences on an individual's deficit. The deficit for some individuals in the group may be due entirely to shared and/or nonshared environment, while for other disabled readers it is likely that the genetic influence is quite strong. The foregoing subtype analyses indicated that the likely proportion of genetic and environmental influence may vary depending on an individual's profile of IQ, general processing speed, and possibly their phonological-surface subtype. These important results bring us a step closer to making more accurate predictions about the genetic and environmental etiology of an individual's reading deficit. Now, we turn to recent evidence from disabled readers' genes (DNA) that may eventually lead to a much more precise specification of individual etiology.

Linkage analyses are being used to search for genetic markers that could ultimately lead to the identification of specific genes associated with individual reading deficits. Markers indicating the presence of a specific DNA pattern have been shown to co-occur significantly more often in relatives that share a reading disorder. These markers are not the specific gene or genes that may contribute to a reading disability, but the markers are close enough to cosegregate with the genes that are responsible. (Adjacent regions on a chromosome tend to be inherited together.) Cardon, Smith, Fulker, Kimberling, Pennington, and DeFries (1994) reported evidence from two independent samples (ordinary sibling pairs and DZ twins) for linkage of a composite measure of reading within a 2-centimorgan region on the short arm of chromosome 6. Gayan, Olson, Cardon, Smith, Fulker, Kimberling, Pennington, and DeFries (1995) subsequently reported evidence in the same DZ twin sample that deficits in word recognition show the strongest linkage in this region, compared to deficits in reading comprehension and spelling.

A new sample of DZ twins in the Colorado study has recently been genotyped with new markers in the same region of chromosome 6 studied by Cardon et al. (1994) and Gayan et al. (1995). Preliminary analyses with this second replication sample have again indicated significant linkage for reading measures in the HLA region of chromosome 6. Moreover, linkage appears to be particularly strong for disabled readers' deficits in phonological decoding, phoneme awareness, and orthographic coding. An independent laboratory has also provided confirming evidence of linkage for deficits in reading and phoneme awareness in the same region of chromosome 6 (Grigorenko, Wood, Meyer, Hart, Speed, Shuster, and Pauls, 1997).

Much more work needs to be done to further verify the above linkage results, to find the specific gene or genes involved in this region as well as other possible regions of the genome, and to understand how the proteins coded by genes associated with reading disabilities ultimately influence brain development and behavior. The independent genetic influences on the phonological and orthographic components of word recognition add to the complexity of these goals. The specific genetic and environmental mechanisms will certainly vary across individuals.

In conclusion, behavioral-genetic analyses of MZ-DZ twin similarities and linkage analyses of data from DZ twins have both indicated a significant genetic influence on the group deficit in word recognition. Subtype analyses suggested that genetic influences were likely to be particularly strong for disabled readers with relatively high IQ and/or general processing speed. Nevertheless, we emphasize now as strongly as before (Olson et al., 1989) that evidence for genetic influences on reading disabilities and the apparent longitudinal stability of phonological deficits (Wagner, Torgesen, and Rashotte, 1994) should not discourage our best efforts in remediation. In the medical field, environmental interventions for largely genetic disorders have been quite successful (e.g., insulin for diabetes, glasses for myopia, diet for PKU, etc.). Although reputable studies of different remedial programs for reading disabilities have not found such simple or complete cures, intense remedial training in reading and phonological skills can result in substantial gains for most disabled readers (see Levy, chapter 3, this volume; Lovett, chapter 4, this volume; Olson and Wise, 1992; Wise and Olson, 1995). The evidence for genetic influence helps explain why additional instructional resources may be required for some children with reading disabilities. Until the specific genetic mechanisms are better understood, a main contribution of behavioral-genetic and linkage evidence may be the early identification of children at risk for reading disability followed by intensive remediation of their phonological and/or orthographic deficits during critical periods of language and reading development.

Acknowledgments

This work was supported in part by program project and center grants from the NICHD (HD-11681 and HD-27802), and RO1 HD-22223. Major projects and principal investigators include the behavioral-genetic analysis of twin and family data (John DeFries), component-skills analyses of reading and language (Richard Olson), executive function and attention deficits (Bruce Pennington), linkage analyses and physical mapping (Shelly Smith), computer-based remediation (Richard Olson and Barbara Wise), and brain morphometry (Bruce Pennington and Pauline Filipek). A common subject population of identical and fraternal twins provides an important link among all of the component projects. The contributions of staff members of the many Colorado school districts that participate in our research, and of the twins and their families, are gratefully acknowledged.

References

Barker, T.A., Wagner, R.K., and Torgesen, J.K. (1992). The role of orthographic processing skills on five different reading tasks. *Reading Research Quarterly*, 334–345.

Berninger, V.W. (1995). Has the phonological recoding model of reading acquisition and reading disability led us astray? A critique of "Cognitive Processes in Early Reading Development." *Issues in Education, 1*, 59–63.

Boder, E. (1973). Developmental dyslexia: A diagnostic approach based on three atypical reading and spelling patterns. *Developmental Medicine and Child Neurology, 15,* 663-687.

Bowers, P.G., and Wolf, M. (1993). Theoretical links among naming speed, precise timing mechanisms and orthographic skill in dyslexia. *Reading and Writing, 5,* 69–85.

Cardon, L.R., Smith, S., Fulker, D., Kimberling, W., Pennington, B., and DeFries, J. (1994). Quantitative trait locus for reading disability on chromosome 6. *Science, 266,* 276–279.

Carroll, J.B. (1993). *Human Cognitive Abilities: A Survey of Factor Analytic Studies.* Cambridge: Cambridge University Press.

Castles, A.E., and Coltheart, M. (1993). Varieties of developmental dyslexia. *Cognition, 47,* 149–180.

Conners, F., and Olson, R.K. (1990). Reading comprehension in dyslexic and normal readers: A component-skills analysis. In D.A. Balota, G.B. Flores d'Arcais, and K. Rayner (eds.), *Comprehension Processes in Reading* (pp. 557–579). Hillsdale, NJ: Erlbaum.

DeFries, J.C., Filipek, P.A., Fulker, D.W., Olson, R.K., Pennington, B.F., Smith, S.D. and Wise, B.W. (1997). Colorado Learning Disabilities Center. *Learning Disabilities, 8,* 7–19.

DeFries, J.C., and Fulker, D.W. (1985). Multiple regression analysis of twin data. *Behavior Genetics, 15,* 467–473.

DeFries, J.C., and Fulker, D.W. (1988). Multiple regression analysis of twin data: Etiology of deviant scores versus individual differences. *Acta Geneticae Medicae et Gemellogiae, 37,* 205–216.

DeFries, J.C., Fulker, D.W., and LaBuda, M.C. (1987). Evidence for a genetic aetiology in reading disability of twins. *Nature, 239,* 537–539.

DeFries, J.C., and Light, J.G. (1996). Twin studies of reading disability. In J. H. Beitchman, N. Cohen, M.M. Konstantareas, and R. Tannock (eds.), *Language, Learning, and Behavior Disorders.* New York: Cambridge University Press.

DeFries, J.C., Olson, R.K., Pennington, B.F., and Smith, S.D. (1991). Colorado reading project: An update. In D. Duane and D. Gray (eds.), *The Reading Brain: The Biological Basis of Dyslexia* (pp. 53–87). Parkton, MD: York Press.

DeFries, J.C., Singer, S.M., Foch, T.T., and Lewitter, F.I. (1978). Familial nature of reading disability. *British Journal of Psychiatry, 132,* 361–367.

Denckla, M.B. and Rudel, R.G. (1976). Rapid automatized naming (R.A.N.): Dyslexia differentiated from other learning disabilities. *Neuropsychologia, 14,* 471–479.

Dunn, L.M., and Markwardt, F.C. (1970). *Examiner's Manual: Peabody Individual Achievement Test,* Circle Pines, MN: American Guidance Service.

French, J.W., Ekstrom, R.G., and Price, L.A. (1963). *Manual for a Kit of Reference Tests for Cognitive Factors.* Princeton, NJ: Educational Testing Service.

Gayan, J., Forsberg, H., and Olson, R.K. (1994). Genetic influences on subtypes of dyslexia. *Behavioral Genetics, 24*, p. 513.

Gayan, J., Olson, R.K., Cardon, L.R., Smith, S.D., Fulker, D.W., Kimberling, W.J., Pennington, B.F., and DeFries, J.C. (1995). Quantitative trait locus for different measures of reading disability. *Behavioral Genetics, 25*, 266.

Gjessing, H.J. (1953). Lese-og skrivevansker [reading and writing difficulties]. Skole og samfunn, 8.

Grigorenko, E.L., Wood, F.B., Meyer, M.S., Hart, L.A., Speed, W.C., Shuster, B.S., and Pauls, D.L. (1997). Susceptibility loci for distinct components of developmental dyslexia on chromosomes 6 and 15. *American Journal of Human Genetics, 60*, 27–39.

Hohnen, B., and Stevenson, J. (1995). Genetic effects in orthographic ability: A second look. *Behavioral Genetics, 25*, 271.

Jackson, N.E., and Butterfield, E.C. (1989). Reading–level–match designs: Myths and realities. *Journal of Reading Behavior, 21*, 387–412.

Manis, F.R., Seidenberg, M.S., Doi, L.M., McBride–Chang, C., and Peterson, A. (1996). On the bases of two subtypes of developmental dyslexia. *Cognition, 58*, 157–195.

Neale, M.C., and Cardon, L.R. (1992). *Methodology for Genetic Studies of Twins and Families.* Dordrecht: Kluwer.

Olson, R.K. (1985). Disabled reading processes and cognitive profiles. In D. Gray and J. Kavanagh (eds.). *Biobehavioral Measures of Dyslexia* (pp. 215-244). Parkton, MD: York Press.

Olson, R.K., Forsberg, H., and Wise, B. (1994). Genes, environment, and the development of orthographic skills. In V.W. Berninger (ed.), *The Varieties of Orthographic Knowledge I: Theoretical and Developmental Issues* (pp. 27–71). Dordrecht, The Netherlands: Kluwer Academic Publishers.

Olson, R.K., Forsberg, H., Wise, B., and Rack, J. (1994). Measurement of word recognition, orthographic, and phonological skills. In G.R. Lyon (ed.) *Frames of Reference for the Assessment of Learning Disabilities: New Views on Measurement Issues* (pp. 243–277). Baltimore: Paul H. Brookes Publishing Co.

Olson, R.K., Kliegl, R., Davidson, B.J., and Foltz, G. (1985). Individual and developmental differences in reading disability. In G.E. MacKinnon and T.G. Waller (eds.), *Reading Research: Advances in Theory and Practice, vol. 4.* (pp. 1-64). New York: Academic Press.

Olson, R.K., Rack, J.P., Conners, F.A., DeFries, J.C., and Fulker, D.W. (1991). Genetic etiology of individual differences in reading disability. In L.V. Feagans, E.J. Short, and L.J. Meltzer (eds.), *Subtypes of Learning Disabilities.* (pp 113–135). Hillsdale,NJ: Lawrence Erlbaum Associates.

Olson, R.K. and Wise, B.W. (1992). Reading on the computer with orthographic and speech feedback: An overview of the Colorado Remedial Reading Project. *Reading and Writing: An Interdisciplinary Journal, 4,* 107–144.

Olson, R.K., Wise, B., Conners, F., Rack, J., and Fulker, D. (1989). Specific deficits in component reading and language skills: Genetic and environmental influences. *Journal of Learning Disabilities, 22,* 6, 339–348.

Pennington, B.F., Gilger, J., Olson, R.K., and DeFries, J.C. (1992). The external validity of age– versus IQ–discrepancy definitions of reading disability: Lessons from a twin study. *Journal of Learning Disabilities, 25,* 562–573.

Plomin, R., DeFries, J.C., and McClearn, G.E. (1990). *Behavior Genetics: A Primer.* San Francisco: W.H. Freeman and Company.

Rack, J.P., Snowling, M.J., and Olson, R.K. (1992). The nonword reading deficit in developmental dyslexia: a review. *Reading Research Quarterly, 27*(1), 28–53.

Shaywitz, B.A., Holford, T.R., Holahan, J.M., Fletcher, J.M., Steubing, K.K., Francis, D.J., and Shaywitz, S.E. (1995). A matthew effect for IQ but not for reading: Results from a longitudinal study. *Reading Research Quarterly, 30,* 894–906.

Siegel, L.S.(1989). IQ is irrelevant to the definition of learning disabilities. *Journal of Learning Disabilities, 22,* 469–479.

Stanovich, K.E. (1986). Cognitive processes and the reading problems of learning disabled children: Evaluating the assumption of specificity. In J.K. Torgesen and B.Y.L. Wong (eds.), *Psychological and Educational Perspectives on Learning Disabilities.* Orlando, FL: Academic Press.

Stanovich, K.E. (1991). Discrepancy definitions of reading disability: Has intelligence led us astray? *Reading Research Quarterly, 26,* 7–29.

Stanovich, K.E., and Siegel, L.S. (1994). The phenotypic performance profile of reading–disabled children: A regression–based test of the phonological–core variable–difference model. *Journal of Educational Psychology, 86,* 24–53.

Stanovich, K.E., and West, R.F. (1989). Exposure to print and orthographic processing. *Reading Research Quarterly, 24,* 402–433.

Tallal, P. (1980). Auditory temporal perception, phonics, and reading disabilities in children. *Brain and Language, 9,* 182–198.

Wagner, R.K., Torgesen, J.K., and Rashotte, C.A. (1994). Development of reading–related phonological processing abilities: New evidence of bidirectional causality from a latent variable longitudinal study. *Developmental Psychology, 30,* 73–87.

Wechsler, D. (1974). *Examiner's Manual: Wechsler Intelligence Scale for Children– Revised.* New York: The Psychological Corporation.

Wise, B.W., and Olson, R.K. (1995). Computer–based phonological awareness and reading instruction. *Annals of Dyslexia, 45,* 99–122.

6
Pure Alexia: Underlying Mechanisms and Remediation

Marlene Behrmann

Letter-by-letter reading, or pure alexia, is a disorder acquired as a result of brain damage in premorbidly literate adults. Although it is only one of a host of different types of reading deficits that result from brain damage, it probably has the longest history of any of them. A little over a 100 years ago, in 1892, Jules Dejerine presented a case of pure alexia to the Biological Society in Paris (Bub, Arguin, and Lecours, 1993). The case, Mr. C, was an established textile merchant who was well educated and enjoyed a rich cultural life in Paris. He had been in excellent health until he suffered a cerebrovascular accident at the age of 68 years. Mr. C presented with a right hemianopsia (field defect in the right visual field) and hemiachromatopsia (failure to see colors in the right visual field), and, he was completely unable to read even though he had no problem communicating or understanding spoken language. Importantly, he retained the ability to write but was then unable to read what he had written. According to Dejerine, the deficit was restricted to an impairment in processing orthographic material as Mr. C was able to identify other kinds of visual stimuli. Since this initial description of pure alexia, there have been many reports of patients with performance profiles very similar to that of Mr. C (see Mayall and Humphreys, 1996, for a review of some of these cases, and the special issue of *Cognitive Neuropsychology*, 1998, devoted to pure alexia).

Because of the apparent selectivity of the reading deficit that characterizes pure alexia, this disorder presents as an interesting testing ground within which to address questions about the organization of the reading system in the normal brain. In the first section, I describe the impairment in further detail and outline several existing explanations that might account for the pattern of reading performance. I then go on to argue that the deficit affects the efficient and normal activation of letters and that, under stringent testing conditions, this letter processing deficit may be uncovered. In the second section, I describe approaches to the remediation of pure alexia and suggest that theoretically motivated rehabilitation studies are important not only because they bring about improvement for the patient but also because they shed light on the mechanisms giving rise to pure alexia.

Pure Alexia or Letter-by-Letter Reading

The term *pure alexia*, as it is used today, refers to disproportionately slow but generally accurate reading of single words and text. Although this characterization is somewhat at odds with Dejerine's report that Mr. C was completely unable to read, the behavioral examination of Mr. C is not sufficiently detailed to know whether he had any residual reading ability whatsoever. The hallmark of pure alexia is the *word-length effect*— an increase in reaction time as the number of letters in the string increases. It is usually associated with lesions to the left occipital lobe, sometimes but not always accompanied by a lesion of white matter tracts such as the splenium of the corpus callosum or forceps major (Black and Behrmann, 1994; Coslett, 1997; Damasio and Damasio, 1983). Patients may require up to 3 or 4 seconds to name even common three-letter words, and for each additional letter, reading time is slowed incrementally (Patterson and Kay, 1982; Warrington and Shallice, 1980). The interpretation of this linear relation between reading time and word length is that pure alexic patients read each letter sequentially. This contrasts with the findings from normal subjects who show rather small word-length effects (Henderson, 1982) and are thought to process the entire letter string in parallel. This sequential or serial behavior producing the word length effect has given rise to the term letter-by-letter (LBL) reading.

Many different accounts have been proposed for the impairment that gives rise to this monotonic relationship between reading latency and string length (for a review, see Behrmann et al., 1998; Saffran and Coslett, 1998). At present, the number of possible interpretations of the mechanism underlying LBL reading almost equals the number of patients who demonstrate the deficit. It may be incorrect to assume a common underlying mechanism for all the patients given the variability both in their reading times and in behaviors such as their ability to access semantics or to show a word superiority effect (Price and Humphreys, 1992, 1995) but a unitary, coherent explanation may still underlie the varying patterns of behavior. One class of explanations of pure alexia proposes that the primary damage is to early prelexical stages of processing during which visual arrays are encoded prior to obtaining an integrated word form. The high proportion of visual errors in LBL reading (Hanley and Kay, 1992; Karanth, 1985) and the interaction between word length and degraded visual input (Farah and Wallace, 1991) lend support to the idea that the locus of the deficit is at early stages of processing. Furthermore, the fact that there is no compelling evidence that any LBL reader shows normal single-letter processing (Behrmann and Shallice, 1995; Behrmann, Plaut and Nelson, 1998) and that these patients also appear to be impaired at processing other visual forms, such as pictures (Behrmann, Nelson and Sekuler, 1998; Friedman and Alexander, 1984) further endorses the claim that the deficit is at an early stage of processing. These more peripheral explanations contrast with interpretations of pure alexia which argue that the word-length effect derives from damage to more central mechanisms such as the visual word-form system (Warrington and Shallice, 1980), access to phonological processing (Arguin, Bub, and Bowers, 1998; Bowers, Arguin, and Bub, 1996), or from the recruitment of the right hemisphere (Coslett and Saffran, 1994; Saffran and Coslett, 1988).

There is, however, growing agreement that the damage is to peripheral stages of reading, affecting prelexical stages of processing (Behrmann, Plaut, and Nelson, 1998). Even within these early stage explanations, there is still no clear consensus about the underlying cause of the deficit. The existing explanations encompass a wide range of possible impairments, including, for example, a general deficit in rapidly switching attention between two components of a visual display (Price and Humphreys, 1992), of distributing attention evenly across the spatial extent occupied by the letter string (Rapp and Caramazza, 1991) or of a loss of the automatic and rapid identification of letters leading to slow and inefficient recognition of orthographic input. The deficit may be restricted to the accurate and efficient identification of single symbols (Arguin and Bub, 1992, 1993; Reuter-Lorenz and Brunn, 1990) or it may be manifest as an inability to access word form representations rapidly and in parallel from multiple letters (Kay and Hanley, 1991; Patterson and Kay, 1982). Below, I explore some of these peripheral views through the detailed study of a single patient with pure alexia and present empirical data to adjudicate between these various alternatives. This work was conducted in collaboration with Tim Shallice (for more details see Behrmann and Shallice, 1995).

Case Report

DS, a 34-year-old right-handed English-speaking female who reads in a LBL fashion has been described in several other studies (Behrmann, Black, and Bub, 1990; Behrmann and Shallice, 1995; Sekuler and Behrmann, 1996). DS suffered an occlusion of the left posterior cerebral artery in October 1986, and a CT scan performed at the time revealed a left occipital lobe infarction (see scan in Behrmann et al., 1990). At onset, DS had a right homonymous hemianopsia (she could not see anything in her right visual field) that resolved to an upper-right quadrantanopsia (she could not see anything only in the upper half of her right visual field) at six months postonset and remained stable thereafter. Throughout the time course of her illness, DS's reading accuracy was relatively good even immediately postonset. Although her reading speed improved dramatically over time, the latency remained slow relative to normal subjects and she still showed a significant word length effect. DS's auditory comprehension and spoken language production were good, although she did show occasional word finding difficulties in spontaneous speech. She had resumed her premorbid lifestyle as a homemaker, taking care of her two young children. She had also enrolled in a typing course but found this extremely difficult. She still found reading laborious and tiresome, and although she had read for enjoyment premorbidly she no longer did so.

DS's Letter and Word-Reading Deficit

The experiments reported here were administered by means of Psychlab software (Bub and Gum, 1988) run on a Macintosh Plus computer. The procedure adopted was identical for most experiments and any deviations from this standard procedure are described where pertinent. Stimuli were presented in bold black uppercase letters, in 24 point Geneva font on a white background. DS sat at a distance of approximately 40 cm from the screen. Each stimulus was preceded by a central black fixation point that remained on the screen for 500 msec and was followed by a 1 second delay. The exposure duration of the stimulus was varied according to the task. All stimuli were presented in DS's intact left visual field and the visual angles subtended for stimuli of 1, 3, 5, and 7 characters in length were 1°, 1.5°, 2.4°, and 3.6°, respectively. On tasks requiring an oral response, reaction time (RT) was measured by a voice activation key, while on tasks requiring a key press, RTs were measured from the keyboard. For most experiments, data were collected from a single age- and education-matched female control subject, RS, using the identical procedures. The first set of experiments provide evidence for the diagnosis of DS as a LBL reader and thereafter her letter processing abilities are investigated.

Word-length effects: Naming latency and lexical decision

To test DS's word-length effect in oral reading, a list of 120 words—40 words of 3, 5, and 7 letters in length—was presented with each word shown individually in lower case, but mixed within a block and in randomized order. Half the stimuli were abstract while the remaining half were concrete. Half the items were low frequency (less than 20 per million, $M = 6.5$, SD 5.2; Francis and Kuçera, 1982) while the second half were high frequency (more than 50 per million, $M = 87$, SD 79). The words were presented once in print and on a second occasion in script.

The same 120 words used for naming latency were presented to DS for lexical decision together with 120 nonwords formed by changing a single letter in the 3 and 5 letter words (e.g., *ape-afe, bribe-blibe*) and 2 letters in the 7 letter words (e.g., *balloon-bafloan*). DS was instructed to use the middle and index fingers of her dominant hand to press the period key for "yes" and the comma key for "no" responses. The strings remained on the screen for an unlimited duration until a response key was depressed.

DS made two errors in print reading both on 3 letter words, yielding an overall accuracy score of 99%, and no errors on script reading. Her accuracy in lexical decision was 93% with an equal number of errors occurring across each string length. Mean naming latencies for the correct responses, plotted as a function of word length for print and script presentation, are shown in figure 6.1a below. Figure 6.1b reflects the mean RTs for both "yes" and "no" responses as a function of string length. DS showed the typical monotonic relationship between word length and RT for words in both fonts. An analysis of variance (ANOVA) with font (print, script), concreteness (abstract, concrete), frequency (high, low), and word length (3, 5, and 7) as within-subject factors showed a significant effect of word length ($F(2,3)=16.52$, $p<.001$) and frequency with faster RTs for high ($M=1209$ msec) than for low frequency words ($M=1306$ ms) ($F(1,2)=5.52$, $p<.001$). There were no other significant main effects nor interactions. The results of the lexical decision data using an ANOVA with string type (word/nonword) and length (3, 5, 7) revealed significantly faster decision times for words than for nonwords ($F(1,8)=9.7$, $p<.01$) as well as a

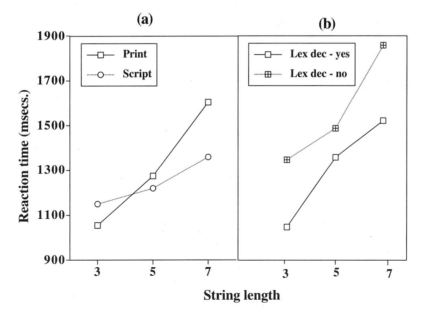

Figure 6.1 DS's response latencies (ms) as a function of string length for (a) reading aloud print and script words and (b) "yes" and "no" responses in lexical decision.

significant effect of string length ($F(2,8)= 6.7$, $p<.05$) and no interaction between them ($p>.05$).

The results of the naming latency and lexical decision tasks demonstrate a monotonic increase in response time as a function of increasing string length. A regression line plotted with DS's naming RT against word length reveals a linear fit with an intercept of 742 msec and a slope of 108 msec for each additional letter in the stimulus. Although DS is a mild LBL reader, the slope of 108 msec contrasts with the finding that normal subjects typically show a maximum increase (if any at all) of 28-30 ms in RT for each additional letter in the string even when presented to the left visual field (Young and Ellis, 1985). The difference between DS and normal readers is perhaps even more dramatic in lexical decision where normal readers typically show a minimal effect of word length (Frederiksen and Kroll, 1976; Koriat and Norman, 1984). On a linear regression analysis with lexical decision RT and word length, DS's "yes" responses revealed an intercept of 717 and a slope of 119 ms for each additional letter. DS's pattern fits the typical profile of a LBL reader with marked effects of word length on reading RT.

Allocating attention to words

One current hypothesis proposed to explain LBL reading suggests that the underlying disorder is an attentional deficit. More precisely, the deficit is thought to be a failure to distribute attention evenly across all the positions of a letter string, resulting necessarily in the sequential allocation of resources to different string positions (Rapp and Caramazza, 1991). An alternative view is that the difficulty is not in the spatial distribution of attention but rather that the problem is one in which DS has difficulty processing a second (and third, etc.) letter irrespective of whether the letters are presented spatially or not. On this latter account, the problem lies not in the spatial but in the ordinal position of the letters. To examine these alternatives, we had DS report two letters from word and nonword stimuli of increasing length: in one condition DS reported the first and last letters (positions 1 and n), whereas in the second she reported the letters from the first and second positions (positions 1 and 2). In this latter condition, there is minimal spatial processing required as the letters are adjacent. The prediction is that if spatial, rather than ordinal, extent affects performance, letter report should be worse when reporting the last letter which requires greater distribution of spatial attention (1/n) than when reporting the second letter (1/2). Performance on the first letter will always be best. In contrast, if the deficit is not in encoding spatial information but rather in the processing of the second-named letter irrespective of its location, then, again, the first letter should be reported best but there should be no difference between DS's reporting of the second and the last letter in the string—the report of the second letter would be equivalent and not affected by spatial location.

To demonstrate that this task is indeed sensitive to a deficit in spatial processing, we also tested a patient with a deficit of visuospatial attention. MG, a 64 year-old, right-handed English speaking retired executive, who suffered a right-middle cerebral artery infarction in August 1990, shows hemispatial neglect across a range of bedside neglect tasks. Because MG has left-sided neglect, position 1 refers to the final right-sided letter in the string (his optimal position), position 2 to the penultimate right-sided letter and position n to the first letter in the string (on the left). We predicted that MG would show an effect of spatial location, reporting letters in position 1 significantly better than those in position 2, and that letters in position 2, in turn, would be reported significantly better than those in position n (left-most letter).

Thirty words and 30 random letter strings (e.g., *ndfme*), each of 3, 4, 5, 6, and 7 letters in length (n=300) were selected. The words were matched for frequency, with one third of the trials each falling below 20 per million, between 30 and 90 per million, and over 110 per million for each word length (Francis and Kuçera, 1982). The stimuli were centered over a point located in the fourth character position from fixation in the left visual field for DS and the right visual field for MG. The subjects were required to report two letters in two different conditions: in the 1/n condition, they were instructed to report the first and last letters (e.g., *ae* in *athlete*). In the 1/2 condition, DS was instructed to report the first and second letters (e.g., *at* in *athlete*) and MG was instructed to report the final two letters (e.g., te in *athlete*, where 1 is the final and 2 is the second last letter). The stimuli were presented blocked and condition of report followed an ABBA order: 1/2 words, 1/n words, then 1/n nonwords and finally, 1/2 nonwords.

The stimuli were presented at a preset exposure duration at which accuracy of report of the first and last letter was 60%. The duration was titrated on a practice set of 30 nonwords of varying lengths. This titration procedure ensured that the testing conditions were equivalent for the two patients. The same experiment was also presented to the normal control subject but even at the briefest possible exposure duration (17 msec, no mask), performance was at ceiling. The exposure selected for DS was 100 msec while the exposure for MG was 200 msec. Since MG was only available for a limited time of testing, only 75 trials were completed in each of the 4 cells (rather than 150 as for DS), for a total of 300 trials for MG and 600 for DS. Two testing sessions were necessary to complete this experiment with DS.

The number and proportion of letters reported correctly from positions 1, 2 and n for MG and DS are shown in table 6.1. Overall, MG reported 73% (438/600) of the letters correctly. Accuracy of final letter report (position 1) was significantly better than that of the second last letter (position 2) ($x^2_{(1)}$ = 39.5, $p<.001$) which, in turn, was reported significantly better than the left-most letter closest to fixation in the right field (position n) ($x^2_{(1)}$ = 14.7, $p<.0001$). This deterioration across serial positions, in particular the contrast between position 2 and position n, is consistent with a deficit in visuospatial attention in which the location of the letter significantly affects performance.

Table 6.1
Number and proportion of letters reported
correctly from positions 1, 2, and n for MG and DS

	MG		DS	
	Number	Proportion	Number	Proportion
Position 1	275/300	.92	551/600	.92
Position 2	94/150	.68	186/300	.62
Position n	69/150	.43	182/300	.61

The pattern shown by DS was markedly different from that of MG although overall accuracy was similar—DS reported 76% (919/1200) of the letters correctly. The left-most letter (position 1) was reported significantly better than the letter in position 2 ($x^2_{(1)}$ = 182.4, $p<.001$) and the letter in position n ($x^2_{(1)}$ = 128.5, $p<.001$), and there was no significant difference between the latter two letters ($x^2_{(1)}$ = 0.112, $p>.10$). Thus, on this analysis, DS's report of the second letter is equally poor irrespective of its spatial location in the string.

The effect of spatial position for MG and the absence of a spatial effect for DS is also apparent from an analysis of the percentage of trials on which both letters are reported correctly (see table 6.2 below). These data might provide a more stringent test of the spatial attention hypothesis since they now reflect the extent to which both of two spatially distant letters are correctly processed. MG reports both letters correctly significantly more often in condition 1/2 (last and second-last letter) than in condition 1/n (last and first letter) ($x^2_{(1)}$= 8.3, $p<.005$), while DS shows no such difference ($x^2_{(1)}$ = 0.112, $p>.05$). The superior performance in the condition of adjacent (1/2) over distant (1/n) letters by MG but not by DS supports the view that spatial extent affects MG's reading but does not influence DS's behavior.

The findings from this experiment show a clear difference between the performance of MG, a patient with left-sided spatial deficit, and DS, a LBL reader. MG is able to identify the right-most letter in a string relatively well but performance drops off markedly across the serial positions with poorest report of the left-

Table 6.2

Percentage of trials on which both letters are reported correctly for
DS and MG as a function of string type and condition of report

	MG: Neglect dyslexia Condition of report		DS: Letter-by-letter Condition of report	
String type	1/2	1/n	1/2	1/n
Words	84	56	69	66
Nonwords	47	25	57	53
Mean	65.5	40.5	63	59.5

most letter. This difference as a function of location reflects the impairment in visuospatial processing that characterizes neglect. In contrast, DS does not show this spatial effect and report of the second letter is worse than the first letter irrespective of its location. The absence of a spatial effect on letter report rules out an attentional explanation for DS's performance and suggests that the impairment underlying her performance is not spatially based.

Letter activation and pure alexia

The results thus far suggest that the deficit underlying DS's reading is not one of impaired spatial distribution of attention nor of inadequate distribution of processing resources across the letter string. Rather, the problem appears to arise in DS's reporting the identity of the second letter independent of its spatial location. In the data thus far, however, there still remains a confound between letter order and spatial position because letters on the left of the word are also on the left of space. In the following experiments, we deconfound these factors and examine in more detail the serial order effect on DS's ability to process letters.

Rapid Serial Visual Presentation (RSVP)

In this experiment, we compare DS's ability to report the first and second letters of a string under conditions where the two letters occupy the exact same spatial position. The strong prediction is that, if the word length effect in reading arises because of a deficit in the rapid and efficient processing of single letters, reporting two letters will still be impaired even in a situation where spatial location is held constant. One possible reason is that if single letter activation is slow and unreliable, additional time will be required to process a letter satisfactorily. If a second letter appears while the first letter is still being processed, this would produce interference and its effects would need to be inhibited by attentional focusing. If this occurs, either of the letters might be processed accurately but not both; strategic factors would determine which. If more time is given, however, so that the first letter is processed relatively well before the second letter appears, processing of the first letter might be completed but activation of the second letter would still need to be inhibited. One would therefore expect that report of the second letter would improve provided that the time interval between the appearance of the two letters was sufficient and enough time was available for processing of the first letter to be completed prior to the arrival of the second letter.

A trial consisted of a string of 15 symbols (2 letters and 13 digits) that appeared individually for 100 msec in rapid serial succession all in the same spatial location. The 120 trials were divided into three conditions: when the two letters appeared either temporally adjacent with 0 digits between them (e.g., 15786FH963172), or when there were 3 (e.g., 35785W267B74219) or 7 (e.g., 943G8357481K749) digits between them. The stimulus onset asynchrony (SOA) between the letters in the 0 digit condition was 100 msec from onset of the first digit, while the SOA in the 3 and 7 digit conditions was 400 and 800 msec respectively. Letters did not appear in either the first or the final three positions of the string so as to avoid primacy and recency effects. Following a central fixation point which remained on the screen for 500 msec, and followed by a 500 msec blank screen, the first item appeared 2 character spaces ($1°$) to the left of fixation followed by the other symbols. DS was instructed to report only the two letters at the end of the trial. The same experiment was presented to the control subject, RS, also at 100 msec and accuracy was recorded.

The data are shown in table 6.3. As is evident from examining the first column of the table that reflects the percentage of overall correct letter report, DS is significantly worse than the control subject at both 100 and 400 ms SOA (100 ms: $x^2_{(1)} = 8.5$, $p<.005$; 400 ms: $x^2_{(1)} = 4.5$, $p<.05$) but not at 800 ms ($x^2_{(1)} = 1.1$, $p>.05$). In considering her performance on the first letter, there is no significant difference between DS and the control except at the 800 ms condition ($x^2_{(1)} = 3.9$, $p<.05$) but, curiously, DS is better than the control subject. The important findings, however, come from consideration of her report on the second item (see the final two columns of the table). She is significantly poorer at reporting the second item than the control subject both at the 100 ms ($x^2_{(1)} = 17.6$, $p<.001$) and 400 ms exposures ($x^2_{(1)} = 4.3$, $p<.04$) but not significantly different from the control at 800 ms. Furthermore, when considering the result for the second item conditionalized on correct report of the first, we see that at 100 ms, if the control subject reports the first item correctly, she always gets the second correct. In contrast, DS's chance of getting the second letter correct when the first item was correct is only 44%. A similar result is observed at the intermediate exposure duration. When sufficient time is permitted, however, such is the case at 800 ms, the deficit is eliminated and DS shows 83% correct report of the second letter.

Table 6.3
Number of letters reported by DS and control on RSVP
presentation as a function of increasing SOA between letters

	SOA	Overall % correct	%1st correct	%2nd correct	%2nd correct| 1st correct
DS					
	100	61.25	62.5	60.00	44.00
	400	63.75	77.5	50.00	45.16
	800	68.75	60.00	77.50	83.33
Control					
	100	82.50	65.00	100.00	100.00
	400	80.00	85.00	75.00	76.47
	800	77.50	82.50	72.50	69.70

These findings demonstrate strong support for the hypothesis that DS's deficit has to do with the close temporal proximity of the letters to be encoded. DS may be able to identify the first letter correctly but she needs time to complete the process prior to the appearance of the second letter. When the interval between the two items is increased, DS's ability to encode the second item is dramatically improved. This paradigm is similar to that used to study the latency of the "attentional blink" or refractory period required by normal subjects in processing successive temporal items (Duncan, Ward, and Shapiro, 1994). The findings from DS, with respect to letter processing, is that the attentional blink or dwell time is larger than that for normal subjects such that she requires a larger refractory period before being able to process a subsequent item accurately. Provided that she has sufficient time to complete the processing of the first letter, she can process the second letter well.

Simultaneous versus sequential letter processing

Given that DS requires more time than normal for letter processing, one would predict that when two letters are presented simultaneously and there is no refractory period between the letters—at 0 ms SOA—she should have particular difficulty matching the letters compared to a situation in which the same two letters are presented sequentially. When the time interval between the letters is sufficient—at least 400 ms as indicated by the previous experiment—she should be able to perform the matching task well. There is, however, one qualification: when she simply has to decide whether the two letters are physically identical (*physical match* condition; e.g., A A) and she does not need to process the letter identity, she might be able to do so even under simultaneous presentation. When the match depends on the identity and use of abstract letter codes (*name match* condition; e.g., Aa), a full description of the letters is necessary and the interval between letters becomes critical. Thus, we might expect an interaction between type of match and SOA with no difference across SOAs for the physical match but better performance at longer than shorter SOAs for the name match. To examine this, we tested DS on simultaneous and sequential presentation of physical and name matches using a variant of the Posner and Mitchell (1967) paradigm employed by Reuter-Lorenz and Brunn (1990) and by Kay and Hanley (1991). Both Reuter-Lorenz and Brunn (1990) and Kay and Hanley (1991) reported an interaction between SOA and condition for their subjects, WL and PD, although the exact form of this interaction was slightly different in their two cases. Nevertheless, the major finding was that performance was poorer for name matches and performance was poorer at shorter SOAs.

Four letters with different upper- and lower-case forms were selected (Aa, Rr, Hh, Gg). The stimuli fell into two conditions where the pairs of letters were the same (n=60) or different (n=60) and DS was required to make same/different judgments. Trials requiring the response "same'" fell into two different conditions. The 30 same *physical match* trials contained two letters that were structurally identical and were divided equally into upper- and lower-case trials (e.g., AA or aa). The 30 same *name match* trials contained two letters which shared a nominal or letter code but not a physical match (e.g., Aa or Rr). The 60 different trials were constructed by pairing two different letters in the same case (e.g., AR, ar) or across case (e.g., Ar, aR) with equal probability.

Following a central fixation point, a single stimulus, subtending a visual angle of 1°, appeared on the screen. Two SOAs were used: in the *simultaneous* condition both members of the pair appeared on the screen (0 ms SOA) while in the *sequential* condition, the first stimulus was presented for 500 ms prior to the appearance of the second letter. Sequential and simultaneous trials were mixed and randomized and two blocks of 120 trials were run. Unlike previous experiments (Reuter-Lorenz and Brunn, 1990; Kay and Hanley, 1991) in which the two letters appeared horizontally adjacent, in this experiment the two letters appeared vertically one directly above the other. This vertical presentation was used since any shift in eye movement with a horizontal display could place one stimulus in the blind field, making the comparison between stimuli more difficult particularly under conditions of limited exposure duration. In both simultaneous and sequential conditions, after presentation, both stimuli remained on the screen until the response key was pressed. DS was instructed to press one key for the "same" (includes physical and name match conditions) and a second key for "different" decisions. Reaction time and accuracy was measured for DS. The control subject also completed in this experiment.

DS and RS made 8/240 and 4/240 errors, respectively. All 8 errors made by DS were on the sequential presentation. A one-way ANOVA with case (lower/upper, e.g., AA and aa) showed no significant difference on DS's RT ($F(1,1)=0.25$, $p>.5$) and thus the data are pooled across case for the rest of the analysis. Mean reaction times for both DS and RS for physical, name, and different trials for simultaneous and sequential conditions are displayed in table 6.4. An ANOVA of the data with trial type (physical, name, and different matches) and condition (simultaneous/sequential) as within-subject variables was conducted separately for DS and for RS. Although the name and physical match conditions are more comparable as they both require "same" responses, the data for the "different" trials are also included in the analysis.

As can be seen from table 6.4, there is a significant effect of condition ($F(2,2)=11.47$, $p<.001$) for the control subject, RS, with faster physical matches than either name or different matches. This pattern holds equally across simultaneous and sequential presentations ($F(1,2)=2.12$, $p>.10$). The most interesting finding for DS is the presence of the predicted interaction between condition and SOA ($F(2,2,)=5.2$, $p<.05$); DS was approximately 100 ms slower to make name matches relative to physical matches in the simultaneous than in the sequential condition. The main effects of condition ($F(1,2)=3.15$, $p>.05$) and of SOA ($F(1,2)=2.12$, $p>.05$) were also significant.

The most interesting result from this experiment is the disproportionate benefit of sequential over simultaneous presentation for the name-match condition for DS. These findings suggest that while DS may be able to make judgments about the physical description of the letters reasonably fast, even under simultaneous presentation, she requires additional time for processing the abstract (name) identity of a single letter. This is compatible with the data from the previous RSVP experiment in which, even at a delay of 400 ms, DS's performance was improving but was not yet at ceiling.

Table 6.4

Mean RT for physical, name and different trials in simultaneous and sequential conditions.

	O ms SOA			500 ms SOA		
	Physical	Name	Different	Physical	Name	Different
DS	840	1198	880	730	1005	880
Control	602	640	625	580	630	634

General discussion: patient DS

To examine the nature of the mechanism underlying the word-length effects in pure alexia, we have taken as our case, DS, a patient with an acquired reading deficit following a left occipital lobe lesion. DS shows relatively preserved single-letter identification (under unlimited exposure duration) and the characteristic monotonic relationship between RT and increasing word length in reading. We initially examined two current hypotheses that have been put forward to explain the underlying deficit in patients with this pattern of behavior. The spatial hypothesis suggests that the increase in RT with word length arises because of a deficit in the distribution of attention to multiple spatial locations in parallel. According to Rapp and Caramazza (1991), the decreasing left-to-right spatial gradient requires that the patient attend serially to each letter to increase letter discriminability and the signal-to-noise ratio. With the alternative view—the letter activation hypothesis—the deficit arises in the processing of single letters, independent of spatial location.

For DS, we first show that report of the second letter, although significantly worse than that of the first letter, is unaffected by the variation in spatial location. This is in marked contrast with the pattern of data obtained from MG, a patient with an attentional deficit (neglect dyslexia). This finding rules out a deficit in the distribution of resources across a spatial array as the mechanism giving rise to DS's serial reading pattern. The alternative hypothesis of an impairment in on-line letter processing was then investigated. Evidence for a letter processing deficit in DS is quite clear—she is disproportionately impaired in name matches over physical matches (also relative to the control subject) even under sequential conditions where only a single stimulus is present at any one time. The results of the letter activation experiments provide converging evidence supporting the hypothesis that DS has an impairment in letter processing with slowing or reduction in the activation of single letters. A second critical result is that even when a single letter appears in isolation without surrounding letters (RSVP and sequential presentation with 500 msec SOA), DS performs more poorly than the normal control subject. Estimates of the additional time required by DS comes from the RSVP experiment where performance is not yet at ceiling at 400 ms SOA. In the simultaneous/sequential matching task, at 500 ms SOA, performance is significantly better than at 0 ms but letter matching (particularly name matching) is still slow relative to normal times. These results support the view that single-letter processing is slowed or reduced relative to normal processing.

DS's LBL reading is well explained by an impairment in letter processing, a position similar to that held by a number of previous authors (e.g., Arguin and Bub, 1993; Bub et al., 1989; Friedman and Alexander, 1984; Howard, 1991; Reuter-

Lorenz and Brunn, 1990; Shallice and Saffran, 1986). We therefore propose that the default explanation for the functional deficit underlying pure alexia should be one of an impairment that results in less efficient letter processing. It is this impairment that gives rise to the sequential reading pattern and the signature word-length effect.

One of the controversial aspects of pure alexia, alluded to even by Dejerine, concerns the extent to which the deficit is restricted to the processing of alphanumeric stimuli. The long-standing and widely accepted view of pure alexia was that the reading deficit was the only major neurobehavioral impairment suffered by these patients—hence the designation "pure" to the disorder. If any additional accompanying deficits existed, (e.g., anomia, color deficits), they were mild and insubstantial. According to this view, the failure to recognize words is specific to orthographic items (*the orthographic view)* and thus, patients are only impaired in the processing of alphanumeric materials (e.g., Dejerine, 1892: in Bub, 1993; Geschwind, 1965; Patterson and Kay, 1982; Shallice and Saffran, 1986; Warrington and Shallice, 1980). The *perceptual view,* on the other hand, claims that a more basic and inclusive visual processing deficit underlies pure alexia (e.g. Farah, 1992, 1991; Farah and Wallace, 1991; Friedman and Alexander, 1984; Kinsbourne and Warrington, 1962). A critical distinction between the two views is made here. Whereas the orthographic view implies that there is a separate process or separate area of the brain dedicated to processing visually presented language-related items, and that this system can be selectively impaired following brain damage, the perceptual view does not require invoking this type of structure.

Although the argument provided in this chapter thus far is that the deficit giving rise to pure alexia is one of slowed letter activation, my colleagues and I do not think the deficit is restricted to letter processing. In two studies, we have investigated the perceptual abilities of several LBL readers using nonorthographic material. Erica Sekuler and I showed that four pure alexic (LBL readers), one of whom was patient DS, were impaired on tasks involving perceptual speed and fluency on nonorthographic material. Furthermore, in contrast to normal controls, these patients relied more on perceptual cues such as symmetry and figural goodness and when these cues were not available, these patients performed even more poorly (Sekuler and Behrmann, 1996). Along similar lines, Erica Sekuler, James Nelson, and I showed that five LBL readers were impaired relative to normal subjects in their ability to name black-and-white line drawings. Even more interesting was that as the visual complexity of these line drawings increased, the patients' deficit was even more evident (Behrmann, Nelson, and Sekuler, 1998). It is important to note that a deficit in letter activation in reading is entirely consistent with this perceptual view.

We would claim that a global perceptual disturbance gives rise to the letter identification deficit. Even though these patients are not floridly agnosic, under taxing testing conditions, this more general perceptual deficit may be elicited and observed.

Rehabilitation of Pure Alexia

Despite the fact that pure alexia was one of the first neurobehavioral deficits to be documented scientifically in the case studies by Dejerine (Bub et al., 1993), and the fact that there has been so much current research attempting to characterize its nature and underlying mechanism, it is still often overlooked in the rehabilitation setting (Marks and De Vito, 1987). When rehabilitation is implemented, the best explored intervention method is the multiple oral rereading (MOR) technique initially developed by Moyer (1979). This technique requires that the patient read the same short text passage daily for approximately one week after which time a second passage is given for a week and so on. This repetitive practice with the same text has proved successful both with pure alexic patients as well as with patients with other forms of acquired dyslexia (Moyer, 1979; Moody, 1988). In one fairly recent study, for example, Tuomainen and Laine (1991) evaluated the single word and text reading speed of three patients with pure alexia all of whom completed a MOR rehabilitation program. The most interesting result from this study is that, while text reading improved for some patients, their performance on lists of single words did not. Based on these results, Tuomainen and Laine (1991; see also Tuomainen and Laine, 1993) argued that the increase in text reading speed may be attributed to top-down processes that provide syntactic and semantic constraints and thereby facilitate the processing of single words. The benefit obtained from the MOR method, therefore, comes not from the direct alteration of the impaired functional system per se; rather, word processing is facilitated by virtue of the concurrent context.

A quite different approach to remediation with a pure alexic patient that also does not affect the putative functional lesion but nevertheless has yielded beneficial results is one in which kinesthetic facilitation accompanies reading. Kashiwagi and Kashiwagi (1989) had their Japanese patient copy characters while reading them aloud. After some time, the copying was phased out and reading practice continued. Following this training, improvement was observed in reading aloud but the change was restricted to the copied and did not extend to the uncopied symbols. Based on these findings, the authors suggested that the kinesthetic images of characters, probably mediated by the intact right hemisphere, contributed to the improvement in reading. A more recent study that also involves kinesthetic feedback was carried out by Nitzberg Lott, Friedman, and Linebaugh (1994). They trained their pure alexic patient, TL, to trace letters onto the palm of his hand while naming them aloud. This training with single letters was particularly critical given that TL was impaired even in single letter visual identification. Following this tactile-kinesthetic intervention, TL showed a 50% improvement in the reading of trained item. Of even more interest is that he also showed a 40% increase in reading untrained words, demonstrating the effectiveness of the treatment program. As is evident, both the MOR procedure and kinesthetic facilitation produced positive and encouraging results for patients with pure alexia. In both cases, however, the damaged mechanism itself was not the focus of therapy. Rather, alternative, compensatory procedures were exploited to retrain word recognition. It remains an open question, therefore, to what extent pure alexia can be rehabilitated by a more direct approach in which the underlying impairment that gives rise to the overt reading deficit is treated.

The deficit in letter activation forces LBL readers to process letters singly at any one time, usually starting from the left and proceeding to the right. Because of this impairment, a marked effect of serial order in letter identification is observed. For example, Kay and Hanley (1991) found that their pure alexic patient, PD, showed a marked drop in the accuracy of single letter report as a function of serial position across a four-letter string. Whereas accuracy of letter report for position 1 was approximately 80%, performance on the fourth letter had dropped to below 20% (Kay and Hanley, 1991, fig. 2, p. 257), irrespective of whether the string was a word, a pseudoword, or a random set of letters. Similarly, Howard (1991) showed a strong effect of serial position in a string on the probability of correct letter report in two cases; patients PM and KW reported 48% and 85% of the first letter in a four-letter string but accuracy dropped to 18% and 5% respectively, for the final letter. In contrast with this dramatic drop-off across the string, single-letter report studies with normal subjects frequently yield M-shaped serial position curves with best performance on letters at both ends and in the middle of the array and poorest performance in the intermediate locations (Bouma, 1987; Mason, 1975, 1982). The benefit for items at the end of a string has also been demonstrated by Merikle, Coltheart, and Lowe (1971) who showed that items in the center, but not at the ends, of a string are adversely affected by the presence of a mask. These end-effects cannot be accounted for by sensory explanations nor by the retinal location of the items—the advantage still obtains even when the string is centered over the fovea and the end letters are furthest from fixation (Mason, 1982). Furthermore, the benefit for end letters applies irrespective of string length. Interestingly, however, this advantage for end letters is not always seen and instead applies only to strings of familiar (e.g., English letters) but not unfamiliar symbols (e.g., Greek letters). Together, these findings suggest that explanations based on lateral inhibition from neighboring letters or from limitations in perceptual analysis are incomplete. Rather, the results suggest that because the initial and final elements are salient and indicate word length, they are given preferential weighting over other letters (Mason, 1982).

An immediate question comes to mind: What is the relationship between the M-shaped letter detection curves and whole-word recognition in normal subjects? Although normal subjects show these M-shaped curves for single-letter report, most models of word recognition assume that all the visual elements are processed simultaneously and spatially in parallel (e.g., McClelland and Rumelhart, 1981). This conclusion is based on findings that normal readers show minimal effects of word length on naming RT when words are presented in free-field (usually foveally) and are not distorted in any way (see Henderson, 1982, for an overview of these studies). The M-shaped curve, however, is not necessarily inconsistent with parallel processing—it may be the case that normal subjects adopt a strategy whereby the end letters are given additional weighting during the process of parallel activation of all letters. The assumption in the pure alexia research, however, has been that patients are forced to use a serial process of letter identification because they cannot use parallel letter recognition processes to drive word recognition. The product of this compensatory serial process, then, is the monotonic linear relationship between word length and reading latency (Howard, 1991). The hypothesis is that if the processes involved in letter identification are related to those used in word recognition, improving the former would have positive consequences for the latter. SI, the subject of this rehabilitation study, for example, demonstrates a linear function for recognizing letters in a string as a function of serial position and shows the typical and expected word length effect in reading. For SI, then, if the sequential compensatory process were to be altered through therapy and replaced with a function that more closely approximated the normal M-shaped letter identification curve, the effect of word length on single-word reading should be minimized as is the case for normal readers. Jean McLeod and I tested this prediction in a study with SI, and readers are referred to Behrmann and McLeod (1995) for further details. A matched control subject, BR, was also tested on many of the same experiments.

Case Report

The subject of this rehabilitation study, SI, is a 46-year-old, right-handed, English-speaking woman who was born in Edinburgh, Scotland, and immigrated to Canada at the age of 15. She received a grade 13 education and was a part-time computer programmer and analyst. SI is a diet-controlled diabetic and had a mitral valve replacement in 1989. In February 1991 she experienced a sudden right quadrantanopsia (which still persisted at the time of testing), a severe headache, and some memory loss. She did not lose consciousness and presented with no other focal neurological deficits. A SPECT scan done at that time showed a large left parieto-occipital perfusion deficit and a normal right hemisphere. A MRI scan in October 1991 revealed a high signal area in the left occipital-temporal region indicating an infarction of the posterior cerebral artery and involving the hippocampus, fusiform, and lingual gyri. A second, smaller lesion of the middle cerebral artery affecting the parietal region was also noted (see Behrmann and McLeod, 1995, for scan).

Prior to the start of this intervention study, in December 1991, SI scored 95/100 on the Reading Comprehension Battery for Aphasia, a test designed to evaluate a person's functional reading skills. Her performance on the functional communication subtest was 6 correct out of 10 items. Despite this reasonably high level of overall accuracy, the total time taken for SI to complete the test, summed over the 10 subtests, was 23 minutes, substantially longer than is normal for someone of her intelligence and education. At this time, SI believed that her reading difficulties were a function of her quadrantanopsia and was distressed to find out that this was not the case—even when the written material was presented in her intact left field, her reading was still slow and labored. In contrast to her reading deficit, SI's spontaneous speech was fluent and comprehension was good and the only problem was a mild word finding difficulty.

SI's relatively isolated reading deficit in the absence of other marked neurobehavioural deficits is consistent with the diagnosis of pure alexia. Although SI had enjoyed reading prior to her stroke and described herself as a '"speed reader", she no longer read for pleasure postmorbidly. She could not provide us with any examples of her premorbid writing but reported that her spelling was excellent. When she was tested in January 1992, however, she made several spelling errors, most of them phonologically plausible renditions of the target. For example, she wrote SIEVE as *syv*, CHAOS as *caos*, CIRCUIT as *circut* and SEIZE as *sceaze*. The coexistence of surface dysgraphia, in which words with irregular sound-spelling correspondences are given a regular form of spelling, with pure alexia has been reported in several cases (Friedman and Hadley, 1992; Patterson and Kay, 1982). SI participated in an occupational therapy program between July 1991 and January 1992 but this was terminated prior to the implementation of her reading therapy which started in January 1992. At this time, she was unable to return to work but was involved in volunteer work at a nearby secondary school. SI was strongly motivated to participate in this study.

The rehabilitation study was a single-subject time series approach in which a pretreatment baseline was obtained followed by the introduction of the intervention procedure. After a nine-week therapy period in which SI was seen twice a week for approximately 90 minutes a session, an in-depth posttherapy evaluation was conducted to determine the extent of change in her performance. The testing material and procedure were generally the same as that reported in the section for DS above.

SI's Letter and Word Reading Deficit

Letter naming

SI was able to report the identity of single letters presented alone or in two-letter arrays at an exposure duration of 17 ms with 100% accuracy. She was also able to identify correctly 83% (75/90) of single letters presented in three-letter arrays (e.g., S V X). Of the 15 letters misidentified, 12 (80%) occupied the third position in the array. These results suggest that single letter identification is generally good even under rather brief exposure durations and that when errors do occur, the majority are on letters occupying the final position of the string.

Naming latency and lexical decision

The material and procedure for naming latency and lexical decision were identical to those used with DS although only the print (but not script) material was used.

SI made 2 errors (PAT-> *pot* and CANDLES -> *candies*) on naming latency both of which involved the substitution of a single letter. She made 21/240 (9%) errors on lexical decision with 16 of the errors on three-letter nonwords. The latencies for correct responses in the naming latency and lexical decision experiments as a function of word length are shown in figures 6.2a and 6.2b. The regression lines of best fit are also depicted on the figure. A one-way ANOVA with word length as a between-subjects factor and trials as a random factor revealed a significant increase in RT with word length for SI ($F(1,116)=11.63$, $p<.001$). This increase with a slope of 178.5 ms for each additional letter is consistent with the pattern of LBL reading. A two-way ANOVA with string type (word, nonword) and length (3, 5, 7) shows that SI's lexical decisions are slowed by 324 ms for each additional letter (calculated on "yes'" responses), again confirming the pattern of LBL reading. The word length effect was particularly evident when SI had to make "no" responses ($F(1, 205)=9.3$, $p<.005$). Main effects for string type ($F(1,205) = 8.2$, $p <.05$) and for length ($F(1,205) = 69.4$, $p<.0001$) were also significant.

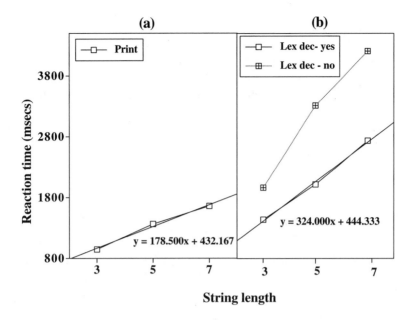

Figure 6.2 SI's response latencies (ms) as a function of string length for (a) reading aloud printed words and (b) "yes" and "no" responses in lexical decision. The lines of best fit are included.

Pretherapy Sequential Processing and Baseline Naming Latency

Measure of sequential processing

Because the goal of the therapy procedure with SI was to facilitate the adoption of a more parallel letter processing procedure, we initially documented her sequential letter processing as a function of serial position in an array. Specifically, the goal was to ascertain whether SI processed strings "ends-in" as is the case for normal subjects (Mason, 1982) or sequentially as is the case for many patients with pure alexia (Howard, 1991; Kay and Hanley, 1991).

A single target letter appeared on the left of the screen (3 spaces to the left of fixation) for 250 msecs, following the presentation of a foveal fixation point. After a 500 ms interval, a string of 5 random letters appeared centered over the position 3 spaces to the left of fixation so that the final letter appeared next to the fixation location. For example, the target "V"'appeared followed by the string "PSXVL". SI was instructed to decide whether or not the target letter was present in the string and to indicate her response using two keys, the comma and period, for present and absent responses respectively. Of the 150 trials, the target was present on 100, with equal probability of occurrence over the 5-letter positions in the string. The target was absent on the remaining 50 trials. Both accuracy and reaction time to detect the presence of the letter was measured.

Overall, SI was correct on 134/150 trials, with most errors (only 12/20 correct) occurring on position 3 of the string. One possibility for this high error rate in position 3 is that the target was presented in this position prior to the presentation of the string. Masking from the target might have affected letter processing in this position. Figure 6.3a and 6.3b show the RTs as a function of serial position for trials on which the target was present for SI and the control subject, BR, respectively. Note the difference in the Y-axis. The control subject, BR, shows the expected M-curve with fastest RT for the two end positions, followed by the middle position. The times are somewhat slower than those usually obtained for normal undergraduate subjects (Mason, 1982) but this is probably because BR is older than the subjects typically tested in these studies. In contrast to this M-shaped curve, SI's RTs form a mostly linear pattern, increasing across the array at the rate of 283 msec per additional letter (see also patient EL, in Behrmann, Nelson, and Sekuler, 1998). Of note is that SI's RT is slowest for those items in positions 4 and 5 which are closest to fixation. This is consistent with the finding that retinal position does not significantly affect serial order effects (Mason, 1982). SI's base RT (and intercept), even for letters in the first position, is slowed relative to BR. This slowing in RT is a common finding in patients with brain damage.

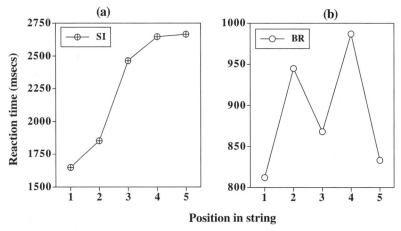

Figure 6.3 Reaction time to detect presence of target letter as a function of serial position in a nonword string of 5 letters for (a) SI and (b) control subject, BR. Y-axes differ for the two subjects.

Ends-in processing for words and nonwords

In the previous experiment, we showed that SI's letter processing is sequential in a random letter string, as reflected in the linear increase in RT with serial order. There is reason to believe, however, that if the display is a word, this may have some special effects on letter processing (McClelland and Rumelhart, 1981; Wheeler, 1970). To determine whether SI also processes legal letter strings sequentially, in this experiment we compare her ability to report the first and last letters (positions 1 and n) of word and random letter strings of increasing length. This procedure is similar to that used with DS and described above.

The material and procedure was identical to that used with DS and the exposure duration selected for SI was 100 msec (see DS, second section, allocating attention to words). Only condition 1/n was run rather than 1/n and 1/2 and a comparison across words and nonwords was made.

The number of letters, both 1 and n, reported correctly for words and nonwords is shown in table 6.5. The trials per word length are too small to obtain reliable effects and thus the data are collapsed across length. Overall, letters are reported better from words than from nonwords ($x^2_1 = 7.01$, $p < .005$) and the first letter is identified better than the last ($x^2_1 = 51.3$, $p < .0001$). Interestingly, there is an interaction such that letter 1 is reported equally well for words and nonwords ($x^2_1 = .23$, $p > .5$) but letter n is reported better for words than for nonwords ($x^2_1 = 4.3$, $p < .05$). This is consistent with the findings of a word superiority effect in some LBL readers (Bub, Black, and Howell, 1989; Kay and Hanley, 1991; Reuter-Lorenz and Brunn, 1990) and has been explained as the result of context effects from higher order orthographic representations (as in the interactive activation model, McClelland and Rumelhart, 1981; Rumelhart and McClelland, 1982). These data suggest, then, that in contrast to normal performance SI is not using an "ends-in" strategy or processing the beginning and ends of words in parallel. Rather, the results are consistent with a sequential left-to-right strategy in which there is some additional benefit obtained for words over nonwords.

Table 6.5
Number correct letter report for letters 1 and n as a function of string type pretherapy

	Words		Nonwords		Total
	Letter 1	Letter n	Letter 1	Letter n	
Pretherapy:	74	57	72	39	242

Pretherapy baseline on word-length effects

To establish that SI's reading performance was not improving spontaneously prior to intervention and that any effects of therapy were specific to the intervention procedure, her reading RTs for words of increasing letter length were measured again prior to therapy. These two testing sessions are compared with each other and with the naming latencies collected from SI two months prior to this (as in figure 6.2).

Two lists of 120 items, each including 40 three-, five- and seven-letter words, were drawn up such that there were an equal number of high- and low-frequency items (above or below 20 per million, Francis and Kuçera, 1982) and an equal number of abstract and concrete items across each word length. Each of the two lists was used once to measure SI's naming latency as a function of word length. The two testing sessions took place a week apart. The lists were randomized across length and a single word was presented on the screen, to the left of fixation, using the same procedure as above. Again, accuracy and RT were measured.

The RTs of the correct trials (120 for each of the two separate sessions and 120 from the earlier session, n=334) was subjected to a three-way ANOVA with length (3, 5, and 7), frequency (high, low) and time (testing session 1, 2, or 3) as between-subject factors and trials as the random factor. Prior to the ANOVA, items for which the RT was more than 2 standard deviations from the mean of its own cell were eliminated from the analysis. The most important result was that there was no significant effect of testing time ($F(2, 322)=.774, p>.5$) on naming latency. RTs increased significantly as a function of length, as documented previously ($F(2, 322)= 17.3, p<.001$), particularly for low-frequency words ($F(1, 322)=7.3, p<.05$). The absence of a significant effect of testing session and no interaction of this with length suggests that SI's reading performance was stable and that the characteristic word-length effect persisted. Having established that SI's performance was not fluctuating and that her performance was not improving spontaneously, the intervention program was implemented.

Therapy Procedure and Results

The intervention procedure and results are described first and thereafter, the outcome measures from the posttherapy testing.

Lists of 20 real words were drawn up, blocked by length for words of 3, 5, and 7 letters. There were five blocks of three-letter words, and ten each of five- and seven-letter words. In each block, half the words were low in frequency, occurring less than 20 times per million, and half were high in frequency, occurring more than 80 times per million (Francis and Kuçera, 1982). Therapy was conducted once a week for 90 minutes over a nine week period. The major goal of therapy was to encourage SI to process the beginning and end letters of words in parallel, that is, "ends-in" by getting her to attend simultaneously to the two ends of a string. The general procedure consisted of presenting a single word on the computer screen for a set exposure duration and instructing SI to report the first and last letters (as in condition 1/n of the sequential processing experiment). Accuracy of report was measured. All items in a block of 20 trials were the same length. When a criterion level of 18/20 correct report of both the first and last letter for two consecutive lists was reached at a particular exposure duration, a list of longer words (to a maximum of 7 letters in length) was presented at that same exposure duration. When the criterion was reached for seven-letter words at an exposure duration, the exposure was decreased by 100 ms and the procedure repeated. If criterion was not reached at one exposure after five successive administrations of a particular list length, lists of shorter word length were reintroduced until criterion was established on the shorter word-length lists. Thereafter, the longer length words were presented once again. If criterion was not reached on a longer list after this, exposure was increased by 50 ms for the words of longer length. When all ten lists of seven-letter words had been used, the lists were repeated with the individual trials randomized. The ultimate goal was to continue gradually decreasing exposure duration and to use words of increasing length until performance reached normal limits. Each session was started at the exposure duration and the list length used at the end of the previous session. The starting exposure duration was 500 ms.

Table 6.6 summarizes the exposure durations and list lengths for which the criterion level was achieved across the nine therapy sessions. A checkmark indicates that criterion of 18/20 correct was reached where as a hyphen indicates that it was not. SI reached criteria for three- and five-letter words with little difficulty at all exposure durations on all testing sessions. The same was not true for seven-letter words. Although she reached criterion for seven-letter words at 500 ms without much difficulty in the first session, she required extensive practice at all other exposure durations. She failed to reach stable performance (18/20 on two consecutive blocks) at 200 ms after two consecutive therapy sessions, the fourth and fifth sessions. The exposure duration was increased to 250 ms and SI achieved criterion level at this duration. When the exposure duration was decreased again to 200 msec, she initially scored 17/20 on two consecutive trials and then reached criterion in the following session. Finally, at 100 ms exposure, she also scored 17/20 on two consecutive trials but did not reach criterion. At this stage, because of time limitations, therapy was terminated and the posttherapy evaluation was conducted. In sum, the intensive drill work on initial- and final-letter identification was relatively

Table 6.6

Summary of exposure durations and criterion reached for different
word lengths in the therapy session

Session	Exposure	Three	Five	Seven
1	500	√	√	√
	400	√	√	-
2	400	√	√	√
	300	√	√	-
3	300	√	√	√
4	300	√	√	√
	200	√	√	-
5	200	√	√	-
6	250	√	√	√
7	200	√	√	-
8	200	√	√	√
9	100	√	√	-

easy for words of 3 and 5 letters in length but not for those of 7 letters. Nevertheless, SI persisted and after a total of 55 blocks, each containing 20 seven-letter words,
some progress was made. Whether SI would have been able to succeed at 100 ms
for seven-letter words if therapy had been continued is dubious in light of the difficulty she was experiencing. A week after the final therapy session, the posttherapy
testing was conducted over two sessions, a week apart.

Posttherapy Results

The posttherapy assessment involved evaluating SI's ability to process letters in
parallel using the same procedures as those conducted pretherapy. In addition, her
single-word reading performance was examined to see whether any transfer from
therapy had occurred.

Sequential letter processing
     The identical procedure used pretherapy was adopted here: a single target
appeared prior to a string of letters and SI made a present/absent judgment on the
target letter.
     Figure 6.4 shows her posttherapy RT to make these decisions. Her pretherapy
data (plotted from figure 6.3a) are included for ease of comparison. As can be seen
from figure 6.4, SI's posttherapy performance looks rather different from her

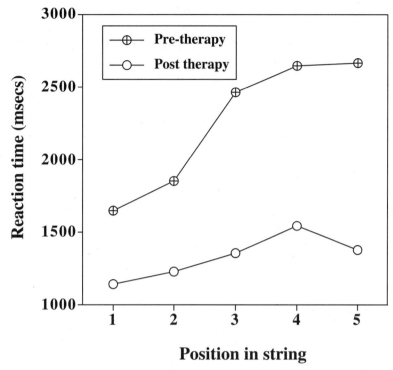

Figure 6.4 Reaction time for SI pre- and posttherapy to detect the
     presence of a target letter as a function of serial position in a
     nonword string.

pretherapy behavior. An ANOVA with time (pre-, posttherapy) and position (1-5) revealed an interaction in the data ($F(2, 269)=9.1$, $p<.001$). Post-hoc Tukey tests at $p<.05$ significance shows that the major differences between pre- and posttherapy RTs arise at positions 3, 4, and 5 of the strings. A main effect of time was also noted with significantly faster detection times after therapy than before. While SI does not yet show a normal M-shaped curve posttherapy, the slope is considerably flatter than it was pretherapy. Therefore, therapy appears to have been effective in altering the nature of the letter processing strategy and in improving SI's ability to detect the final letter.

Ends-in processing for words and nonwords

     The identical procedure adopted to investigate SI's pretherapy processing of letters in word and nonword strings was also repeated posttherapy.

     Table 6.7 shows the number of letters correctly reported for letters 1 and n for words and for nonwords. The posttherapy data are described along with a comparison of the results to the pretherapy scores (See table 6.5). As was the case pretherapy, the posttherapy scores show that SI reported letter 1 significantly better than letter n (x^2_1 = 29.1, p<.0001) and showed no difference in the accuracy of identifying letter 1 in words and nonwords (x^2_1 = .17, p>.5). In contrast to the pretherapy scores, however, posttherapy, SI identified letters in words and nonwords equally well, collapsed across position (x^2_1 =.4, p>.1), and she reported letter n equally well from words and nonwords (x^2_1 = .13, p>.5). The main effect of therapy, therefore, appears to have been in altering SI's performance on reporting the last letter of nonword strings. It is interesting to note that the benefit of therapy was restricted to nonwords, where there was the most room for improvement pretherapy and did not affect the report of letter n in words. These results are consistent with the findings from the previous experiment, showing how the training in therapy increased the accuracy and speed of report of the final letter.

Table 6.7

Number correct letter report for letters 1 and n as a function of string type posttherapy

	Words		Nonwords		Total
	Letter 1	Letter n	Letter 1	Letter n	
Posttherapy:	73	56	71	53	253

Naming latency

The results from the two tests of letter processing both show an improvement in SI's ability to identify and report the final letter. The crucial question is whether this improvement translates into a positive benefit for her word reading and particularly, whether this change alters the slope of the word-length effect. This was done by having SI read the same two lists of 120 words, consisting of words of three-, five- and seven-letters in length, that were used for pretherapy evaluation. Each of the two lists was read in a different session, separated by a week. The words remained on the screen for an unlimited time until SI made a response. RT and accuracy were monitored.

SI made only 3/240 errors. Figure 6.5 below shows the mean RT across the two posttherapy sessions as a function of word length and includes the mean pretherapy baseline data for comparison (collapsed over the three pretherapy sessions). These data were all subject to an ANOVA with time (pre- versus posttherapy) and word length (3,5, or 7) as between-subjects factors. Again, trials that deviated from the cell mean by more than two standard deviations were taken out of the posttherapy data prior to the ANOVA. The analysis revealed that SI improved sig-

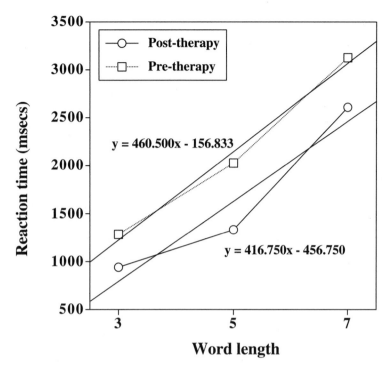

Figure 6.5 The mean RT for SI for pre- and posttherapy naming latency as a function of word length.

nificantly from pre- to posttherapy ($F(1,555)=27$, $p<.0001$) as is evident from the faster RTs seen in figure 6.5. There was a main effect of word length ($F(2,555)=37.3$, $p<.0001$), however, which did not interact with time ($F(2,555)=1.08$, $p>.5$). These results suggest that, although SI did improve in that her base RTs were faster overall as reflected in the intercept change, the absence of the interaction between length and pre/posttherapy indicates that the slope or the word-length effect had not changed from pre- to posttherapy.

General Discussion: Patient SI

This chapter describes an intervention program designed to enhance the parallel processing of letters in a patient, SI, who had an acquired dyslexia following an infarction to the left occipital lobe and surrounding areas. Initially, SI showed the hallmark feature of pure alexia or LBL reading, namely, the increase in RT to read aloud a word with an increase in the number of letters in a string. This word length effect persisted and there was no evidence of spontaneous improvement or fluctuation over time. In addition to the word length effect, pretherapy, SI's accuracy in detecting the presence of a letter in a random string was linearly related to the serial order of the letter in the string. This is consistent with a pattern of sequential processing from the left to right of a string. This linear function is quite different from the M-shaped curve obtained from normal subjects (Mason, 1975, 1982).

The goal of therapy was to facilitate SI's processing of the ends of the string by getting her to report the identity of the first and last letters in words presented for a limited exposure duration. It was hoped that this would bring her letter-report ability across letter strings closer to that observed for normal subjects. Over nine sessions, the length of the string was gradually increased while the exposure duration was gradually decreased. Posttherapy evaluation attested to the beneficial effects of therapy and revealed significantly better identification of the final letter in the string on two different tasks. The most critical but disappointing finding, however, was that despite this improvement SI's word length effect was of the same magnitude as it was prior to therapy, and her mode of word processing did not shift to a more parallel approach after intervention. There are several possible explanations for the lack of transfer from improved final letter identification to word reading. One possibility is that, even though the function of the letter detection curve was flatter following therapy than prior to therapy, it still did not approximate the normal function sufficiently to produce normal reading behavior. Thus, although the final letter was identified faster and more accurately by SI, the shape of the curve was still not quite M-shaped. The prediction that follows from this is that, if therapy could somehow further alter the shape of this curve and bring about a more normal M-shaped curve, the benefits for word reading would then be observed. This outcome appears rather dubious given the effort required to alter SI's performance even to its current level.

A more plausible explanation of the discrepancy between the advantage for end letters in letter detection and the spatially parallel mode of word processing is that the computational properties required for ends-in activation differ from those needed for parallel word processing required for normal reading. Whereas therapy might have served to increase the strength of input activation on the end letter, this still does not guarantee that the temporal dimension—parallel or serial processing—is affected. Thus, increasing the parameter of input strength and spatially parallel processing need not go together and, in spite of this increased activation, the word-length effect could still persist. This pattern is seen in the well-known interactive activation model where manipulating the strength of the input activation, as in the simulations of the serial-order effects, have no bearing on whether or not processing is spatially parallel or sequential (Rumelhart and McClelland, 1982). There is also empirical evidence from neuropsychology to support the independence of input activation and parallel processing. For example, Reuter-Lorenz and Brunn (1990) showed that their pure alexic patient, WL, was most accurate in reporting the letters from the first and last position of a string in a free report task of briefly presented stimuli. This ends-in advantage or stronger activation of the extreme letters resembled the normal pattern of accuracy of report for subjects under lateralized viewing conditions (Bouma, 1987). Despite this seemingly normal letter perception curve, WL showed a robust length effect with an increase in RT from 700 ms for a two-letter word to approximately 3.4 sec for a six-letter word (Reuter-Lorenz and Brunn, 1990, figure 1, p. 4; see also Bub et al., 1989 for a similar result). The presence of an ends-in processing curve concurrently with a sequential LBL reading suggests that these two processes might indeed be separable and independent. The ability to detect end letters with more accuracy or speed than other letters is, therefore, insufficient for eliminating LBL reading.In spite of the rather compelling evidence for a separation between the processes involved in doing ends-in letter detection and parallel word reading, it might still be the case that the same processes are used to accomplish these tasks. Any discrepancies between performance on letter detection and word reading may then arise not from some fundamental difference between the two tasks but from the fact that subjects have available to them multiple strategies that they invoke selectively and differentially to maximize performance on each of the tasks. Howard (1991), for example, reported that his pure alexic patient, KW, could read aloud 75% of the five-letter words presented for 250 ms and then masked. When the task was shifted to letter report, however, KW was only able to report correctly all the letters on a single trial of a four-letter word even when it was not masked. Based on the discrepancy between KW's performance on letter report and word reading, Howard (1991) argued that KW was able to shift from a slow serial letter identification strategy, used in letter report, to a faster, more parallel process for word identification. Along similar lines, Bub and Arguin (1995) showed that their patient, DM, was also able to adopt different modes of processing for different tasks. Whereas DM appeared to rely on an inefficient analysis of letters for some tasks, such as naming and semantic decision, he did not rely on this mechanism for lexical decision. Lexical decisions were made accurately even at brief exposure durations and performance was not affected by word length or by case alternation to the same extent as was seen in KW's performance on tasks such as naming or semantic judgment. The differences in performance in naming and semantic judgment, compared with that on lexical decision, led Bub and Arguin to conclude that more than one method of processing may be available to their patient, DM.

Although the word-length effect on SI's naming latency was not significantly altered, her base reaction time rate was faster following the intervention. A possible explanation for this intercept change is that, following therapy, SI was better at identifying single letters or combinations of the letters but that she had not substantially altered her basic reading procedure. Following the completion of our study, another intervention study with a LBL reader came to our attention, the results of which are remarkably consistent with our findings. After considerable preliminary testing, Arguin and Bub (1994) determined that their patient, DM, was unable to convert letter tokens to letter types. Thus, DM did not benefit from cross-case priming (e.g., A a) even though he was able to identify the individual letters when they were presented in isolation. Based on these results, they argued that the failure to identify letters based on abstract orthographic representations may explain the hallmark word-length effect seen in DM's performance. To encourage DM to use an abstract letter-type process, they trained him to perform cross-case nominal matching (e.g., G g). In addition, to promote the use of letter-type encoding and holistic identification of letter strings, they trained DM to read pronounceable letter strings under time pressure. Although the approach taken by Arguin and Bub in therapy was different from the one adopted with SI, the findings are almost identical. Whereas improvement in the trained tasks was evident and base RT was faster, there was no significant change in the slope of RT's as a function of stimulus length. Arguin and Bub (1994) argued that DM showed an increased rate in letter identity encoding (and this applied to both letters that were trained and letters that were not trained) and that DM had also improved in his ability to assemble individual letters into subword combinations (i.e. bigrams or trigrams). Nevertheless, these changes did not translate into direct improvement in word reading.

The absence of direct transfer from the improvement in letter identification or matching to word recognition suggests that the relationship between letter processing and word reading is not as transparent as one might think. If this is so, then rehabilitation for pure alexia perhaps requires an alternative approach. As discussed previously, compensatory procedures that circumvent the basic deficit are effective. Therapy techniques such as tactile-kinesthetic feedback through copying or repetitive practice of text, which do not address the specific deficit giving rise to LBL but which have proven effective, might provide one solution. An alternative, potentially fruitful approach that does address the defective functional process might be to use the same method as described in this study with SI. To ensure transfer to word reading, however, instead of requiring simply first- and last-letter report, all letters should be reported or better yet, the whole word should be read on each trial. A recent report by Nitzberg Lott and Friedman (1995) is that training word reading under tachistoscopic presentation with feedback is effective for both categorization and oral reading tasks. An alternative which has not yet been considered in the rehabilitation literature concerns the retraining of basic perceptual abilities. Given that patients with pure alexia appear to have a more widespread visual processing impairment than the processing of orthographic code (Behrmann, Nelson, and Sekuler, 1998; Farah, 1991, 1992; Sekuler and Behrmann, 1996), it might be the case that a perceptual training program would also have positive consequences for the acquired reading deficits in these patients.

Concluding Comments

The emphasis of this chapter has been on the study of a rather pure form of acquired dyslexia—pure alexia or letter-by-letter reading. Because of its relative isolation from other neurobehavioral deficits, it provides a unique opportunity for studying reading and its breakdown. Two major lines of work were covered here, the characterization of the underlying deficit and a potential approach to rehabilitation based on the assumption that the patients process letters in a word serially rather than in parallel. The hypothesis advanced from the first section is that the impairment giving rise to LBL reading is one of an inefficiency in identification that forces the patient, DS, to deal laboriously with a single letter at a time in a left-right direction. The therapy program capitalizes on this notion of serial processing and through a systematic drill procedure attempts to alter the performance of a patient, SI, such that letters are treated in parallel. Despite the obvious improvement made in therapy and documented experimentally, SI's reading performance was not significantly different from that observed prior to the intervention. Alternative approaches, including an emphasis not only on letter identification but on word reading, have been suggested as well as a possible perceptual retraining program for patients with LBL reading.

Acknowledgments

I wish to thank David Plaut for his comments and input. Thanks are also due to Jean McLeod, James Nelson, Erica Sekuler, and Tim Shallice for their involvement in various aspects of this research. Special thanks to the patients for their time and cooperation. This research was supported by a scholarship and an operating grant from the Medical Research Council of Canada and by a grant from the National Institutes of Mental Health (MH54746). A version of this paper was presented at the symposium on reading hosted by the Department of Psychology, Dalhousie University, Halifax, in August 1994.

References

Arguin, M., and Bub, D.N. (1992). Letter identification is over tokens, not types in pure alexia. Paper presented at the Academy of Aphasia, Toronto, October.

Arguin, M., and Bub, D.N. (1993). Single character processing in a case of pure alexia. *Neuropsychologia, 31,* 435–458.

Arguin, M., and Bub, D.N. (1994). Pure alexia: Attempted rehabilitation and its implications for interpretation of the deficit. *Brain and Language, 47,* 233–268.

Arguin, M., Bub, D.N. and Bowers, J. (1998). Extent and limits of covert lexical activation in letter-by-letter reading. *Cognitive Neuropsychology, 15*(1/2), 53–92.

Behrmann, M., Black, S.E., and Bub, D.N. (1990). The evolution of letter-by-letter reading. *Brain and Language, 39,* 405–427.

Behrmann, M., and McLeod, J. (1995). Rehabilitation for pure alexia: Efficacy of therapy and implications for models of normal word recognition. *Neuropsychological Rehabilitation, 5*(1/2), 149–180.

Behrmann, M., Nelson, J., and Sekuler, E. (1998). Visual complexity in letter-by-letter reading: "Pure" alexia is not so pure. *Neuropsychologia, 36,* 11, 1115–1132.

Behrmann, M., Plaut, D.C., and Nelson, J. (1998). A literature review and new data supporting an interactive account of letter-by-letter reading. *Cognitive Neuropsychology, 15,* 7–51.

Behrmann, M., and Shallice, T. (1995). Pure alexia: An orthographic not spatial deficit. *Cognitive Neuropsychology, 12,* 4, 409–427.

BLACK, S.E., and Behrmann, M. (1994). Localization in alexia. In A. Kertesz (ed.) *Localization in Neuropsychology.*(pp. 331–376). Academic Press, New York.

Bouma, A. (1987). Serial position curves for the identification of letter strings in visual half–field studies. *Journal of Clinical and Experimental Neuropsychology, 9,* 22.

Bowers, J.S., Arguin, M., and Bub, D.N. (1996). Fast and specific access to orthographic knowledge in a case of letter-by-letter surface alexia. *Cognitive Neuropsychology, 13,* 525–567.

Bub, D.N., and Arguin, M. (1995). Visual word activation in pure alexia. *Brain and Language, 49,* 77–103.

Bub, D.N., Arguin, M., and Lecours, A.R. (1993). Jules Dejerine and his interpretation of pure alexia. *Brain and Language, 45,* 531–559.

Bub, D.N., Black, S.E., and Howell, J. (1989). Word recognition and orthographic effects in a letter-by-letter reader. *Brain and Language, 36,* 357–376.

Bub, D.N., and Gum, T. (1988). Psychlab software. McGill University, Montreal.

Coslett, H.B. (1997). Acquired dyslexia. In T. Feinberg and M.J. Farah (eds.), *Behavioral Neurology and Neuropsychology* (pp. 197–208). New York: McGraw Hill.

Coslett, H.B., and Saffran, E.M. (1994). Mechanisms of implicit reading in alexia. In

M.J. Farah and G. Ratcliff (eds.), *The Neuropsychology of High Level Vision* (pp 299–230). Hillsdale, N.J.:Lawrence Earlbuam Associates.

Damasio, A., and Damasio, H. (1983). The anatomic basis of pure alexia. *Neurology, 33,* 1573–1583.

Duncan, J., Ward, R., and Shapiro, K. (1994). Direct measurement of attentional dwell time in human vision. *Nature, 369,* 313–315.

Everitt, B.S. (1972). *The Analysis of Contingency Tables.* Chapman and Hall: London.

Farah, M.J. (1991). Patterns of co-occurence among the associative agnosias: Implications for visual object recognition. *Cognitive Neuropsychology, 8,* (1), 1–19.

Farah, M.J. (1992). An object is an object is an object. *Current Directions in Psychological Science, 1,* 5, 164–169.

Farah, M.J., and Wallace, M. (1991). Pure alexia as a visual impairment: A reconsideration. *Cognitive Neuropsychology, 8,* 3/4, 313–334.

Francis, W.M., and Kuçera, H. (1982). *Frequency Analysis of English Usage.* Boston: Houghton Mifflin Company.

Frederiksen, J.R., and Kroll, J.F. (1976). Spelling and sound: Approaches to an internal lexicon. *Journal of Experimental Psychology: Human Perception and Performance, 2,* 361–379.

Friedman, R., and Alexander, M.P. (1984). Pictures, images and pure alexia: A case study. *Cognitive Neuropsychology, 9,* 1–23.

Friedman, R., and Hadley, J.A. (1992). Letter-by-letter surface alexia. *Cognitive Neuropsychology, 9,* 1–23.

Geschwind, N. (1965). Disconnection syndromes in animals and man. *Brain, 88,* 237–294.

Hanley, J.R., and Kay, J. (1992). Does letter-by-letter reading involve the spelling system? *Neuropsychologica, 30,* 3, 237–256.

Henderson, L. (1982). *Orthography and Word Recognition in Reading.* London: Academic Press.

Howard, D. (1991). Letter-by-letter readers: Evidence for parallel processing. In D. Besner and G. W. Humphreys (eds.) *Basic Processes in Reading: Visual Word Recognition* (pp.76). London: Lawrence Erlbaum.

Karanth, P. (1985). Dyslexia in a Dravidian language. In K.E. Patterson, J.C. Marshall and M. Coltheart (eds.) *Surface Dyslexia I.* London: Lawrence Erlbaum Associates,

.

Kashiwagi, T., and Kashiwagi, A. (1989). Recovery process of a Japanese alexic without agraphia. *Aphasiology, 3,* 1, 75–91.

Kay, J., and Hanley, R. (1991). Simultaneous form perception and serial letter recognition in a case of letter-by-letter reading. *Cognitive Neuropsychology, 8,* 3/4, 249–273.

Kinsbourne, M., and Warrington, E.K. (1962). A disorder of simultaneous form perception. *Brain, 85,* 461–486.

Koriat, A., and Norman, J. (1984). Reading without vowels: Lexical access in Hebrew. In H. Bouma and D.G. Bouwhuis (eds.) *Attention and Performance X: Control of Language Processes* (pp. 227–242).Hillsdale, NJ.: Lawrence Erlbaum Associates.

Marks, R.L., and De Vito, T. (1987). Alexia without agraphia and associated disorders: Importance of recognition in the rehabilitation setting. *Archives of Physical Medicine and Rehabilitation, 68,* 239–243.

Mason, M. (1975). Reading ability and letter search time: Effects of orthographic structure defined by single–letter positional frequency. *Journal of Experimental Psychology: General, 104,* 146–166.

Mason, M. (1982). Recognition time for letters and nonletters: Effects of serial position, array size and processing order. *Journal of Experimental Psychology: Human Perception and Performance, 8,* 5, 724–738.

Mayall, K., and Humphreys, G.W. (1996). A connectionist model of alexia: Covert recognition and case mixing effects. *British Journal of Psychology, 87,* 355–402.

McClelland, J.L., and Rumelhart, D. (1981). An interaction model of context effects in letter perception: Part 1: An account of the basic findings. *Psychological Review, 88,* 375–807.

Merikle, P.M., Coltheart, M., and Lowe, D.G. (1971). Familiarity and method of report as determinants of tachistoscopic recognition. *Canadian Journal of Psychology, 25,* 167–174.

Moody, S. (1988). The Moyer reading technique re–evaluated. *Cortex, 24,* 473–476.

Moyer, S. (1979). Rehabilitation of alexia: A case study. *Cortex, 15,* 139–144.

Nitzberg Lott, S., and Friedman, R.B. (1995). Semantic treatment for pure alexia revisited. Paper presented at the Academy of Aphasia, San Diego, CA.

Nitzberg Lott, S., Friedman, R.B. and Linebaugh, C. (1994). Rationale and efficacy of a tactile-kinaesthetic treatment for alexia. *Aphasiology, 8,* 2, 181–195.

Patterson, K.E., and Kay, J. (1982). Letter–by–letter reading: Psychological descriptions of a neurological syndrome. *Quarterly Journal of Experimental Psychology, 34A,* 411–441.

Posner, M.I., and Mitchell, R.F. (1967). Chronometric analysis of classification. *Psychological Review, 74,* 392–409.

Price, C.J., and Humphreys, G.W. (1992). Letter-by-letter reading? Functional deficits and compensatory strategies. *Cognitive Neuropsychology, 9:*5, 427–457.

Price, C.J., and Humphreys, G.W. (1995). Contrasting effects of letter–spacing in alexia: Further evidence that different strategies generate word length effects in reading. *The Quarterly Journal of Experimental Psychology, 48A:*3, 573–597.

Rapp, B., and Caramazza, A. (1991). Spatially determined deficits in letter and word processing. *Cognitive Neuropsychology, 8,* 3/4, 275–311.

Reuter–Lorenz, P., and Brunn, J.L. (1990). A pre–lexical basis for letter–by–letter reading: A case study. *Cognitive Neuropsychology, 7*, 1–20.

Rumelhart, D., and McClelland, J.L. (1982). An interactive activation model of context effects in letter perception. Part 2. The contextual enhancement effect and some tests and extensions of the model. *Psychological Review, 89*:1, 60–94.

Saffran, E.M., and Coslett, H.B. (1998). Implicit vs. letter-by-letter reading in pure alexia: A tale of two systems. *Cognitive Neuropsychology, 15*(1/2), 141–165.

Shallice, T., and Saffran, E. (1986). Lexical processing in the absence of explicit word identification: Evidence from a letter–by–letter reader. *Cognitive Neuropsychology, 3*, 429–458.

Sekuler, E., and Behrmann, M. (1996). Perceptual cues in pure alexia. *Cognitive Neuropsychology, 13*(7), 941–974.

Tuomainen, J., and Laine, M. (1991). Multiple oral re-reading technique in rehabilitation of pure alexia. *Aphasiology, 5*, 401–409.

Tuomainen, J., and Laine, M. (1993). Multiple oral rereading in the treatment of slowed reading: Is it necessary to be repetitive? Paper presented at the Academy of Aphasia meeting, Tucson, Arizona, October.

Warrington, E.K., and Shallice, T. (1980). Word-form dyslexia. *Brain, 103*, 99–112.

Wheeler, D.D. (1970). Processes in word recognition. *Cognitive Psychology, 1*, 59–85.

Young, A.W., and Ellis, A.W. (1985). Different modes of lexical access for words presented in the left and right visual fields. *Brain and Language, 24*, 326–348.

7

Phonological Processing Reexamined in Acquired Deep Dyslexia

Lori Buchanan
Nancy Hildebrandt
G. E. MacKinnon

For most of us, reading occurs with little effort, and visual information is translated into an encoded message that allows pronunciation and meaning to be derived from the printed word. Researchers who investigate word recognition are interested in how this translation occurs and how the encoded message accesses stored representations of words. This research has lead to the general agreement that there are at least two ways in which pronunciation can be derived from the printed word (see figure 7.1). In one pathway (A), subword phonological information is pieced together to form an entire pronunciation (i.e., the words are sounded out). In a second pathway (B), whole-word visual information accesses stored representations of both the meaning and the pronunciation. Some researchers also posit a third pathway (C) that can directly access the pronunciation of a word without first activating a semantic representation (see Buchanan and Besner, 1993; Carr and Pollatsek, 1985; Patterson and Coltheart,1987; and Besner, chapter 13, this volume; Masson, chapter 12, this volume and Plaut, chapter 11, this volume for discussions on these pathways). Although figure 7.1 represents relevant features of what is typically known as the "dual-route" model of word recognition, the acceptance of a grapheme-phoneme (or sublexical) conversion and a visual (orthographic or lexical) route is common to most views of word recognition. This chapter, therefore, frames the discussion of deep dyslexia within this pathway model (see Plaut, McClelland, Seidenberg and Patterson, 1996; Besner, this volume; and Plaut, this volume for discussions of theoretical similarities and differences across models).

Word-recognition research is usually conducted on normal, college-aged readers but there are also a number of studies investigating these processes in patients with acquired reading impairments. The possibility that spared processes in these patients can tell us about the normal word recognition system makes the study of acquired dyslexias a potentially rich source of information (see chapters by

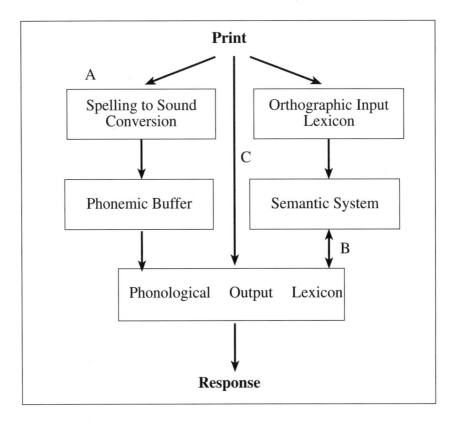

Figure 7.1 The dual-route model

Behrmann, Besner, and Plaut in this volume for related discussions about patients with various reading impairments). These forms of dyslexia are usually defined in terms of the patient's capacity to derive meaning and pronunciation from three different types of printed stimuli. These three types include nonwords (such as *frip*), regular words (i.e., words with consistent spelling sound correspondences, such as *gave, rave* and *save*) and exception words (i.e., words with inconsistent spelling-sound correspondences such as *have*).

There are a number of reports of patients who correctly read aloud regular words and nonwords but who are poor at reading exception words. These patients, referred to as *surface dyslexics*, regularize exception words; they pronounce the words so that the bodies (i.e., the word minus its initial phoneme) rhyme with the bodies of regular words. For example, *have* is pronounced such that it rhymes with *gave*, and *rave* (e.g., Coltheart, Masterson, Byng, Prior, and Riddoch, 1983; Marshall and Newcombe, 1973).

Another reading impairment is demonstrated by patients who can read words but who do so at a painfully slow rate. This rate reduction suggests that the analysis of the printed word occurs at the level of individual letters and not whole-word representations (see Behrmann, this book for a complete discussion of empirical and theoretical issues surrounding this form of *letter by letter dyslexia*).

Still another group of patients appear to rely exclusively on the whole-word procedure that accesses the semantic system since they can derive semantic information from print and can read exception and regular words aloud. These patients, however, are very poor at reading nonwords (such as *frip*). These patients are known as *phonological dyslexics* since they appear unable to process information about subword level phonology (i.e., they cannot "sound out" a nonword) (Beauvois and Derouesne, 1978; Warrington and Shallice, 1979).

A final group of dyslexic patients are also impaired at nonword reading. Unlike phonological dyslexics, however, these patients make semantic errors when reading words aloud (e.g., *poem-singing*). This disorder has been called *deep dyslexia* since the impairment appears to involve something more central to the reading system than either phonology or orthography.

Deep dyslexics produce visual errors, derivational errors, and most importantly, in terms of classification, semantic errors when asked to read words aloud[1]. This chapter focuses on this form of acquired dyslexia. We present data from a series of studies that investigate phonological processing in deep dyslexic patients (from Buchanan, Hildebrandt, and MacKinnon, 1994, 1996; and Buchanan, Burgess, and Lund, 1996), and we briefly describe a model of deep dyslexia that we developed in response to our findings.

Deep Dyslexia: The Syndrome

Deep dyslexia is diagnosed in premorbidly literate adults on the basis of a complex set of reading deficits. The primary reading impairments include the inability to read nonwords aloud and the production of semantic, visually based, and derivational errors when reading words aloud (see table 7.1 for examples of typical error types). In addition to word naming errors deep dyslexics usually show a preference for frequent over infrequent words, nouns over function words, and concrete over abstract words (Coltheart, 1980a).

Deep Dyslexia: The Models

To account for the patients' inability to name nonwords, the traditional hypothesis of the deep dyslexic deficit was that subword phonological processing had been

Table 7.1
Examples of typical errors in deep dyslexia

Error type	Target	Response
Visual	mouth	month
Semantic	heart	blood
Visual and/or semantic	barn	farm
Visual then semantic	ajar	windex (via ajax)
Derivational	sleep	sleeping

Naming data produced by the patient JC in Buchanan, Hildebrandt, and MacKinnon (1994).

eradicated (e.g., Coltheart, 1980b; Glosser and Friedman, 1990; Morton and Patterson, 1980; Plaut and Shallice, 1991, 1993; Newton and Barry, 1997). The models based on this fundamental hypothesis will be reviewed here with the goal of describing how each relies on the assumption that deep dyslexics are entirely unable to derive phonological information from a printed nonword. This review will be followed by a description of recent evidence suggesting a need to reexamine this assumption.

The Right-Hemisphere Hypothesis

Coltheart (1980b) describes a right-hemisphere account of deep dyslexia, in which preserved reading abilities are claimed to reside in a subsidiary reading system in the right hemisphere. This subsidiary system is uncovered subsequent to devastation of the primary reading system in the left hemisphere (see Demb, Poldrack, and Gabrieli, chapter 9, this book, for a review of neuranatomical investigations of reading processes in both normal and impaired readers). The inability to perform phonological decoding of nonwords reflects reliance on this less verbal hemisphere. The claims of this theory were motivated by similarities in performance between deep dyslexic patients and split-brain patients reading with the right hemisphere (e.g., Zaidel, 1978) and by investigations of normals reading with their right hemisphere (e.g., Cohen and Freeman, 1979; Moscovitch, 1976).

Patterson and Besner (1984a), however, dispute the validity of the split brain research upon which this model was based (see also Patterson and Besner, 1984b, but see also Zaidel and Schweiger, 1984, and Rabinowitz and Moscovitch, 1984 for responses to Patterson and Besner). Moreover, direct evidence against the model comes from Roeltgen (1987) who describes a patient who became deep dyslexic following an initial stroke in the left hemisphere and then completely lost his reading ability following a second stroke in the left hemisphere. Further evidence against the model is presented by researchers using fMRI technology to map language processing in deep dylexia (Price et al., 1998). Despite these objections, the right-hemisphere hypothesis remains a widely accepted explanation for deep dyslexia that relies on the observation that phonological processing is severely compromised in the deep dyslexic patient.

The right-hemisphere hypothesis is unique in that it does not depend on an existing model of normal word recognition. Its advantage over other models of deep dyslexia is that it describes the disorder in terms of plausible neurological mechanisms. It presents a potential objection to word-recognition research with deep dyslexic patients, however, in that it implies that the examination of preserved function in deep dyslexia can tell us little about how the normal word-recognition system operates. Despite the possibility that deep dyslexics are not using the preserved parts of the normal word recognition system, the other theories of deep dyslexia described in this chapter adapt normal word-recognition models to fit deep dyslexia data. The advantages of this approach are that the data are usually understood within the confines of a well-specified model of word recognition and, relatedly, (despite Coltheart's objections) that if they turn out to be correct, the data may in turn tell researchers more about how normal people read. Of existing models of deep dyslexia, the Morton and Patterson model (1980) provides one of the best examples of a model with these advantages.

The Morton and Patterson Dual-Route Account

Normal readers process printed words in a number of ways (e.g., see reviews by Carr and Pollatsek, 1985; Patterson and Coltheart, 1987). Within the dual-route framework there exist both an addressed and an assembled routine (see figure 7.1). These routines consist of pathways and lexicons (i.e., mental dictionaries with entries or nodes corresponding to each item in the reader's vocabulary). The orthographic input lexicon contains orthographic descriptions for each word. The phonological lexicons contain knowledge about the sounds of these words. The phonemic buffer stores an assembled whole-word pronunciation and the semantic system contains representations for the meanings of these words. Activation of entries in these lexicons and the transmission of this activation via the pathways forms the basis for reading for meaning and reading aloud.

The assembled routine (pathway A) identifies subword orthographic segments and converts them into subword phonological segments that are in turn combined to provide a pronunciation for the letter string. Since this procedure is assumed to be rule-based, it produces correct pronunciations for both nonwords and words with typical spelling-sound correspondences[2]. English has many of these regular words (such as *lint, mint* and *hint*) but it also has a number of exceptions (such as *pint*).

Since the standard rules of English spelling-sound correspondence cannot produce the correct pronunciation for a word such as *pint*, the assembled routine cannot be used to read it aloud.

In contrast, the addressed routine relies on word-specific knowledge, allowing words like *pint* to be read through pathways B and C. This whole-word information, however, depends on the existence of a representation in the orthographic lexicon. The existence of such a representation requires previous exposure to the word so this routine cannot be used to read nonwords. In this pathway, printed words activate the corresponding representation in the orthographic lexicon. Activation then spreads (through pathway B) from the orthographic input lexicon to the phonological output lexicon via the semantic system. In pathway C, activation of the phonological representation occurs without prior activation of a semantic representation. Reading nonwords is also impossible for this pathway because, like pathway B, it relies on the use of a previously established orthographic representation.

The three pathways differ in that pathway A can read nonwords, but it cannot directly access the semantic system. In contrast, pathways B and C cannot read nonwords, but pathway B can obtain semantic information prior to accessing the phonological code. Since the defining symptoms of deep dyslexia are associated with both, purportedly independent, pathways (nonword reading impairments are associated with pathway A while semantic errors are associated with pathway B), the syndrome presents a challenge to the dual-route theory. Morton and Patterson (1980) provided an answer to this challenge with their dual-route account of deep dyslexia.

In Morton and Patterson's (1980) account, deep dyslexia arises when the normal reading system is damaged in multiple areas of the dual-route model. Of particular interest are the claims that some components of the addressed routine (the semantic system of pathway B) are damaged (to accommodate the presence of semantic errors) and that the grapheme-phoneme conversion routine (pathway A) is destroyed. This latter aspect of the model reflects the assumption that phonological processing of nonwords has been eradicated. If this assumption is erroneous, the model would necessarily require revision.

A Connectionist Approach

Computational modeling of psychological processes addresses the questions of cognitive psychology with the tools of computer science. Computer programs that describe a given psychological theory are written and implemented. Data from these simulations are then compared to data from humans to test whether the theory upon which they were based has validity. One of the strengths of the computational approach is that, to produce an implemented version of the psychological model, every detail must be considered and specified (see Plaut, this volume for a discussion of additional strengths of the computational approach to word recognition research).

Connectionism is a specific type of computational modeling that consists of a massively parallel set of connections. A consequence of this parallel processing is that the performance of the model is difficult to predict. When implementations have been developed, however, they have produced data that closely resemble those produced by humans. This approach has been very fruitful in word-recognition research (e.g., Seidenberg and McClelland, 1989), and it has recently been applied to study questions concerning how deep dyslexia arises in a normal word-recognition system (Hinton and Shallice, 1991; Plaut and Shallice, 1991;1993). Shallice and his colleagues modeled deep dyslexia by producing "lesions" in various locations within connectionist architectures. These networks consist of a number of interconnected layers of nodes that can be used to represent various features of a word. The Hinton and Shallice model, for example, has a layer of semantic nodes and a layer of orthographic nodes.

The orthographic nodes can be likened to input receptors that learn patterns of orthographic information. The nodes of a given layer interact so that a word has a semantic representation, for example, in the form of a pattern of activation across several nodes. Semantic information is coded by giving each node in the semantic system a truth statement (i.e., "it flies"). In such a representation the pattern of truth values across nodes gives information about the meaning of a word (i.e., if the nodes "it flies", "it has feathers", "it is small", "it is brown" are activated, then the summed activation represents *bird*). The summed activation, when the system settles to a steady state, is taken as the response; in this case the word *bird* is produced. The nodes in the semantic layer become associated with various inputs during learning such that semenes (semantic units) that are highly associated (occur together often) are in close proximity in the architecture. This point is critical in that damage to a specific area will have effects on similar semenes. When lesions were produced in the semantic layer of the model implemented by Hinton and Shallice, patterns of data were similar to those obtained with deep dyslexics. A limitation of their model, however, was that it did not have phonological units, so the production of naming errors was impossible.

Plaut and Shallice (1991, 1993) refined the approach of Hinton and Shallice by lesioning architectures with a phonological layer. The phonological layers in these architectures receive input from the semantic layer. Plaut and Shallice report that a single lesion within the system can produce error patterns similar to those produced by deep dyslexics. Since these patterns occur following a single lesion, it may be tempting to conclude that this approach provides a more parsimonious account than previous left-hemisphere theories of deep dyslexia. It should be noted, however, that a primary reason for postulating more than one area of damage in left-hemisphere theories has been the co-occurrence of semantic-visual errors and an inability to read nonwords. Nonword reading was impossible for all of the architectures lesioned by Plaut and Shallice because the phonological layer relied on activation from the semantic system and nonwords have no semantic representation. This inability can, therefore, be likened to a second source of damage in the model and lesions were produced in architectures that were already dyslexic to the extent that they were unable to read nonwords. Nevertheless, Plaut et al. (1996) describe several simulations using models with a much more fully implemented phonological layer. While nonword reading is possible with these newer architectures, they lack a semantic layer and, consequently, cannot be employed to test Plaut and Shallice's (1991,1993) account of deep dyslexia. Like the two previously described models of deep dyslexia, this view is also founded on the assumption that nonword phonological processing is impossible for deep dyslexics.

Continuum Theory of Phonological and Deep Dyslexia

Glosser and Friedman (1990) claim that deep dyslexia is an endpoint on the phonological dyslexia continuum. Their continuum theory of deep and phonological dyslexia is based on an analogy model of word recognition (see Glushko, 1979; Henderson, 1985; Humphreys and Evett, 1985 and Marcel, 1980 for complete descriptions of analogical models). In the Glosser and Friedman analogy model, there are two routes: a semantic route and a nonsemantic route. To that extent the analogy model is similar to the dual-route model (see Patterson and Coltheart, 1987). In the dual-route model, however, the nonsemantic pathway assembles phonology on the basis of a rule-governed process. In contrast, an analogy model obtains pronunciation by an analogical mapping of sublexical orthographic units to specific lexical items (the exact nature of this mapping remains unclear).

In Glosser and Friedman's model, both phonological and deep dyslexics are hypothesized to have a variable degree of impairment to orthography-to-phonology connections. Deep dyslexia arises when this impairment becomes so severe that the reader relies more on a damaged semantically mediated processes. Semantic errors occur because phonology cannot contribute to the response.

Support for the continuum model of deep dyslexia comes from deep dyslexic patients whose impairments have diminished with time. For example, Klein, Behrmann, and Doctor (1994) describe a patient (RL) who initially presented with typical symptoms of deep dyslexia, such as semantic errors, concreteness, and word-class effects. Subsequent testing at eighteen months post onset resulted in a much different picture. RL no longer produced semantic errors; nor did he produce effects of concreteness or word class. He was still unable, however, to pronounce nonwords aloud. The continuum model has been designed to accommodate findings such as this within an analogy model of normal word recognition; the patients' non-semantic processing improves, resulting in less reliance on the impaired semantic pathway. This improvement results in a deep dyslexic patient who no longer makes errors during naming but who is, nonetheless, unable to read nonwords aloud; the patient becomes a phonological dyslexic.

In this model, phonological dyslexia is assumed to arise as a result of an impairment in the nonsemantic pathway. Semantic errors observed in deep dyslexia are hypothesized to occur as the result of both severe impairments to the nonsemantic route and an additional impairment in the semantic route. Hence, like the previously described models, an inability to process sublexical phonology is critical for the continuum hypothesis. In this case, a revision allowing for sublexical processing of nonword phonology would be somewhat problematic. The mechanism by which the analogies are mapped, however, has not been clearly specified so, as will be shown later in this chapter, the model may easily accommodate different types of data depending on how the operations of these mechanisms are characterized.

Summary

In this section we briefly reviewed existing theories of deep dyslexia and suggested that in all cases the underlying assumptions include acceptance of the notion that deep dyslexics are unable to derive useful information about the phonology of nonwords. An examination of the phonological analysis of nonword letter strings in a deep dyslexic patient would therefore be a critical test of these theories. Such examinations will be described in this chapter, but first attention will be focused on recently reported evidence of implicit phonological influences during the processing of words by deep dyslexic patients.

Implicit Phonological Processing of Words in Deep Dyslexia

The basis for every model of deep dyslexia described in this chapter is the assumption that phonological processes are extremely impaired. This assumption has been formed by the repeatedly observed inability of patients to read nonwords aloud. Hildebrandt and Sokol, however, have argued that "... a failure on an explicit test does not necessarily imply that the targeted process is not occurring." (1993, p. 47). This view is echoed by Katz and Lanzoni (1992) who cite dissociations of implicit and explicit processing in other neurological disorders (e.g., memory impairments in Warrington and Weiskrantz, 1968, 1970; and prosopagnosia in de Haan, Young, and Newcombe, 1987) as a basis for their search for such a dissociation in the deep dyslexic they studied. Katz and Lanzoni reported preserved implicit phonological knowledge in a deep dyslexic patient. The deep dyslexic (JA) in this study showed the typical phonological impairments found in other deep dyslexic patients. Despite this, JA produced a normal rhyme advantage in a lexical decision task similar to that of Meyer, Schvaneveldt, and Ruddy (1974) in which subjects had to make lexical decisions about orthographically similar pairs of words, that either rhymed (e.g., *bribe, tribe*) or did not rhyme (e.g., *touch, couch*).

JA's lexical decisions to rhyming pairs like *tribe, bribe* were faster than were his lexical decisions times to nonrhyming pairs such as *touch, couch.* This effect was found for content words but not for function words (e.g., *but, cut* versus *had, wad*). Because word class is a lexical characteristic, this effect prompted Katz and Lanzoni to conclude that the phonological processing must occur in the lexical (addressed) pathway at the phonological output lexicon. In this regard the data fit the standard assumption that sublexical phonology is not encoded by deep dyslexics. They also indicate, however, that deep dyslexics are influenced by phonology (albeit word-level phonology) even in lexical decision (a task that does not specifically require that it be processed).

Further evidence for the influence of phonology is reported by Hildebrandt and Sokol (1993) who examined the phonological regularity effect in their deep dyslexic patient. This effect exists when words with typical spelling-sound correspondences are read with greater speed and accuracy than are words with atypical spelling-sound correspondences (e.g., *gave, rave,* and *save* are read faster than *have*). In general, this effect has been taken to indicate that sublexical phonology is computed during word recognition (e.g., Barron and Strawson, 1976; Parkin, 1982; Waters and Seidenberg, 1985).

Hildebrandt and Sokol (1993) reported a significant regularity effect in lexical decision data from a patient who fit the general deep dyslexic profile. They concluded that this normal regularity effect was evidence for intact sublexical phonological processing. Hildebrandt and Sokol's patient, however, did not produce a normal pseudohomophone effect (elevated RTs and/or greater errors for pseudohomophones relative to nonpseudohomophonic nonwords) in lexical decision. They suggested that an analogy process (following Glosser and Friedman, 1990) might operate on different-sized orthographic units for words and nonwords:

phonological processing of words via whole-word analogy mechanisms and phonological processing of nonwords via subword analogy mechanisms. If so, then other deep dyslexics should show normal regularity effects for words because these arise through use of the intact whole-word analogy mechanism. They should not, however, produce a normal pseudohomophone effect since this effect depends on the impaired subword components in the system.

These two studies have challenged traditional views by demonstrating that phonological processing is preserved in deep dyslexia to a greater extent than was previously assumed. These phonological effects were demonstrated in patients who failed to demonstrate phonological awareness on a number of explicit tasks. The sensitivity to phonological information indicates that the deficits found in deep dyslexic patients are not as encompassing as most models suggest. The data in both cases are limited only to word-level phonology, that could arguably occur in a lexical routine at the phonological output lexicon (via pathways B and C). It may be the case, however, that this knowledge also extends to nonword phonology that is processed via a nonlexical route (pathway A). Three of the experiments we now describe were designed to examine the extent to which phonological awareness for nonwords influences performance in deep dyslexic patients.

Nonword Phonological Effects in Deep Dyslexia

The patients selected for these studies fit the deep dyslexia profile; they produce semantic errors, are severely impaired in nonword reading, and are sensitive to the lexical status and imageability of words. All patients studied were fluent aphasics with speech output disorders but largely preserved speech comprehension. All patients also suffer from right-side paralysis that resulted in a slight limp for GZ and JC and confinement to a wheelchair for PB. In addition, the patients had limited use of their right hands so manual responses were made with the left hand. For all patients this resulted in the use of their previously nondominant hand (see Buchanan, Hildebrandt, and MacKinnon, 1994, 1996, for full descriptions of their patients).

JC, PB, and GZ had impairments in word naming and nonword naming that are typical of deep dyslexic patients: 30% of JC's reading errors were semantic, while PB and GZ both produced approximately 10% semantic errors. They also showed, under standard testing procedures, the typical inability to read nonwords aloud [0/78 on two occasions for JC and GZ and 6/80 and 4/80 for PB on Coltheart's N (Coltheart, Davelaar, Jonasson, and Besner, 1977) list of nonwords]. The question of interest in our studies was whether sensitivity to phonological characteristics of these nonwords could be found in these patients despite their inability to explicitly decode nonword phonology. We addressed this question by examining performance on lexical decision tasks when nonword phonology was manipulated.

The first experiment was designed to examine the extent to which phonological analysis influences processing of nonwords. During lexical decisions, normal readers take more time to reject pseudohomophones than their nonword orthographic controls (e.g., McCann and Besner, 1987). According to the dual-route model, this elevation in RT (i.e., the pseudohomophone effect) results from the presence of conflicting responses to information about the nonword. Orthographic information from the pseudohomophone travels through the lexical pathways (B and C) and produces the correct "no" response. Conversely, a "yes" response is generated when phonological information from the pseudohomophone travels through the subword pathway (A) and feeds back to the semantic system to activate an entry that represents the phonologically identical word. The conflict between these two potential sources of information takes time to resolve and a pseudohomophone effect is produced.

This conflict can only arise if the phonology of the nonword is processed and, accordingly, the pseudohomophone effect is taken to indicate sensitivity to nonword phonology and the operation of the subword phonological pathway (A). A pseudohomophone effect in this experiment would, therefore, provide support for the claim that the subword phonological processing is possible for deep dyslexic patients despite their inability to read these nonwords aloud. It would also pose a serious problem for the models of deep dyslexia described earlier since all assume that nonword phonology cannot be processed by deep dyslexics.

Buchanan, Hildebrandt, and MacKinnon (1994, 1996) presented the three deep dyslexic patients described earlier with a series of words and nonwords in a lexical decision task. The target words were presented in blocks of 60 words in a background of either 60 pseudohomophonic nonwords or 60 non-pseudohomophonic orthographic control nonwords[3]. Each block, therefore, consisted of 60 words and 60 nonwords. The patients received the pseudohomophone block first on one occasion and second on another occasion. The RTs for correct rejection were analyzed and each patient produced a pseudohomophone effect (see table 7.2). This effect indicates that they can process information via the sub-word phonological route since they are sensitive to the phonology of nonwords. This effect is in contrast to findings reported by Patterson and Marcel (1977) and Hildebrandt and Sokol (1993), and it may (as we have argued in Buchanan et al., 1996) be due to our use of a larger, more powerful stimulus set and more sophisticated timing measures).

Table 7.2

Mean rejection RTs and errors as a function of nonword type

| | Pseudohomophones | | Control nonwords | | Pseudohomophone |
	Mean RT	Errors	Mean RT	Errors	Effect
JC	2959±829	42/120	2203±1519	37/120	*t(86) =2.14, p<.05*
PB	1762±703	31/120	1510±442	25/120	*t(104)= 2.21, p<.05*
GZ	1827±1394	40/120	1394±439	29/120	*t(95)=3.65, p<.001*

Nonword Phonology and Semantics in Deep Dyslexia

The pseudohomophone effect from the first experiment indicates that the phonology of nonwords can be processed by deep dyslexics and that this processing extends from the subword phonological routine into the semantic system of the whole-word routine. This argument stems from the observation that pseudohomophones differ from orthographically matched nonwords in that their phonology is linked to a semantic representation. The presence of a semantic representation for these nonwords leads to a conflict in responses that results in the pseudohomophone effect. We hypothesise that the semantic representations of pseudohomophones (such as *taybul*) should also assist readers in a manner similar to that in which the word *table* facilitates processing of the word *chair* in normals (e.g., Neely, 1977, 1991). Such a pseudohomophone priming effect has been reported for normal readers (Buchanan and Besner, 1993; Lukatela and Turvey, 1991) and has been taken as evidence that the subword phonological pathway feeds back to the semantic system during naming. We, therefore, tested the extent to which this phonological activation of semantics occurred in deep dyslexic patients by examining pseudohomophone priming in a lexical decision task with a stimulus set that consisted of target words (e.g., *chair*), pseudohomophone semantic primes (e.g., *taybul*) and their orthographic controls (e.g., *tarbul*). The traditional models of deep dyslexia would predict a null effect of semantic priming since they assume that the ability to process phonological information from nonwords is eradicated and, consequently, that nonword phonology can not activate the semantic system.

In this experiment (reported in Buchanan, et al., 1994, 1996) the stimulus list consisted of 60 letter string sets. Each set contained a target word, a pseudohomophone derived from an associatively related word and an orthographically matched nonword. The patients were tested in a lexical decision task with this stimulus set on two occasions. On the first occasion, half of the target words appeared with their related pseudohomophones and the other half appeared with the nonword controls. On the second occasion, the pairing was reversed such that those

Table 7.3
Mean RTs (ms) and Error Rates as a Function of
Relatedness of Prime to Target

| Patient | Related | | Unrelated | | Difference |
	Mean RT	Errors%	Mean RT	Errors%	(priming effect)
JC	1255±339	3.0	1692±1154	1.0	$t(41)=1.04$, $p=.304$
PB	946±263	1.0	1095±250	0.0	$t(54)=3.89$, $p<.001$
GZ	1099±236	1.3	1148±205	1.5	$t(28)=2.05$, $p<.05$

words that appeared in the related condition on the first occasion appeared with the controls. RTs for the target words appear in table 7.3. Both JC and PB produced significant priming effects.

The results of this experiment indicated that both JC and PB were able to access semantic information from pseudohomophones and that they could benefit from this information in terms of a priming advantage for subsequent words. GZ did not produce a significant effect of semantic relatedness in this experiment. In a subsequent test of pseudohomophone priming, however, all three patients produced significant relatedness effects, being quicker to decide that a target is a word when it followed a semantically related pseudohomophone prime than when it followed an unrelated pseudohomophone prime. This experiment was identical to the preceding one except that the orthographic controls of that stimulus set were replaced with unrelated pseudohomophones (i.e., *chair* would now be preceded by an unrelated pseudohomphone such as *brane* rather than the orthographically similar nonword control for *table*). This manipulation forfeited the orthographic control of the previous experiments but was an important addition because it was possible that the patients simply recognized that psuedohomophones were more word-like and thus the priming may not have been truly semantic. In this experiment, all three patients produced significant relatedness effects with mean RTs for targets preceded by a related pseudohomophone being shorter than that for targets preceded by an unrelated pseudohomophone (see table 7.4). This was taken as additional support that deep dyslexics can obtain semantic information about nonwords on the basis of their phonological similarity to words.

Discussion of Phonological Processing Experiments

The data from Buchanan et al. (1994, 1996) and from other examinations of preserved phonological processing (e.g., Katz and Lanzoni, 1992; Hildebrandt and Sokol, 1993) indicate that phonological processing plays a role in word-recognition processes in several cases of deep dyslexia. While it may be the case that nam-

Table 7.4

Mean RTs (ms) and Error Rates as a Function of
Relatedness of Prime to Target

| Patient | Related | | Unrelated | | Difference |
	Mean RT	Errors%	Mean RT	Errors%	(priming effect)
JC	1195±519	5.0	2103±2077	6.0	$t(37)=2.42$, $p<.05$
PB	1465±218	1.0	1726±432	10.0	$t(54)=3.15$, $p<.05$
GZ	948±1081	6.0	1081±306	5.0	$t(46)=2.24$, $p<.05$

ing of nonwords is impaired, it appears clear that in at least three cases of deep dyslexia pathway A remains intact.

Taken together, the data from the experiments described here suggest that nonword phonological information is available to some patients with deep dyslexia. It may be possible that there exist deep dyslexics who are completely unable to derive phonological information from nonwords. If such patients did exist, however, they would be expected to produce data unlike the pattern described for the patients in the current study. These patients would have a form of deep dyslexia more consistent with Barry and Richardson's (1988) description of input deep dyslexia.

Our view of the patients in the studies described here is that their disorder is related to a disruption in the final, output stage of word recognition. The data from the experiments that examined their phonological processing provide a clear indication that phonology from nonwords enters the system. The challenge that faced us as a consequence of these findings was to account for these data and the data that previously existed for deep dyslexic reading patterns with a new model of deep dyslexia.

Revised Account of Output Deep Dyslexia

Morton and Patterson (1980) describe the nonword reading impairments in deep dyslexia as being a function of a grossly impaired subword phonology routine (pathway A). According to their model of word recognition, this routine is the primary way in which nonword phonology can be derived. If use of this routine was impossible in deep dyslexia, then neither a pseudohomophone effect nor a semantic priming effect with pseudohomophones would be possible. Pseudohomophones differ from nonwords in that the phonology of the word can activate lexical entries. If phonological processing of nonwords is impossible, then the subsequent activation of lexical entries based on that phonology would also be impossible. To accommodate the data reported here, the Morton and Patterson account of deep dyslexia requires substantial revision. For example, pathway A must be available during processing, at least in those cases when a nonword is presented and at least to the point where nonword phonology can feed back to the semantic system.

In normal reading of familiar words, activation spreads through both routines shown in figure 7.1. When presented with the word *life*, for example, the subword phonology is assembled through pathway A, and this assembled representation activates the phonological representations associated with *life* in the phonological output lexicon. Activation in the phonological lexicon then spreads from the target representation to phonological neighbors such as *light* and *wife* . At the same time activation of *life* and orthographically similar items (such as *line* and *wife*) travels through pathway B to activate their representations and representations of their semantic neighbors. Pathway C sends activation from the orthographic input lexicon directly to the phonological output lexicon. Relative levels of activation are gauged and activation from the most promising candidates is sent on to the phonological output lexicon where final selection occurs by assessing the contribution of activation from the three pathways.

In the normal reading system, the most highly activated representation in the phonological output lexicon is selected and the response reflects the representation with input from the most sources. Damage to this selection mechanism (perhaps in the form of random noise, see Hildebrandt, 1994) can result in the naming errors that one sees in deep dyslexia data. This selection impairment view of deep dyslexia has also been suggested by Katz and Lanzoni (1992; 1997), and it has been tested by determining that their patient showed facilitory effects when a phonological clue (e.g., the first phoneme) for a target word was presented. Our view differs from Katz and Lanzoni (1992) in that they suggest that the phonological pathway has been eliminated in deep dyslexia. In contrast, we claim that this subword phonological routine remains intact to the extent that phonological codes can be assembled for both words and nonwords and can enter the phonological output lexicon. Output from this lexicon is compromised, however, by the impaired selection mechanism and would therefore be expected to produce errors during word naming.

Any model of deep dyslexia must account for the inability to name nonwords. Since we believe that the subword, phonological routine remains intact, our explanation for this inability cannot be a straightforward inability to process subword phonological units. In the proposed model, we assume that prior to the pronunciation of a nonword a lexical check occurs whereby the assembled phonology of the nonword enters the phonological output lexicon. The phonological neighbors of these nonwords become activated and this activation is used during an analogical mapping of pronunciations. For normal readers this check results in a "nonmatch" and the assembled phonology is the "best guess" of the system.

In the case of deep dyslexia, the check becomes more demanding as the random activation in the phonological lexicon makes it difficult to be certain that no match is available. Thus, on some trials a word that has received the most activation (i.e., a close neighbor) may be chosen while in other cases the system will "time-out" as the memory demands exceed the amount of time the assembled pronunciation can be held. This would result in a case in which, on some trials, a word is offered in response to a nonword (usually these words have some relationship—phonological—with the nonword, suggesting that a match has been attempted) while on other trials the patient will supply no response. This is precisely the pattern that occurs during most (if not all) reported cases of deep dyslexic nonword naming.

A selection mechanism that responds on the basis of relative levels of activation must have sufficient sensitivity to determine which representation is most activated. If this sensitivity is eliminated, then representations with similar levels of activation would be indistinguishable and selection would be reduced to near chance or chance levels[4]. Thus, variables that affect the number of activated candidates in the phonological output lexicon should have an impact on reading performance in deep dyslexic patients. Two such variables included phonological and semantic neighborhood size. We tested this prediction in a final experiment that examined whether words with a large number of phonological and semantic neighbors resulted in poorer performance than words with few neighbors. Figure 7.2 provides a description of what would happen if, for example, orthographic and phonological neighborhood size was held constant (at one) and semantic neighborhood size varied.

The neighborhood effects were examined in an experiment that required the patients to name 300 one-syllable words that varied in orthographic (ON), phonological (PN), and semantic neighborhood (SN) size, and word length (WL). ON was determined by calculating the total number of words from the Kucera and Francis (1967) corpus that could be produced by changing only one letter of the target item: for example, orthographic neighbors of *sleet* include *sheet, sweet* and *sleep*. PN was determined using the Stone and Van Hoy (Stone, 1995) computerized data set to calculate the number of words in the Kucera and Francis (1967) corpus whose bodies rhyme with the bodies of the words in the list (for example, *cheat, sweet*, and *meat* would all be phonological neighbors of the target word *sleet*). SN was determined by counting the number of different responses generated by 218 University of Waterloo undergraduates when they were asked write down the first word that came to mind for each of 300 items; WL represents the number of letters per word.

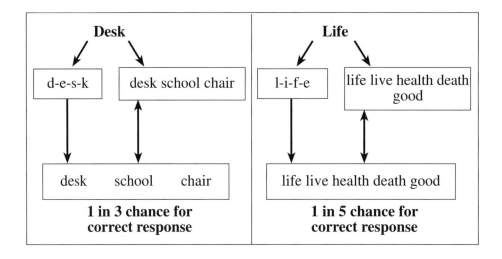

Figure 7.2 Selection probabilities in an impaired phonological output lexicon

Our model resulted in the prediction that both PN and SN would be negatively correlated with performance and ON would be positively correlated with performance since this effect arises at an unimpaired part of the reading system and the normal effect of increased ON is facilatory (e.g., Andrews, 1989). Since the orthographic input lexicon feeds forward to the semantic system prior to sending a candidate on to the phonological lexicon, there is an opportunity for a check with feedback to the orthographic lexicon. Thus, we are postulating that the orthographic input lexicon does not send several candidates onto the phonological lexicon. Consequently, we predict a normal effect of ON despite the obvious correlation between ON and PN (in our list this correlation is: $r=.211$, $t(295)=3.74$, $p=.0002$).

We also investigated the effects of word length since word-length effects are assumed to arise via the subword phonology routine (see Behrmann, this book). The items used in this experiment produce significant negative correlations between WL and naming RTs for normals (Bourassa and Besner, 1998). This effect is commonly used as support for the use of the sub-word phonology route during naming by normal readers. The prediction that length effects occur with these deep dyslexic patients is implied in the present claim that deep dyslexics also process words via this routine.

The patients read these words aloud with no time pressures and RTs were not taken, as the variability in naming RT data from deep dyslexics generally results in uninterpretable data. Correct and incorrect responses were recoded as 1s and 0s, respectively, and these data were entered into point biserial correlations with the neighborhood variables[5]. As predicted, both PN and SN were negatively correlated with performance while ON was positively correlated with performance. As indicated by the regression coefficients reported in table 7.5, however, not all effects were significant for all patients[6]. The data were thus combined to examine whether the trend across individual patients would contribute to statistical significance in a group analysis using Fisher's method of adding logs (Guilford, 1954), with the significance of the combined effect tested using Chi-square. These analyses revealed significant effects of PN ($X^2(6)=15.48$, $p<.05$), ON ($X^2(6)=17.72$, $p<.05$), and an effect that approached significance for the SN variable ($X^2(6)=10.36$, $p=.10$).

In a recent reanalyses of these data, a different measure of semantic neighborhood produced stronger results. Buchanan, Burgess, and Lund (1996) correlated the patients' performance with a measure of semantic neighborhood produced by a computational model of semantic space (Lund and Burgess, 1996). This model produces a measure of semantic density that can be described as the standard deviation of 50 items in the semantic neighborhood defined by both semantic and associative relationships between a corpus of over 100 million words of text. In this study the density measure (SDEN) used in the analysis represents the standard deviation of 50 items in each semantic neighborhood.

Our model predicted that semantic neighborhood size would be negatively correlated with performance since it was assumed to increase the competition for selection during response production. In contrast, a less dense semantic neighbor-

Table 7.5
Correlations between patients' performance
and neighborhood measures

Patient	Variable	r	$t(295)$	p
	PN**	-0.157	-2.74	.003
JC	SN	-0.043	-0.75	.226
	ON*	0.091	1.58	.057
	PN	-0.059	-1.01	.157
PB	SN	-0.028	-0.49	.313
	ON	0.050	0.87	.191
	PN	-0.025	-0.44	.330
GZ	SN**	-0.107	-1.76	.040
	ON**	0.152	2.66	.004

** = $p<.05$ on one tailed test, * = $p<.10$ on one tailed test.

hood should produce fewer competitors in the phonological output lexicon. Thus, the standard deviation of the semantic distances generated from this computational model should be positively correlated with performance. The correlations were stronger when this measure of semantic neighborhood was used and the combined analysis was significant ($X^2(6)=20.59$, $p<.05$), demonstrating that the use of both semantic and associative neighbors provides a better description of semantic space than associations alone.

A final analysis was conducted on the relationship between WL and performance for each patient to test the hypothesized use of the subword phonology routine. JC and GZ's data produced significant negative correlations between WL and correct performance ($r=-0.094$, for GZ and $r=-0.120$, for JC, $p<.05$ in both cases). PB's individual analysis did not result in a significant effect ($r=-.049$), but the direction of the effect supports the hypothesised use of the assembled routine. The Chi-square analysis on the combined WL data produced a significant effect ($X^2(6)=14.96$, $p<.05$).

The PN, SN, and WL correlations are interesting for two reasons: First, PN and SN correlations support the claim that sensitivity is disrupted in the selection mechanism of the phonological lexicon since neighborhood in general has a negative impact; second, the PN and WL correlations provide converging support for our claims regarding intact nonlexical processing since both PN and WL are effects considered to reflect processing in the subword phonological pathway. The ON effect is interesting because it supports our claim that the early part of the system (orthographic input) remains unimpaired. This appears to be the case because all patients produced positive correlations between ON and performance and this effect mimics the effect produced by normals.

The goals of this study were: (1) to provide converging support, via standard word recognition methodology, for the position that deep dyslexics can process nonword phonology; (2) to demonstrate that this processing is nonlexical; and (3) to determine whether a single source of impairment in the phonological lexicon could be responsible for the errors produced by deep dyslexics. With varying degrees of success across patients, these questions were answered.

The data from the first three experiments demonstrate that deep dyslexics can process nonword phonology and the word-length effect in the final experiment shows that this is done via the grapheme-phoneme or assembled phonology pathway. The final experiment tested the predictions generated from our hypothesis about the impaired selection mechanism in the final stage of word reading. The data provide some support for the suggestion but none of the patients produced effects that were statistically significant for all variables. Thus, the model has not been fully supported. Future examinations of neighborhood effects in deep dyslexia are required to provide a complete assessment of the reduction of sensitivity hypothesis. The empirical support for a preserved nonlexical pathway, however, is very compelling and it is clear that revisions of traditional models of deep dyslexia are necessary.

Previous Models and the Present Data

The data from these experiments suggests that previous models of deep dyslexia cannot be correct. All of the models described in this paper rely on the assumption that phonological processing is impossible for deep dyslexics. This section briefly considers why each of these models is inadequate and suggests revisions that may be appropriate in light of these new data.

The Right-Hemisphere Hypothesis

Coltheart et al. (1987) suggest that the right hemisphere "is incapable of translating between orthography and phonology (in either direction) by using mappings between subword orthographic units and subword phonological units" (p. 428). The data reported here have shown that at least some deep dyslexics can translate between orthography and phonology at the subword level. The right-hemisphere hypothesis can, however, accommodate the present findings since one need only claim that the right hemisphere is capable of implicit translation of orthography to phonology but is impaired at explicitly accessing that information. Thus, the two hemispheres may differ in their ability to consciously process phonological information. While this account is not without appeal, there remain serious objections to the right-hemisphere hypothesis (e.g., Patterson and Besner, 1984; Roeltgen, 1987).

The Dual-Route Model

Morton and Patterson (1980) describe the nonword reading impairments in deep dyslexia as being a function of a grossly impaired assembled phonology routine. Since, according to their model of word recognition, the assembled routine (pathway A) is the primary way in which nonword phonology can be derived, the current results are not easily accommodated. If use of the assembled routine was impossible in deep dyslexia, then neither a pseudohomophone effect nor a semantic priming effect with pseudohomophones would be possible. Pseudohomophones differ from nonwords in that the phonology of the word can activate lexical entries. If phonological processing of nonwords is impossible, then the subsequent activation of lexical entries based on that phonology would also be impossible. To accommodate the data reported here, the Morton and Patterson model would have to be revised. This revision would require that the assembled routine be available during processing, at least in those cases when a nonword is presented and at least to the point where nonword phonology can feed back to the semantic system. It is precisely this revision that we described and tested earlier in this chapter, and we believe that future examinations of deep dyslexia within the framework of this model will be very instructive. Our current efforts are aimed at examining the link between the semantic system and the phonological output lexicon via computational and empirical studies.

The Analogy Model

This chapter has discussed how analogy models can accommodate the implicit phonological processing data from previous deep dyslexia studies (i.e., Hildebrandt and Sokol, 1993; Katz and Lanzoni, 1992). This is possible if there are two analogy mechanisms in a system, one that processes word phonology at the lexical level and another that processes the phonology of nonwords at a sublexical level. Hildebrandt and Sokol noted that if deep dyslexic subjects have an impairment to specifically sublexical mechanisms, then other deep dyslexic subjects should also show a normal spelling-to-sound regularity effect for words because that effect arises via the lexical route. They should not, however, produce a pseudohomophone effect since that effect arises via the nonlexical route. Similarly, the Katz and Lanzoni (1992) data can be accommodated within the analogy model since only words with semantic representation produced a phonological effect. Words considered to be bereft of semantics (i.e., function words) did not produce the phonological effect. This could be taken as evidence against nonlexical phonological processing and as such is not problematic for the analogy model. The current data show, however, that the implicit phonological knowledge that was reported by these authors is also present for nonword phonology. Therefore, the hypothesis that deep dyslexic subjects have impairments of sublexical phonological mechanisms used only for nonwords must be rejected and Glosser and Friedman's (1990) hypothesis within an analogy model that orthography-to-phonology connections are impaired in deep and phonological dyslexia cannot be maintained. Moreover, analogy models in general have been rejected as appropriate explanations for normal word recognition because the mechanisms by which the system works are not well specified (Plaut et al., 1996).

Glosser and Friedman (1990) described deep dyslexia as being an endpoint on a continuum of phonological dyslexia. This view has appeal because it can explain the reported pattern of recovery for a number of deep dyslexic patients (Glosser and Friedman, 1990; Job and Sartori, 1984; Klein, et al., 1994; Laine, Neimi, and Marttila, 1990). This continuum view, however, can also be adopted in the model we propose to the extent that that deep dyslexia occurs when a lesion in the relevant areas of the brain introduces noise into the system. This noise is postulated to reside in the phonological output lexicon and results in a loss of sensitivity to the relative activation of a number of nodes. Since these nodes are activated by the semantic system and the assembled routine there are two sources of activation for words and only one for nonwords (the nonlexical or phonological pathway). If the noise were to be reduced (but not completely eliminated) during recovery, then additional activation for the words over nonwords (i.e., the activation from the lexical pathway) may be sufficient for the relevant node to maintain activation beyond the noise level. In the case of nonwords, however, a single unit of activation is introduced into the phonological lexicon and this may be insufficient to boost activation of the relevant nodes beyond that of the nonrelevant nodes. If recovery occurs via a reduction in noise, then a deep dyslexic would produce errors like those seen in phonological dyslexia. Thus, recovery of function as well as the existence of phonological dyslexics can be readily accommodated within our view of deep dyslexia. In this way the current model is similar to the continuum model of deep dyslexia proposed by Glosser and Freidman (1990).

Connectionist Approach

Recent connectionist approaches to the study of deep dyslexia have provided a catalyst for the development of a deeper understanding of acquired reading disorders. The implementations tested by Plaut and Shallice (1993), however, cannot accommodate the data presented here. This is not a consequence of the logic behind the implemented lesion studies themselves but rather it stems from the fact that the architectures tested lacked direct connections from orthography to phonology. The current data suggest that such connections do exist in the reading systems of deep dyslexic patients. At least three deep dyslexics can access the semantic system via phonology. That is not possible in the architectures used in the Plaut and Shallice (1993) study nor is it clear how a connectionist account using computational principles of the newer architectures described by Plaut et al. (1996; see also, Plaut, this volume) could accommodate these findings.

One strength of the computational methodology is that it requires full specification; the assembly of the architectures demand that assumptions are stated and coded in whatever programming language the models are written. Partly because of this strength, these models are a popular means of examining neurological deficits (Allport, 1985; Plaut and Shallice, 1991). Moreover, Farah, O'Reilly, and Vecera (1993) maintain that implicit effects are a natural consequence (i.e., an emergent property) of lesions in connectionist models. The further extension of the examination of these effects in phonological processing of deep dyslexia would appear to be a promising approach.

Future Directions

The model we proposed makes assumptions about the normal system with respect to the selection of representations in the phonological output lexicon and in the semantic system. The test of the model and those assumptions was met with some success. Lund and Burgess (1996), however, provided a much better measure of semantic neighborhoods than the one we had originally used (Buchanan, Burgess, and Lund, 1996). The fact that a measure, including both semantic and associative relationships, produced a stronger correlation than does associativeness alone indicates that the semantic system must contain representations that reflect these relationships. We are currently extending this initial investigation by examining, independently, the associative and semantic relations of target words to semantic errors from eight deep dyslexic patients. We are hopeful that this will provide us with valuable information about both deep dyslexia and the normal semantic system.

Finally, the research that we have described here and data reported by others (Katz and Lanzoni, 1992, 1997; Hildebrandt and Sokol, 1993; Behrmann, chapter 6, this volume) all support the idea that patients with acquired reading disorders show the same type of implicit-explicit dissociation reported in other neurological disorders. This suggests to us that future research in this area should focus on tests that tap preserved implicit knowledge in these patients. Historically, the examination of patients with reading disorders has focused on what they are unable to do. We believe that, for both theoretical and therapeutic reasons, there is more to be gained by concentrating efforts on the abilities that remain.

Notes

[1] Importantly, semantic errors are the symptom that distinguishes the deep dyslexics from other phonological dyslexics. For the purposes of classification, a patient is considered deep dyslexic if he or she makes semantic errors. Thus, the other symptoms, such as concreteness effects, word class effects, visual errors, and the inability to read nonwords aloud are not necessary, nor are they, without the presence of semantic errors, sufficent for the classification of a patient as deep dyslexic. These other

symptoms,however, are usually found in deep dyslexic patients (Coltheart, Patterson, and Marshall, 1986).

[2] There are examples of dual-route models that do not rely on these pronunciation rules (see Masson, chapter 12, this volume for one example).

[3] The critical control in this experiment is the orthographic overlap between the pseudohomophone and the control nonword, since we wanted to be sure that the priming effect was not due to the pseudohomophone being more orthographically similar to the word from which it was derived. This control was checked using Bruck and Water's (1988) overlap ratings and Mayzner and Tresselt (1965) bigram frequency scores.

[4] We do not claim that selection is at chance. We use a chance level for illustrative purposes only.

[5] Because of this coding, a positive correlation means that an increase in N is associated with better performance.

[6] Unfortunately, point biserial correlations are not a particularly robust method of testing effects, particularly when the patients' performance was not at the ideal 50% correct level. PB produced relatively few errors in this experiment (45 versus 135 for GZ and 201 for JC), so the effects may not have been as easily obtained although, in direction at least, they fit the model. GZ's data produced significant effects for the ON and SN variables in the direction predicted by the model. JC's responses produced significant effects on PN and ON. These effects were again in the predicted directions.

References

Allport, D.A. (1985). Distributed memory, modular systems and dysphasia. In S.K. Newman and R. Epstein (eds.). *Current Perspectives in Dysphasia.* England: Churchill Livingston.

Andrews, S.A. (1989). Frequency and neighborhood effects on lexical access: activation or search? *Journal of Experimental Psychology: Learning, Memory and Cognition, 15,* 802–814.

Barron, J. and Strawson, J.C. (1976). Use of orthographic and word–specific knowledge in reading words aloud. *Journal of Experimental Psychology: Human Perception and Performance, 2,* 286–298.

Barry, C. and Richardson, J.T.E. (1988). Accounts of oral reading in deep dyslexia. In H.A. Whitaker (ed.), *Phonological Processes and Brain Mechanisms.* New York: Springer–Verlag.

Beauvois, M.F. and Desrouesne, J. (1979). Phonological alexia: three dissociations. *Journal of Neurology, Neurosurgery and Psychiatry, 42,* 1115–1124.

Bourassa, D. and Besner, D. (1998). When do nonwords activate semantics? *Memory and Cognition*, 26, 61–74.

Bruck, M., and Waters, G., (1988). An analysis of the spelling errors of children who differ in their reading and spelling skills, *Applied Psycholinguistics, 9,* 77–92.

Buchanan, L., and Besner, D., (1993). Reading aloud: Evidence for the use of a whole word non–semantic pathway. *Canadian Journal of Experimental Psychology, 47,* 133–152.

Buchanan, L., Burgess, C., and Lund, K. (1996). Overcrowding in semantic neighborhoods: A computational analysis of deep dyslexia. *Brain and Cognition. 32,* 111–114.

Buchanan, L., Hildebrandt, N., and MacKinnon, G.E. (1994). Phonological processing by a deep dyslexic patient: A rowse is implicitly a rose. *The Journal of Neurolinguistics, 8,* 163–181.

Buchanan, L., Hildebrandt, N., and MacKinnon, G.E. (1994). Implicit phonological processing in deep dyslexia. *Brain and Language, 47,* 435–437.

Buchanan, L., Hildebrandt, N., and MacKinnon, G.E. (1996). Phonological processing of nonwords in deep dyslexia: Typical and independent? *The Journal of Neurolinguistics, 9,* 113–133.

Carr, T.H., and Pollatsek, A. (1985). Recognizing printed words: A look at current models. In D. Besner, T.G. Waller, and G.E. MacKinnon (eds.). *Reading Research: Advances in Theory and Practice (vol.5).* New York: Academic Press.

Cohen, D. and Freeman, R. (1979). Individual differences in reading strategies in relation to handedness and cerebral asymmetry. In J. Requin (ed.), *Attention and Performance VII.* Hillsdale, NJ: Lawrence Erlbaum Associates.

Coltheart, M. (1980a). Deep dyslexia: A review of the syndrome. In M. Coltheart, K. Patterson and J. C. Marshall (eds.), *Deep Dyslexia.* London: Routledge and Kegan Paul.

Coltheart, M. (1980b). Deep dyslexia: A right-hemisphere hypothesis. In M. Coltheart, K. Patterson and J. C. Marshall (eds.), *Deep Dyslexia.* London: Routledge and Kegan Paul.

Coltheart, M., Davelaar, E., Jonasson, J.T., and Besner, D. (1977). Access to the internal lexicon. In S. Dornic (ed.), *Attention and Performance VI* (pp. 535–555). Hillsdale, NJ: Lawrence Erlbaum Associates

Coltheart, M., Masterson, J., Byng, S., Prior, M., and Riddoch, M.J. (1983). Surface dyslexia. *Quarterly Journal of Experimental Psychology,* 35, 469–495.

Coltheart, M., Patterson, K.E., and Marshall, J.C. (1987). Deep dyslexia since 1980. In M. Coltheart, K. Patterson and J. C. Marshall (eds.), *Deep Dyslexia (2nd. ed),* London: Routledge and Kegan Paul.

de Haan, E.H.F., Young, A.W., and Newcomb, F. (1987). Face recognition without awareness. *Cognitive Neuropsychology, 4,* 385–415.

Farah, M.J., O'Reilly, R.C., and Vecera, S.P. (1993). Dissociated overt and covert recognition as an emergent property of a lesioned neural network. *Psychological Review, 100,* 571–88.

Glosser, G., and Friedman, R.B. (1990). The continuum of deep/phonological dyslexia. *Cortex, 26,* 343–359.

Glushko, R.J. (1979). The organization and activation of orthographic knowledge in reading aloud. *Journal of Experimental Psychology: Human Perception and Performance, ,* 674–691.

Guilford, J.P. (1954). *Psychometric Measures.* NY: McGraw-Hill.

Henderson, L. (1985). Issues in the modeling of pronunciation assembly in normal reading. In Patterson, K., Marshall, J.C., and Coltheart, M.(eds.). *Surface Dyslexia: Cognitive and Neuropsychological Studies of Phonological Reading.* London: Lawrence Erlbaum Associates.

Hildebrandt, N. (1994). The Reicher-Wheeler Effect and Models of Deep and Phonological Dyslexia. *Journal of Neurolinguistics, 8,* 1–18.

Hildebrandt, N., and Sokol, S.M. (1993). Implicit sublexical phonological processing in an acquired dyslexic patient. *Reading and Writing. 5,* 43–68.

Hinton, G.E. and Shallice, T. (1991). Lesioning an attractor network: Investigations of acquired dyslexia. *Psychological Review, 98,* 74–95.

Humphreys, G.W., and Evett, L.J. (1985). Are there independent lexical and non-lexical routes in word processing? An evaluation of the dual route theory. In A.S. Reber and D.L. Scarborough (eds.). *Toward a Psychology of Reading: The Proceedings of the CUNY Conferences.* Hillsdale, NJ: Lawrence Erlbaum Associates.

Job, R., and Sartori, G., (1984). Morphological decomposition: evidence from crossed phonological dyslexia. *Quarterly Journal of Experimental Psychology, 36,* 435–458.

Katz, R.B., and Lanzoni, S.M. (1992). Automatic activation of word phonology from print in deep dyslexia. *Quarterly Journal of Experimental Psychology, 45,* 575–608.

Katz, R.B., and Lanzoni, S.M. (1997). Activation of the phonological lexicon for reading and object naming in deep dyslexia. *Brain and Language. 58,* 46–60

Klein, D., Behrmann, M., and Doctor, E. (1994). The evolution of deep dyslexia: Evidence for the spontaneous recovery of the semantic reading route. *Cognitive Neuropsychology,* 11, 579–611.

Kucera, H., and Francis, W.M. (1967). *Computational Analysis of Present–Day American English.* Providence, RI: Brown University Press.

Laine, M., Niemi, P., and Marttila, R. (1990). Changing error patterns during reading recovery: A case study. *Journal of Neurolinguistics, 5,* 75–81.

Lukatela, G., and Turvey, M.T. (1991). Phonological access of the lexicon: Evidence from associative priming with pseudohomophones. *Journal of Experimental Psychology: Human Perception and Performance. 17,* 951–66.

Lund, K., and Burgess, C. (1996). Producing high dimensional semantic spaces from lexical co–occurrence. *Behavior Research Methods, Instruments, and Computers. 28,* 203–208.

Marcel, T. (1980). Surface Dyslexia and beginning reading: A revised hypothesis of the pronunciation of print and its impairment. In M. Coltheart, K. Patterson and J.C. Marshall (eds.), *Deep Dyslexia.* London: Routledge and Kegan Paul.

Marshall, J.C., and Newcombe, F. (1966). Syntactic and semantic errors in paralexia. *Neuropsychologia, 4,* 169–176.

Marshall, J.C., and Newcombe, F. (1973). Patterns of paralexia: A psycholinguistic approach. *Journal of Psycholinguistic Research, 2,* 175–199.

Marshall, J.C., and Newcombe, F. (1980). The conceptual status of deep dyslexia: An historical perspective. In M. Coltheart, K. Patterson and J.C. Marshall (eds.), *Deep Dyslexia.* London: Routledge and Kegan Paul.

Mayzner, M.S., and Tresselt, M.E. (1965). Tables of single-letter and digram frequency counts for various word-length and letter-position combinations. *Psychonomic Monograph Supplements, 1,* 13–32.

McCann, R.S. and Besner, D. (1987). Reading pseudohomophones: Implications for models of pronunciation and the locus of the word-frequency effect in word naming. *Journal of Experimental Psychology: Human Perception and Performance, 13,* 13–24.

Meyer, D.E., Schvaneveldt, R.W. and Ruddy, M.G. (1974). Functions of graphemic and phonemic codes in word recognition. *Memory and Cognition. 2,* 309–21.

Morton, J., and Patterson, K.E. (1980). A new attempt at an interpretation, or, an attempt at a new interpretation. In M. Coltheart, K. Patterson and J. C. Marshall (eds.), *Deep Dyslexia.* London: Routledge and Kegan Paul.

Moscovitch, M. (1976). On the representation of language in the right hemisphere of right-handed people. *Brain and Language, 3,* 47–71.

Neely, J.H. (1991). Semantic priming effects in visual word recognition: A selective review of current findings and theories. In D. Besner and G. Humphreys (eds.) *Basic Processes in Reading: Visual Word Recognition.* Hillsdale, NJ: Lawrence Erlbaum Associates.

Newcombe, F., and Marshall, J.C. (1980). Response monitoring and response blocking. In M. Coltheart, K. Patterson and J.C. Marshall (eds.), *Deep Dyslexia.* London: Routledge and Kegan Paul.

Newton, P.K., and Barry, C. (1997). Concreteness effects in word production but not word comprehension in deep dyslexia. *Cognitive Neuropsychology, 14,* 481–509.

Parkin, A.J. (1982) Phonological recoding in lexical decision: Effects of spelling-sound regularity depend on how regularity is defined. *Memory and Cognition, 10,* 43–53.

Patterson, K.E. (1978). Phonemic dyslexia: Errors of meaning and meaning of errors. *Quarterly Journal of Experimental Psychology, 30,* 587–608.

Patterson, K.E. and Coltheart, V. (1987). Phonological processes in reading: A tutorial review. In M. Coltheart (ed.), *Attention and Performance XII: The Psychology of Reading.* London: Lawrence Erlbaum Associates.

Patterson, K.E. and Besner, D. (1984a). Is the right hemisphere literate? *Cognitive Neuropsychology, 1,* 315–341.

Patterson, K.E. and Besner, D. (1984b). Reading from the left: A reply to Rabinowicz and Moscovitch and to Zaidel and Schweiger. Cognitive Neuropsychology, 1, 365–380.

Patterson, K.E., and Marcel, A.J. (1977). Aphasia, dyslexia and the phonological coding of written words. *Quarterly Journal of Experimental Psychology, 29,* 307–18.

Plaut, D., and Shallice T. (1991). Deep dyslexia: A case study of a connectionist neuropsychology. University of Toronto technical report CRG–TR–913.

Plaut, D., and Shallice, T. (1993). Deep dyslexia: A case study of connectionist neuropsychology. *Cognitive Neuropsychology., 10,* 377–500.

Plaut, D.C., and McClelland, J.L. (1993). Generalization with componential attractors: Word and nonword reading in an attractor network. *Proceedings of the 15th Annual Conference of the Cognitive Science Society* (Erlbaum), pp. 824–829.

Plaut, D.C., Behrmann, M., Patterson, K.E., and McClelland, J.L., (1993). Impaired oral reading in surface dyslexia: Detailed comparison of a patient and a connectionist model. Poster presented at the 34th Annual Meeting of the Psychonomic Society, Washington DC, November 5–7.

Plaut, D.C., McClelland, J.L., Seidenberg, M.S., and Patterson, K.E. (1996). Understanding normal and impaired word recognition: Computational principles in quasi–regular domains. *Psychological Review, 103,* 56–115.

Rabinowicz, B., and Moscovitch, M. (1984). Right hemisphere literacy: A critique of some recent approaches. *Cognitive Neuropsychology, 4,* 343–350.

Roeltgen, D.P. (1987). Loss of deep dyslexic reading ability from a second left hemisphere lesion. *Archives of Neuropsychology, 44,* 346–348.

Seidenberg, M.S. and McClelland, J.L. (1989). A distributed, developmental model of word recognition and naming. *Psychological Review, 96,* 523–568.

Stone, G. (1995). Stone and Van Hoy computerized word-level descriptors. Personal communication.

Warrington, E. and Weiskrantz, L. (1968). New method of testing long-term retention with special reference to amnesic patients. *Nature, 228,* 628–630.

Warrington, E.K. and Shallice, T. (1979). Semantic access dyslexia. *Brain, 102,* 43–63.

Warrington, E. and Weiskrantz, L. (1970). Amnesic syndrome: Consolodation or retrieval? *Nature, 277,* 972–974.

Warrington, E.K. (1981). Concrete dyslexia, *British Journal of Psychology, 72*, 175–196.

Waters, G.S. and Seidenberg, M.S. (1985). Spelling-sound effects in reading: Time-course and decision criteria. *Memory and Cognition, 13*, 557–72.

Zaidel, E. and Schweiger, A. (1984). On wrong hypotheses about the right hemisphere: Commentary on K. Patterson and D. Besner, "Is the right hemisphere literate?" *Cognitive Neuropsychology, 1*, 351–364.

Zaidel, E. (1978). Lexical organization in the right hemisphere. In P. Busner and A. Rouggeul-Buser (eds.), *Cerebral Correlates of Conscious Experience.* Amsterdam: Elsevier.

8

Are there Orthography-Specific Brain Regions? Neuropsychological and Computational Investigations

Martha J. Farah

Pure Alexia: A Brief Description

Patients with pure alexia are impaired at visual word recognition, despite their intact auditory word comprehension, intact ability to produce written language, and apparently intact recognition of visual patterns other than printed words. On the face of things, this combination of abilities and impairment implies the existence of a specialized visual word recognition system, that is implemented in localized neural tissue and thus vulnerable to localized brain damage. In this chapter I will review neuropsychological and computational research on pure alexia to address the following questions: Is there a specialized visual word recognition system in the human brain? And what implications does cerebral specialization for reading have for the nature and origins of cerebral specialization more generally?

Pure alexia is called "pure" because of the apparent sparing of all other linguistic and perceptual functions on which visual word recognition depends. Its defining characteristics are thus largely exclusionary: It is an impairment of visual word recognition that is not secondary to other problems with language or vision and is in this sense pure. The purity of the condition seems especially striking when one sees a patient write a complete sentence with accuracy and ease, and then struggle without success to read it!

Most pure alexic patients are not absolutely incapable of reading. More often they read abnormally slowly, and with errors, but can attempt and sometimes succeed at recognizing printed words. Their attempts at reading usually consist of recognizing one letter at a time, a strategy known as "letter-by-letter" (LBL) reading, which is often very obvious, as the reader will say the letters aloud. Even when reading silently, however, pure alexics take proportionately longer to read words with more letters, consistent with a LBL strategy. Figure 8.1 shows the average single-

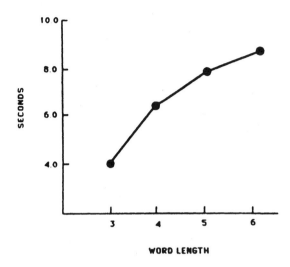

Figure 8.1 Average word-reading latencies for a pure alexic subject with a moderate degree of impairment, with words of different lengths

word reading latencies of one pure alexic as a function of the number of letters in the word. Three-letter words take, on average, four seconds to read and latency increases steeply with additional letters. Not surprisingly, the slope levels off somewhat for the longest words, as their identities can usually be guessed before the very last letter is recognized. More severe pure alexics may require 10 or 20 seconds to recognize even three-letter words, and if pushed to read longer words, they may spend literally minutes at the task.

Three general types of hypothesis have been put forth in neuropsychology to explain pure alexia, each with clear implications for the question: Does the human brain contain a dedicated reading area? In the remainder of this chapter I will review these three hypotheses and add a fourth new hypothesis.

The Visual-Verbal Disconnection Hypothesis

The first attempt to explain pure alexia was originally proposed by Déjerine (1892) and more recently championed by Geschwind (1965). According to this account, reading consists of associating visual information in occipital cortex with language representations in posterior language areas. This is done by way of the left angular gyrus, adjacent to the Wernicke's area, which is hypothesized to contain stored multimodal associations linking the visual and sound patterns of printed words. Thus, pure alexia results from any lesion that disconnects the visual cortex from the left angular gyrus. The neuropathology of pure alexia is generally consistent with this hypothesis (e.g., Damasio and Damasio, 1983; Greenblatt, 1983), often involving a left occipital lesion (causing blindness in the right visual field) and damage to the adjacent splenium (disconnecting left visual field information from the left hemisphere). Despite the anatomical support for this interpretation of pure alexia, it is not an altogether satisfying explanation. For one thing, although it is not in any way inconsistent with the LBL reading strategy of pure alexic patients, it is also not explanatory of this highly characteristic feature of the syndrome.

It is, of course, possible that disconnection may contribute to some particularly severe cases of pure alexia. I recall one patient who was virtually unable to read at all and whose LBL reading often involved letters that bore no relation to the word he was looking at. His oral verbal responses appeared to be running free—independent of orthographic input—with a tendency toward perseveration, and his picture naming had the same unrelated and often perseverative qualities. The total impression was of a disconnection in the pathways that normally link visual input and verbal output. Yamadori (1980) reported two relatively severe cases of pure alexia with what he called "unilateral dyscopia," the inability to copy written characters with one hand. In both cases the right-hand copies were worse than the left, consistent with the inability of visual information to reach the left hemisphere. The more severe case, a person who was entirely unable to read written characters, showed the more complete dissociation in copying between the left and right hands.

The disconnection account, as described by Geschwind, does not involve any reading-specific components. General purpose visual mechanisms are hypothesized to be disconnected from a language center, which is not itself specialized for visual language. Indeed, disconnection accounts in neuropsychology are usually marked by their extreme parsimony, invoking only the most elementary faculties and explaining apparently complex higher level impairments by particular disconnections among these simpler elements. In light of this, it is interesting to note that Déjerine's version of the disconnection account differed from Geschwind's on the issue of reading-specific brain regions. Déjerine proposed that the brain's visual areas do contain reading-specific substrates, and that the relevant disconnection was between these and the auditory language areas (Bub, Arguin, and LeCours, 1993).

The Visual Impairment Hypothesis

According to a second hypothesis, pure alexia results from an impairment of visual perception, which is not limited to the perception of printed words during reading but is merely most obvious in this context. Many authors have noted that pure alexic subjects who are not at all agnosic for real objects may nevertheless misidentify line drawings, particularly if they are complex (e.g., Friedman and Alexander, 1984). When naming letters presented in isolation or identifying them in the context of word reading, pure alexics tend to confuse similar-looking letters (e.g., Patterson and Kay, 1982) and show increased interference in single-letter naming from similar-looking letters (Arguin and Bub, 1993), suggesting that the breakdown occurs at a visual stage of processing. An impairment in visuospatial attention has been discussed in connection with some cases of pure alexia (Rapp and Caramazza, 1991), although it does not appear to be characteristic of pure alexia in general (e.g., Behrmann and Shallice, 1995). A number of investigators have found that pure alexic subjects are impaired at simple letter-matching tasks in which briefly presented pairs of letters must be judged the same or different (Behrmann, chapter 6, this volume; Bub, Black, and Howell, 1989; Kay and Hanley, 1991; Reuter-Lorenz and Brunn, 1990). Although Arguin and Bub (1993) argued against an early visual shape encoding impairment in pure alexia on the basis of their subject's normal performance in a visual feature conjunction task (i.e., a task in which subjects must search for a target stimulus distinguished from nontarget stimuli by a conjunction of two visual features), the feature conjunction they used was black (as opposed to white) and X (as opposed to 0). This is not a conjunction of shape features, but of one-shape feature (straightness) with a color or intensity feature. In contrast, the task they used to assess postperceptual processing required searching for a target letter among other letters and therefore did involve shape-feature conjunction. Thus there exist a number of observations implicating an impairment of visual shape perception and none that strictly absolve this stage of processing in pure alexia. What the foregoing data do not precisely specify is the nature of the shape perception impairment.

The Nature of the Visual Impairment

Marcie Wallace and I attempted to revive interest in a specific hypothesis concerning the perceptual impairment in pure alexia that was first put forth by Kinsbourne and Warrington in 1962 and to find new ways to test this hypothesis (Farah and Wallace, 1991). The initial support for the hypothesis came from a series of elegant tachistoscopic experiments in which the speed of processing single and multiple visual shapes, both orthographic and nonorthographic, could be assessed. These experiments showed that alexics' tachistoscopic recognition thresholds for single forms (letters of simple pictures) were within normal limits, but that their thresholds departed dramatically from those of normals when more than one form had to be recognized. In an ingenious series of experiments, they found that the visual processing bottleneck in these patients was determined solely by the number of separate forms to be recognized. Spatial factors such as size, position, and separation of the stimuli had no effect. They therefore concluded that these patients had a disorder of simultaneous form perception, or "simultanagnosia," and that this disorder was the cause of their alexia. Because they could recognize only one letter at a time, they were forced to read letter-by-letter.

Levine and Calvanio (1978) replicated and extended the findings of Kinsbourne and Warrington with three new cases of what they termed "alexia-simultanagnosia." Among the novel results of their study were three findings that helped to pinpoint the locus of processing impairment more precisely than the original Kinsbourne and Warrington studies. First, Levine and Calvanio demonstrated that the difficulty with multiple stimuli is present even when the task does not involve naming the stimuli but merely judging whether any two of the stimuli in an array are identical or not. This implies that the limitation is truly affecting perception per se and not the process of labeling the percept. Second, subjects made more errors in this matching task when the letters in the display were visually similar (e.g., OCO, as opposed to OXO), again suggesting a visual locus for the processing breakdown. Finally Levine and Calvanio contrasted the effects of position cues presented just before and just after the stimulus array on subjects' performance. If shape recognition per se is limited to just one item, then the precue should improve performance because it allows the subject to recognize the one item that has been cued, but the postcue should not because it comes after the stimulus array has disappeared and thus cannot guide selective perception. In contrast, if the bottleneck is occurring after shape recognition, in some short-term memory buffer or labeling process, then the postcues should also help. Levine and Calvanio found that subjects were helped by the precues: if they knew in advance which letter (indicated by the position of a precue) from a multiletter array they were to report, they could do so accurately, even with the other letters present. If the cue came after perceptual processing has been completed, however, it did not help, again implicating visual recognition per se as the locus of impairment.

Wallace and I found evidence for a limitation of the rapid encoding of multiple visual shapes in nontachistoscopic tasks as well. Ekstrom, French, and Harman (1976) developed a large set of factor-analyzed paper and pencil tasks that tested a range of cognitive and perceptual abilities. Three of these tasks loaded on a factor that came to be labeled "perceptual speed" and required the rapid recognition of multiple shapes. One of the three tests involved searching for occurrences of the letter *e* in printed words, and is therefore not ideal for testing the hypothesis that pure alexics have an impairment beyond their inability to read (although the task does not require reading the words per se). The other two were more informative in that they did not involve verbal materials at all. In one, subjects must determine whether pairs of number strings are identical or differ by one digit. In the other, subjects view rows of small pictures and for each row must find a target picture. We tested a pure alexic subject with these tests and found him to be impaired on all three (Farah and Wallace, 1991). We have subsequently tested three other pure alexic patients, all of whom were impaired. Sekuler and Behrmann (1996) have also replicated these findings with three additional subjects. They have also assessed pure alexics' abilities to make use of grouping processes in perceptual judgments in multielement displays as a further test of the hypothesis. They report that when gestalt factors do not facilitate the grouping of elements in these tasks (the grouping of distractors in a visual search task, or the grouping object parts in a object-based attention task), pure alexics' performance deviates disproportionately from that of control subjects. These results are consistent with the multiple-parts or simultanagnosia hypothesis. Although Sekuler and Behrmann failed to find a monotonically increasing effect of number of parts for the patients, which they interpreted as inconsistent with the specifics of our hypothesis, normal subjects also failed to show this effect, raising the possibility that the visual system's parse of the stimuli differed from the experimenters' intended parse.

The foregoing studies of visual perception in pure alexia are all studies of associations. They are therefore all vulnerable to a particular type of alternative explanation, involving two separate abilities that depend upon neighboring brain regions. Perhaps the perceptual impairment is a separate consequence of the same lesion that causes pure alexia, rather than being causal of the alexia. The ambiguity of associational data provided the motivation for Marcie Wallace and me to manipulate the difficulty of visual perception and assess its effect on the reading of a pure alexic (Farah and Wallace, 1991). We used additive factors logic to identify

point

moral

until

Figure 8.2 Examples of normal and degraded word stimuli.

the stage of reading that gives rise to the abnormal word length effect (i.e., the stage of reading at which the process is forced to proceed LBL) and specifically to test whether it is a visual stage of processing. According to additive factors logic, if two experimental manipulations affect the same stage of processing, their effects will be interactive, whereas if they affect separate stages, their effects will be additive (Sternberg, 1969). We presented our subject with words of varying length to read, printed either clearly or with visual noise superimposed, as shown in figure 8.2. The visual quality of a stimulus is a factor known to affect the stage of visual perception. We found that word length and visual quality interacted in determining reading latency. Specifically, the word-length effect was exacerbated by visual noise, as shown in figure 8.3. This finding is consistent with a perceptual locus for the word-length effect in this experiment and with the more general hypothesis that an impairment in the rapid perception of multiple objects or multipart objects underlies pure alexia.

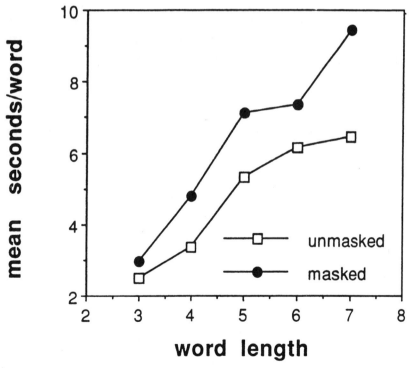

Figure 8.3 Average word-reading latencies of a pure alexic subject for normal and degraded words of different lengths.

A Computational Interpretation of Simultanagnosia

Why might the brain recognize multiple shapes with a distinct and separately lesionable system? Computationally, the recognition of multiple shapes poses a special problem distinct from the problem of recognizing complex shapes or unfamiliar shapes (to mention two other ways in which shape perception can be made difficult). The special problem for multishape recognition is crosstalk or interference among the representation of separate shapes, which will be more severe the more distributed the representation.

Although distributed representation has many computational benefits and is used in a number of brain systems, including the visual object recognition system, it is not well-suited to representing a number of items simultaneously. Once two distributed representations have been superimposed, it is difficult to know which parts of each of the two distributed representations go together. This problem is illustrated in the top part of figure 8.4. The bottom part of the figure shows that one way around this problem is to develop more localist representations. A tentative interpretation of the perceptual impairment of pure alexics is that they have lost a region of cortex in which shape information is represented in a relatively more local manner. This allows for the possibility that word and object recognition differ in degree rather than in kind. Both make use of a common type of visual ability, namely the localist representation of shape that enables multiple shapes to be encoded without crosstalk, although word recognition is relatively more dependent on that ability than object recognition. This conclusion contrasts with the next type of explanation offered for pure alexia that states it is caused by an impairment specific to orthography.

The Orthography-Specific Impairment Hypothesis

There are a number of levels of orthographic representation that could be impaired in pure alexia, including individual letters and whole-word representations. In 1980 Warrington and Shallice proposed that pure alexia was the result of damage to relatively high-level orthographic representations of words and morphemes. They call these representations "word forms" and pointed out that a loss of word forms can explain the characteristic LBL reading of pure alexics, as their visual word recognition cannot make use of word forms and must therefore proceed via individual letter recognition and knowledge of spelling.

The evidence presented by Warrington and Shallice in favor of their hypothesis was of two kinds. First, they assessed various visual capabilities in an attempt to rule out visual perception as the locus of impairment. By a process of elimina-

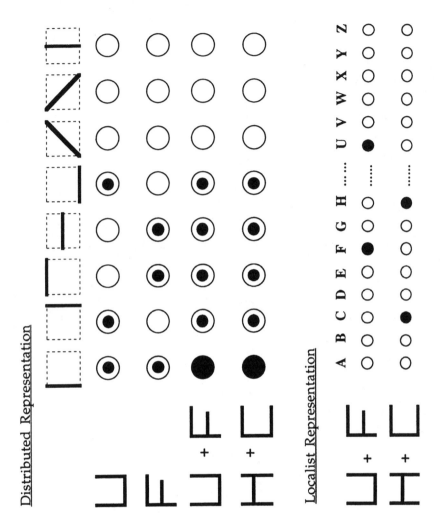

Figure 8.4 Illustration of the problem of cross-talk with distributed representations, as opposed to local, representations.

tion, this would strengthen the case for a word-form impairment. Despite having used a number of different perceptual tasks, however, many of which involved displays of multiple items, none of the tasks specifically taxed the process of rapid perception of multiple shapes, which is the leading alternative hypothesis. For example, some of the tasks were not speeded, some involved foreknowledge of target locations (eliminating the need to recognize all but the target stimuli), and so on (see Farah and Wallace, 1991, for a detailed review of these tasks).

Second, Warrington and Shallice manipulated reading difficulty in two ways that they believed would render subjects relatively more dependent on visual word forms. In one experiment they compared the reading of print to the reading of script and found performance with script to be worse. In a second experiment they compared reading words that had been presented tachistoscopically, for a half second, to reading nontachistoscopic word presentations and found a marked decrement in reading performance with tachistoscopic presentations.

Patterson and Kay (1982) proposed a modification of the word-form hypothesis, according to which the word-form system is intact, whereas its input from letter recognition systems is limited to one letter at a time. This hypothesis can account for all of Warrington and Shallice's data. In fact, both versions of the word-form hypothesis are compatible with all of the data collected by Warrington and Shallice and Patterson and Kay, and both groups acknowledge this (Patterson and Kay, 1982; Shallice, 1988, chapter 4). Patterson and Kay's reasons for preferring their alternative include several indirect and in their words "intuitive" considerations. One of the most compelling is their observation that for some patients "enormous effort was required to identify letters; but, once that had been achieved, moving from letters to the word was virtually automatic" (1982, p. 433). This is the opposite of what one would expect if the word forms themselves were damaged. In terms of the commonality versus specificity of reading and other forms of visual recognition, however, Patterson and Kay's modification of Warrington and Shallice's hypothesis maintains the idea of a visual word-form system specific to orthography.

The Word Superiority Effect and Word Forms in Pure Alexia.

Word-form hypotheses have not fared well in the face of more recent demonstrations that at least some pure alexic subjects show a "word superiority effect." The word superiority effect refers to the facilitation of letter perception when letters occur in the context of a word or pseudoword, relative to a nonword or, in some cases, no flanking letters at all (Reicher, 1969; Wheeler, 1970). The facilitation of letter perception by word or word-like contexts is not simply the result of a bias to guess letters that would make a word, because it is observed even in forced-choice tasks when both choices make a word: for example, when the stimulus is ROAD and subjects are asked whether the second character was an O or an E.

The word superiority effect might appear to be paradoxical at first, for one usually thinks of letters being perceived before words, yet here words are influencing letter perception. Nevertheless, it can be explained using the framework of connectionism. Letters are indeed perceived before words, in the sense that their representations begin to be activated before word representations begin to be activated (Johnston and McClelland, 1980). If we assume that letter activation is not complete, however, by the point at which word representations begin to be activated, and if we also assume that activated words both compete with one another in a winner-take-all manner and that they feed activation back down to their component letter representations, the facilitating influence of words on letter perception no longer appears to be mysterious. McClelland and Rumelhart (1981) present a computational model that accounts in a simple and parsimonious way for most of the findings concerning word superiority in letter perception. Figure 8.5 shows a schematic depiction of part of their model. Because of the importance of this issue to the interpretation of pure alexia, a brief overview of the model will be offered here.

Letter units are initially activated by an amount proportional to the input they receive from the units representing their constituent features. The letter units then pass activation on to the words with which they are consistent. For example, if there appears to be a *t* in the first position, that will cause the words *trap, trip, take,* and *time* to gain activation. In addition, word units are inhibited by the activation of units that are inconsistent with the word. For example, *able* will be inhibited by the unit representing an initial *t,* as activation in these units represents incompatible hypotheses, and *able* will also be inhibited by activation in other word units for the same reason. So far, this model would seem to account for word recognition, but it is not yet clear how it accounts for the word superiority effect, nor is it clear how it accounts for phenomena involving pseudowords, that is, statistical approximations to real words. The word superiority effect is explained by postulating feedback from the word level to the letter level. Switching to a different set of examples from those shown in figure 8.5, if the word shown is *read,* and perception of the letter in the second position is just barely adequate, so that the *e* unit is ever so slightly more activated than the *o* unit, then this will give the edge to the word *read* over the word *road.* Inter-word inhibition will then drive the activation of the *road* unit down, and feedback from the word level to the letter level will therefore consist of greater top-down support for *e* than for *o.* Thus, people will be more accurate at discriminating *e* from *o* in the context of *read* than in a nonword context or alone. Why should pseudowords also give rise to superior letter perception, given that there are no units corresponding to them at the word level? Because pseudowords are sufficiently similar to real words that their constituent letters will at least partially activate some real word units. *yead,* for example, will activate *year, bead, read,* and so on. Once these word units have become activated, they will in-

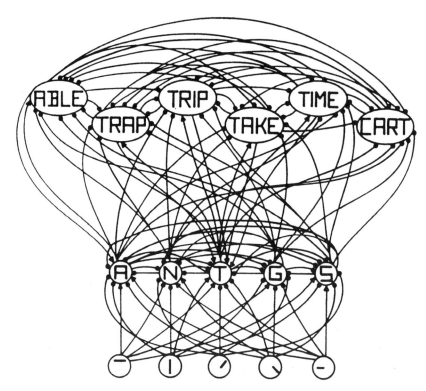

Figure 8.5 An illustration of part of a network hypothesized by Rumelhart
and McClelland (1978) to underly the word-superiority effect.

hibit other word units that are less consistent with the activated letter level units,
and will provide top-down support for the letters that do occur in the words similar to *yead*, including, for example, the *e* in the second position.

The word-form hypothesis appears to predict an absent or at least attenuated
word superiority effect in pure alexic subjects. In contrast, the perceptual impairment hypothesis predicts a normal word superiority effect because however degraded
the visual representation of letters, they will to some degree activate word representations and thus receive top-down support. In two cases pure alexics subjects have
shown word superiority effects, calling into question at least the strongest form of
the word-form hypothesis according to which they lack a visual word-form system
(Bub, Black, and Howell, 1989; Reuter-Lorenz and Brunn, 1990). Bub et al. compared their subject's performance with that of an age-matched nonalexic subject who
had a similar visual field defect, and they found that relative to this control subject,
their pure alexic showed a normal word superiority effect. This suggests that the
word-form system was intact in this pure alexic subject.

In contrast, two pure alexics have not shown word superiority effects (Behrmann, Black, and Bub, 1990; Kay and Hanley, 1991), which might imply that the word form hypothesis is the correct interpretation of some cases of pure alexia but not others. Before we resort to subtyping, however, it is worth considering the ways in which a single underlying condition can manifest itself differently in combination with some other factor that varies from case to case. It is possible that a visual-shape encoding impairment rather than a word-form impairment underlies all cases of pure alexia. We know from research with normal readers that the word superiority effect is greatly diminished or abolished when subjects attempt to read a letter in a particular position rather than distributing their attention more normally across several letter positions (Johnston and McClelland, 1974). Of course, LBL reading consists of just this strategy: first reading the letter in the first position, then reading the letter in the second, and so on.

In the two cases that showed a word superiority effect, analysis of their accuracy as a function of letter position indicated that they had abandoned the LBL strategy in the context of the experiment. Although they required much longer exposure durations than normal subjects to attain the same overall level of performance, consistent with diminished visual recognition capacity, the profile of performance over letter positions was similar to that of normal control subjects: accuracy was highest in the first and last letter positions, while lower in the middle letter positions, consistent with a normal strategy of distributing attention over all letter positions and the normal advantage for end letters. The two cases who did not show a word superiority effect did not abandon their LBL reading strategy in the experiment: Behrmann et al.'s case and Kay and Hanley's case both showed a gradient of performance across letter positions, with best performance in the first position, next best in the second, and so on. Even within one case, there is a correlation between the profile of performance across letter positions and the word superiority effect. In one variant of the experiment, Bub et al.'s case failed to show the word superiority effect, and it also showed the left-to-right gradient in accuracy over letter positions. Thus, the available evidence suggests that it may be the presence versus absence of the LBL strategy while performing the experimental task, rather than the presence versus absence of word form knowledge, that determines whether pure alexics will show a word superiority effect.

In sum, evidence for the word-form hypothesis is, at present, weak. The finding that pure alexics have difficulty reading tachistoscopically presented words, or words written in script, is no more diagnostic of a word-form impairment than of an impairment visual-shape encoding more generally. The variable findings concerning the word superiority effect are also ambiguous. Preservation of the word superiority effect suggests a locus of impairment other than the word-form system and is consistent with a prelexical perceptual impairment. Even when the word superiority effect is not found, independent evidence concerning perceptual strategy in these cases supports an explanation consistent with general (as opposed to orthography-specific) perceptual impairment.

The possibility of an orthography-specific impairment in letter representation, as opposed to word form representation, has received less systematic study. As early as Déjerine's (1892) study of pure alexia, clinicians have noted that some pure alexics appear to have more trouble recognizing single letters than other types of shapes, including single digits. Unfortunately, there has yet to be a well-controlled experimental demonstration of this, and there are many possible confoundings between the letter-nonletter distinction and other factors predictive of recognition difficulty. For example, letter recognition might be worse than digit recognition simply because of the greater uncertainty that results from a larger stimulus set. Intermixing letters and digits circumvents this problem: Thad Polk and I have seen one patient who maintained her advantage of digits over letters under mixed conditions. It is surprising that so little attention has been paid to discrepancies between letter and number recognition in pure alexia, given its relevance to the issue of orthography specificity.

A Fourth Hypothesis: General Visual Impairment Most Severe For Orthography

It appears sensible to divide the space of alternative hypotheses for explaining pure alexia into those that are orthography-specific and those that hypothesize a visual impairment for orthographic and nonorthographic stimuli alike. Indeed, I originally took this to be the basic decision that should sit at the base of our Baconian decision tree for understanding pure alexia (e.g., Farah and Wallace, 1991). But it is possible that mother nature did not design the brain with neat, binary alternatives in mind. There is another, hybrid possibility that I now believe bears scrutiny. It is that pure alexia is the result of a general visual impairment that affects the rapid perception of multiple shapes from any category, but which is most severe for letters. There are both empirical and theoretical reasons to take this hybrid hypothesis seriously. On the empirical side, the apparently worse recognition of letters than numbers in some cases suggests that pure alexia may be partially specific to orthography. On the theoretical side, recent research with artificial neural networks provides a mechanism whereby a generalized impairment with particular severity for orthographic material could arise naturally, without hypothesizing two separate lesions.

Self-Organization of a "Letter Area"

Thad Polk and I have explored some of the ways in which self-organizing systems can respond to statistical regularities in our visual environment, particularly orthographic regularities. By "self-organizing system" I refer to a class of neural network models that learn without a teacher or external source of information, conveying "right" or "wrong." Indeed, in such systems there is no "right" or "wrong" because there is no target pattern to be learned. Rather, the strength of connections among the neuron-like units of such a network is changed simply as a function of the correlations among the activity levels of the units in the network. The best known learning rule for self-organizing systems is the Hebbian rule, which can be poetically summarized as "Neurons that fire together wire together." In other words, when the activity levels of two units are positively correlated, the connection strength between them increases. This increases the likelihood that their activations will be correlated in the future as activation of one will cause the other to become active by virtue of the strengthened connection. In this way, the network develops a repertoire of stable patterns of activation in the sense that activation patterns that are close to the learned pattern (e.g., contain part of it) will be transformed into the learned pattern and tend to remain active. These stable patterns can be viewed as representations of whatever inputs to the network evoke the patterns.

If it is assumed that prior to learning, neighboring neurons have excitatory connections among them such that activating one neuron tends to activate its neighbors, then it is possible to account for a number of aspects of cortical representation by the simple mechanism of Hebbian learning. For example, topographic maps such as the somatosensory homunculus arise because neighboring locations in the input to be represented (locations on the body surface in the case of the homunculus) tend to be activated at the same time. Because of the short-range excitatory connections, this biases neighboring units of the network to represent neighboring regions of the input (e.g., Merzenich, 1987). The emergence of simple feature detectors (e.g., Linsker, 1986), and location-invariant shape representations (Foldiak, 1991) have also been modeled with self-organizing systems.

In the foregoing examples, statistical regularities in the environment interact with correlation-driven learning to give rise to organized cortical representations. For example, the statistical regularity of correlated activity at neighboring locations of the input space leads to topographic mapping of that space. Polk and I reasoned that orthographic statistical regularities in the visual environment would also interact with the correlation-driven learning of self-organizing systems in much the same way. The most obvious aspect of the statistics of orthography is the co-occurrence among letters. If you are looking at one letter, you are probably seeing many other letters and you are unlikely to be seeing a digit. In contrast, if you are looking at a digit, there is a good chance that you are seeing other digits at the same time rather than letters.

We found that, across a number of variations in simple Hebbian-type learning rules and network architectures, the co-occurrence of letters with letters and digits with digits led the network to segregate its letter and digit representations (Polk and Farah, 1995a). In other words, the network developed specialized letter and digit areas as shown in figure 8.6. This is because once a unit in the network has begun to represent one letter, spreading activation will cause its neighbors to become active when that letter is presented. Other items that are presented along with that letter will therefore be biased to come to be represented by the neighbors of the original letter's representing unit because those neighbors will be active during the presentation of the other item. The fact that the co-occurring items will usually be other letters means that other letters' representations will cluster around that first one.

If the statistics of the input are adjusted to take into account the greater co-occurrence of letters with letters than of numbers with numbers, the simulation then tends to organize with letter areas only. Digits and other shapes remain intermixed. This accounts for the observation that letter perception may be worse than digit perception in some pure alexic subjects.

The idea that co-occurrence drives the organization of visual shape representations toward a segregated letter area was tested with a group of subjects whose visual experience with letters and digits conforms to very different statistics. Thad Polk and I tested postal workers who spend eight hours on alternate days sorting Canadian mail by postal code. These codes consist of alternating letters and numbers, for example M5M 2W9. As a measure of the segregation of letter representations from number representations, we used the degree to which letters pop out in a visual search task, against a background of numbers. If letter representations are indeed segregated from number representations, then the presence of a letter can be detected by the presence of activity in the letter area without the need to individually recognize the characters in a display. Letters are indeed detected among numbers faster than among letters (e.g., Jonides and Gleitman, 1972), consistent with the existence of segregated letter representations in normal subjects. As predicted, Canadian mail sorters showed less of a difference between these two conditions than postal worker control subjects (Polk and Farah, 1995b).

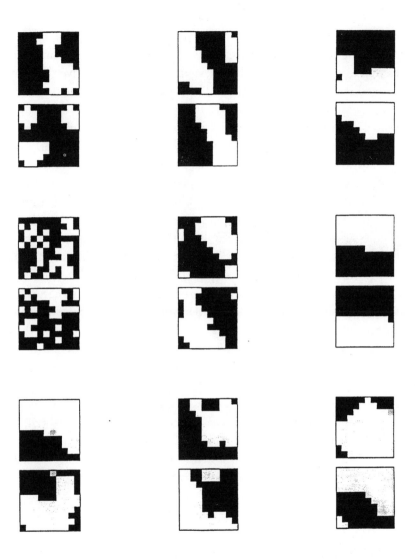

Figure 8.6 Representative results of Polk and Farah's (1995a) self-organizing
system after exposure to letter and digit inputs. Upper boxes in each pair
show the combined representation of all letters learned; lower boxes all
numbers.

Self-Organization of Abstract Letter Identities

A variation on the same type of mechanisms that create segregation of letter areas in self-organizing systems can also create case-invariant letter representations, sometimes referred to as abstract letter identities. Just as correlation-driven learning tends to drive together representations of stimuli that occur at the same time in the previous model because the network is in a similar state when the co-occurring stimuli are presented, it will also drive together the representations of stimuli that occur in similar contexts because the similar contexts will evoke similar network states. For a visual network, "similar" naturally means similar looking. Note, however, that a number of letters do look similar in their upper and lower case forms, for example *C* and *c*, *P* and *p*. Thus, if the network sees *CAP* and *cap*, the similar contexts for *A* and *a* will tend to drive the representations of those shapes together. A variety of simulations bear this out (Polk and Farah,1997); a representative outcome of this learning process is shown in figure 8.7. These simulations demonstrate the computational feasibility of the hypothesis that certain aspects of the statistics of the orthographic environment could not only form a letter area in visual cortex but could form an area representing abstract letter identities. In light of this, it is interesting to note pure alexic subjects are generally disproportionately impaired in visual matching tasks requiring cross-case matching (Behrmann, chapter 6, this volume; Bub, Black, and Howell, 1989; Kay and Hanley, 1991; Reuter-Lorenz and Brunn, 1990).

If letter representations are segregated within the visual system by the type of mechanism proposed here, then our visual system does contain orthography-specific components and pure alexia could follow from damage to such a component. Because this component segregates out within an area that is already specialized for representing multiple shapes simultaneously, however, most lesions would be ex-

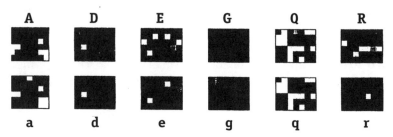

Figure 8.7 Representative result of Polk and Farah's (1997) self-organizing system after exposure to word inputs.

pected to result in some degree of general impairment in the recognition of multiple shapes as well as a more severe impairment for the recognition of orthography and an especially severe impairment for tasks requiring the representation of abstract letter identity, such as cross-case matching.

Conclusions

Does the human brain contain tissue that is dedicated to reading, that is, required for reading and not required for any other tasks? The answer to this question has implications for the genesis of functional brain architecture in general as well as the interpretation of pure alexia more specifically.

Dedicated Neural Systems: How Do they Arise?

Consider some uncontroversial examples of functions known to make use of dedicated brain tissue—color vision, face perception, motor control, and spoken language. Localized brain damage can render a person color blind, prosopagnosic, paralyzed or apraxic, or aphasic. In contrast, evidence has yet to be presented for a localized brain system dedicated to chess playing or ballet. That is, brain damage has never been found to impair chess ability while sparing general intellect, perception, memory as well as poker and canasta playing. It cannot impair ballet while sparing ballroom and belly dance. The following generalization appears to fit these observations as well as most people's intuitions on the issue: Brain tissue becomes dedicated to a particular psychological function through genetic mechanisms. Only abilities that evolved can be carried out by specialized brain regions. Setting aside the example of reading, it appears a plausible empirical generalization that learning within an individual's lifetime cannot create new brain areas.

Of course, learning modifies the brain in the sense that it alters connections between individual neurons. Learning and other forms of experience can even alter the organization of a brain area. The work of Merzenich (1987) in the somatosensory system is probably the best known example of this. After finger amputation, stimulation of the adjacent fingers results in their neural representations taking over the brain tissue that once represented the lost digit. But even this more molar type of experience-driven change in brain organization falls well short of the genesis of a new functionally defined area. Unless one adopts a rather unnatural parse of brain architecture, according to which the representation of each digit in the somatosensory system and each visual field location in the visual system is a separate "area" or "system," no new areas or systems have been created or destroyed as a result of experience in these experiments on plasticity. In contrast, if learning to read leads to the creation of an area specialized for visual word recognition, then experience as well as genetics can play a major role in determining the existence and nature of specialized brain systems.

Perhaps because of their implications for the genesis of functional brain architecture, the acquired dyslexias have recently been scrutinized for evidence of true reading specificity. Surface dyslexia, in which the reading of irregular words (e.g., *leopard*, *yacht*) is impaired, was traditionally interpreted as a loss of whole-word representations, leaving the reader dependent on the use of grapheme-to-phoneme rules which work poorly with irregular words (Coltheart, 1983). More recently, however, it has been suggested that surface dyslexia may result from a loss of semantic representations, a nonreading-specific impairment (Patterson and Hodges, 1992). According to this new view, irregular words are particularly dependent on word recognition, including recognition of the words' semantics for pronunciation. Phonological dyslexia, in which the reading of nonwords is impaired, was traditionally interpreted as a loss of the grapheme-to-phoneme route to word recognition, leaving the reader dependent on whole word-representations, which do not exist for nonwords. This form of dyslexia, however, may also be secondary to a more general linguistic problem, namely impaired phonological representation (e.g., Farah, Stowe, and Levinson, 1996; Coltheart, 1996). In sum, acquired disorders of reading provide important clues to the genesis of functionally specialized brain areas. Although more research is needed to address the issue with certainty, it appears that pure alexia may provide the clearest evidence so far available for localization of a category of knowledge that is fundamentally arbitrary and learned relatively late in life.

The Nature of Pure Alexia

Much of the research on pure alexia in the past ten years has focused on a binary decision: Is it a visual impairment affecting all types of stimuli or is it orthography-specific? Reluctantly, I have come to the conclusion that the truth is probably more complex than either of these two alternatives. Although I was initially impressed with the evidence for a visual impairment that extends beyond orthography, an accumulation of clinical observations suggests that visual letter perception, if not word perception, may be disproportionately impaired in some pure alexics. Both observations can be accommodated by an hypothesis of "specialization within specialization." The more general visual impairments are caused by damage to a brain region specialized for rapid encoding of multiple shapes that may involve a computational strategy of localist representation. Among the shapes most frequently processed in this area are letters, seen mainly in the context of words and by the mechanisms proposed by Polk and myself (Polk and Farah, 1995a,b; 1997), these will segregate out within this multiple-shape encoding area, forming an even more specialized subarea and possibly coming to represent abstract letter identities. Depending upon the exact location of the lesion relative to these areas, pure alexics would be expected to have a visual impairment for rapid encoding of multiple visual shapes with varying degrees of orthography specificity.

References

Arguin, M., and Bub, D.N. (1993). Single character processing in a case of pure alexia. *Neuropsychologia, 31,* 435–458.

Behrmann, M. (1999). Pure alexia: Underlying mechanisms and remediation. In R.M. Klein and P.A. McMullen (Eds.), *Converging Methods for Understanding Reading and Dyslexia.* Cambridge: MIT Press.

Behrmann, M., Black, S.E., and Bub, D.N. (1990). The evolution of pure alexia: A longitudinal study of recovery. *Brain and Language, 39,* 405–427.

Behrmann, M., and Sekuler, E.B. (1996). Perceptual cues in pure alexia. *Cognitive Neuropsychology, 13,* 941–974.

Behrmann, M., and Shallice, T. (1995). Pure alexia: An orthographic not spatial deficit. *Cognitive Neuropsychology, 12,* 409–427.

Bub, D.N., Black, S., and Howell, J. (1989). Word recognition and orthographic context effects in a LBL reader. *Brain and Language, 36,* 357–376.

Bub, D.N., Arguin, M., and Lecours, A.R. (1993). Jules Déjerine and his interpretation of pure alexia. *Brain and Language, 45,* 531–559.

Coltheart, M. (1996). Phonological dyslexia: Past and future issues. *Cognitive Neuropsychology, 13,* 749–762.

Coltheart, M. (1985). Cognitive neuropsychology and the study of reading. In M.I. Posner and O.S.M. Marin (Eds.), *Attention and Performance, XI* (pp. 3–37). Hillsdale, NJ: Lawrence Erlbaum Associates Inc.

Damasio, A.R., and Damasio, H. (1983). The anatomic basis of pure alexia. *Neurology, 33,* 1573–1583.

Déjerine, J. (1892). Contribution a l'étude anatomo–pathologique et clinique des differentes varietés de cecite verbale. *Comptes Rendus Hebdomadaires de Seances et Memoires de la Societe de Biologie, Ninthe series. 4* (pp 61–90).

Ekstrom, R., French, J.W., and Harman, H.H. (1976). *Manual for Kit of Factor-Referenced Cognitive Tests.* Princeton, NJ: Educational Testing Service.

Farah, M.J., and Wallace, M.A. (1991). Pure alexia as a visual impairment: A reconsideration. *Cognitive Neuropsychology, 8,* 313–334.

Farah, M.J., Stowe, R.M., and Levinson, K.L. (1996). Phonological dyslexia: Loss of a reading–specific component of the cognitive architecture? *Cognitive Neuropsychology, 13,* 849–868.

Foldiak, P. (1991). Learning invariance from transformation sequences. *Neural Computation, 3,* 194–200.

Friedman, R.B., and Alexander, M.P. (1984). Pictures, images, and pure alexia: A case study. *Cognitive Neuropsychology, 1,* 9–23.

Geschwind, N. (1965). Disconnexion syndromes in animals and man. Part II. *Brain, 88,* 584–644.

Greenblatt, S.H. (1983). Localization of lesions in alexia. In A. Kertesz (Ed.), *Localization in Neuropsychology.* New York: Academic Press.

Johnston, J.C., and McClelland, J.L. (1994). Perception of letters and word: Seek and ye shall not find. *Science, 184,* 1192–1194.

Johnston, J.C., and McClelland, J.L. (1980). Experimental tests of a hierarchical model of word identification. *Journal of Verbal Learning and Verbal Behaviour, 19,* 503–524.

Jonides, J., and Gleitman, H. (1972). A conceptual category effect in visual search: O as a letter or as a digit. *Perception and Psychophysics, 12,* 457–460.

Kay, J., and Hanley, R. (1991). Simultaneous form perception and serial letter recognition in a case of letter-by-letter reading. *Cognitive Neuropsychology, 8,* 249–273.

Kinsbourne, M., and Warrington, E.K. (1962). A disorder of simultaneous form perception. *Brain, 85.* 461–486.

Levine, D.N., and Calvanio, R. (1978). A study of the visual defect in verbal alexia-simultanagonosia. *Brain, 101,* 65–81.

Linsker, R. (1986). From basic network principles to neural architecture: Emergence of orientation-selective cells. *Proceedings of the National Academy of Sciences, 83,* 8390–8394.

McClelland, J.L., and Rumelhart, D.E. (1981). An interactive activation model of context effects in letter perception: Part 1. An account of basic findings. *Psychological Review, 88,* 345–407.

Merzenich, M.M. (1987). Dynamic neocortical processes and the origins of higher brain functions. In J.P. Changeux and M. Konishi (Eds.), *Neural and Molecular Bases of Learning* (pp. 337–358). Chichester, England: John Wiley and Sons.

Patterson, K.E., and Kay, J. (1982). LBL reading: Psychological descriptions of a neurological syndrome. *Quarterly Journal of Experimental Psychology: Human Experimental Psychology, 34A,* 411–441.

Patterson, K.E., and Hodges, J. (1992). Deterioration of word meaning: Implications for reading. *Neuropsychologia, 30,* 1025–1040.

Polk, T.A., and Farah, M.J. (1995a). Brain localization for arbitrary stimulus categories: A simple account based on Hebbian learning. *Proceedings of the National Academy of Sciences, 92,* 12370–12373.

Polk, T.A., and Farah, M.J. (1995b). Late experience alters vision. *Nature, 376,* 648–649.

Polk, T.A., and Farah, M.J. (1997). A simple co–occurrence account for the development of abstract letter identities. *Neural Computation, 9,* 1277–1289.

Rapp, B.C., and Caramazza, A. (1991). Spatially determined deficits in letter and word processing. *Cognitive Neuropsychology, 8,* 275–311.

Reicher, G.M. (1969). Perceptual recognition as a function of meaningfulness of stimulus material. *Journal of Experimental Psychology, 81,* 275–280.

Reuter-Lorenz, P.A., and Brunn, J.L. (1990). A prelexical basis for LBL reading: A case study. *Cognitive Neuropsychology, 7,* 1–20.

Sekuler, E., and Behrmann, M. (1996). Perceptual cues in pure alexia. *Cognitive Neuropsychology, 13(7),* 941-974.

Shallice, T. (1988). From Neuropsychology To Mental Structure. Cambridge: Cambridge University Press.

Sternberg, S. (1969). The discovery of processing stages: Extensions of Donders' method. *Acta Psychologica, 30,* 276–315.

Warrington, E.K., and Shallice, T. (1980). Word–form dyslexia. *Brain, 103,* 99–112.

Wheeler, D.D. (1970). Processes in word recognition. *Cognitive Psychology, 1,* 59–85.

Yamadori, A. (1980). Right unilateral dyscopia of letters in alexia without agraphia. *Neurology, 30,* 991–994.

9
Functional Neuroimaging of Word Processing in Normal and Dyslexic Readers

Jonathan B. Demb
Russell A. Poldrack
John D.E. Gabrieli

One of the greatest challenges in cognitive neuroscience is an understanding of the relationship between neural activity and language processing. Using the functional neuroimaging techniques positron emission tomography (PET) and functional magnetic resonance imaging (fMRI), psychologists and neuroscientists are beginning to map specific brain areas to the orthographic, phonological, and semantic processes essential for language. Insights into the brain organization of these linguistic processes could contribute to the understanding of language disorders such as dyslexia.

This chapter reviews neuroimaging findings about the processing of single words because most studies have examined language processing at the single-word level. The findings reviewed are further limited to studies using neuroimaging techniques that meet current standards of spatial and temporal resolution. The chapter is organized into three main sections that describe (1) neuroimaging methodology, (2) functional imaging studies of single-word processing, and (3) functional imaging studies of developmental dyslexia. The first section describes the physiological basis of PET and fMRI measurements and experimental characteristics of functional neuroimaging studies. The second section provides an overview of the brain regions activated during orthographic, phonological, and semantic processing of single words. The third section describes functional imaging studies of language abilities and early visual processing in individuals who have developmental dyslexia.

Neuroimaging Methodology

PET and fMRI are functional neuroimaging methodologies that have generated insights into the localization of neural systems involved in language processes. Both techniques indirectly estimate changes in neural activity by measuring properties of blood (i.e., flow or oxygenation) while subjects perform cognitive tasks. Increased neural activity results in increased blood flow to the active region (Fox and Raichle, 1986; Frostig, Lieke, Ts'o, and Grinvald, 1990; Raichle, 1987). Therefore, local changes in blood properties provide an index of local changes in brain activity. Comparison of brain activity during experimental and baseline states allows for a direct correlation between active brain tissue and a putative mental process.

PET and fMRI have high spatial resolutions with localization on the order of millimeters. Temporal resolution is currently limited with these techniques, however, as a result of the temporal delay between neural activity and the correlated hemodynamic response that provides the PET or fMRI signal. Other recording techniques, such as electrical recording with scalp electrodes (see McCandliss and Posner, chapter 10, this volume) or magnetoencephalography (MEG), have high temporal resolutions on the order of milliseconds but poor spatial resolution. Ultimately, a combination of these techniques will lead to an understanding of both the localization and temporal response characteristics of brain systems involved in language (Heinze et al., 1994; Snyder, Abdullaev, Posner, and Raichle, 1995).

Positron Emission Tomography (PET)

PET can be used to track regional cerebral blood flow (rCBF) by measuring a radiolabeled isotope tracer in the brain that is typically inhaled (e.g., $C^{15}O_2$) or injected into a vein in the arm (e.g., $H_2{}^{15}O$) prior to the PET scan. The distribution of rCBF is indexed by accumulated counts of the tracer across the scanning period (typically about one minute), and all levels that occur across this scanning time are averaged into one PET image. The short, two-minute half-life of some radioactive tracers makes possible scans of multiple behavioral conditions within the same session. The limited number of times that subjects can participate in PET studies, however, due to the exposure to radioactive material, often prohibits longitudinal studies that require multiple scanning sessions.

A PET image created during a single condition is not interpretable because it represents both structural and functional determinants of blood flow (e.g., because there is more blood flow in gray than white matter); it resembles a low-resolution anatomical image. Therefore, subtraction images are created by taking the difference between two conditions. This effectively subtracts out the background anatomy and reveals regions differentially activated in the two conditions. Difference image activations are believed to be related to the mental processes that differ between the compared conditions (task subtraction is further discussed in the section on experimental design). To increase the signal-to-noise ratio (SNR) that is inherently low in cognitive studies (Petersen, Fox, Posner, Mintun, and Raichle, 1988), individual difference images are spatially normalized into standardized coordinates from a stereotactic brain atlas (Talairach and Tournoux, 1988), and they are averaged together to form composite group difference images (although individual data can be analyzed if the same conditions are run multiple times in an individual subject, e.g., Watson et al., 1993).

For example, a PET image obtained during a "fixation" condition, during which subjects fixate centrally on a cross, might be subtracted from a PET image obtained during a "word-presentation" condition, during which subjects fixate centrally while words are presented below fixation (Petersen, Fox, Snyder, and Raichle, 1990). The subtraction image (word presentation minus fixation) reveals areas that are more activated during the word-presentation condition relative to the fixation condition. These areas represent brain regions that may be involved in orthographic, phonological, and semantic analysis of the words or other task characteristics (e.g., attentional states). Additional conditions (most PET studies include four to eight conditions) and image subtractions help to further elucidate the functional significance of the activation patterns in the difference images (Petersen et al., 1990).

PET data analysis must assess significant changes in activation across conditions in a large number of comparisons (thousands of cube-shaped "voxels" in multiple brain slices) from a relatively small number of subjects. To address this challenge, many investigators have used statistical parametric mapping that determines voxels in a group difference-image that show a significant change in activation between conditions after correcting for the large number of comparisons (Friston, Frith, Liddle, and Frackowiak, 1991a; Friston et al., 1990). An alternative approach is to separate subjects into two groups and test for regions that show a significant change across conditions in a first group of subjects (i.e., a hypothesis-generating group) that replicate in a second group of subjects (i.e., a hypothesis-testing group, see Buckner et al., 1995a; Fiez et al., 1995). Regions that replicate across the two independent samples are considered reliable.

Functional Magnetic Resonance Imaging (fMRI)

This chapter reviews fMRI studies that measure changes thought to depend on blood-oxygen level (blood oxygen level dependent or BOLD, see Kwong et al., 1992; Ogawa et al., 1992). The BOLD technique has been the preferred fMRI method because it does not require the injection of contrast material (Belliveau et al., 1991), and thus poses no constraint upon the number of studies conducted with the same individual.

BOLD fMRI signal is thought to rely on changes at the capillary level in the local percentage of deoxyhemoglobin (deoxy-Hb), which is paramagnetic relative to oxyhemoglobin (oxy-Hb) and surrounding brain tissue (Ogawa, Lee, Nayak, and Glynn, 1990; Thulborn, Waterton, Matthews, and Radda, 1982). Increased neural activity is accompanied by increased blood flow to the active region that delivers more oxygen than is utilized, resulting in a relative decrease in deoxy-Hb (Fox and Raichle, 1986; Fox, Raichle, Mintun, and Dence, 1988; Frostig et al., 1990). This increase in local oxygenation (i.e., the oxy-Hb/deoxy-Hb ratio) results in a local increase in MR signal relative to a resting state (see Moseley and Glover, 1995).

Although early fMRI studies used subtraction techniques similar to PET studies to analyze activated regions (e.g., Kwong et al., 1992), more recent studies have used other comparison techniques for image analysis (e.g., correlational techniques, general linear model, see Bandettini, Jesmanowicz, Wong, and Hyde, 1993; Engel et al., 1994). In studies that use correlational techniques, subjects typically alternate between two conditions (e.g., task A, task B, task A, task B, etc, see figure 9.1). The time series of each pixel can then be correlated with a square wave or sinusoidal waveform at the task frequency. This type of correlational analysis may enhance SNR compared to the subtraction technique and may reduce signal from larger vessels that are distant from neural activity (Binder et al., 1994b; Lee, Glover, and Meyer, 1995). Also, this technique essentially allows for several comparisons between two conditions due to its reversal design. A limitation of this technique is that correlational analysis assumes independence among data points in the time series, which does not exist due to the sluggishness of the hemodynamic response. Another form of analysis has been developed that avoids this limitation by extending the general linear model to temporally correlated data such as fMRI images (Friston et al., 1995).

Several studies have used fMRI designs in which activation on single trials can be imaged. In one approach, trials are presented very slowly (~18 seconds per trial) to allow the hemodynamic response to rise and then return to baseline following the trial; brain regions that exhibit a response to the trial compared to baseline are considered to be activated (Buckner et al., 1996). In another approach, short groups of trials are presented, and responses to each trial are decomposed using mathematical techniques (Buckner et al., 1998). These "event-related" or "single-trial" fMRI designs allow comparisons of brain activations across different classes of trials. For example, Brewer et al. (1998) performed single-trial fMRI scanning during encoding of stimuli into memory. For analysis, the stimulus trials were separated into those that were later remembered and those that were later forgotten, revealing brain regions whose activity predicted later memory (which included the parahippocampal cortex). Wagner et al. (1998) found similar results using the grouped single-trial approach. The primary weakness of event-related fMRI is that it requires much more

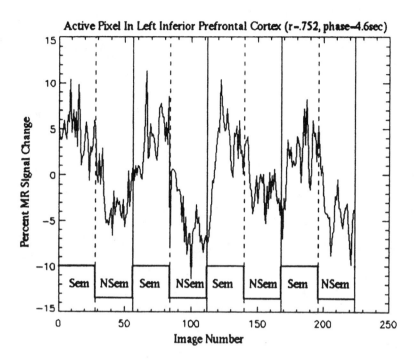

Figure 9.1 Time series from a single active pixel in left-inferior prefrontal cortex expressed as percent MR signal change from the mean response. The fMRI response was greater during semantic (Sem) encoding (abstract/concrete decision) than during non-semantic (NSem) encoding of words (ascending/descending alphabetic decision; see text) that controlled for task difficulty (Demb et al., 1995). 224 fMR images were acquired every 1.5 seconds continuously for 336 seconds (4 task cycles) in a slice in prefrontal cortex. The raw time series of a pixel located in the left-inferior frontal sulcus that was significantly correlated with a sinusoidal reference waveform at the task frequency (i.e., 4/336) is shown. The correlation magnitude was r=.752, and the temporal phase delay (with respect to a sine-wave) was 4.6 seconds, which is within the temporal range of hemodynamic responses associated with small vessels close to the site of neural activity (Lee et al., 1995).

scan time than a blocked design for the same task comparison. Event-related fMRI holds great promise for analyzing the relationship between brain responses and cognitive processing, but it has yet to be extensively applied to questions of language processing.

Experimental Design and Psychological Interpretation

The ideal brain-imaging paradigm involves two tasks that differ by only one mental process. A subtraction of one condition from another would identify regions whose activity reflects the unshared mental process. This ideal situation is made difficult by at least two limitations. First, it is difficult to truly isolate mental processes in behavioral experiments and this difficulty extends to functional imaging studies of mental processes (Sergent, Zuck, Levesque, and MacDonald, 1992). This limitation can be somewhat overcome by providing behavioral data, along with brain imaging results, that demonstrate the behavioral differences between tasks (e.g., Raichle et al., 1994). Still, there is often disagreement about the exact processes elicited by behavioral tasks (Petersen et al., 1988; Wise et al., 1991). A second difficulty in interpreting brain-imaging results is the complexity of brain systems that are highly interactive. For example, subtracting a condition in which subjects read words silently from one in which subjects read words aloud may reveal something besides simply areas involved in speech production. Regions involved in other aspects of the task (i.e., visual perception and lexical analysis) may interact with motor areas and be modulated during speech output even though these regions are not directly related to the motor aspects of speech production. In this example, difference-image activation could misattribute regions as being involved in the motor aspects of speech if a strictly noninteractive, linear system was assumed (see Jennings, McIntosh, Kapur, Tulving and Houle, 1997).

One approach toward avoiding the complexity of interactive brain systems has been the comparison of an active condition during which subjects perform a task to a resting baseline during which subjects perform no task. The logic of this comparison is that the entire neural network engaged in performing a task will be visualized when the active and resting baseline scans are compared. Additional active conditions are then used to characterize the processes mediated by specific components of the entire neural network (Wise et al., 1991). This approach has its merits but also some hazards. Perhaps the greatest hazard is that subjects' minds are not inactive during a rest condition. To the extent that mental processing overlaps between rest and active states, the corresponding brain activation will not appear in the subtraction. In that case, a well-controlled activation baseline may reveal more of the entire neural network than a resting baseline.

   A pertinent example comes from a PET study of memory retrieval tasks that examined activation while subjects attempted to complete word stems (e.g., *gar___*) with words they had seen in a study list (*recall*), completed word stems with the first word that came to mind (*baseline*), or passively viewed a fixation cross (*fixation*) (Buckner et al., 1995a). The recall-baseline subtraction revealed activation in a region of the right prefrontal cortex. Similar right prefrontal regions have been attributed to explicit memory retrieval processes in numerous other studies (see Buckner and Tulving, 1995; Tulving, Kapur, Craik, Moscovitch, and Houle, 1994). This right prefrontal activation, however, was reduced in magnitude in the recall-fixation subtraction. These findings would indicate that passively viewing a fixation cross (which is close to a resting baseline) requires more explicit retrieval than does the baseline condition. A more plausible interpretation, however, is that the subject's attention was drawn to the baseline word completion task and other meaningful thought (including remembering past experiences) was minimized. With little to look at in the fixation condition, the subject's mind was free to wander to various meaningful thoughts. Thus, although the fixation task did not require explicit retrieval, this memory process may have been present due to the lack of an attentionally demanding task. Therefore, a resting baseline or minimally engaging fixation condition may promote mental processing that obscures an important component of an activated condition.

   More generally, certain mental processes may be extraordinarily difficult to image in a subtraction between two conditions. These include ubiquitous processes (e.g., attentional processes) that are present across all or most conditions as well as processes that may become automatized as a consequence of preexperimental experience that can result in reduced activation from a once active region. For example, several studies have reported reduced activation in prefrontal regions initially involved in semantic processing as subjects performed the task repeatedly with the same words (Demb et al., 1995; Gabrieli et al., 1996; Raichle et al., 1994). Activation associated with practiced behavior may decrease or increase depending on the region of the brain being imaged and the amount of practice with the task (Karni et al., 1995; Poldrack et al., 1998).

   The intersubject averaging technique used in most PET studies also merits attention (Steinmetz and Seitz, 1991). Averaging may result in reduced activation because of anatomical variability that leads to reduced overlap of similar functional regions across brains. For example, cortical stimulation mapping has demonstrated a high degree of neuroanatomical variability for perisylvian language areas (Ojemann, 1983; Ojemann et al., 1989). A study of two frontal cytoarchitectonic areas commonly implicated in cognitive abilities showed significant variability in size and location of the areas across subjects (Rajkowska and Goldman-Rakic, 1995). Steinmetz and Seitz (1991) concluded that the activation reported by PET studies may be biased to the largest of activated areas—the areas that demonstrate the least intersubject variability—or to regions that have the highest increases. For example, instead of concluding that a given region of the left temporal lobe was involved in language processing, a more plausible interpretation might be that across subjects and the many areas involved in a given language task, an area in the left temporal lobe showed the greatest overlap across subjects. If a specific mental process was localized more variably across the subjects' brains, activation associated with that process may not appear in a group image subtraction. Imaging studies are able to examine individual subject images as well as group composite images to examine both intersubject variability as well as the most commonly activated regions across subjects (e.g., Demb et al., 1995; Gabrieli et al., 1996; Watson et al., 1993). It is still the case, however, that studies of individual subjects tend to focus on the most consistent regions across subjects and consider these consistencies most reliable. Only when there is an external validation of individual differences, such as Wada-assessment of language lateralization, or a direct measure of reliability, such as within-subject replication, can individual differences in location of activation be interpreted with confidence (Desmond et al., 1995).

Even after determining that a brain activation pattern is reliable and correlated with a specific behavior, it is still uncertain how any given activated region contributes to a specified behavior. A clear example of this problem comes from studies of delay-eyeblink classical conditioning, and has been demonstrated in both electrophysiological studies of animals and brain imaging studies of humans. PET studies found activation associated with delay-eyeblink conditioning in several regions including the cerebellum and hippocampus (Blaxton et al., 1996; Logan and Grafton, 1995). Patients with hippocampal lesions are unimpaired in the delay paradigm (Gabrieli et al., 1995), but patients with cerebellar lesions show impaired conditioning (Daum et al., 1993; Lye, O'Boyle, Ramsden, and Schady, 1988). Thus, only the cerebellar PET activation signaled a process necessary for the measured behavior of delay conditioning. The hippocampus activation signaled a correlated process that is not necessary for conditioning. These studies illustrate that physiological measurements, such as those made in brain imaging, can determine neural activity that is correlated with a particular behavior, but they cannot determine whether that neural activity is involved in the expression of that particular behavior. This is not to say that results from patients with brain lesions provide a better brain-behavior correlation than functional imaging results. Rather, this example illustrates that patient and functional imaging results should be used to provide mutual constraints in interpretation of results from either technique. Studies of patients with acquired brain lesions that affect reading ability are, therefore, highly relevant to the interpretation of brain imaging results of word processing (see Behrmann, chapter 6; Farah, chapter 8, this volume).

The important consequence of the above considerations is not that functional neuroimaging is overshadowed by complexities and ambiguities of interpretation. As will be apparent in the review below, functional neuroimaging studies can visualize the location of mental processes with considerable specificity and reliability. Rather, the above considerations are reminders that determination of what is being visualized in a functional image rests upon the interpretation of what psychological processes are differentially engaged in two tasks.

Functional Neuroimaging Studies of Single-Word Processing

This review of functional neuroimaging studies of single-word processing is organized into sections on orthographic, phonological, and semantic processing. In each section, the type of processing is defined and the anatomy of relevant brain systems is outlined. The appendices provide a comprehensive summary of the studies that relate to each type of processing (see appendices 9.1 to 9.3) as well as studies that investigate components of language that do not fit discretely into one of the above categories (appendix 9.4). The sections draw upon many of the studies provided in the appendices but focus on areas of convergence across studies. This overview should provide a general framework for understanding brain systems involved in language whereas the appendices can be used to follow up on activation differences between individual paradigms.

Orthographic and semantic processes are clearly central to reading. The relation between phonological processes and reading may be less obvious but it is likely that phonological processing plays a key role in the development of reading ability (Wagner and Torgesen, 1987), and phonological processing deficits are evident in subjects with developmental dyslexia (see Farmer and Klein, 1995). Thus, a review of functional imaging of phonological processing will also be useful in understanding reading.

Orthographic Processing

Orthographic processing refers to the visual encoding of written words. Several imaging studies have investigated brain regions involved in the visual processing of words and word-like forms (see appendix 9.1). The studies typically compared activation between two conditions with the same task (e.g., passive viewing) but different types of visual stimuli (e.g., words versus false-font strings). Regions more activated during visual encoding of words relative to control stimuli are believed to be specifically involved in orthographic processing.

Cortical visual perception begins bilaterally in primary visual cortex (i.e., visual area 1 or V1) located posteriorly and medially in the occipital lobes (see figure 9.2). This region is known as striate cortex due to a visible stripe of white matter (the stripe of Gennari) that consists of incoming myelinated axons from the lateral geniculate nucleus (LGN) of the thalamus and other cortical regions. Visual processing continues anteriorly in secondary or extrastriate occipital regions that, in turn, send their outputs toward temporal and parietal cortices specialized for higher level processing of objects and spatial relations (Ungerleider and Mishkin, 1982; Felleman and Van Essen, 1991).

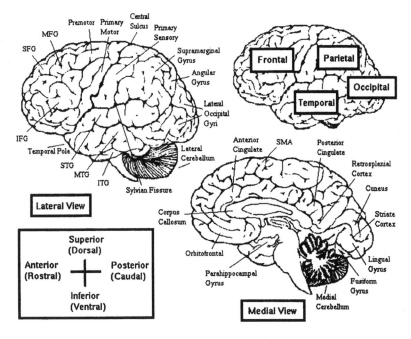

Figure. 9.2 Human neuroanatomy. A lateral (upper-left) and medial view (lower-right) of the human brain are depicted. The regions labeled correspond to activated regions across language studies presented in the apendices. Major lobes are indicated in the upper-right. Abbreviations: SFG=superior frontal gyrus, MFG=middle frontal gyrus, IFG=inferior frontal gyrus, STG=superior temporal gyrus, MTG=middle temporal gyrus, ITG=inferior temporal gyrus, SMA=supplementary motor area.

In terms of orthographic processing, a question of interest is what regions are activated by words as opposed to other similar visual stimuli? In striate cortex, for example, words may not be processed differently than other visual stimuli. Therefore, studies that compare brain activation during word perception relative to viewing a blank field will reveal activation in primary visual areas that are known to be involved in processing many types of visual stimuli as well as other areas that may be specifically involved in orthographic processing (Petersen et al., 1988; 1989). Further, the location of orthographic processing as well as other language abilities may be differentially localized in the left hemisphere, given the typical left-hemisphere dominance for language.

Medial extrastriate cortex

PET studies have indicated that two posterior cortical regions are commonly and specifically involved in orthographic processing. These regions are in left-medial extrastriate cortex and left-lateral temporal cortex (see figure 9.3). Evidence for the left-medial extrastriate region comes from studies by Petersen et al. (1988, 1989, 1990) who investigated orthographic processing by comparing activation for words and word-like stimuli relative to viewing a fixation cross (appendix 9.1). Left-medial extrastriate regions were activated by words and letter strings that obey the rules of English orthography (pseudowords, e.g., *tweal*) (figure 9.3), but not orthographically illegal consonant strings (e.g., *nlpfz*) or false-font strings. Price et al. (1994) found medial extrastriate activation during passive viewing of words relative to false-font strings (see Price et al., 1996) and during articulation of words relative to articulated decisions about false-font strings see figure 9.3).[1] Kapur et al. (1994b) also found activation in this left-medial occipital region as well as other occipital and

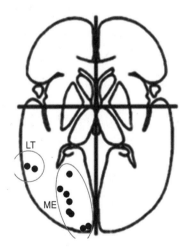

Figure 9.3 Orthographic processing activations are represented as symbols projected onto a horizontal slice (z=0 mm, Talairach and Tournoux, 1988) that indicate the center of the activations. Posterior activations (i.e., y<-40 mm) from z=0 mm to z=8 mm are shown from 4 studies (see appendix 9.1.). There are two regions, one in Medial Extrastriate (ME) cortex and one in Lateral Temporal (LT) cortex, that are activated during orthographic processing across studies.

parietal regions when subjects viewed words and responded if the letter *a* was present relative to responding about word meaning. One fMRI study (Indefrey et al., 1997) found medial extrastriate activation for words and for false-font strings compared to a single false-font character, but it did not find activation in this region for words compared to false-font strings. This suggests that the medial extrastriate activation could result from differences in stimulus extent. Several other studies, however, reported medial extrastriate activation to words relative to control stimuli (rows of x's or false-font strings) matched for visual extent (Price et al., 1994, 1996; Menard et al., 1996). Thus, the majority of the evidence suggests that a medial extrastriate area is activated by word forms.

Subsequent studies examining activation for pseudowords in the medial extrastriate cortex have yielded inconsistent results. For example, Pugh et al. (1996), using fMRI, found that processing real words activated the medial extrastriate region more strongly than pseudowords (for males only) and that activity to pseudowords did not differ from case judgments on consonant strings. Price et al. (1996), on the other hand, found more activation in the medial extrastriate region for pseudowords than for words. It is thus unclear to what extent this region is sensitive to the lexical status of visual stimuli.

Lateral temporal cortex
Evidence for the participation of a left-lateral temporal region in orthographic processing was first reported by Howard et al. (1992). They compared a condition where subjects read words aloud with a control condition where subjects viewed false-font strings and repeated the word *crime* aloud to control for articulation (see figure 9.3). An advantage of this comparison is that both conditions had letter-like forms and articulation. A disadvantage is that the stimulus type (i.e., words or false fonts) and the type of articulation (i.e., saying different words versus the same word repeatedly) were simultaneously changed between conditions. This study found only a trend for activation in the medial extrastriate regions reported by Petersen et al. (1990) but found significant activation in the posterior middle temporal gyrus. Price et al. (1994, 1996) also found left-lateral temporal activation when subjects passively viewed words relative to false-font strings, and Beauregard et al. (1997) found lateral temporal activation for passive reading of words compared to fixation (see figure 9.3).

The discrepancy in some of the above findings regarding lateral temporal activation may be due in part to differences in experimental design. For example, Petersen et al. (1990) used a short stimulus exposure duration (150 ms) and a passive viewing condition, whereas studies that reported lateral temporal activation (Howard et al., 1992; Price et al., 1996; Beauregard et al., 1997) used a longer exposure duration (1000 ms) and some required pronunciation. Price et al. (1994) investigated this possibility by comparing words and control stimuli presented at both exposure durations during both types of task. The conclusion of this study was that activations clearly depended on aspects of experimental design, but that the pattern of results did not suggest systematic changes that could explain the discrepancy between the previous studies.

Although these lateral temporal activations were found in comparisons thought to isolate orthographic processing, there is evidence that they may instead reflect semantic processing. Activation of the left-posterior middle temporal cortex has been found for semantic tasks such as verb generation (e.g., Warburton et al., 1996) and abstract-concrete decision (Wagner et al., 1998). Studies by Martin et al. (1995, 1996) have demonstrated that processing different aspects of word meaning results in activation of different regions in the temporal lobe. For example, generation of action words from line-drawing cues resulted in activation of the left-middle temporal gyrus, whereas generation of color words from the same line drawing cues resulted in activation of the left-fusiform gyrus (Martin et al., 1995). Similarly, Damasio et al. (1996) found that different regions of the lateral temporal cortex were activated by naming tools, animals, and people. These findings suggest that lateral temporal activations may reflect processing of semantic features of words, and that the categorical nature of the stimuli in a particular study may determine the nature of activation evoked by those stimuli.

Phonological Processing

Phonological processing refers here to the encoding or evaluation of auditory word characteristics and can be elicited by speech perception or by tasks that require phonological analysis (e.g., rhyming judgments). Studies examining the brain regions activated during phonological processing may be divided into two general classes (see appendix 9.2). One class (analogous to the studies reviewed in the section on orthographic processing) identifies regions activated during the basic perception of auditory-linguistic stimuli by comparing two conditions with the same task (e.g., passive listening) but different types of stimuli (e.g., speech syllables versus noise bursts). The second class identifies brain regions activated when subjects make judgments about the phonological attributes of stimuli (e.g., monitoring for particular phonemes) and can be performed with either visual or auditory stimuli (e.g., Fiez et al., 1995). In all of these studies, brain regions that are more activated during a condition that requires increased phonological processing, relative to a control condition, are believed to be selectively involved in phonological processing.

Cortical auditory perception begins bilaterally in primary auditory cortices (Heschl's gyri) located on the dorsal surface of the superior temporal gyrus (i.e., the floor of the lateral sulcus, see figure 9.2) which receive subcortical afferent input from the medial geniculate nucleus (MGN) of the thalamus. Auditory input undergoes further analysis in secondary and tertiary association cortices located adjacent to primary auditory cortex (including the planum temporale) on the lateral surface of the superior and middle temporal gyri and extending into the inferior parietal cortex. In terms of hierarchical processing from primary auditory areas to association areas, the key question is when sensitivity to phonology first occurs in auditory processing. Studies that compare brain activation during auditory word perception relative to silence reveal both primary auditory areas known to be involved in processing many types of auditory stimuli as well as other areas that may be specifically involved in phonological processing (Petersen et al., 1988, 1989).

Regions of motor and prefrontal cortex may also be important to phonological processes (see figure 9.2). The motor cortex is located in the posterior frontal lobe on the precentral gyrus, anterior to the central sulcus, and is involved in voluntary movements such as articulatory processes required by speech production (Petersen et al., 1988, 1989). Premotor areas, including the supplementary motor area (SMA) and the premotor cortex, are anterior to the motor cortex on both the medial and lateral surfaces. Premotor areas provide a major input to the motor cortex and are involved in planning and coordinating complex movements. Anterior regions of prefrontal cortex provide an input to premotor areas. Broca's area, a region in left opercular frontal cortex to which lesions can result in expressive ("Broca's") aphasia (see Damasio, 1992), has been implicated in such language processes as articulatory planning and phonological perception (Blumstein, Baker, and Goodglass, 1977).

Brain-imaging studies have revealed several cortical regions associated with phonological processing. In this review, we focus on four left-hemisphere cortical regions where phonological activation is evident in a number of studies. These regions are groupings of focal changes in activation reported by individual studies and are depicted in figure 9. 4. The individual data points have been grouped based on similarities among task comparisons that produced the activations. Each area is discussed separately below with an emphasis on the similarity, across studies, in the task comparisons that produced the activation in each region. Finally, other activations that are near known language regions will be discussed.

Auditory association cortex

Several studies have reported that a region in auditory association cortex is activated during the processing of many linguistic stimuli including words and speech syllables (see figure 9.4). This region is primarily activated during tasks that require attention to phonological features such as phoneme monitoring compared to passive noise listening (Zatorre, Evans, Meyer, and Gjedde, 1992) and phoneme monitoring in pseudowords relative to sequence monitoring in tone triplets (Demonet et al., 1992; Demonet, Price, Wise, and Frackowiak, 1994a). Price et al. (1992) found that activation in this region (as well as primary auditory cortex) increased linearly with increasing word presentation rate (see Binder et al., 1994a; Wise et al., 1991 for similar results). Fiez et al. (1995) found increased activation in this area during a detection task that required subjects to respond to a target stimulus (e.g., a particular word) compared to a passive listening condition with the same

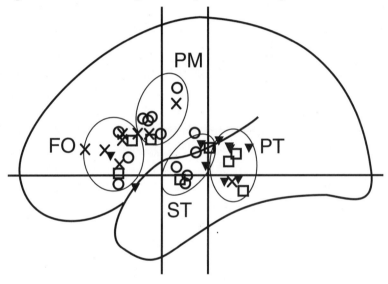

O Auditory phonological tasks
X Visual phonological tasks
▼ Passive listening/repetition
□ Pseudoword tasks

Figure. 9.4 Phonological processing activations are represented as symbols projected onto a lateral view of the left-hemisphere that indicate the center of activations from 10 studies (see appendix 9.2.). Four regions are grouped by the similarity between the tasks that elicited them: Superior Temporal (ST) region (secondary auditory cortex), Posterior Superior- and Middle-Temporal (PT) region (near Wernicke's area), Frontal Opercular (FO) region (near Broca's area, Brodmann's areas 44/45), and Premotor (PM) area (near Brodmann's areas 6/44). See text for details.

stimuli. The above studies suggest that this region is primarily stimulus-driven but may be modulated by stimulus presentation rate and attentional state.

Wernicke's area.

A more posterior temporal-lobe region is activated primarily during the passive presentation of spoken words (see figure 9.4). The studies below have attributed the location of this activation to "Wernicke's area," a region implicated in receptive (Wernicke's) aphasia (see Damasio, 1992). Activation in this region may represent a pattern matching process that links incoming patterns of phonemes to stored patterns that represent words. Howard et al. (1992) found that a region in the posterior temporal cortex was more activated when subjects repeated spoken words aloud than when they listened to reversed speech and repeated the word *crime* to control for articulatory processes. Price et al. (1996) found similar activation for passive listening compared to reversed speech. Schlosser et al. (1998) found activation in this region for native English speakers listening to English sentences relative to listening to Turkish sentences, and Fiez et al. (1995) found activation in this region for passive listening compared to silent fixation. Some studies that examined activation to speech stimuli that were not words (e.g., speech syllables such as *tig)* did not report activation in this region (e.g., Zatorre et al., 1992). Other studies examining auditory presentation of pseudowords compared to rest, however, did find activation near this region (Warburton et al., 1996; Wise et al., 1991). These data suggest that this region may be activated by nonword stimuli if they are sufficiently similar to real words.

A study by Price et al. (1992) reported a posterior temporal region that was activated during the presence of auditory words regardless of word presentation rate (see Wise et al., 1991 for a similar result). This differed from primary and association auditory areas that both showed a linear increase that depended on word presentation rate (see above). Instead, this posterior region demonstrated a nonlinear "signal transformation" such that activation was present during word presentation relative to silence but was similar regardless of word presentation rate (i.e., between 10 to 90 words per minute, see Price et al., 1992). Another study (Dhankar et al., 1997) using fMRI, however, did find that the response of the posterior superior temporal region increased with presentation rate (as did the primary auditory cortex).

Taken together, these studies suggest that a posterior region that may correspond to Wernicke's area is specifically activated by spoken words and word-like stimuli. The proximity of this region to the left-lateral temporal region active for words versus false-font stimuli suggests that there may be modality-specific regions in the posterior temporal lobe that are nearby and that process "lexicality," that is, the matching of incoming visual or auditory patterns to modality-specific word representations.

Inferior frontal lobe

A third area implicated in phonological processing is a frontal-lobe opercular region encompassing Brodmann's areas 44/45 (figure 9. 4). This frontal region appears to be modality independent; activation occurs for both visual and auditory stimuli. Activation in this region usually occurs when the subject is performing a task that requires phonological analysis but sometimes also occurs with passive listening or repetition tasks. Activation of the frontal operculum has been reported with several related task comparisons, including: phonological discrimination and monitoring with nonword syllables relative to passive listening (Zatorre et al., 1992, 1996); phonological monitoring in spoken nonwords relative to sequence monitoring in tone triplets (Demonet et al., 1992, 1994); phonological (rhyme) judgments relative to spatial (orientation) judgments about visually-presented letters (Sergent et al., 1992); generation of a rhyme relative to word repetition (Klein et al., 1995); phonological (syllable counting) judgments relative to semantic judgments (Price et al., 1997); and phonological (rhyme) judgments about visually presented pseudowords relative to orthographic (letter case) judgments about consonant strings (Shaywitz et al., 1995b; Pugh et al., 1996). Shaywitz et al. (1995b) found a gender difference in the activation resulting from this latter task such that females showed bilateral activation but males showed left-lateralized activation. Buckner, Raichle, and Petersen (1995b), however, did not find gender differences in this area with a task that probably had phonological demands.

The inferior frontal region appears to respond equally to words and pseudowords. Studies have found activation of the left inferior frontal region during silent reading of pseudowords compared to rest (Warburton et al., 1996) and compared to reading of real words (Herbster et al., 1997). Activation is also observed during passive listening to words compared to rest (Price et al., 1996b; Warburton et al., 1996). Activation of this region has also been found during rhyme judgments on visually presented pseudowords compared to both perceptual judgments (Shaywitz et al., 1995.; Pugh et al., 1996) and to fixation (Rumsey et al., 1997); activity is also found during phonological decisions on real words such as rhyming judgments (Klein et al., 1996) and syllable counting (Price et al., 1997). This frontal region may be specifically involved in the processing of phonological segments such as phonemes or syllables rather than whole-word phonology (which may be processed by posterior regions such as Wernicke's area). The activation observed here, however, during some passive listening or repetition tasks suggests that intentional word segmentation is not necessary to activate the left-inferior frontal region.

A number of investigators have emphasized the importance of fast temporal processing in analysis of critical phonological information such as stop consonants (Tallal, Miller, and Fitch, 1993). Dyslexic individuals are impaired at tasks that require processing of rapidly successive events in both linguistic and non-linguistic stimuli (Farmer and Klein, 1995; Witton et al., 1998). Fiez et al. (1995) reported that the frontal opercular area was activated during the performance of a detection task on stimuli with rapid temporal changes regardless of linguistic content. The types of stimuli that elicited activation in this region were words, syllables, and tone triplets that changed within a short temporal period (250 msec). Steady-state vowels did not produce activation in this region. Fiez et al. concluded that this region is involved in processing stimuli that involve rapid temporal modulation, including many speech stimuli, but that the presence of rapid temporal changes is more important than a linguistic quality per se (i.e., activation was present during the rapid tone sequences but not during steady-state vowels). There was no detectable activation when the same stimuli were presented without task requirements. In addition, phonological judgments (long-vowel discrimination) but not orthographic judgments (ascending-letter discrimination) about words yielded activation in this region regardless of whether the words were presented in the visual or auditory modality (Fiez et al., 1995). The above studies suggest that the left-frontal opercular region contributes to processing of rapidly successive information, and that it is modality-independent, modulated by task demands, and not sensitive to the lexical status of stimuli.

Premotor cortex

A premotor region has shown activation during phonological monitoring and decision tasks (see figure 9.4) and it may represent a neural correlate of "inner speech." This region was more activated during sequential processing of perceptually challenging stimuli (i.e., detecting the phoneme /b/ with a preceding /d/, as in the pseudoword *redozabu*) relative to sequence monitoring in tone triplets (Demonet et al., 1994a), relative to semantic monitoring in word pairs (Demonet, Price, Wise, and Frackowiak, 1994b), and relative to passive processing of speech syllables (Zatorre et al., 1992). Phoneme monitoring tasks that required nonsequential decisions or used stimuli that are not as perceptually challenging did not yield activation in this area (Demonet et al., 1994a). The premotor region was also active during rhyme decision on nonwords compared to fixation (Rumsey et al., 1997) and during syllable counting judgments compared to semantic judgments (Price et al., 1997). A similar region has been implicated in the "articulatory loop" component of verbal working memory (Baddeley, 1986; Paulesu, Frith, and Frackowiak, 1993). Thus, this region may reflect an inner-speech process that is required in tasks involving mental manipulation of phonological information.

Finally, two other regions are worth mentioning, given their proximity to postulated language zones. The left supramarginal gyrus in the parietal lobe was activated during tasks that also activated the premotor region discussed above (Paulesu et al., 1993; Demonet et al., 1994b; Price et al., 1997; Rumsey et al., 1997). This region may act as a short-term storage buffer for phonological information that interacts with the articulatory loop in working memory models (Paulesu et al., 1993). A more ventral temporoparietal region was strongly activated during rhyming judgments with visually presented words relative to rest (Petersen et al., 1988, 1989). Fiez et al. (1995), however, failed to find activation in this area during phonological processing conditions that were expected to activate it. The processing role of this region is, thus, unclear.

Semantic Processing

Semantic processing refers to the encoding or analysis of word meaning. Imaging studies that investigated regions involved in semantic processing (see appendix 9.3) typically compared two conditions with similar stimuli (e.g., visual words) but different responses (e.g., reading the words versus generating semantically related words). In these studies, brain regions that are more activated during a condition requiring increased analysis of word meaning, compared to a condition that controls for other levels of word analysis, are believed to be selectively involved in semantic processing.

Semantic processing, like many complex cognitive operations, is not related to a specific sensory system in the way that orthographic and phonological processing are inherently related to the visual and auditory system, respectively. The prefrontal cortex, however, is believed to be involved in complex processes unique to humans, and lesions to this region result in a wide array of intellectual deficits including a loss of verbal fluency (Benton, 1968; Kolb and Whishaw, 1990). Lesion evidence suggests that damage to multiple areas of frontal cortex can result in different forms of aphasia and category-specific knowledge impairments, (see Damasio, 1992; Kolb and Whishaw, 1990). Imaging studies have consistently reported left-prefrontal activation during semantic processing tasks. In this review, we concentrate on the prefrontal areas activated during semantic processing in the relevant studies, although other cortical regions (i.e., the anterior cingulate gyrus, posterior temporal cortex, superior prefrontal cortex, lateral cerebellum) have also shown activation across studies (see appendix 9.3).

Several studies have revealed left prefrontal involvement in semantic processing during tasks requiring generation of responses based upon semantic features such as the verb generation task. Petersen et al. (1988), using PET, were the first to use a verb-generation paradigm to explore semantic processing. In the verb-generation condition, subjects generated aloud verbs to presented nouns (e.g., *eat* in response to *cake*). In the noun-repetition control condition, subjects read aloud the presented nouns. Both tasks require that words be read and articulated, but greater semantic analysis is required for verb generation than for word reading (along with other possible differences, such as decision processes). Petersen et al. (1988, 1989) reported left-prefrontal activation during verb generation relative to noun repetition. An inferior prefrontal region was activated with both visual and auditory stimuli, while a more posterior and superior region was activated with visual stimuli only (see figure 9.5). The inferior region was also activated when subjects monitored words for a given category (i.e., dangerous animals) relative to passive word processing (Petersen et al., 1988, 1989). The inferior activation was replicated using fMRI (McCarthy, Blamire, Rothman, Gruetter, and Shulman, 1993). Raichle et al. (1994) chose a region of interest near the center of the prefrontal activation cluster found by earlier studies (Petersen et al., 1988; 1989) and replicated the verb-generation finding in the prefrontal region. Comparing verb generation to rest in a set of four experiments, Warburton et al. (1996) found activation of both the anterior and posterior regions seen in other studies. Activity of the anterior region was also found when subjects generated synonyms to words (e.g., *drink* in response to *beverage*) relative to repeating words (Klein, Milner, Zatorre, Meyer, and Evans, 1995).

Other studies have used semantic decision paradigms to investigate semantic processing. For example, Gabrieli et al. (1996) and Demb et al. (1995) used fMRI and compared semantic and nonsemantic encoding of words while measuring responses in the prefrontal cortex. In both conditions, subjects made decisions about words that were either abstract (e.g., *hope*) or concrete (e.g., *BOOK*) printed in upper- or lower-case letters. In the semantic-encoding condition, subjects decided if words were abstract or concrete, and in the nonsemantic-encoding condition, subjects decided if words appeared in upper- or lower-case letters. Both conditions require subjects to read words and make responses, and both conditions probably induce semantic and perceptual analysis of the words to some degree. More semantic analysis, however, is required for the abstract/concrete decision relative to the upper-case/lower-case decision. The left-inferior prefrontal cortex was more activated during the semantic task relative to the nonsemantic task (see figure 9.5). A num-

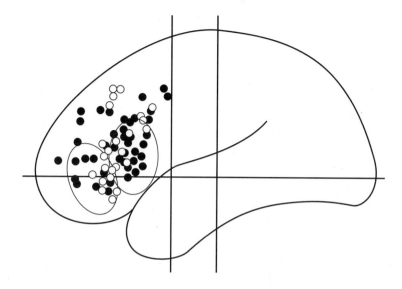

● Semantic generation tasks
○ Semantic decision tasks

Figure 9.5 Semantic processing activations in left-prefrontal cortex are represented as symbols projected onto a lateral view of the left-hemisphere that indicate the center of activations from 7 studies (see appendix 9.3.). This region has been divided into two subregions: an Anterior/Inferior (A/I) region and a Posterior/Superior (P/S) region. See text for details. Other brain regions have shown some consistency across studies (i.e., anterior cingulate gyrus, posterior temporal cortex, superior prefrontal cortex, lateral cerebellum) but are not depicted on the figure.

ber of subsequent studies have replicated this activation in the same task (Poldrack et al., 1999; Wagner et al., 1998). The laterality of activation correlated with side of language dominance in Wada-tested patients who were either left- or right-hemisphere dominant for language (Desmond et al., 1995). A prior PET study also found left-prefrontal cortex activation during semantic relative to nonsemantic encoding (Kapur et al., 1994a, 1994b); activation was not detected in any other region. A similar left-prefrontal region (reported as Brodmann's area 47, Demonet et al., 1992) was activated during a semantic-monitoring condition relative to a tone monitoring condition (Demonet et al., 1992; Binder et al., 1995) and relative to passive word viewing (Petersen et al., 1988, 1989). Several studies found that this left-inferior prefrontal region is activated during semantic processing of pictures as well as words (see Buckner et al., 1998; Vandenberghe et al., 1996, Wagner et al., 1997).

One confound in many and perhaps all of the above studies is the relative difficulty of the semantic and control conditions (with difficulty defined as the time needed to make a response). For example, the semantic encoding tasks have been more difficult than the nonsemantic tasks (Gabrieli et al., 1996; Kapur et al., 1994a), and generating verbs to nouns is more difficult than simply repeating nouns. Therefore, left-prefrontal activation could reflect a response to either semantic processing or task difficulty. To examine whether left-prefrontal activation was related to semantic processing or task difficulty, Demb et al. (1995) compared the semantic-encoding condition (abstract/concrete decision) to both an easy nonsemantic-encoding condition (upper-case/lower-case decision) and a difficult nonsemantic-encoding condition, in which subjects had to decide whether there was an ascending (e.g., *CHAIR*) or descending (e.g., *love*) alphabetic relation between the first and last letter of a word (ascending/descending decision). Response times showed that the easy nonsemantic-encoding condition took the least time, the difficult nonsemantic-encoding condition took the most time, and the semantic-encoding condition took an intermediate time. Only the semantic task, however, required subjects to attend to word meaning. There was increased left-inferior prefrontal cortex response during semantic encoding relative to both the easy and the difficult nonsemantic tasks, and this was evident in both individual subject and group analyses (Demb et al., 1995). This suggests that the left-inferior prefrontal response is related to an aspect of semantic analysis rather than task difficulty.

Analysis of activations for semantic processing across studies (see figure 9.5) suggests that two regions of the left-prefrontal cortex may be involved in separate aspects of semantic processing (see Buckner, 1996; Poldrack et al., 1999). A posterior region, corresponding to the Broca's area region active during phonological tasks (Brodmann's areas 6/44/45), is active primarily during tasks requiring semantic generation. In addition, nonsemantic-generation tasks that require access to lexical knowledge, such as letter fluency (i.e., generate word beginning with the letter F) with overt response (Frith, Friston, Liddle, and Frackowiak, 1991a, 1991b; Friston, Frith, Liddle, and Frackowiak, 1991b) or covert response (Hinke et al., 1993) or baseline word-stem completion (i.e., complete the stem BRE to form a word, see Buckner et al., 1995a) have also yielded activations that occur in this cluster (see appendix 9.4). Activation is also seen in this region during lexical decision (Price et al., 1994; Rumsey et al., 1997) and reading words aloud (Price et al., 1994), both tasks which do not activate the anterior inferior prefrontal cortex. Therefore, this posterior region may be involved in access to lexical knowledge that is necessary for the performance of most semantic or phonological tasks. Activity of this region may not depend on an overt response, as tasks with covert responses have produced activation in this area as well (Hinke et al., 1993; Wise et al., 1991).

A more anterior and inferior region, corresponding to the anterior limb of the inferior frontal gyrus (Brodmann's areas 45/47/10), is active during both semantic-generation and semantic-decision tasks, is active for both visual and auditory semantic tasks, and is not active during phonological tasks. This anterior region may be specifically involved in the processing of semantic information, whereas the posterior region may be involved in processes more directly related to the retrieval of phonological information related to speech production. This anterior region is active when tasks require an overt response but not when there is only a covert response (McCarthy et al., 1993; Wise et al., 1991). This last point suggests that differences in attention required by overt and covert response paradigms may influence activation in this area, or that it may be involved in processes particular to the articulation of a verbal response.

Whereas most studies have assumed that left-frontal activation during semantic tasks was related to retrieval of knowledge from semantic memory, a study by Thompson-Schill et al. (1997) has suggested that the role of the left-inferior prefrontal cortex may lie in the selection of relevant information during semantic retrieval rather than in semantic retrieval per se. In three tasks, semantic processing was compared between low- and high-selection conditions. In low-selection conditions, all features of the stimulus were relevant to task performance. In high-selection conditions, only some features of the stimulus were relevant to the task whereas others had to be ignored. In each task, the posterior/superior section of left-inferior frontal cortex (Brodmann's areas 44/45) was more active for the high-selection condition compared to the low-selection condition. An additional comparison between conditions designed to vary the amount of semantic retrieval while keeping selection constant did not find activation in the left-inferior prefrontal cortex. A study by Desmond et al. (1998) also examined selection by asking subjects to complete word stems that had either few completions (low selection) or many completions (high selection). This study found activation in the middle frontal gyrus for items with many compared to few completions, with no such activation in the inferior frontal cortex.

Although these studies suggest that various left-frontal regions may be particularly sensitive to selection demands, other studies have found left-inferior frontal activation for semantic relative to nonsemantic tasks that had similar selection demands. For example, Vandenberghe et al. (1996) found activation of the left-frontal cortex for judgments of the size of a drawing's referent compared to judgments of the size of the drawing itself. Each of these tasks requires similar selection of the size of the stimulus, but the tasks differ in the necessity of semantic retrieval. Further studies are necessary to examine the particular processes subserved by left-frontal regions in semantic processing.

Functional Neuroimaging Studies in Subjects with Developmental Dyslexia

Developmental dyslexia refers to a specific deficit in learning to read that is not a result of inadequate learning opportunity or acquired brain lesion. Several lines of investigation have suggested structural neuroanatomical abnormalities in developmental dyslexia including *in vivo* brain imaging (i.e., Hynd, Semrud-Clikeman, Lorys, Novey, and Eliopulos, 1990; Rumsey et al., 1986) and postmortem studies (i.e., Galaburda, Sherman, Rosen, Aboitiz, and Geschwind, 1985; Livingstone, Rosen, Drislane, and Galaburda, 1991). In addition, several studies have used functional neuroimaging techniques to explore developmental dyslexia. Reports of regional cerebral blood flow and glucose metabolism measurements in dyslexic and control subjects (i.e., good readers) are listed in appendix 9.5, and the group differences have been emphasized. Some of these studies used now outdated techniques with lower temporal (e.g., scan times around 30 minutes) and spatial resolution (e.g., comparison between hemispheres and major lobes only) than the studies considered in the previous section. Other studies compared dyslexic and control subjects on a single task condition without a control condition (e.g., Gross-Glenn et al., 1991). These studies do not eliminate the possibility that dyslexic and control brains may show differences at rest, in addition to differences seen during task performance as has been reported by more recent studies. In spite of these limitations, these studies have been included here for completeness.

Several methodological complications arise when comparing dyslexic and control subjects. These complications include the tasks used, the subjects under study, and the groups that are compared. First, there could be difficulties in the interpretation of images acquired during a task that is performed differently by dyslexic and control subjects. For example, if dyslexic and control individuals are compared during a condition that requires subjects to read challenging words, dyslexic individuals may show abnormal activation because they are failing at the task rather than differences associated with reading. In that case, differential activation could be a consequence, rather than a cause, of the underlying language difficulty. Many studies control for this problem by using tasks that can be performed approximately equally by the dyslexic and control groups (e.g., Gross-Glenn et al., 1991; Rumsey et al., 1994b; Paulesu et al., 1996). Second, studies of dyslexia have been performed with adults with a history of developmental dyslexia rather than children with dyslexia, because many of the techniques have required administration of radioactive materials that are not routinely used with children. There could be differences in the brains of dyslexic individuals that depend on age. Future studies that use fMRI may provide a safe way to study children with dyslexia (Casey et al., 1995). Finally, because dyslexia is a heterogeneous disorder with multiple proposed subtypes (Castles and Coltheart, 1993; Rispens, van der Stege, and Bode, 1994), it may be fruitful for future studies to compare brain-activation differences in subtypes of dyslexia. For example, Castles and Coltheart (1993) reported surface and phonological subtypes of developmental dyslexia. Surface dyslexics had difficulty reading exception words but could read regular words and nonwords; phonological dyslexics could read regular and irregular words but had difficulty reading unfamiliar words and nonwords. These subtypes may represent different underlying deficits in brain systems involved in orthographic, phonological, or semantic processing. Future imaging studies should compare these subtypes directly to examine this possibility.

Resting state differences.

Several studies reported differences in rCBF between dyslexic and control subjects during resting states (see appendix 9.5). Rumsey et al. (1992) reported that control subjects showed higher resting blood flow than dyslexic subjects in the right-sylvian cortex, while dyslexic subjects showed higher resting blood flow than controls in medial-frontal cortex. Two other studies reported that dyslexic subjects showed reduced blood flow, relative to controls, in a left-hemisphere parietal region near the angular and supramarginal gyri (Rumsey et al., 1994a, 1994b). Given reported difficulties with phonological processing in dyslexia (Farmer and Klein, 1995), it is interesting to note that similar parietal regions have been implicated in phonological processing in nondyslexic subjects (Demonet et al., 1994b; Paulesu et al., 1993; Rumsey et al., 1997).

Orthographic processing

Orthographic processing paradigms have also been used to compare dyslexic and control subjects (see appendix 9.5). Flowers, Wood, and Naylor (1991) used a spelling analysis task that required subjects to listen to nouns and respond only if they were 4-letters long. This task requires orthographic processing to the extent that subjects have to imagine words in their visual form to determine the number of letters in them. Correlations with task accuracy or childhood reading level were computed. In good readers, there was a correlation between task accuracy and overall blood flow in an area near Wernicke's region, an area that was activated by spoken language (e.g., Howard et al., 1992). Poor readers performed the task less well and had less blood flow in Wernicke's region. Poor readers showed more flow than good readers, however, in a temporoparietal region posterior to Wernicke's region. Activation of the temporoparietal region was unrelated to task accuracy and adult reading outcome (i.e., subjects with "persisting" versus "improved" reading ability both showed the effect). Flowers et al. (1991) suggested that certain language functions may be displaced from Wernicke's area to the temporoparietal region in dyslexic subjects. In another study, Gross-Glenn et al. (1991) required dyslexic and control subjects to read aloud written words. This task involves orthographic analysis to the extent that subjects have to decode written words in order to read them aloud. The dyslexic subjects showed higher overall activation in the lingual lobule of the occipital lobe than the control subjects (possibly near ME, see figure 9.3); this was not related to task performance as both groups performed at ceiling due to the easy task of reading familiar words. Greater activation in lingual/fusiform cortex for dyslexic versus control subjects was also found by Rumsey et al. (1997) during pseudoword reading compared to fixation.

Increased occipital activation in dyslexics may reflect more extensive visual analysis of words. A behavioral study showed that dyslexic subjects had better than normal scores on an orthographic awareness task that tests knowledge about orthographic rules, but dyslexic subjects had lower scores than control subjects on a test of phonological skills (Siegel, Share, and Geva, 1995). Dyslexic subjects may be compensating for difficulties with phonological processing by using a strategy that relies heavily on visual processing of word features (Siegel et al., 1995). Thus, the increased occipital activation in a region that may be useful for encoding orthography [see page 253] may reflect an increased reliance on orthographic processing in dyslexia. This reliance may be specific, however, to certain subtypes of dyslexia (e.g., phonological dyslexia) and should be examined in future imaging studies.

Phonological processing

Rumsey et al. (1992) explored phonological processing in dyslexia by comparing a rhyme judgment task minus a resting baseline state in dyslexic and control subjects. The rhyme judgment task required subjects to decide if two auditorily presented words in a pair rhymed. Dyslexic subjects performed the task slightly worse than controls did. A tone task that did not require phonological (or fast temporal) processing (the continuous performance task) was also compared to rest. The tone task required subjects to respond if a low tone was presented, but not if middle or high tones were presented. Dyslexic subjects showed less activation than controls during the phonological task in several left-hemisphere regions, including a temporoparietal (near the angular gyrus), middle-temporal, and posterior frontal region (possibly near FO, see figure 9.4). Similar regions have been implicated in phonological processing in normals [see page 257]. There was no difference between groups in these left-perisylvian areas during the tone task, which did not require fast temporal processing. Thus, phonological tasks, but not auditory tasks generally, elicited functional deficits in these dyslexic individuals.

Hagman et al. (1992) compared activation in dyslexic and control subjects on a consonant-vowel syllable detection task that required fast temporal processing. Dyslexic subjects showed higher metabolism in bilateral medial temporal areas that included both gray and white matter regions. A resting scan, however, which may have differed in the two groups, was not subtracted from the task condition, thus complicating the interpretation of this result. Rumsey et al. (1994a) also compared dyslexic and control subjects on a task that required fast temporal processing of tones minus a resting baseline. Dyslexic subjects performed worse than controls but above chance on this task. Controls showed greater PET activation than dyslexic subjects in several right-hemisphere regions. This difference in activation may reflect right-hemisphere contributions to fast temporal processing or an aspect of task difficulty that reflects the different performance in the two groups.

Several studies have also examined phonological processing with visually presented stimuli. Phonological processing in dyslexic and control subjects was examined in PET using naming, rhyme, and lexical decision tasks by Rumsey et al. (1997). In the naming task, subjects pronounced either nonwords or exception words, two kinds of stimuli that are phonologically demanding. In the rhyme task, subjects decided which of two pseudowords rhymed with a real word, whereas in the lexical decision task the subjects decided which of two items (a word and its pseudoword homophone) was a real word. Each of these tasks was compared to fixation. Across these tasks, dyslexic subjects exhibited less activation in the left-supramarginal gyrus, left-superior temporal, and left-middle temporal cortices. These data were further analyzed by Horwitz et al. (1998), who examined the correlation of all voxels in the brain with a reference voxel in the angular gyrus across subjects. Compared to controls, dyslexics exhibited a significantly lower correlation between activity in the angular gyrus and activity in temporal, occipital, and frontal regions involved in language processing. Together, the findings of Rumsey et al. (1997) and Horwitz et al. (1998) suggest that the angular gyrus is "functionally disconnected" from other language regions. The fact that lesions to the angular gyrus result in impairment of reading ability (alexia with agraphia) provides converging evidence for the importance of this region in reading.

Paulesu et al. (1996) examined rhyming and phonological working memory tasks using PET in compensated dyslexics (i.e., people previously diagnosed with dyslexia who now exhibit normal reading performance). In the rhyming task, rhyme judgments on consonants (e.g., do *b* and *p* rhyme?) were compared to shape judgments on Korean symbols, whereas in the working memory task short-term memory for consonants was compared to short-term memory for Korean symbols. In the rhyming task, the dyslexic subjects exhibited less activation in the superior temporal gyrus (Wernicke's area) and in the left insula (along with several other regions). In the working memory task, dyslexics exhibited less activation in the left-supramarginal gyrus, left-inferior frontal gyrus, left-premotor cortex, left insula, and several other regions. Paulesu et al. (1996) argued that the lack of activation in the left insula suggests that dyslexia may result from the disconnection of posterior language regions (Wernicke's area and inferior parietal cortex) from frontal language areas (inferior frontal cortex), and they speculated that this connection may be normally mediated by the insula. Rumsey et al. (1997) found increased activation, however, in the insula in dyslexics relative to controls during naming tasks, and Horwitz et al. (1998) did not find a decreased correlation between angular gyrus activation and insula activation. This suggests that the findings of Paulesu et al. (1996) may be limited to a subset of compensated dyslexics.

Shaywitz et al. (1998) used fMRI to study phonological processing in dyslexic and control subjects across several conditions that varied in phonological demands: line-orientation judgment, letter-case judgment, single-letter rhyme judgment, nonword-rhyme judgment, and semantic-category judgment. Data were analyzed in several regions of interest (ROIs) determined on the basis of previous studies; a factorial analysis of variance was performed on the number of activated pixels in each ROI across tasks, hemispheres, and subject groups. This analysis is less sensitive to group differences in the intensity of activation than the analyses used by Rumsey et al. (1997) and Paulesu et al. (1996), but it is more sensitive to differences in the extent of activation. The analysis demonstrated group x task interactions in several regions bilaterally, including superior temporal gyrus (including Wernicke's area in the left hemisphere), angular gyrus, striate cortex, and inferior frontal cortex. During rhyme judgments, control subjects exhibited greater activation than dyslexics in posterior brain regions, and dyslexic subjects exhibited greater activation than controls in an inferior frontal region. The difference in posterior brain activity confirms previous PET findings of decreased activation in the inferior parietal region in dyslexia. Large group differences in performance accuracy on the phonological tasks, however, complicate the interpretation of the difference in inferior frontal activation. Paulesu et al. (1996) found greater activation for control than dyslexic subjects in this region during a similar task in which dyslexics performed normally, suggesting that the difference found by Shaywitz et al. (1998) may be related to group differences in task accuracy or some other characteristic of the particular subject group.

Together, the studies of phonological processing in dyslexia reviewed here suggest that a number of perisylvian language regions, including the angular gyrus, supramarginal gyrus, and superior temporal gyrus (Wernicke's area) exhibit significantly less activity in dyslexics than controls during phonological processing.

Semantic processing

Studies have also compared dyslexic and control subjects on semantic processing tasks. Rumsey et al. (1994b) compared dyslexic and control subjects on a test that required subjects to determine if two auditory sentences with syntactic differences had a similar meaning; this was compared to a resting baseline condition. Although there were differences in some regions (see appendix 9.5), both groups showed PET activation in left-middle temporal and inferior frontal regions, as had been found previously in nondyslexic subjects performing semantic processing tasks compared to rest (Wise et al., 1991). Similarly, the results of Shaywitz et al. (1998) appear to suggest that differences between dyslexics and controls were weaker for semantic processing than for rhyme processing (though this statistical comparison was not explicitly reported). These results suggest that abnormal left-perisylvian activations in dyslexic subjects are best elicited by phonological tasks (Rumsey et al., 1994b), and that left-hemisphere regions involved in semantic processing may be normal.

Visual processing

Finally, there have been two recent neuroimaging studies of early visual processing in dyslexia that may be relevant to reading difficulties. The studies examined a specific hypothesis that there is an abnormality in an early pathway between the retina and the brain known as the magnocellular (M) pathway. This hypothesis was based on psychophysical (see Demb, Boynton, Best, and Heeger, 1998a; Williams and Lovegrove, 1992), electrophysiological (Lehmkuhle, Garzia, Turner, Hash, and Baro, 1993; Livingstone et al., 1991), and anatomical evidence (Livingstone et al., 1991) for a deficit in the M pathway.

The M pathway carries information about specific properties of the visual world (i.e., high temporal frequencies, low spatial frequencies) and is relatively more sensitive than other pathways (e.g., the parvocellular or P pathway) under conditions of low mean luminance and low contrast (Merigan and Maunsell, 1993; Purpura, Kaplan, and Shapley, 1988). It is true that many of these characteristics are, if anything, opposite to the characteristics found in printed text in good lighting conditions (i.e., which include higher spatial frequencies, high mean luminance, and high contrast). An intact M pathway, however, may be crucial for the eye movement control or fixational stability that are necessary operations for reading text in most situations (Stein and Walsh, 1997). Alternatively, this deficit in a major fast temporal processing visual pathway may be a marker of a more general deficit in other sensory pathways and brain systems in dyslexia (see Demb, Boynton, and Heeger, 1998b). Deficits of rapid auditory processing in dyslexia are correlated with rapid visual processing deficits (Witton et al., 1998), and these auditory deficits could be the more immediate cause of reading difficulties. Either way, the use of stimuli with visual characteristics not found in the normal reading situation in these studies is useful for isolating the M pathway (which is also sensitive at higher contrast and mean luminance) even though they are not identical to the normal reading situation.

Eden et al. (1996) compared adult dyslexic and control subjects on conditions of viewing low contrast moving dots (M condition) and higher contrast stationary dots (parvocellular pathway or P condition) relative to viewing a blank screen. Both groups showed activity in an early visual area (V1/V2) in the P condition, but only controls showed significant activity in a lateral motion-sensitive visual area (MT+) during the M condition. MT+ is thought to be homologous to monkey area MT and adjacent motion-sensitive areas that receive a dominant M pathway projection (Merigan and Maunsell, 1993). Demb, Boynton, and Heeger (1997, 1998b) found similar results in a study of adult dyslexic and control subjects. They compared activity while subjects viewed either moving sine-wave gratings at low mean luminance across several contrasts (M conditions) or flickering gratings at high mean luminance across several contrasts (control conditions). Dyslexic subjects showed reduced activity compared to controls both in primary visual cortex (V1) and in area MT+ in the M conditions, but V1 activity was similar across groups in the control conditions (MT+ was not scanned in the control conditions). Most importantly, significant positive correlations were found between individual differences in reading rate and brain activity in the M conditions. These results support the hypothesis for an M pathway abnormality in dyslexia and imply a strong relationship between the integrity of the M pathway and reading ability.

Conclusion

Recent advances in functional neuroimaging technology have allowed psychologists and neuroscientists to explore many aspects of human cognition. Among these, language processing has been of particular interest due to the absence of an animal model (but see Fitch et al., 1994), and the wide variety of disorders that affect language, such as dyslexia (Caplan, 1992). The goals of this chapter were to describe functional neuroimaging methodology, review recent studies of single-word processing, and review functional imaging studies of developmental dyslexia. Although there are several limitations to neuroimaging methodology, studies that used PET or fMRI have already proven useful in replicating and extending knowledge about language in the brain. The review of recent studies of single-word processing demonstrated converging evidence for several regions involved in orthographic, phonological, and semantic processing. Differences across studies in experimental design probably add variability to the results. Future research will determine which results are replicable across studies that examine a common process.

There have been relatively few functional imaging studies in dyslexia, but recent studies have converged to suggest abnormalities in perisylvian regions that have been implicated in phonological and orthographic processing in good readers. Neuroimaging studies have also provided evidence for deficits in the processing of rapidly changing visual information. Further studies of dyslexia will continue to elucidate the neural basis of reading disorders. In addition, neuroimaging methods will be important in the evaluation of treatment strategies for dyslexia and other language disorders. One successful strategy for the treatment of developmental language impairments has been to improve processing of rapidly changing auditory information (Merzenich et al., 1996; Tallal et al., 1996). Such training must alter brain processing, and the use of neuroimaging in this situation could provide evidence about how treatment changes the neural processes underlying reading. In this way, functional neuroimaging may both reveal the neural basis of developmental dyslexia and guide the formulation of effective treatment.

Acknowledgments

We thank Randy Buckner, Zenzi Griffin, Ray Klein, Paddy McMullen, Cathy Price, Steve Petersen, and Anthony Wagner for their thoughtful comments on earlier versions of this chapter and Elise Temple for assistance in completing the appendices. Support for the writing of this chapter came from the National Institute of Aging (AG 12995) and the McDonnell-Pew Program in Cognitive Neuroscience.

Notes

[1] Price et al. (1994) reported that their results were not consistent with Petersen et al. (1990), but this may be due to discrepencies between different versions of a commonly used brain atlas (Talairach et al., 1967; Talairach and Tournoux, 1988) that made individual data points appear farther apart than they actually were.

References

Baddeley, A.D. (1986). *Working Memory*. London: Oxford University Press.

Bandettini, P.A., Jesmanowicz, A., Wong, E.C., and Hyde, J.S. (1993). Processing strategies for time-course data sets in functional MRI of the human brain. *Magnetic Resonance in Medicine, 30,* 161–173.

Beauregard, M., Chertkow, H., Bub, D., Murtha, S., Dixon, R., and Evans, A. (1997). The neural substrate for concrete, abstract, and emotional word lexica: A positron emission tomography study. *Journal of Cognitive Neuroscience, 9,* 441–461.

Belliveau, J.W., Kennedy, D.N., McKinstry, R.C., Buchbinder, B.R., Weisskoff, R.M., Cohen, M.S., Vevea, J.M., Brady, T.J., and Rosen, B.R. (1991). Functional mapping of the human visual cortex by magnetic resonance imaging. *Science, 254,* 716–719.

Benton, A.L. (1968). Differential effects of frontal lobe disease. *Neuropsychologia, 6,* 53–60.

Binder, J.R., Rao, S.M., Hammeke, T.A., Frost, J.A., Bandettini, P.A., and Hyde, J.S. (1994a). Effects of stimulus rate on signal response during functional magnetic resonance imaging of auditory cortex. *Cognitive Brain Research, 2,* 31–38.

Binder, J.R., Rao, S.M., Hammeke, T.A., Frost, J.A., Bandettini, P.A., Jesmanowicz, A., and Hyde, J.S. (1995). Lateralized human brain language systems demonstrated by task subtraction functional magnetic resonance imaging. *Archives of Neurology, 52,* 593–601.

Binder, J.R., Rao, S.M., Hammeke, T.A., Yetkin, F.Z., Jesmanowicz, A., Bandettini, P.A., Wong, E.C., Estkowski, L.D., Goldstein, M.D., Haughton, V.M., and Hyde, J.S. (1994b). Functional magnetic resonance imaging of human auditory cortex. *Annals of Neurology, 35,* 662–672.

Blaxton, T.A., Zeffiro, T.A., Gabrieli, J.D.E., Bookheimer, S.Y., Carrillo, M.C., Theodore, W.H., and Disterhoft, J.F. (1996). Functional mapping of human learning: A positron emission tomography activation study of eyeblink conditioning. *Journal of Neuroscience, 16,* 4032–4040..

Blumstein, S.E., Baker, E., and Goodglass, H. (1977). Phonological factors in auditory comprehension in aphasia. *Neuropsychologia, 15,* 19–30.

Bookheimer, S.Y., Zeffiro, T.A., Blaxton, T., Gaillard, W., and Theodore, W. (1995). Regional cerebral blood flow during object naming and word reading. *Human Brain Mapping, 3,* 93–106.

Brewer, J.B., Zhao, Z., Desmond, J.E., Glover, G.H., and Gabrieli, J.D. (1998). Making memories: brain activity that predicts how well visual experience will be remembered [see comments]. *Science, 281*(5380), 1185–1187.

Buckner, R.L. (1996). Beyond hera: contributions of specific prefrontal brain areas to long-term memory retrieval. *Psychonomic Bulletin and Review, 3,* 149–158.

Buckner, R.L., Bandettini, P.A., O'Craven, K.M., Savoy, R.L., Petersen, S.E., Raichle, M.E., and Rosen, B.R. (1996). Detection of cortical activation during averaged single trials of a cognitive task using functional magnetic resonance imaging [see comments]. *Proceedings of the National Academy of Sciences USA 93*(25), 14878–14883.

Buckner, R.L., Goodman, J., Burock, M., Rotte, M., Koutstaal, W., Schacter, D., Rosen, B., and Dale, A.M. (1998). Functional-anatomic correlates of object priming in humans revealed by rapid presentation event-related fMRI. *Neuron, 20*(2), 285–296.

Buckner, R.L., and Tulving, E. (1995). Neuroimaging studies of memory: Theory and recent PET results. In F. Boller and J.Grafman (eds.), *Handbook of Neuropsychology* (v. 10, pp. 439–466). Amsterdam: Elsevier.

Buckner, R.L., Petersen, S.E., Ojemann, J.G., Miezin, F.M., Squire, L.R., and Raichle, M.E. (1995a). Functional anatomical studies of explicit and implicit memory retrieval tasks. *Journal of Neuroscience, 15*, 12–29.

Buckner, R.L., Raichle, M.E., and Petersen, S.E. (1995b). Activation of human prefrontal cortex across different speech production tasks and gender groups. *Journal of Neurophysiology, 74*, 2163–2173.

Caplan, D. (1992). *Language: Structure, Processing, and Disorders.* Cambridge: MIT Press.

Casey, B.J., Cohen, J.D., Jezzard, P., Turner, R., Noll, D.C., Trainor, R.J., Giedd, J., Kaysen, D., Hertz-Pannier, L., and Rapoport, J.L. (1995). Activation of prefrontal cortex in children during a nonspatial working memory task with functional MRI. *Neuroimage, 2*, 221–229.

Castles, A., and Coltheart, C. (1993). Varieties of developmental dyslexia. *Cognition, 47*, 149–180.

Damasio, A.R. (1992). Aphasia. *New England Journal of Medicine, 326*, 531–539.

Damasio, H., Grabowski, T.J., Tranel, D., Hichwa, R.D., and Damasio, A.R. (1996). A neural basis for lexical retrieval. *Nature, 380*, 499–505.

Daum, I., Schugens, M.M., Ackerman, H., Lutzenberger, W., Dichgans, J., and Birbaumer, N. (1993). Classical conditioning after cerebellar lesions in humans. *Behavioral Neuroscience, 107*, 748–756.

Demb, J.B., Boynton, G.M., and Heeger, D.J. (1997). Brain activity in visual cortex predicts individual differences in reading performance. *Proceedings of the National Academy of Sciences USA, 94*, 13363-13366.

Demb, J.B., Boynton, G.M., and Heeger, D.J. (1998b). Functional magnetic resonance imaging of early visual pathways in dyslexia. *Journal of Neuroscience, 18*, 6939–6951.

Demb, J.B., Boynton, G.M., Best, M., and Heeger, D.J. (1998a). Psychophysical evidence for a magnocellular pathway deficit in dyslexia. *Vision Research, 38,* 1555–1559.

Demb, J.B., Desmond, J.E., Wagner, A.D., Vaidya, C.J., Glover, G.H., and Gabrieli, J.D.E. (1995). Semantic encoding and retrieval in the left inferior prefrontal cortex: A functional MRI study of task difficulty and process specificity. *Journal of Neuroscience, 15,* 5870–5878.

Demonet, J.-F., Chollet, F., Ramsay, S., Cardebat, D., Nespoulous, J.L., Wise, R., Rascol, A., and Frackowiak, R. (1992). The anatomy of phonological and semantic processing in normal subjects. *Brain, 115,* 1753–1768.

Demonet, J.-F., Price, C., Wise, R., and Frackowiak, R.S.J. (1994a). A PET study of cognitive strategies in normal subjects during language tasks: Influence of phonetic ambiguity and sequence processing on phoneme monitoring. *Brain, 117,* 671–682.

Demonet, J.-F., Price, C., Wise, R., and Frackowiak, R.S.J. (1994b). Differential activation of right and left posterior sylvian regions by semantic and phonological tasks: A positron-emission tomography study in normal human subjects. *Neuroscience Letters, 182,* 25–28.

Desmond, J.E., Gabrieli, J.D., and Glover, G.H. (1998). Dissociation of frontal and cerebellar activity in a cognitive task: Evidence for a distinction between selection and search. *Neuroimage, 7*(4 Pt 1), 368–376.

Desmond, J.E., Sum, J.M., Wagner, A.D., Demb, J.B., Shear, P.K., Glover, G.H., Gabrieli, J.D.E., and Morrell, M.J. (1995). Functional MRI measurement of language lateralization in Wada-tested patients. *Brain,* 118, 1411–1419.

Dhankar, A., Wexler, B.E., Fulbright, R.K., Halwes, T., Blamire, A.M., and Shulman, R.G. (1997). Functional magnetic resonance imaging assessment of the human brain auditory cortex response to increasing word presentation rates. *Journal of Neurophysiology, 77*(1), 476–483.

Eden, G.F., VanMeter, J.W., Rumsey, J.M., Maisog, J.M., Woods, R.P.,and Zeffiro, T.A. (1996). Abnormal processing of visual motion in dyslexia revealed by functional brain imaging. *Nature,* 382, 66–69.

Engel, S.E., Rumelhart, D.E., Wandell, B.A., Lee, A.T., Glover, G.H., Chilchinsky, E.-J., and Shadlen, M. (1994). fMRI of human visual cortex. *Nature, 369,* 525.

Farmer, M.E., and Klein, R. (1995). The evidence for a temporal processing deficit linked to dyslexia: A review. *Psychonomic Bulletin and Review, 2,* 460–493.

Felleman, D.J., and Van Essen, D.C. (1991). Distributed hierarchical processing in primate cerebral cortex. *Cerebral Cortex, 1,* 1–47.

Fiez, J.A. (1997). Phonology, semantics, and the role of the left inferior prefrontal cortex. *Human Brain Mapping, 5,* 79–83.

Fiez, J.A., Raichle, M.E., Miezin, F.M., Petersen, S.E., Tallal, P., and Katz, W.F. (1995).

PET studies of auditory and phonological processing: Effects of stimulus characteristics and task design. *Journal of Cognitive Neuroscience, 7*, 357–375.

Fitch, R.H., Tallal, P., Brown, C.P., Galaburda, A.M., and Rosen, G.D. (1994). Induced microgyria and auditory temporal processing in rats: A model for language development? *Cerebral Cortex, 4*, 260–270.

Fletcher, P.C., Frith, C.D., Grasby, P.M., Shallice, T., Frackowiak, R.S.J., and Dolan, R.J. (1995). Brain systems for encoding and retrieval of auditory-verbal memory: An in vivo study in humans. *Brain, 118*, 401–416.

Flowers, D.L., Wood, F.B., and Naylor, C.E. (1991). Regional cerebral blood flow correlates of language processes in reading disability. *Archives of Neurology, 48*, 637–643.

Fox, P.T., and Raichle, M.E. (1986). Focal physiological uncoupling of cerebral blood flow and oxidative metabolism during somatosensory stimulation in human subjects. *Proceedings of the National Academy of Sciences USA, 83*, 1140–1144.

Fox, P.T., Raichle, M.E., Mintun, M.A., and Dence, C. (1988). Nonoxidative glucose consumption during focal physiological neural activity. *Science, 241*, 462–464.

Friston, K.J., Jezzard, P., and Turner, R. (1994). Analysis of functional mri time-series. *Human Brain Mapping, 1*, 153–171.

Friston, K.J., Frith, C.D., Liddle, P.F., and Frackowiak, R.S.J. (1991a). Comparing functional (PET) images: The assessment of significant change. *Journal of Cerebral Blood Flow and Metabolism, 11*, 690–699.

Friston, K.J., Frith, C.D., Liddle, P.F., and Frackowiak, R.S.J. (1991b). Investigating a network model of word generation with positron emission tomography. *Proceedings of the Royal Society of London: Biology, 244*, 101–106.

Friston, K.J., Frith, C.D., Liddle, P.F., Dolan, R.J., Lammertsma, A.A., and Frackowiak, R.S.J. (1990). The relationship between global and local changes in PET scans. *Journal of Cerebral Blood Flow and Metabolism, 10*, 458–466.

Friston, K.J., Holmes, A.P., Poline, J.B., Grasby, P.J., Williams, S.C., Frackowiak, R.S., Turner, R. (1995). Analysis of fMRI time-series revisited. *Neuroimage, 2*, 45–53.

Friston, K.J., Jezzard, P., and Turner, R. (1994). Analysis of functional MRI time-series. *Human Brain Mapping, 1*, 153–171.

Frith, C.D., Kapur, N., Friston, K.J., Liddle, P.F., and Frackowiak, R.S.J. (1995). Regional cerebral activity associated with the incidental processing of pseudo-words. *Human Brain Mapping, 3*, 153–160.

Frith, C.D., Friston, K.J., Liddle, P.F., and Frackowiak, R.S.J. (1991a). A PET study of word finding. *Neuropsychologia, 29*, 1137–1148.

Frith, C.D., Friston, K., Liddle, P.F., and Frackowiak, R.S.J. (1991b). Willed action and the prefrontal cortex in man: A study with PET. *Proceedings of the Royal Society of London: Biology, 244*, 241–246.

Frostig, R.D., Lieke, E.E., Ts'o, D.Y., and Grinvald, A. (1990). Cortical functional architecture and local coupling between neuronal activity and the microcirculation revealed by in vivo high–resolution optical imaging of intrinsic signals. *Proceedings of the National Academy of Sciences USA, 87,* 6082–6086.

Gabrieli, J.D.E., Desmond, J.E., Demb, J.B., Wagner, A.D., Stone, M.V., Vaidya, C.J., and Glover, G.H. (1996). Functional magnetic resonance imaging of semantic memory processes in the frontal lobes. *Psychological Science, 7,* 278–283.

Gabrieli, J.D.E., McGlinchey-Berroth, R., Carrillo, M.C., Gluck, M.A., Cermak, L.S., and Disterhoft, J.F. (1995). Intact delay-eyeblink classical conditioning in amnesia. *Behavioral Neuroscience, 109,* 819–827.

Galaburda, A.M., Sherman, G.F., Rosen, G.D., Aboitiz, F., and Geschwind, N. (1985). Developmental dyslexia: four consecutive patients with cortical anomalies. *Annals of Neurology, 18,* 222–233.

Gross-Glenn, K., Duara, R., Barker, W.W., Loewenstein, D., Chang, J.-Y., Yoshii, F., Apicella, A.M., Pascal, S., Boothe, T., Sevush, S., Jallad, B.J., Novoa, L., and Lubs, H.A. (1991). Positron emission tomographic studies during serial word–reading by normal and dyslexic adults. *Journal of Clinical and Experimental Neuropsychology, 13,* 531–544.

Hagman, J.O., Wood, F., Buchsbaum, M.S., Tallal, P., Flowers, L., and Katz, W. (1992). Cerebral brain metabolism in adult dyslexic subjects assessed with positron emission tomography during performance of an auditory task. *Archives of Neurology, 49,* 734–739.

Heinze, H.J., Mangun, G.R., Burchert, W., Hinrichs, H., Scholz, M., Munte, T.F., Gos, A., Scherg, M., Johannes, S., Hundeshagen, H., Gazzaniga, M.S., and Hillyard, S.A. (1994). Combined spatial and temporal imaging of brain activity during visual selective attention in humans. *Nature, 372,* 543–546.

Herbster, A.N., Mintun, M.A., Nebes, R.D., and Becker, J.T. (1997). Regional cerebral blood flow during word and nonword reading. *Human Brain Mapping, 5,* 84–92.

Hinke, R.M., Hu, X., Stillman, A.E., Kim, S.-G., Merkle, H., Salmi, R., and Ugurbil, K. (1993). Functional magnetic resonance imaging of Broca's area during internal speech. *Neuroreport, 4,* 675–678.

Horwitz, B., Rumsey, J.M., and Donohue, B.C. (1998). Functional connectivity of the angular gyrus in normal reading and dyslexia. *Proceedings of the National Academy of Sciences USA, 95*(15), 8939–8944.

Howard, D., Patterson, K., Wise, R., Brown, W.D., Friston, K., Weiller, C., and Frackowiak, R. (1992). The cortical localization of the lexicons. *Brain, 115,* 1769–1782.

Hynd, G.W., Hynd, C.R., Sullivan, H.G., and Kingsbury, T.B. (1987). Regional cerebral blood flow (rCBF) in developmental dyslexia: Activation during reading in a surface and deep dyslexic. *Journal of Learning Disabilities, 20,* 294–300.

Hynd, G.W., Semrud-Clikeman, M., Lorys, A.R., Novey, E.S., and Eliopulos, D. (1990). Brain morphology in developmental dyslexia and attention deficit disorder/hyperactivity. *Archives of Neurology, 47,* 919–926.

Indefrey, P., Kleinschmidt, A., Merboldt, K.D., Kruger, G., Brown, C., Hagoort, P., and Frahm, J. (1997). Equivalent responses to lexical and nonlexical visual stimuli in occipital cortex: a functional magnetic resonance imaging study. *Neuroimage, 5*(1), 78–81.

Jennings, J.M., McIntosh, A.R., Kapur, S., Tulving, E., and Houle, S. (1997). Cognitive subtractions may not add up: the interaction between semantic processing and response mode. *Neuroimage, 5*(3), 229–239.

Kapur, S., Craik, F.I.M., Tulving, E., Wilson, A.A., Houle, S.H., and Brown, G.M. (1994a). Neuroanatomical correlates of encoding in episodic memory: Levels of processing effect. *Proceedings of the National Academy of Sciences USA 91,* 2008–2011.

Kapur, S., Rose, R., Liddle, P.F., Zipursky, R.B., Brown, G.M., Stuss, D., Houle, S., and Tulving, E. (1994b). The role of the left prefrontal cortex in verbal processing: Semantic processing or willed action? *Neuroreport, 5,* 2193–2196.

Karni, A., Meyer, G., Jezzard, P., Adams, M.M., Turner, R., and Ungerleider, L.G. (1995). Functional MRI evidence for adult motor cortex plasticity during motor skill learning. *Nature, 377,* 155–158.

Klein, D., Milner, B., Zatorre, R.J., Meyer, E., and Evans, A.C. (1995). The neural substrates underlying word generation: A bilingual functional–imaging study. *Proceedings of the National Academy of Sciences USA, 92,* 2899–2903.

Kolb, B., and Whishaw, I.Q. (1990). *Fundamentals of Human Neuropsychology.* New York: Freeman.

Kwong, K.K., Belliveau, J.W., Chesler, D.A., Goldberg, I.E., Weisskoff, R.M., Poncelet, B.P., Kennedy, D.N., Hoppel, B.E., Cohen, M.S., Turner, R., Cheng, H.–M., Brady, T.J., and Rosen, B.R. (1992). Dynamic magnetic resonance imaging of human brain activity during primary sensory stimulation. *Proceedings of the National Academy of Sciences USA, 89,* 5675–5679.

Lee, A.T., Glover, G.H., and Meyer, C.H. (1995). Discrimination of large venous vessels in time-course spiral blood-oxygen-level-dependent magnetic-resonance functional neuroimaging. *Magnetic Resonance in Medicine, 33,* 745–754.

Lehmkuhle, S., Garzia, R.P., Turner, L., Hash, T., and Baro, J.A. (1993). A defective visual pathway in children with reading disability. *New England Journal of Medicine, 328,* 989–996.

Livingstone, M.S., Rosen, G.D., Drislane, F.W., and Galaburda, A.M. (1991). Physiological and anatomical evidence for a magnocellular defect in developmental dyslexia. *Proceedings of the National Academy of Sciences USA, 88,* 7943–7947.

Logan, C.G., and Grafton, S.T. (1995). Functional anatomy of human eyeblink conditioning determined with regional cerebral glucose metabolism and positron-emission tomography. *Proceedings of the National Academy of Sciences USA, 92,* 7500–7504.

Lye, R.H., O'Boyle, D.J., Ramsden, R.T., and Schady, W. (1988). Effects of a unilateral cerebellar lesion on the acquisition of eye-blink conditioning in man. *Journal of Physiology, 403,* 58.

Martin, A., Haxby, J.V., Lalonde, F.M., Wiggs, C.L., and Ungerleider, L.G. (1995). Discrete cortical regions associated with knowledge of color and knowledge of action. *Science, 270,* 102–105.

Martin, A., Wiggs, C.L., Ungerleider, L.G., and Haxby, J.V. (1996). Neural correlates of category-specific knowledge. *Nature, 379,* 649–652.

Mazoyer, B.M., Tzourio, N., Frak, V., Syrota, A., Murayama, N., Levrier, O., Salamon, G., Dehaene, S., Cohen, L., and Mehler, J. (1993). The cortical representation of speech. *Journal of Cognitive Neuroscience, 5,* 467–479.

McCarthy, G., Blamire, A.M., Rothman, D.L., Gruetter, R., and Shulman, R.G. (1993). Echo-planar magnetic resonance imaging studies of frontal cortex activation during word generation in humans. *Proceedings of the National Academy of Sciences USA, 90,* 4952–4956.

Menard, M.T., Kosslyn, S.M., Thompson, W.L., Alpert, N.M., and Rauch, S.L. (1996). Encoding words and pictures: a positron emission tomography study. *Neuropsychologia, 34*(3), 185–194.

Merigan, W.H., and Maunsell, J.H.R. (1993). How parallel are the primate visual pathways? *Annual Review of Neuroscience, 16,* 369–402.

Merzenich, M.M., Jenkins, W.M., Johnston, P., Schreiner, C., Miller, S.L., and Tallal, P. (1996). Temporal processing deficits of language-learning impaired children ameliorated by training. *Science, 271*(5245), 77–81.

Moseley, M.E., and Glover, G.H. (1995). Functional MR Imaging: Capabilities and limitations. *Neuroimaging Clinics of America, 5,* 161–191.

Ogawa, S., Lee, T.M., Nayak, A.S., and Glynn, P. (1990). Oxygenation-sensitive contrast in magnetic resonance image of rodent brain at high magnetic fields. *Magnetic Resonance in Medicine, 14,* 68–78.

Ogawa, S., Tank, D.W., Menon, R., Ellerman, J.M., Kim, S., Merkle, H., and Ugurbil, K. (1992). Intrinsic signal changes accompanying sensory stimulation: Functional brain mapping using MRI. *Proceedings of the National Academy of Sciences USA, 89,* 5951–5955.

Ojemann, G.A. (1983). Brain organization for language from the perspective of electrical stimulation mapping. *Behavioral and Brain Sciences, 6,* 89–206.

Ojemann, G.A., Ojemann, J., Lettich, E., and Berger, M. (1989). Cortical language localization in left, dominant hemisphere. An electrical stimulation mapping investigation in 117 patients. *Journal of Neurosurgery, 71,* 316–326.

Paulesu, E., Frith, C.D., and Frackowiak, R.S.J. (1993). The neural correlates of the verbal component of working memory. *Nature, 362,* 342–345.

Paulesu, E., Frith, U., Snowling, M., Gallagher, A., Morton, J., Frackowiak, R.S.J., and Frith, C.D. (1996). Is developmental dyslexia a disconnection syndrome? Evidence from PET scanning. *Brain,* 119, 143–157.

Petersen, S.E., Fox, P.T., Posner, M.I., Mintun, M., and Raichle, M.E. (1988). Positron emission tomographic studies of the cortical anatomy of single-word processing. *Nature, 331,* 585–589.

Petersen, S.E., Fox, P.T., Posner, M.I., Mintun, M., and Raichle, M.E. (1989). Positron emission tomographic studies of the processing of single words. *Journal of Cognitive Neuroscience, 1,* 153–170.

Petersen, S.E., Fox, P.T., Snyder, A.Z., and Raichle, M.E. (1990). Activation of extrastriate and frontal cortical areas by visual words and word-like stimuli. *Science, 249,* 1041–1044.

Poldrack, R.A., Desmond, J.E., Glover, G.H., and Gabrieli, J.D.E. (1998). The neural basis of visual skill learning: An fMRI study of mirror-reading. *Cerebral Cortex, 8,* 1–10.

Poldrack, R.A., Wagner, A.D., Prull, M., Desmond, J.E., Glover, G.H., and Gabrieli, J.D.E. (1999). Functional specialization for semantic and phonological processing in the left interior prefrontal cortex. *Neuroimage,* in press.

Price, C.J., Moore, C.J., Humphreys, G.W., and Wise, R.J.S. (1997). Segregating semantic from phonological processes during reading. *Journal of Cognitive Neuroscience, 9,* 727–733.

Price, C.J., Wise, R.J.S., Warburton, E.A., Moore, C.J., Howard, D., Patterson, K., Frackowiak, R.S.J., and Friston, K.J. (1996a). Hearing and saying: The functional neuro-anatomy of auditory word processing. *Brain, 119,* 919–931.

Price, C.J., Wise, R.J., and Frackowiak, R.S. (1996b). Demonstrating the implicit processing of visually presented words and pseudowords. *Cerebral Cortex, 6*(1), 62–70.

Price, C.J., Wise, R., Ramsay, S., Friston, K., Howard, D., Patterson, K., and Frackowiak, R.S.J. (1992). Regional response differences within the human auditory cortex when listening to words. *Neuroscience Letters, 146,* 179–182.

Price, C.J., Wise, R.J.S., Watson, J.D.G., Patterson, K., Howard, D., and Frackowiak, R.S.J. (1994). Brain activity during reading: The effects of exposure duration and task. *Brain, 117,* 1255–1269.

Pugh, K.R., Shaywitz, B.A., Shaywitz, S.E., Constable, R.T., Skudlarski, P., Fulbright, R.K., Bronen, R.A., Shankweiler, D.P., Katz, L., Fletcher, J.M., and Gore, J.C. (1996). Cerebral organization of component processes in reading. *Brain, 119,* 1221–1238.

Purpura, K., Kaplan, E., and Shapley, R.M. (1988). Background light and the contrast gain of primate P and M retinal ganglion cells. *Proceedings of the National Academy of Sciences USA, 85,* 4534–4537.

Raichle, M.E., Fiez, J.A., Videen, T.O., MacLeod, A.K., Pardo, J.V., Fox, P.E., and Petersen, S.E. (1994). Practice-related changes in human brain functional anatomy during nonmotor learning. *Cerebral Cortex, 4,* 8–26.

Raichle, M.E. (1987). Circulatory and metabolic correlates of brain function in normal humans. In F. Plum and V. Mountcastle (eds.), *The Handbook of Physiology* (v. 5, pp. 643–674). Bethesda, MD: American Physiological Association.

Rajkowska, G., and Goldman-Rakic, P.S. (1995). Cytoarchitectonic definition of prefrontal areas in the normal human cortex: II.Variability in locations of areas 9 and 46 and relationship to the Talairach coordinate system. *Cerebral Cortex, 5,* 323–337.

Rispens, J., van der Stege, H., and Bode, H. (1994). The clinical relevance of dyslexia subtype research. In K.P. van den Bos, L.S. Siegel, D.J. Bakker, and D.L. Share (eds.), *Current Directions in Dyslexia Research* (pp. 71–90). Lisse: Swets and Zeitlinger.

Rumsey, J.M., Horwitz, B., Donohue, B.C., Nace, K., Maisog, J.M., and Andreason, P. (1997a). Phonological and orthographic components of word recognition. A PET-rCBF study. *Brain, 120,* 739–759.

Rumsey, J.M., Nace, K., Donohue, B., Wise, D., Maisog, J.M., and Andreason, P. (1997b). A positron emission tomographic study of impaired word recognition and phonological processing in dyslexic men. *Archives of Neurology, 54*(5), 562–573.

Rumsey, J.M., Andreason, P., Zametkin, A.J., Aquino, T., King, A.C., Hamburger, S.D., Pikus, A., Rapoport, J.L., and Cohen, R.M. (1992). Failure to activate the left temporoparietal cortex in dyslexia. *Archives of Neurology, 49,* 527–534.

Rumsey, J.M., Andreason, P., Zametkin, A.J., King, A.C., Hamburger, S.D., Aquino, T., Hanahan, A.P., Pikus, A., and Cohen, R.M. (1994a). Right frontotemporal activation by tonal memory in dyslexia, and O-15 PET study. *Biological Psychiatry, 36,* 171–180.

Rumsey, J.M., Berman, K.F., Denckla, M.B., Hamburger, S.D., Kruesi, M.J., and Weinberger, D.R. (1987). Regional cerebral blood flow in severe developmental dyslexia. *Archives of Neurology, 44,* 1144–1150.

Rumsey, J.M., Dorwart, R., Vermess, M., Denckla, M.B., Kruesi, M.J.P., and Rapoport, I.L. (1986). Magnetic resonance imaging of brain anatomy in severe developmental dyslexia. *Archives of Neurology, 43,* 1045–1046.

Rumsey, J.M., Nace, K., Donohue, B., Wise, D., Maisog, J.M., and Andreason, P. (1997). A positron emission tomographic study of impaired word recognition and phonological processing in dyslexic men. *Archives of Neurology, 54,* 562–573.

Rumsey, J.M., Zametkin, A.J., Andreason, P., Hanahan, A.P., Hamburger, S.D., Aquino, T., King, A.C., Pikus, A., and Cohen, R.M. (1994b). Normal activation of frontotemporal language cortex in dyslexia, as measured with oxygen 15 positron emission tomography. *Archives of Neurology, 51*, 27–38.

Schlosser, M.J., Aoyagi, N., Fulbright, R.K., Gore, J.C., and McCarthy, G. (1998). Functional MRI studies of auditory comprehension. *Human Brain Mapping, 6*, 1–13.

Sergent, J., Zuck, E., Levesque, M., and MacDonald, B. (1992). Positron emission tomography study of letter and object processing: Empirical findings and methodological considerations. *Cerebral Cortex, 2*, 68–80.

Shallice, T., Fletcher, P., Frith, C.D., Grasby, P., Frackowiak, R.S.J., and Dolan, R.J. (1995). Brain regions associated with acquisition and retrieval of verbal episodic memory. *Nature, 368*, 633–635.

Shaywitz, B.A., Pugh, K.R., Constable, R.T., Shaywitz, S.E., Bronen, R.A., Fulbright, R.K., Shankweiler, D.P., Katz, L., Fletcher, J.M., Skudlarski, P., and Gore, J.C. (1995a). Localization of semantic processing using functional magnetic resonance imaging. *Human Brain Mapping, 2*, 149–158.

Shaywitz, B.A., Shaywitz, S.E., Pugh, K.R., Constable, R.T., Skudlarski, P., Fulbright, R.K., Bronen, R.A., Fletcher, J.M., Shankweiler, D.P., Katz, L., and Gore, J.C. (1995b). Sex differences in the functional organization of the brain for language. *Nature, 373*, 607–609.

Shaywitz, S.E., Shaywitz, B.A., Pugh, K.R., Fulbright, R.K., Constable, R.T., Mencl, W.E., Shankweiler, D.P., Liberman, A.M., Skudlarski, P., Fletcher, J.M., Katz, L., Marchione, K.E., Lacadie, C., Gatenby, C., and Gore, J.C. (1998). Functional disruption in the organization of the brain for reading in dyslexia. *Proceedings of the National Academy of Sciences USA, 95*(5), 2636–2641.

Siegel, L.S., Share, D., and Geva, E. (1995). Evidence for superior orthographic skills in dyslexics. *Psychological Science, 6*, 250–254.

Snyder, A.Z., Abdullaev, Y.G., Posner, M.I., and Raichle, M.E. (1995). Scalp electrical potentials reflect regional cerebral blood flow responses during processing of written words. *Proceedings of the National Academy of Sciences USA, 92*, 1689–1693.

Stein, J., and Walsh, V. (1997). To see but not to read; The magnocellular theory of dyslexia. *Trends in Neuroscience, 20*, 147–152.

Steinmetz, H., and Seitz, R.J. (1991). Functional anatomy of language processing: Neuroimaging and the problem of individual variability. *Neuropsychologia, 12*, 1149–1161.

Talairach, J., and Tournoux, P. (1988). *Co-planar Stereotaxic Atlas of the Human Brain.* Stuttgart: Thieme.

Talairach, J., Szikla, G., Tournoux, P., Prossalentis, A., Bordas-Ferrer, M., Covello,

L., Iacob, M., and Mempel, E. (1967). *Atlas d'Anatomie Stereotaxique due Telencephale.* Paris: Masson.

Tallal, P., Miller, S.L., Bedi, G., Byma, G., Wang, X., Nagarajan, S.S., Schreiner, C., Jenkins, W.M., and Merzenich, M.M. (1996). Language comprehension in language-learning impaired children improved with acoustically modified speech. *Science, 271*(5245), 81–84.

Tallal, P., Miller, S., and Fitch, R. (1993). Neurobiological basis of speech: A case for the preeminence of temporal processing. *Annals of the New York Academy of Sciences, 682*, 27–47.

Thompson-Schill, S.L., D'Esposito, M., Aguirre, G.K., and Farah, M.J. (1997). Role of left inferior prefrontal cortex in retrieval of semantic knowledge: a reevaluation. *Proceedings of the National Academy of Sciences U S A, 94*, 14792–14797.

Thulborn, K.R., Waterton, J.C., Matthews, P.M., and Radda, G.K. (1982). Oxygenation dependence of the transverse relaxation time of water protons in whole blood at high field. *Biochimica et Biophysica Acta, 714*, 265–270.

Tulving, E., Kapur, S., Craik, F.I.M., Moscovitch, M., and Houle, S. (1994). Hemispheric encoding/retrieval asymmetry in episodic memory: Positron emission tomography findings. *Proceedings of the National Academy of Sciences USA, 91*, 2016–2020.

Ungerleider, L.G., and Mishkin, M. (1982). Two cortical visual systems. In D.J. Ingle, M.A. Goodale, and R.J.W. Mansfield (eds.), *Analysis of Visual Behavior* (pp. 549–586). Cambridge, MA: MIT Press.

Vandenberghe, R., Price, C., Wise, R., Josephs, O., and Frackowiak, R.S. (1996). Functional anatomy of a common semantic system for words and pictures . *Nature, 383*(6597), 254–256.

Wagner, A.D., Schacter, D.L., Rotte, M., Koutstaal, W., Maril, A., Dale, A.M., Rosen, B.R., and Buckner, R.L. (1998). Building memories: remembering and forgetting of verbal experiences as predicted by brain activity [see comments]. *Science, 281*(5380), 1188–1191.

Wagner, A.D., Desmond, J.E., Demb, J.B., Glover, G.H., and Gabrieli, J.D.E. (1997). Semantic repetition priming for verbal and pictorial knowledge: A functional MRI study of left inferior prefrontal cortex. *Journal of Cognitive Neuroscience, 9* 714–726.

Wagner, R.K., and Torgesen, J.K. (1987). The nature of phonological processing and its causal role in the acquisition of reading skills. *Psychological Bulletin, 101*, 192–212.

Warburton, E., Wise, R.J., Price, C.J., Weiller, C., Hadar, U., Ramsay, S., and Frackowiak, R.S. (1996). Noun and verb retrieval by normal subjects. Studies with PET. *Brain, 119*(Pt 1), 159–179.

Watson, J.D.G., Myers, R., Frackowiak, R.S.J., Hajnal, J.V., Woods, R.P., Mazziotta, J.C., Shipp, S., and Zeki, S. (1993). Area V5 of the human brain: Evidence from a combined study using positron emission tomography and magnetic resonance imaging. *Cerebral Cortex, 3,* 79–94.

Williams, M.C., and Lovegrove, W. (1992). Sensory and perceptual processing in reading disability. In J. Brannan (ed.), *Applications of Parallel Processing in Vision* (pp. 263–302). Amsterdam: Elsevier Science Publishers.

Wise, R., Chollet, F., Hadar, U., Friston, K., Hoffner, E., and Frackowiak, R. (1991). Distribution of cortical neural networks involved in word comprehension and word retrieval. *Brain, 114,* 1803–1817.

Witton, C., Talcott, J.B., Hansen, P.C., Richardson, A.J., Griffiths, T.D., Rees, A., Stein, J.F., and Green, G.G. (1998). Sensitivity to dynamic auditory and visual stimuli predicts nonword reading ability in both dyslexic and normal readers. *Current Biology, 8,* 791–797.

Zatorre, R.J., Meyer, E., Gjedde, A., and Evans, A.C. (1996). PET studies of phonetic processing of speech: review, replication, and reanalysis. *Cerebral Cortex, 6,* 21–30.

Zatorre, R.J., Evans, A.C., Meyer, E., and Gjedde, A. (1992). Lateralization of phonetic and pitch discrimination in speech processing. *Nature, 256,* 846–849.

Appendix 9.1 Orthographic processing

Activated regions during orthographic processing across studies. Only activations relevant to the Petersen et al. (1990) and Howard et al. (1992) studies are given for the Price et al. (1994) study. Abbreviations: PET=positron emission tomography, fMRI=functional magnetic resonance imaging, L=left, R=right, B=bilateral, Inf=inferior, Post=posterior, Lat=lateral, Mid=middle, Med=medial, Occ=occipital, whole brain=the whole brain or most of brain (often excluding dorsal parietal and/or ventral temporal cortex and cerebellum) was imaged.

Study	Task comparison	Area imaged	Technique	Principle activations
Petersen et al 1988, 1989	word reading - fixation (covert response) (Note: 150 ms duration, 1/1 sec)	whole brain	PET	B striate, B extrastriate R inf lat occipital, L putamen
Petersen et al. 1990	1. word reading - fixation (covert response) 2. pseudowords (e.g., TWEAL) - fixation 3. letter strings (e.g., NLPFZ) - fixation 4. false fonts - fixation 5. words - false fonts 6. pseudowords - false fonts	whole brain	PET	1. B extrastriate, L med extrastriate 2. B extrastriate, L med extrastriate 3. B extrastriate 4. B extrastriate 5. L med extrastriate, L inf prefrontal 6. L med extrastriate
Howard et al. 1992 (Note: 1000 ms duration, 1/1.5 sec on avg.)	word reading - see false fonts and say 'crime' (overt response)	whole brain	PET	L post mid temporal L anterior cingulate L med extrastriate (Note: trend)
Price et al. 1994	1. word reading - false font feature decision (overt response) (both 150 and 981 ms duration) 2. word reading - view false fonts silently (covert response) (both 150 and 1000 ms duration)	whole brain	PET	1. L post lateral sulcus, striate L inf/mid frontal sulcus 2. B mid temporal L post lateral sulcus L inf/mid occipital sulcus L inf frontal

Study	Task / contrast	Region	Method	Activated areas
Kapur et al. 1995b	letter monitoring - semantic monitoring in words	whole brain	PET	B precuneus, B occipitotemporal
Bookheimer et al. 1995	words - random line drawing (silent viewing)	whole brain	PET	L inf temporal, L fusiform, L sup temporal, L inf pareital, B extrastriate, L inf frontal
Shaywitz et al. 1995a	letter-string case judgment - line orientation judgment	3 axial slices (z=-5,10,20)	fMRI	B extrastriate
Menard et al. 1996	words - x's (silent viewing)	whole brain	PET	L medial extrastriate, L inf frontal gyrus, L angular gyrus
Price et al. 1996b	1. letters - false fonts (silent viewing)	whole brain	PET	1. L fusiform, L lateral extrastriate
	2. words - false fonts (silent viewing)			2. medial extrastriate (cuneus), L inf frontal gyrus, B mid temporal
Pugh et al. 1996	1. letter-string case judgement - line orientation judgement	3 axial slices (z=-8,8,20)	fMRI	1. B lateral extrastriate
	2. category judgement - nonword rhyme judgement			2. B medial extrastriate
Beauregard et et al. 1997	1. concrete words - fixation (silent viewing)	whole brain	PET	1. L extrastriate, L mid temporal, L occipito-temporal, L inf frontal, L inf temporal
	2. abstract words - fixation (silent viewing)			2. L striate, L mediate extrastriate, L mid temporal, L inf frontal, L inf temporal
	3. emotional words - fixation (silent viewing)			3. L medial extrastriate, L mid temporal, L inf frontal

Appendix 9.2 Phonological Processing

Activated regions during phonological processing across studies. Abbreviations: Ant=anterior, Sup=superior, hemis=hemisphere, lat=lateral, SMG=supramarginal gyrus, SMA=supplementary motor area, Heschl's=Heschl's gyrus (primary auditory cortex), Wernicke's=Wernicke's area, Broca's=Broca's area, > =greater than. (other abbreviations are same as in appendix 9.1.)

Study	Task comparison	Area imaged	Technique	Principle Activations
Petersen et al. 1988, 1989	word perception (auditory) - fixation (silence)	whole brain	PET	B primary auditory, L ant sup temporal, L temporoparietal, L inf anterior cingulate
Petersen et al. 1989	rhyme judgments - passive viewing of word pairs (e.g., weigh-they)	L temp/par analysis	PET	L temporoparietal
Wise et al. 1991	1. pseudowords (auditory) - rest 2. word presentation rate effect (about 28 or 52 words per minute)	whole brain	PET	1. B B Heschl's, B sup temporal gyri 2. B sup temporal (except Wernicke's) bias to input (i.e., increase with increasing presentation rate) L sup post temporal (Wernicke's) no bias to input
Demonet et al. 1992, 1994b	1. phonological monitoring task (sequential, ambiguous) with nonwords - tone monitoring 2. phonological monitoring task with nonwords - semantic monitoring task with word pairs	whole brain	PET	1. L sup temporal, B mid temporal L Broca's 2. L SMG, L Motor

Study	Task/Contrast	Coverage	Method	Results
Howard et al. 1992	word repetition (auditory) - hear nonwords and say 'crime' (overt response)	whole brain	PET	L sup/mid temporal R striate/cuneus
Price et al. 1992	parametric study of varying presentation rate for auditory words (0, 10, 30, 50, 70, and 90 words per minute)	whole brain	PET	B sup temporal (except Wernicke's) linear increase with increasing presentation rate L sup post temporal (Wernicke's) increase during words not dependent on presentation rate
Sergent et al. 1992	letter-sound task (rhyme decision) - letter-spatial task (orientation decision)	whole brain	PET	L inf/mid frontal, L orbital frontal caudate, L mid temporal
Zatorre et al. 1992	1. passive presentation of speech syllables - noise bursts 2. phonetic judgments - passive processing of auditory speech syllables	whole brain	PET	1. L inf frontal, B sup temporal L post sup temporal 2. L Broca's, L sup parietal, cingulate R striate, L inf temporal gyrus
Mazoyer et al. 1993	word perception (auditory) - rest (silence)	whole brain	PET	L inf frontal (Broca's) B sup temporal
Binder et al. 1994b	phoneme discrimination task - rest (silence) parametric variation of presentation rate (.17-2.5 Hz0)	1 sagittal slice in both hemis. (13 mm from lat. surface)	fMRI	B Heschl's B sup temporal gyri and sulci nonlinear, monotonically increasing signal with increasing presentation rate
Binder et al. 1994b	1. words (auditory) - rest 2. pseudowords (e.g, narb) (auditory) - rest 3. noise - rest	1 sagittal slice in both hemis. (8 mm from lat. surface)	fMRI	1. B dorsal sup temporal gyri/sulci B mid temporal, R mid frontal 2. B dorsal sup temporal gyri/sulci B mid temporal, R mid frontal 3. B dorsal sup temporal (Heschl's)

Study	Task	Coverage	Method	Results
Demonet et al. 1994a	phonological monitoring tasks in nonwords - tone monitoring task (4 stimulus types) 1. nonsequential, unambigious target 2. nonsequential, ambigious target 3. sequential, unambigious target 4. sequential ambigious target	whole brain	PET	1. B sup temporal (Wernicke's) posterior cingulate 2. L sup temporal (Wernicke's) L fusiform, L inf temporal L motor, posterior cingulate 3. L sup temporal (Wernicke's) 4. B sup temporal (Wernicke's) L frontal (Broca's) L inf temporal, L motor
Shaywitz et al. 1995a	rhyme-judgment with pseudowords - letter-case judement case with consonant strings	3 axial slices ($z = -5, 10, 20$)	fMRI	inf frontal gyrus (L for males, B for females) sup and mid temporal
Shaywitz et al. 1995b	generation to phonemic cue - generation to semantic cue (covert response)	2 axial slices ($z = 0, 8$)	fMRI	L ant temporal lobe L insular cortex
Klein et al. 1995	generation to phonological cue - word repetition (overt response)	whole brain	PET	L prefrontal, L sup frontal L inf temporal, L post parietal R cerebellum
Fiez et al. 1995	1. auditory detection task - fixation (e.g., words, syllables, steady-state vowels, tone triplets) 2. linguistic stimulus effect (e.g., words, syllables, steady-state vowels) 3. rapid-temporal-modulation stimulus effect (e.g., tone triplets, words, syllables)	1 to 4 whole brain	PET	1. B sup temporal, B frontal operculum, SMA 2. R post sup temporal 3. L frontal operculum

Study	Task / contrast	Method	Results
	4. task effect: detection - passive listening ascending letter or long vowel discrimination on visual or auditory words - fixation		4. L sup temporal, B frontal operculum, SMA
	5. task effect: long vowel task > ascending letter task	5 and 6 frontal analysis	5. L frontal operculum
	6. presentation modality effect: auditory versus visual stimuli		6. no detectable change
Pugh et al. 1996	rhyme judgment - letter case judgment	3 axial slices (z=-8,8,20) ROI analysis	fMRI	L inf frontal gyrus, B lateral orbital gyrus, B dorsolateral prefrontal, B mid temporal gyrus, B sup temporal gyrus
Warburton et al. 1996	1. passive word listening - rest	whole brain	PET	1. B sup temporal sulcus, L inf frontal sulcus, R anterior insula
	2. silent repetition of auditory pseudowords - rest		2. B sup temporal sulcus, L inf frontal gyrus/operculum/ant insula, L inf temporal gyrus, L motor cortex, R temporal operculum, R ant insula
Price et al. 1996a	1. passive word listening - rest	whole brain	PET	1. B sup temporal gyrus
	2. passive word listening - passive reversed speech listening		2. L inf frontal gyrus, L sup temporal gyrus, L mid temporal gyrus, R inf temporal sulcus
Fiez et al. 1996	1. words (auditory) - rest	whole brain, PET ROI analysis based on previous data	1. L temporoparietal, B auditory cortex
	2. pseudowords (auditory) - rest		2. L temporoparietal, B auditory cortex

Study	Task	Coverage	Method	Activation
Zatorre et al. 1996	1. phonetic discrimination - passive word listening 2. phonetic monitoring - passive word listening	whole brain	PET	1. L inf frontal gyrus 2. L inf frontal gyrus, L precentral gyrus, L supramarginal gyrus, L cerebellum, B occipital, L fusiform
Dhankar et al. 1997	auditory word presentation - rest parametrically varying presentation rate analysis	2 or 4 axial slices - ROI based on anatomy	fMRI	B primary and secondary auditory cortex increased in activation with rate up to 90 words/minute
Rumsey et al. 1997	pseudoword homophone decision (decide which pseudoword sounds like a real word) - fixation	whole brain	PET	L inf frontal, L insula, L lingual, L fusiform, L inf temporal, B inf parietal, B postcentral, L cingulate, R cerebellum, R thalamus
Herbster et al. 1997	read pseudoword - read word	whole brain	PET	L inf frontal
Price et al. 1997	syllable counting - semantic decision (visual presentation)	whole brain	PET	B supramarginal gyrus, R angular gyrus, L precentral gyrus, L occipital
Schlosser et al. 1998	1. auditory English sentences - auditory Turkish sentences (subjects were non Turkish speakers) 2. auditory English sentences - frequency sweeps	7 axial slices or 7 coronal slices	fMRI	1. B sup temporal sulcus, L inf frontal 2. L sup temporal sulcus, L inf frontal

Appendix 9.3 Semantic Processing

Activated regions during semantic processing across studies. Abbreviations: sag=sagittal, AG=angular gyrus, (other abbreviations are same as in appendices 9.1 and 9.2) Studies used visually presented stimuli unless otherwise noted.

Study	Task comparision	Area imaged	Technique	Principal activations
Petersen et al. 1988, 1989	verb generation - noun repetition (overt response)	whole brain	PET	L prefrontal, anterior cingulate R cerebellum
Petersen et al. 1989	semantic monitoring - passive wordq proessing (number of targets = 1/40 or 20/40)	frontal analysis	PET	L prefrontal, anterior cingulate (anterior cingulate increases with increasing number of targets)
Wise et al. 1991	1. verb generation - rest (covert response, slower presentation than Petersen et al, 1988, 1989)	whole brain	PET	1. L temporal (Wernicke's), L frontal (Broca's), SMA
	2. noun-noun semantic comparison - rest			2. B Heschl's, B sup temporal (trends in L Broca's and SMA)
	3. verb-noun semantic comparison - rest			3. B Heschl's, B sup temporal (trends in L Broca's and SMA)
Demonet et al. 1992, 1994a	1. semantic monitoring with words - tone monitoring	whole brain	PET	1. L temporal (widespread) L SMG/AG, L prefrontal L sup prefrontal
	2. semantic monitoring with words - phoneme monitoring with pseudowords			2. B AG, L sup prefrontal posterior cingulate, L mid temporal
McCarthy et al. 1993	1. verb generation (overt response) - rest	axial slice (z=-8mm) L prefrontal analysis	fMRI	1. L inf frontal (also some R-sided)
	2. verb generation (covert response) - rest			2. less/no response
	3. noun repetition - rest			3. less/no response

Study	Task	Coverage	Method	Regions
Raichle et al. 1994	verb generation - noun repetion (overt response, slower presentation than Petersen et al. 1988, 1989)	whole brain	PET	L prefrontal, anterior cingulate L post temporal, R cerebellum
Kapur et al. 1994a,b	semantic monitoring - letter monitoring in words	whole brain	PET	L prefrontal
Shallice et al. 1994, Fletcher et al. 1995	paired-associate encoding during easy distractor - during difficult distractor	whole brain	PET	L prefrontal, retrosplenial
Shaywitz et al. 1995a	semantic category judgments with word pairs - rhyme judgments with pseudoword pairs	3 axial slices (z=-5,10,20)	fMRI	sup and mid temporal gyri
Shaywitz et al. 1995b	generation task to semantic cue - generation to phonemic cue (covert response)	2 axial slices (z=0,8)	fMRI	B inf frontal, L post temporal R occipital
Binder et al. 1995	semantic monitoring - tone monitoring	2 sag slices in each hemi	fMRI	L lateral frontal L temporal-parietal-occipital junction
Klein et al. 1995	synonym generation - word repetition (overt response)	whole brain	PET	L prefrontal, L sup frontal L inf temporal, L post parietal midline occipital, anterior cingulate R cerebellum
Demb et al. 1995, Gabrieli et al, 1996	semantic monitoring - letter case monitoring (letter task less difficult than semantic)	2 coronal slices (y=32,29)	fMRI	L prefrontal, L sup frontal L anterior cingulate
Demb et al. 1995	semantic monitoring - letter alphabetic decision (letter task more difficult than semantic)	2-3 coronal slices (y=32,39,46)	fMRI	L prefrontal, L sup frontal

Study	Task	Imaging region	Modality	Results
Desmond et al. 1995	semantic judgement - letter case judment (epileptic patients undergoing Wada testing)	2 coronal slices (y=32,39)	fMRI	lateralization of inf frontal activation correlated with Wada outcome
Martin et al. 1995	1. color word generation - object naming 2. action word generation - object naming	whole brain	PET	1. L mid frontal gyrus, L orbitofrontal, L inf parietal gyrus, B fusiform, L parahippocampal, R thalamus 2. L inf frontal gyrus, L mid frontal gyrus, L inf parietal gyrus, L mid temporal gyrus, L sup temporal gyrus, R cerebellum
Binder et al. 1995	semantic monitoring - tone frequency monitoring (auditory presentation)	2 sagittal slices (1 in each hemisphere)	fMRI	L inf frontal gyrus, L precentral, L mid temporal gyrus, L angular gyrus L occipito-temporal
Pugh et al. 1996	semantic judgment - letter case judgment ROI analysis	3 axial slices (z=-8,8,20),	fMRI	L inf frontal gyrus, B lateral orbital gyrus, B dorsolateral prefrontal, B mid temporal gyrus, B sup temporal gyrus, B medial extrastriate
Vandenberghe et al. 1996	category matching task - size judgment task	whole brain	PET	L inf frontal gyrus, L mid temporal gyrus, L inf temporal gyrus, L fusiform, L parietal-temporal, L sup occipital, L hippocampus, vermis, R cerebellum
Binder et al. 1996a	semantic judgment - tone frequency judgment (auditory presentation)	3 sagittal slices in left hemisphere	fMRI	L sup temporal sulcus, L mid temporal gyrus, L inf temporal gyrus, L inf frontal gyrus, L angular gyrus

Study	Task	Coverage	Method	Activations
Binder et al. 1996b	semantic judgment - tone frequency judgment (auditory presentation)	whole brain	fMRI	L sup temporal sulcus, L mid temporal gyrus, L inf temporal fusiform/parahippocampal gyri, L inf gyrus, L mid frontal gyrus, L sup frontal gyrus, B angular gyrus, L posterior cingulate/retrosplenial, L caudate/thalamus, R cerebellum
Warburton et al. 1996	1. verb-noun comparison - rest; 2. verb generation - rest (common activations across expts. 1-4)	whole brain	PET	1. B sup temporal sulcus, L inf frontal sulcus, R mid lateral sulcus, thalamus; 2. L mid temporal gyrus, L inf frontal/operculum, R sup temporal sulcus, R ant insula
Jennings et al. 1997	semantic judgment - letter judgment: partial least squares analysis for semantic component common to all response modes	whole brain	PET	L inf frontal gyrus, L orbitofrontal, L occipital, R ant cingulate, R cerebellum
Thompson-Schill et al. 1997	1. verb generation: items w/ dominant response - items without dominant response; 2. semantic comparison by specific attribute - semantic comparison by global similarity; 3. object classification by single attribute - classification by multiple attributes	whole brain	fMRI	1. L inf frontal gyrus, L SMA/cingulate; 2. L inf frontal, B mid frontal, L SMA/cingulate, L mid temporal, L inf temporal, L occipital; 3. B inf frontal gyrus, L SMA/cingulate, L inf temporal, L sup parietal
Wagner et al. 1998	semantic judgment - lettercase judgment	whole brain	fMRI	L inf frontal, L parahippocampal, L fusiform

Appendix 9.4 Other Verbal Tasks

Activated regions during verbal tasks other than those in appendices 9.1 to 9.3. Abbreviations: DLPFC=dorsolateral prefrontal cortex, 4T=4 Tesla magnet (unlike other studies that typically used 1.5 Tesla magnets)(other abbreviations are the same as in appendices 9.1 to 9.3)

Study	Task comparison	Area imaged	Technique	Principal activations
Frith et al. 1991a Friston et al 1991	lexical decision - counting and verbal fluency	whole brain	PET	B sup temporal, L frontal R prefrontal
Frith et al. 1991a, 1991b Friston et al 1991	word generation (letter cue) - counting and lexical decision or repeating words (overt response)	whole brain	PET	L DLPFC, L parahippocampal gyrus L parietal, B anterior cingulate
Hinke et al. 1993	word generation (letter cue) - rest (covert response)	2-3 axial slices	fMRI (4T)	L Broca's area
Price et al. 1994	1. lexical decision - false font feature decision (both 150 and 1000 ms duration) 2. lexical decision - reading aloud (both 150 and 1000 ms duration)	whole brain	PET	1. striate, L hippocampus, L insula SMA, L premotor, B DLPFC 2. SMA, B DLPFC
Buckner et al. 1995	word stem completion (unprimed) - fixation (overt response)	whole brain	PET	L frontal opercular B extrastriate, L rolandic cerebellum, SMA
Rumsey et al. 1997	lexical decision - fixation	whole brain	PET	L inf frontal, L lingual gyrus, B fusiform, R cerebellum,B inf parietal, B postcentral, L precentral, L thalamus, L lentiform, L cingulate

Appendix 9.5 Studies of developmental dyslexia

Activated regions in subjects with developmental dyslexia and control subjects during different language/control tasks and functional imaging methods. Abbreviations: Dys=dyslexics, Con=control subjects, > =greater activation than, < = less activation than, +r = positively correlated, C-V=consonant-vowel, IQ=intelligence quotient, rCBF=regional cerebral blood flow, ^{133}X=133-Xenon, rCMRglc=regional cerebral glucose metabolism rate, FDG=[F-18] 2-fluoro-2-deoxyglucose, $H_2{}^{15}O$=radioactive water, ROIS=regions of interest, LH=left hemisphere, RH=right hemisphere, CPT=Continuous Performance Test (other abbreviations are the same as in appendices 9.1 to 9.4)

Study	Task or task comparison	Area imaged/ comparison	Technique	Group activation differences
Rumsey et al. 1987	1. semantic classification task 2. spatial relations line orientation task (difficult) 3. number matching task (easy)	whole brain LH vs. RH Anterior vs. Posterior	rCBF ^{133}X	1. dys - increased LH>RH asymmetry 2. dys - smaller Ant/Post difference 3. no detectable group differences
Hynd et al. 1987	read narrative text - rest	whole brain/ LH vs. RH	rCBF ^{133}X	surface dys - less RH activation deep dys - lower B activation
Flowers et al 1991	orthographic task (listen to nouns and respond to 4-letter words	whole brain/ 8 ROIS	rCBF ^{133}X	good readers - task accuracy +r with Wernicke's area activation poor readers - displaced activation in temporoparietal area with no r with task accuracy
Gross-Glenn et al. 1991	read aloud written words every 5 secs.	whole brain/ lobes and hemispheres lobule analysis	PET rCMRglc FDG	dys - lower RH frontal activation con - occipital LH>RH dys -occipital LH=RH dys -less RH>LH prefrontal asymmetry con - LH>RH in Lingual lobule

Study	Task	Region	Method	Results
Rumsey et al. 1992	1. rest	whole brain/ 49 ROIS	PET $H_2^{15}O$	dys - RH>LH in Lingual lobule; dys>con in Lingual lobule 1. con> dys in R sylvian; dys>con in med-frontal
	2. rhyme task (auditory words) - rest			2. con>dys in L AG, L mid temporal, L post frontal, R ant frontal; dys>con in L rolandic, R mid temporal; dys - L parietal +r with verbal IQ
	3. tone task (CPT) - rest			3. dys - L ant temporal
Hagman et al. 1992	C-V auditory syllable detection	whole brain	PET rCMRglc FDG	dys>con in B med temporal lobe (gray and white matter)
Rumsey et al. 1994a	1. rest	whole brain/ 49 ROIS	PET $H_2^{15}O$	1. con>dys in L par (AG/SMG area)
	2. syntax test (auditory sentences) - rest			2. con>dys in L par (Note:trend), med occip; dys>con in R ant and med frontal; con - LH>RH in parietal region; dys - RH>LH in parietal region; con - increased LH>RH asymmetry in ant temporal/inf frontal +r with task performance

Rumsey et al. 1994b	1. rest	whole brain/ 49 ROIS	PET $H_2^{15}O$	1. dys -reduced L parietal
	2. tonal memory task (matching) - rest (more difficult than phoneme or syntax tasks in Rumsey et al., 1992; 1994a)			2. con>dys in R mid temporal, 2 R frontal regions
Eden et al. 1996	coherently moving random dot pattern - fixation	surface coils over occipital region - ROI analysis of area MT/V5	fMRI	con>dys in B MT/V5
Rumsey et al. 1997	1. pseudoword pronounciation - fixation	whole brain $H_2^{15}O$	PET	1. con>dys in B inf parietal (SMG), B sup temporal, B med temporal, B fusiform, B precuneus, R pre/postcentral, L orbitofrontal, R uncus dys>con in L lingual/fusiform, B insula, L pre/postcentral, L thalamus, B cerebellum
	2. irregular word pronounciation - fixation			2. con>dys in L inf parietal (SMG), R precuneus, B fusiform, B mid temporal, L sup temporal, R pre/postcentral, L inf frontal, L medial frontal, L cingulate dys>con in L post cingulate, B insula, L pre/postcentral, R orbitofrontal, R thalamus, L cerebellum

	Tasks	Method/Area	Results
	3. pseudoword homophone decision (decide which pseudoword sounds like a real word) - fixation		3. con>dys in L inf parietal (SMG), L precuneus, R mid temporal/AG, B fusiform, B mid temporal, L uncus, L cingulate, R subcallosal white matter dys>con in L inf occipital, L post cingulate, L medial temporal, R insula, R sup frontal, R midfrontal, B cerebellum, B caudate
	4. lexical decision - fixation		4. con>dys in L SMG, L inf temporal/fusiform, B mid temporal, B sup temporal, B uncus, R insula, L inf frontal, L cingulate dys>con in R mid frontal, L cerebellum, B caudate, R thalamus
Paulesu et al. 1997	1. consonant rhyme judgment - shape similarity judgment 2. short-term memory for consonants - short-term memory for visual forms	whole brain PET H$_2$^{15}O	1. con>dys in L sup temporal, L premotor, SMA, L insula, R striatum 2. con>dys in L inf frontal, L SMG, L premotor, L insula, L SMA, cerebellum, R inf frontal, R insula
Shaywitz et al. 1998	5 tasks: line orientation judgment, lettercase judgment, single-letter rhyme judgment, nonword rhyme judgment, semantic judgment	whole brain ROI analysis of activated pixels in selected regions	fMRI con>dys in sup temporal gyrus, angular gyrus, striate cortex dys>con in inferior frontal gyrus

Reference	Task	Analysis	Method	Results
Horwitz et al. 1998	1. pseudoword reading 2. exception word reading	whole brain, correlation analysis of left hemi with left angular gyrus	PET H$_2$^{15}O	1. con>dys: correlation of L AG with inf frontal, cerebellum, mid temporal, inf temporal, sup tempo ral, occipital gyrus, fusiform gyrus 2. con>dys: correlation of L AG with lingual gyrus, cerebellum, fusiform gyrus, sup temporal, mid frontal, inf frontal
Demb et al. 1997, 1998b	low mean luminance, moving sine wave grating at several contrasts - gray field	8 slices, posterior cortex, ROI analysis of MT+, VI and other early visual areas	fMRI	con>dys on contrast response in MT+, VI, and other areas combined group showed correlation between reading rate and activity in MT+, VI and other areas

10
Brain Circuitry During Reading

Michael I. Posner
Bruce D. McCandliss

Almost immediately after your eyes land on each word of this page, patterns of neural activation enable you to access precise information about their meaning and pronunciation. Somehow—through years of careful attention, practice, and learning—we have developed specialized neural circuits that allow us to rapidly access linguistic information through gazing at static visual-othrographic forms. This chapter focuses on how researchers can combine neuroimaging methods within cognitive investigations that center on how this neural circuitry is organized to support reading skill in the normal adult and how this circuitry might be created and modified by attention, practice, and learning.

PET and fMRI research described in the last chapter has been used to draw associations between particular brain regions and cognitive processes associated with orthographic, phonological and semantic information critical to word reading. This chapter reviews recent work that investigates the dynamics of neural activations in real time, during the few hundred milliseconds it takes to read a visual word. We use the term *neural circuitry* to describe the time dynamic interactions between brain areas that support a complex mental skill such as reading. We examine how investigations of the real-time neural activations can lead to insights into the functional organization of reading circuitry in adults, how this neural circuitry can be modified by learning and practice to facilitate processing, and how the organization of this circuitry changes over the course of reading skill development.

At the very outset of considering the time course of a cognitive act such as word recognition, it is critical to establish benchmarks for how long such a process takes in the skilled adult reader. A great deal of information about the time course of reading visual words has been provided by studies that examine eye movements in real time during reading (Rayner and Pollatsek, 1992; Reichle, Pollatsek, Fisher, and Rayner, 1998: Rayner, chapter 1, this volume). Findings from this literature provide important upper limits concerning the amount of time needed for a visual word to activate cortical areas related to stored information about words. During each fixation a skilled reader obtains semantic information from only one or two words. These fixations only last 275 ms. on average. After a fixation starts, the amount of time that elapses before the eye moves on is systematically influenced by the length, meaning and frequency of the word being fixated (Rayner, this volume; Rayner and Pollatsek, 1992; Sereno, Pacht, and Rayner, 1992). The influence of these psychological factors on the duration of eye fixations during reading provides important constraints on the time course of the initial onset of cortical activations related to visual and semantic processes outlined by Demb, Poldrack, and Gabrieli (chapter 9, this volume). Unfortunately, most methods for mapping the spatial organization of brain activity in the human cortex rely on hemodynamic responses which unfold over many seconds, and that makes it difficult to draw strong links between insights from fine-grained temporal studies of reading behavior and brain activity in the normal adult.

The next section describes how methods based on scalp electrical recording can be related to areas of blood-flow change, and how together these two approaches can address issues of real-time activation of cortical areas. These validation studies usually involve simple visual features. We show how these same methods can be applied to the task of reading visual words to reveal information about the time course of activation related to processing the visual and semantic features of words. A great deal of ERP research has demonstrated that the electrical signals recorded at the scalp can be used to trace on-line processes related to integrating word and sentence meanings (see Kutas and Van Petten, 1994 for a review of N400 studies). The discussion here focuses specifically on semantic effects in ERP paradigms that are specifically designed to converge with neuroimaging and chronometric studies of accessing the meanings of individual words. These ERP paradigms provide a link between the temporal precision of chronometric approaches and anatomical precision of the neuroimaging approaches, and together these methods can be used to trace parts of the neural circuitry of reading.

The final section considers how the circuitry involved in word reading changes with experience. On a short time scale this can be examined by looking at how something read a moment ago can influence the brain's response to a visual word (priming). On a slightly longer time scale we examine changes in cortical activations that take place as several weeks of training transform novel words into high-frequency items well integrated into a subject's lexicon. Finally, on a longer time scale, we examine how cortical responses to visual words are influenced by familiarity and orthographic structure at different points in literacy development. These studies attempt to investigate the plasticity of the circuitry involved in reading.

Anatomy to Circuitry

To understand how reading is achieved in the brain it is important to study the time course of activation of the various anatomical areas involved. This requires a method of linking the time course of mental activity with brain activation. PET and fMRI imaging methods rely on measures of hemodynamics (vascular changes) that are physiologically related to electrical activity in the circuits that support mental activity. Although hemodynamic measures lag several seconds behind the neuronal activity that cause them, electrical measures such as ERP do not suffer such a delay. By combining these methods, we have attempted to relate spatially localized cortical changes in hemodynamics to changes in brain electrical activity measured at the scalp.

Methods

To study brain electrical activity, we have used high-density scalp recordings from normal subjects (Tucker et al., 1994). Event related potentials (ERPs) are stimulus-locked averages of the electroencephalogram (EEG) averaged across many presentations of stimuli. The use of ERPs has a long history in cognitive studies (see Hillyard and Anllo-Vento, 1998 for a recent review). These measures provide a continuous record, obtained simultaneously at many different scalp locations, of electrical changes related to on-going cognitive processing. ERP recordings reflect electrical signals produced by activity from cortical areas; however, accurate localization of these sources is difficult for many reasons. For the weak electrical signals produced by any set of neurons to be recorded at the scalp, they must be positioned in a way that allow them to summate to create electric fields that can be conducted through brain tissue, skull, and scalp. (Gevins, 1996). Additionally, any one scalp signature could be consistent with a number of proposed sources if no additional constraints are available. One approach to addressing the difficulties of identifying the cortical areas (generators) that might gives rise to the recorded electrical activity at the scalp is to use the anatomy provided by PET or fMRI studies to help constrain the problem.

An additional complication is that there is no guarantee that the activity of any particular area found active in a PET (or fMRI) study can be observed through electrical recordings at the scalp's surface. Whether the sets of neurons producing the PET signal have an influence that can be detected at the scalp depends on whether they are oriented in a way that allows the current to reach the scalp electrodes. It is largely an empirical matter whether any particular brain area that changes in blood flow during a cognitive task will also produce electrical changes that can be recorded at the scalp.

To increase the likelihood of detecting electrical activations that result in blood flow changes from scalp electrodes, it is important to have available a good sampling of the scalp electrical field. To accomplish this, we have used a geodesic electrode net (Tucker, 1993) that contains 128 electrodes (64 in the prototype version). Each electrode is in the form of a tube of saline solution (see figure 10.1). A sponge at the bottom of each tube rests against the scalp and maintains electrical contact with it. The net is easily applied, and its geodesic shape and elastic tension can be adjusted to conform comfortably to the geometry of each subject's skull. Landmarks on the skull are used as markers to adjust the net in a standard way for each individual.

The signal from each electrode is amplified and the voltage is sampled every 4 or 8 ms and converted to digital form. The samples taken following each stimulus in a category are then averaged. For example, if we are looking at the ERP to the presentation of words, all trials containing words are averaged together, providing an average electrical signal at each time point from 200 ms before presentation of the word to 800 ms after presentation. When the average is computed, the parts of the electrical activity that are not time locked to the word presentation are averaged out. The final average waveform thus represents a near millisecond resolution record of the electrical activity produced in response to the words. We are usually interested in how these average waveforms differ in response to different stimuli. For example, if we want to know when the electrical responses first show evidence of a difference in processing between words and consonant strings, we can compare the two average waveforms recorded at each of the electrode sites time point by time point to find out when they begin to depart from each other and what the scalp signature of that difference looks like and how it changes over time as processing proceeds from recognition to response. In the next section we will turn to issues of relating scalp signatures of such effects to their underlying cortical areas.

Validation

Both PET and fMRI studies began with retinotopic mapping as a means of determining whether blood flow tracks neuronal activity (Fox, Mintun, Raichle, and Miezin, 1986; Schneider, Noll, and Cohen, 1993). In a similar manner the most convincing studies relating anatomical areas active in PET and fMRI studies to time dynamic changes in scalp electrical activity have examined areas of the visual system.

In one such study (Clark and Hillyard, 1996) patterned visual stimuli were presented rapidly to each visual field. Attention was directed either to the left or right visual field in separate blocks of trials. Several important components of the event related potential were analyzed in an attempt to locate the source of the electrical activity. Results of these source localization efforts indicated that a very early potential starting at 50 ms was located within primary visual cortex. The relatively early latency of this ERP effect and the fact that this effect was not modified by attention, (at least under conditions of a relatively empty visual field), fit well with data from cellular recording in the primary visual cortex. A second component (P1) was modified by attention and appeared to come from lateral extrastriate cortex.

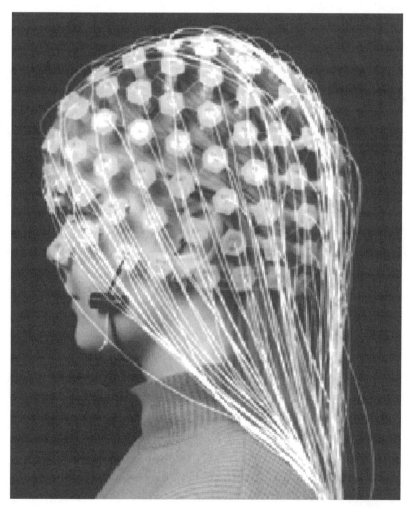

Figure 10.1 A 128-channel geodesic sensory net after Tucker, 1993.

Another study compared PET directly with the scalp signatures found from electrical recording (Heinze et al., 1994). Once again visual stimuli were presented to the left or right visual field and subjects were required to monitor for targets. Separate blocks of attend-left and attend-right allowed the authors to examine the influence of the stimulus separately from its modification by visual attention. The PET study showed that subtraction of the attended from the unattended events produced a single generator along the fusiform gyrus of the attended hemisphere. This extrastriate brain area is in the part of the visual system involved in recognition of object identity. It lies close to areas that have been shown to be selectively activated by letters and words in PET and cellular recording studies (Petersen et al., 1990; Nobre and McCarthy, 1994). As in many previous studies, attention to the stimulus modulates blood flow within the brain areas apparently carrying out the computation. The ERP data showed that attention modulated the P1 component of the ERP, starting at about 80 ms. The authors used an algorithm developed by Scherg in Germany (Scherg and Berg, 1993) to obtain point sources of electrical activity that best fit the obtained distribution of potentials recorded at the scalp from 80 to 120 ms after the stimulus. These sources (generators) of electrical activity were also located on the fusiform gyrus of the hemisphere opposite the stimulus, but somewhat more anterior than the area of PET activation.

One extrastriate area that has been well characterized from cellular studies in the monkey is an area sensitive to visual motion. PET studies have located a similar bilateral area in human beings (de Jong et al., 1994). When scalp electrical activity was induced by fast motion, the ERPs were found first in the motion specific area of the temporal lobe. When changes were induced by slowly moving stimuli, the ERPs indicated that the earliest effects were in primary visual cortex (Ffytche, Guy, and Zeki 1995). These studies show how ERPs can be used to complement PET data and provide information on the speed of input to particular brain systems.

All these studies provide evidence of the ability to relate electrical activity recorded from the scalp to anatomical data provided by neuroimaging and single-cell recording methods. These studies involve relatively simple sensory and cognitive activity. To get adequate characterization of the putative generator of scalp electrical activity, it is important that the number of generators active during any temporal epoch be rather few. One way to accomplish this is to use very simple stimuli and tasks. Thus, the most successful studies have involved clicks that activate primary auditory cortex or simple visual stimuli. Another way to reduce the number of active generators is to perform a subtraction that eliminates most of them. By subtracting the attend-left from attend-right conditions on trials that presented left-visual field stimuli, all the active generators are eliminated except those that reflect the boost of activity that occurs in the recognition pathway of the attended hemisphere. To study the orthography and meaning of words it is obviously necessary to use complex stimuli and tasks, but we have attempted to apply the subtractive method to isolate more limited number of generators involved in each cognitive operation.

Reading Words

The studies we have described so far all used rather simple visual stimuli and visual attention tasks to validate the link between scalp signatures of electrical activity and areas of blood flow. We have built upon these links by examining scalp signatures of electrical activity in tasks used to study word reading in PET studies. We will review related ERP research from our lab that provides some information about the time dynamics of these effects. The two major areas of activation we examine are those based on visual orthography and those related to word meaning.

Orthography

As discussed in the previous chapter, PET studies show that many types of letter strings activate right prestriate and parietal areas, whereas only word-like stimuli activated homologous left-hemisphere areas. In an early ERP (32-channel) study, Compton et al. (1991) presented words and consonant strings under four task conditions: (1) passive viewing, (2) thickened letter segment detection, (3) case mismatch detection, and (4) lexical decision. They observed that the P100 (first positive wave of the ERP with a peak latency of about 100 ms) was larger over right-hemisphere scalp sites than left ones for all types of strings. This amplitude difference occurred in all tasks and started at about 50 ms. Compton et al. suggested that the surface potential asymmetry reflected an analysis of high-level visual features common to the perception of any visual input.

Compton et al. also observed a difference between words and consonants strings in the N1 or first negative wave (consonant strings were more negative), beginning at about 150 ms poststimulus and somewhat lateralized in left-hemisphere scalp sites. Compton et al. proposed that the N1 differences over posterior temporal sites were related to visual word form activations reported in PET studies. A study designed to test changes in ERPs over several weeks (McCandliss, Posner, and Givón, 1997) suggested that the N1 effect in Compton et al.'s study is related to orthographic regularities of letter strings rather than specific familiarity with particular visual words. N1 magnitude was related to the degree to which letters strings approximated the patterns of English orthography rather than the amount of exposure subjects had to particular letter strings (novel versus 50 hours of training). Additional support for a left-posterior locus for word processing within this time window was reported by Dehaene (1995) in which spelled digits activated primarily left-posterior areas while Arabic digits activated bilateral areas. The time course was similar to that reported by Compton et al. In an intracranial ERP study, Nobre and McCarthy (1994) found that particular portions of posterior fusiform gyri produced large negativities around 200 ms to word-like letter strings but not to other visual objects or patterns.

It appears that attention can also influence processing in related visual areas. In a PET study discussed above, Heinze et al. (1994) reported that a visual-spatial attention task (attend-left or attend-right) could change activation of the ipsilateral posterior fusiform gyrus. In an analogous ERP study, Heinze et al. also found a corresponding modulation of the P1 over posterior sites starting at 80 ms. These findings raise the possibility that attention could have a substantial impact on the initial processes of forming a visual code for a word by modulating the activity in this part of the circuitry of reading.

There has been a dispute about PET extrastriate visual word form activation described above reflects processing due to English orthography or whether orthographic computations take place in a left-lateral temporal area closer either to the angular gyrus (Menard, Kosslyn, Thompson, Alpert, and Rauch, 1996) or to Wernicke's area (Howard, Patterson, Wise et al., 1992). It could be that the passive conditions used to study various letter strings in the early PET studies (Petersen, Fox, Posner, Mintun, and Raichle, 1988; Petersen, Fox, Snyder, and Raichle, 1990) allowed differential attention to be paid to the various strings. For example, if subjects paid more attention during the block containing words, this could amplify activity in visual areas that are not necessarily specialized for processing visual words. ERP data is relevant to this issue, even though the spatial resolution of source localization for electrical recordings is not sufficient to resolve debates over which of these two generators is most appropriately related to visual word-form processing. Words and consonant strings produce different electrical activations in posterior sensors within 200 ms after input. This early effect is found even when the two types of input strings are randomly intermixed within the same block, indicating that the effect is likely related to differences in initial processing of each stimulus rather than block effects. Taking the PET and ERP data together implies that the posterior activations are indexing orthographic word-form processing that occurs early enough to influence eye movement during reading.

Word Meanings

As described in the previous chapter, tasks that increase demands on semantic processing, as in the generate-use task compared to simply reading, typically activate a network of areas illustrated in the PET images shown in Figure 10.2. The left frontal (middle row), and left posterior temporal (bottom row) activations. To investigate the time dynamics of the PET activations associated with semantics, Snyder, Abdullaev, Posner, and Raichle (1995) collected ERPs to visual words as subjects either named them aloud or generated a use. ERPs in the naming condition were subtracted from the generate condition. Figure 10.2 third column shows the scalp electrical activity at 200 ms (top), 250 ms (middle) and 650 ms bottom (Abdullaev and Posner, 1998). Abdullaev and Posner used these scalp differences to localize potential neural generators by means of brain electrical source analysis (BESA) algorithms (Scherg and Berg, 1993). These neural source 'dipole' estimates are presented in figure 10.2, second column, at these same points in time.

The top figure in the second column shows that the first significant effect, an increase in frontal positivity starting around 200 ms, was best fit by a single generator on the frontal midline, a location that appeared to fit with the anterior cingulate activation found in PET. The anterior cingulate has been associated with higher level attention systems (Posner and DiGirolamo, 1998).

The significant effects that appeared around 250 ms demonstrated an increased positivity over left-frontal regions, and at this time an additional dipole source was required to account for the scalp signature (second column, middle row). This dipole source was localized to the left-frontal cortex, matching the left-frontal regions activated in PET. Around 600 to 700 ms, ERP differences were found over left temporo-parietal regions (see figure 10.2, third column, bottom panel), and BESA computed a generator matching the PET activation in Wernicke's area (see figure 10.2, second column, bottom panel). Additionally, a late effect around 800 ms appeared over anterior temporal regions (right greater than left) that was apparently related to the PET finding of reduced activity in the insular region during word generation as compared to reading aloud.

The likely time course of activation of the functional anatomy in visual word reading can be estimated through studies of electrical activity. Figure10.3 summarizes some of these results in relation to the time it takes to make an eye movement during reading.

Visual feature analysis occurs from about 50 to 100 ms after input and the perceptual word form is synthesized from letters by about 150 ms. By 180 ms, frontal attentional areas become active and by 220 ms, frontal semantic areas are activated.

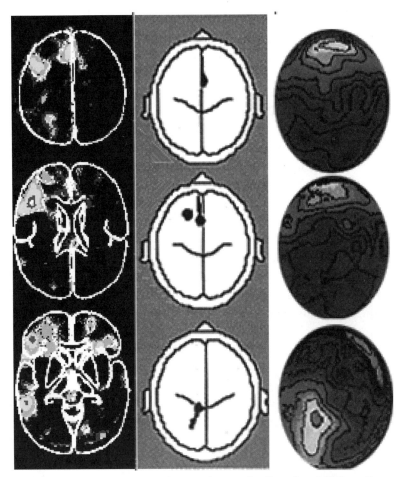

Figure 10.2 Left column indicates the results found in PET studies
of word generation. Top two rows show areas of activation in the
anterior cingulate and left-frontal cortex. Bottom row shows left-
frontal and posterior activation. The second column indicates best
fitting dipoles from EEG studies that match the PET results. The
top row is about 200 ms after input, the middle about 250 ms,
and the bottom about 650 ms. The third column shows the scalp
distributions of electrical activity that produced the dipoles. Bright
areas indicate higher positivity in the generate condition over
reading aloud.

Regions associated with output phonology and Wernicke's area are possibly active later. Exactly when posterior areas related to the semantics of word are active may depend upon the task. In our studies of the generation of word uses, activation in the generate condition only differs from reading aloud after 600 ms. Dehaene (1995, 1996), however, recorded from scalp electrodes during the processing of a variety of semantic categories, including animals and numerals. The task was to monitor a list of words and consonant strings for a particular category such as animals. Nontargets could be consonant strings or members of categories other than the target category for that block. This allowed examination of ERPs to different semantic categories when they were not targets. Significant differences between different categories emerged over posterior sites at around 300 ms.

Overall, these findings suggest that frontal areas involved in the generation of word uses and visual areas related to the visual word form are active early enough to influence on-line eye movement programming during reading. Because previous PET studies have indicated that frontal areas are generally not strongly activated in the routine reading of familiar visual words, it appears likely that eye movement programming is related to activation of a network of posterior visual word-form areas, but this programming could be modified by frontal areas in time to influence fixation time.

Neural Circuitry and Top Down Processing

The time line in figure 10.3 indicates a serial organization of processes during reading; however, this could be misleading. The attention system could be used to reactivate any of these anatomical areas and thus reorder the priority of the cognitive operations involved. These processes reflect top-down attention driven rather than sensory activation of a given brain area. There is by now a great deal of evidence that posterior brain areas—even sensory areas—can be activated either by input or by attention. For example, studies of visual imagery suggest that subjects can activate visual cortex (even primary visual cortex) in the absence of sensory input (Kosslyn, 1995; Kosslyn, Thompson, Kim, and Alpert, 1995). This also appears to be a common aspect of experiments that deal with physical aspects of the stimulus. When subjects are asked to think about the color most associated with a visually presented word (e.g., *banana-yellow*), PET imaging reveals that prestriate areas involved in processing color become active (Martin et al., 1995).

We have attempted to develop methods to study how this form of attention might drive the processes invoked during reading of single printed words (see Posner and Raichle, 1994). In one study, subjects viewed the same stimuli under two different instruction blocks in an attempt to manipulate the order of the cognitive op-

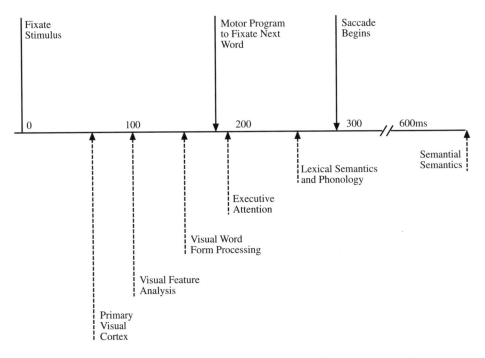

Figure 10.3 Proposed time course of activation of various internal
processes during reading (from Posner et al., 1998).

erations subjects employed in the task. Half of the words had a thickened letter and
half appeared in normal font. In addition, half the words represented manufactured
items and half represented natural ones. In one block, subjects were asked either to
make a "yes" or "no" decision on the basis of a semantic category (manufactured,
e.g., PIANO). In another block the decision was defined on the basis of a sensory
feature (thick letter, e.g., APPLE).

On one day, subjects performed the thick letter task, and later they were asked
to perform a new task that involved pressing the target key only for items that had
a thick letter and were also from the manufactured category. These instructions
together with the subjects experience with the previous task should lead subjects to
first look for the visual feature and then make the semantic analysis. On another
day, subjects performed the simple semantic task and were later asked to perform a
new task of pressing the target key only for items that were manufactured and had
a thick letter. This time the instructions together with their previous experience in
the semantic task placed initial priority on the semantic analysis rather than the
physical feature. In both tasks, however, the overall conjunction of the two deci-

sions was the same. The inputs were identical and the responses (if correct) were identical, but the priorities given to the underlying computations were reversed.

The expectation was that subjects would emphasize and perhaps complete the computation assigned priority somewhat earlier than the other computation. If the subjects were trained on the thick letter task and then asked to respond to targets that had a thick letter and were manufactured items, it was expected they would give priority to the visual search for a thick letter. The reaction times suggested that the instructions were successful in getting the subjects to assign different priorities. When instructed to give priority to the thick letter, subjects were faster to say "no" to items missing the thick letter than they were to those in the wrong category and the reverse held when the semantic category was given priority. In addition, the ERPs recorded over frontal semantic areas showed an earlier amplification of electrical activity when the semantic task was given priority than when the visual task had been given priority. The posterior visual area showed an earlier amplification of electrical activity when the thick letter task was given priority than when the semantic task was given priority.

These results show that subjects are able to reorder the priority of the underlying computations in the conjunction task; this observation may provide us with a basis for understanding how the brain can carry out so many different tasks. By reordering the component computations, we can produce novel thoughts. Some of the underlying computations do not appear to be affected by the instructions at all. The visual attribute area of the right-posterior brain appears to carry out the computation on the input string at 100 ms irrespective of whether the visual features are identified as part of the task or not. When the task is identified as looking for a thick letter, however, these same brain areas are reactivated and presumably carry out the additional computations necessary to make sure that one of the letters has enough thickening to constitute a target. Attention can serve to increase neuronal activity (as measured by ERPs) within particular areas but often appears to do so by reactivating the same area that initially performed the computation, not by activating new higher level association areas.

The conjunction method described above may provide a general tool for exploring the circuitry involved in brain activity. It is often tempting to think of brain circuitry as a set of fixed anatomical connections among brain areas or neurons within an area. However any brain area can be anatomically connected to any other area by either direct or indirect routes, providing multiple possibilities for recombining component operations in novel ways. The act of attending to a particular type of information can be thought of as setting up a temporary circuitry from higher level to lower level areas. It is in this sense that attention can control the order of the computations such as those involved in the thick letter and semantic category tasks. If this hypothesis concerning the brain is correct, conjunctions can be used to explore the relation among remote areas of the brain during specific cognitive tasks. The method uses the person's own attention to illuminate the order of the computations and thus the higher level circuits that execute the task instruction. To test this very general hypothesis, new experiments will be required that will take as their elements anatomical areas shown to be active during simple computations. Subjects can then be asked to assemble these elements in different ways while the impact of this cognitive reorganization on the neural circuitry recruited is measured.

Experience-Related Changes in Activation

So far, most of the research strategies we have discussed for investigating the neural circuitry of reading skill have manipulated either the task instructions or the stimuli to observe the resulting changes in cortical activation. Another important strategy involves holding both task and stimuli constant, but changing the experiences that the subject brings to the experiment. Responses to visual words can be altered by a person's experience within the last few seconds (as in the case of priming) the last few minutes (as in the case of most memory research) over the last several weeks (as in the case of learning new words) or even over several years (as with the case of gaining the ability to read a new language or gaining literacy skill for the first time). Thus, experience-related changes in the brain's response to visual words can be investigated at many time scales. We will examine each of these in turn and consider how such changes in experience might lead to different forms of changes in the neural circuitry of word reading.

Practice, Learning, and Plasticity

Raichle et al. (1994) have shown that practicing the generate-use task on a single list of nouns leads to behavioral evidence of automatization. Reaction times to practiced words were fast, responses became increasingly stereotyped, and subjects found the task easier than for novel words. Changes in brain activations were traced via PET measures before and after practice. Activations in the left-lateral frontal and posterior areas and in the anterior cingulate were reduced with practice. The activation in the insular cortex, however, actually increased so as to become as strong as during the reading aloud task.

Abdullaev and Posner (1998) also studied the role of practice in word generation while recording from scalp electrodes. In the previous PET studies, subjects were asked to generate uses for the same list of 40 items ten times in row and this produced a high level of automatic performance. The ERP study used a list of 100 items and as subjects repeated the list they were instructed to try and produce the same words each time they went through the list. In general, the intense scalp activity found over frontal regions and Wernicke's area was reduced by practice. A clear right-frontal area of positivity, however, was also produced by the practiced condition. This finding of right-prefrontal positivity relates to PET and fMRI findings of right-frontal activation in tasks requiring explicit retrieval of information from memory and has been studied and summarized by Tulving et al. (1994). The electrical activity suggests that the act of contacting a previous memory to obtain explicit information on the stored word starts over right-frontal structures by about 250 ms after input.

After subjects generated words to the same list for four successive trials, we asked them to generate a new, unusual use for the same items. We found that the early frontal positivity found in the original generate task returned, although it appeared to be slightly later in time. Within the later time window, posterior temporo-parietal positivity was as strong and significant as in the first naive use generation task, but it was clearly bilateral with two peaks in symmetrical regions of the left and right hemisphere. Generating the new thought appears to recruit a right-hemisphere area symmetric to Wernicke's area. The left- and right-hemisphere activations tended to alternate from 620 to 820 ms. The left-hemisphere activation was joined by the right temporo-parietal activation twice within this time window; first around 650 ms and then around 720 ms. These results illustrate the temporal relations among brain areas involved in processing semantic associations and confirm the idea arising from cognitive and brain injury studies that unusual associations require additional processing resources from the right hemisphere. In these ERP studies, these resources involve the right temporo-parietal region symmetric to the Wernicke's area and begin about 600 ms after input.

In a related study, Posner and Pavese (1998) used ERP measures to explore functional differences between the left-anterior and left-posterior activations found in the circuitry related to processing word meanings. They proposed that left-frontal areas might be related to accessing semantic associations and details of word meanings and left-posterior areas might be more related to integration of words into propositions. To test this notion, they employed the conjunction method discussed above. In their basic task, subjects viewed a sentence fragment (e.g., "He ate his food with his _____"), a target word (e.g., *fork*), and then a prompt to respond "yes" or "no". Half the target words were related to the sentence meaning and half were not. Additionally, half the target words represented manufactured items and half represented natural objects. In the conjunction task, subjects were to respond "yes" if a target was both manufactured and completed the sentence well. This conjunction task was studied under two conditions: one that gave priority to the word-level decision and one that gave priority to the sentence-level decision. Priority to one or the other type of decision was manipulated by practicing the subject on only the priority task immediately beforehand (i.e., responding "yes" if the target word is manufactured) and also phrasing the instructions to mention the priority task first (i.e., respond "yes" if the target is manufactured and completes the sentence.) This design enabled them to examine the influence of sentence versus word priority within ERPs collected from the same stimuli, with the same motor output and the same stimulus to response mapping. The only thing that differed is whether subjects mentally gave priority to the sentence- or word-level decision. Posner and Pavese found when subjects gave mental priority to word-level information there was an increase in activity over left-anterior areas, and when priority was placed on sentence-level information there was an increase in left-posterior activations. Findings such as these contribute to our understanding of interhemispheric communication, and allow investigations of the precise nature in which the hemispheres contribute to particular cognitive functions.

The results described above reveal a large degree of flexibility in the circuitry recruited to perform simple cognitive tasks that involve producing responses related to the meaning of a word. It has also been shown that within the anterior and posterior semantic areas, different portions are active when processing different semantic categories (Martin et al., 1996; Spitzer et al., 1995). The presence of category-specific semantic areas indicates that the brain might utilize the same principles of mapping to handle semantic relations that are used for dealing with the organization of sensory information, although the exact organization of the individual categories within anterior and posterior semantic brain areas appear to differ from one subject to another. One important implication of this neural mapping principle is that practice that involves a particular region of a map can lead to cortical expansion of that region. For example, evidence collected by cellular recording in monkeys demonstrates that practice on tactile discrimination tasks can lead to expansion of cortical maps in primary somatosensory cortex (Jenkins, Merzenich, and Recanzone, 1990). It appears possible that similar cortical expansion phenomena could occur for higher levels of representation. For example, extensive practice could induce a temporary increase in the amount of neural tissue recruited by a semantic category. If this proves to be the case, it could provide a new explanation for why it is that spending an extended time absorbed in a particular set ideas, be they negative thoughts (as in depression) or brain imaging (as in writing this article) might increase the rate we later find ourselves spontaneously thinking about those topics, and why our thoughts might come to be dominated by just a few semantic categories.

Repetition Priming

Several forms of changes in brain circuitry with practice have been studied in PET, fMRI, and ERP studies. For example, we described above how practicing specific associations in the use generation task led to reduced blood flow and changes in electrical activity in areas originally used to generate the association. The reduction of left-lateral frontal activity with repetition has been confirmed in a fMRI study (Demb et al., 1996). In this study subjects classified words into abstract or concrete categories. Left-frontal regions active in previous word generation studies described above were activated by this task, and this activity was reduced by a single repetition of each word. Thus, even a single prior exposure can lead to measurable changes in brain activation.

Repetition priming effects in behavior have been used to study implicit processes of word recognition as well as explicit memories of recently presented items. Recently, several memory researchers have employed clever instructional manipulations to separate implicit priming from deliberate recall in word-stem completion tasks. In this paradigm, subjects learn a list of words, then generate words in response to word stems (i.e., the first three letters of a word). The experiment is run either with the instruction to generate the first association that comes to mind (priming instruction) or with the instruction to provide the previously learned items starting with those letters (recall instruction). Effects of prior learning are demonstrated when words from the studied list appear as completions more frequently than expected by chance.

These procedures have been successfully used in PET studies (e.g., Buckner et al., 1995; Schacter et al., 1996) to address issues of priming and explicit memory. One intriguing result of these PET studies was that priming reduced activation in right-posterior areas. These brain areas have often been associated with the implicit storage of visual information (Beglieter, Porjesz, and Wang, 1993). If primed items require less neuronal activity in this area, it could indicate that in this paradigm the memory trace of the previously learned word was activated with greater efficiency by the three-letter cue. This improved efficiency would be indexed by a reduction in the neuronal activity needed to reactivate the visual code of the word stored from the prior learning. Since PET does not provide a time course for the changed neuronal activity, however, it is also possible that the reduced blood flow merely means that when a word has been encountered before, less attention and effort is needed to generate a response to the three-letter cue. Less attention to the visual code of the primed word would also result in less blood flow than for unprimed items. In other words, the reduced activation of the right-posterior area might be either bottom-up or top-down. The separation of more automatic pathway activation from attentional control has been common in cognitive studies since the mid-1970s (Posner and Snyder, 1975), however, these methods have not been widely applied to imaging studies.

Electrical recording provides additional ways to investigate whether priming in word-stem completion occurs in an automatic form that influences perception of stems or whether the effects are related to later processes. Badgaiyan and Posner, (1996) replicated the PET studies with high-density electrical recording. Results suggest that the difference between primed and unprimed targets in this paradigm occur between 60 and 200 ms after the three-letter cue is presented. The priming effect occurred in the same place and time under both instruction conditions. The deliberate instruction to recall from the prior list, however, differed from implicit instruction mainly in frontal areas after 250 ms. The ERP data favor an account of priming that occurs early in processing, is largely influenced by automatic, bottom-up processing, and can be described as modulating activations primarily in posterior areas. These results are encouraging for the prospects of applying ERP data to the study of basic cognitive questions such as the automatic nature of priming effects.

Another recent set of studies examined ERP responses to immediately repeated versus nonrepeated words presented in the left or right visual fields. These studies were designed to trace out processing differences between right- and left-hemisphere mechanisms. Left-posterior ERPs distinguished repeated from nonrepeated words after about 150 ms (McCandliss, Curran, and Posner, 1993, 1994). Several aspects of this left-lateralized repetition effect suggest that it might be tapping into mechanisms recruited during the formation of visual word codes. This early repetition priming effect was left lateralized both for word that appeared in either the left visual field or the right visual field. Secondly, the repetition effect did not depend on repetition of superficial visual details—the same robust effect appeared regardless of whether the repeated words occurred in the same or different case and font as the prime. These findings suggest left-posterior mechanisms are sensitive to immediate repetitions of abstract orthographic information that is not restricted to visual features or spatial position. Other ERP repetition priming effects reported in the literature (i.e. Rugg, 1987; Van Petten, Kutas, Kluender, Mitchiner, and McIsaac, 1991) typically report longer latencies for the onset and peak of these effects. It is possible that by recording repetition effects with more electrodes, and thus recording more of the inferior surface of the scalp, our methods are sensitive to effects that might be missed by smaller electrode arrays used in many laboratories (10–20 system). It is also possible, however, that early ERP repetition effects (near 150 ms) are dependent on a number of experimental factors and thus are difficult to replicate across slightly different experimental paradigms. Regardless of these differences, our immediate repetition findings are in general agreement with PET studies showing left-posterior activations associated with processing visual word forms (Howard, Patterson, Wise et al., 1992; Petersen, Fox, Snyder, and Raichle, 1990). Although the anatomy and short latency of the immediate repetition effects demonstrated by McCandliss et al. appear to reflect automatic activation, it is possible that they are also influenced by attention. Future studies that use cognitive methods to more clearly separate automatic and attended activation will allow us to determine the degree of automaticity of such effects. More generally, differences among these immediate repetition effects demonstrating left-lateralized ERP effects and longer term repetition effects demonstrating right-lateralized effects in both PET and ERP for repetition priming in word-stem completions tasks presents a new set of puzzles that might help us tease apart differences between right- and left-posterior contributions to word-reading processes and processes related to visual memories of words.

Neuroimaging provides opportunities to examine the relation between cognitive computations and brain activity. The results to date generally support the view that we can image different types of computational processes, each with its unique anatomy. Specific processes perform computations within limited content domains. For reading words, these include visual, orthographic, phonological, and semantic codes. Attentional modulations arise in quite different anatomical networks and can modify activations within task-specific domains. Priming studies that demonstrate early, bottom-up effects may serve as a key method for separating modulations related to repeating an operation from those related to changes in the amount of attention devoted to those operations. Although many unanswered questions remain concerning priming, the data to date suggest that priming can be used to modulate activity in highly specific anatomical regions by manipulating the type of information shared by the prime and the target.

Learning New Vocabulary

Vocabulary learning represents another level at which experience can modify cortical activations to visual words. Presumably the activations associated with fluently recognizing a well-known word are quite different than the processes we apply when we encounter an unfamiliar word. Through weeks or months of learning, the same visual words which at one time struck us as meaningless can be transformed into rapidly accessible entries in our mental lexicons. Furthermore, several cognitive studies suggest that when enough words of a particular orthography (i.e., English) are learned to the point of rapid recognition, learning related to more abstract orthographic regularities can influence how we process novel strings that either follow or violate that system. Successful learning of abstract orthographic patterns is demonstrated when skilled readers are able to process pseudowords faster than random strings (see Carr and Pollatsek, 1985). Neuroimaging can be used to trace these learning processes over time in different brain systems. Such investigations can track how activations related to semantic content and orthographic patterns change as a set of novel words become increasingly familiar and meaningful, and as new orthographic systems are learned to the point that regularities in that system influence processing.

In a recent study, McCandliss, Posner, and Givón (1997) investigated changes that took place in neural circuitry as subjects spent several weeks learning novel words from another language and came to recognize them as rapidly as English words. The new words being learned were formed by an artificial orthographic rule system that combines letters into word forms according to a limited set of rules. These "words" are fully pronounceable but contain many bigrams and trigrams that are unusual in English, and the word forms appear more like Italian or Spanish than English. Half of the words produced by this orthographic system were used to form a miniature artificial language called Keki. The other half were reserved for testing purposes (Keki control strings). These stimuli provided an opportunity to examine the process of item-specific learning against a group of very well matched control strings.

Each Keki word was assigned a distinct meaning corresponding to a high-frequency English word (i.e., "*gilki*" = bird, "*penka*" = black). Together the set of 68 Keki words formed a small functional language that could be used to convey meaningful sentences. A group of undergraduates learned Keki via a series of computer tutorials (visual and auditory) in a laboratory setting for two hours per day, five days per week, over a period of five weeks. During these two-hour computer tutorials, subjects worked through interactive exercises that stressed reading Keki words in meaningful contexts. Thus, subjects received extensive visual and semantic experience (50 hours over five weeks) with a small word set created by a somewhat novel orthographic system.

A behavioral task (Yang and Givón, 1993) was administered at several points across the training program to trace learning. Two successive visual strings were presented in rapid succession, followed by a same-different judgment. Stimuli were familiar English words, Keki words, and Keki control strings. Subjects demonstrated a consistent reaction time advantage for English words over Keki control strings at all three testing intervals (a form of word superiority effect). Yang and Givón found that a similar benefit for Keki words was not present before training but developed over the course of the five weeks of training. This result supports the notion that after five weeks of training, Keki words were taking on some of the same processing qualities that are present for well-known English words.

In an ERP study McCandliss et al. investigated how early posterior ERP effects related to processing visual word forms were influenced by 50 hours spent learning Keki words. The impact of subjects' processing goals on the ERP responses were examined by presenting all stimuli under three different task blocks. A semantic block required subjects to decide whether each string represented something tangible. A visual feature block also required an active binary decision on each trial but the decision required only a judgment about the presence of a small thickened letter segment embedded somewhere within the stimuli. Finally, a passive block required no response.

ERP measures were collected in response to Keki strings, Keki control strings, and English strings before, during, and after training. In addition, consonant strings were included in the ERP experiments to provide a baseline stimulus set that controlled for the visual input of letters without introducing regular orthographic patterns, familiar patterns at the word level, or semantic meanings. Tracing how ERP responses to Keki strings start to deviate from the consonant string baseline can be used to investigate learning of the structure of the Keki word form, learning of particular whole Keki words, and access to the meaning of the Keki words.

To examine how Keki training influenced visual word-form processes, McCandliss et al. focused on an early ERP visual word form effect over posterior visual areas (see figure 10.4, top panel) originally reported by Compton et al. (1991). When contrasting ERPs to English words and consonant strings, the earliest differences emerge as a positive shift for English words after approximately 200 ms. As discussed above, this ERP effect has been linked to activation of a posterior visual word form system that is sensitive to regular orthographic patterns. McCandliss et al. replicated this effect for English versus consonant strings before, during, and after training. This effect was used to assess word-form processing effects for Keki words. Results indicated that regardless of training, both Keki words and Keki control items produced a positive shift relative to consonant strings around 200 ms in the same posterior channels as English words. The magnitude of this shift, however, was significantly smaller than the shift observed for English words (see figure 10.4, bottom panel). McCandliss et al. argued that this early visual word-form response demonstrated systematic sensitivity to the internal structure of letter strings, demonstrating the largest response to strings that are highly consistent with the

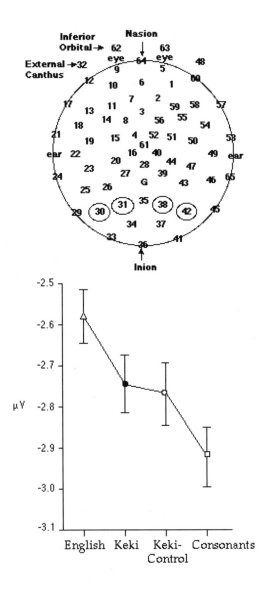

Figure 10.4 Top panel shows the spatial layout of the 64 channels in the
Geodesic Sensor Net. Circled numbers indicate the inferior/posterior
electrodes that demonstrate visual word form effects in adults with 200
ms (McCandliss et al., 1997). Data collected in these channels (bottom
panel) at about 200 ms demonstrate a positive shift for English words
and Keki strings above a consonant string baseline, yet no difference
between Keki words studied for 50 hours and novel Keki control stimuli.

subjects orthographic experiences (English words), a smaller but significant response to strings based on a unique but similar orthography (Keki and Keki control), and the weakest (baseline) responses to unordered consonant strings. This pattern remained stable across all three testing sessions (before, during, and after training) and all three task conditions (passive viewing, semantic judgments, and visual feature judgments).

These same early posterior ERP measures were used to examine the impact of word familiarity on the operation of the visual word form system. McCandliss et al. compared the early posterior ERP response to fully trained Keki words (after 50 hours of training) with untrained Keki control items. Results demonstrated no impact of training. ERP responses were virtually unchanged by 50 hours of familiarization and training. Apparently during the first 200 ms of processing, the visual word-form system in adult readers is uninfluenced by the familiarity of particular word items, yet is highly sensitive to the abstract orthographic structure of both novel and familiar letter strings. Taken together, the effects revealed by the early posterior ERP effects appear to reflect a visual word form system that is sensitive to orthographic regularities, rather insensitive to familiarity for specific visual words, and rather slow to change.

The last goal of the study was to trace word-learning effects in other systems related to word meaning. To examine this type of learning, McCandliss et al. focused on a second ERP effect that emerged when contrasting English words with consonant strings. Approximately 300 ms after presentation, English words demonstrated a negative shift (compared to consonant strings) that was significant under passive viewing conditions, virtually doubled in magnitude under semantic task demands, and was greatly attenuated under the task that required a nonsemantic decision for each stimulus (letter feature judgment). Unlike the earlier orthographic effect that was isolated to posterior areas, this effect had a widely distributed scalp signature, including posterior and frontal regions. Examining the ERP responses for Keki versus Keki control words in the semantic task during this same time window (280 to 360 ms) revealed a set of systematic changes that occurred over the five weeks of training.

In the first session Keki words and Keki control strings did not differ from each other, but both were more positive than English words. Over the course of training, a difference emerged between the Keki and Keki control such that responses to Keki words came to resemble the response to English words, while responses to Keki controls and consonant strings remained more positive than English words. After 50 hours of training, the ERP response to Keki words was equivalent to English words and was significantly different from both Keki control and consonant strings. Like the effect for English words, versus consonant strings, the difference that emerged between Keki words and Keki control strings was broadly distributed over posterior and frontal sites.

Overall, these results demonstrate that human learning can be systematically traced via measures related to neural circuitry, that different aspects of learning can potentially be related to changes in different aspects of the neural circuitry and the results of such learning studies can provide a new approach to understanding the functional organization that supports skilled behavior. Within the first 200 ms of processing, ERP results suggest that the orthography of letter strings can influence processing by posterior brain mechanisms associated with visual word-form information; however, the operation of these mechanisms is not influenced by task demands and these processes do not change noticeably across five weeks of training, indicating that item familiarity has little influence on the system. After about 300 ms of processing, the effects of learning are evident over frontal and posterior sites and this learning effect appears strongest when subjects attend to the meanings of the words. These findings illustrate potential differences in the way brain circuitry changes with experience, suggesting that some aspects of the neural circuitry of reading might be more easily modified by experience than others. We believe that the approach used in this study will allow examination of many questions about how different forms of learning can be understood in terms of changes in the neural circuitry that supports a task.

Initial Literacy

Perhaps the most important domain for understanding how experience influences the neural circuitry of word reading is the area of reading skill acquisition. Reading skill is a cultural invention with a history that is relatively short in the evolutionary history of our species. Studying the relationship between early years of reading experience and the development of the neural circuitry that supports fluent reading could provide a link between studies of experience-dependent changes in cortical function and the development of higher level cognitive skills. Insights into changes in brain circuitry associated with successful acquisition of literacy may aid in understanding both the normal fluent reader as well as neurological problems associated with failures to acquire literacy, as in developmental dyslexia (see chapters 4 and 5, this volume). Little neuroimaging evidence is currently available, however, from children during the years of initial literacy acquisition. Many neuroimaging techniques are considered too invasive to apply to developing children, and the complexity of reading precludes an appropriate animal model for neurological investigations. This situation is likely to change in the near future—increasing numbers of laboratories are beginning to use fMRI to investigate cortical function in normal children as young as five years of age (Casey et al, 1997; Shaywitz et al., 1996). Fortunately the ERP techniques we have described are easily applied to children, and several developmental ERPs studies have been done that investigate how children process visual words.

In general, developmental ERP studies have demonstrated that the basic shape of ERP waveforms change systematically as a function of age. ERP components are generally much larger and somewhat slower in younger children than adults and decrease in amplitude and latency as children progress from age four to age sixteen (Holcomb, Coffey, and Neville, 1992; Johnson, 1989; Courchesne, 1978; Friedman, Boltri, Vaughan, and Erlenmeyer-Kimling, 1985). The larger amplitude of ERPs from children is often thought to be related to developmental changes in the filtering properties of the skull (Gevins, 1966).

A smaller number of developmental studies have investigated age-related changes in ERPs to visual words (Holcomb, Coffey, and Neville, 1992; Holcomb, Ackerman, and Dykman, 1985; Licht et al., 1988, 1992). They have demonstrated that the overall ERP waveforms to visual words also change in latency and amplitude with age. In addition, Holcomb et al. demonstrated that an N400-like component in 8-year-old children was sensitive to whether a word matched or violated the context of a simple written sentence, demonstrating that these techniques hold promise for studying how children derive meaning from looking at visual words.

We have recently conducted a set of high-density ERP experiments with children designed to examine the development of the visual word-form system. In our first set of studies, we collected ERPs as 4 and 7-year-old children watched letter strings on a computer screen. Our initial goal was to demonstrate that we could use our ERP measures with children to study changes in visual processing, so we contrasted ERPs collected when children either passively watched the strings or actively processed them to decide whether a thickened letter segment was present. Although the children's overall waveforms were quite different from adults, the specific differences that emerged between active and passive conditions across both age groups were remarkably similar to the adults in the sense that posterior channels showed an increased positivity during the thickened letter search task. As with many other developmental ERP findings, the latency of this effect generally decreased with age. Presumably these effects are due to attention-related changes in the way visual stimuli are processed, and 4-year-olds and 7-year-olds are very much like adults in their abilities to engage in such attentional modulation of visual ERPs.

A critical aspect of this study was that half of the letter strings in these tasks formed high-frequency words that are common in first grade curricula and the other half were consonant strings. In adults, the earliest indication that the brain processes words and consonant strings differently occurs in posterior channels within the first 200 ms of processing (Compton et al., 1991; McCandliss, Posner, and Givón, 1997; Bentin et al., 1999). In the Keki study this effect was present during both passive viewing and feature search.

Our initial studies with 4- and 7-year-olds showed little difference between words and consonant strings within the posterior channels for which the word form effect was found in adults. 10-year-olds, however, demonstrated an effect of stimulus type that appeared at about 200 ms and diminished by about 300 ms. This word form effect occurred in the same posterior and inferior channels as in the adult data (see figure 10.4, top panel), although the time course was slightly delayed. Unlike the adult ERP response, however, the 10-year-olds showed no evidence of effects related to abstract orthographic encoding. Instead, it appears that this early poste-rior-inferior ERP response in 10-year-olds is sensitive only to the familiarity of the presented letter string (see figure 10.5, top panel)

A different pattern of stimulus effects emerged in more superior channels start-ing at about 300 ms and continuing through to 450 ms (see figure 10.5, bottom panel). These effects indicate no sensitivity to the familiarity of the letter string being processed, but appear to be sensitive to the differences between orthographically regular strings versus consonant strings.

This study shows that early posterior ERP effects in adults and 10-year olds can be used to track the development of the visual word form system. Adults show and early positive shift for both novel and known words relative to consonant strings, demonstrating a form of abstract orthographic encoding in the visual word form system. Although 10-year-olds also demonstrate a visual word form ERP effect with a similar time course and topography, they demonstrate a positive shift for known words, but not for orthographically regular novel words. This suggests that during the first several years of literacy the visual word form system codes specific visual words, and as reading skill approaches adult levels of expertise the visual word form system comes to code more abstract patterns of letter combinations inherent in English orthography.

Our results provide some initial evidence that the neural circuitry that sup-ports the automatic integration of letters into word forms within the visual system develops by initially representing specific word information and then eventually comes to integrate novel word forms that conform to the orthographic patterns of English. During the first several years of literacy children may have the ability to rapidly integrate letters into visual word forms, but this ability appears to be restricted to well known items. For unfamiliar items, they may have to resort to slower pho-

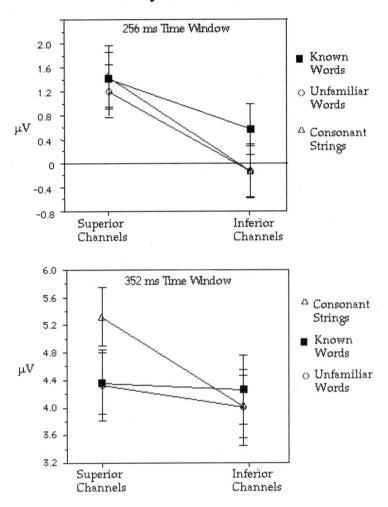

Figure 10.5 Data from 10-year-olds indicating the two disctinct patterns of stimulus effects. Top panel shows an effect of familiarity but not of orthography in the inferior (30, 31, 38, and 42) electrodes at 250 ms. Bottom panel shows differences between words (whether familiar or not) and consonant strings at 350 ms in more superior channels (25, 26, 43, 46) (see figure. 10.4, top panel, for location of numbered electrodes).

nological decoding processes. These phonological processes are potentially related to the ERP effects that emerged after 300 ms in our study of 10-year-olds.

These preliminary results raise important questions for cognitive theories of word recognition and literacy acquisition. What mechanisms account for the transition of the visual word form system from word-specific coding in children to more abstract orthographic coding in adults? One possibility is that the ability of the system to generalize to orthographically regular novel word forms grows as a function of the number of specific words that have been learned. Some connectionist models provide such an account of the development of visual word recognition skills and the ability of the system to generalize processing to novel strings (i.e. McClelland and Rumelhart, 1981). Such models propose that neighborhoods of stored exemplars are fairly sparse during early training, and thus generalization to novel words is poor. Later, as the number of trained exemplars grows, the orthographic neighborhoods become very dense and begin to allow the system to respond to both familiar and novel words in kind. Another possibility is that the visual word form system changes from word-specific processing to more general orthographic processing as a result of increasing fluency in phonemic decoding skills. As children become increasingly fluent in decoding graphemes into phonemes, they may start to alter the top-down processing demands placed on the visual word form system such that there is an increased demand to accurately code smaller orthographic units rather than coding entire visual word forms. Similarly, the development of phonological decoding fluency might encourage children to change the way they attend to visual word forms during encoding and thus alter the bottom-up input to the visual word form system.

It is now possible to use both ERP and neuroimaging techniques such as fMRI to track the development of reading skills in children. Combining these methods with the research strategies described within this chapter, it is possible to gain new insights into the relationship between the development of component reading skills and changes in the dynamics of the cortical circuitry that support these developing skills. Such investigations will allow us to refine theories of the cognitive and cortical mechanisms involved in attending to words, learning to read new words, and developing more general literacy skills

Conclusions

Combining functional methods for brain imaging such as fMRI and PET with high density electrical recording has proven to be an effective way to image the circuitry of high-level skills. In this chapter we have attempted to illustrate the use of this strategy and to apply it to several sources of plasticity in the reading task. Moment-to-moment changes due to shifts of attention or priming can be studied by examining the time course of mental operations. We have also reported changes in brain circuitry due to learning a new language or to the acquisition of the reading skill. We hope that this strategy will be of benefit both in improving our understanding of the cognitive and cortical of skilled reading as well as the learning-related changes that take place over the course of literary aquisition.

Acknowledgments.

This research was supported by grants from the Office of Naval Research N00014-9600273, the James S. McDonnell Foundation 94-48, Pew Memorial Trusts, and W.M. Keck Foundation 901171 in support to the Center for the Cognitive Neuroscience of Attention. The authors are grateful to Sara Sereno, Yalchin Abdullaev, and Rajendra Badgaiyan for their help.

References

Abdullaev, Y.G., and Posner, M.I. (1998). Event related potential imaging of semantic encoding during single word processing. *Neuroimage, 7,* 1–13

Abdullaev, Y.G., and Posner, M.I. (1997). Time course of activating brain areas in generating verbal associations. *Psychological Science, 8,* 51–59.

Badgaiyan, R.D., and Posner, M.I. (1996). Priming reduces input activity in the right posterior cortex during stem completion. *Neuroreport, 7,* 2975–78.

Beglieter, H., Porjesz, B., and Wang, W. (1993). A neurophysiologic correlate of visual short-term memory in humans. *Electroencephalography and Clinical Neurophysiology, 87,* 46–53.

Bentin, S., Mouchetant-Rostaing, Y., Giard, M.H., Echallier, J.F., and Pernier, J. (1999). ERP manifestation of processing printed words at different psycholinguistic levels: time course and scalp distribution. *Journal of Cognitive Neuroscience, 11,* 235–260.

Buckner, R.L., Petersen, S.E., Ojemann, J.G., Miezin, F.M. Squire, L.R., and Raichle, M.E. (1995). Functional-anatomical studies of explicit and implicit memory retrieval tasks. *Journal of Neuroscience, 15,* 12–29.

Carr, T.H., and Pollatsek, A. (1985). Recognizing printed words: A look at current models. In D. Besner, T.G. Waller, and G.E. MacKinnon (eds.), *Reading Research: Advances in Theory and Practice,* volume 5. (pp 1–82) New York: Academic Press.

Casey, B.J., Trainor, R., Giedd, J., Vauss, Y., Vaituzis, C.K., Hamburger, S., Kozuch, P., and Rapoport, J.L. (1997). The role of the anterior cingulate in automatic and controlled processes: a developmental neuroanatomical study. *Developmental Psychobiology, 30,* 61–69.

Clark, V.P., and Hillyard, S.A. (1996). Spatial selective attention affects early extrastriate but not striate components of the visual evoked potential. *Journal of Cognitive Neuroscience, 8*, 387–402.

Compton, P., Grossenbacher, P., Posner, M.I., and Tucker, D.M. (1991). A cognitive anatomical approach to attention in lexical access. *Journal of Cognitive Neuroscience, 3*, 304–312.

Courchesne, E. (1978). Neurophysiological correlates of cognitive development: changes in long-latency event-related potentials from childhood to adulthood. *Electroencephalography and Clinical Neurophysiology, 45*, 468–482.

Dehaene, S. (1995). Electrophysiological evidence for category-specific word processing in the normal human brain. *NeuroReport, 6*(16).

de Jong, B.M., Shipp, S., Skidmore, B., Frackowiak, R.S.J., and Zeki, S. (1994). The cerebral activity related to the visual perception of forward motion in depth. *Brain, 117*, 1039–1054.

Demb, J.B., Desmond, J.E., Wagner, A.D., Vaidya, C.T., Glover G.H., and Gabrieli, J.D.E. (1996). Semantic encoding and retrieval in the left inferior prefrontal cortex: A functional MRI study of task difficulty and process specificity. *Journal of Neuroscience, 15*, 5870–5878.

Ffytche, D.H., Guy, C.N., and Zeki, S. (1995). The parallel visual motion inputs into areas V1 and V5 of human cerebral cortex. *Brain, 118*, 1375–1394.

Fox, P.T., Mintun, M.A., Raichle, M.E., and Miezin, F. M. (1986). Mapping human visual cortex with positron emission tomography. *Nature, 323*, 806–809.

Friedman, D., Boltri, J., Vaughan, H., and Erlenmeyer-Kimling, L. (1985). Effects of age and sex on the endogenous brain potential components during two continuous task performance tasks. *Psychophysiology, 22*, 4, 440–452

Gevins, A. (1966). Electrophysiological imaging of brain function. In A.W. Toga and J.C. Mazziotta (eds.). *Brain Mapping: The Methods.* (pp 259–273) San Diego: Academic Press.

Heinze H.J., Mangun, G.R., Burchert, W., Hinrichs, H., Scholz, M., Münte, T.F., Gos, A., Scherg, M., Johannes, S., Hundeshagen, H., Gazzaniga, M.S., and Hillyard, S.A. (1994). Combined spatial and temporal imaging of brain activity during visual selective attention in humans. *Nature, 372*, 543–546.

Hillyard, S.A., and Anllo-Vento, L. (1998). Event related brain potentials in the study of visual selective attention. *Proceedings of the National Academy of Sciences, 95*, 781–787.

Holcomb, P.J., (1988). Automatic and attentional processing: An event-related brain potential analysis of semantic priming. *Brain and Language, 35*, 66–85.

Holcomb, P.J., Coffey, S.A., and Neville, H.J. (1992). Visual and auditory sentence processing: A development analysis using event-related brain potentials. *Developmental Neuropsychology, 8*, 203–241.

Holcomb, P.J., Ackerman, P., and Dykman, R. (1985). Cognitive event related potentials in children with attention and reading deficits. *Psychophysiology, 22,* 656–667.

Howard, D., Patterson, K., Wise, R., Brown, W.D., Firston, K., Weiller, C., and Frackowiak, R.S.J. (1992). The cortical localization of the lexicons. *Brain, 115,* 1769–1782.

Jenkins, W.M., Merzenich, M.M., and Recanzone, G. (1990). Neocortical representational dynamics in adult primates: implications for neuropsychology. *Neuropsychologia, 28,* 573–584.

Johnson, R. (1989). Developmental evidence for modality-dependent P300 generators: a normative study. *Psychophysiology, 26,* 6, 651–667.

Kosslyn, S. (1995). *Image and Brain.* Cambridge: MIT Press.

Kosslyn, S.M., Thompson, W.L., Kim, I.J., and Alpert, N.M. (1995). Topographical representations of mental images in primary visual cortex. *Nature, 378,* 496–498

Kutas, M. (1993). In the company of other words: Electrophysiological evidence for single words versus sentence context effects. *Language and Cognitive Processes, 8* (4), 533–572.

Kutas, M. and Van Petten, C.K. (1994). Psycholinguistics Electrified: event-related brain potential investigations. In M. A. Gernsbacher (ed.) *Handbook of Psycholinguistics* (pp. 83–143). London: Lawrence Erlbaum.

Licht, R., Bakker, D.J., Kok, A., and Bouma, A. (1992). Grade–related changes in event-related potentials (ERPs) in primary school children: Differences between two reading tasks. *Journal of Child and Experimental Neuropsychology, 14,* 193–210.

Licht, R., Bakker, D.J., Kok, A., and Bouma, A. (1988). The development of lateral event-related potentials (ERPs) related to word naming: A four year longitudinal study. *Neuropsychologia, 26*(2), 327–340.

Martin, A., Wiggs, C.L., Ungerleider, L.G., and Haxby, J.V. (1995). Neural correlates of category-specific knowledge. *Nature, 379,* 649.

McCandliss, B.D. (submitted). Development of the visual word form system in learning to read. *Neuropsychologia.*

McCandliss, B.D., Posner, M.I., and Givón, T. (1997). Brain plasticity in learning visual words. *Cognitive Psychology, 33,* 88–110.

McCandliss, B.D., Curran, T., and Posner, M.I. (1994). Exploring the time course of word recognition for identical and cross-case repetitions. Poster presented to the annual meeting of the Psychonomic Society. St. Louis, MO.

McCandliss, B.D., Curran, T., and Posner, M.I. (1993). Repetition effects in processing visual words: a high density ERP study of lateralized stimuli. *Neuroscience Abstracts, 19,* no. 1807.

McClelland, J.L., and Rumelhart, D.E. (1981) An interactive activation model of context effects in letter perception. Part 1. An account of basic findings.

Psychological Review, 88, 375–407

Menard, M.T., Kosslyn, S.M., Thompson, W.L., Alpert, N.M., and Rauch, S.L. (1996). Encoding words and pictures: A positron emission tomography study. *Neuropsychologia, 34,* 185–194.

Nobre, A.C., and McCarthy, G. (1994). Language-related ERPs: Scalp distributions and modulation by word type and semantic priming. *Journal of Cognitive Neuroscience, 6,* 233–255.

Petersen, S.E., Fox, P.T., Posner, M.I., Mintun, M., and Raichle, M. E. (1988). Positron emission tomographic studies of the cortical anatomy of single word processing. *Nature, 331,* 585–589.

Petersen, S.E., Fox, P.T., Snyder, A.Z., and Raichle, M.E. (1990). Activation of extrastriate and frontal cortical areas by visual words and word-like stimuli. *Science, 249,* 1041–1044.

Posner, M.I., and DiGirolamo, G.J. (1998) Conflict, Target detection and cognitive control. In R. Parasuraman (ed.) *The Attentive Brain.* (pp 401–424) Cambridge: MIT Press.

Posner, M.I., and Pavese, A. (1998). Anatomy of word and sentence meaning. *Proceedings of the National Academy of Sciences, 95,* 899–905.

Posner, M.I., and Raichle, M.E. (1994). *Images of Mind.* New York: Scientific American Library.

Posner, M.I., and Snyder, C.R.R. (1975).Facilitation and inhibition in the processing of signals. In P.M.A. Rabbitt and S. Dornic (eds.), *Attention and Performance V* (pp.669–682). New York: Academic Press

Raichle, M.E., Fiez, J.A., Videen, T.O., MacLeod, A.M.K., Pardo, J.V., and Petersen, S.E. (1994). Practice-related changes in human brain functional anatomy during non–motor learning. *Cerebral Cortex, 4,* 8–26.

Reichle, E.D., Pollatsek, A., Fisher, D.L., and Rayner, K. (1998). Torward a model of eye movment control in reading. *Psychological Review, 105,* 125–157.

Rayner, K., and Pollatsek, A.I. (1992). *The Psychology of Reading.* Englewood Cliffs, NJ: Prentice–Hall.

Rugg, M.D. (1987). Dissociation of semantic priming, word and non-word repetition effects by event-related potentials. *Quarterly Journal of Experimental Psychology, 39A,* 123–148.

Schacter, D.L., Alpert, N.M., Savage, C.R., Rauch, S.L., and Albert, M.S. (1996). Conscious recollection and the human hippocampal formation: evidence from positron emission tomography. *Proceedings of the National Academy of Sciences, 93,* 321-325.

Scherg, M., and Berg, P. (1993). *Brain Electrical Source Analysis.* Version 2.0. NeuroScan, Inc.

Schneider, W., Noll, D.C., and Cohen, J.D. (1993). Functional topographic mapping of the cortical ribbon in human vision with conventional MRI scanners. *Nature, 365,* 150–153.

Sereno, S.C., Pacht, J.M., and Rayner, K. (1992). The effect of meaning frequency on processing lexically ambiguous words: Evidence from eye fixations. *Psychological Science, 3,* 296–300.

Shaywitz, B.A., Shaywitz, S.E., Pugh, K.R., Constable, R.T., Skudlarski, P.l., Fulbright, R.K., Bronen, R.A., Fletcher, J.M. Shankweiler, D.P., Katz, L., and Gore, J.C. (1996). Sex differences in the functional organization of the brain for language. *Nature, 373,* 607–609.

Snyder, A.Z., Abdullaev, Y.G., Posner, M.I., and Raichle, M.E. (1995). Scalp electrical potentials reflect regional cerebral blood flow responses during processing of written words. *Proceedings of the National Academy of Sciences of the U.S.A., 92,* 1689–1693.

Spitzer, M., Kwong, K.K., Kennedy, W., Rosen, B.R., and Belliveau, J.W. (1995). Category-specific brain activation in fMRI during picture naming. *NeuroReport, 6,* 2109–2112.

Tucker, D.M. (1993). Spatial sampling of head electrical fields: The geodesic sensor net. *Electroencephalography and Clinical Neurophysiology, 87,* 154–163.

Tucker, D.M., Liotti, M., Potts, G.F., Russell, G.S., and Posner, M.I. (1994). Spatiotemporal analysis of brain electrical fields. *Human Brain Mapping, 1,* 134–152.

Tulving, E., Kapur, S., Craik, F.I.M., Moscovitch, M.,and Houle, S. (1994). Hemispheric encoding/retrieval asymmetry in episodic memory: PET findings. *Proceedings of the National. Academy of Sciences,* 2016–2020.

Van Petten, C., Kutas, M., Kluender, R., Mitchiner, M., and McIsaac, H. (1991). Fractionating the word repetition effect with event-related potentials. *Journal of Cognitive Neuroscience, 3,* 131–150.

Yang, L., and Givón, T. (1993). *Tracking the acquisition of L2 Vocabulary: The Keki Language Experiment.* (tech. rep. no. 93–11). University of Oregon, Institute of Cognitive and Decision Sciences.

11

Computational Modeling of Word Reading, Acquired Dyslexia, and Remediation

David C. Plaut

Many researchers assume that the most appropriate way to express the systematic aspects of language is in terms of a set of rules. For instance, there is a systematic relationship between the written and spoken forms of most English words (e.g., GAVE => /geIv/), and this relationship can be expressed with a fairly concise set of grapheme-phoneme correspondence (GPC) rules (e.g., G => /g/, A_E => /eI/, V => /v/). In addition to being able to generate accurate pronunciations of so-called *regular* words, such rules also provide a straightforward account of how skilled readers apply their knowledge to novel items–for example, in pronouncing word-like nonwords (e.g., MAVE => /meIv/). Most linguistic domains, however, are only partially systematic. Thus, there are many English words whose pronunciations violate the standard GPC rules (e.g., HAVE => /hæv/). Given that skilled readers can pronounce such *exception* words correctly, GPC rules alone are insufficient. More generally, skilled language performance at virtually every level of analysis–phonological, morphological, lexical, syntactic–requires both effective handling of exceptional items and the ability to generalize to novel forms.

In the domain of reading, there are three broad responses to this challenge. The first, adopted by traditional "dual-route" theories (Besner, chapter 13, this volume; Besner and Smith, 1992; Coltheart, 1978; 1985; Coltheart, Curtis, Atkins, and Haller, 1993; Marshall and Newcombe, 1973; Meyer, Schvaneveldt, and Ruddy, 1974; Morton and Patterson, 1980; Paap and Noel, 1991), is to add to the GPC system a separate, lexical system that handles the exceptions. The second response, adopted by "multiple-levels" theories (Norris, 1994; Shallice and McCarthy, 1985; Shallice, Warrington, and McCarthy, 1983), is to augment the GPC rules with more specific, context-sensitive rules, (e.g., OOK => /Uk/ as in BOOK), including rules that apply only to individual exceptions (e.g., PINT => /paInt/). Both of these approaches retain the general notion that language knowledge takes the form of rules (although such rules may be expressed in terms of connections between localist connectionist units; see, e.g., Norris, 1994; Reggia, Marsland, and Berndt, 1988).

The third response to the challenge, adopted by distributed connectionist theories (Plaut, McClelland, Seidenberg, and Patterson, 1996; Seidenberg and McClelland, 1989; Van Orden, Pennington, and Stone, 1990; Van Orden and Goldinger, 1994) and elaborated here, is more radical. It eschews the notion that the knowledge supporting online language performance takes the form of explicit rules. Of course, such performance can certainly be described approximately with rules, and language users can sometimes even state verbally certain of these "rules" (i.e., "I before E. . . "). The connectionist claim is that the language mechanism itself does not contain a set of rules and a rule interpreter. Rather, language knowledge is inherently graded, and the language mechanism is inherently a learning device that gradually picks up on the statistical structure among written and spoken words and the contexts in which they occur. In this view, there is no sharp division between the regular items that obey the rules and the exception items that violate them. Instead, the emphasis is on the degree to which the mappings among the spelling, sound, and meaning of a given word are consistent with those of other words (Glushko, 1979).[1]

To make this third perspective concrete, consider the connectionist-parallel distributed processing (PDP) framework for lexical processing depicted in figure 11.1, based on that of Seidenberg and McClelland (1989). Orthographic, phonological, and semantic information is represented by distributed patterns of activity over separate groups of simple neuron-like processing units. Within each domain, similar words are represented by similar patterns of activity. Lexical tasks involve transformations among these representations–for example, oral reading requires the orthographic pattern for a word to generate the appropriate phonological pattern. Such transformations are accomplished via the cooperative and competitive interactions among units, including additional hidden units that mediate between the orthographic, phonological, and semantic units. In processing an input, units interact until the network as a whole settles into a stable pattern of activity–termed an *attractor*–corresponding to its interpretation of the input. Unit interactions are governed by weighted connections among them, which collectively encode the system's knowledge about how the different types of information are related. Weights that give rise to the appropriate transformations are learned on the basis of the system's exposure to written words, spoken words, and their meanings.

As figure 11.1 makes clear, the connectionist approach does not entail a complete lack of structure within the reading system. But the distinctions that are relevant relate to the different types of information that must be coordinated–orthographic, phonological, and semantic. Given that such information may be differentially based on input from different modalities (at least for the surface forms), it

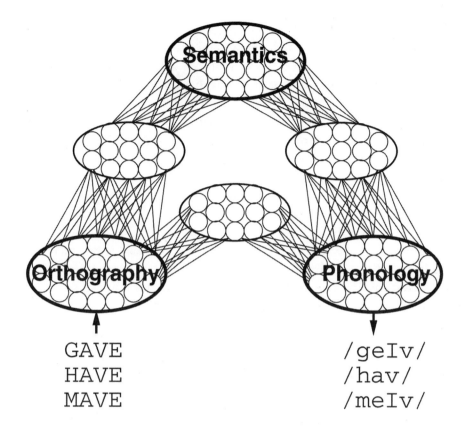

Figure 11.1 A connectionist framework for lexical processing, based on
that of Seidenberg and McClelland (1989).

is natural to assume that the corresponding representations–and hence the pathways among them–are neuroanatomically distinct. In fact, such divisions will turn out to be critical in accounting for data on the selective effects of brain damage on reading. Irrespective of these distinctions among types of representations, however, there is a uniformity in the processing mechanisms by which they are derived and interact. In this way, the distributed connectionist approach is fundamentally at odds with the core tenet of dual-route theories. To be clear, the essence of a dual-route theory is not that it has two pathways from print to sound (in fact, most such theories have three such pathways: sublexical, lexical semantic, and lexical nonsemantic; see Besner, chapter 13, this volume); rather, it is the claim that the mechanism that processes nonwords (typically GPC rules and an interpreter) is functionally distinct from, and operates according to different principles than, the mechanism that processes exception words (typically a look-up table or an associative network). It is this inhomogeneity of processing mechanisms that the distributed connectionist approach rejects.

In this context, it is important to note that it is perfectly feasible to build a dual-route mechanism out of connectionist hardware. For example, Zorzi, Houghton, and Butterworth (1998) have recently described simulations in which direct connections from letter units to phoneme units support the pronunciation of regular words and nonwords, whereas a separate pathway, composed either of hidden units or localist word units, supports the pronunciation of exception words (also see Reggia et al., 1988). Although the mechanisms employed for the two pathways are more homogeneous than in more traditional, rule-based implementations (e.g., Coltheart et al., 1993), the models nonetheless retain a categorical distinction between items that obey spelling-sound rules and items that violate them.

This chapter describes a series of computational simulations based on the framework depicted in figure 11.1. The value of computational modeling is greatest when properties of the formalism guide and constrain simulation work, and lead to insight into counterintuitive findings. Along these lines, one can identify three general computational principles on which the current connectionist approach to word reading is based:

1. *Distributed representation.* Orthography, phonology, and semantics are represented by distributed patterns of activity such that similar words are represented by similar patterns.[2]
2. *Structure-sensitive learning.* Knowledge of the relationships among orthography, phonology, and semantics is encoded across connection weights that are learned gradually through repeated experience with words in a way that is sensitive to the statistical structure of each mapping.
3. *Interactivity.* Mapping among orthography, phonology, and semantics is accomplished through the simultaneous interaction of many units, such that familiar patterns form stable attractors.[3]

These principles are claimed to be general in that versions of them apply across all cognitive domains. The challenge, however, is to apply the principles to account for detailed behavioral data. The goal here is to demonstrate that, when instantiated in a particular domain–single-word reading–these principles provide important insights into the patterns of normal and impaired cognitive behavior. Word reading is a particularly appropriate domain of study because there is a wealth of detailed empirical data on reading acquisition and developmental dyslexia, normal skilled reading, acquired dyslexia from brain damage, and rehabilitation after brain damage. Each of these areas will be noted, but the focus here is on issues in normal reading, acquired dyslexia, and rehabilitation.

Skilled Oral Reading

Although the distributed connectionist framework for word reading depicted in figure 11.1 may appear reasonable at a general level, it reflects a radical departure from traditional theorizing about lexical processing, particularly in two ways. First, there is nothing in the structure of the system that corresponds to individual words per se, such as a lexical entry, localist word unit (McClelland and Rumelhart, 1981) or "logogen" (Morton, 1969). Rather, words are distinguished from nonwords only by functional properties of the system—the way in which particular orthographic, phonological, and semantic patterns of activity interact (also see Plaut, 1997; Van Orden et al., 1990). Second, there are no separate mechanisms for lexical and sublexical processing (*contra* Coltheart et al., 1993), such that, for instance, regular words (e.g., MINT) are pronounced by one route and exceptions (e.g., PINT) by another. Rather, all parts of the system participate in processing all types of input, although the contributions of different parts may be more or less important for different inputs.

In an attempt to demonstrate that the structural reification of words and of lexical-sublexical processing routes is unnecessary to account for skilled oral reading, Seidenberg and McClelland (1989) trained a connectionist network to map from the orthography of about 3,000 monosyllabic English words—both regular and exception—to their phonology (i.e., the bottom portion of the framework in figure 11.1, referred to as the *phonological pathway*). After training, the network pronounced correctly 97.7% of the words, including most exception words. The network also exhibited the standard empirical pattern of an interaction of frequency and consistency in naming latency (Andrews, 1982; Seidenberg, Waters, Barnes, and Tanenhaus, 1984a; Taraban and McClelland, 1987; Waters and Seidenberg, 1985) if its real-valued accuracy in generating a response is taken as a proxy for response time (under the assumption that an imprecise phonological representation would be less effective at driving an articulatory system). The model was much worse than skilled readers, however, at pronouncing orthographically legal nonwords (Besner, Twilley, McCann, and Seergobin, 1990) and at lexical decision under some conditions (Besner et al., 1990; Fera and Besner, 1992). Thus, the model failed to refute traditional claims that localist, word-specific representations and separate mechanisms are necessary to account for skilled reading. More recently, Plaut,

McClelland, Seidenberg, and Patterson (1996, see also Plaut and McClelland, 1993; Seidenberg, Plaut, Petersen, McClelland, and McRae, 1994) have shown that the limitations of the Seidenberg and McClelland model in pronouncing nonwords stems not from any general limitation in the abilities of connectionist networks in quasiregular domains (as suggested by, e.g., Coltheart et al., 1993), but from its use of poorly structured orthographic and phonological representations. The original simulation used representations based on context-sensitive triples of letters or phonemic features. When more appropriately structured representations are used–based on graphemes and phonemes and embodying phonotactic and graphotactic constraints–network implementations of the phonological pathway can learn to pronounce regular words, exception words, and nonwords as well as skilled readers. Furthermore, the networks also exhibit the empirical frequency-by-consistency interaction pattern when trained on actual word frequencies.[4] This remains true if naming latencies are modeled directly by the settling time of a recurrent, attractor network (see figure 11.2, top panel).

Importantly, Plaut et al. (1996) went beyond providing only empirical demonstrations that networks could reproduce accuracy and latency data on word and nonword reading to offer a mathematical analysis of the critical factors that govern why the networks (and, by hypothesis, subjects) behave as they do. This analysis was based on a network that, while simpler than the actual simulations–it had no hidden units and employed Hebbian learning–retained many of the essential characteristics of the more general framework (e.g., distributed representations and structure-sensitive learning). For this simplified network, it was possible to derive an expression for how the response of the network to any input (test) pattern depends on its experience with every pattern on which the network is trained, as a function of its frequency of training, its similarity with the test pattern, and the consistency of its output with that of the test pattern. Specifically, the response $s_j^{[t]}$ of any output unit j to a given test pattern t is given by

$$s_j^{[t]} = \sigma \left(F^{[t]} + \sum_f F^{[f]}\theta^{[ft]} - \sum_e F^{[e]}\theta^{[et]} \right) \quad (1)$$

in which the standard smooth, nonlinear sigmoidal input-output function for each unit, $\sigma(\cdot)$, is applied to the sum of three terms: (1) the cumulative frequency of training on the pattern t itself, $F^{[t]}$; (2) the sum of the frequencies $F^{[f]}$ of the *friends* of pattern t (similar patterns trained to produce the same response for unit j), each

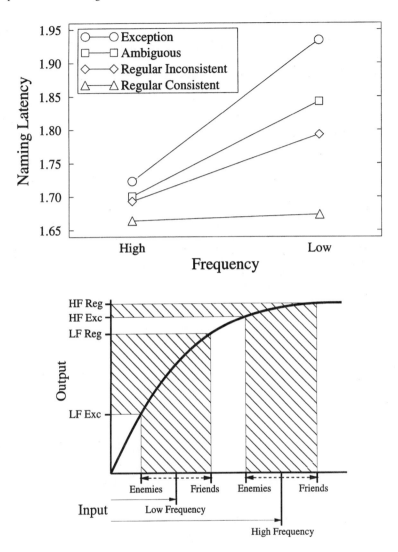

Figure 11.2 The frequency-by-consistency interaction exhibited in the
settling time of an attractor network implementation of the
phonological pathway in pronouncing words of varying frequency and
spelling-sound consistency (Plaut et al., 1996, simulation 3); and its
explanation in terms of additive contributions of frequency and
consistency subject to an asymptotic activation function (only the top
of which is shown).

weighted by its similarity (overlap) with t, $\theta^{[f_i]}$; and (3) minus the sum of the frequencies $F^{[e_i]}$ of the *enemies* of pattern t (similar patterns trained to produce the opposite response), each weighted by its similarity to t, $\theta^{[e_i]}$.

Many of the basic phenomena in word reading can be seen as natural consequences of adherence to this frequency-consistency equation. Factors that increase the summed input to units (e.g., word frequency, spelling-sound consistency) improve performance as measured by naming accuracy and/or latency, but their contributions are subject to "diminishing returns" due to the asymptotic nature of the activation function (see figure 11.2, bottom panel). As a result, performance on stimuli that are strong in one factor is relatively insensitive to variation in other factors. Thus, regular words show little effect of frequency and high-frequency words show little effect of consistency, giving rise to the standard pattern of interaction between frequency and consistency, in which the naming of low-frequency exception words is disproportionately slow or inaccurate. Equation 1 is only approximate, however, for more complex networks—those with hidden units and trained with an error-correcting algorithm like back-propagation. These two aspects of the Plaut et al. (1996) simulations are critical in that they help to overcome interference from enemies (i.e., the negative terms in equation 1), thereby enabling the networks to achieve correct performance on exception words—that is, words with many enemies and few, if any, friends—as well as on regular words and nonwords.

Impaired Oral Reading in Surface Dyslexia

Although Plaut et al. (1996) demonstrated that implementations of the phonological pathway on its own can learn to pronounce words and nonwords as well as skilled readers, a central aspect of their general theory is that skilled reading more typically requires the combined support of both the semantic and phonological pathways see also Harm, 1998; Hillis and Caramazza, 1991; Van Orden and Goldinger, 1994), and that individuals may differ in the relative competence of each pathway (Plaut, 1997; Seidenberg, 1992). Certainly semantic involvement is necessary to pronounce homographs like WIND and READ correctly. Furthermore, a semantic variable—imageability—influences the strength of the frequency-by-consistency interaction in the naming latencies and errors of skilled readers (Strain, Patterson, and Seidenberg, 1995). Moreover, brain damage that impairs lexical semantics—typically to the left-temporal lobe—can lead to an abnormal pattern of reading performance, known as *surface dyslexia* (see Patterson, Coltheart, and Marshall, 1985). In its purest, so-called fluent form (e.g., MP, Behrmann and Bub, 1992; Bub, Cancelliere, and Kertesz, 1985; KT, McCarthy and Warrington, 1986; HTR, Shallice et al., 1983) surface dyslexic patients read nonwords and regular words with normal accuracy and latency, but they exhibit an interaction of frequency and consistency in word reading accuracy that mirrors that shown by normal subjects in their naming latencies. That is, surface dyslexic patients are disproportionately poor at pronouncing low-frequency exception words, often giving a pronunciation consistent with more standard spelling-sound correspondences (e.g., SEW read as "sue," termed a *regularization* error). In fact, there can be a close correlation for individual patients between the lack of comprehension of exception words and their likelihood of being regularized (Graham, Hodges, and Patterson, 1994; Hillis and Caramazza, 1991). Moreover, the surface dyslexic pattern may emerge gradually as lexical semantic knowledge deteriorates in patients with some types of progressive dementia, such as semantic dementia (Graham et al., 1994; Patterson and Hodges, 1992; Schwartz, Marin, and Saffran, 1979) or dementia of the Alzheimer's type (Balota and Ferraro, 1993; Patterson, Graham, and Hodges, 1994).

The framework for lexical processing depicted in figure 11.1 (and the implied computational principles) provides a natural formulation of how contributions from both the semantic and phonological pathways might be integrated in oral reading. At an abstract level, given that phonological units simply sum their inputs from the two pathways, the influence of the semantic pathway can be included in a straightforward manner by adding an additional term, $S^{[t]}$, to the summed input in equation 1. Furthermore, if we assume that this term increases with imageability, this accounts for the three-way interaction of frequency, consistency, and imageability found by Strain et al. (1995). When formulated explicitly in connectionist terms, however, this integration has far-reaching implications for the nature of learning in the two pathways. During training, to the extent that the contribution of one pathway reduces the overall error, the other will experience less pressure to learn. Specifically, if the semantic pathway contributes significantly to the pronunciation of words, then the phonological pathway need not learn to pronounce all of the words by itself. Rather, this pathway will tend to learn best those words high in frequency and/or consistency (i.e., those items with large positive terms in equation 1); on its own it may never master low-frequency exception words completely. Of course, in skilled readers, the combination of the semantic and phonological pathways will be fully competent. But brain damage that reduced or eliminated the semantic pathway would lay bare the latent inadequacies of the phonological pathway, giving rise to surface dyslexia.

In further simulations, Plaut et al. (1996; Plaut, 1997) explored the possibility that the surface dyslexic reading pattern might reflect the natural limitations of an intact but isolated phonological pathway that had learned to rely on semantic support. Given that a full implementation of the semantic pathway was beyond the scope of their work, they approximated the contribution that such a pathway would make to oral reading by providing the output (phoneme) units of the phonological pathway with external input that pushed them toward the correct pronunciation of each word during training. Semantic damage, then, was modeled by weakening or removing this external input. Plaut and colleagues found that, indeed, a phonological pathway trained in the context of support from semantics exhibited the central phenomena of surface dyslexia when semantics was removed and, moreover, that individual differences in the severity of surface dyslexia can arise not only from differences in the amount of semantic damage but also from premorbid differences in the division of labor between the semantic and phonological pathways. This division of labor–and the overall competence of the reading system–would be expected to be influenced by a wide variety of factors, including the nature of reading instruction, the sophistication of preliterate phonological representations, relative experience in reading aloud versus silently, the computational resources (e.g., numbers of units and connections) devoted to each pathway, and the reader's more general skill levels in visual pattern recognition and in spoken word comprehension and production. Thus, the few patients exhibiting mild to moderate semantic impairments without concomitant regularization errors (early WLP, Schwartz et al., 1979; MB, Raymer and Berndt, 1994; DRN, Cipolotti and Warrington, 1995; DC, Lambon Ralph, Ellis, and Franklin, 1995) may have, for various reasons, reading systems with relatively weak reliance on the semantic pathway (see Plaut, 1997, for relevant simulations and discussion).

In summary, Plaut et al. (1996) provided connectionist simulations and mathematical analyses supporting a view of lexical processing in which the distinctions between words and nonwords, and between regular and exception words, are not reflected in the structure of the system but rather in functional aspects of its behavior as it brings all its knowledge to bear in processing an input. An important insight that emerges from this approach is that semantic and phonological processing are intimately related, over the course of reading acquisition, in normal skilled performance, and in the effects of brain damage. Unfortunately, while emphasizing the importance of semantics, the Plaut et al. simulations offer little insight into the specific nature of semantic representations and processes; the simulations of surface dyslexia in particular are limited by the lack of an actual implementation of the semantic pathway (see, however, Harm, 1998). Moreover, without such an implementation, Plaut et al. were also unable to remedy the limitations of the Seidenberg and McClelland (1989) model in performing lexical decision.

In fact, given that the relationship between a (monomorphemic) word and its meaning is essentially arbitrary, it might appear that an implementation of the semantic pathway would require the use of word-specific representations. Implementations of the semantic pathway using distributed representations have, however, been pursued on a smaller scale in the context of modeling semantic and associative priming in lexical decision (Plaut, 1995b), impaired reading via meaning in deep dyslexic patients (Plaut and Shallice, 1993), and remediation of semantics by retraining after damage (Plaut, 1996). The next three sections take up the issues in each of these domains.

Semantic and Associative Priming in Lexical Decision

In a variety of lexical tasks, including naming and lexical decision, subjects are faster and more accurate to process a word, such as BUTTER, when it is preceded by a semantically related word like BREAD relative to an unrelated word like HOUSE (e.g., Meyer and Schvaneveldt, 1971, see Neely, 1991, for a review). This semantic priming effect is influenced by a number of stimulus factors, including perceptual factors like visual quality (greater for visually degraded stimuli; see, e.g., Becker and Killion, 1977; Meyer, Schvaneveldt, and Ruddy, 1975), lexical factors like word frequency (greater for low-frequency targets; see, e.g., Becker, 1979), and semantic factors like category dominance (greater for high-dominance exemplars; see, e.g., Lorch, Balota, and Stamm, 1986). Priming also varies with the stimulus onset asynchrony (SOA) between prime and target, and it is subject to both facilitation and inhibition effects (e.g., Neely, 1977). Such findings are taken by many theorists as reflecting fundamental properties of the organization of semantic knowledge.

To provide an account for these findings, Plaut (1995b) trained a distributed attractor network on an artificial version of the task of deriving the meanings of written words (i.e., mapping orthography to semantics in figure 11.1). As is standard in distributed network models (e.g., Kawamoto, 1988; Masson, 1991; 1995; McRae, de Sa, and Seidenberg, 1993; Sharkey and Sharkey, 1992), semantic relatedness among words was reflected in the degree of overlap of their semantic features. These models typically employ only a single, symmetric manipulation–pattern overlap–to encode word relatedness, so there is no opportunity for different types of relations among words to behave differently. In particular, one can distinguish an associative relation among words (e.g., as measured by free association norms; Postman and Keppel, 1970) from a purely semantic relation (i.e., having similar meanings, such as category co-ordinates). These two types of relations have been shown to give rise to different empirical effects in a number of contexts (e.g., Becker, 1980; Glosser and Friedman, 1991; Moss and Marslen-Wilson, 1993; Moss, Ostrin, Tyler, and Marslen-Wilson, 1995; Seidenberg, Waters, Sanders, and Langer, 1984b). In Plaut's (1995b) simulation, semantic relatedness was encoded by degree of pattern overlap (as in most distributed models) but an association from one word to another was encoded in a different manner in the likelihood that the one follows the other during training (see Moss, Hare, Day, and Tyler, 1994, for a similar approach).

Semantic patterns were constructed to form categories by generating eight random prototype patterns (e.g., *bird*), such that each feature had a probability of 0.1 of being active. Sixteen category exemplars were then generated from each prototype by randomly changing some of its features; fewer for high-dominance exemplars (e.g., *robin*) than for low-dominance exemplars (e.g., *goose*). The resulting 128 semantic representations were randomly assigned orthographic representations consisting of patterns of activity over 20 orthographic units. These patterns were generated randomly such that each unit had a probability of 0.1 of being active, with the constraint that every pattern had at least two active units and all pairs of patterns differed in the activities of at least two units. No attempt was made to model orthographic relatedness among words; the orthographic patterns simply guaranteed that the written forms of words were fairly sparse and were discriminable from each other. The critical property of the task was that, although there were systematic relationships among word meanings, there was no systematic relationship between the written form of a word and its meaning.

During training, the network started from the final activity pattern produced by the previous word in processing the next word. Often the next word chosen was the associate of the previous word. On the remaining trials, the probability that words were selected for training depended on their assigned frequency such that high-frequency words were twice as likely to be trained as low-frequency words. To encourage robust performance, each orthographic pattern was corrupted slightly with Gaussian noise (*SD*=0.05) when presented for training. The network was trained with a continuous version of back-propagation through time (Pearlmutter, 1989) to activate the word's semantic features as quickly as possible when presented with its orthography.

After training, the network was tested for priming effects by presenting a prime word for some specified duration, then replacing it with the target word and allowing the network to settle to the appropriate semantic representation for the target. The prime could be semantically related, associatively related, or unrelated to the target. The reaction time (RT) of the network to the target was defined as the time it took the network to settle to the point where no semantic unit changed it state by more than 0.001. The difference in RT values for unrelated versus related primes constitutes a measure of (semantic or associative) priming.

When trained and tested in this manner, the network exhibited two empirical effects that have posed problems for other distributed network theories of priming (e.g., Kawamoto, 1988; Masson, 1991; 1995; McRae et al., 1993; Sharkey and Sharkey, 1992): much stronger associative priming than semantic priming (e.g., Becker, 1980; Shelton and Martin, 1992), and significant associative priming across an intervening unrelated item (e.g., Joordens and Besner, 1992; McNamara, 1994).[5] It also reproduced the empirical findings of greater priming for low-frequency targets, degraded targets, and high-dominance category exemplars.

Although not reported by Plaut (1995b), the network's performance on words provides a reliable basis for performing lexical decision (LD). A natural way to perform LD is on the basis of some measure of the familiarity of the stimulus (Balota and Chumbley, 1984). A commonly used measure of familiarity in distributed networks is the negative of the energy, $\Sigma_{i<j} s_i s_j w_{ij}$ (Hopfield, 1982), that reflects the degree to which unit states satisfy the soft constraints imposed by the weights. A number of researchers (e.g., Besner and Joordens, 1995; Borowsky and Masson, 1996; Masson and Borowsky, 1995; Rueckl, 1995, see also Masson, chapter 12, this volume) have proposed recently that it may be possible to perform LD on the basis of differences in the energy of words versus nonwords. A serious drawback of this measure, however, is that it requires decision processes to have explicit access to the weights among units (analogous to synaptic strengths between neurons), which is far less neurobiologically plausible than a procedure that need only access unit states. An appropriate alternative measure, termed stress, is based only on the states of units. Specifically, the stress S_j of unit j is a measure of the information content (entropy) of its state s_j, corresponding to the degree to which it is different from rest:

$$S_j = s_j \log_2(s_j) + (1 - s_j) \log_2(1 - s_j) - \log_2(0.5) \quad (2)$$

The stress of a unit is 0 when its state is 0.5 and approaches 1 as its state approaches either 0.0 or 1.0. The target semantic patterns for words are binary vectors (i.e., consist of 1s and 0s) and thus have maximal stress. Since over the course of training the semantic patterns generated by words increasingly approximate their target patterns, the average stress of semantic units approaches 1 for words. By contrast, nonwords are novel stimuli that share orthographic features with words that have conflicting semantic features. As a result, nonwords typically fail to drive semantic units as strongly, producing semantic patterns with much lower average stress. Thus, the average stress of semantic units, here termed simply *semantic stress*, forms a reliable basis for performing LD.[6]

To demonstrate the adequacy of this approach, 128 nonwords were created by generating new orthographic patterns in the same manner as the trained patterns, ensuring that each nonword differs from every word by at least two units (i.e., the same constraint that applies between any two words). These patterns function as nonwords in that they have the same statistical structure as the orthographic patterns for words but were never presented to the network during training. The performance of the network was tested on each word and nonword as target when preceded by each unrelated word as prime (over a range of prime durations). Using a response criterion by which a "yes" response was given if the semantic stress after settling exceeded 0.945, the network made only 0.70% misses and 0.38% false alarms in LD, yielding a d' of 5.12 (see figure 11.3). Thus, a distributed network that maps orthography to semantics can account for the ability of skilled readers to reliably distinguish word from word-like nonwords based on a measure of the degree to which semantic units receive strong input that drives them to near-binary states.

More recently, Plaut (1997) has successfully applied this approach to model

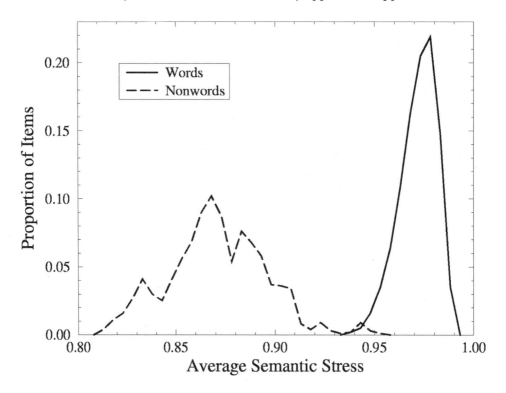

Figure 11.3 The distributions of average stress of semantic units for words and nonwords exhibited by the Plaut (1995b) network.

LD on actual word and nonword stimuli. A feed-forward network was trained to map from the orthographic representations of the 2,998 monosyllabic words in the Plaut et al. (1996) corpus to their phonological representations and to artificially created semantic representations like those described above. After 1,300 epochs of training, the network accurately derived the phonology and semantics of each word when presented with its orthography. It was then tested for its ability to distinguish these words from 591 pronounceable nonwords (Seidenberg, Plaut, Petersen, McClelland, and McRae, 1994) on the basis of the levels of semantic stress produced by each type of stimuli. When a "yes" criterion of 0.955 was adopted, the network produced only 0.90% (27/2998) misses and 1.52% (9/582) false alarms, corresponding to a d' of 4.53. In a second test involving 64 pseudohomophones (PH; e.g., JOAK) and closely matched nonpseudohomophone (nonPH) control nonwords (e.g., HOAK; Seidenberg, Petersen, MacDonald, and Plaut, 1996), the network produced reliably higher semantic stress values–and thus poorer discrimination from words–for the pseudohomophones (means: PH = 0.9246, nonPH = 0.9184; paired t[63] = 2.408, p = .019). Thus, the network exhibited accurate performance overall as well as the empirical finding of a pseudohomophone disadvantage in LD (see Besner,chapter 13, this volume; Coltheart, Davelaar, Jonasson, and Besner, 1977; McCann and Besner, 1987).

    The Plaut (1995b) and Plaut (1997) simulations focus on normal skilled performance of lexical decision. Other simulations of the operation of the semantic pathway have attempted to address patterns of impaired performance among certain types of brain-damaged patients and how such impairments might be remediated.

Impaired Reading via Meaning in Deep and Phonological Dyslexia

As one might expect from the name, patients with *deep dyslexia* (see Coltheart, Patterson, and Marshall, 1980) have reading impairments that are in many ways opposite to those with surface dyslexia in that they appear to read almost entirely via semantics. Deep dyslexic patients are thought to have severe (perhaps complete) damage of the phonological pathway, as evidenced by their inability to read even the simplest of pronounceable nonwords (but see Buchanan, Hildebrandt, and MacKinnon, 1994a; 1994b; 1996; chapter 7, this volume). They also have impairments in reading words that suggest additional partial damage to the semantic pathway. In particular, the hallmark symptom of deep dyslexia is the occurrence of semantic errors in oral reading (e.g., reading CAT as "dog"). Strangely, these semantic errors co-occur with a peculiar combination of other symptoms. Central among these are other errors that involve visual similarity: pure visual errors (e.g., CAT =>

"cot"), mixed visual-and-semantic errors (e.g., CAT => "rat"), and even mediated visual-then-semantic errors (e.g., SYMPATHY => "orchestra", presumably via symphony). Furthermore, the likelihood that a word is read correctly depends on its part-of-speech (nouns > adjectives > verbs > function words) and its concreteness or imageability (concrete, imageable words > abstract, less imageable words). Finally, differences across patients in written and spoken comprehension, and in the distribution of error types, suggest that the secondary damage to the semantic pathway may occur before, within, or after semantics (Shallice and Warrington, 1980).

Deep dyslexia is closely related to another type of acquired dyslexia–so-called *phonological dyslexia* (Beauvois and Derouesne, 1979). The defining characteristic of phonological dyslexic patients is that they have a selective impairment in reading nonwords compared with reading words. Although such patients do not produce above-chance rates of semantic errors, they can be quite similar to deep dyslexic patients in other respects. In fact, Glosser and Friedman (1990; see also Buchanan, Hildebrandt, and MacKinnon, chapter 7, this volume) argued that deep and phonological dyslexic patients fall on a continuum of severity of impairment with deep dyslexia at the most severe end. Moreover, Friedman (1996; see also Klein, Behrmann, and Doctor, 1994) has argued that the symptoms in deep dyslexia resolve in a particular order over the course of recovery, reflecting the continuum of impairment. The occurrence of semantic errors is the first symptom to resolve, constituting a somewhat arbitrary transition from deep to phonological dyslexia). The concreteness effect is the next symptom to resolve, followed by the part-of-speech effect, then the visual and morphological errors, and only lastly the impaired nonword reading. A similar pattern of recovery has been documented in deep dysphasic patients, who make semantic errors in repetition (see Martin, Dell, and Schwartz, 1994; Martin and Saffran, 1992; Martin, Saffran, and Dell, 1996).

Hinton and Shallice (1991) reproduced the co-occurrence of visual, semantic, and mixed visual-and-semantic errors in deep dyslexia by damaging a connectionist network that mapped orthography to semantics. During training, the network learned to form attractors for 40 word meanings across five categories, such that patterns of semantic features that were similar to a known word meaning were pulled to that exact meaning over the course of settling. When the network was damaged by removing some units or connections, it no longer settled normally; the initial semantic activity caused by an input would occasionally fall within a neighboring attractor basin, giving rise to an error response. These errors were often semantically related to the stimulus because words with similar meanings correspond to nearby attractors in semantic space. The damaged network also produced visual errors due to its inherent bias toward similarity: visually similar words tend to produce similar initial semantic patterns, which can lead to a visual error if the basins are distorted by damage (see figure 11.4).

Plaut and Shallice (1993) extended these initial findings in a number of ways. They established the generality of the co-occurrence of error types across a wide range of simulations, showing that it does not depend on specific characteristics of the network architecture–the learning procedure– or the way responses are generated from semantic activity. A particularly relevant simulation in this regard involved an implementation of the full semantic pathway–mapping orthography to phonology via semantics–using a deterministic Boltzmann machine (Hinton, 1989; Peterson and Anderson, 1987). Lesions throughout the network gave rise to both

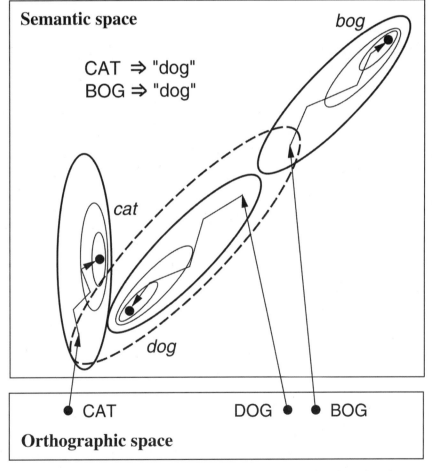

Figure 11.4 How damage to attractors (dashed oval) can give rise to both semantic and visual errors.

visual and semantic errors, with lesions prior to semantics producing a bias toward visual errors and lesions after semantics producing a bias toward semantic errors. Thus, the network replicated both the qualitative similarity and quantitative differences among deep-dyslexic patients. The network also exhibited a number of other characteristics of deep dyslexia not considered by Hinton and Shallice (1991), including the occurrence of visual-then-semantic errors, greater confidence in visual as compared with semantic errors, and relatively preserved lexical decision with impaired naming.

Plaut and Shallice carried out further simulations to address the influences of concreteness on the reading performance of deep-dyslexic patients. Another full implementation of the semantic pathway, shown in figure 11.5, was trained to pronounce a new set of words consisting of both concrete and abstract words. Concrete words were assigned far more semantic features than were abstract words under the assumption that the semantic representations of concrete words are less dependent on the contexts in which they occur (Saffran, Bogyo, Schwartz, and Marin, 1980; Schwanenflugel, 1991). As a result, the network developed stronger attractors for concrete than abstract words during training, giving rise to better performance in reading concrete words under most types of damage, as observed in deep dyslexia (see figure 11.6, left). Surprisingly, severe damage to connections implementing the attractors at the semantic level produced the opposite pattern in which the network read abstract words better than concrete words (see figure11.6, right). This pattern of performance is reminiscent of CAV, the single, enigmatic patient with *concrete word dyslexia* (Warrington, 1981). The double dissociation between reading concrete versus abstract words in patients is often interpreted as implying that there are separate modules within the cognitive system for concrete and abstract words. The current simulation demonstrates that such a radical interpretation is unnecessary: the double dissociation can arise from damage to different parts of a distributed network in which parts process both types of items but develop somewhat different functional specializations through learning (see Plaut, 1995a, for further results and discussion).

The Plaut and Shallice (1993) simulations of deep dyslexia provide strong support for characterizing the operation of the semantic pathway, and lexical semantic processing more generally, as a distributed network that learns to form attractors for patterns of semantic features that correspond to word meanings. It should be pointed out, however, that it is possible to model similar phenomena using word-specific representations. For example, Dell (1986; 1988) used a connectionist network with localist units to model semantic and phonological influences in speech production errors, and Martin et al. (1994) replicated aspects of deep dysphasia

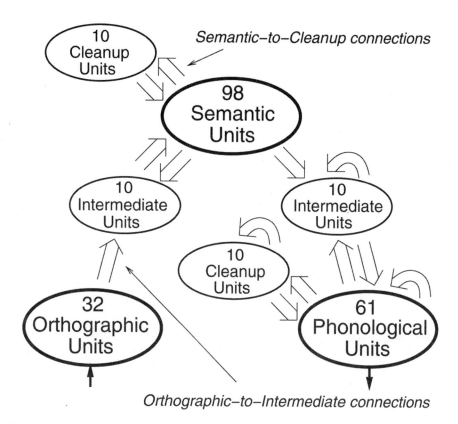

Figure 11.5 The architecture used by Plaut and Shallice (1993) to model
the effects of concreteness in deep dyslexia. The network constitutes a
full implementation of the semantic pathway of figure 11.1 with the
addition of extra "cleanup" units that allow the network to learn
stronger semantic and phonological attractors.

(Howard and Franklin, 1988; Katz and Goodglass, 1990; Martin and Saffran,
1990), including semantic and phonological errors in word repetition, by introducing abnormally rapid decay of lexical activation in the Dell model. The advantage
of the distributed approach in the current context is that the properties of normal
and impaired semantic processing arise out of the same computational principles
that operate in the rest of the lexical system.

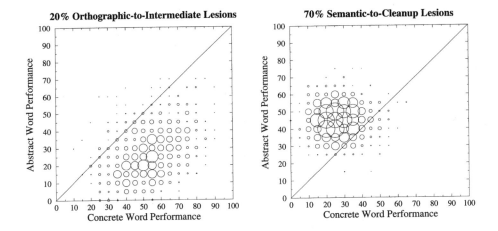

Figure 11.6 Percent correct performance on concrete versus abstract words of the Plaut and Shallice (1993) simulation after (left) 1000 lesions of 20% of orthographic-to-intermediate connections and (right) 1000 lesions of 70% of semantic-to-cleanup connections, as depicted in figure 11.5. The radius of each circle is proportional to the number of lesions yielding the performance levels indicated by the position of the circle. The diagonal lines correspond to equal levels of performance on concrete and abstract words.

Rehabilitating Reading via Meaning

An important but often neglected motivation for theoretical analyses of normal cognitive processing and its breakdown following brain damage in individual patients is that such analyses may lead to the design of more effective therapy to remediate cognitive impairments (Howard and Hatfield, 1987). Attempts at cognitive rehabilitation of the mapping between orthography and semantics (e.g., Behrmann, 1987; Coltheart and Byng, 1989; Scott and Byng, 1989; Weekes and Coltheart, 1996) have resulted in considerable improvement in performance on treated words and significant generalization to untreated but related words, although there is little understanding of the underlying mechanisms by which this occurs. Furthermore, the degree and breadth of recovery and generalization can vary considerably across patients: Some patients show generalization in some semantic categories but not others (e.g., CH, Behrmann and Lieberthal, 1989), some learn the treated items well but show no generalization to untreated items (e.g., PS, Hillis, 1993), still others have difficulty learning the treated items themselves. As Hillis (1993) points out, what is needed is a theory of rehabilitation that provides a detailed specification of the impaired cognitive system, how it changes in response to treatment, and what factors are relevant to the efficacy of the treatment.

With the goal of contributing to such a theory, Plaut (1996) investigated the degree of recovery and generalization produced when networks that read via meaning are retrained after damage. In one experiment, a replication of the Hinton and Shallice (1991) network was trained until it was fully accurate on all 40 words. It was then subjected to damage either near orthography, or within semantics, and retrained on half of the words. Performance was measured both for those treated words and for the untreated words. For comparison, performance of the network when retrained on all 40 words was also measured. Plaut found that retraining produced rapid improvement on treated words and substantial generalization to untreated words only after lesions within semantics; when retraining after lesions near orthography, treated improvement was erratic and there was no generalization to untreated words (see figure 11.7). This difference is due to the relative degree of consistency in the mapping performed at different levels of the network. Figure 11.8 presents a graphical depiction of this effect using vectors (arrows) to represent weight changes. Within semantics, similar words require similar interactions so that the weight changes caused by retraining on some words will tend also to improve performance on other, related words (i.e., the optimal weight changes for words are mutually consistent). By contrast, similar orthographic patterns typically must gen-

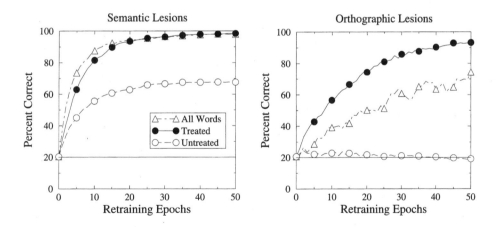

Figure 11. 7 Correct performance in pronouncing treated and untreated items when retraining the Plaut (1996) network that maps orthography to semantics after (a) lesions within semantics (i.e., 50% of cleanup-to-semantics connections), and (b) lesions near orthography (i.e., 30% of orthographic-to-intermediate connections; see figure 11.5). Performance when retraining on all 40 words is also shown for each condition.

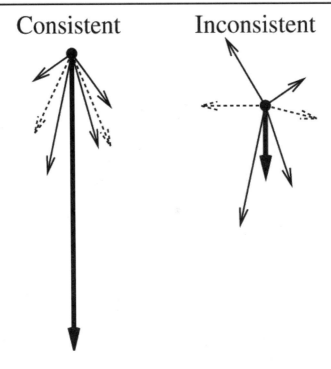

Figure 11.8 Depiction of the effect of consistent versus inconsistent weight changes on the extent of recovery and generalization in relearning. In each condition, the small solid arrows represent directions of weight change induced by treated words; the large solid arrow is the (vector) sum of these smaller arrows, representing the actual weight changes administered to the network. The length of this vector reflects the speed of relearning the treated words. The dotted arrows represent directions of weight change that would be optimal for untreated words if they were trained—to the extent that these point in the same direction as the actual weight-change vector, retraining on the treated words will also improve performance on the untreated words.

erate very different semantic patterns. As a result, when retraining after lesions near orthography, the weight changes for treated items are unrelated to those that would improve the untreated items and there is no generalization. These finding provide a basis for understanding the mechanisms of recovery and generalization in patients and may help explain the observed variability in their recovery.

A theory of rehabilitation should provide guidance in selecting items for treatment so as to maximize generalized recovery. In a second experiment, Plaut (1996) used an artificial version of the task of mapping orthography to semantics to investigate whether generalization was greater when retraining on high- versus low-dominance category exemplars. Somewhat surprisingly, although retraining on high-dominance exemplars produced greater recovery on treated items, retraining on low-dominance exemplars produced greater generalization to untreated items. These findings can be understood in terms of the relative adequacy with which the sets of high- versus low-dominance exemplars approximate the range of semantic similarity among all of the words. In the simulation, high-dominance words accurately estimate the central tendency of a category but provide little information about the ways in which category members can vary. By contrast, each low-dominance word indicates many more ways in which members can differ from the prototype and yet still belong to the category. Thus, collectively, the semantic representations of low-dominance words cover more of the features needed by the entire set of words than do the representations of high-dominance words. At the same time, the average affects of retraining on low-dominance words provides a reasonable estimate of the central tendency of the category, yielding generalization to high-dominance words (as found in human category learning by, e.g., Posner and Keele, 1968).

In a final simulation, Plaut (1996) used the failure of the network in replicating the error pattern of recovering deep-dyslexic patients to constrain the underlying theory of normal and impaired word reading. Plaut measured the changes in the distribution of error types brought about by retraining an orthography-to-semantics network after damage. Rather than semantic errors being the first to drop out, visual and unrelated errors were eliminated earliest. Semantic and mixed visual-and-semantic errors were eliminated only at the very end of retraining. Thus, the changes in the pattern of errors produced by the network in recovery to near normal levels of correct performance failed to reproduce the transition from deep to phonological dyslexia observed in patients (Friedman, 1996; Klein et al., 1994). This discrepancy between the behavior of the network and that of patients can be understood if recovery in the patients involves more than relearning in the semantic route alone. In particular, the findings suggest that within the current approach the transition from deep to phonological dyslexia must also involve some improvement in the operation of the phonological pathway (or in phonology itself). Such improvement would produce a greater reduction in semantic errors relative to other types of error because even partial correct phonological information about the stimulus would be sufficient to rule out most semantic errors (Newcombe and Marshall, 1980).

It must be kept in mind that the Plaut (1996) findings relate to patient therapy only in the most general way, given that the version of the task of mapping orthography to semantics it performs is much simpler than the task performed by patients. Nonetheless, the principles that emerge as central to understanding the nature of relearning and generalization in the networks may provide the foundations for understanding the nature of recovery in patients.

Conclusion

The traditional way of thinking about the mechanisms subserving word reading (and other lexical tasks) involves stipulating rather complicated and domain-specific structures and processes. Thus, there are representations that apply only to specific words, or to words but not to nonwords, or to concrete words but not abstract words, and so forth. And there are separate sets of rules or pathways that process words but not nonwords, or only regular words but not exception words, and so forth.

This chapter has attempted to articulate and support an alternative view of lexical knowledge and processing: that they develop through the operation of general learning principles as applied to written and spoken words and their meanings. Distinctions between words and nonwords, and among different types of words, are not reified in the structure of the system but rather reflect the functional implications of the statistical structure among and between the relevant types of information—orthographic, phonological, and semantic. The structural divisions within the system—which are critical in accounting for specific patterns of acquired dyslexia—arise from the neuroanatomic localization of input and output modalities, not from differences in the content of representations (see Farah, 1994; Farah and McClelland, 1991, for similar arguments).

The simulations described here illustrate how connectionist computational principles—distributed representation, structure-sensitive learning, and interactivity—can provide insight into central empirical phenomena in normal skilled reading, its breakdown due to brain damage, and its remediation following damage. This is not to say that the models are fully adequate and account for all of the relevant data in sufficient detail—this is certainly not the case. In fact, given that they are models, they are abstractions from the actual processing system and are certainly wrong in their details. Nonetheless, their relative success at reproducing key patterns of data in the domain of word reading, and the fact that the very same computational principles are being applied successfully across a wide range of linguistic and cognitive domains, suggests that these models capture important aspects of representation and processing in the human language and cognitive system.

Acknowledgments

This work was supported by NIH/NIMH Grant MH47566 and the McDonnell-Pew Program in Cognitive Neuroscience Grant T89-01245-016. I'd like to thank Jay McClelland, Karalyn Patterson, Mark Seidenberg, and Tim Shallice for their contributions to the work described in this chapter, and Marlene Behrmann, Derek Besner, Max Coltheart, Joe Devlin, Geoff Hinton, and Eamon Strain for helpful discussions and comments.

Notes

1. The relationship between regularity and consistency is often a source of confusion. *Regularity* is a dichotomous variable that expresses whether or not the pronunciation of a given word obeys a particular set of spelling-sound correspondence rules. Such rules are most typically described as grapheme-phoneme correspondence (GPC) rules, although the only set of spelling-sound rules that have been implemented (Coltheart et al., 1993) involve a considerably greater degree of context sensitivity. By contrast, *consistency* is a continuous variable that expresses the degree to which the pronunciation of a word agrees with those of similarly spelled words. Here, similarity is typically cast in terms of word endings or *bodies* (i.e., the vowel and any following consonants), in part on the basis of empirical evidence that this unit accounts for considerable variance in monosyllabic word pronunciations (see Treiman, Mullennix, Bijeljac-Babic, and Richmond-Welty, 1995). Of course, similarity in terms of smaller orthographic and phonological units—including graphemes and phonemes—would also be expected to influence performance. Consequently, although the terms regularity and consistency entail rather different theoretical commitments concerning the nature of spelling-sound knowledge, their empirical implications are notoriously difficult to distinguish.

2. A representation is *localist* if there is a one-to-one relationship between processing units and entities in the domain; it is *distributed* if the relationship is many-to-many (i.e., each entity activates many units and each unit participates in representing many entities). Thus, a representation is localist or distributed only relative to a specific set of entities. For example, the letter layer of the Interactive Activation model (McClelland and Rumelhart, 1981) is localist with respect to letters but distributed with respect to words. Despite the terminology used by Besner (chapter 13, this volume), both localist and distributed models can be "connectionist" in the sense that the system's knowl-

edge is encoded in terms of weights on connections between simple, neuron-like processing units (Feldman and Ballard, 1982).

3. An attractor is a stable pattern of activity within a network such that unit interactions cause similar patterns to move toward and settle into the exact attractor pattern.

4. Seidenberg and McClelland (1989) trained their model using logarithmically compressed word frequencies to ensure sufficient sampling of the lowest frequency words. Plaut et al. (1996) avoided this problem by using word frequency to scale weight changes directly.

5. Consistent with Plaut's (1995b) account, Masson (1995 and this volume) considered the possibility that the intervening word might be processed only partially, leaving residual semantic activation from BREAD to influence BUTTER. Using a Hopfield (1982) network, Masson simulated the small priming effect across unrelated words in a naming task by basing the network's response on the activity of phonological units which were updated more frequently than semantic units. However, the simulations used a very small vocabulary (only three pairs of semantically related items), and no independent justification was provided for why phonological and semantic units should behave differently.

6. It is assumed that LD responses are actually generated by a stochastic decision process (e.g., Ratcliff, 1978; Usher and McClelland, 1995) that computes stress by integrating over semantic unit states and that adopts a decision criterion such that stress values farther from the criterion are responded to more quickly and accurately. In a given experimental context, a specific criterion is chosen that allows fast responding with acceptable error rates depending on the composition of the word and nonword stimuli.

References

Andrews, S. (1982). Phonological recoding: Is the regularity effect consistent? *Memory and Cognition, 10,* 565–575.

Balota, D., and Ferraro, R. (1993). A dissociation of frequency and regularity effects in pronunciation performance across young adults, older adults, and individuals with senile dementia of the Alzheimer type. *Journal of Memory and Language, 32,* 573–592.

Balota, D.A., and Chumbley, J.I. (1984). Are lexical decisions a good measure of lexical access? The role of word frequency in the neglected decision stage. *Journal of Experimental Psychology: Human Perception and Performance, 10,* 340–357.

Beauvois, M.-F., and Derouesne, J. (1979). Phonological alexia: Three dissociations. *Journal of Neurology, Neurosurgery, and Psychiatry, 42,* 1115–1124.

Becker, C.A. (1979). Semantic context and word frequency effects in visual word recognition. *Journal of Experimental Psychology: Human Perception and Performance, 5*, 252–259.

Becker, C.A. (1980). Semantic context effects in visual word recognition: An analysis of semantic strategies. *Memory and Cognition, 8*, 493–512.

Becker, C.A., and Killion, T.H. (1977). Interaction of visual and cognitive effects in word recognition. *Journal of Experimental Psychology: Human Perception and Performance, 3*, 389–401.

Behrmann, M. (1987). The rites of righting writing: Homophone remediation in acquired dysgraphia. *Cognitive Neuropsychology, 4*, 365–384.

Behrmann, M., and Bub, D.N. (1992). Surface dyslexia and dysgraphia: Dual routes, a single lexicon. *Cognitive Neuropsychology, 9*, 209–258.

Behrmann, M., and Lieberthal, T. (1989). Category–specific treatment of a lexical semantic deficit: A single case study of global aphasia. *British Journal of Communication Disorders, 24*, 281–299.

Besner, D. (this volume). Basic processes in reading: Multiple routines in localist and connectionist models. In R.M. Klein, and P.A. McMullen (eds.), *Converging Methods for Understanding Reading and Dyslexia*. Cambridge, MA: MIT Press.

Besner, D., and Joordens, S. (1995). Wrestling with ambiguity–further reflections: Reply to Masson and Borowsky (1995) and Rueckl (1995). *Journal of Experimental Psychology: Learning, Memory, and Cognition, 21*, 515–301.

Besner, D., and Smith, M.C. (1992). Models of visual word recognition: When obscuring the stimulus yields a clearer view. *Journal of Experimental Psychology: Learning, Memory, and Cognition, 18*, 468–482.

Besner, D., Twilley, L., McCann, R.S., and Seergobin, K. (1990). On the connection between connectionism and data: Are a few words necessary? *Psychological Review, 97*, 432–446.

Borowsky, R., and Masson, M.E.J. (1996). Semantic ambiguity effects in word identification. *Journal of Experimental Psychology: Learning, Memory, and Cognition, 22*, 63–85.

Bub, D., Cancelliere, A., and Kertesz, A. (1985). Whole-word and analytic translation of spelling-to-sound in a non-semantic reader. In K. Patterson, M. Coltheart, and J. C. Marshall (eds.), *Surface Dyslexia* (pp. 15–34).Hillsdale, NJ: Erlbaum.

Buchanan, L., Hildebrandt, N., and MacKinnon, G.E. (1994a). Implicit phonological processing in deep dyslexia. *Brain and Language, 47*, 435–437.

Buchanan, L., Hildebrandt, N., and MacKinnon, G.E. (1994b). Phonological processing of nonwords by a deep dyslexic patient: A rowse is implicitly a rose. *Journal of Neurolinguistics, 8*, 163–181.

Buchanan, L., Hildebrandt, N., and MacKinnon, G.E. (1996). Phonological processing of nonwords in deep dyslexia: Typical and independent? *Journal of Neurolinguistics, 9*, 113–133.

Buchanan, L., Hildebrandt, N., and MacKinnon, G.E. (this volume). Effects of phonology on deep dyslexia. In R.M. Klein, and P.A. McMullen (eds.), *Converging Methods for Understanding Reading and Dyslexia*. Cambridge, MA: MIT Press.

Cipolotti, L., and Warrington, E.K. (1995). Semantic memory and reading abilities: A case report. *Journal of the International Neuropsychological Society, 1*, 104–110.

Coltheart, M. (1978). Lexical access in simple reading tasks. In G. Underwood (ed.), *Strategies of Information Processing* (pp. 151–216). New York: Academic Press.

Coltheart, M. (1985). Cognitive neuropsychology and the study of reading. In M.I. Posner, and O.S.M. Marin (eds.), *Attention and Performance XI* (pp. 3–37). Hillsdale, NJ: Erlbaum.

Coltheart, M., and Byng, S. (1989). A treatment for surface dyslexia. In X. Seron, and G. Deloche (eds.), *Cognitive Approaches in Neuropsychological Rehabilitation* (pp. 159–174). Hillsdale, NJ: Erlbaum.

Coltheart, M., Curtis, B., Atkins, P., and Haller, M. (1993). Models of reading aloud: Dual-route and parallel-distributed-processing approaches. *Psychological Review, 100*, 589–608.

Coltheart, M., Davelaar, E., Jonasson, J., and Besner, D. (1977). Access to the internal lexicon. In S. Dornic (ed.), *Attention and Performance VI* (pp. 535–555). Hillsdale, NJ: Erlbaum.

Coltheart, M., Patterson, K., and Marshall, J.C. (eds.). (1980). *Deep Dyslexia*. London: Routledge and Kegan Paul.

Dell, G.S. (1986). A spreading-activation theory of retrieval in sentence production. *Psychological Review, 93*, 283–321.

Dell, G.S. (1988). The retrieval of phonological forms in production: Tests of predictions from a connectionist model. *Journal of Memory and Language, 27*, 124–142.

Farah, M.J. (1994). Neuropsychological inference with an interactive brain: A critique of the locality assumption. *Behavioral and Brain Sciences, 17*, 43–104.

Farah, M.J., and McClelland, J.L. (1991). A computational model of semantic memory impairment: Modality-specificity and emergent category-specificity. *Journal of Experimental Psychology: General, 120*, 339–357.

Feldman, J.A., and Ballard, D.H. (1982). Connectionist models and their properties. *Cognitive Science, 6*, 205–254.

Fera, P., and Besner, D. (1992). The process of lexical decision: More words about a parallel distributed processing model. *Journal of Experimental Psychology: Learning, Memory, and Cognition, 18*, 749–764.

Friedman, R.B. (1996). Recovery from deep alexia to phonological alexia. *Brain and Language, 52*, 114–128.

Glosser, G., and Friedman, R.B. (1990). The continuum of deep/phonological alexia. *Cortex, 26,* 343–359.

Glosser, G., and Friedman, R.B. (1991). Lexical but not semantic priming in Alzheimer's disease. *Psychology and Aging, 6,* 522–527.

Glushko, R.J. (1979). The organization and activation of orthographic knowledge in reading aloud. *Journal of Experimental Psychology: Human Perception and Performance, 5,* 674–691.

Graham, K.S., Hodges, J.R., and Patterson, K. (1994). The relationship between comprehension and oral reading in progressive fluent aphasia. *Neuropsychologia, 32,* 299–316.

Harm, M.W. (1998). *Division of labor in a computational model of visual word recognition.* Ph.D. thesis, Department of Computer Science, University of Southern California, Los Angeles, CA.

Hillis, A.E. (1993). The role of models of language processing in rehabilitation of language impairments. *Aphasiology, 7,* 5–26.

Hillis, A.E., and Caramazza, A. (1991). Category-specific naming and comprehension impairment: A double dissociation. *Brain, 114,* 2081–2094.

Hinton, G.E. (1989). Deterministic Boltzmann learning performs steepest descent in weight-space. *Neural Computation, 1,* 143–150.

Hinton, G.E., and Shallice, T. (1991). Lesioning an attractor network: Investigations of acquired dyslexia. *Psychological Review, 98,* 74–95.

Hopfield, J.J. (1982). Neural networks and physical systems with emergent collective computational abilities. *Proceedings of the National Academy of Science, USA, 79,* 2554–2558.

Howard, D., and Franklin, S. (1988). *Missing the Meaning?* Cambridge, MA: MIT Press.

Howard, D., and Hatfield, F.M. (1987). *Aphasia Therapy.* Hillsdale, NJ: Erlbaum.

Joordens, S., and Besner, D. (1992). Priming effects that span an intervening unrelated word: Implications for models of memory representation and retrieval. *Journal of Experimental Psychology: Learning, Memory, and Cognition, 18,* 483–491.

Katz, R.B., and Goodglass, H. (1990). Deep dysphasia: Analysis of a rare form of repetition disorder. *Brain and Language, 39,* 153–185.

Kawamoto, A. (1988). Distributed representations of ambiguous words and their resolution in a connectionist network. In S.L. Small, G.W. Cottrell, and M.K. Tanenhaus (eds.), *Lexical Ambiguity Resolution: Perspectives from Psycholinguistics, Neuropsychology, and Artificial Intelligence.* San Mateo, CA: Morgan Kaufmann.

Klein, D., Behrmann, M., and Doctor, E. (1994). The evolution of deep dyslexia: Evidence for the spontaneous recovery of the semantic reading route. *Cognitive Neuropsychology, 11,* 579–611.

Lambon Ralph, M., Ellis, A.W., and Franklin, S. (1995). Semantic loss without surface dyslexia. *Neurocase,* 1, 363–369.

Lorch, R.F., Balota, D., and Stamm, E. (1986). Locus of inhibition effects in the priming of lexical decisions: Pre- or post-lexical access? *Memory and Cognition, 14*, 95–103.

Marshall, J.C., and Newcombe, F. (1973). Patterns of paralexia: A psycholinguistic approach. *Journal of Psycholinguistic Research, 2*, 175–199.

Martin, N., Dell, G.S., and Schwartz, M.F. (1994). Origins of paraphasias in deep dysphasia: Testing the consequences of a decay impairment to an interactive spreading activation model of lexical retrieval. *Brain and Language, 47*, 609–660.

Martin, N., and Saffran, E.M. (1990). Repetition and verbal STM in transcortical sensory aphasia: A case study. *Brain and Language, 39*, 254–288.

Martin, N., and Saffran, E.M. (1992). A computational account of deep dysphasia: Evidence from a single case study. *Brain and Language, 43*, 240–274.

Martin, N., Saffran, E.M., and Dell, G.S. (1996). Recovery in deep dysphasia: Evidence for a relation between auditory-verbal-STM capacity and lexical errors in repetition. *Brain and Language, 52*, 83–113.

Masson, M.E.J. (1991). A distributed memory model of context effects in word identfication. In D. Besner, and G. W. Humphreys (eds.), *Basic Processes in Reading* (pp. 233–263). Hillsdale, NJ: Erlbaum.

Masson, M.E.J. (1995). A distributed memory model of semantic priming. *Journal of Experimental Psychology: Learning, Memory, and Cognition, 21*, 3–23.

Masson, M.E.J. (this volume). Interactive processes in word identification: A computational approach. In R.M. Klein, and P.A. McMullen (eds.), *Converging Methods for Understanding Reading and Dyslexia*. Cambridge, MA: MIT Press.

Masson, M.E.J., and Borowsky, R. (1995). Unsettling questions about semantic ambiguity in connectionist models: Comment on Joordens and Besner (1994). *Journal of Experimental Psychology: Learning, Memory, and Cognition, 21*, 509–514.

McCann, R.S., and Besner, D. (1987). Reading pseudohomophones: Implications for models of pronunciation and the locus of the word-frequency effects in word naming. *Journal of Experimental Psychology: Human Perception and Performance, 13*, 14–24.

McCarthy, R., and Warrington, E.K. (1986). Phonological reading: Phenomena and paradoxes. *Cortex, 22*, 359–380.

McClelland, J.L., and Rumelhart, D.E. (1981). An interactive activation model of context effects in letter perception: part 1. An account of basic findings. *Psychological Review, 88*, 375–407.

McNamara, T.P. (1994). Theories of priming II: Types of primes. *Journal of Experimental Psychology: Learning, Memory, and Cognition, 20*, 507–520.

McRae, K., de Sa, V., and Seidenberg, M.S. (1993). Modeling property interactions in accessing conceptual memory. In *Proceedings of the 15th Annual Conference of the Cognitive Science Society* (pp. 729–734). Hillsdale, NJ: Erlbaum.

Meyer, D.E., and Schvaneveldt, R.W. (1971). Facilitation in recognizing pairs of words: Evidence of a dependence between retrieval operations. *Journal of Experimental Psychology, 90*, 227–234.

Meyer, D.E., Schvaneveldt, R.W., and Ruddy, M.G. (1974). Functions of graphemic and phonemic codes in visual word recognition. *Memory and Cognition, 2*, 309–321.

Meyer, D.E., Schvaneveldt, R.W., and Ruddy, M.G. (1975). Loci of contextual effects on visual word recognition. In P.M.A. Rabbitt, and S. Dornic (eds.), *Attention and Performance V*. New York: Academic Press.

Morton, J. (1969). The interaction of information in word recognition. *Psychological Review, 76*, 165–178.

Morton, J., and Patterson, K. (1980). A new attempt at an interpretation, Or, an attempt at a new interpretation. In M. Coltheart, K. Patterson, and J.C. Marshall (eds.), *Deep Dyslexia* (pp. 91–118). London: Routledge and Kegan Paul.

Moss, H.E., Hare, M.L., Day, P., and Tyler, L.K. (1994). A distributed memory model of the associative boost in semantic priming. *Connection Science, 6*, 413–427.

Moss, H.E., and Marslen–Wilson, W.D. (1993). Access to word meanings during spoken language comprehension: Effects of sentential semantic context. *Journal of Exerimental Psychology: Learning, Memory, and Cognition, 19*, 1254–1276.

Moss, H.E., Ostrin, R.K., Tyler, L.K., and Marslen–Wilson, W.D. (1995). Accessing different types of lexical semantic information: Evidence from priming. *Journal of Experimental Psychology: Learning, Memory, and Cognition, 21*, 863–883.

Neely, J.H. (1977). Semantic priming and retrieval from lexical memory: Roles of inhibitionless spreading activation and limited capacity attention. *Journal of Experimental Psychology: General, 106*, 226–254.

Neely, J.H. (1991). Semantic priming effects in visual word recognition: A selective review of current findings and theories. In D. Besner, and G. W. Humphreys (eds.), *Basic Processes in Reading* (pp. 264–336). Hillsdale, NJ: Erlbaum.

Newcombe, F., and Marshall, J.C. (1980). Transcoding and lexical stabilization in deep dyslexia. In M. Coltheart, K. Patterson, and J.C. Marshall (eds.), *Deep Dyslexia* (pp. 176–188). London: Routledge and Kegan Paul.

Norris, D. (1994). A quantitative multiple-levels model of reading aloud. *Journal of Experimental Psychology: Human Perception and Performance, 20*, 1212–1232.

Paap, K.R., and Noel, R.W. (1991). Dual route models of print to sound: Still a good horse race. *Psychological Research, 53*, 13–24.

Patterson, K., Coltheart, M., and Marshall, J.C. (eds.). (1985). *Surface Dyslexia*. Hillsdale, NJ: Erlbaum.

Patterson, K., Graham, N., and Hodges, J.R. (1994). Reading in Alzheimer's type dementia: A preserved ability? *Neuropsychology, 8*, 395–412.

Patterson, K., and Hodges, J.R. (1992). Deterioration of word meaning: Implications for reading. *Neuropsychologia, 30,* 1025–1040.

Pearlmutter, B.A. (1989). Learning state space trajectories in recurrent neural networks. *Neural Computation, 1,* 263–269.

Peterson, C., and Anderson, J.R. (1987). A mean field theory learning algorithm for neural nets. *Complex Systems, 1,* 995–1019.

Plaut, D.C. (1995a). Double dissociation without modularity: Evidence from connectionist neuropsychology. *Journal of Clinical and Experimental Neuropsychology, 17,* 291–321.

Plaut, D.C. (1995b). Semantic and associative priming in a distributed attractor network. In *Proceedings of the 17th Annual Conference of the Cognitive Science Society* (pp. 37–42). Hillsdale, NJ: Erlbaum.

Plaut, D.C. (1996). Relearning after damage in connectionist networks: Toward a theory of rehabilitation. *Brain and Language, 52,* 25–82.

Plaut, D.C. (1997). Structure and function in the lexical system: Insights from distributed models of naming and lexical decision. *Language and Cognitive Processes, 12,* 767–808.

Plaut, D.C., and McClelland, J.L. (1993). Generalization with componential attractors: Word and nonword reading in an attractor network. In *Proceedings of the 15th Annual Conference of the Cognitive Science Society* (pp. 824–829). Hillsdale, NJ: Erlbaum.

Plaut, D.C., McClelland, J.L., Seidenberg, M.S., and Patterson, K. (1996). Understanding normal and impaired word reading: Computational principles in quasi-regular domains. *Psychological Review, 103,* 56–115.

Plaut, D.C., and Shallice, T. (1993). Deep dyslexia: A case study of connectionist neuropsychology. *Cognitive Neuropsychology, 10,* 377–500.

Posner, M.I., and Keele, S.W. (1968). On the genesis of abstract ideas. *Journal of Experimental Psychology, 77,* 353–363.

Postman, L., and Keppel, G. (1970). *Norms of Word Associations.* New York: Academic Press.

Ratcliff, R. (1978). A theory of memory retrieval. *Psychological Review, 85,* 59–108.

Raymer, A.M., and Berndt, R.S. (1994). Models of word reading: Evidence from Alzheimer's disease. *Brain and Language, 47,* 479–482.

Reggia, J.A., Marsland, P.M., and Berndt, R.S. (1988). Competitive dynamics in a dual-route connectionist model of print-to-sound transformation. *Complex Systems, 2,* 509–547.

Rueckl, J.G. (1995). Ambiguity and connectionist networks: Still settling into a solution-Comment on Joordens and Besner (1994). *Journal of Experimental Psychology: Learning, Memory, and Cognition, 21,* 501–508.

Saffran, E.M., Bogyo, L.C., Schwartz, M.F., and Marin, O.S.M. (1980). Does deep dyslexia reflect right-hemisphere reading? In M. Coltheart, K. Patterson, and J.C. Marshall (eds.), *Deep Dyslexia* (pp. 381–406). London: Routledge and Kegan Paul.

Schwanenflugel, P.J. (1991). Why are abstract concepts hard to understand? In P.J. Schwanenflugel (ed.), *The Psychology of Word Meanings*. Hillsdale, NJ: Erlbaum.

Schwartz, M.F., Marin, O.S.M., and Saffran, E.M. (1979). Dissociations of language function in dementia: A case study. *Brain and Language, 7,* 277–306.

Scott, C., and Byng, S. (1989). Computer assisted remediation of a homophone comprehension disorder in surface dyslexia. *Aphasiology, 3,* 301–320.

Seidenberg, M.S. (1992). Beyond orthographic depth: Equitable division of labor. In R. Frost, and K. Katz (eds.), *Orthography, Phonology, Morphology, and Meaning* (pp. 85–118). Amsterdam: Elsevier.

Seidenberg, M.S., and McClelland, J.L. (1989). A distributed, developmental model of word recognition and naming. *Psychological Review, 96,* 523–568.

Seidenberg, M.S., Petersen, A., MacDonald, M.C., and Plaut, D.C. (1996). Pseudohomophone effects and models of word recognition. *Journal of Experimental Psychology: Learning, Memory, and Cognition, 22,* 48–62.

Seidenberg, M.S., Plaut, D.C., Petersen, A.S., McClelland, J.L., and McRae, K. (1994). Nonword pronunciation and models of word recognition. *Journal of Experimental Psychology: Human Perception and Performance, 20,* 1177–1196.

Seidenberg, M.S., Waters, G.S., Barnes, M.A., and Tanenhaus, M.K. (1984a). When does irregular spelling or pronunciation influence word recognition? *Journal of Verbal Learning and Verbal Behaviour, 23,* 383–404.

Seidenberg, M.S., Waters, G.S., Sanders, M., and Langer, P. (1984b). Pre- and postlexical loci of contextual effects on word recognition. *Memory and Cognition, 12,* 315–328.

Shallice, T., and McCarthy, R. (1985). Phonological reading: From patterns of impairment to possible procedures. In K. Patterson, M. Coltheart, and J.C. Marshall (eds.), *Surface Dyslexia* (pp. 361–398). Hillsdale, NJ: Erlbaum.

Shallice, T., and Warrington, E.K. (1980). Single and multiple component central dyslexic syndromes. In M. Coltheart, K. Patterson, and J.C. Marshall (eds.), *Deep Dyslexia* (pp. 119–145). London: Routledge and Kegan Paul.

Shallice, T., Warrington, E.K., and McCarthy, R. (1983). Reading without semantics. *Quarterly Journal of Experimental Psychology, 35A,* 111–138.

Sharkey, A.J., and Sharkey, N.E. (1992). Weak contextual constraints in text and word priming. *Journal of Memory and Language, 31,* 543–572.

Shelton, J.R., and Martin, R.C. (1992). How semantic is automatic semantic priming? *Journal of Experimental Psychology: Learning, Memory, and Cognition, 18,* 1191–1210.

Strain, E., Patterson, K., and Seidenberg, M.S. (1995). Semantic effects in single-word naming. *Journal of Experimental Psychology: Learning, Memory, and Cognition, 21*, 1140–1154.

Taraban, R., and McClelland, J.L. (1987). Conspiracy effects in word recognition. *Journal of Memory and Language, 26*, 608–631.

Treiman, R., Mullennix, J., Bijeljac-Babic, R., and Richmond-Welty, E.D. (1995). The special role of rimes in the description, use, and acquisition of English orthography. *Journal of Experimental Psychology: General, 124*, 107–136.

Usher, M., and McClelland, J.L. (1995). On the time course of perceptual choice: A model based on principles of neural computation (technical report PDP.CNS.95.5). Pittsburgh, PA: Carnegie Mellon University, Department of Psychology.

Van Orden, G.C., and Goldinger, S.D. (1994). Interdependence of form and function in cognitive systems explains perception of printed words. *Journal of Experimental Psychology: Human Perception and Performance, 20*, 1269.

Van Orden, G.C., Pennington, B.F., and Stone, G.O. (1990). Word identification in reading and the promise of subsymbolic psycholinguistics. *Psychological Review, 97*, 488–522.

Warrington, E.K. (1981). Concrete word dyslexia. *British Journal of Psychology, 72*, 175–196.

Waters, G.S., and Seidenberg, M.S. (1985). Spelling-sound effects in reading: Time course and decision criteria. *Memory and Cognition, 13*, 557–572.

Weekes, B., and Coltheart, M. (1996). Surface dyslexia and surface dysgraphia: Treatment studies and their theoretical implications. *Cognitive Neuropsychology, 13*, 277–315.

Zorzi, M., Houghton, G., and Butterworth, B. (1998). Two routes or one in reading aloud? A connectionist "dual-process" model. *Journal of Experimental Psychology: Human Perception and Performance, 24*, 1131–1161.

12
Interactive Processes in Word Identification: Modeling Context Effects in a Distributed Memory System

Michael E. J. Masson

The development of connectionist or neural-network models has provided a new and promising way of understanding cognitive functions. Reading processes, particularly those associated with the identification of words, have been the subject of extensive study through computational modeling with connectionist systems. The general goal of this enterprise has been to develop a theory of skilled word-recognition processes, including accounts of the development of that skill (Seidenberg and McClelland, 1989) and of neurological damage that leads to disorders of reading ability (Hinton and Shallice, 1991; Plaut, McClelland, Seidenberg, and Patterson, 1996; Plaut and Shallice, 1993). Connectionist models of these phenomena have come to rely on a division of labor among different sources of knowledge to account for patterns of successful and impaired word-reading performance (e.g., Plaut et al., 1996). The general theme pursued in this chapter is the issue of how knowledge sources interact to bring about fluent word reading.

The proposition that multiple knowledge sources interact in the process of identifying words has been of fundamental importance in the development of reading models (e.g., Lesgold and Perfetti, 1981; Massaro, 1979; Masson and Sala, 1978; Plaut and Shallice, 1993; Rumelhart, 1977). Not surprisingly, the nature of this interaction is a source of controversy for it cuts to the heart of the defining principles of differing views of cognitive architecture, such as the debate about whether perceptual input systems are modular, and therefore unaffected by higher level knowledge (e.g., Fodor, 1983; Rueckl and Oden, 1986; Seidenberg and Tanenhaus, 1986), or nonmodular and consequently influenced in a direct way by nonperceptual information (e.g., Rhodes, Parkin, and Tremewan, 1993).

This chapter describes a simple computational model of the knowledge sources that are assumed to interact during the course of performing various word-identification tasks. The model constitutes a particular view of how this interaction takes place. It provides an account of performance in various word-identification tasks, especially the influence of contextual information on task performance. Context effects are a crucial source of empirical evidence regarding the interaction of knowledge sources and they provide constraints on model development.

The model has been implemented with a distributed representation of knowledge and its processing assumptions are in the connectionist or parallel distributed-processing tradition. The distributed representation of knowledge leads to an account of word-identification phenomena that is qualitatively different from that of models that assume a localist representation. In a localist representation, each concept is represented by a single processing unit and an arbitrary number of units can be simultaneously active to any degree, depending on assumptions about how the units interact (e.g., Anderson, 1983; Collins and Loftus, 1975; McClelland and Rumelhart, 1981). In contrast, a distributed representation places natural constraints on the simultaneous activation of multiple concepts. In a distributed representation scheme, knowledge about words is represented as connection weights between processing units. This knowledge constitutes a "potential" for various known words to come to mind. For a specific word to come to mind, which can be caused by presentation of its visual form, its unique pattern of activation across a set of processing units must be invoked. How a word's pattern of activation is instantiated is discussed below, but for now the important point is that full activation of a word requires setting all of the processing units to the activation values dictated by that word. Thus, it is not possible for two different words to be fully activated at the same time (see McClelland, 1985, for a suggestion regarding how two simultaneously presented words might be processed in a connectionist model). Multiple words are partially activated, however, if the processing units form a pattern that is similar but not identical to the corresponding patterns of activation for those words. Moreover, a change in any subset of the processing units affects the degree of activation of all words known to the system. As shown below, these characteristics of distributed representation provide for a natural account of context effects such as semantic priming.

A second important aspect of the model is that the influence of different knowledge sources operates in a cascaded fashion (McClelland, 1979), providing for continuous change in the availability or activation of knowledge about specific words. The continuous influence of different sources of knowledge is combined over time to allow the model to generate responses. For example, in the task of reading aloud printed words, the model accumulates knowledge about a word's phonology by computing the correspondence between orthographic and phonological patterns, and also by computing the meaning associated with an orthographic pattern, then computing the phonological pattern associated with that meaning. These two sources of influence on the generation of a phonological code operate simultaneously and have a combined influence over time on the construction of a phonological code (see also Plaut et al., 1996; Seidenberg and McClelland, 1989).

This approach to reading a word aloud resembles models that assume there are independent routes to pronunciation such as a direct route from orthography to phonology and an indirect route either through semantics or an orthographic lexicon (e.g., Besner, chapter 13, this volume; Besner and Smith, 1992; Coltheart, Curtis, Atkins, and Haller, 1993; Paap and Noel, 1991). These multiple-route models characterize word reading as a race between independent routes that yield either the same response or differing responses (as in the case of exception words such as *have*). If the two routes deliver identical phonological responses, the faster route can drive the response. But in the case of exception words, the routes produce opposing responses that must be competitively resolved. In the connectionist model described here, as in other connectionist models of word identification, however, the semantic and orthographic routes to phonology are trained to produce compatible phonological patterns even for exception words. Rather than implementing general pronunciation rules in the orthography to phonology route, connectionist models employ learning rules that capitalize on the statistical structure that characterizes the relation between orthographic and phonological patterns (e.g., Seidenberg and McClelland, 1989). In principle, the correct pronunciation for both regular and exception words can be generated by the orthographic route in connectionist models.

In the next section of this chapter, a full specification is provided of the connectionist model that I have been using to account for how knowledge sources interact to produce a range of context effects. A review is then provided of recent applications of the model to simulate semantic context effects (including tests of informational encapsulation), semantic ambiguity effects, and masked priming effects. Finally, a number of unresolved issues and new directions for development of the model are considered.

Architecture of the Distributed Memory Model

The connectionist model I have developed (henceforth referred to as the *distributed memory model*) adopts the general architecture proposed by Seidenberg and McClelland (1989) in which separate sets or modules of processing units are devoted to representing a word's orthographic, phonological, and semantic information. Although the original version of the distributed memory model (Masson, 1991) consisted of only two sets of processing units—called perceptual and conceptual— a third set (phonological) was later added to permit simulation of the word-naming task (Masson, 1995). The implementation of semantic information in the distributed memory model is constrained so that there is no feedback from semantics to orthography. Thus, there is no top-down influence of semantic knowledge on orthographic processing. Semantic knowledge, once activated by orthography, influences the development of a phonological representation and thereby contributes to performance on word naming tasks. A schematic representation of the model is presented in figure 12.1. Flow of activation among modules is indicated by arrows. Furthermore, each unit within the semantic and phonological modules is connected to all other units in its module.

The model is implemented as a Hopfield network (Hopfield, 1982), in which each unit in the network is connected to all other units. The only modification made in creating the distributed memory model is that units responsible for representing orthography are affected only by visual input, not by one another nor by units in the semantic or phonological modules. This constraint on connectivity means that

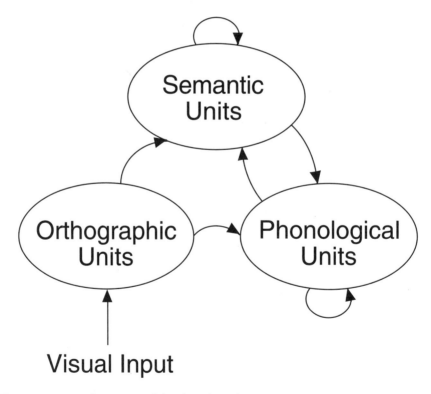

Figure 12.1 Architecture of the distributed memory model. Each type of word knowledge is represented as a pattern of activation across a set of processing units. Arrows indicate flow of activation within and between sets of units.

the distributed memory model assumes informational encapsulation of visual word input in the sense proposed by Fodor (1983). Although this restriction on input to orthographic units is not intended as a crucial assumption of the model, it has been useful in the examination of issues associated with context effects, particularly the question of what kind of evidence may be taken as evidence against the informational encapsulation assumption.

Knowledge Representation

A fundamentally important property of the distributed memory model is that word knowledge of all types is represented in a distributed fashion. For example, knowledge about a particular word's orthography is represented as a pattern of activation across all units in the orthographic module. A word's phonology and meaning are similarly represented as patterns of activation across the phonological and semantic units. Each unit can take on one of two values, 1 or −1, so a word's pattern of activation consists of a vector of ±1 values across all the units in the network. No assumptions have been made regarding correspondence of particular processing units or subsets of units to specific letters, letter positions, phonemes, or semantic features. In models such as those of Plaut et al. (1996), Plaut and Shallice (1993), and Seidenberg and McClelland (1989), the objective has been to develop a computation model of the mapping of orthography to phonology or orthography to semantics for specific English words. In contrast to these models, the goal for the distributed memory model has been more modest; namely, to examine general properties of a system in which multiple knowledge sources converge to generate a representation in response to input. For this purpose, it has not been necessary to incorporate details of, for example, English orthography and phonology. Neither has it been necessary to posit a particular set of semantic features (see Hinton and Shallice, 1991; McRae, de Sa, and Seidenberg, 1997; Plaut and Shallice, 1993) in representing word meaning. It has been sufficient to use arbitrarily (even randomly) constructed patterns to represent each word's orthography, phonology, and semantics.

The use of arbitrary patterns to represent word knowledge does not imply a rejection of the ideas put forth in models designed to capture aspects of language such as grapheme-phoneme correspondences or the specification of semantic features. To the contrary, the distributed memory model embraces the notion, developed by Seidenberg and McClelland (1989), that pronunciation of both the regular and exception words can, in principle, be computed by a single pathway between a distributed representation of orthography and a distributed representation of phonology. Because the goal of developing the distributed memory model was not to account for aspects of linguistic competence such as these, it has been possible to use a simpler representational scheme involving arbitrary patterns of activation for each word.

Learning

The distributed memory model uses a learning rule derived from Hebb (1949) and discussed by Hopfield (1982) in which the connection weight between any pair of units is changed as a function of the activation states the units take on when a pattern to be learned is instantiated. When a specific pattern of activation (representing a particular word) is learned, the connection weight between each pair of units is adjusted. In particular, if the pattern of activation calls for two units to be in the same activation state, the connection weight between them is increased; if the pattern dictates different activation states for the two units, the connection weight between them is decreased. The formula for this learning rule is presented in the appendix to this chapter.

The effect of this learning rule is to increase the connection weight between two units that typically are in the same activation state across the various patterns of activation (words) that the system learns. For two units that typically are in different states, the connection weight is decreased (i.e., becomes negative). If, across the entire vocabulary of words, a pair of units is about equally often in different states and in the same state, the net weight change will be close to zero. Thus, the learning rule allows connection weights to capture correlations between pairs of units that hold over the full set of words.

The disadvantage of using this simple learning rule is that the distributed memory model is capable of learning only a small set of words. I have found, however, that even with a vocabulary of 6 to 12 words, the model is able to provide an account of a range of interesting word-identification phenomena.

Pattern Completion

A crucial feature of Hopfield networks is their ability to complete a partial pattern instantiated in the network to form a previously learned pattern of activation (Hopfield, 1982). In particular, Hopfield networks are attractor networks in that learned patterns of activation lie at the bottom of basins of attraction in a multidimensional space consisting of all possible patterns of activation across the network's units. The process of pattern completion begins by instantiating part of a previously learned pattern of activation across a subset of the network's units. This subset of units is fixed, or clamped, in this pattern, then the network is allowed to update the activation states of its other units. A unit's activation state is determined by computing the input coming into that unit from all other units in the network. The input received by a unit will cause it to take an activation state of either +1 or −1. The formula for computing the input to a unit and the rule for using input to determine a unit's activation state are provided in the appendix. Over time, as units are sampled and their states computed, the network moves step-by-step into the learned pattern dictated by the initial, partial pattern that was instantiated in the network.

Once the network has fully instantiated a learned pattern, it will normally remain in that state until a new partial pattern is instantiated in the network. Thus, learned patterns are sometimes referred to as stable states. The progress of the network as it moves down a basin of attraction toward a learned pattern can be tracked by computing a measure known as *energy*. As the network moves more deeply into a basin, energy is reduced (takes on a larger and larger negative value), achieving a maximal negative value when the bottom of the basin is reached and the learned pattern is fully instantiated. The formula for computing energy is provided in the appendix. An important interpretation of the energy of the network is that of goodness of fit: A large negative value of energy indicates that the current pattern of activation across the units constitutes a good fit between the current pattern and the connection weights in the network. That is, pairs of units that have positive connections tend to be in the same state and those with negative connections tend to be in opposite states. Energy can be computed across the entire network or within a subset of the modules, depending on which sources of information are assumed to be used in performing a particular task.

Word Identification

The distributed memory model simulates word identification as a pattern completion process in which a word's orthographic pattern is instantiated in the network and the remaining processing units are updated to complete the target word's pattern. In the applications for word-identification tasks described here, various criteria have been applied in simulating responses, depending on the nature of the task. For example, simulation of the word-naming task involves instantiating a word's orthographic pattern, then updating the semantic and phonological units until the latter set of units forms a pattern of activation that corresponds to the target word's phonology. The number of updating cycles required to simulate a response is taken as a measure of response latency. Although it is not clear what function ought to be used to map the number of updating cycles to response latency, it has proven adequate to assume there is a linear relation between number of updates and response latency.

Converging sources of influence

As indicated in figure 12.1, the model includes two sources of influence on phonological units that originate outside the phonological module: an influence from orthography and another from semantics. Similarly, the instantiation of a word's meaning is affected by two sources outside the semantic module: orthography and phonology. With two converging sources of input influencing the reconstruction of a phonological or a semantic code, questions arise as to the relative strength and the timing of the two influences.

Two factors together determine the strength of a module's influence on a particular unit in the network (either within that module or within a different module). The first is the number of units in a module. The more units in a module, the larger will be that module's contribution to the net input to a unit. In the simulations described below, the typical numbers of units in the three modules were 130 orthographic units, 80 semantic units, and 40 phonological units. The values were determined primarily by practical constraints. First, using a large number of orthographic units is one way of making it likely that the rest of the processing units will form the correct pattern of activation when a particular word's orthographic pattern is instantiated. (A similar effect could be accomplished with fewer orthographic units by implementing a form of gain control on the weights connecting orthographic units with other units.) Second, to keep the time needed for running simulations within reasonable bounds, the number of phonological units was made relatively small. By using fewer units, the average number of processing cycles needed to reach a stable state across the entire phonological module was kept to a reasonable value. Finally, the choice of the number of semantic units was determined in part by the need to provide for different words that have similar semantic patterns so that semantic priming effects could be simulated. With 80 semantic units, there is freedom to examine a range of semantic similarity.

The second factor that determines a module's influence on a unit in the network is the rate at which the module's units are updated. Different modules have the potential to have their units updated at different rates. In the simulations reported by Masson (1995), it was assumed that when a word was visually presented, its orthographic units immediately took on the relevant pattern of activation, then the phonological and semantic units began updating. The immediate instantiation of a word's orthographic pattern was used only for convenience; in later simulations, orthographic units were updated over time rather than immediately shaped to the correct pattern. It is also assumed that phonological units update at a higher rate than semantic units, allowing phonological units to have an early influence on instantiation of the word's meaning. This approach is consistent with empirical results suggesting that phonological recoding of words occurs early during word reading and contributes to the access of meaning (e.g., Lukatela and Turvey, 1994; Perfetti and Bell, 1991; Perfetti, Bell, and Delaney, 1988; Van Orden, Johnston, and Hale, 1988; Ziegler and Jacobs, 1995). Because the orthographic module is larger than the phonological module and is either fully instantiated at the start of a trial or updated at a higher rate than units in any other module, however, orthographic units will have the dominant influence on units in the network. In this sense, the model is sensitive to findings that indicate orthography can have a direct influence on access to word meaning (Daneman, Reingold, and Davidson, 1995; Jared and Seidenberg, 1991).

Lexical access versus pattern formation

Nondistributed or localist models of word identification typically assume that word knowledge is represented in some form of lexicon (Coltheart et al., 1993; Forster, 1976; Jacobs and Grainger, 1992; Johnson and Pugh, 1994; Morton, 1969). The lexicon contains an entry for each known word and word identification consists of accessing the appropriate entry in the lexicon. Localist models provide for the possibility that multiple words can be accessed or activated at the same time. When multiple lexical entries become active simultaneously, one means of determining which active entry corresponds to the target word is to invoke an inhibitory process that permits the correct entry to be selected against the background of similar, active entries. For example, in the interactive activation model, it is assumed that lexical entries mutually inhibit one another so that the entry most strongly supported by orthographic evidence eventually wins out (e.g., Jacobs and Grainger, 1992; McClelland and Rumelhart, 1981).

In the distributed memory model, and in other models that assume a distributed representation of word knowledge, knowledge about multiple words can become "activated" simultaneously, but only partially so. A distributed network can move into patterns of activation that partially match a number of known words. A word is activated to the extent that its pattern is instantiated in the network's units. Only one word at a time, however, can have its full pattern instantiated across the entire network. Thus, a distributed network provides a natural solution to the problem of distinguishing among a number of competing candidates: as the network forms a pattern of activation in response to presentation of a word, it eventually settles into the target word's pattern and in so doing moves away from patterns associated with other words. Cohorts, neighbors, or other related words that might have become partially activated during early processing of a target word lose their activation as the target pattern takes hold. This natural suppression of related words is a consequence of the shared representational space constituted by the network of processing units.

To illustrate this property of the distributed memory model, a simulation was run in which a vocabulary of nine items was learned. The items constituted three triplets, each consisting of a target word and two related words. One related word was similar to the target only with respect to orthography and the other was similar to the target only with respect to meaning. In the distributed memory model, similarity between words is defined as similar patterns of activation across a set of units. Two words that are, for example, orthographically similar, would have a high proportion of orthographic units in the same activation state (± 1) when their respective orthographic patterns are instantiated in the network. In the simulation described here, orthographically similar pairs shared the same activation states in 90 of the 130 orthographic units. Unrelated words shared activation states in an average of 65 orthographic units (half of 130). Similarly, words that were semantically related had the same activation states in 55 of the 80 semantic units. After learning, each target word was presented to the network multiple times. On each presentation, the network was run for 2,000 updating cycles, allowing the network to approach formation of the full pattern of activation for the target word.

To simulate the construction of a word's orthographic pattern over time, the orthographic units were not clamped to the appropriate pattern at the beginning of a trial. Instead, they were initially set to a random pattern, just as all other units in the network, then randomly sampled for updating with high probability (0.60). When sampled, an orthographic unit was clamped to its appropriate state. If the orthographic module was not sampled on a cycle, then a unit from the phonological module was sampled with probability 0.60, otherwise a semantic unit was sampled. Thus the simple probabilities of sampling orthographic, phonological, and semantic units were 0.60, 0.24, and 0.16, respectively.

The degree of activation over time (updating cycles) of orthographic, phonological, and semantic aspects of a target word is shown in figure 12.2a. Activation of knowledge about a word was taken as the proportion of units in a module (e.g., orthographic) that were in states that correspond to that word's learned pattern. Once a word is fully instantiated in the network, all units meet this criterion and so the activation value reaches its asymptote of 1.0. The effect of using different probabilities for sampling units from the three modules is apparent in figure 12.2a. The relatively high sampling rate for the orthographic units resulted in a rapid rise to asymptotic activation for those units. The small number of phonological units combined with a higher sampling rate than the rate for semantic units, produced a rapid rise in activation of a target's phonological representation. Both the ortho-

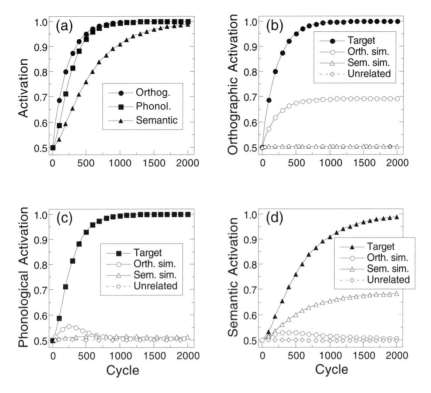

Figure 12.2 Activation over time of orthographic, phonological, and
    semantic knowledge about a word whose orthographic pattern is
    presented to the network (a). Activation is measured as the proportion
    of units in a module that are in a state that corresponds to target word's
    pattern. Activation of target word knowledge within each module is
    compared with activation of knowledge about an orthographically
    related, a semantically related, and an unrelated word that occurs as a
    byproduct of processing the target word (b, orthographic module; c,
    phonological module; d, semantic module).

graphic and phonological patterns were fully formed before the semantic pattern
was completely instantiated.

   The activations of each type of knowledge (orthographic, phonological, and
semantic) are shown separately in figures 12.2b to 12.2d. Each plot shows activation for the target word and its related words. Only external input affects the orthographic units, so only the target and its orthographically related word show any
sign of activation. The related item's orthographic pattern reaches a level of activa-

tion that corresponds to its degree of similarity to the target's orthographic pattern. In the phonological module, the orthographically similar word's phonological pattern is initially activated as the orthographic units begin to form the target's pattern. This activation occurs because the orthographically similar word's orthographic pattern is partially instantiated and the target's pattern is not yet completely instantiated. As the target's orthography becomes more fully established, however, the phonological module is dominated by the target, and activation of the orthographically related word's phonology dies away. No attempt was made to incorporate correlations between orthographic and phonological patterns in the items learned by the network, so the target's orthographic pattern offers no support whatever to the phonological pattern of its orthographic neighbor.

In the semantic module, the semantically related word's pattern of activation grows along with the target's activation, although it reaches a lower asymptote. The semantic pattern of the orthographically related word is also activated during the early stages of processing the target, although this activation eventually dies out. Although the orthographic neighbor has no stronger semantic similarity to the target than does an unrelated word, the pattern of activation in the orthographic units (which are somewhat compatible with the orthographic neighbor) initially push the semantic units toward a pattern that is similar to the orthographic neighbor. As the target's pattern comes to dominate the network, however, any semantic activation of semantically unrelated words dissipates.

In general, the activation of the relevant aspect of a related word grows to a moderate asymptotic value but does not subsequently drop to the original resting level. Related words will be simultaneously active with the target just to the extent that they share patterns of activation with the target. Although activation of relevant aspects of related words does not die away, figures 12.2c and 12.2d make it clear that temporary activation of other aspects of related words can be short-lived and does eventually fall back to resting level as the target's pattern comes to dominate the network. This elimination of activation occurs despite the fact that the distributed memory model has no mechanism for directly inhibiting activation of word knowledge. Instead, the loss of activation occurs as a natural consequence of the network's distributed architecture. As one pattern comes to dominate the network, unrelated patterns recede gracefully into the background.

Applications of the Distributed Memory Model

This section provides an account of semantic priming within the distributed memory model then briefly reviews a number of applications of the model related to priming and other semantic effects in word identification. Then a new set of simulations are described in which the model was used to account for results from masked priming experiments.

Semantic Priming

Semantic priming effects generally involve enhanced performance on a target word (e.g., shorter response latency) when presentation of the target is preceded by presentation of a related prime word relative to when the prime word is unrelated to the target (e.g., Meyer, Schvaneveldt, and Ruddy, 1972; Neely, 1977). In the distributed memory model, semantic priming effects are a natural consequence of the assumption that semantically related words consist of similar patterns of activation across the semantic units. Priming arises because presentation of a prime word causes the semantic units to begin to form that word's pattern of activation. When a related target is then presented, the pattern of activation in the semantic units is closer to the target word's pattern than would be the case had an unrelated prime, or no word at all, been presented. Therefore, fewer changes need be made to the semantic units to form the target word's semantic pattern (see Sharkey, 1989, 1990, for a similar account of semantic priming). Even if responding to the target does not require the target word's semantic pattern to be fully formed, the head start into the target's semantic pattern will be beneficial for various measures of the model's progress toward identifying the target (e.g., settling of the phonological units to simulate a word-naming response).

Semantic versus associative priming

Before discussing the distributed memory model's account of specific experimental results involving semantic priming, some consideration of the distinction between semantic and associative priming is warranted. Semantic priming refers to cases in which words that have similar meanings prime one another in a word-identification task. In contrast, associative priming refers to priming effects that obtain when words are associatively related, as measured by free association norms (e.g., Postman and Keppel, 1970), but not semantically related (e.g., *milk* and *cow*). Shelton and Martin (1992) found that under conditions intended to prevent the use of expectancy and postlexical checking, associatively related word pairs generated a priming effect in lexical decision, whereas semantically related pairs did not.

The Shelton and Martin (1992) result poses a problem for the class of models, including the distributed memory model, that assume semantic priming effects are a consequence of similarity in the patterns of activation for semantically related words. More recent empirical studies, however, have produced evidence for automatic semantic priming. First, Moss, Ostrin, Tyler, and Marslen-Wilson (1995) found that under conditions like those used by Shelton and Martin semantically related words that share a functional relationship (e.g., *broom-floor*), but are not associatively related, produce a reliable priming effect. Thus, automatic semantic priming can occur in the absence of an associative relationship. Second, McRae and Boisvert (1998) showed that pairs of words that were rated by subjects as highly similar in meaning, but that were not associatively related, produced reliable semantic priming using the Shelton and Martin procedure (see Thompson-Schill, Kurtz, and Gabrieli, 1998, for a similar result). McRae and Boisvert also replicated the lack of a priming effect with the items originally used by Shelton and Martin, and they showed that those pairs were rated as less similar than the pairs that yielded a priming effect. These new results support the proposal that semantic priming effects arise from semantic similarity between pairs of words and therefore support accounts of priming effects that are based on semantic similarity.

Influence of an intervening item

An important implication of the distributed memory model's representation of word knowledge is that priming effects occur because processing of the prime moves the network's pattern of activation into a state that is favorable to the upcoming target. This basis for priming is susceptible to interference from presentation of an event that intervenes between the prime and the target. In particular, if a word were to be presented just after a prime, but before a related target, and if that intervening word were unrelated to either prime or target, then processing of that word would move the network's pattern of activation away from the pattern that was established by the prime. That is, the preliminary work done by the prime would be dismantled in the course of processing the intervening word, thereby reducing or eliminating the priming effect. Whether the effect is entirely eliminated would depend on the amounts of processing time devoted to the prime and the intervening word. As more time is devoted to the intervening word, the effect of the prime begins to disappear.

The distributed memory model is not the only type of model that predicts this effect of an intervening word on semantic priming. This phenomenon is also predicted by the compound-cue model proposed by Ratcliff and McKoon (1988, 1995). In that model, binary decision tasks, such as lexical decision, are performed by assessing the familiarity in memory of a target stimulus. In paradigms that involve presentation of a prime in conjunction with a target item, the prime and target are assumed to form a compound stimulus that becomes the object of the familiarity assessment. Semantic priming effects in this model emerge from the relatively high degree of familiarity of a prime-target compound that consists of a related pair of words, compared to the familiarity of a compound consisting of two unrelated words. By presenting an unrelated word between a related prime-target pair (e.g., *cat-spy-DOG*), a new compound is formed consisting of the unrelated, intervening item and the target. The familiarity of this compound would be about the same as for any pair of unrelated words, leading to the disappearance of the priming effect.

Empirical evidence about the effect of an intervening word has been mixed; some studies find that priming still occurs (e.g., McNamara, 1992; Meyer et al., 1972) and others find that priming is eliminated (e.g., Dannenbring and Briand, 1982; Ratcliff and McKoon, 1988, 1995). Using a word-naming task, I found that an unrelated intervening stimulus reduces or eliminates semantic priming and reported a simulation of the result using the distributed memory model (Masson, 1995). These effects are not simply due to the presentation of any stimulus between the prime and target because robust priming effects occur if the intervening item is a neutral stimulus such as a row of x's or a word that occurs on many trials (e.g., *ready*).

The intervening stimulus effect is important not only because it supports the predictions of the distributed memory and compound cue models, but also because it is contrary to what would be expected by the Collins and Loftus (1975) model of semantic priming that was based on localist representation of knowledge. In that model, activation spreads automatically from a prime word to all related words, independently of activity in other parts of the network.

Thus, presentation of an unrelated intervening word should have no effect on activation that is spreading in a distant area of the network. A more sophisticated localist representation model, the ACT* model of Anderson (1983), can account for the disruptive effects of an intervening item in the following way. Activation of a prime is assumed to decay once the prime stimulus disappears unless attention to the prime is maintained. The pattern of priming effects found when the intervening stimulus is an unrelated word versus a neutral stimulus can be explained if it is assumed that activation of the prime decays during processing of an unrelated intervening word but is maintained by attention when the intervening item is a neutral stimulus. A similar proposal involving automatic spreading activation combined with attentional allocation in semantic memory was made by Posner and Snyder (1975). Thus, although the intervening stimulus effect does not provide a means of discriminating between the distributed memory and compound-cue models on one hand, and all versions of spreading activation models on the other hand, it does constitute support for important predictions of the first two models while contradicting predictions of classic spreading activation models.

A related result that might be taken as a challenge to the distributed memory model was reported by Joordens and Besner (1992). In a continuous word-naming task, they embedded pairs of target words in the list that were semantically related but separated by an intervening unrelated target. All targets were named as quickly as possible, and a small but reliable priming effect was observed despite the fact that an unrelated word intervened between related targets. This result was problematic for the original version of the distributed memory model (Masson, 1991) because that model simulated only a generic word identification task and did so by requiring the entire set of conceptual units to settle into a stable state. Any advantage created by a related target would be completely destroyed by processing and responding to an unrelated word because the latter word's pattern of activation would completely take over the conceptual units, leaving no vestige of the related target's processing.

A more realistic simulation of word naming was developed in the modified version of the distributed memory model (Masson, 1995), as described above. In the modified version of the model, settling of phonological units is the criterion for word naming. Because the phonological units are fewer in number and update at a faster rate than conceptual units, naming an intervening word did not completely change the pattern of activation in semantic units created by the previous target. Therefore, when the critical target was presented, some of the work in the semantic units done by the earlier related target was still in place. Processing of the related target was able to take advantage of this weak semantic pattern, producing a small priming effect.

Evidence for top-down effects of priming

A fundamental question that models of priming must consider is whether or not conceptual knowledge has a direct influence on lower levels of processing (e.g., development of an orthographic representation or identification of letters). On the view of interactive models, such as the interactive activation models of McClelland and Rumelhart (1981) and McClelland (1991), such top-down influences are a key part of the models' architecture. For example, in the interactive activation model, McClelland and Rumelhart accounted for superior identification of a target letter when embedded in a word as compared to a nonword by assuming that activation is passed from the level of word units back down to the level of letter units. Others have proposed that top-down activation of this kind does not occur, and that higher level knowledge interacts with perceptual information only during a decision stage, as in the fuzzy logical model of perception (e.g., Massaro, 1979, 1989; Rueckl and Oden, 1986). The latter perspective is compatible with the notion of informational encapsulation (e.g., Fodor, 1983), in which it is assumed that input modules are affected only by direct perceptual input but not by higher level knowledge.

The distributed memory model, as described here and in Masson (1991, 1995) adopts the view that conceptual knowledge does not affect perceptual processing. As shown in figure 12.1, the model's architecture does not provide for any influence of semantic or phonological knowledge on the development of an orthographic pattern. Only direct visual input affects the state of the orthographic units. Although this aspect of the model could easily be modified, it has been instructive to examine the model's performance under the assumption that no top-down influences are in effect. This version of the model has been particularly useful in the evaluation of two results that could be taken as support for the proposition that higher level knowledge influences perceptual processing.

First, it has been found that context effects on lexical decision and word-naming tasks are amplified when targets are degraded (e.g., Becker and Killion, 1977; Besner and Smith, 1992; Borowsky and Besner, 1991; Meyer, Schvaneveldt, and Ruddy, 1975). To examine the model's performance under conditions of degraded input, a version of the model like that used to produce the data in figure 12.2 was used to simulate four word naming conditions representing a factorial combination of related versus unrelated prime and clear versus degraded target. Target degradation was simulated by probabilistically setting an orthographic unit to its correct state when it was sampled for updating. The result of this perturbation in the development of a target's orthographic pattern was generally to slow the rate at which that pattern was formed, and therefore to increase the number of cycles to settle the phonological pattern, just as degradation generally slows responding in humans. The model also produced an enhanced effect of context when the targets were degraded, as shown in figure 12.3. This interaction follows the pattern observed in human data and is generated because the noisy orthographic influence on phonology gives the semantic units a greater opportunity to influence the state of the phonological units. Thus, the effect of semantic priming is amplified under conditions of degraded visual input.

It should be acknowledged that the interaction between context and degradation may not be as straightforward as depicted here. Recent evidence reported by Stolz and Neely (1995) indicates that there are conditions under which context and degradation do not interact in the lexical decision task. In particular, these two factors were additive when the proportion of trials on which the prime was related to the target was low (.25). The potential for degradation and context to be additive poses a significant challenge to connectionist models in general because of their highly interactive character. A possible solution would be to introduce a mechanism that would, under certain circumstances, delay inputs from orthographic to other modules until the orthographic pattern of activation reaches some criterion level of completeness (e.g., Joordens, Masson, and Besner, 1995). This approach would create a stage-like process that might result in additivity between degradation and context.

A second result that supports the proposal that context influences perceptual processes in a top-down manner is the demonstration that accuracy in identifying words, measured using signal detection, can be increased by semantic priming. Following Farah's (1989) argument that signal detection measures of sensitivity reflect perceptual processing, whereas measures of bias reflect attentional and semantic processes, Rhodes et al. (1993) showed that word-nonword discrimination accuracy, measured using A', the nonparametric signal detection version of sensitivity, was significantly greater when the target was preceded by a related prime. Rhodes et al. interpreted this result to mean that priming semantic knowledge had improved the perceptual processing of the targets, constituting a clear example of a

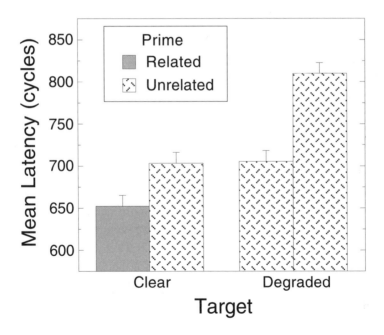

Figure 12.3. Mean cycles to settle phonological units under conditions of clear and degraded visual input. The effect of semantic priming is increased when degraded input is used. Error bars indicate the 95% within-subjects confidence interval for the means.

top-down influence of context.

Contrary to that conclusion, however, Norris (1995) was able to simulate the effect of context on sensitivity using a criterion-bias model in which each word is represented as a logogen and the effect of a related context word is to reduce the recognition threshold for logogens related to that context word. In the criterion-bias model, context has no effect on the acquisition of stimulus information but the lowered threshold means that less stimulus information is required for a primed logogen to reach the level of activation needed to exceed that threshold. Crucially, a prime lowers the thresholds only of words related to the prime, so in the case of an unrelated prime the target word's threshold is not lowered. The resulting difference in the amount of stimulus information needed to reach threshold in the related and unrelated conditions produces the observed sensitivity effect.

Like the criterion-bias model, the distributed memory model is also able to simulate the sensitivity effect in word identification. Masson and Borowsky (1998) simulated the lexical decision task used by Rhodes et al. (1993) with the distributed memory model by assuming that decisions in this task are based on a feeling of familiarity generated when the target is processed (e.g., Balota and Chumbley, 1984; Besner and Johnston, 1989). We assumed that familiarity corresponds to how well the network's current pattern of activation across all processing units conforms to the constraints imposed by the connection weights. As described above, the energy function provides a measure of this constraint satisfaction (see the formula in the appendix) and we assume that larger negative energy values correspond to a feeling of familiarity.

Using familiarity (energy) as a basis for the model's lexical decisions, we found that the model produced a robust effect of semantic priming on sensitivity in the simulation of the masked lexical decision task. The reason for the model's prediction is that familiarity was computed across all units and connections in the network thereby integrating all sources of knowledge in the model: semantic, phonological, and orthographic. Without ever directly affecting perceptual processes or the formation of the orthographic pattern of activation, semantic knowledge had a strong influence on lexical decisions because that knowledge converged with other knowledge sources, including orthographic knowledge, to determine the value of energy. This approach is compatible with the fuzzy logical model of perception (Massaro, 1979; Rueckl and Oden, 1986) that assumes semantic and perceptual information are integrated at a decision stage, without semantic knowledge affecting perceptual processing.

Masson and Borowsky (1998) also conducted two experiments using a probe-matching identification task. In this task, target words were presented briefly and followed by a mask, then a probe word. The task was to decide whether the probe matched the target. The targets were preceded by a related or unrelated prime in the form of either a word or a line drawing. Both types of related prime—word or line drawing—led to increased accuracy as measured by signal detection. The distributed memory model was used to simulate this effect by assuming that degraded information about the target is held in a temporary buffer and compared against the fully instantiated representation of the probe word. If the similarity between the buffer contents and the probe reached some criterion, a positive decision was made.

The effect of semantic priming in this case was to allow the model to develop more of the target's pattern of activation in the semantic units during the brief time the target was processed. Improved accuracy in the semantic units would also contribute to an improvement in the phonological units. When the target's pattern was loaded into the buffer at the completion of target processing, the pattern would be more accurate with respect to the target's semantic and phonological patterns following a related rather than an unrelated prime. When these two sources of information are combined with orthographic information about the prime to make a comparison against the probe word, accuracy is improved because of the enhanced semantic and phonological aspects of the target's representation. This improvement accrues in the model despite the fact that orthographic information about the target is unaffected by priming. Thus, the probe-matching task yielded a reliable effect of priming on accuracy. Once again, however, this result cannot be taken as clear evidence that semantic knowledge affects perceptual processes because the distributed memory model successfully accounts for the result without assuming any top-down influences on perception.

The implications of the model's successful simulation of the sensitivity effect are clear. The results obtained by Rhodes et al. (1993) cannot be taken unequivocally as evidence that semantic knowledge affects perceptual processing. The model provides an existence proof that sensitivity effects can be generated by a modular system, as long as perceptual and semantic sources of knowledge are integrated when making a response.

Lexical Ambiguity

An interesting problem faced by models of word identification, particularly models that use a distributed representation for semantic knowledge, is the resolution of lexical ambiguity. Many words have multiple, unrelated meanings (e.g., *bat*, *chest*), yet we typically are able to retrieve one meaning or another without conjuring up bizarre mutations consisting of bits of meaning drawn from the different interpretations of the ambiguous word. The difficulty confronting models of word identification is that a single orthographic input pattern is associated, on different occasions during learning, with different semantic patterns. In the distributed memory model, this difficulty is evident because the model forms basins of attraction that represent a blend of the two meanings of an ambiguous word (Joordens and Besner, 1994), and the model often fails to form basins of attraction that conform to the learned meanings of that word. When presented with the orthographic pattern of an ambiguous word, the model's semantic units move into a blend state rather than into a state corresponding to one of the word's assigned meanings.

To make it more likely that the distributed memory model would form basins of attraction for the learned meanings of ambiguous words, Borowsky and Masson (1996) implemented a version of the model that had a substantial number of semantic units (140) relative to orthographic units (70). With this version of the model, we were able to simulate results of three experiments we conducted involving ambiguous and unambiguous words in the lexical decision and word-naming tasks as well as a result involving gaze duration during reading comprehension (e.g., Duffy, Morris, and Rayner, 1988; Rayner and Frazier, 1989). The relevant empirical results and the simulation of those results are shown in table 12.1.

For the word-naming task, we found no evidence when testing human subjects of a difference between ambiguous and unambiguous words. In contrast, an advantage for ambiguous words was found in the lexical decision task, but only when pronounceable nonwords were used; no effect was found when nonwords were consonant strings. Gaze-duration data from Duffy et al. (1988) and Rayner and Frazier (1989) show that subjects spend more time fixating ambiguous than unambiguous words when these items are presented in neutral context and the two meanings of each ambiguous word are of about equal frequency.

Examination of the model's settling of phonological and semantic units during processing of ambiguous and unambiguous targets showed that the phonological units settled at about the same rate for both types of target (hence there was no effect of ambiguity on word naming). On the other hand, activation of word meaning was initially higher for one of the two meanings of an ambiguous target than for the meaning of an unambiguous target. By 250 cycles of processing, however, this situation had reversed and the meaning of an unambiguous target was more active than either meaning of an ambiguous target. The early advantage of ambiguity in activating meaning arose because on each trial the network was started in a random state, and it is more likely that the starting state will be closer to one of the two meanings of an ambiguous word than to the one and only meaning of an unam-

biguous word. That advantage, however, did not benefit the activation of phonological units because the connection weights between semantic and phonological
units were more strongly determined by the learning of unambiguous words than
by the learning of ambiguous words. This differential influence of semantics on
phonology was due to the training regimen in which the meaning of an ambiguous word was presented once, whereas the meaning of an unambiguous word was
presented twice to ensure that both types of word were equated with respect to frequency of presentation of their respective orthographic patterns. Thus, the semantic units had a somewhat greater influence on phonological units when unambiguous targets were presented, counteracting the greater activation of semantics by
ambiguous targets during the early stages of processing.

In the lexical decision task, responses were based on energy computed across
the orthographic and semantic units. If energy reached a threshold value before a
specified time limit, the target was classified as a word, otherwise it was classified as
a nonword. To simulate the experiment with pronounceable nonwords, nonword
orthographic patterns were constructed to be similar to learned words, whereas to
simulate the results involving consonant string nonwords, the nonword patterns
were very different from the learned words. As shown in table 12.1, there was an
ambiguity advantage, but only when "pronounceable" nonwords were used.

The reason for the ambiguity advantage is the proximity effect discussed above:
the random starting state of the meaning units is likely to be somewhat closer to

Table 12.1 Mean response latency and error percentage as a function of lexical
ambiguity

Data source and task	Response latency Ambig. Unambig.		% Error Ambig. Unambig.	
Results from human subjects				
Word naming	494	495	4.1	5.1
Lexical decision				
Pronounceable nonwords	637	647	3.2	4.3
Consonant string nonwords	569	567	2.3	2.6
Results from simulations				
Word naming	291	290	3.7	3.7
Lexical decision				
Pronounceable nonwords	116	119	3.2	5.2
Consonant string nonwords	54	54	3.6	4.0
Gaze duration during				
comprehension	689	629	0.8	0.0

Note. Latencies for human data are in milliseconds and latencies for simulated data are in cycles.
Source: Borowsky and Masson (1996).

one of the two meanings of an ambiguous word than it is to the one and only meaning of an unambiguous word. When updating of units begins for an ambiguous word, the influence of the orthographic units will push the meaning units toward the meaning favored by the random starting state of the meaning units. In the early stages of processing, then, ambiguous words will make faster gains in energy than unambiguous words, affording a slight advantage, mirroring the effect Borowsky and Masson (1996) obtained when subjects performed lexical decision task. By using nonwords that permit an easier and earlier discrimination (i.e., nonwords with orthographic patterns very different from those of learned words), however, the ambiguity advantage disappears. In this case, words can be discriminated very early during processing, before the meaning units have been driven very far from their starting state and before the ambiguity advantage has a chance to establish itself.

To simulate gaze duration during comprehension, we took the number of updating cycles for the meaning units to reach a stable state as a measure of gaze duration. This assumption is based on the idea that the eyes remain on a word until sufficient processing of meaning has occurred (the immediacy assumption of Just and Carpenter, 1980). As shown in table 12.1, the model took longer to reach a stable state in its meaning units when an ambiguous word was presented, indicating a longer average gaze duration for ambiguous words. The ambiguity disadvantage arises from two different meanings associated with an ambiguous orthographic pattern competing with one another for control of the semantic units.

Although the distributed memory model was capable of capturing the pattern of ambiguity effects across three different tasks by adopting plausible definitions of task performance, the ordering of these tasks along the model's measure of processing time (updating cycles) was quite different from the ordering of these tasks with respect to human latency data. Whereas the model's response latency in the lexical decision task was less than in the naming task, which in turn was less than average gaze duration, just the reverse ordering is true in human data. But the ordering across tasks generated by the model is not easy to interpret because the model is intended to simulate only some of the component processes that contribute to response latencies or gaze durations. For example, in the lexical decision task, the model does not simulate time taken to compute familiarity or preparation and execution of a manual response. In the naming task, the model does not simulate the process of translating a phonological representation into an articulatory code nor the time required to initiate articulation.

The important contribution of the distributed memory model to understanding lexical ambiguity effects is the model's characterization of two counteracting forces. First, as originally suggested by Joordens and Besner (1994), a potential advantage for ambiguous words arises in the model due to the proximity of the random starting state of semantic units to one of an ambiguous word's meanings. By chance alone, the random starting pattern in the semantic units is likely to be closer to one of two meanings of an ambiguous word than to the one and only meaning of an unambiguous word. Second, a disadvantage of ambiguity arises from competition between the two different meanings of an ambiguous word in the pattern of activation that is formed across the semantic units. An ambiguous word's orthographic pattern supports two unrelated semantic patterns and competition between them for the same representational space makes retrieval of meaning less efficient. To the degree that word processing tasks are determined primarily by one or the other of these two phenomena—proximity or competition—either an advantage or a disadvantage due to ambiguity may be obtained.

Masked Priming

An important aspect of the distributed memory model, as in most connectionist models of its kind, is the highly interactive nature of the processing units. The interactive character of this class of model means that additive effects of independent variables can pose a significant challenge to these models, as discussed earlier with respect to context and degradation. The distributed memory model, however, has been able to simulate an additive effect involving word frequency and masked primes. In the masked priming paradigm (e.g., Forster and Davis, 1984), a target word is preceded by a briefly presented prime which itself is preceded by a mask. The prime, then, is masked both before and after its presentation, making its very presence difficult to detect. Forster and Davis compared identity and unrelated primes using high- and low-frequency words. Because the prime was presented in lowercase and the target in uppercase, the identity prime was orthographically, not physically, identical to the target (e.g., *avoid-AVOID*). Forster and Davis found that when primes were presented very briefly (60 ms), the advantage of an identity prime over an unrelated prime in a lexical decision task was of the same magnitude for high- and for low-frequency target words (see also Bodner and Masson, 1997).

The distributed memory model was used to simulate this result using a variant of the energy measure, *scaled harmony*, to discriminate between words and nonwords. Generally speaking, scaled harmony is the inverse of energy, scaled to have a maximum value equal to the number of learning trials; it is described in greater detail in the appendix.

To simulate the masked priming task, the network was trained on a set of unrelated word patterns. High-frequency words were given four learning trials each, and low-frequency words were given three learning trials each. On each lexical decision trial, a prime was presented for 40 updating cycles, then was replaced by the target. In this simulation, the network was updated as in the simulations whose results are shown in figures 12.2 and 12.3. The value of scaled harmony was monitored during target processing and if the criterion value of .15 was reached before 1,500 updating cycles had occurred, the target was classified as a word. The number of cycles required to reach the criterion was taken as a measure of response latency. With this decision rule, very few errors were made (less than 0.5%), so no error data are reported. Nonword targets were constructed by perturbing the orthographic patterns of learned words. In the case of an identity prime, processing the prime was just the same as giving the network a head start at identifying the target item because the network's orthographic representation makes no distinction between upper- and lowercase, the feature that distinguished primes and targets in the masked priming experiments.

Consideration was also given to the nature of the unrelated prime used when high- versus low-frequency target words were presented. In the case of an unrelated prime, the network moves into a basin of attraction that is not compatible with the upcoming target and additional processing cycles are required for the network to settle into the target's basin of attraction, relative to what would be required had the network been in a random state when the target was presented. The network generally requires more processing cycles to move away from the pattern of activation associated with a high-frequency word and into the target's pattern than it does when moving away from a low-frequency word. Moreover, the network moves more quickly into the basin of attraction for high-frequency targets than it does for low-frequency targets (the basic word-frequency effect). Consequently, priming effects should be enhanced when high-frequency unrelated primes are paired with low-frequency targets, but reduced when low-frequency unrelated primes are paired with high-frequency targets.

Forster and Davis (1984) did not specify whether unrelated primes were matched to identity primes with respect to word frequency. Therefore, simulations were run with primes matched on frequency and again with frequency of unrelated primes allowed to vary. When unrelated primes varied in frequency relative to the target items, an interaction between prime and target frequency was found: there was more priming for low-frequency targets. When unrelated primes were matched to the targets on frequency, however, priming and frequency were additive, as in the Forster and Davis data. The results of the simulation in which primes and targets were matched on frequency are shown in figure 12.4. The growth of scaled harmony as a function of updating cycles is shown in figure 12.4a, beginning with the presentation of the masked prime 40 cycles prior to the onset of the target. Notice, first, that harmony grows much faster for the word patterns, particularly for high-frequency words than for the nonword patterns. It is these differences in harmony that produces the discrimination between words and nonwords and the word-frequency effect.

The harmony functions for nonword targets also show an effect of priming. In contrast, Forster and Davis (1984) found no identity priming effect for nonwords in the lexical decision task and attributed that lack of priming to the hypothesis that identity priming arises from activation of a lexical entry. On the Forster and Davis account, because nonwords have no entry, there is no basis for priming. Alternatively, it is possible that even the benefit of priming apparent in figure 12.4a might be part of human experience, but the increment in familiarity due to priming supports an incorrect response (Bodner and Masson, 1997). Thus, the benefit of priming might be canceled by the conflict in response selection that it creates. The distributed memory model does not have a detailed mechanism for simulating response

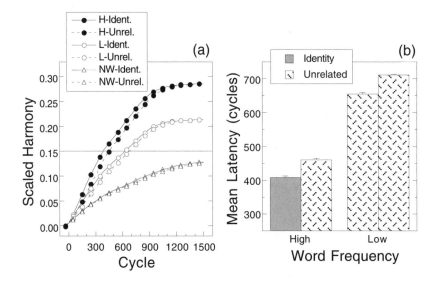

Figure 12.4. Growth of scaled harmony over processing cycles (a) and mean cycles to reach harmony criterion (b) for the simulation of masked identity priming in lexical decision. The harmony criterion for making a positive lexical decision was set at .15, as shown in section a. The error bars in section b represent the 95% within-subjects confidence interval for the means.

selection and therefore does not provide an account of this process.

The mean number of cycles required for word targets to reach criterion is shown in figure 12.4b. Response latency was less for high-frequency than for low-frequency words, and was reliably reduced by presentation of an identity prime, relative to an unrelated prime of the same frequency. Moreover, word frequency and priming were additive, in line with the results obtained by Forster and Davis (1984) and Bodner and Masson (1997). The reason for this additivity stems from the fact that the identity prime provides the network a head start that is uniform across words of varying frequency, akin to shifting the harmony function (as seen in figure 12.4a) to the left. By using unrelated primes of different frequencies, however, the uniformity of the comparison between identity and unrelated primes breaks down and an interactive pattern emerges from the model.

Limitations and Future Directions

The distributed memory model described here suffers from a number of limitations, some of which were revealed by its application to various word-identification paradigms. Other limitations, however, are more general and are shared by other models of the connectionist class, as well as by models of other types. I begin by considering some limitations specific to the distributed memory model and some ideas for overcoming those constraints. I conclude by considering an issue of broader concern to formal models of word reading.

Facilitation Versus Interference

In a recent critique of the distributed memory model (and attractor network models more generally), Dalrymple-Alford and Marmurek (1999) claimed that the semantic priming effects generated by the model when simulating the word-naming task were due to interference rather than facilitation. To support this claim, they used an unprimed presentation of a target word as a baseline condition. Dalrymple-Alford and Marmurek found that a related semantic prime did not produce shorter simulated naming latencies in the model than did the target-alone baseline condition and sometimes the related prime condition even produced interference relative to this baseline. At the same time, however, unrelated primes generated longer simulated naming latencies than related primes. It was concluded that semantic primes, whether related or unrelated, produce only interference effects. More generally, Dalrymple-Alford and Marmurek argued that attractor networks with fully interconnected units, such as the distributed memory model, could not generate facilitative priming in which one set of units (i.e., semantic) improves processing in another set (i.e., phonological).

In response to this claim about attractor networks, I showed that the lack of facilitative semantic priming when the target-alone condition is used as the baseline depends on what happens to the network between trials (Masson, 1999). In their simulations (as in earlier simulations my colleagues and I have conducted), Dalrymple-Alford and Marmurek reset the network to a random pattern of activation after each trial. When the patterns of activation in the network's semantic and phonological modules are random, units in those modules send little, if any, coherent input to units that are selected for updating. Rather, they send a random pattern of input that usually has no systematic influence on the updating of a unit. As units within a module take on a more coherent pattern of activation, they send a stronger more coherent input signal to other units in the network, causing the network to move into a stable pattern of activation that corresponds to a learned word. One way of measuring the coherence of the pattern of activation within a module, and hence the coherence of the input it sends to other units, is to compute the energy within that module's units. This can be done using the formula for energy shown in the appendix, but applying it only to the units and connection weights within the module in question.

When the energy of units in the semantic and in the phonological modules is computed, it becomes apparent why a related prime generally fails to produce shorter simulated naming latencies than the target-alone baseline condition. At the start of a target-alone trial, the network is in a random state and energy within the semantic and phonological modules is close to zero. On a primed trial, however, at the onset of the target the network already has moved into a pattern of activation corresponding to the prime that has just been processed. Therefore, the energy in the semantic and phonological modules has grown to some large negative value, depending on how long the prime was processed. Those modules consequently send coherent input signals to the network's units in support of the prime's pattern of activation. When the prime is unrelated to the target, these coherent input signals are not compatible with the target's pattern and they conflict with the input signals generated by the orthographic units when the target pattern is presented. This conflict slows the network's progress into the target's pattern of activation. As figure 12.5a shows, this effect increases as a function of energy in the semantic units at the time the target's orthographic pattern is presented to the network. Large negative energy values indicate a more complete instantiation of the prime's pattern of activation. Data in figure 12.5a were obtained by presenting an unrelated prime for varying durations and computing energy in the semantic units at the moment the target was presented and computing the number of updating cycles needed for the phonological units to settle on the target's phonological pattern. A relation similar to that shown in figure 12.5a also holds for the energy in the phonological units, but in that case it is a weaker relation because there is a relatively small number of phonological units so their state at target onset has a smaller effect on the network's behavior.

When the prime is semantically related to the target, the input of semantic units to phonological units is somewhat compatible with the target pattern as well, leading to a reduction or elimination of the interference effect. The net result is a priming effect as assessed by the difference between related and unrelated prime conditions. The advantage of semantic relatedness, however, is not great enough to generate a facilitation effect relative to the target-alone condition in which there is no competing source of coherent input to semantic and phonological units.

The distributed memory model is capable of producing a facilitation effect relative to the target-alone condition, however, if the network is not reset to a random state at the start of each trial. By starting each trial with the network in the state it reached at the end of the previous trial, even on target-alone trials the network's semantic and phonological modules are in coherent patterns of activation (energy values are large and negative) at the time the target is presented. Under these conditions, Masson (1999) found that a related prime led to shorter simulated naming latency than the target-alone condition and that this facilitation ef-

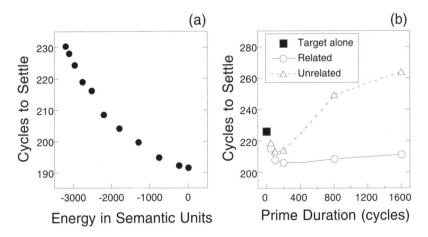

Figure 12.5. Relation between energy in semantic units at target onset and cycles to settle on the target's phonological pattern when an unrelated prime is presented (a) and mean cycles to settle on a target's phonological pattern as a function of prime condition when the network is not reset to a random state at the start of each trial (b).

fect increased as a function of how long the prime was processed, at least up to a point (see figure 12.5b). With longer prime durations, the facilitation effect began to decrease somewhat because the network moved very deeply into the prime's basin of attraction. As can be seen in figure 12.5b, the unrelated primes also produce a facilitation effect at the shortest prime durations. Although this effect appears to be counterintuitive, in the absence of data from experiments with human subjects it can be taken as an interesting prediction of the model.

Other Types of Primes

As an attractor network, the distributed memory model is designed specifically to react to external input by settling in the nearest basin of attraction. A disadvantage of this "single-mindedness" is revealed in the model's response to three types of primes that differ from the typically used related and unrelated primes. First, Dalrymple-Alford and Marmurek (1999) showed that a neutral prime, coded as a random pattern of activation in the orthographic units, had a systematic effect on the distributed memory model's behavior. By starting the semantic and phonological units in a random state, then presenting the network with a random orthographic pattern, the network will eventually move into a pattern of activation correspond- ing to the word whose pattern was most similar to the random starting state of the network. Thus, using a random orthographic pattern as a neutral prime did not cause the network to remain in some indeterminate state. Second, Bourassa and Besner (1998) used the model to simulate the influence of nonword primes that were or- thographically very similar to learned words. In the related prime condition, the nonword prime was orthographically similar to a learned word that was semanti- cally similar to the target word; in the unrelated prime condition the nonword prime was orthographically similar to a word that was semantically unrelated to the tar- get (actual counterparts might be *deg-CAT* versus *deg-SKY*). They found that the model produced a semantic priming effect when this type of prime was used and that the size of this effect increased with longer prime durations, just as occurred for word primes. In contrast, they found that in experiments with human subjects nonword primes generated a priming effect only when they were presented briefly and masked. They found no priming effect with nonwords when the primes were clearly visible to subjects. Third, some priming experiments with human subjects have used a single word as a neutral prime (e.g., *blank* or *ready*). By presenting the chosen word frequently, always followed by an unrelated target, subjects came to react differently to such a prime than to unrelated primes seen only once (e.g., McNamara, 1994; Ratcliff and McKoon, 1988, 1995).

    Some additional mechanism(s) would be required for the network to react in a more noncommittal manner to neutral primes, to be unresponsive to clearly presented nonword primes, and to learn to respond differently to primes that are repeatedly presented with unrelated targets. One approach, proposed by Bourassa and Besner as a means of simulating the nonword priming effect, would be to add a verification process in which the familiarity of an orthographic pattern is assessed. If the pattern is found to be unfamiliar, the network would deconstruct the pattern of activation in semantic units created by that pattern.

An alternative and more general idea is to place a constraint on updating semantic and phonological units. Before an orthographic pattern of activation exerts an influence on semantic and phonological units, an assessment is done regarding that pattern's familiarity. When a familiar pattern is detected (as indicated, for example, by a large negative energy value in the orthographic units), semantic and phonological units begin updating. The thoroughness of this assessment would depend on the availability of orthographic information. With a brief, masked presentation, orthographic information would be minimal and the assessment might be preempted or curtailed, allowing a word-like stimulus to influence semantic and phonological units. A gating mechanism of this sort might also be used to prevent a prime word that is repeatedly presented with unrelated targets from influencing semantic and perhaps phonological units, akin to a semantic satiation effect (e.g., Esposito and Pelton, 1971). A learning mechanism would have to be incorporated as well, however, that would be sensitive to the events in which particular words take part. In general, it appears likely that a more accurate simulation of the effects of various neutral and nonword primes will require the implementation of a mechanism that influences and perhaps gates the reaction of semantic and phonological units to orthographic input and perhaps even to input from themselves.

Stimulus Coding

The final issue to be considered is of general concern in models that are intended to explain responses to externally presented stimuli: How should one represent stimulus input in a model? In many models of word reading, the typical approach has been to finesse this question by taking as the starting point an orthographic representation. Although this approach has the advantage of allowing models to move quickly to issues of higher level processing (such as phonological recoding and semantic processing), it has two serious drawbacks. First, it constrains in arbitrary ways the possible means of simulating the effects on stimulus processing that would occur prior to the formation of an orthographic code, such as stimulus degradation or peripheral neurological disorders. Second, and more important, there may be a high price associated with the convenience of adopting such coding schemes.

These coding schemes typically are crafted with downstream processing in mind, as in the conversion of orthographic representations to phonological representations that motivated the Plaut et al. (1996) modifications to the Seidenberg and McClelland (1989) model. Empirical evidence is beginning to emerge that challenges the typical implementation of a word's visual form as a linear orthographic string (Tainturier and Caramazza, 1996).

Rather than using consequences for higher order coding as the primary factor in determining how stimuli ought to be coded, significant attention should be directed toward honoring the constraints of perceptual processing and toward how an adaptive system discovers which features of its environment are important in rendering an internal description of that environment (see Rumelhart and Zipser, 1985, for an approach to this problem). By working with an internal coding scheme that ignores this set of constraints, we risk moving model development along seriously misguided trajectories. The argument here is that very careful consideration needs to be given to alternative methods of coding stimulus events and to the differences in subsequent processing implied by these alternative methods.

Conclusion

The distributed memory model described in this chapter has been a useful tool in efforts to account for the interaction among orthographic, phonological, and semantic knowledge. Its simple representational and learning assumptions have permitted an early glimpse of the effects that semantic knowledge can have on word-reading tasks that are the foundation of our empirical knowledge concerning word-reading processes. At the same time, however, the model's shortcomings in addressing the subtleties of word characteristics that have dominated much theorizing in other quarters (e.g., Besner, chapter 13, this volume; Besner, Twilley, McCann, and Seergobin, 1990; Plaut, chapter 11, this volume; Plaut and Shallice, 1993; Plaut et al., 1996) has made it difficult for the distributed memory model to make contact with that body of literature. In future development of the model, emphasis will be placed on the construction of more principled representations of knowledge and on methods of governing the network's task performance to achieve the flexibility of processing that is so clearly evident in word-reading performance.

Acknowledgment

Preparation of this chapter was supported by a research grant from the Natural Sciences and Engineering Research Council of Canada. I am grateful to Derek Besner, Ron Borowsky, and Steve Joordens for their many contributions to the collaborative research reported here and to Derek Besner for comments on an earlier version of this chapter.

References

Anderson, J.R. (1983). *The Architecture of Cognition.* Cambridge, MA: Harvard University Press.

Balota, D.A., and Chumbley, J.I. (1984). Are lexical decisions a good measure of lexical access? The role of word frequency in the neglected decision stage. *Journal of Experimental Psychology: Human Perception and Performance, 10,* 340–357.

Becker, C.A., and Killion, T.H. (1977). Interaction of visual and cognitive effects in word recognition. *Journal of Experimental Psychology: Human Perception and Performance, 3,* 389–401.

Besner, D., and Johnston, J.C. (1989). Reading and the mental lexicon: On the uptake of visual information. In W. Marslen-Wilson (ed.), *Lexical Representation and Process* (pp. 291–316). Cambridge, MA: MIT Press.

Besner, D., and Smith, M.C. (1992). Models of visual word recognition: When obscuring the stimulus yields a clearer view. *Journal of Experimental Psychology: Learning, Memory, and Cognition, 18,* 468–482.

Besner, D., Twilley, L., McCann, R.S., and Seergobin, K. (1990). On the association between connectionism and data: Are a few words necessary? *Psychological Review, 97,* 432–446.

Bodner, G.E., and Masson, M.E.J. (1997). Masked repetition priming of words and nonwords: Evidence for a nonlexical basis for priming. *Journal of Memory and Language, 37,* 268–293.

Borowsky, R., and Besner, D. (1991). Visual word recognition across orthographies: On the interaction between context and degradation. *Journal of Experimental Psychology: Learning, Memory, and Cognition, 17,* 272–276.

Borowsky, R., and Masson, M.E.J. (1996). Semantic ambiguity effects in word identification. *Journal of Experimental Psychology: Learning, Memory, and Cognition, 22,* 63–85.

Bourassa, D.C., and Besner, D. (1998). When do nonwords activate semantics? Implications for models of visual word recognition. *Memory and Cognition, 26,* 61–74.

Collins, A.M., and Loftus, E.F. (1975). A spreading-activation theory of semantic processing. *Psychological Review, 82,* 407–428.

Coltheart, M., Curtis, B., Atkins, P., and Haller, M. (1993). Models of reading aloud: Dual-route and parallel-distributed-processing approaches. *Psychological Review, 100,* 589–608.

Dalrymple-Alford, E.C., and Marmurek, H.H.C. (1999). Semantic priming in fully recurrent network models of lexical knowledge. *Journal of Experimental Psychology: Learning, Memory, and Cognition, 25,* 758–775.

Daneman, M., Reingold, E.M., and Davidson, M. (1995). Time course of phonological activation during reading: Evidence from eye fixations. *Journal of Experimental Psychology: Learning, Memory, and Cognition, 21,* 884–898.

Dannenbring, G.L., and Briand, K. (1982). Semantic priming and the word repetition effect in a lexical decision task. *Canadian Journal of Psychology, 36,* 435–444.

Duffy, S.A., Morris, R.K., and Rayner, K. (1988). Lexical ambiguity and fixation times in reading. *Journal of Memory and Language, 27,* 429–446.

Esposito, N.J., and Pelton, L.H. (1971). Review of the measurement of semantic satiation. *Psychological Bulletin, 75,* 330–346.

Farah, M.J. (1989). Semantic and perceptual priming: How similar are the underlying mechanisms? *Journal of Experimental Psychology: Human Perception and Performance, 15,* 188–194.

Fodor, J. (1983). *The Modularity of Mind.* Cambridge, MA: MIT Press.

Forster, K.I. (1976). Accessing the mental lexicon. In R. J. Wales and E. W. Walker (eds.), *New Approaches to Language Mechanisms* (pp. 257–287). Amsterdam: North-Holland.

Forster, K.I., and Davis, C. (1984). Repetition priming and frequency attenuation in lexical access. *Journal of Experimental Psychology: Learning, Memory, and Cognition, 10,* 680–698.

Hebb, D.O. (1949). *The Organization of Behavior.* New York: Wiley.

Hinton, G.E., and Shallice, T. (1991). Lesioning an attractor network: Investigations of acquired dyslexia. *Psychological Review, 98,* 74–95.

Hopfield, J.J. (1982). Neural networks and physical systems with emergent collective computational abilities. *Proceedings of the National Academy of Science, 79,* 2554–2558.

Jacobs, A.M., and Grainger, J. (1992). Testing a semistochastic variant of the interactive activation model in different word recognition experiments. *Journal of Experimental Psychology: Human Perception and Performance, 18,* 1174–1188.

Jared, D., and Seidenberg, M.S. (1991). Does word identification proceed from spelling to sound to meaning? *Journal of Experimental Psychology: General, 120,* 358–394.

Johnson, N.F., and Pugh, K.R. (1994). A cohort model of visual word recognition. *Cognitive Psychology, 26,* 240–346.

Joordens, S., and Besner, D. (1992). Priming effects that span an intervening unrelated word: Implications for models of memory representation and retrieval. *Journal of Experimental Psychology: Learning, Memory, and Cognition, 18,* 483–491.

Joordens, S., and Besner, D. (1994). When banking on meaning is not (yet) money in the bank: Explorations in connectionist modeling. *Journal of Experimental Psychology: Learning, Memory, and Cognition, 20,* 1051–1062.

Joordens, S., Masson, M.E.J., and Besner, D. (1995, November). Connectionist models and additive effects: Are distinct stages of processing necessary? Paper presented at the annual meeting of the Psychonomic Society, Los Angeles, CA.

Just, M.A., and Carpenter, P.A. (1980). A theory of reading: From eye fixations to comprehension. *Psychological Review, 87,* 329–354.

Lesgold, A.M., and Perfetti, C.A. (eds.). (1981). *Interactive Processes in Reading.* Hillsdale, NJ: Erlbaum.

Lukatela, G., and Turvey, M.T. (1994). Visual lexical access is initially phonological: 1. Evidence from associative priming by words, homophones, and pseudohomophones. *Journal of Experimental Psychology: General, 123,* 107–128.

Massaro, D.W. (1979). Letter information and orthographic context in word perception. *Journal of Experimental Psychology: Human Perception and Performance, 5,* 595–609.

Massaro, D.W. (1989). Testing between the TRACE model and the fuzzy logical model of speech perception. *Cognitive Psychology, 21,* 398–421.

Masson, M.E.J. (1991). A distributed memory model of context effects in word identification. In D. Besner and G.W. Humphreys (eds.), *Basic Processes in Reading: Visual Word Recognition* (pp. 233–263). Hillsdale, NJ: Erlbaum.

Masson, M.E.J. (1995). A distributed memory model of semantic priming. *Journal of Experimental Psychology: Learning, Memory, and Cognition, 21,* 3–23.

Masson, M.E.J. (1998). Creating a level playing field generates semantic priming in a recurrent network. Manuscript submitted for publication.

Masson, M.E.J. (1999). Semantic priming in a recurrent network: Comment on Dalrymple-Alford and Marmurek (1999). *Journal of Experimental Psychology: Learning, Memory, and Cognition, 25,* 776–794.

Masson, M.E.J., and Borowsky, R. (1998). More than meets the eye: Context effects in word identification. *Memory and Cognition, 26,* 1245–1269.

Masson, M.E.J., and Sala, L.S. (1978). Interactive processes in sentence comprehension and recognition. *Cognitive Psychology, 10,* 244–270.

McClelland, J.L. (1979). On the time relations of mental processes: An examination of systems of processes in cascade. *Psychological Review, 86,* 287–330.

McClelland, J.L. (1985). Putting knowledge in its place: A scheme for programming parallel processing structures on the fly. *Cognitive Science, 9,* 113–146.

McClelland, J.L. (1991). Stochastic interactive processes and the effect of context on perception. *Cognitive Psychology, 23,* 1–44.

McClelland, J.L., and Rumelhart, D.E. (1981). An interactive activation model of context effects in letter perception: part 1. An account of basic findings. *Psychological Review, 88,* 375–407.

McNamara, T.P. (1992). Theories of priming: I. Associative distance and lag. *Journal of Experimental Psychology: Learning, Memory, and Cognition, 18,* 1173–1190.

McNamara, T.P. (1994). Theories of priming: II. Types of primes. *Journal of Experimental Psychology: Learning, Memory, and Cognition, 20*, 507–520.

McRae, K., and Boisvert, S. (1998). Automatic semantic similarity priming. *Journal of Experimental Psychology: Learning, Memory, and Cognition, 24*, 558–572.

McRae, K., de Sa, V.R., and Seidenberg, M.S. (1997). On the nature and scope of featural representations of word meaning. *Journal of Experimental Psychology: General, 126*, 99–130.

Meyer, D.E., Schvaneveldt, R.W., and Ruddy, M.G. (November 1972). Activation of lexical memory. Paper presented at the annual meeting of the Psychonomic Society, St. Louis, MO.

Meyer, D.E., Schvaneveldt, R.W., and Ruddy, M.G. (1975). Loci of contextual effects on visual word recognition. In P.M.A. Rabbitt and S. Dornic (eds.), *Attention and Performance V* (pp. 98–118). San Diego, CA: Academic Press.

Morton, J. (1969). Interaction of information in word recognition. *Psychological Review, 76*, 165–178.

Moss, H.E., Ostrin, R.K., Tyler, L.K., and Marslen-Wilson, W.D. (1995). Accessing different types of lexical semantic information: Evidence from priming. *Journal of Experimental Psychology: Learning, Memory, and Cognition, 21*, 863–883.

Neely, J.H. (1977). Semantic priming and retrieval from lexical memory: Roles of inhibitionless spreading activation and limited–capacity attention. *Journal of Experimental Psychology: General, 106*, 226–254.

Norris, D. (1995). Signal detection theory and modularity: On being sensitive to the power of bias models of semantic priming. *Journal of Experimental Psychology: Human Perception and Performance, 21*, 935–939.

Paap, K.R., and Noel, R.W. (1991). Dual–route models of print and sound: Still a good horse race. *Psychological Research, 53*, 13–24.

Perfetti, C.A., and Bell, L. (1991). Phonemic activation during the first 40 ms of word identification: Evidence from backward masking and masked priming. *Journal of Memory and Language, 30*, 473–485.

Perfetti, C.A., Bell, L., and Delaney, S. (1988). Automatic phonetic activation in silent word reading: Evidence from backward masking. *Journal of Memory and Language, 27*, 59–70.

Plaut, D.C., McClelland, J.L., Seidenberg, M.S., and Patterson, K.E. (1996). Understanding normal and impaired word reading: Computational principles in quasi-regular domains. *Psychological Review, 103*, 56–115.

Plaut, D.C., and Shallice T. (1993). Deep dyslexia: A case study of connectionist neuropsychology. *Cognitive Neuropsychology, 10*, 377–500.

Posner, M.I., and Snyder, C.R.R. (1975). Attention and cognitive control. In R. L. Solso (ed.), *Information Processing and Cognition* (pp. 55–85). Hillsdale, NJ: Erlbaum.

Postman, L., and Keppel, G. (eds.). (1970). *Norms of Word Association*. New York: Academic Press.

Ratcliff, R., and McKoon, G. (1988). A retrieval theory of priming in memory. *Psychological Review, 95*, 385–408.

Ratcliff, R., and McKoon, G. (1994). Retrieving information from memory: Spreading-activation theories versus compound-cue theories. *Psychological Review, 101*, 177–184.

Ratcliff, R., and McKoon, G. (1995). Sequential effects in lexical decision: Tests of compound-cue retrieval theory. *Journal of Experimental Psychology: Learning, Memory, and Cognition, 21*, 1380–1388.

Rayner, K., and Frazier, L. (1989). Selection mechanisms in reading lexically ambiguous words. *Journal of Experimental Psychology: Learning, Memory, and Cognition, 15*, 779–790.

Rhodes, G., Parkin, A.J., and Tremewan, T. (1993). Semantic priming and sensitivity in lexical decision. *Journal of Experimental Psychology: Human Perception and Performance, 19*, 154–165.

Rueckl, J.G., and Oden, G.C. (1986). The integration of contextual and featural information during word identification. *Journal of Memory and Language, 25*, 445–460.

Rumelhart, D.E. (1977). Toward an interactive model of reading. In S. Dornic (ed.), *Attention and Performance VI* (pp. 573–603). Hillsdale, NJ: Erlbaum.

Rumelhart, D.E., and Zipser, D. (1985). Feature discovery by competitive learning. *Cognitive Science, 9*, 75–112.

Seidenberg, M.S., and McClelland, J.L. (1989). A distributed, developmental model of word recognition and naming. *Psychological Review, 96*, 523–568.

Seidenberg, M.S., and Tanenhaus, M.K. (1986). Modularity and lexical access. In I. Gopnik and M. Gopnik (eds.), *From Models to Modules: Studies in Cognitive Science from the McGill Workshops* (pp. 135–157). Norwood, NJ: Ablex.

Sharkey, N.E. (1989). The lexical distance model and word priming. In G.M. Olson and E.E. Smith (eds.), *Proceedings of the Eleventh Annual Conference of the Cognitive Science* Society (pp. 860–867). Hillsdale, NJ: Erlbaum.

Sharkey, N.E. (1990). A connectionist model of text comprehension. In D. A. Balota, G. B. Flores d'Arcais, and K. Rayner (eds.), *Comprehension Processes in Reading* (pp. 487–514). Hillsdale, NJ: Erlbaum.

Shelton, J.R., and Martin, R.C. (1992). How semantic is automatic semantic priming? *Journal of Experimental Psychology: Learning, Memory, and Cognition, 18*, 1191–1210.

Stolz, J.A., and Neely, J.H. (1995). When target degradation does and does not enhance semantic context effects in word recognition. *Journal of Experimental Psychology: Learning, Memory, and Cognition, 21*, 596–611.

Tainturier, M.-J., and Caramazza, A. (1996). The status of double letters in graphemic representations. *Journal of Memory and Language, 35,* 53–73.

Thompson-Schill, S.L., Kurtz, K.J., and Gabrieli, J.D.E. (1998). Effects of semantic and associative relatedness on automatic priming. *Journal of Memory and Language, 38,* 440–458.

Van Orden, G.C., Johnston, J.C., and Hale, B.L. (1988). Word identification in reading proceeds from spelling to sound to meaning. *Journal of Experimental Psychology: Learning, Memory, and Cognition, 14,* 371–385.

Ziegler, J.C., and Jacobs, A.M. (1995). Phonological information provides early sources of constraint in the processing of letter strings. *Journal of Memory and Language, 34,* 567–593.

Appendix: Implementation of the Distributed Memory Model

The learning rule used in the distributed memory model is a version of the Hebb (1949) learning rule in which connection weights between units are adjusted as a function of the activation states of the two units when a target pattern is instantiated in the network. Each time a pattern is presented for a training trial, the connection weight between a pair of units is changed according to the formula

$$\Delta w_{ij} = n_i n_j,$$

where w_{ij} is the connection weight between units i and j, and n_i and n_j are the activation states for those units when a target pattern is instantiated. For example, if the pattern of activation for a given word calls for two particular orthographic units to take on the value of 1, the connection weight between them will increase by $(1)(1) = 1$.

During pattern completion, part of a learned pattern is instantiated in the network while the remaining units in the network are set to randomly determined states. The units that represent the partial pattern are clamped (i.e., fixed at their assigned activation states) and the remaining units are sampled and their activation states updated. A unit's activation state is updated by computing the net input coming into that unit from all other units in the network, according to the formula

$$net_i = \sum_{i \neq j} w_{ij} n_j,$$

where net_i represents the net input received by unit i. A nonlinear activation function is used to convert the net input into the unit's activation state of 1 or –1. The function is the threshold function

$$\text{if } net_i > 0, \text{ then } n_i = 1, \text{ else } n_i = -1.$$

This updating rule normally causes the pattern of activation across the network's units to move into a stable pattern of activation matching the target pattern that was partially instantiated.

The movement of the network into a learned pattern of activation is a form of gradient descent into a basin of attraction that can be described quantitatively as moving the network into a local minimum of an energy function, E, defined as

$$\underset{i>j}{E} = -\sum w_{ij}\, n_i\, n_j \,,$$

In a three-dimensional analogy, E corresponds to depth in the landscape and has a local minimum at the bottom of a basin of attraction (corresponding to a learned pattern). Each time a unit is updated and its activation state computed, the network has the opportunity to move further down the basin it has entered, reducing E. Whenever the updating of a unit causes its state to change, E is reduced. On some occasions, the input coming into a unit and the threshold function dictate that a unit take on the same activation value it already holds (i.e., the unit does not change state). In these cases, changing the unit's state of activation would cause E to increase. Thus, when the network eventually enters a pattern of activation that corresponds to learned pattern, the updating rule will call for none of the units to change state (i.e., E will have reached a local minimum). We refer to this situation as reaching a stable state.

As an alternative to energy, one can use an inverse of that measure generally known as harmony. The simulations of masked priming described here used a particular version of this measure, scaled harmony (Joordens et al., 1995). This measure is a scaled inverse of energy,

$$H_s = \sum_{i>j} c_{ij}\, w_{ij}\, n_i\, n_j \,,$$

where c_{ij} is a constant equal to the reciprocal of the number of connection weights of the same type as w_{ij} (e.g., semantic unit to semantic unit, or orthographic unit to phonological unit). The scaled harmony measure adjusts the contributions of the three different modules of the network and the connections among them so that all three modules have an equal influence on harmony, independently of differences in number of units in the modules. Without the scaling constant, modules with more units play a greater role in determining the value of harmony. By scaling the w_{ij} values to take into account the number of connection weights of each type (both within and across modules), the potentially arbitrary differences in number of units in the modules will not affect the harmony measure. Although the decision to allow each module to contribute equally to harmony is also arbitrary, it was deemed a reasonable starting assumption. Variations in task demands and materials may affect the validity of this assumption. The maximum value that scaled harmony can take on is equal to the total number of learning trials, and it is attained only if exactly the same pattern is learned on each trial. As different patterns are learned, the Hebbian learning rule leads to connection weights that vary in strength, reducing the maximum value of scaled harmony the network can attain.

13

Basic Processes in Reading: Multiple Routines in Localist and Connectionist Models

Derek Besner

The last decade has seen a major debate between parallel distributed processing (PDP) approaches to cognitive processing and traditional symbolic accounts. This debate has been particularly vigorous in language processing (e.g., see Rumelhart and McClelland, 1986 versus Pinker and Prince, 1988; Pinker, 1991) and, in keeping with the theme of the present book, in reading (e.g., Seidenberg and McClelland, 1989; Plaut, McClelland, Seidenberg, and Patterson, 1996; Plaut, chapter 11, this volume, versus Besner, Twilley, McCann, and Seergobin, 1990; Coltheart, Curtis, Atkins, and Haller, 1993). Within the reading domain, this debate shows little sign of waning despite a conceptual shift such that some of the PDP approaches now look more similar to the classical dual-route account than they did a decade ago. Further, there remains the issue of which approach best reflects what it is that humans do when they recognize words, as opposed to "existence proof by simulation." These issues are addressed in the present chapter.

First, a brief review is presented of some of the background to the debate between these two approaches. This is followed by a selective sampling of the experimental literature as it bears on some of the issues, and a new quantitative analysis of how well several of the implemented models actually perform. The overall conclusion is that, to date, a three-route model provides a better account of performance than either the single or the dual-route models favored by many theorists of the connectionist persuasion[1]. Finally, a localist framework provides a sufficient account, but this is not to deny that one or more of the routines that convert spelling to sound might be well described by models with distributed representations (e.g., in the form of a hidden unit layer).

Introduction

The Received View: Localist Representations and Three Routes

A standard view, spanning the last 35 years or so, is that representations for words in memory are localist in that a single node stands for a single word (e.g., Treisman, 1960; Morton, 1969; Collins and Loftus, 1975; McClelland and Rumelhart, 1981; Coltheart et al., 1993). The more words a reader knows the more lexical nodes they have. A further, often associated view, is that printed words can be read aloud in several different ways (e.g. Patterson and Morton, 1980; Patterson and Coltheart, 1987; Paap and Noel, 1991; Coltheart et al, 1993; Ellis, 1984; Buchanan and Besner, 1995). This view is summarized in the three-route model reviewed by Besner and Smith (1992) and shown in figure 13.1.

For present purposes, the main elements of this view are that (1) there are distinct sublexical, lexical, and semantic levels of representation, (2) these representations, and the processes that operate on them, are in many instances "stand-alone" devices that are revealed by studying patients with an acquired dyslexia (discussed later), and (3) there are multiple ways of using these different knowledge sources to read aloud. Briefly, the orthographic input lexicon consists of lexical entries for the spellings of all words known to a reader. Following Morton and McClelland, it is assumed that neither semantics nor phonology is represented here, and there are no lexical-lexical associations (see also Stolz and Besner, 1996a). The semantic system represents meaning (with no commitment to the nature of the underlying representation, i.e., localist versus distributed). The phonological input and output lexicons consist of lexical entries that represent all the words that a reader knows specified in terms of their phonology. Finally, the phonemic buffer holds information about phonemes.

One way to name a word is via semantics (pathway A-B). When a word is presented to the word-recognition system, it activates its lexical entry in the orthographic input lexicon. This in turn leads to activation in the semantic system, and then in the phonological output system. A second way to name a word is for the orthographic input lexicon to directly activate the phonological output lexicon (pathway D). A third way is to use the assembled routine. Here the reader utilizes spelling-sound correspondence knowledge to translate subword orthographic segments into subword phonological segments, which are then assembled into a speech program. This, in its simplest form, is carried out via pathway E. All three ways of naming a word involve activation of the phonemic buffer; pathway E does so directly, whereas the other two methods do so via the phonological output lexicon

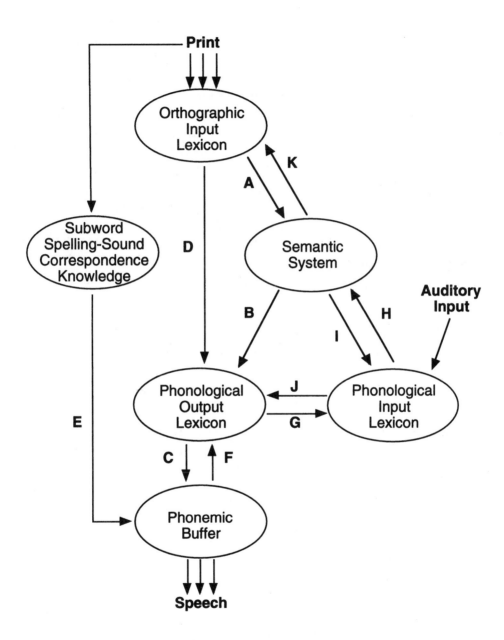

Figure 13.1 A three-route model of visual word recognition and production.

(pathway C). Which particular routine will dominate performance depends on a host of factors (e.g., word length, word frequency, spelling-sound consistency and regularity, lexical status, imageability, context, and mental set).

The remaining central points about this framework concern the nature of the response that a pathway can produce in response to particular stimuli. Thus, nonwords that resemble words orthographically and phonologically (but do not sound identical to real words) will result in some activation in the orthographic and phonological lexicons as well as in semantics (e.g., see Besner, Dennis, and Davelaar, 1985; Bourassa and Besner, 1998), but the resulting semantic activation will not likely be strong enough to drive an overt naming response in intact subjects (at least, I know of no evidence that it can). In contrast, the presentation of either a word or a nonword can result in the assembled route (pathway E) producing a response. In the case of words with unusual spelling-sound correspondences (e.g., HAVE, PINT) the output of the assembled route on its own would rhyme with WAVE and MINT because this system applies the most typical spelling-sound correspondences. The lexical-semantic routes (pathways D, and A-B) can produce a correct response to all words, regardless of their spelling-sound correspondences. Finally, the presentation of a word will also activate other words in the lexical and semantic system that resemble these words, although their activation will not be as strong as the presented word.

An Alternative View: A Single Route PDP Model

The classical view presented above was challenged with the publication of Seidenberg and McClelland's (1989) single-route PDP model. The important points are that the representations are distributed, and that in the implemented model there is only a single way of translating print into sound. Regular words, exception words, and nonwords are thus all read aloud by recourse to a common pathway. The general approach instantiated in this model has been widely promulgated and has captured the imagination of many cognitive scientists. To date, Seidenberg and McClelland's seminal work has been cited over 200 times according to the Social Sciences Citation Index. This is a remarkable achievement in that few paradigm shifts in cognitive psychology have received such an immediate and enthusiastic reception. Still, being a cautious soul, I would like to examine some of the specific claims that have been made in a more deliberate fashion. This chapter thus considers some of the issues that continue to be of concern when attempting to determine which of the current connectionist and localist accounts of visual word recognition provides the best framework for understanding how humans recognize words.

Evaluating A Single Route PDP Model

The Seidenberg and McClelland (1989) model reads virtually all exception and regular words correctly through the action of a single routine. There is little that is theoretically new in that demonstration, however, given that both the lexical and the semantic routes in the classical three-route model can also read these words. A more interesting achievement is that this single-route model simulates the oft reported interaction between regularity and word frequency in naming that has standardly been interpreted in the traditional two- or three- route model described above (e.g., Coltheart and Rastle, 1994). Also new and important was Seidenberg and McClelland's claim that the single routine responsible for reading both regular and exception words also reads nonwords. If true, this would provide an existence proof that different mechanisms are not necessary for reading exception words and nonwords (see Patterson and Coltheart, 1987; Besner and Smith, 1992; Paap and Noel, 1991; Coltheart et al., 1993; Coltheart and Rastle, 1994).

Unfortunately, this PDP model fails to read many nonwords correctly. Besner et al. (1990) showed that, across several stimulus sets, the model preferred the correct phonological representation between 50 and 65% of the time, whereas humans produced the correct reading considerably more often (over 85%) in the context of a speeded naming task. Besner et al. therefore suggested that the model's performance resembled a patient with phonological dyslexia rather than an intact reader. Clearly, a model that reads like a brain- damaged patient needs development if it is to be taken seriously as an account of how intact skilled readers perform. A further problem noted by Besner et al. (1990) and Coltheart et al. (1993) is that Seidenberg and McClelland's (1989) single-routine model can not simulate the pattern of performance seen in so called "surface dyslexia" where some patients read nonwords aloud more accurately than exception words such as YACHT or HAVE. Given that the intact PDP model reads words more accurately than nonwords, it is difficult to see how lesioning the model would lead to more accurate reading of nonwords than words if a single mechanism were responsible for reading both.

Similarly, in one form of "phonological" dyslexia the patient is unable to read nonwords aloud but word reading is well preserved (e.g., see Funnell, 1983; Coltheart, 1995, among other reports). This also presents a problem for any model that reads both words and nonwords with only a single routine.

In reply to Besner et al.'s observations, Seidenberg and McClelland (1990) conceded that the model reads nonwords quite poorly, but they argued that the model's poor performance in this domain was primarily due to the fact that its vocabulary was only 3,000 words. This claim has at least one obvious implication;

children with vocabularies the size of the model's should read nonwords as well as the model does. One might have expected to see Seidenberg and McClelland pursue this issue as their model is represented as a developmental one, but they did not do so. Instead, this issue was investigated by V. Coltheart and Leahy (1992) who concluded that young children read nonwords with better accuracy than the model does. The PDP model reads some nonwords extremely well, but does very poorly on others, depending in part upon the degree of orthographic overlap between the nonword and the words that the model was trained on. Unfortunately, Coltheart and Leahy never investigated exactly what the model produced in response to the specific nonwords that the children were asked to read. In the absence of such data there is no basis for deciding whether Coltheart and Leahy's conclusions are correct.

More generally, it was not clear at this stage in the development of PDP models of visual word recognition whether there was something inherent in the theoretical formalism that led to poor nonword reading, or whether something else was amiss. Besner and colleagues were therefore cautious in their conclusions:

> The issue that future work will need to address is whether these failures merely represent resolvable difficulties associated with the current implementation of the model (e.g., inadequate encoding schemes, too many hidden units, or both) or whether they represent more fundamental problems with the formalism of distributed representations as applied to the study of visual word recognition. Besner et al. (1990, p. 432)

This can be contrasted with the view of those working with the model at that time:

> By way of summary, the model in its current form does a good job of accounting for what we might term the first order phenomena in naming, the performance of normal subjects in reading different types of words, and nonwords. The model provides the only quantitative account of normal performance; moreover, the fit between simulation and behavioural data is quite close. Patterson, Seidenberg, and McClelland (1989, p. 176)

This chapter returns later to the claim that "the fit between the simulation and behavioural data is quite close" when the original model is re-assessed along with one of the new models implemented by Plaut, McClelland, Seidenberg, and Patterson (1996). By way of preview, the conclusions offered here are that (1) the characterization of "fit" as "quite close" is surprising, given the small amount of variance in human naming time accounted for by the model in item level analyses, and (2) a new model performs even more poorly in this regard than the original model.

Newer PDP Models

McClelland and his colleagues (Plaut and McClelland, 1993; see also Seidenberg, Plaut, Peterson, McClelland, and McRae, 1994; Plaut, McClelland, Seidenberg, and Patterson, 1996) have since developed a new set of PDP models that read both words and nonwords about as accurately as intact humans do. It is therefore clear that there is nothing inherently wrong with the connectionist formalism, at least as it pertains to getting a network to produce the correct phonemes in response to the orthographic presentation of monomorphemic words and many nonwords.[2]

These successes raise fundamental questions. Probably the most basic question concerns whether this success is simply an existence proof that a PDP model can read nonwords, regular words, and exception words by recourse to only a single procedure, or whether it represents the stronger, more interesting, and more important proposition that this is the way that humans read.

A reading of this PDP group's various papers make their belief clear: a dual route connectionist model simulates what humans do when they read. The remainder of this chapter, therefore, (1) notes a basic distinction between the issue of how many routines there are, and whether all of the knowledge sources used to read alphabetic English are distributed or not, (2) addresses the broader issue of whether the experimental literature is consistent with the currently implemented PDP models, and (3) contrasts these PDP models with an implemented version of part of the classical three-route localist model described in figure 13.1. The general conclusion offered here is that, despite the fact that some connectionist models now read both words and nonwords about as accurately as humans, there is little convincing evidence that they do so in the way that humans do. Further, at this point in their development there are still a number of basic findings that these PDP models have difficulties explaining. In contrast, these findings currently appear easiest to reconcile with a three-route framework that uses localist representations for lexical and sublexical knowledge.

One, Two, and Three Routines as Distinct from the Issue of Whether Some, All, or None of the Processing is Distributed

There are at least two logically distinct issues that are often conflated in many discussions of the localist versus connectionist debate. The first has to do with how many separable routines mediate print to sound translation. The second concerns the nature of these routines. That is, whether they are all distributed, all localist, or whether some might be distributed and others localist. In this vein, Zorzi, Houghton, and Butterworth (1998) report some simulations of a model which can be described as having two nonsemantic "routes," in that one pathway maps orthography to phonology via a set of hidden units whereas the other pathway involves a mapping between orthography and phonology in the absence of mediating hidden units.

Acquired Dyslexia

Evolution: From a One-Route Model to a Two-Route Model

The proponents of the original single-route PDP model rejected the received idea that the reading of exception words and nonwords must rely on distinct mechanisms. The original model was only partially successful in this regard in that its nonword reading performance was very poor. Plaut and McClelland (1993), Seidenberg et al. (1994), and Plaut et al. (1996), however, subsequently showed that several new versions of the model that employ a somewhat different architecture and a different coding scheme for both orthographic and phonological levels read both words and nonwords about as well as do intact college students. Despite this success, these connectionists do not (now) appeal to a single-route model to account for phonological dyslexia in which words are correctly read more often than nonwords (e.g., as in Funnell, 1983) or that form of surface dyslexia in which nonwords are correctly read more often than low-frequency exception words (e.g., as in Coltheart et al. 1993). Instead, the double dissociation between these two forms of acquired dyslexia is explained in terms of two distinct routines. In one of these routines orthography is mapped onto phonology through a set of hidden units (what they term the direct route. which should not be confused with Zorzi et al.'s "direct route" which does not involve any hidden units). In the other routine, orthography is mapped to semantics through a different set of hidden units and then to phonology through another set of hidden units (the semantic route).

Damage to the direct route can produce a form of phonological dyslexia because the spared semantic pathway can read words but not nonwords. Damage to the semantic pathway can produce that form of surface dyslexia in which the cardinal symptom is the regularization of low-frequency exception words provided that, in those patients, the direct routine never learns to read low-frequency exception words very well. This "division of labor" hypothesis has been advanced by Seidenberg (1992a)[3] and Plaut et al. (1996) and is discussed below.

It can thus be seen that the single-route connectionist account has evolved into a dual-route account in an attempt to deal with both surface and phonological dyslexia. This evolution of the connectionist model raises an obvious question: If both connectionist and localist accounts are now multiroute, then what pattern of performance by normal or impaired readers, if any, distinguishes between them?

Phonological Dyslexia Revisited

As noted earlier, there are several reports of patients with an acquired dyslexia who cannot read any nonwords aloud, but whose word reading is quite intact (e.g., Funnell, 1983; Coltheart, 1995, among others). This suggests that the direct route in the PDP model is compromised, as is the assembled routine in the localist model. Some of these patients, however, also have seriously impaired comprehension abilities for single content words (e.g., Coltheart, 1995). This suggests that the semantic system is damaged and, at least for dual-route models, leads to the obvious prediction that, as in deep dyslexia, semantic errors should be observed when these patients read words aloud, or that the patient cannot read a word. This does not happen, or at least happens only very infrequently (see Coltheart, 1995; Coltheart et al. 1996, versus Plaut et al. 1996, pp. 102-103).

This form of phonological dyslexia is not problematic for the three-route localist model because the patient can read words aloud via the undamaged lexical route shown in figure 13.1 (route D). This is the classical interpretation that has been discussed a number of times (e.g., Besner and Smith, 1992; Funnell, 1983; Coltheart et al., 1996; Coltheart, 1995; Coltheart et al., 1993).

Plaut et al.'s two-route connectionist model may have a problem simulating this form of phonological dyslexia. If these patients are not reading words via the damaged semantic system (because they do not make semantic errors), nor via the direct route (because that is the only other route in this model and it is seriously compromised given the patients inability to read any nonwords), then how can this PDP model simulate this form of phonological dyslexia? Plaut et al. have suggested that interactive activation between the damaged direct route and a damaged semantic route provides a way to produce the proper pattern (zero nonword reading accompanied by good word reading in the absence of semantic errors). If the direct route can produce even a single phoneme correctly, this would suffice to veto an incorrect output from the semantic route and hence prevent semantic errors. This important idea has been suggested a number of times before in the neuropsychological literature but has yet to be explored formally in a simulation.[4]

Surface Dyslexia Revisited

Another reason that the single route PDP model evolved into a dual- route model is because the single-route version could not simulate the performance of surface dyslexic patients (see Plaut et al., 1996, for extended discussion). According to the division of labor hypothesis advanced by Seidenberg (1992a) and elaborated by Plaut et al. (1996), premorbid reading ability will determine whether a patient will present with a form of surface dyslexia following brain damage. As reading skill increases, low-frequency exception word reading comes to rely more on a contribution from semantics, and the direct route learns less about the proper pronunciation of these low- frequency exception words than it does about regular words. This notion predicts that patients who were highly literate premorbidly will be strongly surface dyslexic following semantic damage. Patients such as WLP (at least early in her dementing illness, see Schwartz, Saffran, and Marin, 1980) and DRN (Cipolotti and Warrington, 1995) should therefore be strongly surface dyslexic because they have a profound semantic impairment. These patients are indeed dyslexic in their impaired comprehension of print, but they read low-frequency exception words aloud almost entirely without error. This appears to present a problem for the division of labor hypothesis as currently formulated (but see Plaut, 1997).

This discussion of the acquired dyslexias has revolved in large part around the issue of whether there are one, two, or three routines because in their current form the PDP models examined here do not have a nonsemantic routine for producing a phonological output representation just for words. Another way of attempting to discriminate between localist and certain distributed models is to consider how consistent patients are when their failure to make an overt response (e.g., in picture naming) can not be attributed to a semantic deficit. The discussion turns now to a brief consideration of whether a particular representation (output phonology) should be best thought of as localist in nature, or distributed.

Individuated Nodes in the Phonological Output System?

All current theories of speech production assume a distinction between the phonological level and a semantic level. Localist accounts of the phonological level (e.g., Morton, and Dell, among others) make some simple predictions in response to brain injury at that level. That is, it should be possible to find patients who are consistently unable to produce specific words in speech because they have lost specific entries in the phonological output lexicon. In contrast, the phonological form of a word (output phonology) in models like Seidenberg and McClelland (1989) and Plaut et al. (1996) consists of a distributed pattern of activation. One of the important characteristics of distributed systems is that they are generally resistant to small amounts of damage.As the amount of damage increases, however, there is a general decrement in performance rather than the loss of specific lexical items. Following brain damage then, and provided that there are good grounds for believing that the deficit is not in semantics, distributed models would likely have difficulty accounting for the consistent inability of a patient to produce specific word forms.

Howard (1995) reports a case of lexical anomia, that speaks to this issue. This patient is characterized by a serious deficit in speaking specific words that are nevertheless easily understood in speech. This word-specific deficit is quite consistent and is not ameliorated by the provision of phonemic cues or additional time for retrieval. This deficit is easily accounted for by a localist account in which specific lexical entries in the phonological input system are intact, but the same entries in the phonological output system have been lost or are impaired. In contrast, this result is not in accord with what one would expect to see in a distributed phonological system as in the models discussed here. It remains to be seen whether a nondeterministic PDP model can produce the pattern of deficits observed in this patient. To my knowledge, there is no PDP work that presently addresses this issue.

Conclusion

This concludes the section on those acquired difficulties in reading and speech production, that appear challenging to currently implemented PDP models of visual word recognition and production. In contrast, the three-route localist framework offers a straightforward account of these phenomena (e.g., see Besner and Smith, 1992; Coltheart et al. 1993; Coltheart et al. 1996).

Experiments with Intact Subjects

The chapter turns now to the experimental literature on intact subjects in which the primary question is, again, whether there are phenomena that address the localist versus distributed representation issue and whether a three- as opposed to a dual-route model provides a better account of the data.

Naming Nonwords: Individuated Nodes in the Phonological Output System?

McCann and Besner (1987) reported that nonwords, which sound like words, are named faster than nonwords, which do not sound like real words (e.g., BRANE (from brain) versus FRANE). This pseudohomophone effect (PHE) is easy to understand in the context of the localist account shown in figure 13.1. The assembled routine activates the phonemic buffer (route E) which is engaged in interactive activation with individuated lexical entries in the phonological output lexicon (routes F, C). In essence, it assumes the same kind of interactions between the phoneme level and the (phonological) word level that McClelland and Rumelhart (1981) emphasized between the (orthographic) letter level and word level in the interactive activation model. Despite this, the PHE has consistently exercised the PDP group (e.g., see Plaut et al. 1996; Seidenberg, 1992b; Seidenberg and McClelland, 1989, 1990; Seidenberg et al. 1996).

> Pseudohomophone effects would seem to be a problem for our model because it lacks word level representations; there does not seem to be a way for the spelling or pronunciation of BRAIN to directly influence BRANE because there is no lexical entry for BRAIN. Seidenberg and McClelland (1989, p. 555).

Seidenberg and McClelland (1989) took the view that the pseudohomophones in the McCann and Besner (1987) experiments were more orthographically similar to the base words than were the controls, and they reported some experiments of their own in which they claimed that no PHE resulted when the stimuli were properly matched. In reply, Besner et al. (1990) pointed out that Seidenberg and McClelland's experiments were flawed on various methodological grounds (for example, 25% of Seidenberg and McClelland's control stimuli were actually pseudohomophones), and they reported some new analyses of the McCann and Besner data that served to reject the "orthographic similarity" argument advanced by Seidenberg and McClelland (1989).

Seidenberg and McClelland (1990) replied with a new argument that the McCann and Besner stimuli were not equated across conditions on initial phoneme and attributed the PHE in McCann and Besner's experiment to this factor. This argument has no force, given that McCann and Besner (1987) addressed this issue with an experiment that maintained the different initial phonemes (e.g., BRANE versus FRANE) but changed an internal vowel (e.g., to BRONE versus FRONE). The logic of this experiment is that if BRANE is faster than FRANE because of the initial phoneme, rather than because BRANE sounds like BRAIN, then BRONE should also be named faster than FRONE. This did not happen; FRONE type items were named as fast as BRONE type items.[5] Ignoring this finding, Seidenberg and McClelland did a post hoc analysis of the McCann and Besner experiment in which they selected 54 pairs out of the original 80 pairs such that the pseudohomophones and controls were matched for initial phoneme and length in terms of number of letters. This analysis failed to yield a significant PHE, and Seidenberg and McClelland (1990) therefore again questioned whether a PHE exists.

Seidenberg and McClelland's post hoc analysis of the McCann and Besner data is unconvincing in that it selects items that are matched for initial phoneme and letter length but consequently leaves the bodies to vary. This means, for example, that items like BINJE (from BINGE) are compared to items like BLEEF.

In short, Seidenberg and McClelland are more willing to accept the null hypothesis from their post hoc analysis of 54 pairs than to accept McCann and Besner's interaction between BRANE versus FRANE as compared to BRONE versus FRONE in which the bodies are closely matched in all 80 pairs, and despite the fact that there is a higher probability of a type 2 error in Seidenberg and McClelland's analysis than the probability of a type 1 error in the McCann and Besner analysis.

The above not withstanding, Seidenberg and McClelland (1990) went on to note that in their larger (unimplemented) model there are feedback connections to other parts of the system (semantics) which could, in principle, accommodate a PHE. This makes sense (how else would one know that BRANE sounds like a real word that refers to mind?), but it would also mean that more knowledge is brought to bear on the pronunciation of nonwords than just spelling-sound correspondences as Seidenberg and McClelland (1989) originally claimed.

Seidenberg and McClelland's concerns about orthographic similarity and initial sound segment do not apply to an experiment on reading Japanese reported by Besner and Hildebrandt (1987). In this experiment the pseudohomophones were generated by taking words normally written in Kanji, the ideographic script, and transcribing them so that they were printed in Katakana, the syllabic Japanese script. These transcriptions are never seen in this orthography but when converted into phonology they are words. There is therefore no obvious sense in which the pseudohomophones are more orthographically similar to their base words than the controls. The control items were matched to individual pseudohomophones in that they had the same initial sound segment and were also derived from Kanji words that had been transcribed into Katakana. A medial syllable was changed, however, so as to render it a nonword. For present purposes the main result is that the pseudohomophones were named 82 ms faster and 5.4% more accurately than the control items, suggesting that–as in English–some form of lexical or semantic knowledge contributes to their pronunciation.[6]

Besner and Hildebrandt's experiment has not been discussed by Seidenberg and his colleagues. This PHE could again arise from interactions between a distributed phonological output system and semantics, or because of an interaction between the phonemic buffer and a localist phonological output system as shown in figure 13.1. In the latter case there may also be semantic involvement.

Two other results warrant mention.[7] First, Taft and Russell (1992) reported a PHE in naming for slow, but not fast readers. This is understandable in two different ways. In one, the relative speed of assembling a pronunciation from the information in the phonemic buffer is critical. If this assembly process is fast relative to interactive activation between the phonological lexicon and the phonemic buffer, then no PHE will be seen. It may also be that the degree to which the semantic system interacts with the phonological system is systematically related to reader speed, with fast readers less affected by such interactive activation than slower readers are.

Finally, Seidenberg et al. (1996), after another lengthy methodological analysis of the original McCann and Besner (1987) experiments, reported a new experiment in which the pseudohomophones and controls were matched to their satisfaction. They found a PHE in the online naming condition, but failed to find that it was significantly reduced in the delayed naming condition. They consequently concluded that the PHE is *entirely* attributable to production components of the naming task occurring at the articulatory level.[8] An obvious problem for the Seidenberg et al. account is that Taft and Russell (1992) [unfortunately not cited in Seidenberg et al., 1996] found a PHE in online naming for slow readers, but no effect in the delayed naming condition. Taft and Russell also found no PHE in either online or delayed naming for the faster readers in the same experiment. These results are problematic for Seidenberg et al. in that their account does not explain why there is no PHE for either fast or slow readers in Taft and Russell's delayed naming condition.

The delayed naming condition also merits more attention. One issue concerns whether subjects are properly prepared in this condition. Typically, subjects are hundreds of milliseconds faster in delayed naming than in the online condition. This need not mean, however, that subjects are well prepared all of the time. If subjects are not well prepared, then the observation of a PHE under delayed naming need not mean that the PHE genuinely arises during articulation. How could we know whether subjects are well prepared or not across different experiments? One clue is offered by looking at the ratio of delayed naming time to online naming times. As Rastle (1997) has noted, that ratio is approximately .4 for the McCann and Besner, and Taft and Russell studies, but .7 for the Seidenberg et al. studies, despite the fact that the absolute times for online naming are often quite comparable. This index suggests that subjects were better prepared for the delayed naming condition in the former than the latter studies. If so, then failing to find a larger PHE online than in delayed naming, as in the Seidenberg et al. studies, can be attributed in part to inadequate preparation during delayed naming.

Converging evidence for this view comes from the results of an unpublished experiment in my lab. Following Monsell et al. (1989) recommended delayed naming procedure, subjects named Seidenberg et al.'s pseudohomophones and control items under a delayed naming condition. The twist is that subjects named each item twice, in immediate succession, thus ensuring that they are most likely to be fully prepared on the second presentation. The data from the first presentation looked like Seidenberg et al.'s data, in that pseudohomophones were named faster than controls (although the effect was much larger–about 28 ms). On the second delayed naming trial, however, there was a nonsignificant 2 ms difference between conditions. Further, virtually all the movement in the data across trials came from the control condition, which speeded up. The two-way interaction between first versus second naming, and pseudohomophones versus controls, was significant (p < .01).

My reading of the literature is that two separate issues are sometimes confused here. Contrary to Seidenberg and colleagues, the central issue is not whether pseudohomophones ever make contact with memory representations associated with their real-word counterparts during online naming. The answer to that question is clear, given that a related context facilitates naming time to a pseudohomophone target relative to an unrelated context (Buchanan and Besner, 1995; Lukatela and Turvey, 1991). (Parenthetically, (1) the methodological issues that have exercised Seidenberg and his colleagues are not an issue here because the same target item is being compared across related and unrelated priming conditions, and (2) neither of these papers are referenced by Seidenberg and his colleagues.) Instead, the central issue here is whether a PHE ever occurs in the absence of an interaction with semantics. If it did occur, this would be consistent with individuated nodes in the phonological output system, but I know of no evidence that such an effect can be simulated by a PDP model with distributed representations.

Another puzzle concerns why Seidenberg and colleagues do not address the fact that patients with that form of acquired phonological dyslexia marked by poor nonword reading are more successful at reading pseudohomophones aloud than nonword controls (e.g. Beauvois and Derouesne, 1979; Sasanuma, Ito, Patterson, and Ito 1996; Patterson, Suzuki, and Wydell, 1996). This accuracy based PHE can also be quite dramatic in terms of its magnitude; Sasanuma et al. (1996) and Patterson et al. (1996) have reported that when nonword reading is virtually zero, pseudohomophones are read with better than 80% accuracy. Patterson et al. explain this PHE in terms of the effects of stimulus familiarity (pseudohomophones sound like real words) on a distributed phonological level in addition to this level interacting with the semantic level (pseudohomophones derived from high imageability words are read aloud more accurately than pseudohomophones derived from low imageability words).

By way of a summary, it is clear that a PHE is seen in the reading of both intact and dyslexic readers, and that this effect is not attributable solely to articulatory level processing, contrary to Seidenberg et al. (1996) and Herdman et al. (1996).

For present purposes the most important theoretical issue is whether a PHE ever occurs in the absence of an interaction with semantics. The published data that bear most directly on this issue come from McCann and Besner's (1987) experiment, and experiments 1, 2, and 3 in Marmurek and Kwantes (1996). Provided that pseudohomophones and nonword controls are intermixed in the same block of trials, there is no evidence that the frequency of the pseudohomophone's base word affects performance. Each of these four experiments (with three different stimulus sets) also produced faster naming times to pseudohomophones than to controls. In contrast, Marmurek and Kwantes report additional data to show that when pseudohomophones were either blocked, or mixed with words, a base-word frequency effect occurred in which pseudohomophones derived from high frequency words were named faster than ones derived from low frequency words in four experiments. What do all these data mean?

The presence of a pseudohomophone effect when it is coupled with the *presence* of a base-word frequency effect can be understood as a marker for interactions between the assembled routine and other parts of the word recognition system (i.e., semantics). Dual-route localist models and dual-route PDP models have no problem accommodating such findings.

In contrast, the view taken here is that the presence of a pseudohomophone advantage in the *absence* of a base-word frequency effect implies that the output of the assembled route interacts with the localist phonological output lexicon which is frequency insensitive, but it does not interact with semantics. That is, the standard account that word frequency affects uptake in the orthographic and phonological input-output lexicons is eschewed. This (nonstandard) account has been offered a number of times (see Besner and McCann, 1999; Besner and Smith, 1992a, b; Baluch and Besner, 1991; Borowsky and Besner, 1993).

The negative implications of such data appear quite straightforward as far as the PDP model with distributed representations are concerned. Frequency of occurrence affects the weights on connections throughout the system. PDP modelers thus need to explain how such a system could produce a pseudohomophone advantage without also producing an effect of the base word's frequency.

Evidence for a Third Reading Route in Intact Subjects?

Naming Words in Shallow Orthographies

If there is anything that marks human beings it is their cognitive flexibility. Indeed, this flexibility is often the bane of experimentalists who want to establish how subjects do x or y, only to find to their chagrin, often many years later, that x is done

one way under condition z, but quite another way given conditions q, r, and t. Visual word recognition is no exception to this general observation. Recognizing this, some investigators have begun to explore how context influences the way that readers recognize words. Some findings that are relevant to the present debate are noted below.

In shallow orthographies such as Italian, Spanish, Dutch, Serbo-Croatian, Turkish, Persian, and the Japanese Kana script, the spelling-sound correspondences are typically one-to-one such that a character is virtually always pronounced the same way. This contrasts with orthographies like English that have many exception words (e.g., COUGH, ROUGH, BOUGH, THOROUGH). The fact that the spelling-sound correspondences are so consistent in shallow orthographies has led some theorists to claim that reading in these scripts never occurs via the lexical route as in figure 13.1, but always relies upon computing sublexical spelling-sound correspondences (e.g., Allport, 1979; Katz and Feldman, 1983; Turvey et al. 1984; Bridgeman, 1987; see also the review by Besner and Smith, 1992, which challenges this view, and the revisionist account provided by Katz and Frost, 1992). Indeed, some investigators have gone so far as to suggest that an orthography to semantic route never develops in these orthographies (e.g., see Turvey et al, 1984; Bridgeman, 1987, among others).

More recent work is consistent with the interpretation that readers in these shallow orthographies rely on different routines to read aloud, depending on the nature of the stimuli in the experiment. For example, Hudson and Bergman (1985) reported that Dutch readers showed a word frequency effect in naming when the stimulus set consisted only of words, but that the word-frequency effect disappeared when nonwords were included. This same result has been reported when native readers name words in Turkish (Raman, Baluch, and Sneddon, 1996). Tabossi and Laghi (1992) reported that Italian readers showed semantic priming effects in naming provided that only words were present; semantic priming disappeared when nonwords were included. Related experiments using both word-frequency and semantic-priming manipulations with native readers of Persian were reported by Baluch and Besner (1991). A similar outcome was observed in that both semantic-priming and word-frequency effects were observed when only words were present. In contrast, both semantic-priming and word-frequency effects were eliminated when nonwords were also named.

The above observations are consistent with a three-route localist account, given the assumption that subjects shift their reliance from one route to another depending upon the nature of the items in the experiment. In this model the lexical route reads words but not nonwords, and the assembled route correctly reads nonwords and words with regular spelling-sound correspondences as in the experiments discussed above. The default setting relies on the lexical route because this is what characterizes skilled readers (sensitivity to word frequency). When many of the items to be read are novel, (i.e., nonwords), however, the word recognition system falls back on the assembled route to read both words and nonwords. The immediate consequence of this is that the word frequency and semantic priming effects seen before with these same words now disappear.

This account is clear. All that is necessary is to implement some form of control system responsible for looking after route selection that is not a disguised homunculus (e.g., Hawkins, Reicher, Rogers, and Peterson, 1976; see also Carr and Pollatsek's, 1985, discussion). The fact that virtually no implemented model contains such a control system is not without interest (those with a flair for modeling and in need of a thesis topic take note). It is a curious fact that, at least in the word-recognition literature, processes deemed "automatic" often receive more theoretical and empirical attention than issues surrounding mental set. One has only to look at the Stroop literature for one prominent example of this (see MacLeod's 1991 review; in contrast, see Bauer and Besner 1997; Besner, Stolz, and Boutilier, 1997; Besner and Stolz, 1999).

At first glance the dual-route PDP model can also account for the data reviewed above. One way is for subjects to rely on the orthography-semantics-phonology route when only words are present in the experiment, but to switch to the direct route when nonwords form a large part of the stimulus set. One difficulty with this account is that it begs the question of why subjects would switch between these two different routes when with the direct route they can read both words and nonwords (unlike the lexical route in the localist model which cannot read nonwords). A further problem concerns the assumption that subjects typically read aloud by reference to the orthography-to-semantics-to-phonology route. If subjects typically did so, there would be no reason to see the standard effects of spelling-sound consistency observed in English that Plaut et al. (1996) have spent so much time and effort simulating.

A different way to think about the dual-route PDP model as it applies to naming in shallow orthographies is to assume that subjects read aloud by recourse to the direct route. What varies in response to the presence-absence of nonwords in the experiment, however, is the probability that there is interactive activation between the phonological system and semantics. When only words are in the experiment such interaction occurs (the issue of how the control structure ensures this is finessed here), whereas when nonwords are intermixed with the words this interaction does not occur. This would imply that the interaction with semantics is responsible for producing both word- frequency and semantic-priming effects, and the absence of this interaction is associated with the disappearance of these effects. The presence-absence of semantic effects are self evident in this analysis. The disappearance of the word-frequency effect when there is no interaction with semantics is more counterintuitive, but it is consistent with what is known about the relationship between word frequency and consistency in connectionist networks. Plaut et al. (1996) and Seidenberg (1992a) have shown that when the words that are learned by the orthography-to-phonology part of the network are consistent in their spelling-sound correspondences, the word-frequency effect is extremely small.[9] It is only when some of the spelling-sound correspondences are inconsistent (as in English) that large effects of word frequency are produced by the direct route in the PDP model.

This account of the comings and goings of the word-frequency and semantic-priming effects in the naming of words in a shallow orthography by a connectionist model is coherent; however, it leads to a counterintuitive prediction. Namely, when only words are present in the experiment, and a word frequency effect occurs because of the interaction between phonology and semantics, an imageability effect should also result because of this same interaction with semantics. This prediction is counterintuitive because when intact subjects read aloud words printed in English, an effect of imageability is seen only for low-frequency exception words. High-frequency exception words, and high- and low-frequency words that are regular in their spelling-sound correspondences are not affected by imageability according to Strain et al. (1995). It would be very surprising to find that, in intact subjects, the phonological system typically interacts with semantics when reading words aloud in a shallow orthography, (thus producing an imageability effect) but eschews such an interaction when reading regular words in a deep orthography (and thus does not produce an imageability effect).

This apparent conundrum for the PDP account remains to be resolved. In contrast, the three-route localist framework provides a sufficient account of the data, provided that an executive system is implemented that controls route selection and interactions among processing components.

That said, a pair of important papers by Jared (1997) and Lupker, Brown, and Columbo (1997) dispute the idea that there is contextual control over which route is selected in the naming task. Their argument is that what looks like evidence for route selection can be accounted for by the assumption that subjects try and homogenize their naming RTs by adopting similar release points during articulation. Both sets of authors report evidence supporting this view.

This argument, as applied here, is that including nonwords could serve to pull the fast RTs toward the mean of all the conditions at the same time as pulling the slow RTs (i.e., the nonwords) toward the mean of all the conditions. Inserting nonwords in a list could thus serve to eliminate the word-frequency effect by pulling fast RTs associated with high-frequency words toward the release point associated within nonword naming. Indeed, Raman, Baluch, and Besner's (1998) data are consistent with this account. They observed that when subjects read a block of words printed in Turkish aloud (a shallow script) a word-frequency effect was observed, but when nonwords were mixed in with the words the word-frequency effect was eliminated. Route selection (as in Baluch and Besner, 1991) could account for these data but has more difficulty with the results of another experiment in which nonwords were selected that were fast to name. When these items were mixed together with words in a single block, the words produced a word-frequency effect.

Clearly, the effect(s) of blocking versus mixing words and nonwords together in the naming task is open to a number of competing explanations. Jared, and Lupker et al. have thus made an important empirical discovery (predicated on Poulton's, 1975 warnings about range effects in within subject designs) that will force a number of investigators to reassess whether their data provide strong evidence for changes in the routes that subjects rely on when naming print. Our own data (noted above) suggest that a timing account provides a sufficient account of at least some data. Nonetheless, I doubt that we have heard the last word on this topic. For example, Baluch and Besner (1991) reported that semantic-priming and word- frequency effects are both present and absent in the same within-subject within-block experiment, depending on the kind of word being read (opaque or transparent). It is not immediately obvious why a route selection account is not viable for these data, and it is unclear how the Jared and Lupker et al. account would explain these data. Further, the presence of nonwords in the list when reading English aloud does not eliminate the semantic priming effect (e.g., Tabossi and Laghi, 1992). Finally, Rastle and Coltheart (1999) report data in a naming task that is consistent with a route selection account, but not with a timing account.

A Whole Word Nonsemantic Pathway in the Reading of Japanese Katakana

Written Japanese has three scripts. Kanji is the ideographic script that evolved from pictograms. Katakana, the shallow syllabic script, is used to represent foreign loan words, whereas Hiragana, another shallow syllabic script, is used to represent grammatical morphemes. A word normally written in Hiragana can be transcribed into Katakana and easily read aloud by the assembled route. Similarly, a word normally written in Katakana can be transcribed into Hiragana and read aloud by the assembled route. In both cases these transcribed strings are pseudohomophones much like as in English (e.g., BRANE versus BRAIN).

Several experiments on the naming of orthographically familiar versus orthographically unfamiliar words have been reported. The first observation is that subjects name words normally written in Hiragana faster than the same word transcribed into Katakana, and they name words normally written in Katakana faster than the same word transcribed into Hiragana (Besner and Hildebrandt, 1987; Besner and Smith, 1992; Buchanan and Besner, 1995). This result is consistent with the interpretation that the orthographically familiar words are named faster than their transcriptions because the former can use any or all of the assembled, lexical, or semantic routes but the latter must rely on the assembled route.

Buchanan and Besner (1995) reported an experiment on Japanese readers in which semantic-priming effects for the naming of single targets were modulated by the presence-absence of pseudohomophone type transcriptions as targets. When pseudohomophone and orthographically familiar word targets are randomly intermixed, semantic priming was observed for pseudohomophones but not for the orthographically familiar words. A priming effect for these words was observed in a second experiment, however, where the pseudohomophones were deleted from the test list. The gist of the account provided by Buchanan and Besner was that the orthographically familiar target words were processed by the lexical route which is insulated from semantics following prime processing by activation blocks at various levels in the word-recognition system attributable to the presence of the pseudohomophones in the experiment. When only words were present in the experiment there were no activation blocks and semantic priming is observed. Buchanan and Besner went on to note that the idea of an activation block is quite general (and opposed to the notion of "automatic" interactive activation between levels of representation) and has been invoked to account for a number of findings (see also Stolz and Neely, 1995; Chiappe, Smith and Besner, 1996; Besner, Stolz, and Boutilier, 1997; Stolz and Besner, 1996b; 1998). That said, it should be noted that Lupker et al. offer a different explanation of the Buchanan and Besner data.

These results are difficult to understand in the context of the dual route PDP model. If the orthographically familiar words are not being read via the direct route in experiment 1, then they must be read via semantics, in which case they cannot avoid a semantic-priming effect. On the other hand, if the orthographically familiar words are being read via the direct route, then at the point where they activate phonology they are indistinguishable from pseudohomophones and therefore must be subjected to the same processing and also cannot avoid a semantic-priming effect.

Naming nonwords in a shallow orthography

The consistency effect refers to the fact that the time to name both words and nonwords is affected by how their orthographic neighbors are pronounced (Glushko, 1979). Thus, words that have an inconsistent neighbor (e.g., CAVE has the inconsistent neighbor HAVE) are pronounced more slowly than words whose neighbors are all pronounced the same way. Job, Peressotti, and Cusinato (1998) reported a consistency effect for the naming of nonwords in Italian (e.g., a real word such as DELICATO was used to generate two nonwords (DELICOTO [where the c is pronounced /k/], and the inconsistent DELICETO [where the c is pronounced / ch/] given the context sensitive rules for how the grapheme c is to be pronounced). The observation of a consistency effect when reading nonwords is, of course, not new. Instead, interest centers on Job et al.'s observation that this consistency effect disappeared if the nonwords were named in the context of a list in which words did not appear. This observation appears to be problematic for the PDP models discussed here because in these models consistency effects arise through the connection weights between orthography and phonology. There is currently nothing in these models to suggest that these weights would (or could) change due to list composition, particularly when the words that are included are unrelated to the nonwords.

In contrast, the presence-absence of a nonword consistency effect is understandable in the context of the three-route localist model in that the nonword produces weak activation in the orthographic input lexicon, which in turns produces weak activation in the phonological output lexicon and the phonemic buffer. This potential pronunciation will compete with the products of the assembled route when different. If list composition (e.g., presence-absence of words in the list) affects the availability of a route (e.g., if the withdrawal of "attention" serves to dampen activation in a pathway), then the disappearance of the consistency effect is not surprising.

Do Multiple Mechanisms Underly the "Exception" Effect in Naming?

It is well known that there is an interaction between regularity and word frequency when subjects name words printed in English. Low- frequency exception words (e.g., HAVE) are named slower than low- frequency regular words (e.g., GAVE), but higher frequency words yield little systematic difference (e.g., Paap and Noel, 1991; Waters and Seidenberg, 1985). The classic dual-route account assumes that regular words can be read correctly by either the lexical-semantic routines or the assembled routine, but that exception words can only be correctly read by the lexical-semantic routines. The output from the assembled route regularizes the pronunciation of an exception word. Thus, when assembled output is fast enough relative to output from the lexical route, competition results from the two different pronunciations. For high-frequency words there is typically no exception effect; the lexical route appears too fast relative to the time course of the assembled route to result in competition. For low-frequency words, however, the output from the assembled route occurs in time to compete with the lexical route. Resolving this competition incurs a time cost, and if not properly resolved it also produces a regularized or incorrect pronunciation.

The simulations from the original Seidenberg and McClelland model are impressive in that they produce the standard word-frequency x regularity interaction without appealing to a distinction between lexical and assembled routines. Instead, the interaction arises as a result of the weights on the connections between orthography and phonology acquired through training. Given this existence proof, the question is whether there is a way to determine which of these two explanations provides a better description of what it is that humans do when they read regular and exception words.

Coltheart and Rastle (1994) selected a set of low frequency exception words in which the position of the irregularly pronounced segment varied from left to right in the word and compared naming times to these words against a set of matched regular words. Coltheart and Rastle predicted that the size of the exception effect should decline as the position of the exceptional segment moved from left to right. This prediction was based on the assumption that the assembled route involves a serial mechanism that converts spelling to sound left to right, whereas the lexical route operates on the letters in parallel. Therefore, maximum interference should arise when the exceptional segment is produced early rather than late in processing, because the later it is produced the higher the probability that the output from the lexical routine has been completed. Coltheart and Rastle found that the largest exception effect was produced when the exceptional segment was in the first position and declined monotonically as this segment moved to the right.

Coltheart and Rastle argue that the PDP models implemented by McClelland and his colleagues have no basis for predicting that the position of the exceptional segment should be systematically related to the size of the regularity effect because they operate on the letters in the word in parallel. They therefore concluded that their result is consistent with the classical dual-route architecture and inconsistent with the PDP class of model discussed here.

Plaut et al. (1996) were unable to assess the Coltheart and Rastle effect in a simulation because the stimuli were two syllable and this PDP model is only trained on single syllable items to date.Plaut et al. speculated, however, that it is not the spatial position of the exceptional segment that produces Coltheart and Rastle's effect, but the degree of consistency between the presented words and orthographically related words that they activate in the reading system (see Plaut et al.'s discussion on pages 105–106).

Rastle and Coltheart (1999) replied to this criticism by carrying out an experiment that utilized single syllable words controlled for consistency at each of five orthographic segments. The same pattern as reported by Coltheart and Rastle (1994) emerged. The regularity effect was most pronounced when the position of the exceptional segment was early in the word and decreased to zero when the third position was considered. Finally, the implemented version of dual-route, cascaded (DRC) produced the same pattern when tested with the same stimuli. Rastle and Coltheart therefore conclude that the data are consistent with a dual-route model in which the nonlexical routine operates serially in left to right fashion, and the lexical routine operates concurrently in parallel fashion across all the letters in the array.

These data thus provide an interesting challenge for the PDP class of model. It remains to be seen whether any model of this class can be modified so as to simulate this regularity x serial position interaction in naming.

More about Serial and Parallel Processing: Letter Length Effects in Naming

Converging evidence for the idea that there is a serial processing mechanism involved in naming comes from the well-documented observation that the number of letters in a word or nonword strongly affects the time it takes to name it. The longer the stimulus, the slower the naming time (see Henderson's, 1982, summary in table 11, p. 185). More recently, Weekes (1997) has reported that the length effect in the naming of 4-, 5-, and 6-letter words disappears when the effect of the number of orthographic neighbors is partialled out. In contrast, a letter-length effect for the naming of nonwords survives in the same experiment when the effects of orthographic neighbors are partialled out. The effect of letter length on nonword naming result is consistent with the serial operation of the assembled route. The lexical route processes letters in parallel and therefore need not produce letter length effects.

It is not obvious how any of the currently implemented PDP models reviewed here can produce the combination of a length effect for nonwords in the absence of such an effect for words when neighborhood size is partialled out.[10]

Case Alternation Effects on Naming

CaSe AlTeRnAtIoN slows naming time for both words and nonwords. It generally has a larger effect on low-frequency words than on high-frequency words and affects nonwords more than words (e.g., see Besner and McCann, 1987; Besner and Johnston, 1989; Besner, Davelaar, Alcott, and Parry 1984; Herdman, Chernecki, and Norris, 1999).[11] These general observations are qualified by the observation that when subjects are only presented with exception words, case alternation and word frequency have additive effects on naming time (Besner, 1990; but see Herdman et al., 1999). All of these results are understandable in terms of two assumptions. The first is that case alternation slows the operation of a letter-identification stage that subserves the lexical-semantic routines in the three-route model. The second is that case-alternated stimuli impair the operation of the assembled route because it normally treats graphemes like CH, EE, EA, GH as perceptual units. On this account, nonwords are more affected than words because of the standard assumption that the assembled route plays more of a role in nonword than word naming. Similarly, low-frequency words are more affected than high-frequency words because the assembled route makes more of a contribution to naming in the case of low- than high-frequency words. Finally, case alternation can have additive effects with word frequency when reading a pure list of exception words if the assembled routine can be slowed, shut off, or if its products are not utilized (e.g., Baluch and Besner, 1991; Monsell et al. 1992).

In contrast, it is not clear how any of the PDP models discussed here can produce additive effects of word frequency and case alternation for exception words but an interaction between word frequency and case alternation for regular words. The major problem is that even in the dual-route PDP model, a single orthographic processing module is common to both semantic and nonsemantic routes.

The pattern(s) described above are also problematic for localist dual-route models (i.e., Coltheart and colleagues' DRC model) in so far as all of the routines which process words (and nonwords) assume that individual letters are the only perceptual units used by humans. I predict that we shall see more papers on the use of such supraletter features during visual word recognition, and that all simulation models will in large part ignore these facts because it is less than straightforward to implement representations that can detect such features in these models.

Morphological Effects in English

The three-route localist model assumes that the orthographic input lexicon represents words, or morphemes, as originally suggested by Morton (1968). One way to argue for the proposition that there is a lexical representation independent of semantics is to find some manipulation that eliminates semantic processing but spares morphological processing.

It is well known that lexical decision performance is faster when the preceding prime word is semantically related to the target as compared to when it is not (e.g., see Neely's, 1991 review). Less well known is that this semantic-priming effect can be eliminated by having subjects search the prime word for a letter (e.g., Smith et al., 1983; Friedrich et al., 1991). It has been suggested that this elimination of semantic priming arises because letter search on the prime leads to competition between the resources needed for explicit letter identification and semantic activation (Stolz and Besner, 1996b; Chiappe, Smith, and Besner, 1996). Explicit letter identification (as in letter search) may need more activation at the letter level than is needed when letters are only implicitly processed (as in word naming, lexical decision, or semantic categorization). Consequently, when less activation is needed at the letter level, lexical level processing more easily activates semantics.

Whether this particular account is correct or not is less important than the fact that the letter search paradigm can be used to dissociate morphological and semantic processing. If morphology is represented lexically, such that it is distinct from semantic processing, and if letter search on the prime prevents semantic processing but not lexical level processing, then letter search on the prime should eliminate semantic priming but spare morphological priming under conditions when the subject makes a lexical decision to the target. This is exactly what is observed (e.g., MARKED primes its morphological relative MARK over and above any contribution from orthography and phonology as reflected in a morphologically unrelated prime like MARKET; see Stolz and Besner, 1998).

The presence of morphological priming in the absence of semantic priming following letter search on the prime in the same experiment is consistent with the three-route localist model in which there is a distinction between lexical and semantic representations. It remains to be seen whether this dissociation can be obtained in the naming task, and, if so, how a PDP approach can maintain its commitment to the claim that nonwords and words are read by recourse to the same routine, while also explaining other phenomena, reviewed above, suggesting processing differences between words and nonwords.

How Well Do the Different Models Predict Human Word-Naming Performance?

Clearly, there are a number of phenomena that the PDP models do not handle particularly well. We do not yet know whether implementing other processes and representations (e.g., some form of attentional control system; a semantic representation) will help the models to deal with some of these problems. Still other phenomena may turn out to be particularly difficult to deal with (e.g., lexical anomia).

These problems notwithstanding, both the Seidenberg and McClelland (1989) model and the Plaut et al. (1996) model produce the correct pronunciation of virtually all the words that they were trained on. A natural question is whether this successful performance reflects how intact humans read single words. The ability of the PDP models to simulate human naming performance at the item level is therefore directly assessed. The approach is straightforward; the naming scores from the various models are entered into a regression analysis to determine how much variance in human naming time these scores account for (e.g., see Besner and Bourassa, 1995; 1996). This approach has also been used by Seidenberg and McClelland (1990), Besner et al. (1990), and Fera and Besner (1992).

The details of these experiments need not concern us here other than to note that 30 university students named 300 words in an online naming task and another set of 30 subjects named the same words in a delayed naming task. In a second experiment yet another 30 subjects named the same 300 words mixed together with 300 nonwords. The naming time for items in the delayed naming task was subtracted from the corresponding items in the online naming task because this serves to partial out the powerful effect of the initial phoneme on the time to trip the voice key (e.g., Forster and Chambers, 1973). These difference scores were then correlated with the models and with various predictor variables (see below). The 300 words varied in word frequency (1 to 217 occurrences per million words of text as indexed by the Kucera and Francis count), length (3 to 6 letters), number of neighbors (1 to 17) and spelling to sound regularity (approximately 85% of the words are regular).

All the analyses reported here are item analyses. The correlation between the two online naming experiments RTs is .75; this gives a sense of how stable the human naming data are. Subjects made too few errors to allow a formal analysis (the overall error rate is between 1 and 2%). The scores produced by each model in response to the presentation of a word were separately entered first into a regression equation against the naming time for the 300 words. This gave each of the models its best shot at accounting for variance in human naming time.

Model 1: Seidenberg and McClelland (1989)

The zero-order correlation between Seidenberg and McClelland's phonological error scores for each item and the corresponding human naming time was significant but small. The best it did across experiments was $r = .18$, $p < .001$. This model accounts for about 3.5 % of the variance. In contrast, when word frequency, length, and number of neighbors were entered on the second step of a regression analysis, they accounted for an additional 12% of the variance. In other words, even after the model was given the best chance to account for variance, significantly more variance was accounted for by those same factors (word frequency, neighbors, length) that the model claims to have already incorporated in its performance.

How does this compare with the data reported by Seidenberg and McClelland (1990)? They report a .29 zero order correlation between the phonological error scores from the model and human naming times from the Seidenberg and Waters (1989) 3,000 word corpus. This correlation is larger than the one reported here, but there is a simple explanation. The correlation reported here is based on the difference scores between online and delayed naming times. The simple correlation between online naming times and the phonological error scores for this sample is .26, a value quite close to Seidenberg and McClelland's .29. It thus appears that when a sample of 300 words is used it produces an estimate of the variance accounted for in human naming by this model that is quite close to the one obtained when the sample size is ten times larger.

Model 2: Plaut, McClelland, Seidenberg, and Patterson (1996)

There are at least two reasons why it is interesting to ask how well the new model does by how well it predicts human naming time. Most obviously, is it the case that the new orthographic and phonological coding schemes enable this model to perform better than the original model? Or, might it be the case that there is a tradeoff between improving the accuracy of nonword reading and how well word reading predicts human naming time? That is, have the changes made to the model to produce more accurate nonword reading resulted in a decreased ability to predict humans naming times to words the model was trained on?

The answer to these questions is that is that the attractor network described by Plaut et al. (1996) performs about as poorly as Seidenberg and McClelland's model. The best zero order correlation between the model's naming times and the human naming times across experiments was .17, p < .001. This new model thus accounts for less than 3% of the variance in human naming time to these 300 items. When length, word frequency and number of neighbors were entered together on step 2 of a regression analysis they accounted for an additional 13% of the variance. Further analyses were carried out in which the exception words were omitted from the analyses because of Plaut et al.'s argument that semantics might play a role in naming such words. Including such items in the analysis would be unfair to the model because it has no semantic representation at the present time. Deleting these items failed to change the magnitude of any of the correlations reported above.

At the risk of belaboring the point, one would expect that after the model has had its best shot at accounting for variance in the naming data from humans, the factors that the model is supposed to represent should not account for any variance. The observation that the vector comprising word length, word frequency, and neighborhood size accounts for approximately four times as much of the variance as the model does is therefore problematic for any claim that the model accurately captures what it is that humans do when item level performance is measured.

It should be noted that Spieler and Balota (1997) have also examined the relationship between the naming times from Plaut et al.'s attractor network and human subject's online naming time. It is comforting to note that despite a much larger sample size (2,800 items) the correlation they obtained was no larger than the one observed here. Spieler and Balota also found that word frequency and letter length accounted for a significant amount of the variance in human naming time, just as observed here.

It is clear that the current implementations of these PDP models do very poorly when attempting to predict human naming time at the level of individual items. There are a number of factors that might contribute to this poor performance (e.g., corpus size, the fact that these models are deterministic, inadequate orthographic representations, the fact that the phonological representations are acquired through reading rather than listening and speaking as in normal development, etc.). It might also be that performance will improve when more attention is paid to the issue of deciding when the model should actually emit a response (as when simulating naming RT, given that the system is settling into a solution over time).

The fact that semantics is currently not part of the implemented model in any serious sense is an additional important factor in light of several observations. The first is Bourassa's (1996) report that naming time to words with *regular* spelling-sound correspondences are affected by their status on the imageability dimension when there is a high ratio of exception to regular words in the experiment. The second is Hino, Lupker, and Besner's (1998) report that, in the shallow Japanese scripts, low-frequency words with many meanings are named faster than low-frequency words with fewer meanings. The third is Hino and Lupker's (1996) report that polysemy facilitates the naming of low-frequency words in English.

It will be interesting to see how the next generation of models perform. For the present, it is suggested that the currently implemented versions of these models are best viewed as existence proofs of how a reading system could be organized rather than as adequate models of how humans read single words aloud at the level of individual items.

Model 3: Coltheart et al. (1993)

It appears only fair to subject one of the implemented localist model of word recognition and reading aloud to the same assessment as carried out on the PDP models. I therefore chose to examine the Coltheart et al. (1993) model because it has been discussed a number of times in the literature, and because it produces a number of phenomena observed in the literature on normal and impaired readers word-recognition abilities.

Space restrictions do not permit a full description of this model aside from noting that it consists of three implemented components: (1) McClelland and Rumelhart's (1981) orthographic word-recognition system (feature level, letter level, word level) married to (2) the speech-production system implemented by Dell and his associates, along with (3) a rule-based nonlexical routine for translating spelling to sound developed in Coltheart's lab. A semantic system also forms part of the model but has yet to be implemented.

Interest here centers on the lexical routine because the argument throughout the chapter has been that this routine underlies at least some of the naming performance seen in normal and dyslexic patients, and because it has been argued that there is nothing like this routine in the currently implemented PDP models. RTs from the operation of the model's lexical route in response to each of the 300 words were therefore obtained from Max Coltheart and correlated with the human naming times to these words. The zero order correlation was significant (r = .37, p < .001), accounting for about 13% of the variance. Entering other factors on step 2 of a regression analysis (length, neighborhood size, and word frequency) accounted for a small amount of additional variance (3%).

The performance of this model leaves room for improvement, but at the same time it is noticeably better than the performance of the two PDP models tested here. It will be interesting to see whether implementing a semantic system will increase the amount of variance accounted for.

Comment

It might be objected that a comparison of this localist model with the PDP models is like comparing apples and oranges because the effects of word frequency are imposed on this model by hand setting the resting activation levels in the word-detector system based on word-frequency norms, whereas the PDP models learn the appropriate connection weights through training. This objection is a serious one, but given that there is no learning algorithm associated with the localist model, we work with what we have. We should not lose sight of the fact, however, that a major selling feature of the PDP models is that they are supposed to learn. The fact that a large effect of word frequency is present in the naming data after the PDP models' contribution to performance have been factored out suggests that these models are not learning adequately. Further, this objection to the localist model does not apply to the effects of the number of neighbors on naming performance, and it should be noted that although the simple correlation between naming time and number of neighbors is fair sized (-.33) there is no unique effect of neighborhood size on human naming time once the localist model's RTs have been partialled out of the human naming data.

The fact that Plaut et al.'s PDP model accounts for only 2 to 3% of the variance in word naming also needs to be understood in the context of the fact that the combined effects of length, word-frequency, and neighborhood size on naming latency is only on the order of 15% of the variance as well as in the context of the fact that the cross experiment correlation for items using different subjects is around .75. Certainly, the model needs to do a better job of accounting for the variance attributable to the major variables affecting spelling-sound translation. Still, there is likely considerable variance in naming time that belongs to the production end of processing (see Spieler and Balota, 1997). The models discussed here have virtually nothing to say about such processing at the present time.

Reading Nonwords Aloud

Studying how the different models fare in dealing with nonwords is also important. Rastle and Coltheart (1997a) submitted the nonwords from the Weekes (1997) experiment to both DRC and to the Plaut et al. model, and they then correlated these models' measures with the RTs produced by human subjects in Weekes' experiment. DRC accounted for 38% of the variance, whereas the Plaut et al. model accounted for less than 1%.

Rastle and Coltheart (1997b) went on to investigate how nonwords are named. In DRC, nonword naming is accomplished by a serial, left to right spelling-sound translation process. If this is how humans name nonwords then a straightforward prediction is that as length increases so should naming time. Of course, it is well known that as letter length increases, so does naming time (see Henderson, 1982). What is not known, however, is whether this is due to letter length or phoneme length (in Weekes' sample of items these factors are moderately correlated).

Rastle and Coltheart reported an experiment that held letter length constant and varied the number of phonemes. Nonwords with fewer phonemes were named slower than items with more phonemes. DRC's nonlexical routine produced the same pattern; it took more cycles to produce a pronunciation in the case of nonwords with fewer phonemes. This seemingly counterintuitive result in the human data is given a principled explanation in the operation of the nonlexical routine as instantiated in DRC. Consider the two nonwords FOOPH and FROLP. Because the nonlexical spelling-sound translation process operates left to right on one letter at a time, the first o in FOOPH activates /o/ in the phonological output lexicon, which subsequently must be overridden when the second o is detected because oo is pronounced as /u/ not /o/. The activation for /u/ is slow because of lateral inhibition, a principle in the model (within level inhibition). Similarly, the initial activation in the phonological output lexicon for p is /p/, which needs to be overridden when /h/ is detected because ph should activate /f/ not /p/. In short, because single phonemes are encoded initially, this leads to activation in the phonological output lexicon that is incorrect and needs to be replaced by the correct phoneme. The activation of phoneme in a specified position inhibits the activation of other phonemes in the same position, and it thus takes additional time to overcome this inhibition. This does not happen with FROLP because the correct phonemes are activated on the first pass.

It can thus be seen that a serial process (DRC's nonlexical routine) provides a simple account of nonword naming. It remains to be seen whether any PDP model can account for as much variance in nonword naming time as DRC does, and further, if the development of activation is tracked over time, whether such models initially activate the particular incorrect phonemes as discussed in the example above.

Summary

Considerable ground has been covered in this review; it is therefore useful to briefly summarize the main arguments and conclusions.

Many cognitive scientists hunger for a closer connection between brain and mind. A PDP approach to many issues in cognition and perception has proven enormously popular, in part because the models learn, because performance degrades gracefully following simulated lesions, and because of the intuition that the nodes and the connections among them resemble neurons and synapses in the brain in some way. In contrast, traditional symbolic accounts rarely address the learning issue in their implementations, there is little work on simulated lesions, and the representations that are used rarely make theoretical contact with brain structure. That said, the argument advanced here is that, in the context of providing an explanation of how intact readers and readers with acquired dyslexia read aloud, the single- and dual-route PDP models that are currently implemented face a variety of difficulties not encountered by a three-route framework.

In summary, these PDP models currently have some difficulties (sometimes severe, other times one can imagine how an account might evolve) in providing an account for:

1. How patients with a form of phonological dyslexia read aloud.
2. How patient with a form of surface dyslexia read aloud (but see Plaut, 1997).
3. The fact that there is a consistent deficit in speech production for specific words that are well understood in speech (lexical anomia).
4. Pseudohomophone effects whereby items that sound like real words (e.g., BRANE) are read faster (in intact subjects) or more accurately (in patients) than control items (e.g., FRANE) when coupled with the observation that base-word frequency does not affect naming time.
5. The presence-absence of a word-frequency effect when reading words aloud in a shallow orthography.
6. The presence-absence of a consistency effect when reading nonwords aloud in a shallow orthography.
7. The exception effect in reading aloud as a function of the position of the exceptional segment.
8. The absence of letter-length effects in reading words aloud coupled with the presence of letter-length effects when reading nonwords aloud.
9. Case alternation effects on reading aloud. (This is also a problem for a three-route model such as DRC.)

Finally, although the best developed PDP model reads both words and nonwords about as accurately as humans, it performs poorly at the item level in that it accounts for less than 3% of the variance in human naming time for words and no variance in the naming of nonwords. In contrast, a localist three-route model accounts for about 12% of the variance in naming time to the same set of words as the PDP model was tested on and 38% of the variance in naming time to the same set of nonwords as the PDP model was tested on

Future Directions

Where is the ongoing debate between localist and distributed models headed? It appears clear that both modeling efforts and empirical investigations will continue to influence each other. Some people believe that neuroscience (PET, ERP, fMRI) will also make a contribution to this debate; that remains to be seen.

Certainly, the observation of (1) an imageability effect on the naming of words with regular spelling-sound correspondences in English (Bourassa, 1996) and (2) a homograph effect in the naming of low-frequency words in the shallow Japanese scripts (Hino, Lupker, and Besner, 1998) and (3) an imageability effect for both high- and low-frequency opaque words in Persian (Baluch and Besner, 1999) points to a larger role for semantics in naming by intact subjects than has been envisioned to date. An adequate simulation model of word naming will thus need an implemented semantic system.

There is also the issue of demonstrating that PDP models can *discover* the appropriate mappings between orthography and phonology rather than, as currently done, implementing coding schemes for orthographic and phonological knowledge that already do a lot of this work.

I also expect to see PDP models address the issue of how letter length effects in naming arise when neighborhood effects are partialled out. The data reported by Weekes (1997) suggest that this length effect is restricted to *nonwords* when neighborhood effects are partialled out, a fact that is currently handled by the (serial) assembled routine in the three-route localist model (see also Rastle and Coltheart, 1997a, b). Of course, there is nothing that prevents PDP models from producing serial behaviour.

In short, I am not arguing that there is something intrinsic to PDP models per se that renders them incapable of accommodating much of the data discussed here but rather that PDP models will have to evolve substantially to deal with the issues raised here.

Conclusions

This chapter has briefly touched on acquired dyslexia in several forms, lexical anomia, and a variety of manipulations on intact readers in an attempt to determine whether a two- or a three-route model best describes the data, and in an attempt to determine whether a model with localist or distributed representations best describes the data. The ability of several implemented PDP models and one implemented localist model to predict human naming performance at an individual item level was also assessed. These different lines of investigation converge on the same conclusion. At this point in their respective development, a three-route model in which the lexical and assembled routines consist of localist representations offers a better account of human reading performance at the single-word level and at an individual item level than any of the single- or dual-route PDP models developed by Plaut, Seidenberg, McClelland, and Patterson. To put it another way:

> We see no reason to abandon the view that when humans engage in the oral
> reading of regular words, exception words, and nonwords, they rely at least in
> part upon multiple, dissociable, nonsemantically mediated routines. We are

nevertheless attracted to a distributed representation because it learns and degrades gracefully, among other virtues. We would not be surprised to see, in the next few years, a distributed word recognition model that includes nonsemantic multiple routines that interact with one another.[12] To state it another way, one of these routines will probably resemble what is currently referred to as the lexical route. Besner et al., (1990, p. 445)

My hunch is that a three-route model will continue to provide a better description of naming than two route models. Whether these routines (in humans) are localist, distributed, or hybrid is likely a more difficult question to resolve.

Acknowledgments

This work was supported by Grant A0998 from the Natural Sciences and Engineering Research Council of Canada. The chapter was written in late 1995, and updated in October 1998 and again in 1999. I thank Mark Seidenberg for providing the Seidenberg and McClelland (1989) model, Dave Plaut for simulation data from the Plaut et al. (1996) model, and Max Coltheart for simulation data from the DRC model. I also thank Max Coltheart, Rob McCann, Mike Masson, Jennifer Stolz, Martha Roberts, Ray Klein, and Paddy McMullen for comments on the manuscript.

Notes

1. The terms "connectionist-connectionism" are confusing because they are often used as synonyms for parallel distributed processing. McClelland and Rumelhart's (1981) interactive activation model is an example of a connectionist model but its representations are localist, not distributed, and there are no hidden units. On the other hand, processing is parallel and distributed in the sense that multiple knowledge sources are being processed in parallel. In the present chapter, I arbitrarily label models with hidden units among all levels as connectionist models (i.e., Seidenberg and McClelland, 1989; Plaut et al., 1996), models without hidden units as localist (i.e., DRC), and models where some pathways have hidden units and other pathways do not, as hybrid (i.e., Zorzi et al., 1998). In short, in the present context the term connectionist refers to the nature of some of the representations rather than to the idea that multiple knowledge sources are concurrently active.

2. It is important to bear in mind that not all the representations in these new models are distributed (see Plaut et al., 1996; Coltheart et al., 1996 for discussion). Further, the modelers finesse some of the difficult issues surrounding orthographic and phonological coding schemes. For example, the model does not convert a string of letters to a string of graphemes; the input submitted to the model is already coded into

graphemes. Masson (chapter 12, this volume) comments on this general issue.

3. There is one obvious concern with Seidenberg's (1992a) conjecture concerning the role of the number of hidden units as it relates to the division of labor hypothesis. Seidenberg assumes that a larger number of hidden units is associated with good exception word reading but restricted ability to generalize, hence poor nonword reading. Therefore, on this account, it makes sense for the semantic route to learn to handle the low frequency exception words, leaving the direct route to handle regular words and nonwords. One difficulty with this argument, however, is that Plaut and McClelland's (1993) model has half the number of hidden units that Seidenberg and McClelland's (1989) has, but it reads nonwords much better than the original model without sacrificing accuracy on the low- frequency exception words. It should also be noted that there is nothing in the "division of labor" idea that demands the division be between semantic and nonsemantic pathways. This is illustrated by Zorzi et al.'s (1998) simulations in which a self-organizing division of labor occurs within the module that maps spelling onto sound without reference to semantics.

4. The success of this account depends heavily on whether one believes that there is enough residual functioning in the direct route. For example, zero nonword reading might be taken as evidence that the direct route is seriously compromised, but this could be misleading because the patient might get a single phoneme right in most attempted readings. On the other hand, Funnell's (1983) phonological dyslexic patient read no nonwords correctly but also scored 0/12 at trying to produce the correct phoneme in response to the presentation of a single letter.

5. This cross-experiment interaction is significant but was not reported in the original paper. Skeptics can compute this for themselves; the data appear in the appendix of McCann and Besner (1987).

6. This experiment also included a delayed naming control. After subtracting the delayed naming condition from the online condition, the remaining 16 ms PHE was not reliable but the accuracy advantage remained. I am inclined to the view that there is also a genuine PHE here in RT when delayed RT is subtracted from online RT but that it is obscured by the poor choice of delay interval (too short; see the discussion in Besner and Hildebrandt).

7. There is also a pseudohomophone naming experiment by Herdman, LeFevre, and Greenham (1994) with some rather unusual results. Unfortunately, a cross-table comparison shows that the error rates in the delayed-naming condition are larger than in the online-naming condition, rendering the authors' interpretation of their RT data problematic. This problem has gone unremarked. A further paper by Herdman, LeFevre, and Greenham (1996) asserts that the PHE arises entirely during articulation.

The problem with this conclusion is that it is based on a naming latency experiment that does not include a delayed-naming condition. It is therefore impossible to decide whether their PHE arises during phonological processing, articulation, or both. In any case, Herdman et al.'s conclusion that the PHE arises entirely in articulation is inconsistent with the observation that naming time for pseudohomophone targets is facilitated by a related semantic context (Buchanan and Besner, 1995; Lukatela and Turvey, 1991). To my knowledge, no one has ever claimed that semantic priming effects in naming arise only during articulation.

8. Although Seidenberg et al. reported no reliable interaction in which the PHE in their experiment was larger online than in delayed naming– the online effect was 50% larger. It is unfortunate that Seidenberg et al. do not report a power test of their experiment's ability to detect this critical interaction. It should also be noted that the Seidenberg et al. stimulus set has been the object of some criticism (Borowsky and Masson, 1998; Marmurek, 1997). Finally, Marmurek reports that a better controlled stimulus set than Seidenberg et al.'s produces a 28 ms PHE in the delay condition, and a 46 ms PHE online under conditions similar to Seidenberg et al's.

9. The word-frequency effects seen when naming words in a shallow orthography can be quite substantial [e.g., 50 ms in Serbo-Croat (Besner and Smith, 1992), 35 ms in Persian (Baluch and Besner, 1991), 52 ms in Turkish (Raman et al., 1996), and 30 ms in Dutch (Hudson and Bergman, 1985)].

10. Though note that Plaut et al. (1996, p. 106) are clearly moving in the direction of implementing a sequential process (but the motivation is not to deal with length effects for single syllable words or nonwords).

11. Mayall and Humphreys (1996) report some results that do not quite square with some of those reported by Besner and colleagues. My suspicion is that some of these apparent contradictions represent a type 2 error. More generally, one difficulty with using case alternation as a manipulation is that it renders some words more difficult to recognize than others because of letter confusability (as in the case of I's and l's; e.g. whItTle; tIle). The account offered here as to why case mixing and word frequency have additive effects on naming performance when all the items are exception words is not without its own problems in that Herdman et al. (1999) find the same pattern when exception words and regular words are randomly mixed together in the same block of trials. One noteworthy feature of the Herdman et al. data is that under these conditions, high-frequency exception words are slower than high-frequency regular words, provided that both types of words are case alternated. There is no difference between these two word classes when they appear in lower case (the standard finding). Norris'es multiple-level model appears to simulate this result, but it is not transparent as to why this occurs. Another problem with the Herdman et al. account (i.e., what Norris'es simulation model

produces) is that there is nothing in the model that would allow it to produce the standard result: larger case mixing effects for nonwords than for words.

12. Zorzi, Houghton, and Butterworth (1998) have implemented a network with representations of orthography and phonology that are localist. Critically, there are two pathways that connect orthography to phonology. One of them is direct, meaning that there are no hidden units involved. The second pathway, however, connects the orthographic layer to the phonological layer through a set of hidden units. The most important finding, arguably, is that under appropriate conditions (i.e., a particular number of hidden units) the implemented model self organizes, such that it "decomposes the reading task into two different procedures, one extracting sublexical spelling-sound relations (the direct path) and the other (the mediated path) forming word-specific representations (albeit distributed, given the use of backpropagation in training)." In essence, the path that maps inputs to outputs through a set of hidden units is functionally a lexicon. This model clearly has two routes that are not semantically mediated. That said, there are two problems that come immediately to mind. First, this model will not, in its currently implemented form, produce letter-length effects when nonwords are named at the same time as producing no length effect when words are named. In short, it does not simulate the data reported by Weekes (1997). Relatedly, given that both pathways in the model operate in a parallel mode, it is difficult to see how the interaction of regularity x serial position reported by Coltheart and Rastle (1994; Rastle and Coltheart, 1999) can be accommodated.

References

Allport, D.A. (1979). Word recognition in reading: A tutorial review. In P.A. Kolers, H. Bouma, and M. Wrolstad (eds.), *Processing of Visible Language.* New York: Plenum Press.

Baluch, B., and Besner, D. (1991). Visual word recognition: Evidence for strategic control of lexical and nonlexical routines in oral reading. *Journal of Experimental Psychology: Learning, Memory, and Cognition, 17,* 644–652.

Baluch, B., and Besner, D. (1999). Single word naming: Orthography to semantics to phonology (in preparation).

Bauer, B., and Besner, D. (1997). Processing in the Stroop task: Mental set as a determinant of performance. *Canadian Journal of Experimental Psychology, 51,* 61–68.

Beauvois, M.F. and Derouesne, J. (1979). Phonological alexia: Three dissociations. *Neurosurgery and Psychiatry,* 42 1115–1124.

Besner, D., Davelaar, E., Alcott, D., and Parry, P. (1984). Wholistic reading of alphabetic print: Evidence from the FDM and the FBI. In L. Henderson (ed.),

Orthographies and Reading: Perspectives from Cognitive Psychology, Neuropsychology, and Linguistics. Hillsdale, NJ: Lawrence Erlbaum Associates.

Besner, D. (1990). Does the reading system need a lexicon? In D.A. Balota, G.B. Flores d'Arcais, and K. Rayner (eds.) *Comprehension Processes in Reading.* Hillsdale, NJ: Lawrence Erlbaum Associates.

Besner, D., Dennis, I., and Davelaar, E. (1985). Reading without phonology? *Quarterly Journal of Experimental Psychology,* 37A, 477–492.

Besner, D., and Hildebrandt, N. (1987). Orthographic and phonological codes in the oral reading of Japanese kana. *Journal of Experimental Psychology: Learning, Memory, and Cognition,* 13, 335–343.

Besner, D., and McCann, R.S. (1990). What does the processing of BRANE reveal about the architecture of MIND? (in preparation)

Besner, D., and McCann, R.S. (1987). Word frequency and pattern distortion in visual word identification and production: an examination of four classes of model. In M. Coltheart (ed.), *The Psychology of Reading*: Attention and Performance 12.Hillsdale, NJ: Lawrence Erlbaum Associates.

Besner, D., and Johnston, J.C. (1989). Reading and the mental lexicon: On the uptake of visual information. In W. Marslen-Wilson (ed.), *Lexical Representation and Process.* Cambridge: MA. MIT Press.

Besner, D., and Stolz, J. (1999). What kind of attention modulates the Stroop effect? *Psychonomic Bulletin and Review, 6,* 99–104.

Besner, D., Twilley, L., McCann, R.S., and Seergobin, K. (1990). On the association between connectionism and data: Are a few words necessary? *Psychological Review,* 97, 432–446.

Besner, D., and Smith, M.C. (1992). Basic processes in reading: Is the orthographic depth hypothesis sinking? In R. Frost and L. Katz (eds.) *Orthography, Phonology, Morphology and Meaning.* North Holland Press.

Besner, D., and Bourassa, D. (1995). Localist and parallel distributed processing models of visual word recognition: A few more words. Paper presented at Brain, Behaviour, and Cognitive Science Society, June 24, Halifax, Canada.

Besner, D., Stolz, J.A., and Boutilier, C. (1997). The Stroop effect and the myth of automaticity. *Psychonomic Bulletin and Review, 4,* 221–225.

Borowsky, R. and Besner, D. (1993). Visual word recognition: A multi-stage activation model. *Journal of Experimental Psychology: Learning, Memory and Cognition, 19,* 813–840.

Borowsky, R., and Masson, M.E.J. (1996). Frequency effects in word and pseudohomophone naming. Paper presented at the thirty seventh annual meeting of the Psychonomic Society, Chicago.

Bourassa, D. (1996). Context effects in visual word recognition. Poster presented at Canadian Society for Brain, Behaviour and Cognitive Science, Montreal.

Bourassa, D., and Besner, D. (1998). When do nonwords activate semantics: implications for models of visual word recognition. *Memory and Cognition*, 26, 61–74.

Bridgeman, B. (1987). Is the dual route theory possible in phonetically regular languages? *Behavioral and Brain Sciences*, 10, 331–332.

Buchanan, L., and Besner, D. (1995). Reading aloud: Evidence for the use of a whole word nonsemantic pathway. In J.M. Henderson, M. Singer, and F. Ferreira (eds.), *Reading and Language Processing*. Hillsdale, NJ: Lawrence Erlbaum Associates.

Carr, T.H., and Pollatsek, A. (1985). Recognizing printed words: A look at current models. In D. Besner, T.G. Waller, and G.E. MacKinnon (eds.) *Reading Research: Advances in Theory and Practice*. Academic Press.

Chiappe, P.R., Smith, M.C., and Besner, D. (1996). Semantic priming in visual word recognition: activation blocking and domains of processing. *Psychonomic Bulletin and Review*, 3, 249–253.

Cipolotti, L., and Warrington, E.K. (1995). Semantic memory and reading abilities: A case report. *Journal of the International Neuropsychological Society*, 1, 104–110.

Collins, A.M., and Loftus, E.F. (1975). A spreading activation theory of semantic processing. *Psychological Review*, 82, 407–428.

Coltheart, M., Curtis, B., Atkins, P., and Haller, M. (1993). Models of reading aloud: Dual route and parallel distributed processing approaches. *Psychological Review*, 100, 589–608.

Coltheart, M., and Rastle, K. (1994). Serial processing in reading aloud: Evidence for dual-route models of reading. *Journal of Experimental Psychology: Human Perception and Performance*, 20, 1197–1211.

Coltheart, M. (1995) Lexical but nonsemantic reading. Paper presented at the thirty sixth annual meeting of the Psychonomics Society, Los Angeles, CA.

Coltheart, M., Langdon, R., and Haller, M. (1996) Computational neuropsychology and acquired dyslexia. In B. Dodd, L. Worral, and R. Campbell. *Models of Language: Illuminations from Impairment*. London: Whurr Publishers.

Coltheart, V., and Leahy, J. (1992). Childrens' and Adults' reading of nonwords: Effects of regularity and consistency. *Journal of Experimental Psychology: Learning, Memory, and Cognition*, 18, 718–729.

Derouesne, J., and Beauvois, M.F. (1985). The "phonemic" stage in the nonlexical reading process. Evidence from a case of phonological alexia. In K.E. Patterson, J.C. Marshall, and M. Coltheart (eds.), *Surface Dyslexia*. Hillsdale, NJ: Lawrence Erlbaum Associates.

Ellis, A. (1984). *Reading, Writing, and Dyslexia: A Cognitive Analysis*. Hillsdale, NJ: Lawrence Erlbaum Associates.

Fera, P. and Besner, D. (1992). The process of lexical decision: More words about a parallel distributed processing model. *Journal of Experimental Psychology: Learning Memory and Cognition, 18,* 749–764.

Forster, K.I., and Chambers, S.M. (1973). Lexical access and naming time. *Journal of Verbal Learning and Verbal Behavior,* 12, 627–635.

Friedrich, F.J., Kellogg, W., and Henik, A. (1991). Automatic processes in lexical access and spreading activation. *Journal of Experimental Psychology: Human Perception and Performance,* 17, 792–806.

Funnell, E. (1983). Phonological processing in reading: New evidence from acquired dyslexia. *British Journal of Psychology,* 74, 159–180.

Glushko, R.J. (1979). The organization and activation of knowledge in reading aloud. *Journal of Experimental Psychology: Human Perception and Performance,* 5, 674–691.

Hawkins, H.L., Reicher, G.M., Rogers, M., and Peterson, L. (1976). Flexible coding in word recognition. *Journal of Experimental Psychology: Human Perception and Performance,* 2, 380–385.

Henderson, L. (1982). *Orthography and Word Recognition in Reading.* London: Academic Press.

Herdman, C.M., LeFevre, J., and Greenham, S.L. (1994). Implicating the lexicon: Base word frequency effects in naming pseudohomophones. *Journal of Experimental Psychology: Human Perception and Performance,* 20, 575–590.

Herdman, C.M., LeFevre, J., and Greenham, S.L. (1996). Base word frequency and pseudohomophone naming. *Quarterly Journal of Experimental Psychology,* 49A, 1044–1061.

Herdman, C.M., Chernecki, D., and Norris, D. (1999). Naming cAsE aLtErNaTeD words. *Memory and Cognition, 27,* 254–266.

Hino, Y. and Lupker, S.J. (1996). Effects of polysemy in lexical decision and naming: An alternative to lexical access accounts. *Journal of Experimental Psychology: Human Perception and Performance, 22,* 1331–1356.

Hino, Y. Lupker, S.J. and Besner, D. (1998). Polysemy effects in naming of Japanese Katakana words in their Hiragana transcriptions. Poster presented at the 39th Annual Meeting of the Psychonomics Society.

Howard, D. (1995). Lexical anomia: Or the case of the missing lexical entries. *Quarterly Journal of Experimental Psychology,* 48A, 999–1023.

Hudson, P.T.W., and Bergman, M.W. (1985). Lexical knowledge in word recognition: word length in naming and lexical decision tasks. *Journal of Memory and Language,* 24, 46–58.

Jared, D. (1997). Evidence that strategy effects in word naming reflect changes in output timing rather than changes in processing route. *Journal of Experimental Psychology: Learning, Memory and Cognition,* 23, 1424–1438.

Job, R., Peressotti, F., and Cusinato, A. (1998). Lexical effects in naming pseudowords in shallow orthographies: Further empirical data. *Journal of Experimental Psychology: Human Perception and Performance*, 24, 662–630.

Katz, L., and Feldman, L. (1983). Relation between pronunciation and recognition of printed words in deep and shallow orthographies. *Journal of Experimental Psychology: Learning, Memory and Cognition*, 9, 157–166.

Katz, L., and Frost, R. (1992). The reading process is different for different orthographies: The orthographic depth hypothesis. In R. Frost and L. Katz (eds.) *Orthography, Phonology, Morphology, and Meaning*. North Holland Press.

Lukatela, G., and Turvey, M.T. (1991). Phonological access of the lexicon: Evidence from associative priming with pseudohomophones. *Journal of Experimental Psychology: Human Perception and Performance*, 17, 951–966.

Lupker, S.J., Brown, P., and Columbo, L. (1997). Strategic control in a naming task: Changing routes or changing deadlines? *Journal of Experimental Psychology: Learning, Memory and Cognition*, 23, 570-590.

MacLeod, C.M. (1991). Half a century of research on the Stroop effect: An integrative review. *Psychological Bulletin*, 109, 163–203.

Marmurek, H.H., and Kwantes, P.J. (1996). Reading words and wirds: Phonology and lexical access. *Quarterly Journal of Experimental Psychology*, 49A, 3, 696–714.

Marmurek, H.H. (1997). List context effects in reading pseudohomophones. Poster presented at the thirty eighth annual meeting of the Psychonomics Society, Philadelphia.

Masson, M.E.J. (1999). Interactive processes in word identification: A computational approach. In P.A. McMullen and R.M. Klein (eds.), *Converging Methods for Understanding Reading and Dyslexia*. Cambridge, MA: MIT Press.

Mayall, K., and Humphreys. G.W. (1996). Case mixing and the task sensitive disruption of lexical processing. *Journal of Experimental Psychology: Learning, Memory, and Cognition*, 22, 278–294.

McCann, R.S., and Besner, D. (1987). Reading pseudohomophones: Implications for models of pronunciation and the locus of the word-frequency effects in word naming. *Journal of Experimental Psychology: Human Perception and Performance*, 13, 14–24.

McClelland, J.L., and Rumelhart, D.E. (1981). An interactive activation model of context effects in letter perception: Part 1. An account of basic findings. *Psychological Review*, 88, 375-40.

Monsell, S., Doyle, M.C. and Haggard, P.N. (1989). Effects of frequency on visual word recognition tasks: Where are they? *Journal of Experimental Psychology: General*, 118, 43–71.

Monsell, S., Patterson, K.E., Graham, A., Hughes, C.H., and Milroy, R. (1992). Lexical and sublexical translation of spelling to sound: Strategic anticipation of lexical status. *Journal of Experimental Psychology: Learning, Memory, and Cognition*, 18, 452–467.

Morton, J. (1968). Grammar and computation in language behaviour. In J.C. Catford (ed.), *Studies in Language and Language Behaviour*. Centre for Research in Language and Language Behavior. Progress report no. VI. Ann Arbor, MI. University of Michigan.

Morton, J. (1969). Interaction of information in word recognition. *Psychological Review*, 76, 165–178.

Neely, J.H. (1991). Semantic priming effects in visual word recognition: A selective review of current findings and theories. In D. Besner and G.W. Humphreys (eds.) *Basic Processes in Reading: Visual Word Recognition*. Hillsdale, NJ: Lawrence Erlbaum Associates.

Norris, D. (1994). A quantitative multiple-levels model of reading aloud. Journal of Experimental Psychology: Human Perception and Performance, 20, 1212–1232.

Paap, K.R. and Noel, R.W. (1991). Dual route models of print to sound: Still a good horse race. *Psychological Research, 53*, 13–24.

Patterson, K.E. and Morton, J. (1980). A new attempt at an interpretation, or, an attempt at a new interpretation. In M. Coltheart, K. E. Patterson, and J.C. Marshall, (eds.), *Deep Dyslexia*, London: Routledge and Kegan Paul.

Patterson, K.E., and Coltheart, V. (1987). Phonological processes in reading: A tutorial review. In M Coltheart (ed.) *The Psychology of Reading. Attention and Performance 12*. Hillsdale, NJ: Lawrence Erlbaum Associates.

Patterson, K.E., Seidenberg, M.S., and McClelland, J.L. (1989). Connections and disconnections: Acquired dyslexia in a computational model of reading processes. In R.G.M. Morris (ed.) *Parallel Distributed Processing: Implications for Psychology and Neuroscience*. London: Oxford University Press.

Patterson, K.E., Suzuki, T., and Wydell, T.N. (1996). Interpreting a case of Japanese phonological alexia: The key is in phonology. *Cognitive Neuropsychology*, 13, 803–822.

Pinker, S. (1991). Rules of language. *Science*, 253, 530-535.

Pinker, S. and Prince, A. (1988). On language and connectionism: Analysis of a parallel distributed processing model of language acquisition. *Cognition*, 28, 73–193.

Plaut, D.C. (1997). Structure and function in the lexical system: Insights from distributed models of word reading and lexical decision. *Language and Cognitive Processes, 12*, 765–805.

Plaut, D.C., and McClelland, J.L. (1993). Generalization with componential attractors: Word and nonword reading in an attractor network. In *Proceedings of the 15th Annual Conference of the Cognitive Science Society*. Hillsdale, NJ: Lawrence Erlbaum Associates.

Plaut, D.C., McClelland, J.L., Seidenberg, M.S., and Patterson, K.E. (1996). Understanding normal and impaired word reading: Computational principles in quasi-regular domains. *Psychological Review*, 103, 56–115.

Poulton, E.C. (1975). Range effects in experiments on people. *American Journal of Psychology*, 88, 3–22.

Raman, I., Baluch, B., and Sneddon, P. (1996). What is the cognitive system's preferred route for deriving phonology from print? *European Psychologist*, 1, 3, 221–227.

Raman, I., Baluch, B., and Besner, D. (1998). Unpublished experiments.

Rastle, K. (1997). Processes in skilled reading: Behavioural and computational studies. Unpublished doctoral thesis, Macquarie University.

Rastle, K., and Coltheart, M. (1997a). Whammy and double whammy: Inhibitory effects in reading aloud. Paper presented to the thirty eighth annual meeting of the Psychonomic Society, Philadelphia.

Rastle, K., and Coltheart, M. (1997b). Whammies and double whammies: The effect of length on nonword reading. *Psychonomic Bulletin and Review*, 5, 277–282.

Rastle, K., and Coltheart, M. (1999). Serial and strategic effects in reading aloud. *Journal of Experimental Psychology: Human Perception and Performance, 25*, 482–503.

Rumelhart, D.E., and McClelland, J.L., and the PDP Research Group (1986). *Parallel Distributed Processing: Explorations in the Microstructure of Cognition: Volume 1. Foundations.* Cambridge, MA: MIT Press.

Sasanuma, S., Ito, H., Patterson, K.E., and Ito, K. (1996). Phonological alexia in Japanese: A case study. *Cognitive Neuropsychology*, 13, 823–848.

Schwartz, M.F., Saffran, E.M., and Marin, O.S.M. (1980). Fractionating the reading process in dementia: Evidence for word specific print to sound associations. In M. Coltheart, K.E. Patterson, and J.C. Marshall (eds.), *Deep Dyslexia*. London: Routledge and Kegan Paul.

Seidenberg, M.S. (1992a). Beyond orthographic depth in reading: Equitable division of labour. In R. Frost and L. Katz (eds.), *Orthography, Phonology, Morphology, and Meaning*. North Holland Press.

Seidenberg, M S. (1992b). Dyslexia in a computational model of word recognition in reading. In P.B. Gough, L C. Ehri, and R. Treiman (eds.), *Reading Acquisition*. Hillsdale, NJ: Lawrence Erlbaum Associates.

Seidenberg, M.S., and McClelland, J.L. (1989). A distributed, developmental model of word recognition and naming. *Psychological Review*, 96, 523–568.

Seidenberg, M.S., and McClelland, J.L. (1990). More words but still no lexicon: Reply to Besner et al. (1990). *Psychological Review*, 97, 447–452.

Seidenberg, M.S., Peterson, A.M., MacDonald, M.C. and Plaut, D.C. (1996). Pseudohomophone effects and models of word recognition. *Journal of Experimental Psychology: Learning, Memory and Cognition*, 22, 1–13.

Seidenberg, M.S., Plaut, D.C., Peterson, A.S., McClelland, J.L., and McRae, K. (1994). Nonword pronunciation and models of word recognition. *Journal of Experimental Psychology: Human Perception and Performance*, 20, 1177–1196.

Smith, M.C., Theodor, L., and Franklin, P.E. (1983). The relationship between contextual facilitation and depth of processing. *Journal of Experimental Psychology: Learning, Memory, and Cognition*, 9, 697–712.

Smith, M.C., and Besner, D. (1998). Manuscript in preparation.

Spieler, D.H., and Balota, D.A. (1997). Bring computational models of word naming down to the item level. *Psychological Science*, 8, 411–416.

Stolz, J.A., and Neely, JH. (1995). When target degradation does and does not enhance semantic context effects in word recognition. *Journal of Experimental Psychology: Learning, Memory and Cognition*, 21, 596–611.

Stolz, J.A., and Besner, D. (1996a). Semantic priming and spreading activation in the context of the interactive activation framework: A rapprochement. (unpublished manuscript).

Stolz, J.A., and Besner, D. (1996b). The role of set in visual word recognition: activation and activation blocking as non-automatic processes. *Journal of Experimental Psychology: Human Perception and Performance*, 22, 1166–1177.

Stolz, J.A., and Besner, D. (1997). Visual word recognition: Effort after meaning, but not (necessarily) meaning after effort. *Journal of Experimental Psychology: Human Perception and Performance*, 23, 1314–1322.

Stolz, J.A., and Besner, D. (1998). Levels of representation in visual word recognition: A dissociation between morphological and semantic processing. *Journal of Experimental Psychology: Human Perception and Performance, 22*, 1166–1177.

Strain, E., Patterson, K.E., and Seidenberg, M.S. (1995). Semantic effects in single word naming. *Journal of Experimental Psychology: Learning, Memory and Cognition*, 21, 1140–1154.

Tabossi, P., and Laghi, L. (1992). Semantic priming in the pronunciation of words in two writing systems: Italian and English. *Memory and Cognition*, 20, 315–328.

Taft, M., and Russell, B. (1992). Pseudohomophone naming and the word frequency effect. *Quarterly Journal of Experimental Psychology, 45A, 51–71.*

Treisman, A.M. (1960). Contextual cues in selective listening. *Quarterly Journal of Experimental Psychology*, 12, 242–248.

Turvey, M.T., Feldman, L.B., and Lukatela, G. (1984). The Serbo-Croatian orthography constrains the reader to a phonologically analytic strategy. In L. Henderson (ed.) *Orthographies and Reading: Perspectives from Cognitive Psychology, Neuropsychology, and Linguistics*. Hillsdale, NJ: Lawrence Erlbaum Associates.

Waters, G.S. and Seidenberg, M.S. (1985). Spelling-sound effects on reading: Time course and decision criteria. *Memory and Cognition, 13*, 557–572.

Weekes, B. (1997). Differential effects of letter number on word and nonword naming latency. *Quarterly Journal of Experimental Psychology, 50A,* 439–456.

Zorzi, M., Houghton, G., and Butterworth, B. (1998). Two routes or one in reading aloud? A connectionist dual process model. *Journal of Experimental Psychology: Human Perception and Performance,* 24, 1131–1161.

14

Trying to Understand Reading and Dyslexia: Mental Chronometry, Individual Differences, Cognitive Neuroscience, and the Impact of Instruction as Converging Sources of Evidence

Thomas H. Carr

In 1908, E. B. Huey wrote "And so to completely analyze what we do when we read would almost be the acme of a psychologist's achievements, for it would be to describe very many of the most intricate workings of the human mind, as well as to unravel the tangled story of the most remarkable specific performance that civilization has learned in all its history." Since Huey's proclamation, psychologists have attacked the problem of how to analyze and understand reading in many ways, from many different perspectives. This commentary begins from the perspective of cognitive psychology. First I describe my take on cognitive psychology in general. Next the various attempts at connectionist modeling of cognitive processes are discussed. After that I bring to bear other approaches represented in this volume dealing with individual differences, cognitive neuroscience, and the impact of instruction. Finally, all of these approaches are put together in a discussion of research on the "visual word-form system" which I believe to be one of the early great achievements of the multidisciplinary perspective envisioned by the editors of this volume.

Mental Chronometry and the Human "Reading Machine"

Cognitive psychologists commonly apply the experimental techniques of mental chronometry (Lachman, Lachman, and Butterfield, 1979; Luce, 1986; McClelland, 1979; Meyer, Yantis, Osman, and Irwin, 1988; Posner, 1978). When they study reading, they try to draw conclusions about the architecture and operation of the reading system—a hypothetical information processing machine residing in the mind of the reader. Evidence for their conclusions comes from the speed and accuracy of responses in specially crafted laboratory tasks such as lexical decision (see

Masson, chapter 12, and Plaut, chapter 11, both this volume) or speeded pronunciation (see Masson, Plaut, and also Besner, chapter 13). Additional evidence comes
from patterns of eye movements observed while reading text for comprehension or
memory—what words are fixated, how long each fixation lasts, and how far the eyes
move from one fixation to the next (see Rayner, chapter 10, this volume). Sometimes more global measures of reading under less constrained circumstances are used
as well—for example, total time to read a text as a function of variations in the properties of the text or the goals of the reader (as in Carlson-Radvansky, Alejano, and
Carr, 1991; Carr, Brown, and Charalambous, 1989; Jacoby, Levy, and Steinbach,
1992). In all cases, however, choices about what task to use, what experimental manipulations to make, and what measurements to take are driven by the theoretical
questions being asked about the architecture and operation of the human "reading
machine."

Conceptual Theories and Formal Models

Traditionally, the conclusions of mental chronometry have been stated verbally, as
a conceptual theory of the way the reading system is organized and the way it works.
More and more frequently these days, the conclusions are embodied in a formal
model consisting either of a set of mathematical equations that map measured properties of stimuli onto measured properties of responses, or a computer program that
takes input representing the stimuli a human reader would see in a task, simulates
what is hypothesized to happen in the mind of the reader, and produces output that
is supposed to mimic the reader's responses. The latter "simulation" approach to
modeling is followed by Plaut, Masson, and also Farah (chapter 8) in this volume.

    Systematically evaluating the success of either end product—conceptual theory
or formal model—is complicated, and it is often contentious. Good evaluation
produces a thorough, well-justified decision as to whether a particular conceptual
theory or formal model should live, get modified, or die. The best evaluation places
judgments about a particular theory or model in the context of a search for general
principles of cognition that need to be honored by all theories and models (as in
Besner, Plaut, or Masson, all in this volume; see also Jacobs and Grainger, 1994;
Stone and Van Orden, 1994; Simon and Kaplan, 1989). This is akin to what's called
the "credit assignment problem" in computer science. When a simulation succeeds
or fails, we want to know why so that we can take away larger lessons about what
kinds of approaches will or will not work in trying to understand a complex human capability like reading. Such evaluative considerations of the modeling presented in this volume are considered next.

Is the Human Reading Machine Made from Connectionist Networks?

It is not entirely clear that the world needs another commentary on the assumptions, variations, merits, and demerits of connectionism, but four of the chapters in this volume — by Plaut, Masson, Farah and Besner — make it hard to resist, especially if the focus is on trying to take away larger lessons from the evaluation of particular models. Let's take a look at these authors' strategies for applying connectionist principles and what the authors say about the successes, failures, and possible limits of this theoretical approach.

A good place to begin is Plaut's discussion of what can be learned from the successes of a parallel-distributed-processing version of connectionism as an approach to modeling speeded pronunciation. Plaut provides a very positive evaluation both of the general principles embodied in PDP connectionist models and of the specific achievements of particular PDP models that Plaut and his colleagues have applied to pronouncing printed words, to making lexical decisions, and to the semantic priming phenomena that occur when two words are processed in succession.

Plaut identifies three general principles that he believes to be the most crucial ones in defining what is unique, insightful, and productive about the PDP approach: (1) distributed representation (and its theoretically crucial corollary, that the representations of similar items are themselves similar and partially overlapping), (2) structure-sensitive learning in which correlations among events in the external world are incorporated into the representations of those events in the mental world, and (3) interactivity in which component processes of the reading system exchange information cooperatively to mutually benefit one another's computations.

According to the principle of distributed representation, linguistically relevant properties of letter strings are represented by patterns of activity across large numbers of encoding units. Each unit may be part of the representation of many different words, with the simple but theoretically generative result that similar words are represented by similar patterns of activity in which many of the same processing units are active. The implication is that previous experience at processing one word can help with processing another, similar word, because processing either word involves large parts of the representational activity involved in processing the other. From this principle Plaut derives readers' abilities to pronounce unfamiliar words and pseudowords—though the stimulus has not been seen before, it is similar in spelling and pronunciation to many other stimuli that have been seen before. When the unfamiliar stimulus is encountered, it partially activates the representations of the already-known stimuli, and these partial activations amalgamate into a representational pattern of the unfamiliar stimulus.

Plaut and also Masson use this same principle of representational similarity or overlap to account for a number of the empirical properties of semantic priming. The literature on semantic priming deals with two rather different types of relations between words that can facilitate processing, one involving similarity in meaning and the other involving association. Thus *dog* will not only prime *cat*, with which it shares elements of meaning but also *bone*, with which it is associated despite the fact that the meanings of *dog* and *bone* are not at all alike. Masson derives both types of priming from the principle of similarity or overlap of representation. Plaut, however, uses similarity of representation only to account for priming due to similarity of meaning. He derives associative priming from the second general principle of the PDP approach, structure-sensitive learning.

Structure-sensitive learning refers to the fact that in PDP networks, correlations among features that tend to occur together are learned gradually through repeated experience with words. The learning mechanism responds to and encodes statisical correlation so that stimulus properties that occur together in the world become associated and tend to elicit one another in the patterns of activity that represent those stimuli in the mind.

Plaut uses sensitivity to statistical structure to account for consistency effects in speeded pronunciation. Here the speed and accuracy of pronouncing a word that contains a particular spelling pattern is influenced by the degree to which that spelling pattern is pronounced the same way in every word in which it occurs or is pronounced differently in different words. Farah (chapter 8, this volume) relies on the same notion, but expressed anatomically as well as computationally, to account for the emergence of specialized regions of the visual system that encode letters and sequences of letters that are common in English spelling. To get across the flavor of what she believes is going on, Farah relies on Hebb's famous description of plasticity in the nervous system: "Neurons that fire together wire together." For similar ideas about the development of functional specializations in neural tissue, see Jacobs (1997).

Plaut uses sensitivity to another aspect of statistical structure, the sequential probability of encountering various stimuli, one after another in temporal succession, in his explanation of associative priming. In this respect Plaut's application of PDP principles to priming differs from that of Masson, who relies upon representational overlap exclusively to account for all priming phenomena. This difference in the origins of associative priming means that at least one of these specific models of priming is wrong, or perhaps each is incomplete and they need to be combined. If one or even both of these specific models turned out to be a failure, however, it would not necessarily cast doubt on the general approach. The difference between the specific model of priming generated by Plaut and the specific model generated by Masson could be pursued for quite a while, through competitive hypothesis generation and testing, without leaving the general universe of PDP models.

The third PDP principle is interactivity. Plaut describes this principle by saying that "mapping among orthography, phonology, and semantics is accomplished through the simultaneous interaction of many units, such that familiar patterns form stable attractors." This way of stating the principle emphasizes the coherence that characterizes the processing of familiar, well-learned stimuli—activation of one part of the pattern helps to activate other parts so that once processing of a familiar item begins, it develops a sort of momentum that speeds it on to completion.

This momentum accounts for a very interesting property of PDP models, a property called "pattern completion." If a PDP network is presented with parts of a familiar stimulus, it will tend to activate the entire representational pattern appropriate to the whole stimulus rather than stopping with a partial representation of just those parts that are perceptually available. This property is not strongly relied upon in any direct way by Plaut, but Masson uses it in accounting for semantic priming from masked words and Farah touches on it in discussing the word-recognition deficits of pure alexics. Thus the explanatory moves made in each modeling effort can be directly traced to the general principles that define the PDP class of connectionist models.

Plaut concludes his chapter with a summary assessment. Though he is careful not to attribute perfection to the PDP approach, he is quite happy with its successes.

> This is not to say that the models are fully adequate and account for all of the relevant data in sufficient detail—this is certainly not the case. In fact, given that they are models, they are abstractions from the actual processing system and are certainly wrong in their details. Nonetheless, their relative success at reproducing key patterns of data in the domain of word reading, and the fact that the very same computational principles are being applied successfully across a wide range of linguistic and cognitive domains, suggests that these models capture important aspects of the representation and processing in the human language and cognitive system.(Plaut, chapter 11, page 362, this volume)

Masson offers a counterpoint. Consider Masson's discussion of the strengths, weaknesses, successes, and failures of his PDP attempt to model semantic memory, semantic priming, and the effects of orthographic neighborhood organization that occur in lexical decision and speeded pronunciation. In contrast to Plaut's primarily positive report, Masson gives a frank assessment of changes that need to be made in almost every major characteristic of his modeling. The limitations he identifies are instructive.

First, the storage capacity of Masson's model is woefully small compared to the vocabulary of a human being. To move beyond the status of a "toy" model and scale up to the status of a legitimate hypothesis about human capabilities, the model would need to be able to learn and to retrieve a much larger vocabulary.

Unfortunately, the second area of difficulty is that the representational format used in the model is inadequate to support larger vocabularies. Masson discusses the possibility that the format is too distributed, allowing representations to share so many features that similar words can no longer be efficiently discriminated from one another as vocabulary size increases. Masson notes that this problem could be reduced by making representations sparser so that each feature participates in fewer different word representations. Ironically, then, one possible fix of Masson's PDP approach to semantic memory is to reduce or eliminate the "D" in PDP, moving toward localist rather than distributed representations. Such a move would play poorly with Plaut. Plaut's representational format, however, is rather different from Masson's. Plaut's representations of orthography and phonology are crafted specifically to the orthographic and phonological properties observed in English spelling and pronunciation. Masson does not try to do anything remotely like this in his treatment of meaning. He assumes a large pool of abstract and arbitrary features that are not assigned specific referents. In Masson's semantic memory, the meaning of each word is represented by a random string of binary features constrained only by the assumption that the feature vectors of related words are correlated whereas the feature vectors of unrelated words are uncorrelated. Thus there is no semantic content at all to these representations. As Masson puts it, "No assumptions have been made regarding correspondence of particular processing units or subsets of units to specific letters, letter positions, phonemes, or semantic features."

This simple approach supplies a surprising amount of power in accounting for the speed and accuracy of processing the second of a pair of related or unrelated words, and admittedly it sidesteps a morass of problems that have plagued semantic analysis in linguistics and philosophy. Still, this approach can never be sufficient if one is interested in the more traditional semanticist's goal of identifying the content of human semantic processing—the representational calculus in which meaning is captured and manipulated in the mind. For this reason, I find the arbitrary nature of the representational format rather unsatisfying. At one level this criticism is completely discountable. There is no reason why Masson should share my prejudices about what counts as a satisfying approach to modeling semantics. At another level, however, the criticism may be more telling. Plaut succeeds in large part because he does try to identify effective referential instantiations of features in the representational domains he is trying to model. Masson may need to do this, too, and it may be that the need for concrete representational assumptions is a larger lesson we can take away from our exercise examining these connectionist models. A basic tenet of connectionism is that the mind is empiricist—it learns what is in the particular world with which it is interacting. Connectionist models need to do the same.

The third area of difficulty for Masson is that his model's learning algorithm, which is a form of unsupervised Hebbian learning, is too simple and would need to be changed to some form of error-correction-based learning to support larger vocabularies. Computationally, this move is very straightforward. Making it, however, would mean that the standard problems of ecological validity that arise with error-correction algorithms would need to be faced. If learning requires a "teacher" to tell the system when it has failed, a source of such teaching must be identified in either the environmental experience or the internal processing activity of the learner before one can be confident that the algorithm is a reasonable hypothesis about how humans learn. Whether this ecological requirement could be met in the domain of learning in semantic memory remains to be seen.

This kind of ecological validity is not just Masson's problem. It becomes relevant any time someone touts the ability to learn as a primary theoretical virtue of his or her model and uses error-correction-based learning algorithms to get the job done. In light of this, one might want to inspect the learning algorithms used by other investigators in this volume, with an eye to determining whether they are well-suited to the kinds of learning opportunities actually available to people learning to read. Such inspection reveals that Farah is explicit about using unsupervised Hebbian learning as a means of mastering of the co-occurrences among letters that define orthographic structure. Plaut's chapter, however, is never very clear about how his networks learn. He often refers, however, to what they achieve "after training." This terminology suggests an error-correction algorithm, which means that Plaut needs to meet the same challenge as Masson. If one proposes that networks are trained or taught rather than learning on their own, one must explicitly identify the teacher.

Returning to Masson's modeling of semantic memory, there is more to say about his learning algorithm. Besides supporting too small a vocabulary, the Hebbian learning rule as currently employed just plain works too fast to be a reasonable model of human learning in semantic memory. As Masson says, "Using a simple learning rule enables the model to master a set of words in a very short time (in a single learning trial, rather than thousands of trials)." A simple and fast-acting learning algorithm is highly beneficial for the practical purposes of getting simulation work done in the laboratory. But as shown by Dagenbach, Horst, and Carr (1990; see also Tulving, Hayman, and MacDonald, 1991), learning in semantic memory proceeds much more slowly than this, taking closer to the thousands of trials Masson wants to avoid before new vocabulary items are mastered sufficiently well to produce priming effects at short prime-target SOA's and without conscious attempts by the reader to predict the target from the prime. It may be that the representational and learning assumptions made by Masson are appropriate to episodic priming effects that occur when readers have time to retrieve newly encountered or weakly learned word meanings into working memory, but they do not seem appropriate to priming that arises more automatically within semantic memory itself. For an interesting and provocative discussion of this and related issues, see McClelland, McNaughton, and O'Reilly's (1995) "Why there are complementary learning systems in the hippocampus and neocortex: Insights from the successes and failures of connectionist models of learning and memory."

Finally, Masson points out the difficulties with task analysis—with identifying algorithmic strategies that enable the model to compute task-relevant decisions and determining whether the model's way of carrying out a task corresponds to the human way. This is a very big issue in cognitive psychology. It is faced by everyone, not just by modelers who take the PDP approach. But solving it is a necessary ingredient of successful theory building—indeed, given the topic matter of cognitive psychology, solving it is the definition of successful theory building. For Masson, the big difficulty was figuring out how to get his model to make lexical decisions. He tried two different algorithmic strategies, one based on the "harmony" of the network, which is the extent to which the activity pattern on the semantic output units matches what would be expected simply on the basis of the learned connection weights between those output units and the various input units connected to them. That is, for a given pair of units a positive connection between them suggests they should be in the same state, whereas a negative connection says they should not. Harmony is high when the stimulus presented to the model is a familiar word that it has learned. Harmony is lower when the stimulus is an unfamiliar word or pseudoword that has not been learned. Hence harmony provides a variable that the model can use in a signal-detection-like fashion to decide whether a stimulus it is processing is or is not a word it knows. Harmony worked well for Masson in simulating a number of lexical decision results but failed in simulating others. Success in simulating these others was achieved when Masson switched to another algorithm, one that calculated how closely the pattern of activity across the output units corresponded to each of the ideal patterns that would be expected for the various words that the model had been taught.

Is there anything general we can extract from this need to give up on harmony and switch to an algorithm based on the identities of the particular words known to the model? Like the possibility of making representations sparser to reduce the confusability among representations of similar words, this proposal is a move toward reducing the "D" in PDP, a move toward building more explicitly localized lexical knowledge into the model. To determine whether any given pattern of activity across the output units matches a pattern that represents a word the system has been taught, the system must know what patterns correspond to what words—that is, it must have some sort of word-by-word listing of the patterns it has learned. Functionally, this listing constitutes a localized lexical representation analogous to the word nodes found in activation models of word recognition like Morton (1969) or McClelland and Rumelhart (1981) and in spreading activation models of semantic memory like Collins and Loftus (1975) or Anderson (1983). Thus questions about the extent to which representations can be distributed appear to be building.

Let's turn for a moment to Plaut's attempt to model lexical decision. Plaut also considered harmony as a possible basis for this judgment, but he rejected it in favor of a different algorithmic strategy based on a different property of network operation that we've not yet encountered, called "stress." Stress is the extent to which the output units of the network differ from their resting states and hence represents a measure of the information content of the activated network. Like harmony, stress will be high when the network is processing a known word that it has learned, and it will be lower when it is processing an unknown word or pseudoword. Plaut was able to achieve considerable success modeling lexical decision as a judgment based on stress.

At this point we can draw what I hope will prove to be a very informative contrast between the approaches taken by Masson and Plaut. They both expressed considerable concern about choosing from among the algorithmic strategies that were possible within their models the one that performed the best computationally—that could be made to account for the largest amount of variance in the observed data. Masson and Plaut differed, however, in the extent of their concern about whether the algorithm that performed the best was also the most appropriate or valid as a model of human lexical decision making. Plaut raised this concern only in passing, choosing stress over harmony on the basis of an intuitive appeal to neurobiological plausibility. It appeared more likely to Plaut that decision processes might be able to gain access to information about the states of the output units than to information about the weights on connections buried inside the network. Masson discussed concerns about appropriateness and validity at greater length, raising the possibility that people might make decisions in multiple ways and that models might need to take into account the conditions that lead people to implement one strategy or another.

Masson's discussion of strategic variability and the difficulties it introduces appears to be very well placed. Between Masson and Plaut, we have three different variables that might be the basis for a lexical decision: harmony, stress, and lexical activation. The first two—harmony and stress—are global properties of the entire PDP network, whereas the third—lexical activation—is a local property of each particular stimulus representation that the network has learned, and as we've already seen, using the third one constitutes a move away from fully PDP toward more localist representation.

How do these three variables map onto existing theories of lexical decision? Computing harmony and computing stress might be regarded as different ways of instantiating within a PDP architecture one of the three processes recently proposed by Grainger and Jacobs (1996) in their "multiple read-out model" of how the lexical decision task is done by people. This is the "summed activity" process which is to monitor the amount of activity in lexical memory as a whole, summed across all representational units, and respond "yes" if activity is high. Computing lexical activation, as was done by Masson, is a way of instantiating another of Grainger and Jacobs' three processes—the "unit activity" process—which is to respond "yes" if the amount of activity in any individual lexical unit or word node exceeds a criterion. Grainger and Jacobs' third process is not used by either of these PDP modelers, though it has a venerable history in the cognitive literature (see Coltheart, Davelaar, Jonasson, and Besner, 1977). The third process is to respond "no" by default if time since stimulus onset exceeds a deadline criterion without a "yes" response having been delivered by either the summed activity process or the unit activity process. Grainger and Jacobs amass a substantial amount of evidence that all three of these processes are required to model lexical decision performance, and that how much each process is relied upon relative to the others varies with stimulus properties, instructions, and other task conditions. The unavoidable conclusion is that if Grainger and Jacobs are right, then neither of the PDP approaches to lexical decision presented in this volume is correct. And to the extent that the "D" is a defining part of PDP, it may be that no PDP approach can account for human performance in this task without compromising (to some as yet unknown degree) on the principle of distributed representation. Thus we are finally led to the edge of the PDP universe and invited to step outside.

Nevertheless, despite Masson's extended discussion of weaknesses, failures, and required modifications, which I've amplified a bit by bringing in related considerations from the rest of the literature, Masson expresses no doubts of a more ultimate kind. Specific implementations may prove inadequate, but Masson's commitment to the PDP approach is unwavering.

Perhaps this commitment will be shaken a bit by Besner's chapter, which is the next step in our exercise in evaluating connectionist models. Besner is approximately as critical of major features of the PDP approach to modeling pronunciation as Plaut is complimentary. In particular, Besner attacks the same PDP principle that was just called into question with respect to lexical decision—that localist representation is not needed—and he quarrels with the basic "triangle" architecture assumed in most PDP modeling, in which there is one orthographic network, one phonological network, and one semantic network, each of which communicates with the others through at most a single set of connections (see Plaut's figure 11.1 and Masson's figure 12.1 for two variations on this architectural theme).

Besner summarizes his arguments about speeded pronunciation as follows

> This chapter has briefly touched on acquired dyslexia in several forms, lexical anomia, and a variety of manipulations on intact readers in an attempt to determine whether a two- or a three-route model best describes the data, and in an attempt to determine whether a model with localist or distributed representations best describes the data. The ability of several implemented PDP models and one implemented localist model to predict human naming performance at an individual item level was also assessed. These different lines of investigation converge on the same conclusion. At this point in their respective development, a three-route model in which the lexical and assembled routines consist of localist representations offers a better account of human reading performance at the single-word level and at an individual item level than any of the single- or dual-route PDP models developed by Plaut, Seidenberg, McClelland, and Patterson. (Besner, chapter 13, p. 446)

What are we to make of all this? We have three analysts—Plaut, Masson, and Besner—each seeking to take away larger lessons from the successes and failures of the PDP approach to building formal models of word recognition. One is very enthusiastic in all respects, one is cautious about achievements to date but committed to the approach, and one is highly critical. This exercise demonstrates the complexity—and the potential for disagreement—involved in building and evaluating formal models. Each of the three chapters musters empirical evidence and constructs tightly reasoned arguments. Still, the three chapters reach very different conclusions about how well a popular approach to formal modeling is doing as a tool for trying to understand reading.

This situation might be disconcerting to people from other disciplines who are looking for quick insights that can be easily extracted from the research of cognitive psychologists and imported into their own work on reading. It is tempting to decide that if these cognitive psychologists can't agree any better than what we've seen, perhaps their discipline doesn't have much to offer.

Such a reaction would be short-sighted (or so I hope!). Mental chronometry has been extremely successful in uncovering regularities of human performance, and PDP simulations have been quite powerful in generating hypothetical explanations of these regularities. But neither is a magic bullet and much work remains to be done. As the preceding discussion illustrates, some of this work involves settling questions that are currently under debate at the cutting edge of the field.

Expanding the Bounds of Cognitive Analysis

Other work that remains to be done is highlighted by other chapters in this volume. This work involves finding ways of taking into account factors that practitioners of mental chronometry and simulation modeling have tended largely to ignore. The first of these factors is the existence of individual differences.

Individual Differences

Mental chronometry is a behavioral-computational approach in which the primary data are (1) descriptions of task demands, (2) descriptions of stimuli, and (3) measurements of observable responses intended to satisfy the task demands given the stimuli. Note that something obvious is missing—descriptions of the readers themselves, who are often taken rather for granted or treated as interchangeable replications of one another. Exceptions are easy to find, but the large majority of cognitive psychologists have gravitated toward studying mature reading competence as expressed in the average performance of groups of normal young adults treated as representative samples of generic human beings. Most cognitive psychologists have avoided extended forays into individual differences and developmental change (Ashcraft, 1994; Gardner, 1985; Lachman, Lachman, and Butterfield, 1979; Reisberg, 1997).

Once thinking turns to such issues, attention is readily captured by dramatic examples—a brain-injured adult who speaks, listens, and writes but is unable to read except by naming the letters of each word out loud and painfully putting them together into some semblance of a pronunciation (see Behrmann, chapter 6, this volume, and Farah, chapter 8, this volume); another brain-injured adult who looks at the word *chicken* and reads it as *turkey* or *egg* (see Buchanan, Hildebrandt, and MacKinnon, chapter 7, this volume); an active and loquacious fourth- or fifth-grader who is spatially and mathematically talented but reads like a first-grader (see Lovett, chapter 4, this volume).

These dramatic examples are highly visible but subtler variation can also be found. Even when academic accomplishments are similar, substantial differences in reading speed exist among normal college students (Carr, 1986; Graesser, Hoffman, and Clark, 1980; Jackson and McClelland, 1979; Rayner, chapter 1, this volume). Some of this variation is accounted for by higher level conceptual and linguistic knowledge, but much of it derives from more basic components of the cognitive apparatus such as the speed of word recognition operations (Cunningham, Stanovich, and Wilson, 1990) or the capacity of working memory (Daneman and Carpenter, 1980; Daneman and Tardif, 1987). These are the kinds of cognitive components that mental chronometry tries to isolate and characterize. Measures of skill at basic component processes, often taken directly from the cognitive psychologist's laboratory, can be combined into a battery of measures that can be used to predict overall reading speed and accuracy. The goal of such "component skills analysis" is to determine which components of the reading system exert the most impact on individual differences in system performance and which components change their impact with reading development (Carr and Levy, 1990).

There are no examples of component skills analysis in this book. I regret the omission but it is a direction in which more research might profitably go. Good work on individual differences is not easy to do (for a cautionary tale of woe revolving around a search for individual differences in the architecture of phonological recoding, see three papers: Pexman and Lupker, 1998, Paap and Herdman, 1998, and Bernstein, DeShon, and Carr, 1998). The potential rewards of the work, however, and its sheer generative interest value are great, as I hope to illustrate later in this chapter using as an example an fMRI-based investigation of phonological recoding by Pugh et al. (1997). Discovering systematic relationships among the characteristics of individual readers and the cognitive processes identified by mental chronometry enriches our understanding of the reading system and enlarges the enterprise of cognitive psychology.

Cognitive Neuroscience

The structure, function, health, and integrity of the nervous system have become topics of skyrocketing interest during the last decade or so. A few years ago, I suggested in a paper on automaticity and word recognition (Carr, 1992) that a 30-year-long era of cognitive research I called the "age of cognition", with its focus on abstract computational theories and models based on behavioral data from mental chronometry, would soon give way to an "age of cognitive neuroscience" in which computational theories and models would be mapped onto the anatomical and physiological constructs of neural theories and models. I was behind the times. By 1992, cognitive neuroscience had already made great inroads into the study of reading and has continued to grow in impact.

Modern cognitive neuroscience includes work on task performance by people who have suffered brain damage (represented in this volume by Farah, Behrmann, and Buchanan et al.). The recent exponential growth of cognitive neuroscience, however, is not much because of increased interest in damaged brains. It owes instead to advances in measuring the structure and function of normal brains.

Some of these advances involve the use of PET to measure changes in blood flow across the brain and the use of fMRI to measure changes in blood oxygenation. These measures are used as indicators of where in the brain neuronal activity increases or decreases during one task performance compared to another (for reviews, see Demb, Poldrack, and Gabrieli, chapter 9, this volume, as well as Cabeza and Nyberg, 1997; Carr and Posner, 1995; Frackowiak et al., 1997; Posner and Raichle, 1994; Posner and Carr, 1992).

Other advances lie in more sophisticated applications of electroencephalography and magnetoencephalograpy to measure moment-by-moment changes in the electromagnetic fields generated by the brain. Processes of stimulus encoding, decision making, response planning, and response execution involved in task performance cause small alterations in the time-varying electromagnetic fields that are continuously generated by the ongoing metabolic activity of the brain. The timing of these "event-related potentials" (ERP's) is used as an indicator of when in the time-course of the brain's neuronal activity a particular stimulus property is processed or task-related decision is made (see Posner and McCandliss, chapter 10, this volume). Combining the blood-flow-based methods of PET and fMRI with these electromagnetically based ERP methods allows the neural loci of particular component operations to be determined with more confidence than is warranted by either method alone, and the relative timing of operations jointly identified by the combination of methods can then be extracted from the electrical or magnetic ERP measures (besides Posner and McCandliss, see also Mangun, Hopfinger, Kussmaul, Fletcher, and Heinze, 1997, or Hillyard, Hinrichs, Tempelmann, Morgan, Hansen, Scheich, and Heinze, 1997, for excellent examples of this approach).

Cognitive neuroscience provides techniques for localizing the brain's information processing activities in both space and time—which brain structure or structures are involved in computing different kinds of linguistic information and when they do it. When I was in graduate school, students of cognition largely ignored the brain basis of cognitive activities. Now they heed the brain and the result is a further enrichment of their enterprise. The mutual maturation of cognitive psychology and human neuroscience, making possible the emergence of the "age of cognitive neuroscience," is far and away the single most exciting development to take place during my career as a psychologist.

Biological Preparation and Cultural Engineering

A striking feature of reading is that it is a culturally engineered form of language rather than a biologically prepared one. The input modality for written language is visual rather than auditory as with speech, and while written language can be read out loud, its output modality for initial production is manual rather than articulatory. Learning to read commonly requires explicit instruction and supervised practice of a type that is rarely observed in the acquisition of spoken language. Modern societies invest massive resources in school instruction, much of which is directly aimed at reading. Even so, reading is not nearly so certain to be acquired as is spoken language. Many children who are good speakers and listeners turn out to be much less competent readers. These vagaries of learning are a defining feature of reading as an artifact of cultural engineering rather than a product of biology. By providing language users with technological prosthetics—stylus and clay tablet, pen and paper, typewriter, computer keyboard, plus a symbol system for using these prosthetics as encoding devices—new frontiers of linguistic function have been opened up and the communicative powers of language have been greatly extended. These benefits, however, have not come for free. They have been achieved at a cost to ease and universality of acquisition, to the "naturalness" with which the brain masters the task (Liberman, 1995; Pinker, 1994). Reading attempts to interface the phonological, semantic, syntactic, and pragmatic core components of the naturally occuring linguistic system to new sensory and motor systems whose biological specializations are for quite different functions. Establishing the interface is not easy (Carr and Posner, 1995; Liberman, 1995; Rozin, 1976; Rozin and Gleitman, 1977). A substantial amount of evidence suggests that the success of this developmental process, especially in an alphabetic writing system, depends crucially on the reader's mastery of the writing system's "orthographic structure"—not just the individual letters, but the sequential dependencies among them and how the sequential dependencies that exist in spelling reflect the sequential dependencies that exist in phonology (see, e.g., Bowey and Hansen, 1994; Haynes and Carr, 1990; Manis,

Szeszulski, Holt, and Graves, 1990; Rieben and Perfetti, 1991; Wimmer and Goswami, 1994). Some spelling patterns are quite common, some are more rare, and some sequences of letters never occur at all. In an alphabetic writing system, the sequential dependencies among spelling patterns in writing follow the sequential dependencies among sound patterns in pronunciation. As discussed by Goswami (chapter 2, this volume; see also Treiman, Mullennix, Bijeljac-Babic, and Richmond-Welty, 1995; Zorzi, Houghton, and Butterworth, 1997), there are different ways in which these two sets of sequential dependencies can be parsed and mapped back and forth between one another. Ultimately, the efficiency of the reading system varies with the nature of the mapping rules that are instantiated in the vision-language interface. It has become quite clear that to a first approximation, the best vision-language interface is one that uses phonological structure as a guide in determining how to encode orthographic structure.

The interface problem makes reading very interesting theoretically, which is one of the prime reasons that the cognitive neuroscience of reading is such an active area of investigation. Because the interface problem increases the difficulty of learning and the variability of acquisition, it also makes the impact of instruction an extraordinarily telling measure of how the reading system operates.

The Impact of Instruction

Suppose that some forms of instruction are found to work in teaching reading but others do not, or that one form of instructions works better with one type of reader but another form works better with some other type of reader. If so, then a careful analysis of the differences between forms of instruction and their impact on reading performance will throw bright light on the configuration and operating characteristics of the underlying information-processing system. Investigations that measure instructional impact contribute greatly to understanding reading, and they do so in ways that can not be achieved within the standard confines of mental chronometry or cognitive neuroscience. The power of using the impact of instruction as a window onto the reading system is clearly demonstrated in the chapters in this volume by Levy and by Lovett.

The focus in these studies is on word recognition and, in particular, on whether orthography should be mapped onto phonology word-by-word, onset and rime by onset and rime, or phoneme by phoneme. One might also ask whether any kind of focus on words and their internal organization is important. Perhaps reading instruction should emphasize sentence and text-level processes that take place well beyond the vision-language interface instead of processes that span the interface itself. This question, which forms the basis for an ongoing and often heated debate between proponents of whole-language and phonics-based reading instruction, is extremely controversial in educational circles. For one possible empirical approach to the question, see Evans and Carr (1985), who took advantage of a natural experiment in first- and second-grade curriculum development conducted by a large Canadian school system. Their investigation combined classroom observation with both standardized and laboratory-like testing to compare an extreme version of whole-language reading instruction with a heavily word-oriented curriculum supplementing phonics training with supervised practice at inferring the possible meaning of a new word from context. Reading development was assessed in a variety of ways, and by all measures the word-oriented curriculum won. Perhaps the most striking result involved formal measures of spoken language skill such as mean length of utterance and syntactic complexity. In the word-oriented classrooms, these measures were positively related to reading development, as just about any theory of cognitive and psycholinguistic skill acquisition would predict. In the whole-language classrooms, these same measures correlated negatively with reading development. Evans and Carr drew the rather straightforward conclusion that if early reading instruction does not focus on establishing an effective vision-language interface founded on analytic word recognition, then very strange things can happen.

A difficulty with instructional studies is that the choice of particular skills or subskills to be taught and particular techniques to use in teaching them is often catch-as-catch-can, resulting in inefficient research and slow progress toward understanding. How might one go about picking high-likelihood targets of training and high-probability-of-success techniques of teaching to be examined in studies of instructional impact? Here help might come from another branch of neuroscience called "behavioral genetics." Knowledge of the extent to which various components of the reading system are defined by the reader's biology or can be sculpted by environmental experience, and what kinds of interactions occur between genotypic raw materials and instructional environment, allow advance predictions to be made about which forms of instruction are likely to work on which component skills and why. This information is obviously important educationally, and it also expands our theoretical understanding of reading. The best work of this type is currently being done by Olson and his colleagues; an account appears here in chapter 5.

Crafting Better Scientific Stories and Making Better Instructional Recommendations

So far, I have defined several sources of evidence on reading that are represented in this volume and suggested that they can be combined and interrelated to craft better stories about how reading works and to make better recommendations about how reading should be taught than would be supported by any one of them taken by itself. The sources are mental chronometry, individual differences, cognitive neuroscience, and the impact of instruction. The rest of this chapter attempts to illustrate the benefits to scientific story-telling of having all of these sources of evidence available at once, relying on the work in this volume for inspiration.

A number of different themes could serve as vehicles to illustrate the value of having multiple sources of converging evidence, while at the same time showing off the high-quality work the authors have produced here. Possibilities include the necessary ingredients for a good reading curriculum, the properties of skilled reading by normal readers, the cognitive processes involved in pronouncing written words, and the nature of the "vision-language interface". Of these themes, I have chosen the last one to explore, mainly because it is a theme I have thought about before, not because it is in any way more important, more interesting, or more integrative than the others. A few historical comments are given on the business of trying to attribute mental computations to localized neural structures, then the discussion turns to recent research that has pursued the concept of the "visual word-form system" (VWFS). The story to be told is that a critical step in learning to read involves mastering the perceptual properties of written language so that the visual system can talk effectively to the language system. The product of this learning is a new set of computational structures in the prestriate visual cortex that did not exist prior to reading.

Old-Time Phrenology, Pioneering Neurology, and Their Modern Reincarnation

As currently practiced, the functional neuroimaging methodologies of PET and fMRI constitute techniques for generating and testing hypotheses that can be phrased as questions about localization of function. In this respect, they follow in a long line of scientific footsteps that can be traced back to pioneers of neurology and even to the much maligned but also much misunderstood "phrenologists" of the first half of the 19th century. As a group, the phrenologists—among them famous names in the early history of neurology like Gall, Spurzheim, Broca, and Wernicke— pursued three hypotheses about brain structure and function. The first was that different functions—what cognitive psychologists now call mental operations or component skills—might be carried out relatively independently of one another. Strong versions of this functional or computational hypothesis are now advanced under the banner of "modularity."

The second hypothesis was that each mental operation might have its own relatively independent neural substrate—that modularity of brain underlies modularity of mind. Strong versions of this structural or anatomical hypothesis require strict localization, with a one-to-one mapping between mental operations and brain structures, while weaker versions deal in the possibility that different mental operations might be implemented by distributed (and perhaps partially overlapping) networks of structures rather than by single structures each completely dedicated to a single operation.

The first two phrenological hypotheses sound quite current and in fact they are. The third hypothesis is unfortunately the one for which phrenology is now remembered, and it was the movement's undoing—or at least, it was the reason why respectable 19th-century brain scientists ultimately wanted to be called neurologists instead. This was the "doctrine of the skull," a proposal that individual differences in brain function might arise from variation in the relative size of different brain structures, and that the relative size of different brain structures might be divined from the details of the external shape of the skull. A comparatively large region of brain tissue might push the skull out a bit compared to other people whereas a comparatively small region might leave the skull relatively depressed. Unlike the first two hypotheses, the doctrine of the skull proved to be quite wrong and was quickly discredited. Details of the skull's surface are not determined in any direct way by details of the brain underneath.

Ordinarily this would simply have been a scienfitic hypothesis proven wrong, but the doctrine of the skull had been picked up by vaudeville personologists—high-visibility quacks who charged money to feel people's heads and make pronouncements about their strengths and weaknesses. Discrediting the doctrine of the skull ended this part of vaudeville, and in the process, through a kind of guilt by association, it also discredited the scientific enterprise of phrenology. This does not diminish, however, the scientific legacy of the first two hypotheses—modularity and localization of function—which have thrived to the present day in neurology, neuropsychology, and cognitive neuroscience.

The "Visual Word-Form System": Modern Phrenology at Work

A case study in modern phrenology can be found in the attempt that cognitive psychologists and neuroscientists have made during the last two decades to verify the existence of the so-called "Visual Word-Form System" (VWFS), a term coined by Warrington and Shallice (1980). The VWFS is a hypothetical entity whose computational function is to take information about visual features as input and produce as output a representation of the orthography or spelling of a letter string that might be a word. This orthographic representation (or "visual word-form") is shipped to phonological and semantic processors that compute a pronunciation and a meaning appropriate to the spelling.

At the time of Warrington and Shallice's work, a substantial amount of chronometric evidence from tasks requiring either same-different matching of two letter strings or search for a prespecified target letter in a single letter string converged on the conclusion that the visual system "knows" the orthographic structure of the written language—those sequences of letters that commonly occur in the spelling of printed words. Performance in these tasks is faster and more accurate when the stimuli are words or pseudowords than when the stimuli are random letter strings that do not follow the spelling patterns of the language. The conclusion drawn from this chronometric evidence was that the visual system uses its knowledge of the likelihood of seeing various letter sequences to speed the construction of spelling-based representations of words and pseudowords (for reviews, see Carr, Pollatsek, and Posner, 1981, Carr and Pollatsek, 1985, and Henderson, 1982).

Of course, the purpose of being able to use orthographic knowledge to facilitate the representation of well-structured letter strings is not so that people can carry out laboratory tasks for cognitive psychologists. Well-structured letter strings possess the right visual organization to be words and hence deserve to be rapidly inspected by higher level phonological and semantic encoding operations. According to hypothesis, the visual system has learned to process these "word candidates" very efficiently as a contribution to the overall efficiency of the reading system.

Warrington and Shallice went beyond the chronometric evidence on which this computational argument was based, using neuropsychological evidence concerning the location of brain damage resulting in pure alexia to conclude that the mental function of orthographic encoding has a localized neural substrate in the posterior cortex. Warrington and Shallice's hypothesis about localization of function was taken a step further by Petersen, Fox, Posner, Mintun, and Raichle (1989). Using PET, Petersen and colleagues found that blood flow in a region of the left-medial prestriate occipital cortex increased relative to a baseline fixation condition in a variety of tasks that required judgments about visually presented words, but not in tasks that required similar judgments about auditorily presented words. They proposed that the specific region of occipital tissue showing these increases was the neural substrate of the VWFS.

A critical experiment testing this proposition was conducted by Petersen, Fox, Snyder, and Raichle (1990) who also used PET. Compared to a fixation baseline, they found that looking at words and looking at pseudowords both activated the left-medial prestriate occipital cortex but looking at random letter strings and looking at strings of unfamilar but letter-like shapes did not. Similar results were reported by Price, Wise, Watson, Patterson, Howard, and Frackowiak (1994), and additional findings consistent with the proposition were reported by other investigators using other tasks that involved judgments about spelling (for a review, see Demb, Poldrack and Gabrieli's chapter 9 in this volume). Here, then, was direct evidence from changes in blood-flow-based metabolism that a localized region of the brain's visual system responds to well-structured letter strings in just the manner proposed by the theory of the VWFS.

What additional evidence might one bring to bear? If the VWFS occupies the place it is supposed to occupy in the architecture of the reading system, then it ought to be activated relatively quickly in the time-course of word recognition, and this early activation ought to occur in a wide range of word processing tasks—orthographic encoding starts the ball rolling, so to speak, and hence should be found early and often. ERP evidence supporting early activation of the left-posterior cortex that distinguished words and pseudowords from random letter strings was reported by Ziegler, Besson, Jacobs, Nazir, and Carr (1997). In two quite different word-processing tasks, left-inferior posterior ERPs to words and pseudowords diverged from ERPs to random letter strings within 200 ms after stimulus onset. One of these tasks required letter search as in the original chronometric experiments on orthographic encoding. The other task required category-membership decisions that were semantic rather than orthographic.

What about the interface problem that I described earlier? One might imagine that a region of brain tissue with the functional capabilities and the anatomical location of the VWFS might be a critical component—perhaps the critical component—of the interface between the visual system and the core components of the preexisting language apparatus. If so, then establishing the VWFS would be necessary for proper and efficient functioning of the reading system and might be a rate-limiting factor in reading development. Carr and Posner (1995) developed this idea into a proposal they called the "primary gateway hypothesis," backing it up with an argument showing that the same kinds of word and pseudoword advantages over random letter strings seen in the neuroimaging studies of the adult visual system developed behaviorally in children performing same-different matching and letter search tasks during the first three or four years of reading instruction.

Carr and Posner's circumstantial chronometric argument for the development of something like the VWFS has been supported by neural evidence gathered in training studies with adults learning artificial writing systems. As described by Posner and McCandliss (chapter 10, this volume), McCandliss, Posner, and Givón (1997) obtained ERP results showing that after a small amount of training, words written in the symbols of the artificial writing system partially activate the appropriate region of the left-posterior cortex rather early in processing, approximately 200 ms or so after stimulus onset. This effect remained much the same, however, in the face of 50 more hours of practice with the artificial writing system. In contrast to this early posterior effect, a later ERP component, peaking at 300 ms rather than 200 ms and distributed broadly rather than confined to left posterior regions, changed dramatically over the 50 hours of practice. Early on this component distinguished already-known English words from both random strings of English letters and words written in the artificial writing system. Later in practice this component was approximately the same for the artificial words as for English words. At first glance these results are hard to reconcile with Carr and Posner's ideas. But if one distinguishes between a slowly consolidating orthographic system represented by the early ERP component and a somewhat faster changing system sensitive to lexical familiarity represented by the somewhat later ERP component, one can find confirmatory evidence in the rest of the work reported by Posner and McCandliss (this volume).

In addition to the training studies with adults, Posner and McCandliss examined ERP responses in children who were being taught to read in school. The stimuli included familiar words that had been practiced in school instruction, unfamiliar words that were unknown to the children and had not been encountered in school instruction, and random letter strings. The unfamiliar words served the same role in this study as was served by pseudowords in Petersen et al.'s (1990) PET study— as a test of whether processing activity was orthographic or lexical. Patterns of activity in which unfamiliar words behaved like familiar words and both were different from random letter strings were taken to indicate generalizable orthographic processing that can be applied to any well-structured letter string, regardless of familiarity. Patterns of activity in which only familiar words were different while unfamiliar words looked like random letter strings was taken to indicate lexical processing specific to particular words that have been practiced.

Results from 7-year-olds showed that although the familiar words could be successfully read aloud, electrical activity measured over the left-inferior posterior cortex in the vicinity of the supposed VWFS did not distinguish any of the three types of stimuli from one another. Among 10-year-olds, ERP's over the left-inferior posterior cortex discriminated familar words from random letter strings, but there was no difference between random letter strings and unfamiliar words.

Thus even by ten years of age, after four or five years of reading instruction, the full adult pattern of electrical activity indicative of rapid and efficient—perhaps automatic—orthographic encoding had not yet appeared. Posner and McCandliss's results suggest that establishing of the VWFS proceeds slowly over the first few years of reading instruction, with the system first relying on stored knowledge about specific words that have been experienced perceptually and gradually developing the ability to respond to unfamiliar stimuli with similar orthographic structure. This pattern mimics the progression shown in the chronometric data, where advantages in speed and accuracy of task performance appear earlier for familiar words than for unfamiliar words and pseudowords. Therefore the conclusion to be drawn from the ERP data is generally consistent with the developmental arguments of Carr and Posner (1995), and also with related arguments about developmental progression from larger to smaller units of orthographic and phonological analysis made by Goswami (chapter 2, this volume). It is noteworthy, however, that the electrical evidence derived from coherent brain activity detectable by scalp electrodes suggest a somewhat slower developmental course to VWFS establishment than the chronometric data. It may be that consolidation of neural structures that support performance lags behind the first appearance in performance of the effects of the structures being established.

Just how specialized are these structures? Calling the left-medial extrastriate region the "visual word form system" implies dedication to reading. Studies comparing word recognition and object recognition, however, have observed activation from pictures of objects in much the same vicinity as activation from words (e.g., Bookheimer et al., 1995; Menard et al., 1996; Vandenberghe et al., 1996; see Frackowiak, et al., 1997, for a succinct review). It remains to be seen whether a single neural network provides a "visual front end" for both types of stimuli, as these results might be taken to suggest, or whether a network specialized for words and a network specialized for objects are intertwined or lie too close together in the prestriate cortex to be separated given the resolution of current neuroimaging methods. Whatever the architecture of the visual encoding of words and objects, it must be consistent with the well-established pattern in which traumatic brain damage can debilitate reading without doing much harm to object recognition and vice versa (see McCarthy and Warrington, 1990). Combining this evidence for separable networks with the neuroimaging evidence that words and pictures activate proximal regions of prestriate cortex rather severely constrains the architectures that can be considered. Computational and neuropsychological arguments for a high degree of specialization of VWFS, and a discussion of how this specialization might arise from experience, appear in Farah (chapter 8, this volume).

The body of evidence reviewed here on the existence and function of the VWFS is wide-ranging, reasonably consistent, and reasonably compelling, but it is piecemeal—chronometric data from some studies, neural data from other studies, most of the chronometric data tapping into the naturally acquired reading skills of either children or adults but much of the neural data derived from training studies done with adults learning artificial materials. It remains to put all these techniques together—to nail the story down by combining analytic mental chronometry with blood-flow and electrical neuroimaging in a single investigation to track the joint behavioral and neural development of orthographic processing in children during the first few years of naturalistically occurring reading instruction. Such projects, taking full advantage of the tools of cognitive psychology and cognitive neuroscience put to work in the context of instructional intervention, are just getting underway. One is being conducted by McCandliss, Schneider, Perfetti, Beck, and colleagues at the University of Pittsburgh. Another is being conducted by Pugh, Shaywitz, Gore, and colleagues at Haskins Laboratories and Yale Medical School. There are probably others of which I am not aware.

What about individual differences? The proposition being investigated is that the "primary gateway" represented by the VWFS is a culturally engineered, instructionally created kluge—a bridge between two neural systems that do different jobs and usually do not talk to one another. If this proposition is correct, then one might imagine that there could be room for variation in how the interface problem gets solved, room for individual differences in the final form of the bridge that gets built. Such a possibility has recently been explored by the Pugh-Shaywitz-Gore group, who argue that readers differ systematically in the size of the units of analysis into which letter strings are parsed for the purpose of mapping orthography onto linguistic knowledge about phonology and semantics. Early in their research, this group found that several tasks requiring phonological decisions about visually presented words activate left- and right-prestriate, temporoparietal, and prefrontal structures. Prestriate and prefrontal activation tended to be strongly left-lateralized for males but more bilateral for females. This striking sex difference was reported in *Nature* (Shaywitz et al., 1995).

Later evidence (Pugh et al., 1996, 1997) suggested that the sex difference arises because males and females tend to rely on different strategies for computing phonology from orthography. One strategy involves a direct paired-associate retrieval process in which orthographic codes for words act as visual retrieval cues for phonological representations of words that are already stored in memory, and this "large-unit" process takes place largely in the left hemisphere. VWFS processing localized in the left-prestriate cortex creates orthographic representations at the level of the whole letter string (or perhaps at a just slightly more analytic level at which the letter string is parsed into two units, one representing the initial consonants that spell the word's onset and the other representing the remaining vowels and consonants that spell the word's rime. For a discussion of the onset-rime distinction and its potential importance in reading and reading development, see Goswami's chapter 2, this volume, as well as Treiman et al., 1995, Zorzi, Houghton, and Butterworth, 1998a,b , and Andrews and Scarratt, 1998). These relatively simple orthographic representations are mapped onto analogously simple phonological representations in a set of computations that reading instructors might call "look-say." The constrasting strategy involves grapheme-phoneme correspondences rather than relations between whole-word or onset-rime representations. This "small-unit" process instantiates the heuristic rules of phonics that map particular letters or letter groups onto particular phonemes. Hence, it corresponds more to what reading instructors would call "sounding words out." Parsing letter strings into larger numbers of smaller orthographic units is more demanding of the VWFS and ends up recruiting a wider spread, more bilateral network of prestriate tissue to get the job done. Similarly, the phonological representation onto which this ordered orthographic string is mapped also consists of larger numbers of smaller units and hence is more demanding of phonological processes. These processes are carried out by prefrontal and temporoparietal structures, and at least in the case of the prefrontal structures, their activation is also wider spread more bilateral.

Pugh et al. (1996) derived support for these hypotheses in a sophisticated example of how neural measures of brain activation and chronometric measures of performance in word-recognition tasks can be combined to draw inferences about the functional anatomy of information processing. Readers, both male and female, who showed greater chronometric evidence of "sounding words out" to help them make lexical decisions showed more bilateral prestriate and prefrontal activation (as well as lower levels of temporoparietal activation in both hemispheres), whereas readers who showed little evidenc of relying on the rules of phonics showed left-lateralized prestriate and prefrontal activation (as well as higher levels of temporoparietal activation in both hemispheres). The chronometric evidence for "sounding words out" consisted of (1) slower correct rejections of "pseudohomophonic" nonwords that were not spelled like any word but sounded like a word when pronounced, plus (2) length effects in which lexical decision times were longer for one-syllable letter strings that contained more letters. The first piece of evidence indicated that letter strings were being recoded from orthography to phonology and that the resulting phonological code was playing a part in lexical decision. The second piece of evidence suggested a serial process in which small units of analysis were mapped one-by-one (for similar arguments relating length and serial position effects to the operation of a grapheme-phoneme-based encoding process, see Coltheart and Rastle, 1994, and Rastle and Coltheart, in press). Females were more likely than males to sound words out, and once variation in the laterality of neural activation was taken into account, sex no longer explained any variance in performance. Thus sex differences in the likelihood of adopting a small-unit strategy for representing orthography and mapping it onto phonology could account for the sex difference in laterality that had been reported in *Nature*.

To summarize, then, the data from Pugh and colleagues suggest two broad conclusions. First, computing phonology from orthography relies on a complex and highly distributed set of processes involving occipital, temporal, parietal, and frontal regions of both cortical hemispheres. Depending on what is called a "mental operation," then, one might conclude either that spelling-to-sound translation for printed words is not localized but involves most of the brain, or that while there is localization of function in the system that achieves spelling-to-sound translation, the localized functions are rather specialized computations that must be defined at a highly detailed level of task analysis. Second, there appear to be two quite different strategies for computing phonology, with different brain structures supporting them. One of these strategies is left-lateralized and appears to rely on large units of analysis—whole-word codes for orthography computed by prestriate occipital cortex and whole-word codes for pronunciation computed by more anterior structures. The other strategy is bilateral and appears to rely on smaller units of analysis—orthographic representations of individual letters or small groups of letters and phonological representations of individual phonemes.

The conclusion about strategies invites thoughts about reading instruction, since the look-say methods employed in whole-language curricula try to teach large units of analysis, whereas the grapheme-phoneme methods employed in phonics curricula try to teach small units of analysis. Levy (this volume) and Lovett (this volume) describe very exciting attempts to use the outcome of instruction in large-unit versus small-unit analysis to determine the relative importance and utility of these two strategies in early reading development. How far an instructional hypothesis could be carried in accounting for Pugh et al.'s data, however, is not certain. The sex difference, in which the large-unit strategy appears to be more likely among males whereas the small-unit strategy appears to be more likely among females, would appear to cut across differences in instructional experience and hence invites an interpretation in terms of underlying sexual dimorphisms in brain organization. Thus we have a model system for exploring classic issues of nature, nurture, and their interaction.

Obviously Pugh and colleagues' conclusions are speculative, but the individual differences in brain activation patterns on which they are based appear to be robust and replicable. To me, there appears little doubt that careful pursuit of this fascinating individual difference will enlighten our understanding of the way in which the reading system recruits neural structures to perform desired computations. At this point, it does not matter much (except perhaps to the egos of particular scientists!) whether the theoretical interpretation in terms of reliance on large versus small units of orthographic and phonological analysis stands or is eventually replaced by a more powerful hypothesis that reduces more of the data that will be generated by researchers pursuing this question. A lot will be learned by combining mental chronometry, cognitive neuroscience, individual differences, and instructional intervention, regardless of how the answer comes out.

Postscript

If you are convinced by the preceding couple of sentences, then this commentary has achieved its goal. I firmly believe that scientific story telling will be greatly enriched by combining the methods represented in the chapters of this volume. I further believe that the relevance and applicability of scientific stories to real-world problems will be greatly enhanced by taking such a multimethodological, multidisciplinary approach. The end result of the approach represented in this volume is a much more defensible, much more satisfying, and much more useful understanding of reading than any single method or any single discipline could possibly achieve by itself.

References

Anderson, J.R. (1983). *The Architecture of Cognition.* Cambridge, MA: Harvard University Press.

Andrews, S., and Scarratt, D.R. (1998). Rule and analogy mechanisms in reading nonwords: Hough dou peapel rede gnew wirds? *Journal of Experimental Psychology: Human Perception and Performance, 24,* 1052–1086.

Ashcraft, M.H. (1994). *Human Memory and Cognition.* (2nd ed.). New York: HarperCollins.

Behrmann, M. (1999). Pure alexia: Underlying mechanisms and remediation. In R.M. Klein and P.A. McMullen (eds.), *Converging Methods for Understanding Reading and Dyslexia.* Cambridge, MA: MIT Press.

Bernstein, S.E., DeShon, R.P., and Carr, T.H. (1998). Concurrent task demands and individual differences in the architecture of reading: Discriminating artifacts from Real McCoys. *Journal of Experimental Psychology: Learning, Memory, and Cognition, 24,* 822–844.

Besner, D. (1999). Basic processes in reading: Multiple routines in localist and connectionist models. In R.M. Klein and P.A. McMullen (eds.), *Converging Methods for Understanding Reading and Dyslexia.* Cambridge, MA: MIT Press.

Bookheimer, S.Y., Zeffiro, T.A., Blaxton, T., Faillard, W., and Theodore, W. (1995). Regional cerebral blood flow during object naming and word reading. *Human Brain Mapping, 3,* 93–106.

Bowey, J.A., and Hansen, J. (1994). The development of orthographic rimes as units of word recognition. *Journal of Experimental Child Psychology, 58,* 465–488.

Buchanan, L., Hildebrandt, N., and MacKinnon, G.E. (1999). Phonological processing re–examined in acquired deep dyslexia. In R.M. Klein and P.A. McMullen (eds.), *Converging Methods for Understanding Reading and Dyslexia.* Cambridge, MA: MIT Press.

Cabeza, R., and Nyberg, L. (1997). Imaging cognition: An empirical review of PET studies with normal subjects. *Journal of Cognitive Neuroscience, 9*(1), 1–26.

Carlson-Radvansky, L.A., Alejano, A.R., and Carr, T.H. (1991). The level of focal attention hypothesis in oral reading: Influence of strategies on the context specificity of lexical repetition benefits. *Journal of Experimental Psychology: Learning, Memory, and Cognition, 17,* 924–931.

Carr, T.H. (1986). Perceiving visual language. In K. Boff, L. Kaufman, and J.P. Thomas (eds.), *Handbook of Perception and Human Performance* (vol. 2, pp. 1–92). New York: John Wiley.

Carr, T.H. (1992). Automaticity and cognitive anatomy: Is word recognition "automatic"? *American Journal of Psychology, 105*(2), 201–237.

Carr, T.H., Brown, J.S., and Charalambous, A. (1989). Repetition and reading: Perceptual encoding mechanisms are very abstract but not very interactive. *Journal of Experimental Psychology: Learning, Memory, and Cognition, 15,* 763–778.

Carr, T.H., and Levy, B.A. (eds.). (1990). *Reading and its Development: Component Skills Approaches.* San Diego: Academic Press.

Carr, T.H., and Pollatsek, A. (1985). Recognizing printed words: A look at current models. In D. Besner, T. G. Waller, and G. E. MacKinnon (eds.), *Reading Research: Advances in Theory and Practice* (vol. 5, pp. 1–82). Orlando: Academic Press.

Carr, T.H., Pollatsek, A., and Posner, M.I. (1981). What does the visual system know about words? *Perception and Psychophysics, 29,* 183–190.

Carr, T.H., and Posner, M.I. (1995). The impact of learning to read on the functional anatomy of language processing. In B. de Gelder and J. Morais (eds.), *Speech and Reading: A Comparative Approach* (pp. 267–301). Hove, UK: Erlbaum (UK) Taylor and Francis.

Collins, A.M., and Loftus, E.F. (1975). A spreading-activation theory of semantic processing. *Psychological Review, 82,* 407–428.

Coltheart, M., Curtis, B., Atkins, P., and Haller, M. (1993). Models of reading aloud: Dual-route and parallel-distributed-processing approaches. *Psychological Review, 100*(4), 589–608.

Coltheart, M., Davelaar, E., Jonasson, J.T., and Besner, D. (1977). Access to the internal lexicon. In S. Dornic (ed.), *Attention and Performance VI* (pp. 535–555). London: Academic Press.

Coltheart, M., and Rastle, K. (1994). Serial processing in reading aloud: Evidence for dual-route models of reading. *Journal of Experimental Psychology: Human Perception and Performance, 20*(6), 1197–1211.

Cunningham, A.E., Stanovich, K.E., and Wilson, M.R. (1990). Cognitive variation in adult college students differing in reading ability. In T.H. Carr and B.A. Levy (eds.), *Reading and its Development: Component Skills Approaches* (pp. 129–159). San Diego: Academic Press.

Dagenbach, D., Horst, S., and Carr, T.H. (1990). Adding new information to semantic memory: How much learning is enough to produce automatic priming? *Journal of Experimental Psychology: Learning, Memory, and Cognition, 16*, 581–591.

Daneman, M., and Carpenter, P.A. (1980). Individual differences in working memory and reading. *Journal of Verbal Learning and Verbal Behavior, 20*, 450–466.

Daneman, M., and Tardif, T. (1987). Working memory and reading skill re-examined. In M. Coltheart (ed.), *Attention and Performance XII: The Psychology of Reading*. Hove, UK: Lawrence Erlbaum.

Demb, J.B., Poldrack, R.A., and Gabrieli, J.D.E. (1999). Functional neuroimaging of word processing. In R.M. Klein and P.A. McMullen (eds.), *Converging Methods for Understanding Reading and Dyslexia*. Cambridge, MA: MIT Press.

Evans, M.A., and Carr, T.H. (1985). Cognitive abilities, conditions of learning, and the early development of reading skills. *Reading Research Quarterly, 20*, 327–350.

Farah, M.J. (1999). Are there orthography-specific brain regions? Neuropsychological and computational investigations. In R.M. Klein and P.A. McMullen (eds.), *Converging Methods for Understanding Reading and Dyslexia*. Cambridge, MA: MIT Press.

Frackowiak, R.S.J., Friston, K.J., Frith, C.D., Dolan, R.J., and Mazziotta, J.C. (1997). *Human Brain Function*. San Diego: Academic Press.

Gardner, H. (1985). *The Mind's New Science: A History of the Cognitive Revolution*. New York: Basic Books.

Goswami, U. (1999). Integrating orthographic and phonological knowledge as reading develops: Onsets, rimes and analogies in children's reading. In R.M. Klein and P.A. McMullen (eds.), *Converging Methods for Understanding Reading and Dyslexia*. Cambridge, MA: MIT Press.

Graesser, A.C., Hoffman, N., and Clark, L.F. (1980). Structural comopnents of reading time. *Journal of Verbal Learning and Verbal Behavior, 19*, 135–151.

Grainger, J., and Jacobs, A.M. (1996). Orthographic processing in visual word recognition: A multiple read-out model. *Psychological Review, 103*(3), 518–565.

Haynes, M., and Carr, T.H. (1990). Writing system background and second language reading: A component skills analysis of English reading by native speaker–readers of Chinese. In T.H. Carr and B.A. Levy (eds.), *Reading and its Development: Component Skills Approaches* (pp. 375–421). San Diego: Academic Press.

Henderson, L. (1982). *Orthography and Word Recognition in Reading*. New York: Academic Press.

Hillyard, S.A., Hinrichs, H., Tempelmann, C., Morgan, S.T., Hansen, J.C., Scheich, H., and Heinze, H.J. (1997). Combining steady-state visual evoked potentials and fMRI to localize brain activity during selective attention. *Human Brain Mapping, 5*(4), 287–292.

Huey, E.B. (1908/1968). *The Psychology and Pedagogy of Reading*. Cambridge, MA: MIT Press.

Jackson, M.D., and McClelland, J.L. (1979). Processing determinants of reading speed. *Journal of Experimental Psychology: General, 108*, 151–181.

Jacobs, A.M., and Grainger, J. (1994). Models of visual word recognition-Sampling the state of the art. *Journal of Experimental Psychology: Human Perception and Performance, 20*(6), 1311–1334.

Jacobs, R.A. (1997). Nature, nurture, and the development of functional specializations: A computational approach. *Psychonomic Bulletin and Review, 4*(3), 299–309.

Jacoby, L.L., Levy, B.A., and Steinbach, K. (1992). Episodic transfer and automaticity: Integration of data-driven and conceptually-driven processing in rereading. *Journal of Experimental Psychology: Learning, Memory, and Cognition, 18*, 15–24.

Lachman, R., Lachman, J.L., and Butterfield, E.C. (1979). *Cognitive Psychology and Information Processing: An Introduction*. Hillsdale, NJ: Lawrence Erlbaum.

Levy, B.A. (1999). Whole words, segments, and meaning: Approaches to reading education. In R.M. Klein and P.A. McMullen (eds.), *Converging Methods for Understanding Reading and Dyslexia*. Cambridge, MA: MIT Press.

Liberman, A.M. (1995). Speech processing, its specificity and its relation to reading. In B. de Gelder and J. Morais (eds.), *Speech and Reading: A Comparitive Approach* (17–88). Hove, UK: Erlbaum (UK), Taylor and Francis.

Lovett, M.W. (1999). Defining and remediating the core deficits of developmental dyslexia: Lessons from remedial outcome research with reading disabled children. In R.M. Klein and P.A. McMullen (eds.), *Converging Methods for Understanding Reading and Dyslexia*. Cambridge, MA: MIT Press.

Luce, R.D. (1986). *Response Times: Their Role in Inferring Elementary Mental Organization*. New York: Oxford University Press.

Mangun, G.R., Hopfinger, J.B., Kussmaul, C.L., Fletcher, E.M., and Heinze, H.-J. (1997). Covariations in ERP and PET measures of spatial selective attention in human extrastriate visual cortex. *Human Brain Mapping, 5*(4), 273–279.

Manis, F.R., Szeszulski, P.A., Holt, L.K., and Graves, K. (1990). Variation in component word recognition and spelling skills among dyslexic children and normal readers. In T.H. Carr and B.A. Levy (eds.), *Reading and its Development: Component Skills Approaches* (pp. 207–259). San Diego: Academic Press.

Masson, M.E.J. (1999). Interactive processes in word identification: Modeling context effects in a distributed memory system. In R. M. Klein and P. A. McMullen (eds.), *Converging Methods for Understanding Reading and Dyslexia.* Cambridge, MA: MIT Press.

McCandliss, B.D., Posner, M.I., and Givón, T. (1997). Brain plasticity in learning visual words. *Cognitive Psychology, 33*, 88–110.

McCarthy, R.A., and Warrington, E.K. (1990). *Cognitive Neuropsychology: A Clinical Introduction.* New York: Academic Press.

McClelland, J.L. (1979). On the time relations of mental processes: An examination of systems of processes in cascade. *Psychological Review, 86*, 287–330.

McClelland, J.L., McNaughton, B.L., and O'Reilly, R.C. (1995). Why there are complementary learning systems in the hippocampus and neocortex: Insights from the successes and failures of connectionist models of learning and memory. *Psychological Review, 102*(3), 419–457.

McClelland, J.L., and Rumelhart, D.E. (1981). An interactive-activation model of context effects in letter perception: Part I. An account of basic findings. *Psychological Review, 88*, 375–407.

Menard, M.T., Kosslyn, S.M., Thompson, W.L., Alpert, N.M., and Rauch, S.L. (1996). Encoding words and pictures: A positorn emission tomography study. *Neuropsychologia, 34*, 185–194.

Meyer, D.E., Osman, A.M., Irwin, D.E.,and Yantis, S. (1988). Modern mental chronometry. *Biological Psychiatry, 26*, 3–67.

Morton, J. (1969). Interaction of information in word recognition. *Psychological Review, 76*, 165–178.

Olson, R.K., Forsberg, H., Gayan, J., and DeFries, J. (1999). A behvioral–genetic analysis of reading disabilities and component processes. In R.M. Klein and P.A. McMullen (eds.), *Converging Methods for Understanding Reading and Dyslexia.* Cambridge, MA: MIT Press.

Paap, K.R., and Herdman, C.M. (1998). Phew phonological recoders and frequent failures to direct attention: Two plausible reasons for Pexman and Lupker's failure to replicate Paap and Noel. *Journal of Experimental Psychology: Learning, Memory, and Cognition, 24*, 845–861.

Petersen, S.E., Fox, P.T., Posner, M.I., Mintun, M., and Raichle, M.E. (1989). Positron emission tomographic studies of the processing of single words. *Journal of Cognitive Neuroscience, 1*, 153–170.

Petersen, S.E., Fox, P.T., Snyder, A.Z., and Raichle, M.E. (1990). Activation of extrastriate and frontal cortical areas by visual words and word-like stimuli. *Science, 249*, 1041–1044.

Pexman, P.M., and Lupker, S.J. (1998). Word naming and memory load: Still searching for an individual differences explanation. *Journal of Experimental Psychology: Learning, Memory, and Cognition, 24,* 803–821.

Pinker, S. (1994). *The Language Instinct: How the Mind Creates Language.* New York: William Morrow.

Plaut, D.C. (1999). Computational modeling of word reading, acquired dyslexia, and remediation. In R.M. Klein and P.A. McMullen (eds.), *Converging Methods for Understanding Reading and Dyslexia.* Cambridge, MA: MIT Press.

Posner, M.I. (1986). *Chronometric Explorations of Mind.* (2nd ed.). New York: Oxford University Press.

Posner, M.I., and Carr, T.H. (1992). Lexical access and the brain: Anatomical constraints on cognitive models of word recognition. *American Journal of Psychology, 105*(1), 1–26.

Posner, M.I., and McCandliss, B.D. (1999). Brain circuitry during reading. In R.E. Klein and P.A. McMullen (eds.), *Converging Methods for Understanding Reading and Dyslexia.* Cambridge, MA: MIT Press.

Posner, M.I., and Raichle, M.E. (1994). *Images of Mind.* New York: Scientific American Library.

Price, C., Wise, R., Watson, J.D.G., Patterson, K., Howard, D., and Frackowiak, R. (1994). Brain activity during reading: The effects of exposure duration and task. *Brain, 117,* 1255–1269.

Pugh, K.R., Shaywitz, B.A., Constable, R.T., Shaywitz, S.E., Skudlarski, P., Fulbright, R.K., Bronen, R.A., Shankweiler, D.P., Katz, L., Fletcher, J.M., and Gore, J.C. (1996). Cerebral organization of component processes in reading. *Brain, 119,* 1221–1238.

Pugh, K.R., Shaywitz, B.A., Shaywitz, S.E., Shankweiler, D.P., Katz, L., Fletcher, J.M., Skudlarski, P., Fulbright, R.K., Constable, R.T., Bronen, R.A., Lacadie, C., and Gore, J.C. (1997). Predicting reading performance from neuroimaging profiles: The cerebral basis of phonological effects in printed word identification. *Journal of Experimental Psychology: Human Perception and Performance, 23*(2), 299–318.

Rastle, K., and Coltheart, M. (1999). Serial and strategic effects in reading aloud. *Journal of Experimental Psychology: Human Perception and Performance, 25,* 482–503.

Rayner, K. (1999). What have we learned about eye movements during reading? In R.M. Klein and P.A. McMullen (eds.), *Converging Methods for Understanding Reading and Dyslexia.* Cambridge, MA: MIT Press.

Reisberg, D. (1997). *Cognitive Psychology.* New York: Norton.

Rieben, L., and Perfetti, C.A. (eds.). (1991). *Learning to Read: Basic Research and its Implications.* Hillsdale, NJ: Lawrence Erlbaum.

Rozin, P. (1976). The evolution of intelligence and access to the cognitive unconscious. In J.M. Sprague and A.H. Epstein (eds.), *Progress in Psychobiology and Physiological*

Psychology. New York: Academic Press.

Rozin, P., and Gleitman, L. (1977). The structure and acquisition of reading: II. The reading process and acquisition of the alphabetic principle. In A.S. Reber and D.L. Scarborough (eds.), *Toward a Psychology of Reading*. Hillsdale, NJ: Lawrence Erlbaum.

Shaywitz, B.A., Shaywitz, S.E., Pugh, K.R., Constable, R.T., Skularski, P., Fulbright, R.K., Ronen, R.A., Fletcher, J.M., Shankweiler, D.P., Katz, L., and Gore, J.C. (1995). Sex differences in the functional organization of the brain for language. *Nature, 373*, 607–609.

Simon, H.A., and Kaplan, C.A. (1989). Foundations of cognitive science. In M.I. Posner (ed.), *Foundations of Cognitive Science* (pp. 1–47). Cambridge, MA: MIT Press.

Stone, G.O., and Van Orden, G.C. (1994). Building a resonance framework for word recognition using design and system principles. *Journal of Experimental Psychology: Human Perception and Performance, 20*(6), 1248–1268.

Treiman, R., Mullennix, J., Bijeljac-Babic, R., and Richmond-Welty, E.D. (1995). The special role of rimes in the description, use and acquisition of English orthography. *Journal of Experimental Psychology: General, 124*, 107–136.

Tulving, E., Hayman, C.A.G., and MacDonald, C.A. (1991). Long-lasting perceptual priming and semantic learning in amnesia: A case experiment. *Journal of Experimental Psychology: Learning, Memory, and Cognition, 17*, 595–617.

Vandenberghe, R., Price, C.J., Wise, R., Josephs, O., and Frackowiak, R.S.J. (1996). Functional anatomy of a common semantic system for words or pictures. *Nature, 383*, 254–256.

Warrington, E.K., and Shallice, T. (1980). Word-form dyslexia. *Brain, 103*, 99–112.

Wimmer, H., and Goswami, U. (1994). The influence of orthographic consistency on reading development: Word recognition in English and German children. *Cognition, 51*(91–103).

Ziegler, J.C., Besson, M., Jacobs, A.M., Nazir, T.A., and Carr, T.H. (1997). Word, pseudoword, and nonword processing: A multitask comparison using event-related potentials. *Journal of Cognitive Neuroscience, 9*(6), 758–775.

Zorzi, M., Houghton, G., and Butterworth, B. (1998a). The development of spelling-sound relationships in a model of phonological reading. *Language and Cognitive Processes*, 13, 337–372..

Zorzi, M., Houghton, G., and Butterworth, B. (1998b). Two routes or one in reading aloud? A connectionist dual-process model. *Journal of Experimental Psychology: Human Perception and Performance*, 24, 1131–1161.

Author Index

Subject Index

A

Abstract letter identities 164, 184, 238
Additive factors logic 226
Alexia 9, 153–186, 193, 221–241
  attentional blink 163
  comorbidity with surface dysgraphia 171
  conjunction search task performance 224
  D.M. (patient) 183
  D.S. (patient) 155–165
  deficits
    nonorthographic 167, 234
    orthographic vs. perceptual 167–168
    orthography-specific 238
    restriction to alphanumeric stimuli 167–168
    serial order effects 169–170
  definition 154
  "ends-in" processing 175
  hypotheses
    distribution of attention 155
    ordinal processing deficit 158
    orthographic view 167
    orthography-specific impairment hypothesis 228
    perceptual processing deficit 232
    perceptual view 167
    prelexical processing 154–155
    spatial attention allocation 158–161
    visual impairment hypothesis 223–224
    visual impairment most severe for orthography 12, 234–239
    visual-verbal disconnection hypothesis 222–223
    word-form hypothesis 228–230, 232
  K.W. (patient) 183
  letter processing
    matching task 163–165
    naming latency 172, 224
    sequential 233
    sequential - words vs.nonwords 173–174
    simultaneous form perception 225
    simultaneous vs. sequential 163
  lexical decision tasks 172
  localist model 228
  Mr. C (patient) 153
  multishape recognition 228
  nonword processing 175
  nonword vs. word processing 175
  perceptual grouping processes 226
  perceptual speed 225
  remediation 168–186
    "ends-in" therapy 176, 178–180, 182–185
    future approaches 184–185
    kinesthetic intervention 168–169
    MOR (mutiple oral rereading) 168
    practice 168
  RSVP task performance 161
  S.I. (patient) 170–179
  visual noise effects 226
  visuospatial attention 224
  W.L. (patient) 183
  word length effect 154, 156, 161, 170, 172, 181, 182, 226–227
  word naming 172
  word superiority effect 154, 175, 230, 233
Ambiguious sentences
  eye movements during 38–40, 393
Analogical model of reading aquisition 4
Analogies 115, 119
  development of reading 4, 62–69, 81, 82–83, 92, 115
  in dyslexic reading 116–117
Analogy model of deep dyslexia 212
Angular gyrus 222, 271, 272–273, 312
Anomia 423
Anterior cingulate 313, 318
Associative priming 385
Attention 3, 155, 166, 308, 310, 312, 315, 329
  alexia 224
  attentional blink 163
  spatial attention allocation 159, 166